ANTITRUST LAW IN CHINA, KOREA AND VIETNAM

ANTITRUST LAW IN CHINA, KOREA AND VIETNAM

Mark Furse

OXFORD
UNIVERSITY PRESS

OXFORD
UNIVERSITY PRESS

Great Clarendon Street, Oxford OX2 6DP

Oxford University Press is a department of the University of Oxford.
It furthers the University's objective of excellence in research, scholarship,
and education by publishing worldwide in

Oxford New York

Auckland Cape Town Dar es Salaam Hong Kong Karachi
Kuala Lumpur Madrid Melbourne Mexico City Nairobi
New Delhi Shanghai Taipei Toronto

With offices in

Argentina Austria Brazil Chile Czech Republic France Greece
Guatemala Hungary Italy Japan Poland Portugal Singapore
South Korea Switzerland Thailand Turkey Ukraine Vietnam

Oxford is a registered trade mark of Oxford University Press
in the UK and in certain other countries

Published in the United States
by Oxford University Press Inc., New York

First published 2009

British Library Cataloguing in Publication Data
Data available

Library of Congress Cataloging in Publication Data
Data available

Typeset by Cepha Imaging Private Ltd, Bangalore, India
Printed in Great Britain
on acid-free paper by
CPI Antony Rowe

ISBN 978–0–19–928586–0

1 3 5 7 9 10 8 6 4 2

CONSULTING EDITORS

China	Li Junfeng, Lecturer, School of Law, Shanghai University
Hong Kong	Thomas Cheng, Assistant Professor, Faculty of Law, The University of Hong Kong
Taiwan	Stephen Wu, Lee and Li (Attorneys at Law), Taiwan
Korea	Dr Youngjin Jung, Yulchen (Attorneys at Law), Seoul
Vietnam	Alice Pham, Director, Hanoi Resource Centre, CUTS International

PREFACE

It is no longer the case that antitrust law[1] is the prerogative only of Western States with highly developed economies. As Haley has noted, the 'enactment of competition legislation has become a global phenomenon'.[2] The adoption by China in 2007 of a general antitrust law—the Anti-Monopoly Law—has attracted significant attention from the antitrust community at all levels, and has been the subject of symposia and conference presentations and discussion, and of a wide range of publications. The focus of the present book is on the practice of antitrust law in the five jurisdictions covered, rather than on antitrust policy, although the latter is not neglected given that practice will often follow policy. It is my hope that the many hours of work I have put into this will reduce the workload of busy practitioners grappling with the increasingly complex antitrust issues that may arise in the regimes covered.

I decided to embark on this project when, on a business trip to China in 2004, I picked up the English language *China Daily* newspaper in my hotel lobby to find the lead article on page one was headed, 'China Speeds Progress to Competition Law'. For a competition lawyer with a strong history of engagement in China this proved an irresistible temptation. I have spent, with the support of many people only some of whom are directly thanked below, a significant part of the last four and a half years researching this book, and have spent in total over a year in the jurisdictions covered collecting information, and speaking with those engaged in competition law. From July 2008 to January 2009 I worked exclusively in the jurisdictions on a period of research leave granted by my employer, the School of Law of the University of Glasgow, and I am indebted to the School for its support. This work was in part funded by a research grant from the Sino-British Fellowship Trust, and could not have been completed without that financial support.

---

1 With apologies to European readers the decision has been taken to use the term 'antitrust' consistently throughout this book. As used here the word refers to the control of anti-competitive agreements, abuse of dominant positions and monopolization, merger control, and related procedures. It does not extend to aspects of 'fair competition', such as false representations, and passing-off, although these are often to be found in 'competition' laws.

2 Haley, JO, 'Competition Law for the Asia-Pacific Economic Cooperation Community: Designing Shoes for Many Sizes' (2002) *Washington University Global Studies Law Review*, vol 1, (1 & 2), 1 at 1.

Some explanation is required of the approach taken in this book and the choice of jurisdictions covered—there are other States in East and Southeast Asia which maintain antitrust law regimes. The law of China is at the heart of this book, which deals also with the proposed new law of the Special Administrative Region (SAR) of Hong Kong, and the law of Taiwan. The legal relationship between Taiwan and China is not discussed here; although this is a sensitive issue it should not concern the antitrust practitioner advising clients as to the legality of their commercial arrangements, or the legal risks they face in this area. The law of Taiwan, which enacted a Fair Trade Act in 1991, is the most developed of these three jurisdictions, and many aspects of this law will appear familiar to those schooled in EC or US antitrust law. In Hong Kong the decision was taken in 2007 to introduce a general antitrust law, although earlier policy had been determined on the basis that the economy was so open as to be self-correcting in the face of abuses of market power. The evidence suggests however that this is not the case. At the time of writing in early 2009 this law has not yet been brought forward, but the likely shape of the law is discussed in Part 3 of this book. While officially the two developments are unrelated, it is likely that Hong Kong policy-makers, having undergone a 'Damascene conversion' at least had an eye on moves in China. That China has adopted a general law of antitrust is remarkable given the history of the country over the last 50 years. The market reform processes and legal steps that have led to the adoption of the new law are discussed in Chapter 1-1 of this book, which introduces in broad outline the antitrust policies and legal regimes of the jurisdictions covered. Korea is a very near neighbour of China, and it is likely that those advising companies trading in and doing business with China will also be involved in advising companies on Korean law. Korea enacted antitrust law in 1980, and is thus in possession of what is by some way the oldest regime of those covered in this book. Like Korea, Vietnam is a close neighbour of China and the same considerations have applied to its inclusion here. Vietnam is also a relatively new member of the antitrust family, having adopted its antitrust law in 2004. However, the law in Vietnam is flawed, and although the sincerity of the Vietnamese Government in enacting the law can hardly be doubted, there is in practice little application of the law.

The structure of this book is to deal in Part 1 with the regimes in outline, addressing broader policy issues, and briefly presenting the development and current state of the antitrust law in each jurisdiction. Chapter 2 of this Part presents an overview of antitrust law in the US and in the EC, and is designed to provide a reference point to standard practices for those who are new to antitrust law. Some reference is made to this chapter throughout the text where the approach in the jurisdictions covered is related back to these more mature regimes. The text however is not a comparative one, and Parts 2–6 deal, in order, with the law in China, Hong Kong, Taiwan, Korea, and Vietnam. In each case I have taken as consistent an approach as is possible given the differences in the regimes, first introducing the regime and its institutional structure, then agreements, monopoly control, merger control, and finally procedure. Where there are idiosyncratic approaches in a particular regime that do not fit particularly well into this standard model I have inserted these at what appears to be the most appropriate juncture, but have signalled these elsewhere in the text as necessary.

As will be clear the maturity of the law in each of the jurisdictions covered differs significantly. At the time of completing this book the ink of the Hong Kong law is not yet on the page, whereas in Taiwan and Korea there is a substantial body of legislation, guidance, and, importantly, examples of implementation of the law. China's law has been in force for six months, and has not yet been implemented to any significant degree. Vietnam lies someway in between, but is more hesitant in its development of the law. This has had a substantial impact on the level of detail in this book, which is dependent on the information available. I have avoided speculating as to the development of the law and the way in which it will be applied where this is not yet clear, and have preferred to stick to the facts, although in the case of China some speculation has been unavoidable. This means that whereas the parts of the book dealing with Korea and Taiwan incorporate discussion of secondary materials and of decided cases and policy decisions, the treatment of the law in China and Vietnam is directed more towards explaining the legislation and the rules relating to its application published to date. I have also taken the decision not to deal with the legal systems in general, save where some understanding of these is essential to understanding the respective antitrust laws. Some have doubted the sincerity of the respective States in adopting antitrust law, and have questioned whether the law will be fairly and consistently applied, or indeed if it will be applied at all. In this book I have taken the approach, perhaps naively, of taking the laws at face value, and have discussed, I believe fairly, their content.

Where materials are published in English translations are not usually official. I have adopted a convention of relying first on materials published in English that emanate from the respective antitrust authorities. Where this is the case I have accepted their terms, albeit sometimes with reluctance. I have made minor corrections to English quotes of these materials in this book where the English is clearly incorrect (as, for example, in the dropping of the definite article), but have not rewritten the materials into fluent English as long as the original translated text is clear. Any lawyer who works regularly with foreign language jurisdictions will be aware of the difficulties that translation can give rise to. Some terms simply do not translate, and others may have different acceptable translations. Where the latter is the case I have used a consistent term, but have indicated in a footnote that there are other standard translations which may be encountered in different materials or texts.

The difficulties of writing a practitioner text dealing with the laws of four jurisdictions in which English is not the official language, and in which very different legal and political cultures affect the transparency of the operation of the legal regimes, have been substantial. I have received most generous assistance from numbers of people in each jurisdiction who are engaged in antitrust law and who are able to work in English. The consultant editors, listed on the preliminary pages of this book, have provided invaluable assistance. Assistance has also been provided by graduate students in China during my many teaching visits to the country, and by my own PhD students at the University of Glasgow.

Thanks are due to all of those who have assisted me in this research over the last five years, including those whose work I have read, and those who have been generous with their time in discussing with me aspects of antitrust law in the regimes covered here. The consultant editors have been most supportive of this project, and without their assistance this book could not have been completed. In China I would like to thank in particular Professor Xiaoye Wang of the Chinese Academy of Social Sciences, Dr Heng Wang of the South West University of Political Science and Law, and Miss Yun Lei of the South West University of Finance and Economics, for providing invaluable help and support. The School of Law of Sichuan University, Chengdu, provided me with a base in August and September 2008. Dr Zhou Zhaofeng contributed greatly to my discussion of Chinese antitrust policy during the course of his PhD studies at the University of Glasgow, and I have drawn in parts from his unpublished PhD thesis. In Hong Kong thanks are due in particular to the Asian Institute of International Financial Law at the School of Law of Hong Kong University, which hosted me in the autumn of 2008. In Korea thanks go to Professor Hyun Yoon Shin, of Yonsei University, Seoul who kindly facilitated a stay at Yonsei University as a visiting scholar, and effected introductions to the antitrust community in Korea. Yo Sop Choi, a PhD candidate at the University of Glasgow, has provided invaluable assistance, and has greatly helped in the writing of the Part of the book dealing with the law in Korea. Miss Sarah Louise Melaney, a final year LLB student at the University of Glasgow, provided sterling research assistance at the commencement of this project. Finally thanks must go to the staff at Oxford University Press who contributed to the production of this book, and who showed the patience of Job during its long gestation. All errors and omissions in this text are my sole responsibility.

This book is dedicated to my colleagues at the University of Glasgow who have provided an invigorating intellectual environment and support during its writing; to all of those who have contributed to the development of antitrust law in China, Hong Kong, Taiwan, Korea, and Vietnam and to my knowledge of it; and to Tim Frazer whose encouragement, guidance, and support has been fundamental to my career.

I have endeavoured to ensure that this text is accurate and up to date, and as inclusive as possible given the difficulties of gathering material and information. It is my hope that this book will be followed by future editions, and I would be very grateful for any comments from readers of this book. In particular details of cases or developments would be most gratefully received. I may be contacted either through Oxford University Press, or through the University of Glasgow (m.furse@law.gla.ac.uk).

The law in this book is intended to be up to date as at 15 January 2009, although some later developments may have been incorporated into footnotes.

Mark Furse, BA, LLM, MSc, PhD
Professor of Competition Law and Policy,
School of Law, University of Glasgow

Adjunct Professor, South West University of
Political Science and Law, Chongqing
15 January 2009

CONTENTS—SUMMARY

Table of Cases xxiii
Table of Legislation xxix
Table of International Co-operation/Trade Agreements xli
List of Abbreviations xliii

PART 1 INTRODUCTION

1-1 Introduction 3
1-2 Standards in Antitrust Law 29

PART 2 CHINA

2-1 The Chinese Antitrust Law Regime 67
2-2 China Agreements 79
2-3 China Monopoly and Abuse of Dominance 87
2-4 China Merger Control 97
2-5 China Procedure 111

PART 3 HONG KONG

3-1 Antitrust in Hong Kong 123

PART 4 TAIWAN

4-1 The Taiwan Antitrust Law Regime 135
4-2 Taiwan Agreements 145
4-3 Taiwan Monopoly and Abuse of Dominace 169
4-4 Taiwan Merger Control 177
4-5 Taiwan Procedure 199

PART 5 KOREA

5-1 The Korean Antitrust Law Regime 215

5-2 Korea Agreements 225

5-3 Korea Monopoly and Abuse of Dominance 245

5-4 Korea Merger Control 263

5-5 Korea Procedure 289

PART 6 VIETNAM

6-1 The Vietnamese Antitrust Law Regime 305

6-2 Vietnam Agreements 313

6-3 Vietnam Monopoly and Abuse of Dominance 321

6-4 Vietnam Merger Control 329

6-5 Vietnam Procedure 337

Appendices 353

Bibliography 449

Index 455

CONTENTS

Table of Cases	xxiii
Table of Legislation	xxix
Table of International Co-operation/Trade Agreements	xli
List of Abbreviations	xliii

PART 1 INTRODUCTION

1-1 Introduction

Antitrust Law in China	1-1.06
Antitrust Law in Hong Kong	1-1.16
Antitrust Law in Taiwan	1-1.24
Antitrust Law in Korea	1-1.26
Antitrust Law in Vietnam	1-1.32

1-2 Standards in Antitrust Law

Introduction	1-2.01
The Control of Anti-competitive Agreements	1-2.04
Forms of agreements	1-2.06
The rule of reason, exemptions, and exceptions	1-2.10
Horizontal agreements	1-2.13
Vertical agreements	1-2.18
Monopolization and Abuse of Dominant Position	1-2.21
Markets and market power	1-2.22
Condemned conduct	1-2.25
Predatory pricing	1-2.27
Price discrimination	1-2.30
Excessive pricing	1-2.31
Refusals to supply and the essential facilities doctrine	1-2.32
Full line forcing, bundling, and tie-in sales	1-2.34

Merger Control 1-2.35
Application of Economic Principles and Evidence 1-2.45
International Cooperation 1-2.52

PART 2 CHINA

2-1 **The Chinese Antitrust Law Regime**
Introduction 2-1.01
The Anti-Monopoly Law 2-1.03
The Institutional Structure 2-1.08
Information sources 2-1.15
General Exemptions 2-1.16
Territorial Application 2-1.19
International Cooperation and Agreements 2-1.21
Pre-2007 Legislation 2-1.22

2-2 **China Agreements**
Introduction 2-2.01
Horizontal Agreements 2-2.02
Vertical Agreements 2-2.03
Trade Associations 2-2.04
Exemptions 2-2.05
Penalties 2-2.09

2-3 **China Monopoly and Abuse of Dominance**
Introduction 2-3.01
The Assessment of Dominance 2-3.02
Abuse of Dominant Position 2-3.06
Intellectual property 2-3.09
Abuse of Administrative Power 2-3.10

2-4 **China Merger Control**
Introduction 2-4.01
Jurisdiction 2-4.05
'Foreign mergers' 2-4.10

Procedures 2-4.12
Notification requirements 2-4.12
Expedited review 2-4.16
Pre-notification review 2-4.17
The Substantive Test 2-4.18
Efficiencies and the Failing Firm Defence 2-4.21
Remedies and Penalties 2-4.22

2-5 China Procedure
Introduction 2-5.01
Investigations by the AMEA 2-5.02
Business secrecy 2-5.06
Complaints 2-5.07
Final Decisions 2-5.08
Commitments and undertakings 2-5.09
Penalties 2-5.10
Appeals 2-5.15
Third Party Rights 2-5.18

PART 3 HONG KONG

3-1 Antitrust in Hong Kong
Introduction 3-1.01
The *Proposals* 3-1.04
Substantive provisions 3-1.06
Agreements 3-1.08
Abuse of substantial market power 3-1.09
Exclusions, exemptions, and *de minimis* provisions 3-1.10
Merger control 3-1.13
Procedures 3-1.14
Institutional arrangements 3-1.15
Public enforcement 3-1.17
Penalties, remedies, and leniency 3-1.20
Private enforcement 3-1.25

PART 4 TAIWAN

4-1 The Taiwan Antitrust Law Regime

Introduction 4-1.01
The Fair Trade Commission 4-1.05
Information sources 4-1.08
General Exemptions 4-1.09
Territorial Application 4-1.11
International Cooperation and Agreements 4-1.17

4-2 Taiwan Agreements

Introduction 4-2.01
Horizontal agreements 4-2.02
Approvals 4-2.08
Trade associations 4-2.19
Vertical agreements 4-2.20
Multi-level sales 4-2.22
Intellectual property licensing 4-2.25
Unfair Competition as it Relates to Horizontal and Vertical Agreements 4-2.33
Penalties for Breach 4-2.41

4-3 Taiwan Monopoly and Abuse of Dominance

Introduction 4-3.01
Assessing dominance 4-3.03
Abusive conduct 4-3.07
Remedies and penalties 4-3.12
Case examples 4-3.13

4-4 Taiwan Merger Control

Introduction 4-4.01
Jurisdiction 4-4.06
'Foreign mergers' 4-4.11
Procedures 4-4.13
Pre-merger contacts and review 4-4.13
Notification 4-4.14

Application of the Substantive Test 4-4.20
General review 4-4.21
Market definition 4-4.24
Market power assessment 4-4.25
Horizontal mergers 4-4.26
Vertical mergers 4-4.30
Conglomerate mergers 4-4.31
Efficiencies and the failing firm defence 4-4.32
The case record 4-4.34
Remedies and Penalties 4-4.38

4-5 Taiwan Procedure
Introduction 4-5.01
Investigations 4-5.03
Complaints 4-5.11
Hearings and Access to File 4-5.12
Corrective Measures and Penalties 4-5.21
Leniency 4-5.30
Appeals 4-5.31
Third Party Rights and Damages 4-5.32

PART 5 KOREA

5-1 The Korean Antitrust Law Regime
Introduction 5-1.01
The Fair Trade Commission 5-1.06
Information sources 5-1.08
General Exemptions 5-1.09
Territorial Application 5-1.10
International Cooperation and Agreements 5-1.13

5-2 Korea Agreements
Introduction 5-2.01
Chapter 4, MRFTA—'Improper Cartels' (Horizontal Agreements) 5-2.02
Horizontal agreements 5-2.17
Enforcement examples 5-2.17

Chapter 6, MRFTA—Enterprisers' Organizations (Trade Associations)	5-2.22
Enforcement examples	5-2.25
Chapter 7, MRFTA—Resale Price Maintenance	5-2.26
Enforcement examples	5-2.27
Chapter 8, MRFTA—International Contracts	5-2.28
Vertical Agreements	5-2.29
Penalties for Breach	5-2.31
Franchise Agreements	5-2.34
5-3 Korea Monopoly and Abuse of Dominance	
Introduction	5-3.01
Abuse of Dominant Position	5-3.04
Assessing dominance	5-3.05
Abusive conduct	5-3.08
Remedies and penalties	5-3.19
Case examples	5-3.20
Unfair Trade Practices	5-3.24
5-4 Korea Merger Control	
Introduction	5-4.01
Jurisdiction	5-4.08
'Foreign mergers'	5-4.08
Procedures	5-4.09
Pre-merger contacts and review	5-4.09
Notification	5-4.10
Foreign mergers	5-4.19
Powers of the KFTC	5-4.21
Application of the Substantive Test	5-4.22
General Review	5-4.23
Market definition	5-4.24
Market power assessment and the competitive effects of the merger	5-4.30
Competitive assessment	5-4.31
Horizontal mergers	5-4.32
Vertical mergers	5-4.40

Conglomerate mergers 5-4.42
Efficiencies and the failing firm defence 5-4.46
Remedies 5-4.50

5-5 Korea Procedure
Introduction 5-5.01
Investigations 5-5.04
Hearings, Access to File, and Secrecy 5-5.09
Complaints 5-5.11
Corrective Measures and Penalties 5-5.13
Leniency 5-5.21
Appeals 5-5.24
Damages 5-5.28
Arbitration 5-5.29

PART 6 VIETNAM

6-1 The Vietnamese Antitrust Law Regime
Introduction 6-1.01
Institutional Arrangements 6-1.08
Vietnam Competition-Administration Department ('VCAD') 6-1.10
Vietnam Competition Council 6-1.14
General Exemptions 6-1.15
Acts of the State 6-1.17
Territorial Application 6-1.18
International Cooperation and Agreements 6-1.20
Intellectual Property 6-1.21

6-2 Vietnam Agreements
Introduction 6-2.01
Horizontal Agreements 6-2.02
Trade associations 6-2.04
Exemptions 6-2.06
Vertical Agreements 6-2.10
Multi-level sales 6-2.11

6-3 Vietnam Monopoly and Abuse of Dominance

Introduction 6-3.01

The Assessment of Dominance and Monopoly 6-3.02

The determination of the relevant market 6-3.02

The assessment of dominance 6-3.05

Conduct Prohibited 6-3.10

State-monopolized domains 6-3.15

6-4 Vietnam Merger Control

Introduction 6-4.01

Concentrations 6-4.02

Exemption 6-4.05

Notification and Procedure 6-4.08

Remedies 6-4.13

Other investigations 6-4.14

Territorial Application 6-4.15

6-5 Vietnam Procedure

Introduction 6-5.01

Investigations and Evidence 6-5.06

Hearings 6-5.19

Complaints 6-5.21

Other third parties 6-5.24

Rights of the Parties 6-5.25

Remedies and Penalties 6-5.27

Leniency 6-5.34

Third Party Rights 6-5.35

Appeals 6-5.36

Appendix 1 China: Anti-Monopoly Law 355

Appendix 2 Taiwan: Fair Trade Act of 2002 365

Appendix 3 Korea: Monopoly Regulation and Fair Trade Act 377

Appendix 4 Vietnam: Law on Competition 419

Bibliography 449

Index 455

TABLE OF CASES

China	xxiii
European Community	xxiii
Korea	xxiv
Taiwan	xxv
United Kingdom	xxvi
United States	xxvi

CHINA

CocaCola Corpn—Huiyuan Juice Company, Notice of the Ministry of Commerce of the PRC [2008] 2-4.25

InBev NV/SA—Anheuser-Busch Companies Inc, Notice of the Ministry of Commerce of the PRC [2008] No 95 . . . . 2-4.11, 2-4.24

EUROPEAN COMMUNITY

Commission Decisions

BBI/Boosey & Hawkes 87/500 [1987] OJ L286/36 . . . . 5-3.14

Publishers' Association—Net Book Agreements 89/44 [1989] OJ L22/12. . . . . 5-2.26

Sundbusserne Sverige AB, Case Comp/A.36.568/D3 [2006] 4 CMLR 22. . . . . 1-2.31

UK Tractors Information Agreement 92/157 [1992] OJ L68/19 . . . . 1-2.17

Virgin/British Airways, Commission Decision 2000/74 [2000] OJ L30/ 1-2.24, 1-2.48–1-2.51

Wood Pulp 85/202 [1985] OJ L85/1 . . . . 5-2.13

X/Open Group, Commission Decision 87/69 [1987] OJ L35/36 . . . . 1-2.16

Court of First Instance

Airtours plc v Commission, Case T-342/99 [2002] ECR II-2585, [2002] 5 CMLR 7 . . . . 1-2.39

British Airways plc v Commission, Case T-219/99 [2004] 3 CMLR 19. . . . . 1-2.24

European Night Services v Commission, Joined Cases T-374/94 etc [1998] ECR II-3141 . . . . 1-2.45

Gencor Ltd v Commission, Case T-102/96 [1999] ECR II-753, [1999] 4 CMLR 971. . . . 1-2.43

Independent Music Publishers and Labels Association (Impala) v Commission [2006] 5 CMLR 19. . . . . 1-2.39

Metropole Television (M6) v Commission, Case T-112/99 [2001] ECR II-2459. . . . . 1-2.10

Microsoft Corporation v Commission, Case T-201/04 [2005] 4 CMLR 28. . . . . . 1-2.32, 5-2.29

Tetra Pak Rausing SA v Commission, Case T-51/89 [1991] 4 CMLR 334. . . . . 1-2.01

Court of Justice

A. Ahlström Oy v Commission, Cases C-89, 104, 114, 116, 117 and 125-129/85 [1993] 4 CMLR 407. . . . . 1-2.08, 5-2.13

AKZO Chemie BV v Commission, Case C-62/86 [1993] 5 CMLR 215 . . . . 1-2.24, 1-2.30

Establissements Consten Sarl and Grundig-Verkaufs, GmbH v Commission, Cases 56, 58/64 [1966]1 CMLR 418 . . . . 1-2.19
Hoffmann-La Roche & Co AG v Commission, Case 85/76 [1979] 3 CMLR 211 . . . . 1-2.22, 1-2.24, 1-2.26
ICI v Commission, Case 48/69 [1972] 1 CMLR 557 . . . . 1-2.07
IMS Health GmbH & Co OHG v NDC Health GmbH & Co KG, Case C-418/02 [2004] 4 CMLR 28 . . . . 1-2.32
Nederlandsche Banden-Industrie Michelin NV v Commission, Case 322/81 [1985] 1 CMLR 282 . . . . 1-2.26
Oscar Bronner GmbH & Co KG v Mediaprint Zeitungs-und-Seitschriftenverlag GmbH & Co KG, Case C-7/97 . . . . 1-2.32, 5-3.11
Radio Telefis Eireann and Independent Television Publications Ltd v Commission, Cases C-241-242/91P [1995] 4 CMLR 718. . . . . 1-2.32
Tetra Pak v Commission (no 2), Case C-333/94P [1997] 4 CMLR 662. . . . . 1-2.29
Coöumnlautperatieve Vereniging 'Suiker Unie' UA v Commission, Cases 40-48/73, 50/73, 54-56/73, 111/73, 113-114/73 [1976] 1 CMLR 295 . . . . 1-2.07
United Brands Continental BV v Commission, Case 27/76 [1978] ECR 207, [1978] 1 CMLR 429. . . . . 1-2.21, 1-2.22, 1-2.30, 1-2.31, 1-2.32, 5-3.14

KOREA

Fair Trade Commission

Beckton Dickinson Korea Holding Inc/Shindongbang Medical Co, Decision 2000-38. . . . . 5-4.30, 5-4.53
Decision of 4 June 2008, KFTC Newsletter, 4 July 2008 . . . . 5-2.30
Decision of 30 April 2008, KFTC Newsletter, 4 July 2008 . . . . 5-2.14
Decision 2002-07, 4 April 2002 . . . . 5-1.10
Decision 2003-098, 29 April 2003 . . . . 5-1.12
Decision 2005-080, 24 June 2005 . . . . 5-2.18
Decision 2005-129, 18 August 2005. . . . . 1-1.31
Decision 2005-161, 18 August 2005, KFTC News, 2005-9 . . . . 5-2.25
Decision 2005-163, 31 October 2005. . . . . 5-2.27
Decision 2005-232, 22 November 2005 . . . . 5-2.19
Decision 2005-331, 15 December 2005 . . . . 5-2.20
Decision 2006-042, 24 February 2006 . . . . 5-3.16
Decision 2007-281, 18 May 2007 . . . . 1-1.31
Decision 2007-351, 3 July 2007 . . . . 5-4.41
Decision 2007-504, 24 October 2007. . . . . 1-1.31
Decision 2008-57, 21 February 2008 . . . . 5-3.23
Decision 2008-079, 5 March 2008 . . . . 5-2.18
Decision 2008-137, 2 May 2008 . . . . 5-2.20
Decision 2008-215, 25 July 2008 . . . . 5-3.17
Delphinium Enterprise PTE Ltd/Hansol Co/Shinho Paper Co, Decision 98-269 . . . . 5-4.54
Eland Retail Co and KDF Ltd Distribution Co Ltd/Carrefour Korea, Decision 2000-38. . . . . 5-4.53
Gillette Co/Rocket Korea Co, Decision 98-282 . . . . 5-4.28, 5-4.55
Hite Beer Co/Jinro Distilling Co, Decision 2006-9. . . . . 5-4.24, 5-4.29, 5-4.45, 5-4.55
Hyundai Motor Co, Decision 2007-281, 18 May 2007. . . . . 5-3.06, 5-3.10
Incheon Steel Co/Sammi Steel Co, Decision 2000-151 . . . . 5-4.28, 5-4.30
INI Steel Co/Hyundai Hysco Co/Hanbo Steel Co, Decision 2004-285. . . . . 5-4.28
Intel, KFTC Newsletter, 4 July 2008. . . . . 5-2.29
Kia Motors/Asia Motors, Decision 99-43 . . . . 5-4.55
Kolon Industries Inc/Kohap Co Nylon Film, Decision 2003-018 . . . . 5-4.28, 5-4.53

Korea Customs Brokers Association v Fair Trade Commission,
2001*Du*175, 15 June 2001 . . . . . 5-2.23
Korea Oil Station Association (KOSA), KFTC News, 2005-10 . . . . . 5-2.04
Muhak Co/Daesun Distilling Co, Decision 2003-28 . . . . . 5-4.29, 5-4.52
Owens Corning/Saint-Gobain Vetrotex, 2008 Annual Report p 72 . . . . . 5-4.20, 5-4.34
P&G/Ssangyong Papers Co, Decision 98-84 . . . . . 5-4.53
POSCO/POSTEEL/Korea, 2008 Annual Report p 68 . . . . . 5-4.09, 5-4.49, 5-4.57
Samick Musical Instruments Co/Youngchang Piano Co, Decision 2004-271 . . . . . 5-4.28
SK Inc/DOPCO, Decision 2001-090 . . . . . 5-4.28
SK Telecom/Hanaro Telecom, Decision 2008-105, 13 March 2008 . . . . . 5-4.44, 5-4.54, 5-4.56
Songwon Co/Daehan Special Chemicals Co, Decision 82-24 . . . . . 5-4.52

Seoul High Court

Case 96*Gu*25137, 4 November 1997 . . . . . 5-3.25
Case 98*Nu*11214, 28 April 1999 . . . . . 5-2.12
Case 2000*Nu*3278, 17 May 2001 . . . . . 5-2.22
Case 2002*Nu*6127, 26 August 2003 . . . . . 5-1.11, 5-2.08, 5-2.21
Case 2003*Nu*9000 . . . . . 5-1.12
Case 2005/3174, decision of March 2006 . . . . . 5-4.28

Supreme Court of Korea

Daewoo Co Ltd v Fair Trade Commission, 2001*Du*2935, 14 October 2004 . . . . . 5-3.25
Decision 92*Nu*8040, 13 November 1992 . . . . . 5-1.09
Decision 98*Du*5849, 23 February 1999 . . . . . 5-2.03
Decision 99*Du*6514, 99*Du*6521, 15 March 2002 . . . . . 5-2.12
Decision 2002*Du*7456, 28 October 2004 . . . . . 5-2.09
DPK International, Decision 2000-163, 15 November 2000 . . . . . 5-2.30
General successor of Park Hwa-sam, supervisor for the reorganizing
stock company Mona Lisa v Fair Trade Commission, Decision 2000
*Du*1386, 28 May 2002 and 2000*Du*7872, 8 May 2001 . . . . . 5-2.03, 5-2.09
Han-Song Motors Corporation v Fair Trade Commission,
Decision 2000*Du*3184, 2 May 2002 . . . . . 5-2.29
Hyundai Information Technology Corporation v Fair Trade Commission,
Decision 99*Du*4686, 12 June 2001 . . . . . 5-3.27
Korean Medical Association Inc v Fair Trade Commission, Case 2001*Du*5347,
20 February 2003 . . . . . 5-2.22, 5-2.24, 5-5.15
Pasteur Dairy Industry Co v Fair Trade Commission,
Case 97*Nu*19427, 9 June 2000 . . . . . 5-3.25
POSCO v Korea Fair Trade Commission, Supreme Court of Korea,
Case 2002*Du*8626, 22 November 2007 . . . . . 5-1.01, 5-3.01, 5-3.04, 5-3.05,
5-3.12, 5-3.13, 5-3.14, 5-3.24, 5-3.27
Showa Denko KK v Korea Fair Trade Commission, Case 2004
*Du*11275, 24 March 2006, appeal from Seoul High Court,
2002*Nu*6127, 26 August 2003 . . . . . 5-1.11, 5-2.08, 5-2.21, 5-5.03, 5-5.19

TAIWAN

Board of Directors of the Tourist Bus Association of Taiwan Province,
TFTC Competition Policy Newsletter, 2:11, 30 April 2007 . . . . . 4-2.06
Bristol-Myers Squibb Australia Pty, TFTC Competition Policy Newsletter,
4:11, 31 August 2007 . . . . . 4-2.35
CD-R Patent Licensing Arrangements in Taiwan by Royal Philips Electronics,
Sony Corporation (Japan) and Taiyo Yuden Co Ltd (Japan),
20 April 2006 . . . . . 4-2.32, 4-3.09, 4-3.11

Chinese Petroleum Corporation, 7 March 2002 .... 4-3.08, 4-3.10
Citi Group Inc/Bank of Overseas Chinese, 24 May 2007 .... 4.29
Crown Ltd, 25 January 2007 .... 4-4.34
Domestic Airlines, 26 October 2006 .... 4-2.08
Domestic Ferry Operators, 16 November 2006 .... 4-2.08
Estar Cable TV Corporation, 14 June 2001 .... 4-4.34
Family Mart Co/Niko Mart, 23 August 2007 .... 4-4.29
Far Eastern Department Stores, 21 December 2006 .... 4-4.01
Far Eastern Telecommunications Co Ltd/Yuan Her Telecommunications Co Ltd/KG Telecommunication Co Ltd, 4 December 2003 .... 4-4.32
Great Taipei Gas Corp, 9 May 2000 .... 4-3.03, 4-3.09, 4-3.16, 4-5.10
Holiday Entertainment Co Ltd/Cashbox Partyworld Co Ltd, 8 March 2007 ..... 4-4.24, 4-4.35
Holiday Group Co/Young Sound Multimedia Co, 29 July 2004 .... 4-4.39
Holiday Limited Co/Cashbox Party World Karaoke Parlours, 3 July 2003 .... 4-4.42
Intel Corp/TXC Corp, 11 March 1998 .... 4-4.12
King Cable TV and Everlasting Cable TV, TFTC Competition Policy Newsletter, 3:10, 30 June 2006 .... 4-2.07
Lite-On Technology Corporation/Lite-On Enclosure Inc, 16 October 2003 .... 4-4.32
Lockheed Martin Corporation/Northrop Grumman Corp, 5 November 1997 .... 4-4.12
Nanyi Bookstore, 25 September 1999 .... 4-5.28
National Petroleum Corporation, 13 September 2007 .... 4-4.01
Nestlé Corp/Borden Corp, 18 March 1998 .... 4-4.12
Non-Life Assurance Association of the ROC, 25 January 2007, TFTC Competition Policy Newsletter, 2:11, 30 April 2007 .... 4-2.06
Sin Tai Bei Cable System Co Ltd/Li Guan Cable System Co Ltd. Da An Wen Shan Cable System Co Ltd/Wan Hsiang Cable System Co Ltd, 1 April 2004 .... 4-4.01, 4-4.35
Taipei County Jewellers' Association, TFTC Competition Policy Newsletter, 3:11, 30 June 2007 .... 4-2.06
Taiwan Broadband Communication Consultant Co, 18 August 1999 .... 4-4.24
Taiwan Mobile Co/Taiwan Fixed Network/Tai-Hsin International Telecommunications Co Ltd, 12 April 2007 .... 4-4.25
Taiwan Salt Industrial Co Ltd, 18 January 2007, TFTC Competition Policy Newsletter, 2:11, 30 April 2007 .... 4-2.35
Tyco International Ltd/CIT Group Inc, 31 May 2001 .... 4-4.06
Uni-President Enterprises Corporation, Wei Chuan Corp and Kuang Chuan Dairy Co Ltd, TFTC Competition Policy Newsletter, 5:11, 31 October 2007 .... 4-2.40, 4-4.01, 4-4.42
United Daily News/Economic Daily News/Min Sheng News/ United Evening News/Star News, 19 May 2005 .... 4-4.10
Wen Chiu Inc/China Petroleum Corporation, 12 October 2000 .... 4-3.08, 4-3.14
Yahoo! Taiwan Inc/Wretch, 29 March 2007 .... 4-4.07, 4-4.10, 4-4.42

UNITED KINGDOM

Napp Pharmaceutical Holdings Ltd v Director General of Fair Trading [2002] Comp AR 13 .... 5.11
Net Book Agreement, 1957, Re [1962] 3 All ER 751 .... 5-2.26
Net Book Agreement, 1957 (M and N), Re [1997] LS Gaz R 29 .... 5-2.26

UNITED STATES

Aspen Skiing Co v Aspen Highlands Skiing Corp 105 S.Ct. 2847 (1985) 1-2.32
BF Goodrich Co 110 FTC 207 (1988) 1-2.39

Broadway Delivery Corp v United Parcel Service of America Inc
651 F.2d 122 (2d Cir.) 102 S Ct 512 (1981) 1-2.24
Brooke Group Ltd v Brown & Williamson Tobacco Corp 113 S Ct 2578 (1993). 1-2.27
Chicago Board of Trade v United States (1918) 246 US 231 . . . . 1-2.10
Interstate Circuit v United States 306 US 208 (1939) 1-2.08
Leegin Creative Leather Products, Inc v PSKS, Inc 127 S.Ct 2705 (2007) 1-2.18
Matsushita Electric Industrial Co v Zenith Radio Corp 475 US 574 (1986) 1-2.08, 1-2.26
Richards v Neilsen Freight Lines 810 F.2d 904 (9th Cir, 1987) 1-2.08
Souza v Estate of Bishop 821 F.2d 1332 (9th Cir, 1987) 1-2.08
Spectrum Sports Inc v McQuillan 506 US 447 (1993) 1-2.25
Standard Oil Co of New Jersey v United States (1911) 221 US 1 . . . . 1-2.10
United States v Colgate & Co 39 S.Ct. 465 (1919) 1-2.32
United States v El DuPont de Nemours & Co 351 US 377 . . . . 1-2.22, 1-2.48
United States v Grinnell Corp 384 US 563 (1966) 1-2.25
United States v United States Gypsum Co 438 US 422 (1978) 1-2.17
Valley Liquors v Renfield Importers 822 F.2d 656, 108 S Ct 488 (1987) 1-2.24
Verizon Communications Inc, v Law Office of Curtis v
Trinko LLP 124 S.Ct 872 (2004) 1-2.21, 1-2.31, 1-2.32

TABLE OF LEGISLATION

China	xxix
European Community	xxxi
Germany	xxxii
Hong Kong	xxxii
Korea	xxxii
Taiwan	xxxiv
United Kingdom	xxxvi
United States	xxxvi
Vietnam	xxxvi

CHINA

Administrative Litigation Law 1989 . . . . 2-5.16
Administrative Measures on Organizational Structure of Administrative Organs of the State Council 1997
  art 6 . . . . 2-1.09
  art 10 . . . . 2-1.09
Administrative Review Law. 2-5.16
Anti-dumping Regulation 2001 . . . . . 1-1.09
Anti-Monopoly Law 2008 . . . App. 1, 1-1.06, 1-1.07, 1-1.09, 1-1.10, 1-1.11, 1-1.13, 1-1.14, 1-1.15, 1-2.14, 2-2.02, 2-1.02, 2-1.03, 2-1.08, 2-2.08, 2-1.09, 2-1.10, 2-1.11, 2-1.13, 2-1.15, 2-1.16, 2-1.18, 2-1.22, 2-1.24, 2-3.10, 2-3.11, 2-4.01, 2-4.10, 2-4.19, 2-4.20, 2-5.04, 2-5.09, 2-5.10, 2-5.17, 2-5.18, 2-5.21, 3-1.01
  chap II 2-2.01
  chap III 1-1.05, 2-3.01
  chap IV 1-1.0, 2-4.10, 2-4.14, 2-4.23
  chap V 1-1.05, 2-1.16, 2-3.01, 2-3.10
  chap VI 2-5.01
  chap VII. 2-5.01, 2-5.08
  art 1 . . . . . . 1-2.01, 1-1.06, 2-1.05, 2-1.06
  art 2 . . . . . . 1-1.12, 2-1.19, 2-3.02, 2-4.10
  art 3 . . . . 2-1.06
  art 4 . . . . 2-1.04
  art 5 . . . . 2-4.02
  art 7 . . . . 1-1.12, 2-1.16
  art 9 . . . . 2-1.09
  art 10 . . . . 2-1.13
  art 11 . . . . .2.04
  art 12 . . . . 2-1.07, 2-3.03
  art 13 . . . . .1-1.05, 2-2.02, 2-2.03, 2-2.06, 2-2.07
  art 14 . . . . . 1-1.05, 2-2.03, 2-2.06, 2-2.07
  art 14(1). 2-2.03
  art 14(2). 2-2.03
  art 15 . . . . 2-2.05
  art 16 . . . . 2-2.04
  art 17 . . . . 2-3.02, 2-3.06
  art 17(1). 2-3.08
  art 17(2). 2-3.02
  art 17(7). 2-3.06
  art 18 . . . . 2-3.04
  art 18(6). 2-3.04
  art 19 . . . . 2-3.02
  art 19(3). 2-3.05
  art 20 . . . . 2-4.03
  art 21 . . . . 2-4.03, 2-4.05
  art 22(1). 2-4.03
  art 22(2). 2-4.03
  art 23 . . . . 2-4.13
  art 24 . . . . 2-4.13
  art 25 . . . . 2-4.14
  art 26 . . . . 2-4.14, 2-4.15
  art 27 . . . . 2-4.18
  art 28 . . . . .2-4.02, 2-4.18, 2-4.21, 2-5.15

Anti-Monopoly Law 2008 (*cont.*)
art 29 . . . . 2-4.15, 2-4.22, 2-5.15
art 30 . . . . 2-1.15, 2-4.15
art 31 . . . . 2-4.10, 2-4.20
art 32 . . . . 2-3.10, 2-3.11
art 33 . . . . 2-3.10, 2-3.12
art 34 . . . . 2-3.10, 2-3.13
art 35 . . . . 2-3.10, 2-3.13
art 36 . . . . 2-3.10, 2-3.13
art 37 . . . . 2-3.10, 2-3.13
art 38 . . . . 2-5.02, 2-5.07
art 39 . . . . 2-5.03
art 41 . . . . 2-5.06
art 42 . . . . 2-5.05
art 43 . . . . 5.04
art 44 . . . . 2-5.08
art 45 . . . . 2-5.09
art 46 . . . . 2-2.09, 2-5.08, 2-5.10, 2-5.11, 2-5.12, 2-5.13
art 47 . . . . 2-5.08, 5.10, 2-5.13
art 48 . . . . . 2-4.22, 2-4.23, 2-5.10, 2-5.14
art 49 . . . . 2-5.10
art 50 . . . . 2-5.18
art 51 . . . . 2-1.16, 2-3.15
art 52 . . . . 2-5.05
art 53 . . . . 2-5.15
art 54 . . . . 2-5.06
art 55 . . . . 2-2.03, 2-1.17, 2-3.09, 4-3.09
art 56 . . . . 2-1.18
Bidding Law 1999 . . . . 1-1.09
art 2 . . . . 2-2.02
art 5 . . . . 2-2.03
art 6 . . . . 2-2.03
art 32 . . . . 2-2.03
Circular on Issues Related to Transferring State-owned Shares and Institutional Shares of Listed Companies to Foreign Investors 2002 . . . . 1-1.09
Circular on Key Points of Filing Procedures in Listed Companies Transferring State-owned Shares to Foreign Investors and Foreign Invested Enterprises 2004. . . . . 1-1.09
Civil Aviation Law 1995 . . . . 1-1.09
Commercial Bank Law 1995. . . . . 1-1.09
Company Law 1993 . . . . 1-1.09
Company Law 2005 . . . . 2-4.04
art 217(2) 2-4.04
art 217(3) 2-4.04
Constitution
art 15 . . . . 1-1.06
art 123 . . . . 2-5.18
Consumer Protection Law 1993 . . . . . 1-1.09
Contract Law 1999
art 52 . . . . 2-2.01
art 329 . . . . 2-3.09
Countervailing Regulation 2001. . . . . 1-1.09
Electric Power Law 1995. . . . . 1-1.09
Foreign Trade Law 1994 . . . . 1-1.09
Government Procurement Law 2002 . 1-1.09
Highway Law 1997 . . . . 1-1.09
Insurance Law 1995 . . . . 1-1.09
Interim Measures Governing National Hi-Tech Industry Development Projects 2006 . . . . 1-1.09, 1-1.15
Interim Measures for the Management of the Service Price of Commercial Banks 2003 . . . . . . 1-1.09
Interim Provision Concerning the Banning of Conspiracies in Bid Rigging 2-2.02
Interim Provisions on Mergers and Acquisitions of Domestic Enterprises by Foreign Investors 2003 . . . . 1-1.09
Interim Provisions on Preventing the Activities of Price Monopoly 2003 . . . . 1-1.09
Interim Provisions on State-owned Enterprises' Utilising of Foreign Investment for Reorganising 1998 . . . . 1-1.09
Law on Chinese-Foreign Contractual Joint Ventures 1988 . . . . 1-1.09
Law on Chinese-Foreign Equity Joint Ventures 1979 . . . . 1-1.09
Law for Countering Unfair Competition 1993 . . . . 1-1.09, 1-1.10, 2-1.24, 2-3.06
art 6 . . . . 2-1.23
art 11 . . . . 2-3.06
art 12 . . . . 2-3.06
art 15 . . . . 2-2.02, 2-1.23
art 23 . . . . 2-1.23
art 27 . . . . 2-2.02
Law on Foreign-capital Enterprises 1986. . . . . 1-1.09
Law on Invitation and Submission of Bids 1999 . . . . 1-1.09
Law on Promoting Small and Medium-Sized Enterprises 2002. . . . . . . 1-1.09, 1-1.15
Measures on the Takeover of Listed Companies 2006 . . . . 1-1.09

Patent Law 1984 . . . . 1-1.09
Postal Law 1986 . . . . 1-1.09
Price Law 1997 . . . . . . 1-1.09, 2-1.02, 2-3.06
art 3 . . . . 1-1.09
art 14 . . . . 1-1.09, 2-2.02
art 14(2) 2-3.06
art 14(5) 2-3.06
art 40 . . . . 1-1.09
Provision Concerning the Administrative Punishment for Illegal Pricing Act 1999 . . . . 2-3.06
Provisional Merger and Acquisition Rules, March 2003 . . . . 2-1.02
Provisional Regulation Concerning the Development and Protection of Socialist Competition Mechanism 1980 . . . . 1-1.09
Provisions on Administrative Punishment against Price Violation Activities 1999 . . . . 1-1.09
Provisions on the Establishment of Investment Companies by Foreign Investors 2004 . . . . 1-1.09
Railway Law 1990 . . . . 1-1.09
Regulation on the Administration of Insurance Companies with Foreign Investment 2001 . . . . . . 1-1.09
Regulation of Price of Manufacturing Material 1987 . . . . 1-1.09
Regulation on Telecommunication Industry 2000 . . . . 1-1.09
Regulations on the Administration of Financial Institutions with Foreign Investment 2001 . . . . . . 1-1.09
Securities Law 1998 . . . . 1-1.09
State Council Provision on Prohibiting Regional Blockade in Market Economic Activities 2001 . . . . . . 1-1.09
State Decree No 529 . . . . 2-4.10
art 3 . . . . 2-4.05, 2-4.07
art 3(2) 2-4.06
art 4 . . . . 2-4.07
Supplementary Provisions to the Provisions on the Establishment of Investment Companies by Foreign Investors 2004 . . . . 1-1.09
Tang Code
art 33 . . . . 1-1.06

EUROPEAN COMMUNITY

Notices, Agreements and Guidelines

Guidelines on Vertical Restraints [2000] OJ C29/1 . . . . 1-2.20
Notice on the Definition of the Relevant Market for the purposes of Community competition law [1997] OJ C372/5 . . . . 1-2.46, 1-2.47
Notice on Immunity from Fines and Reduction of Fines in Cartel Cases [2006] OJ C298/17 . . . . 1-2.15

Regulations

Regulation 4064/89 on the control of concentrations between undertakings [1989] OJ L395/1
art 2(2) 1-2.37
Regulation 2658/2000 on the application of art 81(3) of the Treaty to categories of specialisation agreements [2000] OJ L304/3 . . . . 1-2.16
Regulation 2659/2000 on the application of art 81(3) of the Treaty to categories of research and development agreements [2000] OJ L304/7 . . . . 1-2.16
Regulation 1/2003 on the implementation of the rules on competition laid down in Articles 81 and 82 of the Treaty OJ 2003 L1/1 . . . . 1-2.11, 2-5.03
Regulation 139/2004 on the control of concentrations between undertakings [2004] OJ L24/1 . . . . 1-2.38, 1-2.41
art 1(2) 1-2.37
art 1(3) 1-2.37
Regulation 772/2004 on the application of Article 81(3) of the Treaty to categories of technology transfer agreement [2004] OJ L123/11
art 2 . . . . 1-2.20
art 3 . . . . 1-2.20

Treaties

arts 28–30 . . . . 2-3.10
EC Treaty 1-2.21
art 81 . . . . 1-2.04, 1-2.06, 1-2.08, 1-2.09, 1-2.10, 1-2.14, 2-1.01, 2-2.07, 2-1.19, 5-2.01, 5-2.04, 5-2.26
art 81(1) 1-2.04, 1-2.10, 1-2.11, 1-2.13, 1-2.16, 1-2.18, 4-2.17
art 81(1)(c) 2-2.02
art 81(2) 1-2.04, 1-2.10

EC Treaty (*cont.*)
art 81(3) 1-2.04, 1-2.10, 1-2.11, 1-2.12, 1-2.13, 1-2.20, 2-2.05
art 82 . . . . 1-2.21, 1-2.22, 1-2.28, 1-2.30, 1-2.34, 2-1.19, 2-3.06, 2-3.07, 4-3.07, 4-3.09
art 82(c) 1-2.30, 1-2.31, 2-3.06
art 82(d) 1-2.34

GERMANY

Act Against restraints of Competition
s 3 . . . . 2-2.07

HONG KONG

Broadcasting Ordinance 1-1.16
Telecommunications Ordinance 1-1.16

KOREA

Banking Act 5-4.01
Civil Act
art 750 . . . . 5-5.28
Constitution
art 119 . . . . 5-3.13
art 119(1) 5-1.01
art 119(2) 5-1.01
Copyright Act 5-1.09
Design Act 5-1.09
Enforcement Decree of the Monopoly Regulation and Fair Trade Act 1980 . . . . 5-1.03, 5-5.21
art 5 . . . . 5-3.08
art 5(3) 5-3.11
art 5(4) 5-3.11
art 11 . . . . 5-4.16, 5-4.53
art 12(3) 5-4.06
art 12 . . . . 5-4.10
art 12–2 . . . . 5-4.06
art 12–4 . . . . 5-4.02
art 18 . . . . 5-4.10, 5-4.11
art 18(3) 5-4.11
art 35(1)(5) 5-5.21
art 65 . . . . 5-4.14
art 65(3) 5-4.14
Fair Franchise Transactions Act 2002, amended by Law 8630, 3 August 2007 . . . . 5-1.05, 5-2.34, 5-2.38, 5-3.29, 5-5.29
chap 2 . . . . 5-2.36
art 1 . . . . 5-1.05
art 2(1) 5-2.35
art 2(2) 5-2.35
art 2(3) 5-2.35
art 4 . . . . 5-2.36
art 5 . . . . 5-2.36
art 5(6) 5-2.36
art 6 . . . . 5-2.36
art 6(11) 5-2.36
art 12 . . . . 5-2.36
art 12(1) 5-2.37
art 23 . . . . 5-2.36
art 23(1) 5-2.36
art 23(3) 5-2.36
art 23(4) 5-2.36
art 23(5) 5-2.36
art 33 . . . . 5-2.37
art 38 . . . . 5-2.36
Fair Subcontract Transactions Act 1984 . . . . 1-1.29
Government Organization Act
art 2 . . . . 5-1.06
Indirect Investment Act 5-4.13
Korea Technology Credit Guarantee Fund Act 5-4.13
Legal Person Tax Act 5-4.13
Leniency Programme Notification 5.21
art 5 . . . . 5-5.22
art 6(2) 5-5.21
Medical Service Act
art 2(4) 5-2.22
Monopoly Regulation and Fair Trade Act 1980 . . . . App. 3, 1.09, 1-1.26, 1-1.29, 1-1.30, 1-1.31, 1-2.30, 5-1.01, 5-1.03, 5-1.04, 5-1.05, 5-1.06, 5-1.07, 5-1.10, 5-2.01, 5-2.04, 5-2.21, 5-3.01, 5-3.02, 5-4.01, 5-4.08, 5-4.20, 5-5.08, 5-5.13
chap 1 . . . . 5-1.02
chap 2 . . . . 1-1.05, 5-1.02, 5-3.02, 5-3.04, 5-3.05
chap 3 . . . . 5-1.02
chap 4 . . . . 1-1.05, 5-1.02, 5-2.01, 5-2.02–5-2.21, 5-2.17
chap 5 . . . . 1-1.05, 5-1.02, 5-2.01, 5-2.16, 5-3.02, 5-3.24
chap 6 . . . . 1-1.05, 5-1.02, 5-2.01, 5-2.22, 5-2.25, 5-3.02
chap 7 . . . . 1-1.05, 5-1.02, 5-2.01, 5-2.26, 5-2.27
chap 8 . . . . 1-1.05, 5-1.02, 5-2.28
chap 9–2 . . . . 5-1.02
chap 10–2 . . . . 5-5.17
chap 11 . . . . 5-1.02

art 1 . . . . 1-1.26, 5-1.01
art 1(1). 5-2.06
art 2 . . . . 5-1.11
art 2(1). 5-1.04
art 2(1)(7) 5-4.06
art 2(4). 5-2.22
art 2(6). 5-2.26
art 2(7). 5-3.05
art 2(8). 5-3.05
art 2–2 . . . . 5-1.10
art 3 . . . . 5-3.03
art 3–2 . . . . .5-2.29, 5-3.04, 5-3.19, 5-3.20, 5-5.20
art 3–2(1)(1) 5-3.08
art 3–2(1)(2) 5-3.09
art 3–2(1)(3) 5-3.08, 5-3.10, 5-3.11, 5-3.12, 5-3.13, 5-3.14
art 3–2(1)(4) 5-3.15
art 3–2(1)(5) 5-3.15, 5-3.16, 5-3.17
art 3–2(2). 5-3.08
art 3–2(4). 5-3.14
art 4 . . . . .5-3.04, 5-3.05, 5-3.17, 5-4.06
art 5 . . . . 5-3.04, 5-3.19
art 5–6(2). 5-5.28
art 6 . . . . 5-3.04, 5-3.19
art 7 . . . . 5-4.02, 5-4.03
art 7(1). 5-4.02, 5-4.09, 5-4.21, 5-5.20
art 7(1)(3) 5-4.10
art 7(1)(5)(a) 5-4.16
art 7(1)(5)(b) 5-4.16
art 7(2). 5-4.02, 5-4.46
art 7(2)(1) 5-4.46
art 7(2)(2) 5-4.02, 5-4.49
art 7(3). 5-5.20
art 7(4). 5-4.06, 5-4.34
art 7(4)(1)(1)(a) 5-4.34
art 7(4)(1)(1)(b) 5-4.34
art 7(4)(1)(1)(c) 5-4.34
art 7–2 . . . . 5-4.02
art 8–2(2). 5-5.20
art 8–2(3). 5-5.20
art 8–2(5). 5-5.20
art 9 . . . . 5-5.20
art 10(1). 5-5.20
art 10–2(1). 5-5.20
art 12 . . . . 5-4.10, 5-4.20
art 12(1). 5-4.10
art 12(1)(1) 5-4.10
art 12(1)(1)–(5) 5-4.10
art 12(2). 5-4.10
art 12(3). 5-4.13
art 12(3)(1) 5-4.13
art 12(3)(2) 5-4.13
art 12(3)(3) 5-4.13
art 12(6). 5-4.09, 5-4.13, 5-4.18
art 12(7). 5-4.18
art 12(8). 5-4.09, 5-4.41
art 12(9). 5-4.09
art 12–2 . . . . 5-4.10
art 16 . . . . 5-4.21, 5-4.50
art 16(1). 5-4.50
art 16(1)(8) 5-4.21
art 16(2). 5-4.21, 5-4.50
art 19 . . . . .5-2.04, 5-2.09, 5-2.11, 5-2.29, 5-2.31
art 19(1). 5-2.02, 5-2.03, 5-2.23, 5-2.31, 5-5.20
art 19(1)(8) 5-2.14
art 19(2). 5-2.04, 5-2.23
art 19(3). 5-2.23
art 19(5). 5-2.07, 5-2.09
art 19–2 . . . . 5-2.14
art 21 . . . . 5-2.31
art 22 . . . . 5-2.31
art 22–2 . . . . 5-2.31
art 22–2(2). 5-2.31
art 23 . . . . .5-2.29, 5-2.30, 5-2.36, 5-3.20, 5-3.24, 5-3.25
art 23(1). 5-2.23, 5-2.29, 5-2.36, 5-3.28, 5-3.29, 5-5.20, 5-5.29
art 23(1)(1) 5-3.13, 5-3.27
art 23(1)(1)–(5) 5-3.28
art 23(1)(2) 5-3.27
art 23(1)(7) 5-3.25, 5-3.28, 5-5.07
art 23(1)(8) 5-3.25
art 23(4). 5-2.36, 5-3.26
art 23(5). 5-2.29, 5-2.36, 5-3.26
art 24 . . . . 5-3.28, 5-5.29
art 26 . . . . 5-2.23
art 26(2). 5-2.23
art 26(3). 5-2.23, 5-2.24
art 27 . . . . 5-2.24
art 28 . . . . 5-2.24
art 29(1). 5-2.26, 5-2.36, 5-5.20
art 29(2). 5-2.26
art 29(3). 5-2.26
art 30 . . . . 5-2.26
art 31 . . . . 5-2.32
art 31–2 . . . . 5-2.32
art 32 . . . . 5-2.27, 5-2.28
art 32(1). 5-2.28, 5-2.33, 5-5.20
art 33 . . . . 5-2.28
art 34 . . . . 5-2.33
art 35 . . . . 5-1.06

Monopoly Regulation and
Fair Trade
Act 1980 (*cont.*)
art 35(1) 5-1.06
art 36(6) 5-1.06
art 36–2 . . . . 5-1.13
art 36–2(1) 5-1.13
art 36–2(2) 5-1.13
art 36–2(3) 5-1.13
art 37–3(1) 5-1.06
art 37(3) 5-1.06
art 43(1) 5-5.10
art 48–2 . . . . 5-3.29, 5-5.29
art 48–3 . . . . 5-5.29
art 48–6 . . . . 5-5.29
art 48–8 . . . . 5-5.29
art 49(1) 5-5.04
art 49(2) 5-5.04, 5-5.11
art 49(3) 5-5.11
art 49(4) 5-5.04
art 50 . . . . 5-5.04
art 50(1)(1) 5-5.05
art 50(1)(2) 5-5.04
art 50(1)(3) 5-5.04
art 50(2) 5-5.05
art 50(3) 5-5.05
art 50(4) 5-5.05
art 50(5) 5-5.07
art 50(6) 5-5.07
art 50–2 . . . . 5-5.04
art 50–3 . . . . 5-5.08
art 51 . . . . 5-5.13, 5-5.29
art 52 . . . . 5-5.08
art 52(2) 5-5.09
art 52–2 . . . . 5-5.10
art 53–2 . . . . 5-5.25
art 53–2(2) 5-5.25
art 53 . . . . 5-1.06, 5-5.11, 5-5.24
art 53(2) 5-5.24
art 54 . . . . 5-5.26
art 55–3 . . . . 5-5.17
art 55–3(2) 5-5.17
art 55–4 . . . . 5-5.18
art 55–4(1)(2) 5-5.18
art 55–6 . . . . 5-5.18
art 55–7 . . . . 5-5.26
art 56(1) 5-5.28, 5-5.29
art 56–2 . . . . 5-5.28
art 57 . . . . 5-5.28
art 57(1) 5-5.28
art 59 . . . . 5-1.09
art 62 . . . . 5-5.10
art 63 . . . . 5-1.07
art 64(1) 5-5.07
art 64(2) 5-5.07
art 64(3) 5-5.13
art 64-2 . . . . 5-5.12
art 66 . . . . 5-5.20
art 67 . . . . 5-5.20
art 67(6) 5-3.19
art 69(1) 5-5.07
art 69(2) 5-5.10
art 69–2 . . . . 5-4.14
art 71 . . . . 5-5.20
Monopoly Regulation and Price
Stability Act 1975 . . . . 1-1.26
Patent Act 5-1.09
Price Stabilisation Act 1973 . . . . 1-1.26
Private Investment for
Infrastructure Act 5-4.13
Real Estate Investment Act 5-4.13
Securities and Exchange Act 5-4.10
Specialized Credit Financial
Business Act 5-4.13
Support for Small and Medium Enterprise
Establishment Act 5-4.13
Telecommunications Business Act 5-4.01
Trademark Act 5-1.09
Utility Models Act 5-1.09

TAIWAN

Administrative Procedure Law 4-5.31
chap 1, s 10 . . . . 4-5.15
Business Organizations Law 4-2.19
Code of Civil Procedure 4-1.15, 4-5.37
Company Law
art 167(1) 4-4.06
Consumer Protection Law 1994 . . . . . 4-5.32
Copyright Law 4-2.25
Criminal Code 4-2.37
art 304 . . . . 4-2.36
Enforcement Rules to the Fair
Trade Act 4-2.10, 4-2.11,
4-3.02, 4-4.01
art 3 . . . . 4-3.06
art 4 . . . . 4-3.06
art 6 . . . . 4-4.08
art 7 . . . . 4-4.14
art 8 . . . . 4-4.17
art 9 . . . . 4-4.17
art 10 . . . . 4-4.06
art 11 . . . . 4-4.17
art 12 . . . . 4-4.17
art 14(1) 4-2.10
art 16 . . . . 4-2.11
art 17 . . . . 4-2.12
art 18 . . . . 4-2.13

art 19 . . . . 4-2.14
art 20 . . . . 4-2.15
art 21 . . . . 4-2.16
art 23 . . . . 4-2.17
art 24 . . . . 4-2.10
art 26 . . . . 4-2.36
art 27 . . . . 4-2.36
art 30 . . . . 4-5.11
art 31(2). 4-5.05
art 32 . . . . 4-5.05
art 33 . . . . 4-5.05
art 34 . . . . 4-5.06
art 35 . . . . 4-5.06
art 36 . . . . 4-5.27

Fair Trade Act 2002 . . . . .App. 2, 1-1.05, 1-1.24, 1-1.25, 4-1.01, 4-2.21, 4-4.11, 4-4.43, 4-5.01, 6-2.11
chap I. 4-1.02
chap II 4-1.02
chap III 1-1.05, 4-1.02, 4-2.01, 4-2.21, 4-2.33, 4-2.34
chap IV 4-1.02, 4-5.01
chap V 4-1.02, 4-5.02
chap VI 4-1.02, 4-5.02
art 1 . . . . 1-1.24, 4-1.02
arts 1–9 . . . . 4-1.02
art 2 . . . . 4-1.03, 4-4.02
art 3 . . . . 4-3.06
art 4 . . . . 4-1.04
art 5 . . . . 4-3.02, 4-3.03, 4-3.04
art 5–1 . . . . 4-3.02, 4-3.03, 4-3.04, 4-3.05
art 6 . . . . 4-4.01
art 6(1). 4-4.11
art 6(1)(4) 4-4.01
art 6(2). 4-4.01
art 7 . . . . 4-2.03, 4-2.36
art 8 . . . . 4-2.22, 4-4.15
art 10 . . . . .1-1.05, 4-2.32, 4-3.01, 4-3.07, 4-3.10, 4-3.13, 4-3.16, 4-5.15, 4-5.21, 4-5.25
arts 10–17 . . . . 4-1.02
art 10(1). 4-3.14
art 10(2). 3.10, 4-3.16
art 10(4). 4-3.07, 4-3.08, 4-3.11
art 11 . . . . 4-4.06, 4-4.14, 4-4.38
arts 11–13 . . . . 1-1.05, 4-4.01
art 11(1). 4-4.39, 4-4.40, 4-5.15
art 11(1)(3) 4-4.08
art 11(3). 4-4.17, 4-4.39, 4-4.40, 4-5.15
art 11(5). 4-4.17
art 11(5)(2) 4-4.39
art 11–1 . . . . 4-4.06
art 12 . . . . 4-4.20, 4-4.32, 4-5.15
art 13 . . . . 4-4.38, 4-4.39, 4-4.40
arts 13–25 . . . . .4-2.10, 4-2.11, 4-2.34, 4-3.02
art 14 . . . . .1-1.05, 1-2.09, 4-2.01, 4-2.08, 4-2.10, 4-2.20, 4-2.28, 4-2.32, 4-2.36, 4-5.15, 4-5.21, 4-5.25
art 14(1)(2) 4-2.12
art 14(1)(4) 4-2.13
art 14(1)(5) 4-2.14
art 14(1)(6) 4-2.15
art 14(1)(7) 4-2.16
art 14(2). 4-2.10, 4-2.12
art 16 . . . . 4-2.17
art 18 . . . . 4-2.08, 4-2.35
arts 18–24 . . . . 4-1.02
art 19 . . . . .4-2.08, 4-2.20, 4-2.30, 4-2.33, 4-2.36, 4-2.37, 4-5.21, 4-5.25
art 19(1)(iv) 4-2.29
art 19(1)(vi) 4-2.28
art 19(4). 4-2.36
art 19(5). 4-2.36
art 19(6). 4-2.36
art 20 . . . . 4-2.20
arts 20–22 . . . . 4-2.35
art 23 . . . . 4-2.22, 4-5.25
art 23–1 . . . . 4-2.23
art 23–1(2). 4-2.24
art 23–2 . . . . 4-2.23, 4-4.06
art 23–2(2). 4-2.24
art 23–3 4-23
art 23–3(2). 4-2.24
art 23–4 . . . . 4-2.22, 4-2.23
art 24 . . . . 4-2.22, 4-2.38, 4-2.40
art 25 . . . . 4-2.17, 4-5.01
arts 25–29 . . . . 4-1.02
art 25(3). 4-5.01
art 26 . . . . 4-5.03
art 27 . . . . . 4-1.14, 4-2.37, 4-5.07, 4-5.20
art 27(1). 4-5.03
art 27(1)(2) 4-5.03
art 27(1)(3) 4-5.03
art 27(2). 4-5.06, 4-5.07
art 28 . . . . 4-5.01
art 30 . . . . 4-4.43, 4-5.33
arts 30–34 . . . . 4-1.02, 4-5.33
art 31 . . . . 4-4.43, 4-5.33
art 32 . . . . 4-5.34
art 33 . . . . 4-5.35
art 34 . . . . 4-5.36
art 35 . . . . . 4-2.24, 4-2.41, 4-5.25, 4-5.26
arts 35–37 . . . . 4-5.21
arts 35–44 . . . . 4-1.02

Fair Trade Act 2002 (*cont.*)
art 36 . . . . 4-5.25, 4-5.26, 4-5.27
art 38 . . . . 4-5.26
art 40 . . . . 4-2.41, 4-5.23, 4-5.24
art 41 . . . . .4-3.12, 4-5.21, 4-5.22, 4-5.24, 4-5.25
art 42 . . . . 4-2.24, 4-5.24
art 42–1 . . . . 4-2.24
art 43 . . . . 4-5.08, 4-5.24
art 44 . . . . 4-5.25
art 45 . . . . 4-1.10
art 46 . . . . 4-1.09
art 47 . . . . . 4-1.11, 4-1.13, 4-2.25, 4-5.11
Financial Holding Company Law
art 4 . . . . 4-4.06
Financial Institution Merger Law
art 4 . . . . 4-4.06
Holiday Group Co/Young Sound Multimedia Co, 29 July 2004 . . . . 4-4.39
Industrial Organizations Law 4-2.19
Organic Statute of the Fair Trade Commission. 4-1.05
art 14 . . . . 4-1.07
Patent Law 4-2.24
Regulation Governing Access to Materials and Files of the Fair Trade Commission, Order 0910003769, 1 May 2002 . . . . . 4-5.20
art 3 . . . . 4-5.20
art 8 . . . . 4-5.20
art 9 . . . . 4-5.20
art 10 . . . . 4-5.20
Securities and Exchange Law
art 28–2 . . . . 4-4.06
Supervisory Regulations Governing Multi-Level Sales 4-2.23
chap 3 . . . . 4-2.23
art 11 . . . . 4-2.23
chap 4 . . . . 4-2.23
chap 5 . . . . 4-2.23
Telecommunications Law. 4-1.01
Trademark Law. 4-2.25

UNITED KINGDOM

Competition Act 1998 . . . . . . 2-2.02, 3-1.01
Enterprise Act 2002 . . . . 3-1.14

UNITED STATES

Clayton Act 1-2.38, 5-5.28
s 2a. 1-2.30
Federal Trade Commission Act
s 5 . . . . 5-2.29
Foreign Trade Antitrust Improvements Act 1982. . . . . 1-2.37, 2-1.19, 4-4.11
Robinson Patman Act 1936 . . . . 1-2.25, 1-2.30
s 2a. 1-2.30
Sherman Act 1890 . . . . .1-2.03, 1-2.21, 2-1.19
s 1 . . . . .1-2.04, 1-2.06, 1-2.09, 1-2.10, 1-2.13, 2-1.01, 2-2.07, 5-2.01
s 2 . . . . .1-2.03, 1-2.21, 1-2.22, 1-2.24, 1-2.25, 1-2.26, 1-2.32, 1-2.33, 1-2.34, 1-2.42, 2-1.01, 4-3.07
Webb-Pomerene Export Act 1914 . . . . 1-2.14, 4-2.09

VIETNAM

Civil Code
art 94 . . . . 6-4.01
art 95 . . . . 6-4.01
Company Law (1990). 6-4.01
Constitution
art 16 . . . . 1-1.32
Decree on Competition, 15 September 2005. . . . .6-1.05, 6-2.02, 6-3.12, 6-5.01
section 4. 6-3.08
art 4(2). 6-3.02
art 4(5)(c). 3.03
art 5 . . . . 6-3.03
art 6 . . . . 6-3.02, 6-3.03
art 7 . . . . 6-3.04
art 8 . . . . 6-3.04
arts 9–12 . . . . 6-3.06
art 13(2). 6-4.03
art 13(3). 6-4.03
art 14 . . . . 6-2.02
art 15 . . . . 6-2.02
art 16(1). 6-2.02
art 17(2). 6-2.02
art 18 . . . . 6-2.02
art 19 . . . . 6-2.02
art 22 . . . . 6-3.08
art 23 . . . . 6-3.11
arts 23–26 . . . . 6-3.11
art 23(2). 6-3.11
art 27 . . . . 6-3.11
art 27(2). 6-3.11
art 28(1). 6-3.11
art 28(2). 6-3.11
art 28(3). 6-3.11
art 29 . . . . 6-3.11
art 30 . . . . 6-3.11

art 31 . . . . 6-3.11
art 32 . . . . 6-3.13
art 33 . . . . 6-3.13
art 34 . . . . 6-4.02
art 35 . . . . 6-4.02
art 38 . . . . 6-2.11
art 40 . . . . 6-2.07, 6-4.05, 6-4.06
art 40(2). 6-4.05
art 41 . . . . 6-4.07
art 45 . . . . 6-5.21
art 48(1). 6-5.25
art 53 . . . . 6-5.03
art 68 . . . . 6-5.08
arts 69–73 . . . . 6-5.08
art 74(1). 6-5.21
art 75 . . . . 6-5.07
art 78(1). 6-5.10
art 78(2). 6-5.10
art 80 . . . . 6-5.14
art 85 . . . . 6-5.34
art 85(2). 6-2.06
art 88 . . . . 6-5.11
art 88(4). 6-5.11
arts 89–95 . . . . 6-5.11
art 94 . . . . 6-5.11
art 101 . . . . 6-5.19
arts 101–130 . . . . 6-5.19
Decree on Dealing with Breaches in the Competition Sector, 30 September 2005. . . . . .6-1.05, 6-5.01, 6-5.30
chap II 6-5.29
aet 29 . . . . 6-5.29
art 3(a) 6-5.02
art 4 . . . . 6-5.28
art 4(3). 6-5.28
art 4(4). 6-5.32
art 6 . . . . 6-5.35
art 6(1). 6-5.35
art 7 . . . . 6-5.29
art 9(2). 6-5.06
art 10(1). 6-5.29
art 10(2). 6-5.29
art 11(1). 6-5.29
art 11(2). 6-5.29
art 12(1). 6-5.29
art 12(2). 6-5.29
art 13(1). 6-5.29
art 13(2). 6-5.29
art 14(1). 6-5.29
art 14(2). 6-5.29
art 15(1). 6-5.29
art 15(2). 6-5.29
art 16(1). 6-5.29
art 16(2). 6-5.29
art 17(1). 6-5.29
art 17(2). 6-5.29
arts 18–23 . . . . 6-5.32
art 18(1). 6-5.29
art 18(2). 6-5.29
art 18(3). 6-5.29
art 19(1). 6-5.29
art 19(2). 6-5.29
art 19(3). 6-5.29
art 20(1). 6-5.29
art 20(2). 6-5.29
art 20(3). 6-5.29
art 20(4). 6-5.32
art 21(1). 6-5.29
art 21(2). 6-5.29
art 21(3). 6-5.29
art 22(1). 6-5.29
art 22(2). 6-5.29
art 22(3). 6-5.29
art 23(2). 6-5.29
art 23(3). 6-5.29
art 24 . . . . 6-5.29
art 24(2)(b) 6-5.32
art 25 . . . . 6-4.13
art 25(1). 6-5.29
art 25(2). 6-5.29
art 26(1). 6-5.29
art 26(2). 6-5.29
art 27 . . . . 6-4.13
art 27(1). 6-5.29
art 27(2). 6-5.29
art 28(1). 6-5.29
art 28(2). 6-5.29
art 32 . . . . 6-3.14
art 32(2). 6-3.14
art 34 . . . . 6-3.14
art 37 . . . . 6-2.05
art 39(1). 6-5.30
art 39(2). 6-5.30
art 41 . . . . 6-5.29
art 55 . . . . 6-5.33
art 56 . . . . 6-5.33
Decree on the establishment, functions, duties, powers and organizational structure of the Vietnam Competition Council, 9 January 2006. . . . . . . 6-1.05
Decree on functions, duties, powers and organizational structure of the Vietnam Competition Administration Department, 9 January 2006 . . . . 6-1.05, 6-1.20

Electricity Law (2004) 6-3.11
Enforcement Decree
art 3 . . . . 6-5.10
Law on Bankruptcy
art 36 . . . . 6-4.05
Law on Bidding (2005). 6-2.02
Law on Competition (2004) . . . . App. 4, 1-1.32, 1-1.34, 6-1.01, 6-1.02, 6-1.03, 6-1.04, 6-1.05, 6-1.06, 6-1.11, 6-1.12, 6-1.21, 6-2.11, 6-3.03, 6-3.14, 6-4.14, 6-5.06, 6-5.27, 6-5.29
chap 1 . . . . 6-1.03, 6-1.18
chap 2 . . . . 6-1.03
chap 2–2 . . . . 6-3.01
chap 2–3 . . . . 6-4.01
chap 2–4 . . . . 6-2.06
chap 3 . . . . 6-1.03
chap 4 . . . . 6-1.03
chap 5 . . . . 6-1.03
chap 5–7 . . . . 6-5.36
chap 6 . . . . 6-1.03
arts 1–7 . . . . 6-1.03
art 2 . . . . 6-1.06, 6-1.18
art 2(1). 6-4.15
art 2(2). 6-2.04
art 3(1). 6-3.02
art 3(2). 6-1.06
art 3(5). 6-2.03, 6-3.06
art 3(6). 6-2.03
art 3(7). 6-3.11
art 3(8). 6-5.01
art 3(10) 6-5.26
art 3(11). 6-2.11
art 4 . . . . 6-1.02
art 4(1). 6-1.01
art 4(2). 6-1.01, 6-1.02
art 4(3). 6-1.02
art 5(1). 6-1.15
art 5(2). 6-1.16
art 6 . . . . 6-1.17
art 6(3). 6-2.04
art 7 . . . . 6-1.08
art 7(2). 6-1.22
art 7(3). 6-1.08
art 8 . . . . 1-1.05, 6-2.01, 6-2.02
arts 8–38 . . . . 6-1.03
art 8(1). 6-2.02
art 8(1)-(5) 6-2.06
art 9(1). 6-2.03
art 9(2). 6-2.03
art 10 . . . . 6-2.03, 6-2.06
art 11 . . . . 6-3.08, 6-3.09
art 11(1). 6-3.06
art 11(2). 6-3.07
art 12 . . . . 6-3.09
art 13 . . . . . 1-1.05, 6-3.07, 6-3.10, 6-3.11
art 13(2). 6-3.10, 6-3.11
art 14 . . . . 1-1.05, 6-3.10
art 15 . . . . 6-1.06, 6-3.01, 6-3.15
art 16 . . . . 1-1.05, 6-4.01, 6-4.02
arts 16–24 . . . . 6-4.01
art 17 . . . . 6-4.08
art 17(1). 6-4.02
art 17(2). 6-4.02
art 17(3). 6-4.02
art 17(4). 6-4.02
art 18 . . . . 6-4.03, 6-4.10
art 19 . . . . 6-4.03, 6-4.05, 6-4.06
art 19(1). 6-4.05, 6-4.07
art 19(2). 6-4.05, 6-4.07, 6-5.36
art 20(1). 6-4.08
art 20(2). 6-4.06
art 21 . . . . 6-4.09
art 22 . . . . 6-4.09
art 23(2). 6-4.10
arts 25–38 . . . . 6-2.05
arts 25–39 . . . . 6-2.01
art 25(1). 6-2.07
art 26 . . . . 6-4.06
art 27 . . . . 6-2.07, 6-4.06
art 28 . . . . 6-2.07
art 28(2). 6-2.07
art 30 . . . . 6-4.06
art 30(2). 6-2.07
art 31 . . . . 6-4.06
art 32 . . . . 6-2.07, 6-4.07
art 32(2). 6-2.07
art 33 . . . . 6-2.07
art 34 . . . . 6-4.07
art 34(1). 6-2.08
art 34(2). 6-2.08
art 34(3). 6-4.07
art 35(c) 6-2.08
art 37 . . . . 6-2.09
art 37(2). 6-2.08
arts 39–48 . . . . 6-1.03
art 42 . . . . 1-1.05, 6-2.01, 6-2.10, 6-3.14
art 44 . . . . 1-1.05, 6-2.10, 6-3.14
art 47 . . . . 1-1.05, 6-2.05
art 48 . . . . 6-2.11
arts 49–52 . . . . 6-1.09
arts 49–55 . . . . 6-1.03
art 49(2). 6-1.10
art 50 . . . . 6-1.12
art 51 . . . . 6-1.12

art 53 . . . . 6-1.14
arts 53–55 . . . . 6-1.09
art 54(3). 6-5.15
art 55(1). 6-1.14
art 56 . . . . 6-5.02
arts 56–121 . . . . 6-1.03
art 56(1). 6-5.25
art 56(3). 6-5.25, 6-5.26
art 57 . . . . 6-1.19
art 58 . . . . 6-5.20, 6-5.21, 6-5.22
art 59 . . . . 6-5.22
art 60(2)(a). 6-5.10
art 61 . . . . 6-5.22, 6-5.27
art 61(2)(a). 6-5.22
art 61(3). 6-5.22
art 61(4). 6-5.11
art 61(5). 6-5.11
art 62 . . . . 6-5.03
art 63 . . . . 6-5.03
art 63(3). 6-5.22
art 65 . . . . 6-5.06
art 66 . . . . 6-5.25
art 66(1). 6-5.25
art 66(2). 6-5.23
art 66(2)(b) 6-5.21
art 66(3). 6-5.13
art 67 . . . . 6-5.13
art 67(1). 6-5.13
art 68 . . . . 6-5.14
art 68(2)(e). 6-5.14
art 69 . . . . 6-5.14
art 69(2)(g). 6-5.14
art 71 . . . . 6-5.24
art 72 . . . . 6-5.14
art 76 . . . . 6-5.09
art 76(6). 6-5.11
art 77 . . . . 6-5.10
art 77(4). 6-5.11
art 78(1). 6-5.10, 6-5.12
art 78(2). 6-5.10, 6-5.12
art 78(3). 6-5.12
art 79(4). 6-5.11
art 80(1). 6-5.15
art 80(2). 6-5.16
art 81 . . . . 6-5.17
art 82 . . . . 6-5.17
art 83 . . . . 6-5.25
art 85 . . . . 6-5.29
art 86 . . . . 6-5.06
arts 86–88 . . . . 6-5.08
art 87(1). 6-5.08
arts 88–90 . . . . 6-5.08
art 89 . . . . 6-5.08
art 89(2). 6-5.08
art 91 . . . . 6-5.12
art 92 . . . . 6-5.14
art 93(1). 6-5.12
art 93(2). 6-5.12
art 96 . . . . 6-5.15
art 97 . . . . 6-5.12
art 98 . . . . 6-5.19
art 99 . . . . 6-5.15
art 99(2). 6-5.16
art 99(3). 6-5.20
art 100 . . . . 6-5.16
art 101 . . . . 6-4.16, 6-5.31
art 102(1). 6-5.20
art 103 . . . . 6-5.20
art 104(1). 6-5.20
art 105 . . . . 6-5.18
art 107 . . . . 6-5.18
art 110 . . . . 6-5.37
art 111 . . . . 6-5.37
art 112 . . . . 6-5.38
art 113 . . . . 6-5.38
art 115 . . . . 6-5.39
art 117 . . . . 6-5.27
art 117(1)(b) 6-5.32
art 117(2). 6-5.28
art 117(3). 6-5.32, 6-5.35
art 118(1). 6-5.29
art 118(2). 6-5.30
art 119(3). 6-1.21
art 121 . . . . 6-5.33
art 123 . . . . 6-1.03
art 130 . . . . 6-1.22
Law on Cooperatives (1997)
art 44 . . . . 6-4.01
Law on Intellectual Property
Rights (2005) 6-1.22
art 7(2). 6-1.22
art 130 . . . . 6-1.22
art 145 . . . . 6-1.22
Telecommunications Law (2002) 6-3.11
Law on Science and Technology 6-4.05
Law on State-Owned
Enterprises (1995) 6-4.01
Law on Technology Transfer 6-1.22
Ordinance on Dealing with Administrative
Offences, 2 July 2002 . . . . 6-1.05

TABLE OF INTERNATIONAL CO-OPERATION/ TRADE AGREEMENTS

Chile/Korea 5-1.14
chap 14, art 14:2(1) 1-2.52
Japan/Vietnam (2008) 6-1.22
Korea/Australia,
29 September 2002. . . . . 5-1.14
Korea/EFTA, 2003. . . . . 5-1.14
Korea/EFTA, 2005. . . . . 5-1.14
Korea/Latvia/Romania,
17 September 2003. . . . . 5-1.14
Korea/Singapore, 2005. . . . . 5-1.14
Korea/United States, 2007 . . . . 5-1.14

LIST OF ABBREVIATIONS

AMC	Anti-Monopoly Committee (China)
AMEA	Anti-Monopoly Law Enforcement Agency (China)
APEC	Asia-Pacific Economic Cooperation
APM	Administrative Preventive Measures (Vietnam)
ASEAN	Association of Southeast Asian Nations
CCHC	Competition Case Handling Council (Vietnam)
CFA	Court of Final Appeal (Hong Kong)
CFI	Court of First Instance of the European Community
COMPAG	Competition Policy Advisory Group (Hong Kong)
CEDB	Commerce and Economic Development Bureau (Hong Kong)
CPRC	Competition Policy Review Committee (Hong Kong)
CR	Concentration ratio
DDB	Decree on Dealing with Breaches in the Competition Sector (Vietnam)
DOF	Decree on functions, duties, powers and organizational structure of the Vietnam Competition Administration Department
DOJ	Department of Justice (US)
EC	European Community
ECJ	European Court of Justice
ECMR	EC Merger Regulation
EDLB	Economic Development and Labour Bureau (Hong Kong)
FDI	Foreign Direct Investment
FFTA	Fair Franchise Transactions Act (Korea)
FTCA	Federal Trade Commission Act (US)
HHI	Herfindahl-Hirschmann Index
HKCC	Competition Commission (Hong Kong) [Proposed body]
ICN	International Competition Network
IP	Intellectual property
JV	Joint venture
KFSC	Korean Financial Supervisory Commission
KFTC	Korean Fair Trade Commission
KFTMC	Korean Fair Trade Mediation Committee
MIC	Ministry of Information and Communication (Korea)
MIT	Ministry of Industry and Trade (Vietnam)
MOFCOM	Ministry of Commerce (China)
MRFTA	Monopoly Regulation and Fair Trade Act (Korea)
NDRC	National Development and Reform Commission (China)
OECD	Organisation for Economic Cooperation and Development

OFT	Office of Fair Trading (UK)
R&D	Research and Development
RPM	Resale Price Maintenance
SAIC	State Administration for Industry and Commerce (China)
SAR	Special Administrative Region
SETC	State Economic and Trade Commission (China)
SME	Small and medium-sized enterprise
SSNIP	Small but significant non-transitory increase in price
SOE	State-owned enterprise
TFTA	Taiwan Fair Trade Act
TFTC	Taiwan Fair Trade Commission
UCRAM	Unfair Competition Regulatory Authority of Mongolia
US	United States
VCAD	Vietnam Competition Administration Department
VCC	Vietnam Competition Council
VLOC	Vietnam Law on Competition
WTO	World Trade Organization

Part 1

INTRODUCTION

1-1.	**Introduction**	3
1-2.	**Standards in Antitrust Law**	29

1-1

INTRODUCTION

Antitrust Law in China	1-1.06	**Antitrust Law in Korea**	1-1.26
Antitrust Law in Hong Kong	1-1.16	**Antitrust Law in Vietnam**	1-1.32
Antitrust Law in Taiwan	1-1.24		

Introducing the inaugural volume of the *Washington University Global Studies Law Review*, which dealt with antitrust law in the Asia-Pacific area, Haley drew attention to the fact that '[t]he enactment of antitrust legislation has become a global phenomenon. Antitrust law has, in effect, become the latest fashion.'[1] The reasons for this are complex, but are at least related to an increasingly generalized acceptance that liberal market economies (privatized where State ownership was common) are to be preferred over managed (socialist) economies. This trend is particularly prominent in East Asia, although there may remain uneasy tensions between the operation of the market and the retention by the State of relatively close management of economic objectives and actors. The relationship between antitrust policy and wider industrial policies is demonstrated in part by the response to the Asian economic crisis in 1998.[2] In September of that year Frederic Jenny suggested that: **1-1.01**

> . . . the financial crisis has led to an economic crisis because not enough attention has been paid in the past in these countries to market competition as a means to promote economic efficiency and, on the other hand, that in order to restore the necessary confidence in their economies, East Asian governments must not only reform their financial sectors but also adopt a more comprehensive plan of market-oriented reforms. . . .

[1] Haley, JO, 'Competition Law for the Asia-Pacific Economic Cooperation Community: Designing Shoes for Many Sizes', (2002) *Washington University Global Studies Law Review*, vol 1, (1 & 2), 1. See also Wu, P and Thomas, C, 'Taiwan's Fair Trade Act: Achieving the "Right" Balance?' (2005–2006) 26 *Northwestern Journal of International Law and Business* 643: 'Adopting competition laws is part-and-parcel of a global trend' (at 643).

[2] See generally (1999) 1:2 *OECD Journal of Competition Law and Policy*.

> Only lip service was given to competition as a means to promote an economically efficient industrial sector. It was generally considered that international competition was sufficient to force the export oriented firms to perform well. However, these firms were occasionally basing their export growth on easy credit facilities, cheap labour and domestic protection rather than on efforts to achieve high levels of productivity. . . . At the domestic level, it was generally considered to be more important to promote employment than to protect consumers against monopolistic practices. Concentrated domestic markets, sheltered to a certain extent from either domestic or international competition emerged.[3]

Later in this keynote speech (given at a symposium held in Seoul) Jenny made explicit the link between antitrust policy and sound economic development:

> To be sustainable in the long run, economic development has to be based on sound financial and economic principles rather than on the systematic promotion of short run growth. Therefore some disciplining mechanism is necessary, both in the financial area and on goods and services markets, to ensure an efficient allocation of resources among firms and industries. Government intervention is not entirely reliable to provide such a mechanism . . . To a large extent, market competition provides such a disciplining mechanism . . . the importance of permitting sufficient competition to allow market forces to guide the allocation of resources cannot be underestimated. Developing market competition . . . means allowing businesses to operate in an institutional and legal environment which will make it possible . . . for challengers, whether national or foreign, to confront incumbents and which will not allow either the undue exercise of market power or the indefinite protection of inefficient firms. In other words, what is required is an environment guaranteeing competition on the merits rather than through political clout.[4]

1-1.02 International organizations, including the World Trade Organization ('WTO'), are influential in pressing the case for competition law, and the relationship between trade and competition is now recognized to be an important one. All the States whose regimes are discussed in this book are members of the WTO. Although China, whose adoption of antitrust law is discussed below, was not compelled by virtue of its accession to the WTO to adopt antitrust law, there is a clear link between the two events, and China speeded up progress towards the enactment of a general law of antitrust alongside the development of its membership of the WTO.[5]

---

[3] Jenny, F, 'Competition Policy and the Asian Economic Crisis' (1999) 1:2 *OECD Journal of Competition Law and Policy* 13 at 14.

[4] Ibid at 17–18.

[5] See, eg Wang, X and Tao, Z, 'WTO Competition Policy and Its Influence in China' (2004) *Social Sciences in China*, Spring, 43; Wang, X, 'China's Accession to WTO and the Formulation of Competition Law' (2003) *Legal Research* vol 2; Li, KX and Du, M, 'Does China Need Competition Law?' (2007) *Journal of Business Law* 182 at 186; Wu, Z, 'Perspectives on the Chinese Anti-Monopoly Law' (2008) 75 *Antitrust Law Journal* 73 at 79: 'The [Anti-Monopoly Law] should reflect the opening-up policy and adapt to China's WTO entry and the new trend in economic globalization.' While China's accession into the WTO did not create a legal obligation to enact antitrust law a number of States expressed concerns as to the difficulties China 'would face . . . in complying with

The introduction of a general antitrust law in the People's Republic of China (hereinafter 'China') on 30 August 2007, taking effect on 1 August 2008, is perhaps the most significant evidence of this trend. While the policy reasons that led to the adoption of the new law, the substantive provisions of which are discussed in some detail in Part 2 of this book, are not entirely transparent, and although the efficacy and consistency with which the law will be applied may be doubted,[6] this development is undoubtedly an important one. Harris has noted that 'it is difficult to overstate the potential importance, to China and the world economy, of China's adoption, implementation, and rigorous and fair enforcement of a modern competition law'.[7] In March 2007 the Special Administrative Region of Hong Kong (hereinafter 'Hong Kong') announced that it too was to enact a general law of antitrust, following a period in which this policy had been expressly discarded in favour of a sectoral approach on the basis that the Hong Kong economy was so open as itself to regulate and mitigate against anti-competitive conduct, whether 1-1.03

the WTO's requirements of transparency and non-discrimination' (Harris, SH, 'The Making of an Antitrust Law: The Pending Anti-Monopoly Law of the People's Republic of China' (2006–2007) 7 *Chicago Journal of International Law* 169 at 176). These concerns were not lessened by reports within China that one of the spurs for a new Anti-Monopoly Law lay in the abuses of dominant positions being perpetrated by foreign companies trading in China. *China Daily* reported on 25 May 2004 ('Monopoly law badly needed, says report') that Tetra Pak, Microsoft, and Kodak in particular were identified as monopolists acting anti-competitively. See also *Wall Street Journal*, 11 June 2004, A7, 'China Hurries Antitrust Law', in which it was reported that a number of international firms were concerned that they would be the first to face action under the Law. If WTO obligations are to be complied with China will be required to apply the Anti-Monopoly Law in a non-discriminatory manner wherever there is a nexus between the application of the Anti-Monopoly Law and international trade.

It is also the case that the move to the enactment of antitrust law in Taiwan was affected by pressure brought from its trading partners 'to balance trade, including the adoption of more effective mechanisms to prevent unfair competition . . .' (Liu, LS, 'Fostering Competition Law and Policy: A Façade of Taiwan's Political Economy' (2002) *Washington University Global Studies Law Review*, vol 1, (1 & 2), 77 at 78). In the event Taiwan enacted the Taiwan Fair Trade Act ('TFTA') some eleven years before joining the WTO.

[6] See in particular, Williams, M, *Competition Policy and Law in China, Hong Kong and Taiwan* (Cambridge: Cambridge University Press, 2005). Williams, an academic based at the Polytechnic University of Hong Kong with significant expertise in the region, is particularly sceptical of the ability of China to apply its competition law with rigour and consistency. However, Williams accepts that while '[c]ompetition law is clearly no panacea for China's economic problems . . . it might form a valuable component in the ongoing reformation of the Chinese economic system, if implemented fairly and competently' (at 119). See also Dabbah, MM, 'The Development of Sound Competition Law and Policy in China: An (Im)possible Dream?' (2007) 30:2 *World Competition* 341, who is critical of the Anti-Monopoly Law and notes in particular that 'China's clear aim of instituting an effective system of competition law will not be achieved with the mere enactment of the [Anti-Monopoly Law]' (at 363).

[7] Harris, n 5, above, at 229. See also Robertson, JR, 'Symposium: The Anti-Monopoly Law of the People's Republic of China—Editor's Note' (2008) 75 *Antitrust Law Journal* 67, at 68: 'That China now has an [Anti-Monopoly Law] to help it regulate competition within its massive economy is nothing short of amazing'; and Fox, EM, 'An Anti-Monopoly Law for China—Scaling the Walls of Government Restraints' (2008) 75 *Antitrust Law Journal* 173, at 174: 'China has adopted a major law that promises to anchor its markets in a pro-competitive environment.'

multi- or unilateral. At the time of writing Hong Kong has yet to bring forward this new law and Part 3 of this book discusses the likely developments in the light of material currently available. Part 4 deals with the law in Taiwan, which is, for the purposes of this text, treated as a separate jurisdiction from that of China.[8] The decision has also been taken in this text to deal with the law of China's near neighbours, and fellow 'tiger' economies, South Korea and Vietnam. The former, the law of which is discussed in Part 5, has operated its present antitrust law regime (albeit subject to frequent amendment along the way) since 1980. Vietnam introduced a law of antitrust in 2004 (taking effect in 2005), although at the time of writing it has not completed the process of fully developing the necessary framework—both institutional and legal—for the new law to operate effectively and with rigour. There are substantial disparities in the regimes covered in this book, in terms of size, economic development, and legal cultures, and these factors will have an impact on the shape and operation of the antitrust regimes in the respective States. Table 1-1.1 sets out basic economic data.

1-1.04 In each Part of this book, where the law is sufficiently developed, a consistent approach has been adopted. The relevant regime will be introduced, and its broad structure and legal framework set out; the substantive areas relating to the control of agreements, monopolies, and mergers will be explained; and finally the relevant procedural law, including both public powers and private rights, if these exist, will be dealt with. All relevant legislation (the core legislation is reproduced as appendices), guidelines, and other official materials (including preparatory materials) will be referred to as appropriate, and where possible relevant cases will be discussed. Inconsistencies in the depth of analysis provided in this text reflect both different levels of development of the relevant regimes, and differences in the transparency with which the regimes operate. International agreements which relate to the operation of antitrust law, and approaches to territorial jurisdiction will also be dealt with as appropriate. Some reference will be made to relevant literature, and an extensive bibliography is given at the end of the book, but this text is primarily intended for the practitioner, rather than the academic community,

[8] The relationships, both *de jure* and *de facto*, between China and Taiwan are deliberately excluded from consideration in this book. For the purposes of the application of competition law they may be treated, at the present, as being functionally separate regimes. The Nationalist regime in China was replaced by the Communist Regime on 1 October 1949. The island of Taiwan remained in the control of the Nationalist Party under the leadership of Chiang Kai Shek. There is general consensus in international law that Taiwan does not constitute a 'State' but it does, *de facto*, operate as a distinct legal and economic regime. Note that although Taiwan is excluded from membership of many international bodies (but not from membership of the WTO in its capacity as a customs territory), the Taiwan Fair Trade Commission ('TFTC') has entered into a number of bilateral arrangements relating to the application of antitrust law.

Table 1-1.1 Core economic data

	China	Hong Kong	Taiwan	Korea	Vietnam
Population (m)	1,321.3	7.0	22.7	49.0	85.9
GDP (US$bn)	3,241.8	206.7	383.3	969.8	70.7
FDI (% of GDP)	3.0	18.0	0.4	0.8	5.2
Leading markets	US, Hong Kong, Japan	China, US, Japan	China, Hong Kong, US	China, US, Japan	US, Japan, Australia
Leading suppliers	Japan, South Korea, Taiwan	China, Japan, Taiwan	Japan, China, US	China, Japan, US	China, Singapore, Japan

Source: Economist.com, Country Briefings. Figures actual or estimated for 2007.

such that reference to secondary literature will be less than would be the case in an academic monograph.

This chapter provides a broad introduction to the antitrust law regimes of the five jurisdictions dealt with, and sets out the relationship of that antitrust law to the wider legal regime. Table 1-1.2, below, sets out the schema of discussion of the substantive areas of law, excluding Hong Kong in respect of which the discussion is a speculative one. It is, of course, not possible here to provide a full treatment of the five legal regimes in their entirety. There are similarities between the regimes under discussion, although the extent of that similarity varies. Reasons for this similarity include the common purposes of antitrust law, common external legal influences (such as the models of other regimes, and the advocacy of the same international bodies), and some shared cultural traditions, particularly in the case of Taiwan and Korea, and to a slightly lesser extent China, where Confucian traditions of governance are commonly held. Chapter 1-2 provides a general **1-1.05**

Table 1-1.2 Antitrust provisions and coverage in text

	China	Taiwan	Korea	Vietnam
Horizontal agreement	AML, arts 13, 16 [2-2]	TFTA, art 14 [4-2]	MRFTA, chs 4, 6, 8 [5-2]	VLOC, arts 8, 47 [6-2]
Vertical agreement	AML, art 14 [2-2]	TFTA, ch III [4-2]	MRFTA, chs 5, 7 [5-2]	VLOC, arts 8, 42, 44 [6-2]
Abuse of dominance/ monopoly	AML, chs III, V [2-3]	TFTA, art 10 [4-3]	MRFTA, ch 2 [5-3]	VLOC, arts 13, 14 [6-3]
Merger control	AML, ch IV [2-4]	TFTA, arts 11–13 [4-4]	MRFTA, ch 2 [5-4]	VLOC, arts 16–24 [6-4]

introduction to antitrust law, with particular reference to the regimes of the United States ('US') and the European Community ('EC'), both of which have been influential on the development of antitrust law elsewhere.[9]

Antitrust Law in China[10]

1-1.06 Following reforms introduced by Deng Xiaoping after the end of the rule of Mao Tse Tung China is, today, a socialist market economy: art 1 of the Anti-Monopoly Law of the People's Republic of China makes reference to the need to promote 'the healthy development of the socialist market economy'. This is in accordance with the Chinese Constitution, art 15, first sentence, which, following an amendment in 1993, replaced the concept of central planning with that of the socialist market economy. China remains an economy in transition: rapidly industrializing, developing and exploiting high-tech industries, and admitting both private ownership of the means of production and inward foreign investment. It has been noted that until as recently as 'the late 1970s, China possessed a planned and highly centralised economy . . . the market played virtually no role, and competition itself was out of the question, let alone a government policy encouraging such competition'.[11]

---

[9] It is clear, for example, that some jurisdictions will be influenced not only by the broad policies adopted in the US and the EC, but also by the terms in which that policy finds expression. See for example Liu, n 5, above, at 96: 'Foreign practices, such as various US Department of Justice and Federal Trade Commission guidelines also influenced the [Taiwan Fair Trade Law]'. The results in particular cases may also be influenced by overseas actions. The approach taken by the Korean Free Trade Commission ('KFTC') to Microsoft Corp's bundling of Media Player with the Windows operating system in 2006 was remarkably similar to that adopted by the EC Commission. In its reporting of the KFTC action the *Financial Times* noted that the approach taken by the KFTC 'closely followed the precedent' set by the EC (23 August 2006). In that case the KFTC fined Microsoft Won33bn for abusing its market position, Microsoft agreed a US$30m settlement with a complainant, and released a version of Windows XP compliant with the KFTC's Decision. It is worth noting that in Taiwan an administrative settlement agreement was entered into between the TFTC and Microsoft, which in part imported into Taiwan the terms of the US consent decree entered into by Microsoft. These two cases clearly demonstrate the extent to which less well developed jurisdictions may rely on case precedents from the more developed jurisdictions of the EC and US.

[10] The difficulties encountered when working with legal texts produced in a language other than English was noted in the preface to this book. Particular note should be made in regard to the difficulties in working with translations of Chinese texts. Not only are many terms vague in the original, but translating such vague terms may compound problems of understanding: 'the laws and rules in existence contain a number of inadequately defined terms and concepts, and often in practice the meaning of these terms is distorted when translating from Chinese to English. This, in turn, leads to inconsistency when attempting to understand the same rule by reading it in both Chinese and English' (Dabbah, n 6, above, at 351).

[11] Jiang, X, 'Promoting Competition and Maintaining Monopoly: Dual Functions of Chinese Industrial Policies during Economic Transition' (2002) *Washington University Global Studies Law Review*, vol 1, (1 & 2), 49. For a general discussion of changes in China see Gittings, J, *The Changing Face of China: From Mao to Market* (Oxford: Oxford University Press, 2006).

Notwithstanding the scale of the changes which have been made in recent years, the legacy of this planned and highly centralized economy remains. This finds expression primarily in the relatively high number of state-owned enterprises ('SOEs')—it is believed that approximately one-third of Chinese GDP flows from SOEs[12]—and also in the number of economic activities exclusively reserved to the State, or other legal authorities that in other economies would be left to the private sector to undertake in a competitive fashion. It is also evidently the case that China suffers from regional protectionism, where local enterprises are supported in the face of competition coming from those outside the area.[13] It is the case in particular that a significant proportion of local taxation revenues may derive from locally based firms, providing an incentive for local governments to insulate them from vigorous competition. This issue is addressed to some extent in the provisions relating to the abuse of administrative monopoly in the new Anti-Monopoly Law (see further Chapter 2-3, below). **1-1.07**

It has long been recognized that China's economy has been a victim of widespread anti-competitive practices which have been endemic domestically, although the spur to the recent legislation has been at least in part as a response to a perceived unfairness of conduct engaged in by international companies trading into, and within, China. Thus in 1995 it was noted that: **1-1.08**

> Cartel activities have been widely reported in the official press and have been growing in frequency and influence . . . agreements for jointly setting prices, dividing the market, limiting production, and bid-rigging are also prevalent.[14]

Although the enactment of the Anti-Monopoly Law in 2007 is without precedent in modern times the concept of the regulation of competition is not new to China. See Liu, n 5, above, at 83:

> . . . competition policy is not a foreign import to traditional China. Before the First Emperor unified China, scholars such as Guan Chung already had warned the Prince of the threat posed to the throne, farmers and small businessmen by merchants owning thousands of gold bullion. The Tang Dynasty saw the first codification of some form of competition policy: the criminal prohibition against cornering the market. Article 33 of the miscellaneous provisions of the Tang Code, enacted in 737 AD, prohibited any person selling or buying goods from forcibly creating a barrier of entry into the marketplace, fixing the prices of goods they would buy or sell, or misrepresenting the prices of such goods. A violation could lead to eighty floggings and mandatory disgorgement of the offender's illegal profits. (Internal footnotes omitted)

[12] Harris, n 5, above, writes that 'a large percentage of these entities have not, in any meaningful sense, been transitioned into participants in the market economy'. Although noting that there have been reforms and that 'the formerly robust relationship between the government and SOEs has weakened, and money-losing SOEs have been bankrupted or privatized' it remains the case that 'many of the largest and most profitable SOEs have been retained in state hands and represent a substantial share of the Chinese economy' (at 174). Some of the strongest of China's firms are SOEs, even though these may take the form of joint-stock companies. Examples include China Mobile, Sinopec, and Lenovo.

[13] See, for example, Hu Weiwei, 'Anti-monopoly law is a necessity in China' (1995) 3 *Jurisprudence* 35.

[14] Bing, S, 'Competition Policy in a Transitional Economy: The Case of China' (1995) 31 *Stanford Journal of International Law* 387 at 401.

As late as 1998 the State Economic and Trade Commission ('SETC') officially approved the practice of industries adopting 'self-disciplinary' practices—in effect price-fixing cartels.[15]

1-1.09 It was in the mid-1980s that discussions first began in China relating to the enactment of an antitrust law that adhered to international standards. This however did not find expression in a comprehensive single piece of legislation. Prior to the enactment of the 2008 Anti-Monopoly Law there existed in China a plethora of legislative instruments which related to competitive conduct, some general in nature, and some either practice- or sector-specific.[16] The new legislation has not immediately repealed this. For example, the Price Law of the People's Republic of China was brought into effect on 1 May 1998.[17] Article 14 of this law provides that business operators may not 'collude with others to manipulate the market

---

[15] SETC, *Opinions on Self-Disciplinary Prices Adopted by Some Industries*, 17 August 1998.

[16] The following list of Chinese legislation 'with competition relevance' prior to the enactment of the Anti-Monopoly Law is given by Dabbah, n 6, above, at 346–7: 'Law on Chinese-Foreign Equity Joint Ventures 1979; Provisional Regulation Concerning the Development and Protection of Socialist Competition Mechanism 1980 [this was the first attempt in China to introduce provisions relating to competition; art 3 states that 'in economic activities, with the exception of products exclusively managed by state-designated departments and organisations, monopolisation or the sole proprietary management of other products is not allowed']; Patent Law 1984; Law on Foreign-capital Enterprises 1986; Postal Law 1986; Law on Chinese-Foreign Contractual Joint Ventures 1988; Railway Law 1990; Anti-Unfair Competition Law 1993; Consumer Protection Law 1993; Company Law 1993; Foreign Trade Law 1994; Insurance Law 1995; Commercial Bank Law 1995; Civil Aviation Law 1995; Electric Power Law 1995; Highway Law 1997; Price Law 1997; Securities Law 1998; Interim Provisions on State-owned Enterprises' Utilising of Foreign Investment for Reorganising 1998; Provisions on Administrative Punishment against Price Violation Activities 1999; Law on Invitation and Submission of Bids 1999; Regulation on Telecommunication Industry 2000; Countervailing Regulation 2001; State Council Provision on Prohibiting Regional Blockade in Market Economic Activities 2001; Anti-dumping Regulation 2001; Regulations on the Administration of Financial Institutions with Foreign Investment 2001; Regulation on the Administration of Insurance Companies with Foreign Investment 2001; Law on Promoting Small and Medium Sized Enterprises 2002; Government Procurement Law 2002; Circular on Issues Related to Transferring State-owned Shares and Institutional Shares of Listed Companies to Foreign Investors 2002; Interim Provisions on Mergers and Acquisitions of Domestic Enterprises by Foreign Investors 2003; Interim Measures on Preventing the Activities of Price Monopoly 2003; Interim Measures for the Management of the Service Price of Commercial Banks 2003; Circular on Key Points of Filing Procedures in Listed Companies Transferring State-owned Shares to Foreign Investors and Foreign Invested Enterprises 2004; Provisions on the Establishment of Investment Companies by Foreign Investors 2004; Supplementary Provisions to the Provisions on the Establishment of Investment Companies by Foreign Investors 2004; Interim Measures Governing National Hi-Tech Industry Development Projects 2006; Measures on the Takeover of Listed Companies 2006. Dabbah notes both that this is 'a fragmented framework with a high number of laws and regulations being used', and that, perhaps more importantly, 'the framework is interwoven with uncertainty, inconsistency and unenforceability'.

[17] Article 3 of the Price Law states that:

> The State implements and is gradually perfecting a mechanism whereby prices are mainly determined by the market, while subject to economic adjustment and control at the macro level. The setting of prices shall conform to the laws of value. The prices of the great majority of merchandise and services shall be market-adjusted prices, whereas the prices of a very

price, thus harming the lawful rights and interests of other business operators or consumers'. Article 40 provides that anyone in breach of article 14 may be required to pay damages, or have any illegal gains confiscated, and may be fined up to five times the sum of the illegal gains. A law of 1999 makes it illegal to engage in collusive tendering practices.[18] However, the most significant such law is the 1993 Law Against Unfair Competition.[19] This law contains measures which are targeted at combating monopoly practices, but also contains measures relating to consumer protection, and matters such as false trading and passing off. The range of conduct prohibited under the Law led a number of Chinese commentators to argue that such a legislative amalgam was inappropriate.[20] Wang Cunxue was not alone in arguing that this Law was incapable of dealing effectively with cartel practices, and that the patchwork of other relevant legislation, such as the Regulation of the Price of Manufacturing Material of 1987, was ineffective.

It is also clear that the monopoly provisions of the Law Against Unfair Competition have been little used in practice.[21] A number of examples are given in *Anti-Inappropriate Competition Law: Understanding, Application and Case Studies*[22] and *Anti-Inappropriate Competition Law Cases*.[23] In both of these works cases that would be classed as 'antitrust' cases within the western understanding of the word are interspersed with cases relating to unfair or inaccurate advertising, the defamation of the company bringing the case, the giving of discounts to encourage custom (by companies with no market power), and other **1-1.10**

small number of merchandise and services shall be subject to government-guided prices or government-fixed prices.

[18] The Bidding Law of the People's Republic of China.

[19] The Law of the People's Republic of China for Countering Unfair Competition is the usual translation given to the relevant legislation by Chinese government sources published in English.

[20] In the leading work dealing with the legislation there are, for example, sections headed 'bribery and kickback' and 'false and misleading publicity' (Jin, C and Luo, W, *Competition Law in China* (Buffalo NY: William S Hein & Co Inc, 2002). See also Gao, Y and Cao, D (eds), *Anti-Unfair Competition Law: Understanding, Application and Case Studies* (Beijing: Peoples Court Publishing House, 2nd edn, 1997). For a concise and accurate discussion of the pre-Anti-Monopoly Law regime see Li and Du, n 5, above.

[21] See, eg, Harris, n 5, above, at 175: '. . . as enacted and enforced, the [Law Against Unfair Competition] was essentially limited to the protection of trademarks and "passing off" offences, primarily because counterfeit goods were seen as the most pressing issue prompting repeated complaints from various countries, including the US. Efforts to include any "core" antitrust content in the statute were considered unnecessary and ultimately abandoned, at least in part because of disagreements over which agency or agencies would implement and enforce such laws.' See also Li and Du, n 5, above, at 188: 'Although the [Law Against Unfair Competition] contains provisions against monopolistic behaviour, it is primarily a law against unfair trading practices. The [Anti-Monopoly Law] is supposed to focus specifically on monopolistic practices and problems of market concentration. Therefore . . . there will be a clear distinction between laws against unfair trade practices and laws against monopoly in China.'

[22] Gao and Cao (eds), n 20, above.

[23] Huang, Q, Cao, Q, and Tu, T (eds), (Hunan People Publishing House, 1998).

similar matters. In the first work for example, only three of the reported cases would be classed as antitrust cases in the US, or as breaches of antitrust law in the EC. All of the reported cases however could be classed in Chinese law as breaches of the Law Against Unfair Competition, which may perhaps be better characterized as a law relating to consumer protection rather than a law about antitrust.

1-1.11 Many within China advocated the adoption of a new antitrust law, although some of the arguments made in favour of the adoption of a new law were somewhat sweeping.[24] In 1993 preparations began more seriously on a new law, and a working group was set up to draft this. The group comprised officials from the State Administration for Industry and Commerce ('SAIC'), and the SETC. A significant number of parties from outside China commented on the work undertaken, and advocated for particular approaches, and particularly for China to conform to recognizable international standards in any new law.[25] Wu states that:

> The principal drafters had the following goals for the [Anti-Monopoly Law]. The Chinese anti-monopoly legislation should meet the objectives of establishing a unified, open, competitive, orderly, and modern market system in China and of perfecting the socialist market economy system. It should not only be based on the Chinese situation, but it should also borrow from the practical experiences and results of foreign anti-monopoly laws. The law should meet the specific requirements of

---

[24] For example, Fa Zhen of the Chinese Committee of Economy and Trade argued that there were four reasons to adopt a new anti-monopoly law: (1) the objective demand of accelerating the construction of the socialist market economy; (2) developing the socialist law system; (3) deepening the reform of enterprise and stimulating government to change its functions; (4) integrating Chinese approach with international practice and laws (Zhen, F, 'An economic constitution; a discussion of some ideas and problems in legislating a Chinese anti-monopoly law' (1998) 4 *Intertrade* 4).

[25] The process of drafting of the Anti-Monopoly Law is comprehensively discussed by Harris, n 5, above. A particularly good examination of the background is given by Williams, n 6, above. See also Huang, Y, 'Pursuing the Second Best: The History, Momentum, and Remaining Issues of China's Anti-Monopoly Law' (2008) 75 *Antitrust Law Journal* 117 whose analysis is prefaced with the following warning (at 118):

> . . . China which has a culture thousands of years old, with an ideology that is extremely conservative and even feudalistic, is a country undergoing a painful transition from command economy to market orientation. Under these circumstances, it is essential to examine the answers to these questions: What is the backstory to the creation of China's [Anti-Monopoly Law]? What is the driving force behind China's [Anti-Monopoly Law]? What were the controversies that held up the legislative process, and to what extent were they resolved?
>
> These questions may well puzzle the antitrust practitioners and policy makers outside of China, and even more puzzling are the answers that their Chinese counterparts give. To comprehend the answers to these questions, Western scholars have to stand in the shoes of the Chinese and possess a deep understanding about the political and economical reality of the country's past and present, as well as specific characteristics of the Chinese marketplace. Only against this backdrop can those antitrust scholars in the West comprehend the driving forces in the legislative process, the mission of the Chinese [Anti-Monopoly Law], and the major challenges facing this legislation.

> China, promote the orderly development of the socialist market economy, and comply with common international practices and regulations.[26]

The majority of those advocating change appeared to accept that a law could be drafted which took China's special circumstances into account. It was widely recognized that the prevalence of SOEs was a problem, but commentators were quick to point out that other economies which do successfully operate an antitrust law regime also contain within them SOEs, although not to the extent that is the case in China. In the event the approach to be taken to SOEs was one of the most hotly debated issues surrounding the enactment of the new law. The issue has been only partially resolved: Article 2 of the law appears to suggest that it does apply to SOEs and administrative monopolies,[27] stating simply that the law 'is applicable to monopolistic conduct in economic activities within [China]', making no reference to a general exclusion for SOEs. However, art 7, discussed in Chapter 2–3, makes further provision in respect of 'industries controlled by the state-owned economy' providing that the State 'regulates and controls their business operations and the prices of their commodities and services so as to safeguard the interests of consumers and promote technical progress'.[28] It is reasonable to anticipate that the role played by SOEs will diminish over time as private enterprise grows within China, although given the continued importance of the SOEs to the State this is likely to be a slow process. **1-1.12**

---

[26] Wu, Z, 'Perspectives on the Chinese Anti-Monopoly Law' (2008) 75 *Antitrust Law Journal* 73 at 78.

[27] 'Administrative monopoly refers to monopolistic activities initiated by government agencies at all levels by abusing their administrative powers, both legal and extra legal, to promote, manipulate, impede or prevent economic activities. Administrative monopoly includes a wide variety of activities such as legal monopoly and explicitly prohibited ultra vires measures. To a great extent administrative monopoly is a special legacy of socialist countries such as China, a relic of a centrally planned economy. Administrative monopoly manifests itself in various ways, ie as regional monopoly, industry monopoly and compulsory trading' (Li and Du, n 5, above, at 199). Li and Du also note that 'the use of competition law to control administrative monopoly has so far turned out to be a total failure' (ibid at 204). See also Fox, n 7, above.

[28] It has been argued, in reference to an earlier draft of the law, that: 'Dealing with the problem of administrative monopolies is one of the major goals of China's proposed antitrust law. Given China's current structure, administrative monopolies are seen as posing a far more significant problem to China's burgeoning market economy than monopolies created by private enterprises' (Owen, BM, Sun, S, and Zheng, W, 'Antitrust in China: The Problem of Incentive Compatibility' (2005) 1 *Journal of Competition Law and Economics* 123 at 131). For a good discussion of the issue of the problems raised by China's publicly owned utilities see Wen, X, 'Market Dominance by China's Public Utility Enterprises' (2008) 75 *Antitrust Law Journal* 151. At 169:

> . . . it appears to be highly unlikely that the promulgation of the law itself will solve the problem of privileged market status abuse completely. . . . part of the reason for [public utility monopolies] in China is due . . . to the creation of an administrative monopoly by the government. . . . without a separation between the government and the [utilities] it is hard to see how the antitrust law enforcement agencies could enforce the new [Anti-Monopoly Law] independently. It is simply not practical for the government to sue itself—or for that matter for private litigants to sue the government.

1-1.13 The Anti-Monopoly Law went through a substantial number of drafts before finally being enacted in the form discussed in this book. Reference is made to earlier drafts here only when this is considered necessary to highlight features of the law as enacted. There is a substantial literature dealing with the drafting process, and a large range of comment on the various drafts. It is clear from the text of the Anti-Monopoly Law that while no single regime has served as a unique model for the Chinese law the EC regime has been more influential on the drafting of the legislation than that of the US.[29]

1-1.14 The fact that the Anti-Monopoly Law is in many places imprecise, and contains lacunae, has been noted above. It has, however, been stated that the Law 'only articulates the broad principles that will guide antitrust enforcement in China'[30] and that further guidance will provide the necessary detail.

1-1.15 Some comment has been distinctly pessimistic as to the chances of a Chinese antitrust law operating effectively. The most substantial work on antitrust policy in China published in English is Williams' 2005 *Competition Policy and Law in China, Hong Kong and Taiwan*.[31] While Williams recognized that antitrust law 'might form a valuable component in the ongoing reformation of the Chinese economic system',[32] he argued forcefully that 'should a competition law be

---

[29] Harris, n 5, above, points to a number of examples which demonstrate this throughout the text of the Anti-Monopoly Law. Dabbah, n 6, above, argues that the approach of seeming to choose *either* the US *or* the EC model was inappropriate, noting that '[t]here is a need to appreciate that the adoption and development of competition law and policy in a particular country is very much related to and depends on the culture and type of economy of that country as well as on various socio-economic and socio-political circumstances prevailing in such country' (at 354). A similar argument is made in Furse, M, 'Competition Law Choice in China' (2007) 30:2 *World Competition* 323.

[30] Deng, F and Leonard, GK, 'Incentives and China's New Antimonopoly Law' (2008) *Antitrust*, Spring, 73. See also Owen et al, n 28, above, at 141: 'It would be inappropriate to evaluate the proposed law as if it were, as it would be in the US, a set of instructions intended for the judiciary to interpret'. See *contra*, Wang, X, 'Highlight's of China's New Anti-Monopoly Law' (2008) 75 *Antitrust Law Journal* 133 at 144: '. . . in China, laws are more specific [than in the US] and are usually carried out to the letter. Thus what the law expressly states is fundamental.'

[31] Williams, n 6, above. Throughout his book Williams offers a severe critique of the willingness or ability of the Chinese Government to introduce and apply competition law given the current structure of the economy, the inherent weaknesses of the economy, the commitment to a socialist market economy (for example, 'intellectual gymnastics of a sophisticated kind are needed to reconcile socialism with market competition', at 125), and the lack of expertise in the judiciary and government in this area. See in particular, at 426:

> . . . can China administer a competition law? The answer to this must be no. China lacks sufficient competent personnel and its state institutions are notoriously susceptible to corruption of both the political and/or financial type. . . .
>
> . . . can China enforce a competition law? Again the answer is no. China does not have robust legal institutions and cannot ensure that administrative or legal decisions are faithfully carried into effect because of the structure of Chinese political society, local protectionism and a very weak legal system . . .
>
> Thus it is suggested that China cannot implement an effective pro-competition policy regime, even though one might be legislated.

[32] At 119.

enacted, grave doubt exists as to whether it can be implemented'.[33] Harris also raises concerns about the capacity of China to implement the new law effectively, while at the same time noting that 'China has approached the drafting of its Anti-Monopoly Law with remarkable openness and a willingness to hear and consider the views and experiences of Chinese experts as well as foreign antitrust agencies, academics, economists and practitioners'.[34] Nevertheless Harris points to concerns relating to the transparency of the judicial system, institutional capabilities, uncertainty in relation to the political control over the new Anti-Monopoly Law Enforcement Agency ('AMLEA') set up to administer the Law, and in some instances to the text of the legislation itself. There are indeed many lacunae in the legislation, and in particular a great number of terms, which may be important in practice, which are not defined.[35] While implementing regulations have been promised these have been slow to appear, such that at present there remains significant uncertainty as to how the Anti-Monopoly Law will be applied in practice.[36]

Antitrust Law in Hong Kong

The decision to adopt a general law of antitrust in Hong Kong was taken on 20 March 2007. That Hong Kong rejected calls for a general antitrust law prior to this was in part because the Government argued that the open nature of the economy rendered such a general policy unnecessary. This view was not universally shared.[37] In response to an APEC-OECD survey the Government indicated that: **1-1.16**

> [Hong Kong] is fully committed to the promotion of free trade and competition. The fact that its traders and producers are exposed to acute international competition is a good illustration of [Hong Kong] as an open and free economy. The approach to promoting competition is grounded on the basic economic philosophy of

---

[33] Ibid. See also Owen et al, n 28, above, at 123: '. . . our major difficulty with the new law is that, in the absence of a tradition of reliance on the rule of law, Chinese and foreign competitors will find it very difficult to rely on the antitrust statute or the actions of the courts in China as a basis for predicting the antitrust liability that might result from various business practices.'

[34] n 5, above, at 228.

[35] This is not just a feature of the Anti-Monopoly Law. A significant amount of Chinese legislation is drafted with imprecision. Dabbah, n 6, above, notes, for example, that both the Interim Measures Governing National Hi-Tech Industry Development Projects 2006 and the Law on Promoting Small and Medium Sized Enterprises 2002 contain 'a clear absence . . . of objective or workable criteria' (at 348).

[36] I am more optimistic than is Williams as to the likely success of China's new Anti-Monopoly Law. It is however likely that the learning process will be a difficult one—as it has been for antitrust authorities in the West. Williams notes, in relation to the experience in Taiwan, that: 'In any jurisdiction adopting a new competition law, with no previous experience of such legislation, it is to be expected that the enforcement learning curve will be a steep one and that almost inevitably errors will be made' (n 6, above, at 398).

[37] See for example the views of The Frontier and the Hong Kong Democratic Foundation as expressed in *Competition Policy in Hong Kong* (1993).

> minimum government intervention in market forces. In the case of [Hong Kong] which is a small and externally-oriented economy, this approach is regarded as the best means of enhancing competition and efficiency on the one hand and keeping costs and prices down on the other.[38]

Thus it had been noted that: '[u]nder Hong Kong's free trade policy, almost every good can be imported free of duties. The policy has made Hong Kong extremely competitive for goods and services that are traded in the global market.'[39] Instead of a general law in Hong Kong the Government had adopted a sector-specific approach to antitrust issues. For example, both the Telecommunications Ordinance and the Broadcasting Ordinance contain measures designed to frustrate anti-competitive practices.

1-1.17 More generally antitrust 'law' in Hong Kong operated, and at the time of writing continues to operate, on a system of persuasion without the support of sanctions. This futile system is utterly toothless and may be disregarded, such that the treatment of it here is cursory.

1-1.18 In December 1997 the Government created the Competition Policy Advisory Group ('COMPAG') under the chairmanship of the Financial Secretary, which is responsible for the supervision of competition policy in Hong Kong, and to which competition-related complaints are to be referred. In May 1998 COMPAG published the *Statement on Competition Policy*, which serves as the overarching framework in this area for Hong Kong. Paragraph 4 of the Statement is in the following terms:

> *Pro-competition Principles*
>
> All government entities, and public- and private-sector bodies are encouraged to adhere to the following pro-competition principles for the purpose of enhancing economic efficiency and free trade—
>
> (a) maximizing reliance on, and minimizing interference with, market mechanism;
> (b) maintaining a level-playing field;

---

[38] APEC-OECD Integrated Checklist on Regulatory Reform: Addressing Regulatory, Competition Policy, and Market Openness Policy Issues—Hong Kong, China, 2006/SOM3/EC/015, 23. The Government also stated that: 'When a business practice limits market accessibility or market contestability and impairs economic efficiency or free trade, to the detriment of the overall interest of [Hong Kong], the Government will take appropriate remedial action' (ibid). In fact the ability of the Government to take 'appropriate remedial action' was somewhat limited. Cartels could, for example, operate quite lawfully and will be able to do so until the introduction of the new law. The former Governor of Hong Kong, Chris Patten, had announced his intention to bring forward competition law in 1992, but this was abandoned (see generally Chen, AHY, 'Competition Law and Hong Kong' (1993) 23(3) *Hong Kong Law Journal* 412).

[39] Cheng, LK and Wu, C, *Competition Policy and the Regulation of Business* (Hong Kong: City of Hong Kong University Press, 1998) 225. This is one of a series of useful, although slightly dated, works published in the Hong Kong Economic Policy Studies Series. Other titles are: Lam, P-L, *Competition in Energy* (1997); Lam, P-L and Chan, Y-C, *Privatizing Water and Sewage Services* (1997); and Fung, KC, *Trade and Investment, Mainland China, Hong Kong and Taiwan* (1997).

(c) minimizing uncertainty and fostering confidence in system fairness and predictability by—
  (i) consistent application of policies;
  (ii) transparent and accountable operations; and
  (iii) adherence to equitable and non-discriminatory standards and practices.

It will be noted that this policy is directed towards all bodies, both public and private, and therefore extends to private enterprise.

Specific examples of practices 'which may warrant further examination' are given **1-1.19** as price fixing, bid rigging and market allocation or sales and production quotas, joint boycotts and unfair or discriminatory standards. Some examples of abusive conduct are predatory behaviour, setting retail price minimums, and tying. The approach taken, and the implementation of the policy, are set out in paras 8–13. As far as the private sector is concerned the goal set out at para 10(d) is that of 'encouraging the private sector to embrace competition and its stated objective of enhancing economic efficiency and free trade'. This is further supported in paras 12–13, wherein:

> The Government calls upon all businesses to cease existing, and refrain from introducing, restrictive practices that impair economic efficiency or free trade on a voluntary basis. Where justified, the Government will take administrative or legal steps as appropriate to remove such practices as necessary.
>
> Alleged restrictive practices in the public and private sectors may be referred to the concerned policy bureau or government department for consideration. Separately, the COMPAG Secretariat will keep track of all referrals and bring these to the attention of COMPAG should there be substantial policy or systemic implications.

Alongside the Statement COMPAG published in 2003 *Guidelines to maintain a competitive environment and define and tackle anti-competitive practices*. These add little of substance to the Statement. COMPAG has dealt with a number of complaints, details of which may be found in its annual reports, but its effect has been negligible.

There has been international criticism of the approach taken by the Hong Kong Government to antitrust policy. The Secretariat of the WTO, for example, reporting in 2002, noted that a

> lack of coherent measures to address anti-competitive practices in all but a few sectors could constitute an obstacle to greater competition . . . The efficiency of Hong Kong, China's 'sector-specific' approach to competition, as a substitute for a comprehensive competition policy is open to question.[40]

[40] WTO Secretariat, *Trade Policy Review: Hong Kong, China*, WT/TPR/S/109, at III(1)(4).

1-1.20 Some commentators, notably Williams,[41] have also been highly critical of the policy. Williams labelled Hong Kong's earlier refusal to introduce a general law of antitrust as 'very perplexing', and 'intellectually dishonest'.[42] More strongly he argued that:

> The concentration of economic and effective political power in the hands of a small economic, oligarchic elite that benefits from collusive economic practices and would suffer from a competitive market, is the real reason for the government's overt and illogical hostility to regulation, in the public interest, in this field.[43]

1-1.21 It has been argued elsewhere that:

> The Hong Kong economy suffers from a dichotomy. The external sector of the economy—its exporting firms—operates in the highly competitive global environment; the firms are among the world's leaders. On the strength of its external sector, Hong Kong rightly earns high rankings in surveys of external competitiveness . . . However, in Hong Kong's internal sector the picture is very different. Many of Hong Kong's internal markets are not very contestable. Through a variety of mechanisms such as governmental franchises, arrangements to fix prices, and outright collusion many markets are uncompetitive. Examples include electricity supply, domestic water heating and cooking fuel, supermarkets, petrol supply and shipping services.[44]

1-1.22 In June 2005 a Competition Policy Review Committee ('CPRC') was established by COMPAG 'to review the effectiveness of Hong Kong's competition policy and to report to COMPAG on its findings'.[45] A wide ranging consultation exercise was conducted, at the end of which the CPRC recommended that new legislation should be introduced, which should apply to all, but that it should '*not* target market structures, nor seek to regulate "natural" monopolies or mergers and

[41] n 6, above. See generally Chapters 6 and 7. See also Williams, M, 'Cartels and Collusion: Failing Competition Policy in Hong Kong' (2005) 28:3 *World Competition* 313.

[42] n 6, above, at 225.

[43] Ibid. This led Williams to the conclusion 'that unless Hong Kong institutes constitutional reforms to commit to introducing a "functioning democracy", comprehensive competition law will be most unlikely to reach the statute book, save for a Damascene conversion of the vested interest groups that hold effective political power to an active role for government in competition regulation' (at 428); and at 427 '. . . the possibility of comprehensive competition legislation is remote'. The reasons underlying the 'Damascene conversion' of the Hong Kong legislature remain unclear, but the fact is that it appears that in 2009 or 2010 Hong Kong will operate a comprehensive system of antitrust law. Williams does not doubt Hong Kong's ability to implement and operate such a system effectively.

[44] n 37, above (Executive summary). For examples of cartelization see Williams, n 41, above, at 320.

[45] CPRC, *Report on the Review of Hong Kong's Competition Policy*, June 2006, para 2. See, on the early stages of the reform process, Furse, M, 'Competition Law and Reform in Hong Kong' (2007) *European Competition Law Review* 401.

acquisitions'.[46] In November 2006, based in part on the CPRC proposals, a discussion document, *Promoting Competition—Maintaining our Economic Drive* ('*Promoting Competition*'), was published by the Economic Development and Labour Bureau ('EDLB'). Although the need to review the policy in Hong Kong was recognized in *Promoting Competition* there was no commitment expressed in the document to making substantial reform. Four benefits were identified in *Promoting Competition* as possibly flowing from the adoption of a general antitrust law: (1) current policy could be implemented more effectively by *inter alia* allowing for more effective sanctioning; (2) the institutional framework for antitrust policy would be strengthened; (3) the business environment would be improved and a level playing field promoted; (4) long-term relative competitiveness would be improved.

Comment in Hong Kong on the proposal to introduce antitrust law was widespread, with the balance in favour of the adoption of such a regime, although some responses were openly hostile, with particular fears expressed that the regime might criminalize certain conduct (but this was always going to be unlikely), or might open the floodgates to frivolous or vexatious litigation. The response to *Promoting Competition* was set out in the EDLB *Report on Public Consultation on the way forward for Hong Kong's Competition Policy* published in March 2007.[47] At paras 5–8 of Chapter 3 of the Report the EDLB set out 'the way forward', with work to take place on drafting the appropriate legislation, with it being envisaged that this would include: **1-1.23**

(a) the definition of anti-competitive conduct to be covered and the introduction of an appropriate prohibition against such conduct;
(b) the establishment of a Competition Commission as the regulatory authority;
(c) a mechanism for exempting from the application of the law conduct that was considered to be in the wider economic or public interest;
(d) provisions related to confidentiality and a leniency programme; and
(e) the penalties that are applicable to a breach of the prohibition against anti-competitive conduct, refusal to cooperate with investigations, or unauthorized disclosure of confidential information.

A detailed proposal was put out to public consultation in May 2008. This is discussed in Chapter 3-1, below, which addresses the reform process as it stood at January 2009.

---

46 CPRC, n 45, above, para 5.

47 The complete submissions made during the consultation process are posted on the EDLB website, at <http://www.edlb.gov.hk>.

Antitrust Law in Taiwan

1-1.24 Compared to China and Hong Kong Taiwan's antitrust law has assumed a functioning and effective maturity. Williams states that:

> Taiwan has achieved notable success in its progress towards operating a more efficient, flexible and responsive economy, to which end the competition law has been a not insignificant contributor. The commitment of politicians, the long-term public advocacy of competition policy and the effective implementation of the new law by the [TFTC] have been impressive.
>
> The results have not always been perfect but the system and those who operate it have shown themselves to be both reflective and responsive. The law has been amended to improve deficiencies and the bureaucracy has matured in its approach to enforcement.[48]

In common with the majority of regimes covered in this book Taiwan has undergone substantial changes to its economic organizing principles—it is now a mixed economy, and 'Taiwan's private sector is clearly at the centre stage of its economy'.[49] Under the regime of 'authoritarian capitalism' that operated in Taiwan through to the 1970s up to nearly 60 per cent of industrial production was accounted for by Government-owned enterprises. That figure fell dramatically by the 1980s and reflected a determination on the part of the Government to move to a more liberal, market-based economy, although the Government continued to maintain monopolies in many important sectors, including most of the utilities, steel production, and petroleum. Taiwan's antitrust law, now contained in the Fair Trade Act, was drafted originally in the early 1980s as part of a wider process of both market liberalization and a drive for increased international economic engagement.[50] It has been noted that antitrust law in Taiwan 'has been an important element of the program of economic reforms that moved the economy from centrally directed emphasis on manufacturing and exports to a market-driven emphasis on services and high technology'.[51] Like the law in China the process was

[48] n 6, above, at 410–11. See also Liu, n 5, above, at 79: '. . . the pressure of globalization fostered general sentiments in favour of competition policy. The [TFTA] reinforced those sentiments, but its first ten years also demonstrate a checkered history of enforcement.' For an early overview of the development and operation of the regime see Lee, LLC, 'Taiwan's Antitrust Statutes: Proposals for a Regulatory Regime and Comparison of US and Taiwanese Antitrust Law' (1995–1996) 6 *Indiana International and Comparative Law Review* 583. For a more recent perspective see Wu, P and Thomas, C, 'Taiwan's Fair Trade Act: Achieving the "Right" Balance?' (2005–2006) 26 *Northwestern Journal of International Law and Business* 643.

[49] Liu, n 5, above, at 82.

[50] See Williams, n 6, above, at 366–411. See also Liu, n 5, above. In particular in 1984 it was announced by the recently-appointed Premier Yu that Taiwan would pursue a policy of 'internationalisation, liberalization and institutionalization' (see Liu, n 5, above, at 77).

[51] OECD, *Chinese Taipei—Peer Review of Competition Law and Policy 2006*, OECD (2006), 3.

somewhat lengthy, with five years spent drafting the legislation, and a further five years of deliberation. The Fair Trade Act was finally promulgated on 4 February 1991[52] (eleven years before Taiwan joined the WTO as a customs territory in 2002) and has since been amended on a number of occasions.[53] The Act extends to a wide range of conduct, encompassing areas falling within the purview of more mature antitrust regimes, such as those of the US and the EC,[54] but it also extends to unfair trade practices, including counterfeiting, false or misleading advertising, and deceptive practices that might affect the trading order.[55] Article 1 of the Fair Trade Act states that the law was enacted for the purposes of 'maintaining trading order, protecting consumers' interests, ensuring fair competition, and promoting economic stability and prosperity'.

The primary body charged with administering the law is the Taiwan Fair Trade Commission ('TFTC'), which is responsible for 'drafting fair trade policy, laws, regulations, and investigating and handling various activities impeding competition, such as monopolies, mergers, concerted actions, and other restraints on competition or unfair trade practices on the part of enterprises'.[56] The TFTC is, under the terms of the Taiwan Fair Trade Act ('TFTA'), required to function independently of government, and although its Chairman is a member of the Cabinet, the TFTC operates with substantial independence. An OECD peer review process noted that its decisions are not subject to 'revision or reversal based on effects on other policy interests'.[57] Appeal procedures that are in place under the Administrative Appeal Law mean that the TFTC powers are subject to robust judicial control. The TFTC was created in 1992 and has, in its sixteen-year history, drafted amendments to the TFTA, the first of which, in 1993, significantly raised the penalties that were available to it in order to bring the enforcement of the TFTA more in line with that of the US and EC. The TFTC has also produced **1-1.25**

[52] In the words of Liu, n 5, above, at 79, the TFTA was enacted 'without much deliberation. In the frenzy for full political participation, what politician in his right mind would oppose legislation billed as being "fair"?' The OECD has noted that: 'Fair competition appears to be the dominant objective [in the TFTA]. The definition of competition implies that the law is more concerned about process and fairness than about welfare effects' (OECD, n 51, above, at 12).

[53] It should be noted that the TFTA was drafted while martial law was still in force, but that by the time it was enacted martial law had been lifted. This had an impact on institutional arrangements, such as the decision to give the enforcement body an independent status, rather than following the earlier proposal under which the TFTC would have been a part of the Ministry of Economic Affairs.

[54] The German influence on the legislation is also clear: '. . . the [TFTA] draft was the result of [a Ministry of Economic Affairs]-commissioned academic study by the German-worshipping Law Faculty of National Taiwan University' (Liu, n 5, above, at 87).

[55] Although the TFTC is active in its enforcement activity the majority of its case load continues to be taken up with cases brought in relation to deceptive and unfair marketing practices.

[56] Fair Trade Commission website, <http://www.ftc.gov.tw>.

[57] n 51, above, at 7.

guidelines based on its acquired experience in enforcing the legislation. These are referred to in the substantive chapters dealing with Taiwan's antitrust law in Part 4, below. The TFTC is relatively active in its enforcement activity, and in some years has made over 200 formal decisions, although many of these decisions are made after a relatively short procedure. There have also been ongoing advocacy efforts directed, in particular, at the local business community. The TFTC is also relatively active internationally, and Taiwan is an observer member of the OECD, and has been subject to peer review by the OECD, most recently in 2006.[58] Taiwan has entered into formal agreements with the Australian and New Zealand antitrust authorities, and with the French *Conseil de la Concurrence*, and has held bilateral consultation meetings with a number of other antitrust authorities. The TFTC created and maintains the Asia-Pacific Economic Cooperation ('APEC') Competition Policy and Law database, which remains an important source of information in relation to the antitrust regimes of the APEC members.

Antitrust Law in Korea

1-1.26 The core antitrust legislation in Korea now is the Monopoly Regulation and Fair Trade Act ('MRFTA'), the short title of which (often encountered in the relevant materials) is the Fair Trade Act. The Act, which was passed in 1980, has a wide scope, extending to fair trade, antitrust, competition, consumer protection, and (de)regulation.[59] It has been noted that 'in general, Korean competition law resembles that of the European Union rather than that of the United States'.[60] Article 1 of the MRFTA provides that the purpose of the Act is to:

> . . . promote fair and free competition such that creative enterprising activities are fostered, to protect consumers, and to strive for the balanced development of the national economy by preventing the abuse of market dominance by enterprisers and excessive concentration of economic power and by regulating improper cartels and unfair business practices.

58 See OECD, n 51, above. At the time of this review the following recommendations for change were made: implementation of a formal leniency programme; abandonment of special treatment of price fixing and other agreements among SMEs; raising of sanctions; merger notifications to be based on objective criteria, rather than on market share; rights of private claimants should be improved. The review also raised the risk 'that rules based on a cultural tradition of fairness might lead to interventions to correct differences in bargaining power, which could dampen competition rather than promote it' (ibid, Foreword).

59 Anecdotal evidence suggests that there remain tensions between the operation of the antitrust law regime and the operation of regulatory regimes in Korea, with institutional conflicts occasionally manifesting themselves. For a good overview of the development of antitrust in Korea, and its practice up to 2005 see Jung, Y and Chang, SW, 'Korea's Competition Law and Policies in Perspective' (2005–2006) 26 *Northwestern Journal of International Law and Business* 687.

60 Lee, MH, 'Recent Developments in the Treatment of Collusion by the Korean Courts' (2005) 4:2 *Journal of Korean Competition Law* 155 at 157.

Notwithstanding the wide range of activity that may be regulated under the terms of the MRFTA it is clear even from this first article that it incorporates a traditional antitrust approach, with particular attention paid to monopoly conduct, multilateral anti-competitive conduct, and mergers, all of which are dealt with in Part 5 below.

The MRFTA has been amended on many occasions since its enactment, most recently in February 2008.[61] The enforcement agency is the Korea Fair Trade Commission ('KFTC'), which was established in 1981 as an independent quasi-judicial organ, although it has been noted that 'the KFTC retains the character of an administrative organisation due to its important policy-making functions'.[62] The structure of the KFTC is dealt with more fully in Part 5-1 below. The KFTC maintains a website which incorporates substantial English-language information and materials. Unless otherwise indicated extracts from Korean antitrust legislation used throughout this book are taken directly from this website (<http://www.ftc.go.kr>). The MRFTA itself replaced earlier rudimentary legislation dealing with certain aspects of antitrust law. The first such law was the Price Stabilisation Act of 1973, and this was replaced by the Monopoly Regulation and Price Stability Act of 1975. This history of employing the law to control prices, which emerged out of the 1973 oil crisis, continued to haunt the early years of the operation of the MRFTA, and attracted criticism.

It is not possible to make sense of Korean antitrust policy without understanding **1-1.27** the role of the '*chaebol*'—a distinctive industrial conglomerate entity—which collectively are very powerful and prominent in the Korean economy, and whose existence has been highly influential on the development of antitrust policy in Korea. At the end of the Second World War the Korean economy was exceptionally weak and had suffered from nearly 40 years of Japanese colonial rule. The economy was further damaged by the Korean War (1950–1953). In 1962 under the Park Chung Hee administration a five-year plan, the first of several such initiatives, was introduced, and 'a remarkable transformation of the economy took place'.[63] *Chaebols* were deliberately fostered by the Government in the early 1960s as part of the drive towards the development of a modern industrial economy that could compete globally. The result was the emergence of a number of entities with holdings in many different sectors, including heavy industry, chemicals,

[61] The consolidated text of the MRFTA reproduced in Appendix 3 incorporates all amendments at present in force. Not all of the reforms made in 2008 have entered into force at the time of writing.

[62] Kim, Y-H, 'A Guide to Korean Antitrust Law' (2002) 2 *Journal of Korean Law* 161 at 167.

[63] Lee, H-H, 'Korea's Competition Policy and Its Applications to Other Asian Economies', in Hoa, TV (ed), *Competition Policy and Global Competitiveness in Major Asian Economies* (Cheltenham: Edward Elgar, 2003) at 89. See generally Chung, Y-I, *South Korea in the Fast Lane: Economic Development and Capital Formation* (Oxford: Oxford University Press, 2008) Chapter 2.

manufacture, extending through to banking and retail distribution. While the government initiative was successful in transforming the nature of the Korean economy, it has been noted that the 'pattern of industrialisation led by *chaebols* accelerated the monopolistic and oligopolistic concentration of capital and economically profitable activities in the hands of a limited number of conglomerates'.[64] At the start of 2007 for example Samsung, the largest of the *chaebols*, which had in excess of 60 affiliated companies, with interests ranging from petrochemicals to hotels, accounted for nearly 25 per cent of the total of the Korean stock market value, and was responsible for approximately one-fifth of Korea's exports. Jenny pointed to the *chaebols'* damaging role in the Korean economy:

> The development of the *chaebols* went unchecked from the 1960s to at least the middle of the Eighties resulting in a high level of market concentration. The *chaebols* pursued a policy of diversification and over-expansion sometimes with little regard for profitability. With the support of successive governments they were able to get preferential loans to pursue their development. On the contrary, firms which did not belong to a *chaebol*, irrespective of their productivity or profitability had a difficult time getting loans to expand their business. As a result, the *chaebols* accumulated huge debts which made them particularly vulnerable to any slowdown in their export capacity. Well-known scandals revealed the cosy relationship between some *chaebols* and the political elite and the way in which political influence was used by them to secure new sources of financing, even for dubious projects.[65]

1-1.28 Although Korean antitrust law has clearly borrowed in parts from US antitrust law it is closer in spirit to the law of the EC, and there are a number of peculiarities in the system—particularly in relation to merger control—which are explained by the need to take into account the presence of the *chaebols* in the market, and in particular their ability to cross-subsidize activities from one sector to another. The question of the approach that should be taken towards the *chaebols* continues to influence the development of antitrust law in Korea. In February 2007 for example it was reported that although the Government intended to reduce the controls on cross-shareholdings the move was opposed by the Chairman of the KFTC who argued that 'the *chaebols* have become too powerful', and that the proposed move would further ease the position of the *chaebols*.[66]

1-1.29 The role of the *chaebol* has also led to greater steps to protect small and medium-sized enterprises ('SMEs') than may be the case in other jurisdictions. While the EC for example has on occasion pointed to the role of antitrust law in protecting and nurturing SMEs the US is generally silent on such a policy. In Korea SMEs account for in excess of 80 per cent of employment, notwithstanding the power of

---

64 Kim, n 62, above, at 168.

65 Jenny, n 3, above, at 16.

66 'S Korea ties to clip wings of the chaebol', *Financial Times*, 4 February 2007. Provisions of the law which are aimed almost exclusively at curbing *chaebol* power are not dealt with in this book.

the *chaebols*, and a large part of the turnover of the SMEs flows from sub-contracting transactions. The KFTC is particularly concerned in this environment to ensure that 'fair cooperative relationships' are built between large companies and such enterprises. There is some influence of this policy in the MRFTA and in the application of Korean antitrust law, alongside wider protections in dedicated legislation, such as the Fair Subcontract Transactions Act.[67]

Antitrust policy in Korea has not been static since the enactment of the MRFTA, **1-1.30**
as is shown in part by the number of amendments to the MRFTA. In December 2003 for example the KFTC published a *Three-year Market Reform Roadmap* which set out a policy agenda of market reform, the ultimate aim of which was 'to increase efficiency in resource allocation'. This would be achieved by enhancing transparency and fairness in the market, which would 'facilitate the functioning of the market, leading to technological innovation through market competition and the emergence of new growth engines'.[68] Government regulation was to be reduced 'on a gradual basis'. The bulk of this reform programme was addressed to company and financial transactions law and regulation, but the KFTC also announced that it was to carry out a review of the antitrust laws, and that it would look in particular at improving the mergers review system, and facilitate private lawsuits for antitrust damage. The KFTC was also to propose legislative change to regulations which hindered market entry and competition under the umbrella heading of 'The Omnibus Cartel Repeal Act', an earlier version of which had effected change in approximately 20 regulations, including for example areas such as prohibiting previously legal fee-setting arrangements in the professions, including lawyers and tax accountants. At an early stage of the second version of this exercise some 174 anti-competitive regulations were identified as raising possible concern. Particular attention too was placed on the detection and deterrence of cartels, with the KFTC arguing in favour of an enhanced penalty system of up to ten per cent of turnover to align Korean penalties with those of the EC. This policy was subsequently supported, and the penalties permitted under the MRFTA have now been increased.

The antitrust law regime in Korea is active and a version of the effects doctrine is **1-1.31**
applied such that its reach may be extraterritorial. It is with some regularity that enforcement action undertaken by the KFTC is reported, and the powers of the KFTC should not be underestimated. In 2005, for example, the KFTC dealt with a staggering 707 cases violating the MRFTA (the majority of which—481—related to the provisions of the MRFTA dealing with unfair business practices),

[67] No 3799, 31 December 1984; amended by Law No 7107, 20 January 2004.

[68] KFTC, *The Three-Year Market Reform Roadmap*, December 2003, 2. See also KFTC, *Direction of Competition Policy in 2004*, part III.

imposing penalties in excess of Won259bn.[69] More recent activity includes: a probe into Hyundai Card following concerns that the credit card company had received unfair financial support from its parent, Hyundai Motor Group;[70] an investigation into seven of the country's largest supermarket chains to determine whether the retailers were unfairly using their purchasing power;[71] an investigation into possible collusion amongst eleven banks (including Citibank and Standard Chartered) in relation to fee-setting;[72] and an investigation into Hyundai Motor following allegations that the company exerted unlawful pressure on suppliers to impose territorial restrictions.[73] That such actions are more than paper exercises can readily be shown. In May 2006, for example, the three mobile telecommunications providers in the country were fined a combined Won1.78bn (US$1.8m) following a finding that they had colluded in price-setting. In 2005 the KFTC had imposed penalties totalling Won116bn on fixed-line telecommunications providers in relation to similar breaches. Commentators have identified a 'tougher' stance being taken by the KFTC towards anti-competitive activity of large Korean firms in recent cases. In 2007, the KFTC reported, penalties imposed in respect of breaches of the MRFTA amounted to some Won423bn (US$408m), of which cartel infringements accounted for Won307bn.[74]

Antitrust Law in Vietnam

1-1.32 The policy of *doi moi* entered into by Vietnam in 1986 committed the State to the development of a 'socialist oriented market economy',[75] and foreign direct investment was accepted in 1988. The development of a comprehensive antitrust law—something new to Vietnam—was seen as an integral tool for the achievement of this policy. Vietnam introduced an antitrust law in 2004 (the Vietnam Law on Competition ('VLOC')), which entered into force on 1 July 2005, and a number of relevant implementing laws are in place, although the application of these remains undeveloped. This law takes precedence over any other laws regarding

[69] See KFTC, *Annual Report on Competition Policy Development in Korea*, September 2006, 10.

[70] *Financial Times*, 1 November 2006; KFTC Decision 2007-504, 24 October 2007.

[71] *Financial Times*, 31 October 2006.

[72] *Financial Times*, 2 June 2006; KFTC Decision 2005-129, 18 August 2005.

[73] KFTC Decision 2007-281, 18 May 2007.

[74] KFTC Newsletter, 4 July 2008. In respect of cartels punished in 2007 the KFTC imposed penalties against: a synthetic resin cartel (US$101.3m); a non-life insurance cartel (US$48.8m); a sugar making cartel (US$50.7m); and an oil refining cartel (US$50.7m).

[75] Article 16 of the Constitution of Vietnam of 1992 (as amended) states that:

> All economic sectors are important components of the socialist-oriented market economy. Organizations and individuals of all economic sectors may conduct production and business activities not prohibited by law, striving for long-term development, co-operation, equality and competition under law.

anti-competitive practices and applies to all business enterprises and professional and trade associations in Vietnam, including overseas enterprises and associations registered in Vietnam (see further Chapter 6-1, below). State administrative bodies, public utilities, and state monopolies are also subject to the law. Article 1 of the law states that it extends to 'competition-restricting acts' and 'unfair competition acts', and also sets out relevant procedures, although many of the provisions of the law are supplemented by decrees (discussed in further detail in Part 6). As will be discussed in Part 6, although the law is in parts based on the EC model it is also highly distinctive, differing in many places from the standards advocated by bodies such as the International Competition Network ('ICN'), and in practice may be difficult to apply due to the rigidity of the legal provisions. When it can be applied its application may not always be sensitive to competitive realities.

While China's antitrust law has been brought forward in part to facilitate relationships with the WTO, Vietnam was not yet a member of the WTO at the time its law was brought forward. The membership to which Vietnam aspired was granted in January 2007, when Vietnam became the 150th member of the WTO. It has been pointed out however that other international relationships may have played a role in the drafting of the law, and that under a bilateral trade agreement with the US Vietnam is 'committed to improving the quality of its laws and the consistency of its legislative framework'.[76] Although the Vietnamese economy remains characterized by low productivity and inefficiency there have nevertheless been some remarkable successes in the fostering of business. In 2000 there were some 42,000 businesses in Vietnam. By the end of 2007 this number had risen to over 183,000, with nearly 60,000 new businesses being registered in 2007 alone. This growth may be attributed in part to the Enterprise Law of 2005. A large number of SOEs have been equitized, but the State retains a large degree of equity ownership in many of these firms.[77] Throughout 2007 merger and acquisition activity was expanding rapidly in Vietnam. In 2006 there were 38 deals reported with a value of US$299m, whereas in 2007 some 113 deals with a value of US$1.753bn were reported by PricewaterhouseCoopers. In a majority of the larger deals the target was a Vietnamese company, and the acquirer purchased the entirety of the assets. Many purchasers were foreign firms, although there were some mergers in which Vietnamese firms purchased foreign firms. **1-1.33**

[76] McBratney, A, 'The Nine Lives of Vietnam's new Competition Law' (2004) *European Competition Law Review* 485. For a discussion of some of the complexities surrounding the law in Vietnam see generally Pham, A, 'The Development of Competition Law in Vietnam in the face of Economic Reforms and Global Integration' (2005–2006) 26 *Northwestern Journal of International Law and Business* 547.

[77] VCAD, *Report on Economic Concentration in Vietnam in 2008—Current situation and outlook* (2009) [draft, nyp].

1-1.34 There is an unfortunate element of political intervention in the antitrust law system in Vietnam. The primary enforcement agencies are a part of the Ministry of Industry and Trade; a number of key decisions can be taken only by the Minister, and some may only be taken by the Prime Minister. It has, however, been suggested that the Ministry 'is the only place where knowledge and expertise on competition issues is available'.[78] The relationship between the State and the competitive process is further clouded by the presence of a sizeable state-owned sector, with state-owned enterprises ('SOEs') being prevalent (although their performance has, historically, tended to be poor), and a number of important industries remain subject to state-controlled monopolization. A number of these SOEs are highly vertically integrated, and the market generally, in part because of its relatively small size, remains very concentrated, which appears to be a matter of some concern to the Vietnam Competition Administration Department ('VCAD'). Over 50 per cent of industry top-three firms remain state-owned at the end of 2008. Unlike the law in Korea, however (see above), there are no special provisions in the VLOC to deal with conglomerate structures which possess substantial market power, and which may have the ability to hinder entry. Further cultural difficulties exist in the operation of an antitrust regime. As discussed in Chapter 6-3, below, some provisions of the Law are very prescriptive, and it has been noted that there is in Vietnam a 'deep-rooted command and control system'[79] notwithstanding attempts to liberalize markets in accordance with the *doi moi* policy. Further, VCAD itself has recognized that as Vietnam 'is just moving toward a market-oriented economy, both the private sector and regulatory agencies are still inadequately aware of issues that may arise in connection with a modern market mechanism'.[80]

[78] CUTS International, *A Guide to Competition Issues in Vietnam*, at 69.

[79] CUTS International, *Promoting Competition Policy & Law in Vietnam*, at 13. There are a number of legislative instruments which are highly interventionist, including in particular an Ordinance on Price (2002).

[80] See n 77, above, Part IV.

1-2

STANDARDS IN ANTITRUST LAW

Introduction 1-2.01
The Control of Anti-competitive Agreements 1-2.04
Forms of agreements 1-2.06
The rule of reason, exemptions, and exceptions 1-2.10
Horizontal agreements 1-2.13
Vertical agreements 1-2.18
Monopolization and Abuse of Dominant Position 1-2.21
Markets and market power 1-2.22
Condemned conduct 1-2.25
Predatory pricing 1-2.27
Price discrimination 1-2.30
Excessive pricing 1-2.31
Refusals to supply and the essential facilities doctrine 1-2.32
Full line forcing, bundling, and tie-in sales 1-2.34
Merger Control 1-2.35
Application of Economic Principles and Evidence 1-2.45
International Cooperation 1-2.52

Introduction

Antitrust law exists in part (or, depending on one's view, exclusively) to address **1-2.01**
economic concerns relating to the harms that flow from the existence and exercise of market power, and there is a significant degree of consistency in the legal approach taken across different regimes as those economic concerns are consistent. Certainly it is intuitive that the adviser seeking to provide advice in this area will make international comparisons, and draw on experiences gained in other jurisdictions. However, although this chapter is in part based on this premise, it is not the case that all antitrust laws are identical, dealing with the same issues in the same way, and even where similarities are evident it may be dangerous to presume that these support a close reliance on the experience or practice in another jurisdiction. As Advocate General Kirschner noted in the EC case of *Tetra Pak Rausing SA v Commission*:

> Many valuable ideas for the interpretation of Community law can be derived from the discussions going on on the other side of the Atlantic and from the solutions found by the American courts. However, prudence must be counselled in transferring concepts and theories from one legal system to the other. There are substantial

> differences between the various elements going to make up US law and those going to make up Community law . . .[1]

While the US applies an approach based exclusively around an objective efficiency standard the same is not true in the case of the EC, where antitrust law is tainted by policy objectives that extend beyond the attainment of a pareto optimum efficient outcome.[2] Particular attention must be paid in the part of the world covered by this book to the fact that the underlying political and economic assumptions driving policy may be different to those that apply in the West. It is worth noting in particular that both China and Vietnam purport to be, to varying degrees, *socialist* market economies. Article 1 of the Chinese Anti-Monopoly Law makes reference to its operation in the context of a 'socialist market economy', and Vietnam's official title is 'the Socialist Republic of Vietnam'. One of the aims of the relevant Parts of this book is to explain the extent to which these wider political stances will affect the operation of antitrust law. It would be naive to presume that there will be *no* effect. Notwithstanding this caveat the rest of this section addresses, in outline, the approach taken to antitrust law in the US and the EC, and the extent to which common standards have emerged and are being promoted in international organizations, whether formally or informally.

1-2.02 Antitrust—or in the EC 'competition'—law typically addresses three different broad heads of conduct: agreements, monopolistic practices/abuses of dominant positions, and mergers. Broadly the concern driving the law forward is the same in respect of all heads of substantive conduct, and is that the exercise of market power may lead to a loss of welfare—to lower output, higher prices, reduced choice, and reduced quality. Agreements generally raise more concern when they are horizontal, such that competitors substitute cooperation (whether formal or informal) for competition, than when they are vertical, although in some situations (for example resale price fixing) the latter may also be treated as harmful. The view is generally taken that it is not appropriate to seek to prevent the emergence of monopolies where these are the result of victories achieved during a lawful competitive process, but that the strategies by which power is gained, and conduct once power has been gained, may be curtailed. Merger control, the most complex of the areas dealt with under antitrust law, provides an opportunity to curtail the growth of market power which is not the result of internal growth, and for that reason it is usually horizontal mergers between competitors which attract more scrutiny than vertical mergers or mergers which are not between competitors. A number of regimes have taken the choice to eschew merger control, and to focus just on anti-competitive agreements and monopoly issues. While this

---

[1] Case T-51/89 [1991] 4 CMLR 334 at 343–4.

[2] For an overview of antitrust law in the US and EC see Alese, F, *Federal Antitrust and EC Competition Law Analysis* (Aldershot: Ashgate Publishing Limited, 2008).

position is demonstrably illogical (a cartel between five competitors may be banned, but the same five competitors would lawfully be allowed to merge) neither the US nor the EC operated merger control from the outset of their respective antitrust law regimes—indeed, it took the EC thirty-two years before an effective system of merger control was introduced. Hong Kong took the decision in 2007 not to introduce merger control as part of its general antitrust law, although that position may be reviewed in the future.

The two most prominent antitrust law regimes are those of the US and the EC. **1-2.03**
The former, introduced by the Sherman Act in 1890, is the older and the more focused on an efficiency standard, while the law of the EC has been criticized by some for incorporating within its analysis non-efficiency objectives. The Chinese regime has been clearly influenced by EC antitrust law, while the Korean has more similarities to that of the US in its structure, although not necessarily in the wider policy underlying much of the application of the law. Differences and similarities between the operation of the regimes discussed in this book and those of the US and EC will be addressed where it is useful to do so. The following section assumes no prior knowledge of the antitrust law of either the US or EC.

The Control of Anti-competitive Agreements

The control of anti-competitive agreements is addressed primarily by s 1 of the **1-2.04**
Sherman Act in the US, and art 81 of the Treaty in the EC. Section 1 is a unitary provision, and states in part that:

> Every contract, combination in the form of trust or otherwise, or conspiracy, in restraint of trade or commerce among the several States, or with foreign nations, is declared to be illegal. Every person who shall make any contract or engage in any combination or conspiracy hereby declared to be illegal shall be deemed guilty of a felony . . .

Article 81 EC is structured differently, being in three paragraphs, the first of which sets out a prohibition, the second of which states the effect of that prohibition, and the third paragraph of which provides a mechanism to avoid the effect of the prohibition where the relevant agreement meets specified criteria. In full, art 81 EC is as follows:

> 1. The following shall be prohibited as incompatible with the common market: all agreements between undertakings, decisions by associations of undertakings and concerted practices which may affect trade between member states and which have as their object or effect the prevention restriction or distortion of competition within the common market, and in particular those which:
> (a) directly or indirectly fix purchase or selling prices or any other trading conditions;
> (b) limit or control production, markets, technical development, or investment;

(c) share markets or sources of supply;
(d) apply dissimilar conditions to equivalent transactions with other trading parties, thereby placing them at a competitive disadvantage;
(e) make the conclusion of contracts subject to acceptance by the other parties of supplementary obligations which, by their nature or according to commercial usage, have no connection with the subject of such contracts.

2. Any agreements or decisions prohibited pursuant to this Article shall be automatically void.
3. The provisions of paragraph 1 may, however, be declared inapplicable in the case of:
— any agreement or category of agreements between undertakings;
— any decision or category of decisions by associations of undertakings;
— any concerted practice or category of concerted practices;
which contributes to improving the production or distribution of goods or to promoting technical or economic progress, while allowing consumers a fair share of the resulting benefit, and which does not:
(a) impose on the undertakings concerned restrictions which are not indispensable to the attainment of these objectives;
(b) afford such undertakings the possibility of eliminating competition in respect of a substantial part of the products in question.

Although the prohibitions of s 1 and art 81 EC are broadly similar in their effect, the differences in the structure of the two provisions has led to substantial differences in the way in which the law operates.

1-2.05 Neither provision provides comprehensive definitions of key terms and concepts: when an 'agreement' may be found to exist, or who should be engaged in such agreements, or the form such agreements may take. Instead it has been left to the courts and the enforcing public authorities to develop such definitions on a case-by-case approach based on experience. In both cases the law applies to agreements which range from taking the form of clearly drafted contracts to 'gentlemen's agreements', although the latter are particularly difficult to deal with. Both laws extend to vertical as well as to horizontal agreements, although the approach to vertical agreements in the EC is somewhat stricter than is the approach in the US. The definitions of 'persons' in the US, and 'undertakings' in the EC are both wide, encompassing economic actors operating in markets, independent of ownership, legal structure, or status.

Forms of agreements

1-2.06 Article 81 EC makes express reference to agreements, decisions by associations, and to concerted practices, and s 1 of the Sherman Act refers to contracts, combinations in restraint of trade, or to conspiracies. In both cases a wide range of conduct is caught by the terms of the legislation. It should be unquestionable that agreements taking the form of contracts between companies are capable of infringing antitrust law. More questions arise however in respect of the actions of business associations, and in respect of cooperation which falls short of a formal agreement.

In respect of coordinated action which is not evidenced by the existence of an explicit agreement the position is very difficult. In the EC the term 'concerted practice' has been addressed by the European Courts on a number of occasions. The leading statement is that set out in the *Suiker Unie* case, where the European Court of Justice ('ECJ') held that: **1-2.07**

> [t]he concept of a 'concerted practice' refers to a form of co-ordination between undertakings which, without having been taken to the stage where an agreement properly so-called has been concluded, knowingly substitutes for the risks of competition co-operation in practice between them which leads to conditions of competition which do not correspond to the normal conditions of the market, having regard to the nature of the products, the importance and number of the undertakings as well as the size and nature of the said market. Such co-operation in practice amounts to a concerted practice *inter alia* when it enables the persons concerned to consolidate established positions to the detriment of effective freedom of movement of the products in the Common Market and of the freedom of consumers to choose their suppliers.[3]

While this is an attractive definition, its application in practice has raised continuous problems for antitrust enforcement. The question arises as to what extent companies in an oligopoly may be condemned for recognizing, quite legitimately, their mutual interdependence. This question was addressed by the Court in *ICI v Commission,* where the Court held that:

> while it is permissible for each manufacturer to change his prices freely and to take into account for this purpose the behaviour, present and foreseeable, of his competitors, it is, on the other hand, contrary to the competition rules of the Treaty for a manufacturer to co-operate with his competitors, in whatever manner, to determine a co-ordinated course of action relating to an increase in prices.[4]

In both the EC and the US regime mere parallel behaviour cannot, without further evidence, constitute a breach of antitrust law. In the US for example it has been held that 'the fact that many, if not all, firms in an industry react similarly to a particular practice does not evidence an industry wide agreement when there is a legitimate business purpose for each firm's behaviour'.[5] Equally an agreement **1-2.08**

[3] *Coöperatieve Vereniging 'Suiker Unie' UA v Commission* Cases 40–48/73, 50/73, 54–56/73, 111/73, 113–114/73 [1976] 1 CMLR 295 at paras 26–7.

[4] Case 48/69 [1972] 1 CMLR 557 at para 118.

[5] *Richards v Neilsen Freight Lines* 810 F2d 904 (9th Cir, 1987).

cannot be inferred from the mere existence of a 'follow my leader pattern'.[6] In the EC in the case of *Wood Pulp* it was held that:

> . . . parallel conduct cannot be regarded as furnishing proof of concertation unless concertation constitutes the only plausible explanation for such conduct. It is necessary to bear in mind that, although Article [81 EC] prohibits any form of collusion which distorts competition, it does not deprive economic operators of the right to adapt themselves intelligently to the existing and anticipated conduct of their competitors.[7]

The question of whether 'conscious parallelism' is condemned will be determined by the amount of the evidence available. The leading US case of *Interstate Circuit v United States*[8] for example dealt with a situation in which film distributors agreed to terms put forward by a large cinema chain. Discussing the issue of what conditions had to be satisfied to demonstrate a meeting of the minds between the distributors the Court held that the knowledge, motive, as well as the substantial unanimity among the distributors was important in this respect. In the words of the Court 'it was enough that, knowing that concerted action was contemplated and invited the distributors gave their adherence to the scheme and participated in it'. In *Matsushita Electric Industrial Co v Zenith Radio Corp*[9] the Court held that for conspiracy charges to survive on the basis of indirect or circumstantial evidence the conspiracies must make economic sense and evidence must establish that the defendants were not acting independently.

1-2.09 The activities of trade associations may also be subject to scrutiny under antitrust laws relating to anti-competitive agreements. The position is consistent in both the EC and the US in that, normally, the mere formation of a trade association will not be condemned. There is a recognition in this approach that trade associations may do much that is pro-competitive or that has no impact on competition. However, where an association acts as a conduit for the organization of concerted actions by its members—for example by making recommendations as to the prices at which its members sell their goods or services—both the trade association itself and its constituent members may face condemnation under art 81 EC or s 1 of the Sherman Act. There have been a relatively large number of cases in Taiwan dealt with under the Taiwan Fair Trade Act in which trade associations and their members have been condemned for breaches of art 14 of the Act (see further Chapter 4-2, below).

[6] *Souza v Estate of Bishop* 821 F2d 1332 (9th Cir, 1987).

[7] *Re Wood Pulp Cartel: A. Ahlström Oy v Commission* Cases C–89, 104, 114, 116, 117, and 125–129/85 [1993] 4 CMLR 407, para 71.

[8] 306 US 208 (1939).

[9] 475 US 574 (1986).

The rule of reason, exemptions, and exceptions

Taken literally the terms of s 1 of the Sherman Act could extend to a huge range of multilateral conduct taking place in markets. Many agreements contain within them restrictions on competition. However, many of these restrictions may be justified as being pro-competitive. For example the seller of a business who accepts a non-compete obligation requested by the purchaser may find it harder to sell the business without such an obligation being present; the retailer who acts as a distributor of a manufacturer's products may wish for a degree of protection from nearby outlets also offering the products for sale. In the application of s 1 the courts early on developed the concept of the 'rule of reason', first introduced in *Standard Oil Co of New Jersey v United States*.[10] In the leading case Justice Brandeis held that the: **1-2.10**

> true test of legality is whether the restraint imposed is such as merely regulates and perhaps thereby promotes competition or whether it is such as may suppress or even destroy competition. To determine that question the court must ordinarily consider the facts peculiar to the business to which the restraint is applied; its condition before and after the restraint was imposed; the nature of the restraint and its effect, actual or probable. The history of the restraint, the evil believed to exist, the reason for adopting the particular remedy, the purpose or end sought to be attained, are all relevant facts.[11]

Under this US approach restraints or types of agreements may be categorized as being either *per se* prohibited, or as falling within the rule of reason. Where the rule of reason applies it is for the plaintiff to demonstrate that in the case in question the restraint operates so as to likely damage competition. Where the *per se* rule applies it is for the defendant to justify the operation of the restraint as being pro-competitive or efficiency enhancing. Over time the boundaries of the rule have shifted, and restrictions which were once found to be *per se* unlawful may now fall within the rule of reason. There are, for example, no vertical restraints which fall within the *per se* category. In the EC the approach is very different, as the structure of the core legal provision is different. Where s 1 of the Sherman Act required judicial moderation in its application, art 81 EC provides expressly for a system of exempting or excepting agreements from the application of art 81(1) EC where they fall within that prohibition. As a result of this difference in structure the Court of First Instance ('CFI') has held that the rule of reason does not operate in EC antitrust law.[12] In the EC the art 81(1) rubric is cast widely, bringing within the scope of the prohibition many agreements which contain restrictions within them, some of which would be found to fall within the rule of

10 (1911) 221 US 1.

11 *Chicago Board of Trade v United States* (1918) 246 US 231 at 238.

12 *Metropole Television (M6) v Commission* Case T-112/99, 18 September 2001.

reason in the US. Article 81(2) then provides that these agreements are void. However, any party seeking to rely on, enforce, or defend an agreement subject to the strictures of art 81(1) may then argue that the cumulative conditions set out in art 81(3) apply. In essence there are two ways in which such a case may be made. The easier is to rely on any one of a number of 'block exemption regulations' enacted by the EC Commission; the second is to argue that although the agreement in question may not benefit from the terms of one of the block exemption regulations it individually satisfies the conditions for the grant of an art 81(3) exception. Block exemption regulations exist in relation to categories of both horizontal and vertical agreements, and are a generalized application of the principles that apply to art 81(3) generally, based on the experience and practice of the EC Commission. These are binding on courts and National Competition Authorities, as well as on the parties to agreements themselves, such that they may be safely relied on as a defence to an action based in competition law where the terms of an agreement fall entirely within the scope of a relevant block exemption regulation.

1-2.11 Although it might appear that there is, in substance, little difference between the operation of the US rule of reason, and the operation of the art 81(3) requirements in the EC, the difference in the shape that the regime takes as a result of the difference in structure is considerable. From the entry into force of the EC antitrust regime, until the reforms introduced by Regulation 1/2003, as part of the 'modernization' of EC antitrust law, the EC Commission had exclusive jurisdiction to apply art 81(3). This meant in particular that in a case brought before a national court, or by a national competition authority, the defendant could not rely on art 81(3) individually, but instead had to rely either on the terms of a block exemption regulation or had to apply for an exemption from the EC Commission directly. While this process gave the EC Commission considerable power, and allowed it to develop centrally an approach to the various categories of agreements that might be found to fall within art 81(1), it also led to considerable backlogs in the application of antitrust law. Finding that it did not have the time and resources to respond formally to all art 81(3) exemption requests made to it, the EC Commission relied instead on informal case resolutions, which spawned a degree of legal uncertainty. Arguments may be made in favour of both systems. The application of a rule of reason is attractive in that as soon as it becomes clear that a particular practice falls within the rule of reason companies may reasonably rely on the prima facie legitimacy of such arrangements, and are likely to face legal challenge only in extreme cases. If cases are brought by private parties these are likely to be quickly dismissed unless the claimant brings forward at an early stage good evidence of a strong claim of antitrust injury. Those in favour of an exemption and exception system would argue that such a procedure allows for more considered development of antitrust law, and that this is particularly appropriate in the early years of a regime, or in a regime where expertise, particularly at the judicial level, is not robust or well developed. However, where the authority charged with operating an exemption-style system is itself limited in resources and/or expertise then the system may become quickly paralysed unless effective block exemption regulations are published. It was pointed out in the EC context that one of the key problems with the first and second generation of block exemption regulations was that in order to benefit from the attractive legal certainty offered by the regulations companies would, in effect, treat the very detailed exemption regulations as standard form contracts, even where such an approach may not have been best for the business. The 'modernized' block exemption regulations, adopted since 1999, are more flexible and less prescriptive in their approach.

Even where a choice is made to adopt a rule of reason approach there may be differences between regimes as to which agreements are found to fall within the rule of reason, and which are to be *per se* condemned from regime to regime. It is certainly the case, as will be discussed below, that there exist categories of agreements which in some circumstances do not benefit from the application of art 81(3) in the EC, but which do fall within the rule of reason in the US. **1-2.12**

Horizontal agreements

It has been noted above that antitrust regimes are likely to take a far more cautious approach to horizontal agreements (agreements between companies operating at the same level of the chain of production) than they are towards vertical agreements. While horizontal agreements are not necessarily restrictive of competition, they are, almost by definition, agreements between competitors. Some categories of horizontal agreements are generally considered to be relatively benign, and may either not be subject to the strictures of antitrust law at all, or may invite condemnation only in exceptional circumstances, or where the parties possess considerable market power. This might in particular be the case in respect of agreements which define standards (including for example environmental standards), are specialization agreements, or research and development agreements. It may be the case that in order to support such pro-competitive agreements the companies party to them are also required to exchange information, whereas in other circumstances information exchanges between competitors might be frowned upon. In other cases horizontal agreements are almost always likely to invite condemnation. This is particularly the case in respect of agreements which are often described as 'hard-core' restrictions: price fixing, output restricting, market sharing, or bid rigging agreements. The OECD has issued a recommendation to its members that strong action be taken against such practices,[13] and several of the OECD **1-2.13**

[13] *Recommendation of the Council Concerning Effective Action Against Hard Core Cartels*, 25 March 1998 [C/M(98)7/PROV]. Note that Korea is an OECD member.

member countries have criminalized such conduct. In the US such agreements fall within the *per se* prohibition of s 1 of the Sherman Act, and in the EC these may be found on their very terms to fall within art 81(1) EC, and there is very little likelihood of exceptions being awarded under art 81(3).

1-2.14 While neither the rule of reason nor exceptions are likely to apply in the case of these hard-core restrictions, some regimes may accept the operation of output or price fixing cartels where the intent is to generate exports, or to assist the cartel to cope with a crisis in the industry. Neither of these situations has ever been accepted in the EC, although to the extent that EC antitrust law applies exclusively to conduct which may affect trade within the member states, a cartel that had *no* impact within the EC would not be caught by art 81. In the US the Webb Pomerene Export Act of 1914 provides that conduct which would be unlawful if it had an impact in the US would not be unlawful where there was no domestic effect. The Chinese Anti-Monopoly Law makes express provision for the acceptance of export cartels.

1-2.15 Legally the position in respect of hard-core cartels is generally clear, and the only issue is that of whether an enforcement authority has the evidence required to bring a case, or whether a private party can establish the existence of the cartel and that damage has been incurred. A particularly visible trend in recent years has been internationally coordinated activity against cartels. A prominent example is that of the vitamins cartel, which led to criminal prosecutions in the US, as well as massive fines imposed by the Department of Justice ('DOJ'), and to the imposition of then record penalties in the EC. Members of this cartel were also punished in Korea, with the KFTC imposing penalties of US$3m in 2003. Earlier, in 2002, the KFTC had imposed penalties of US$7m on members of the graphite electrodes cartel. Cartel members may, however, take highly sophisticated steps to prevent detection, to the extent of employing personnel charged exclusively with managing cartel proceedings. Early economic literature dealing with cartels suggested that cartels were inherently unstable. This was the position adopted by Stigler in a highly influential article in 1964, in which he argued that any cartel faced serious, and perhaps insurmountable, difficulties in agreeing on its terms, detecting cheating once the terms were agreed, and enforcing the terms if cheating occurred.[14] The empirical evidence, however, in part furnished from evidence gained by antitrust authorities, suggests that cartels can be negotiated, and may be sustainable. This evidence is consistent with more recent economic work which applies game theory to cartel situations, recognizing that in open-ended games a cartel may indeed be theoretically sustainable. A recent study suggests that the difference between the competitive price and a cartel price may be as high as

[14] Stigler, GJ, 'A Theory of Oligopoly' (1964) 72 *Journal of Political Economy* 44.

40 per cent, a figure which is much higher than earlier estimates of the consumer detriment flowing from cartel conduct.[15] Along with internationally coordinated investigative processes the detection of cartels has in more recent times come to rely increasingly on a system of extremely high penalties, coupled in some regimes to the threat of personal criminal sanctions, along with a leniency system which rewards cartel members who either disclose the existence of a cartel or who cooperate with an investigation. Such leniency programmes are operated, on slightly different terms, by the US and EC antitrust authorities, and have proven to be very successful. In particular once one cartel is uncovered members of that cartel may disclose the existence of other cartels in which they are participants in the fear either that another member of that cartel will disclose its presence and thus be the party to benefit from lenience, or in the fear that the cartel will in any event be uncovered during the course of the first investigation. A cascade effect is thereby created, and in some industries many such cartels have been revealed by such methods. There is strong evidence for believing that the key ingredient of a successful leniency programme is that it offers a certainty of reduction of penalty on clearly defined terms. In the EC for example in order to benefit from 100 per cent leniency the undertaking must be the first to come forward, and must provide the Commission with sufficient evidence to allow the Commission to 'carry out a targeted inspection' or to 'find an infringement'.[16]

As noted above, outside these hard-core arrangements the situation with horizontal restraints may be more sensitive to a case-by-case analysis, with pro-efficiency arguments legitimately being advanced to support the existence of the agreement. In the US, for example, standards setting agreements, research and development agreements, and specialization agreements may all benefit from the application of the rule of reason, and in the EC the latter two are covered by block exemption regulations. Standards setting arrangements in the EC will not be considered to fall within the prohibition of art 81(1) where the standards are objectively justifiable and are 'open' such that the terms of the standard are accessible to all.[17] Research and development ('R&D') agreements are unlikely to be condemned in either the US or the EC regimes where they are 'pure' R&D agreements which do not extend to production or marketing, and where there remain other R&D opportunities available to competitors. The closer the R&D partners are to operating their agreement to the final market (ie, where they engage in production of the fruits of the agreement, or production and marketing) the more likely it is that the agreement will be found to be in breach of antitrust law, although even in the **1-2.16**

[15] Connor, JM and Bolotova, Y, 'Cartel Overcharges: Survey and meta-analysis' *International Journal of Industrial Organisation* (2006) vol 24, 1109.
[16] *Notice on Immunity from Fines and Reduction of Fines in Cartel Cases* [2006] OJ C298/17. The US Department of Justice policy may be found on the DOJ website.
[17] See, eg *X/Open Group* Commission Decision 87/69 [1987] OJ L35/36.

case of an agreement which incorporates both production and marketing, condemnation is unlikely unless the parties have considerable market power. Specialization agreements, under which two parties each agree to forego production of a different item, with the other specializing in that item, and then to cross-supply, allowing for the attainment of economies of scale and perhaps a better standard of production, are also generally treated favourably, although these may raise somewhat more concern than R&D agreements. In the EC this is reflected in the relevant block exemption regulation setting lower market thresholds to apply in order for the exemption to apply automatically.[18] In the US the DOJ has published horizontal collaborator guidelines.[19]

1-2.17 Another concern of antitrust is the exchange of information between competitors. There is not normally a blanket prohibition on information exchange, but where the purpose of the exchange is to facilitate, for example, price-fixing, or the allocation of customers, exchanges will be condemned. The approach in the EC, which is mirrored in the US, is to permit exchanges of information which are aggregated and historical, but not that of information which relates to future conduct, or which allows competitors to have a detailed insight into the trading activities of their customers.[20]

Vertical agreements

1-2.18 As indicated above there is far more diversity in respect of the treatment of vertical restraints in EC and US antitrust law than there is in respect of the treatment of horizontal restraints. That this is so is attributable to the somewhat different aims of the two regimes, and in particular flows from the concern of the EC authorities to enforce and support the creation and maintenance of a 'single European market'. It has been argued elsewhere that this concern may be a relevant factor in the application of Chinese antitrust policy, where an historical legacy, combined with the size of the territory, a poor transport infrastructure, and a tradition of regional protectionism means that similar issues may be applicable.[21] Vertical restraints, unlike horizontal restraints, are an essential ingredient of commercial activity, and are daily applied in distribution systems. Broadly, restraints in distribution systems may relate to a territory in which, or to the terms and conditions

---

[18] See in the EC Regulation 2658/2000 on the application of art 81(3) of the Treaty to categories of specialisation agreements [2000] OJ L304/3, and Regulation 2659/2000 on the application of art 81(3) of the Treaty to categories of research and development agreements [2000] OJ L304/7.

[19] Federal Trade Commission and Department of Justice, *Antitrust Guidelines for Collaborations Amongst Competitors* (April, 2000).

[20] In the EC see for example *UK Tractors Information Agreement* Case 92/157 [1992] OJ L68/19. In the US see *United States v United States Gypsum Co* 438 US 422 (1978).

[21] See, eg Hu, W, 'Anti-monopoly law is a necessity in China' (1995) 3 *Jurisprudence* 35.

under which a retailer is to sell the products or services covered by the agreement. In the US there is now no form of vertical restraint which does not fall within the rule of reason. Most recently in 2007 the Supreme Court held in *Leegin*[22] that minimum price requirements imposed by a manufacturer or wholesaler on a retailer were to fall within the rule of reason. Such requirements would fall within art 81(1) EC, and their imposition is expressly precluded within the terms of the block exemption regulation dealing with vertical agreements.[23]

The treatment accorded to territorial restraints, and in particular to exclusive distribution agreements, has been a distinctive facet of the operation of EC antitrust policy. Economists would generally support the existence of exclusivity awarded to a distributor on the grounds that this gives the distributor an incentive to invest in the product, and avoids the free-rider problem. The argument is made that no harm flows as long as the restriction affects only intra-brand competition, with competition being available at the inter-brand level. However, in the seminal case of *Consten and Grundig*[24] the ECJ held that while 'competition between producers is generally more noticeable than that between distributors of the same make, it does not thereby follow that an agreement tending to restrict the latter kind of competition should escape the prohibition'. For the ECJ the key factor appeared to be that consumers in the EC should be able to benefit from *both* inter-brand and intra-brand competition. The judgment has been criticized as subsuming efficiency considerations in favour of a wider single market policy objective, but remains of fundamental importance for the operation of EC antitrust policy. Although a pure efficiency approach would eschew such an application of antitrust law the fact remains that where other policy objectives are clearly enunciated antitrust law may be applied to address these concerns. **1-2.19**

The EC approach to vertical restraints is now most clearly expressed in the block exemption regulation and in the *Guidelines on vertical restraints*.[25] There is a considerable difference between the most recent version of the block exemption regulation and earlier versions (which have dated back to 1967), reflecting a development of the policy and the experience gained from the operation of the earlier versions. The same is true of the block exemption regulations dealing with intellectual property licensing, which have also undergone significant revisions. In the case of Taiwan, however, the TFTC has borrowed heavily, both in terms of content and of format, from the now-replaced version of the EC block **1-2.20**

[22] *Leegin Creative Leather Products, Inc v PSKS, Inc*, 127 S Ct 2705 (2007).

[23] Regulation 2790/99 on the application of art 81(3) of the Treaty to categories of vertical agreements and concerted practices [1999] OJ L336/21.

[24] *Etablissements Consten Sarl and Grundig-Verkaufs-GmbH v Commission* Cases 56, 58/64 [1966] 1 CMLR 418.

[25] [2000] OJ C29/1.

exemption regulation dealing with technology transfer arrangements. As noted above the earlier versions of the vertical agreements regulation were criticized as being far too detailed and both pre- and proscriptive such that they formed a straitjacket for business. The 1999 version of the regulation is far shorter than its predecessors. It first defines broadly those vertical agreements which may be presumed to fall within its terms, and then states at art 2 that:

> Article 81(1) shall not apply to agreements or concerted practices entered into between two or more undertakings each of which operates, for the purposes of the agreement, at a different level of the production or distribution chain, and relating to the conditions under which the parties may purchase, sell or resell certain goods or services ('vertical restraints').

Article 3 of the regulation provides that the exemption shall apply as long as the market share held by the supplier does not exceed 30 per cent, and as long as the agreement in question does not have one of four specified objectives: (1) minimum price setting; (2) territorial restrictions which preclude parallel imports; (3) restricting cross-supplies in a selective distribution system; and (4) setting restrictions in relation to non-approved users of spare parts or repairers. There are now no prescriptive conditions in the regulation. Vertical agreements which do not benefit from the application of the block exemption regulation (as would be the case for example where the market share of the supplier is in excess of 30 per cent) may still be defended on the basis of an individual application of art 81(3).

Monopolization and Abuse of Dominant Position

1-2.21 The key provisions in the Sherman Act and the EC Treaty relating to the control of anti-competitive monopoly[26] conduct are set out in s 2 and art 82 respectively. Section 2 of the Sherman Act is, in part, in the following terms:

> Every person who shall monopolize, or attempt to monopolize, or combine or conspire with any other person or persons, to monopolize any part of the trade or commerce among the several States, or with foreign nations, shall be deemed guilty of a felony.

Article 82 EC provides that:

> Any abuse by one or more undertakings of a dominant position within the common market or in a substantial part of it shall be prohibited as incompatible with the common market in so far as it may affect trade between member states.

[26] The term 'monopoly' is used loosely here. Neither regime limits itself to the control of monopolies in the strict economic sense of the word (a single supplier of a product or service in a relevant market), and the two regimes take different approaches to the degree of market power that must be held before the law can be applied (discussed below).

> Such abuse may, in particular, consist in:
> (a) directly or indirectly imposing unfair purchase or selling prices or unfair trading conditions;
> (b) limiting production, markets or technical developments to the prejudice of consumers;
> (c) applying dissimilar conditions to equivalent transactions with other trading parties, thereby placing them at a competitive disadvantage;
> (d) making the conclusion of contracts subject to acceptance by the other parties of supplementary obligations which, by their nature, or according to commercial usage, have no connection with the subject of such contracts.

It will be noted at the outset that neither of these provisions condemn the existence of a monopoly or dominant position *per se*. It is 'monopolization' that is the offence provided for in s 2, and the 'abuse' of a dominant position that constitutes an infringement of art 82 EC. There are subtle differences in the substance of these two provisions which flow from the wording used. The US condemnation of 'monopolization' is directed towards practices which are exclusionary or which seek to maintain monopoly power, while the EC emphasis on 'abuse' allows the extension of control over practices by which the already successful monopolist may exploit their power. A clear example of the difference between the two approaches is that in the US s 2 of the Act cannot be used to form the basis of an attack on 'excessive' monopoly prices, whereas in the EC art 82 may be relied on to condemn such pricing.[27] In the case of *Trinko* the Supreme Court held that the

> mere acquisition of monopoly power, and the concomitant charging of monopoly prices, is not only not unlawful; *it is an important element of the free market system.* The opportunity to charge monopoly prices—at least for a short period—is what attracts 'business acumen' in the first place; it induces risk taking that produces innovation and economic growth.[28]

In the US, and indeed in the EC, there has been criticism of the more inclusive nature of EC antitrust law, although there continues to be a substantial body of argument in favour of the application of antitrust law to exploitative conduct, in particular where the monopolist is entrenched.

Markets and market power

The first question to be asked in the application of both provisions is that of **1-2.22**
whether the company whose conduct is under scrutiny is a monopolist or in a dominant position for the purposes of the relevant provision. Although the

[27] See, eg in the US, *Verizon Communications Inc v Law Offices of Curtis V Trinko LLP,* 124 S Ct 872 (2004) and in the EC, *United Brands Company and United Brands Continentaal BV v Commission*, Case 27/76 [1978] ECR 207, [1978] 1 CMLR 429.

[28] Ibid, at para III(2) (emphasis added).

approach to the determination of this question is consistent in both the US and the EC there are different thresholds of market power at which the law applies, with the US setting a significantly higher threshold. In the EC it has been held that:

> [t]he dominant position referred to in [art 82] relates to a position of economic strength enjoyed by an undertaking which enables it to prevent effective competition being maintained on the relevant market by giving it the power to behave to an appreciable extent independently of its competitors, customers and ultimately of its consumers.[29]

The ability to act 'independently' 'does not preclude some competition . . . but enables the undertaking which profits by it, if not to determine, at least to have an appreciable influence on the conditions under which that competition will develop, and in any case to act largely in disregard of it'.[30] In the US the traditional definition of monopoly for the purposes of Sherman Act s 2 enforcement is that it is the 'power to control market prices or exclude competition'.[31]

1-2.23 Whether a company enjoys a monopoly is dependent on the amount of market power wielded by the company, and that can be assessed only in relation to a 'relevant market', the determination of which may not always be straightforward. Markets exist in three dimensions: product, geography, and time, with the temporal aspect being in most cases the least important, and in some cases this element may be overlooked. The analysis here is an economic one, although antitrust law can provide a legally sanctioned framework in which the analysis is to take place. The emphasis here is on the approach in the EC, there being little difference in methodology between the two regimes. The approach taken towards the definition of the relevant market is considered further below.

1-2.24 Defining the relevant market in all its dimensions is only the first of two stages in determining the market power of a company, the second being to consider the extent of its power in that relevant market. A number of factors are relevant to determining market power, the most important of which is the market share of the company in question. In the EC for example in the leading case in this respect the Court stated that:

> although the importance of the market shares may vary from one market to another the view may legitimately be taken that very large shares are in themselves, and save in exceptional circumstances, evidence of the existence of a dominant position. An undertaking which has a very large market share and holds it for some time, by means of the volume of production and the scale of the supply which it stands for—without those having much smaller market shares being able to meet rapidly the

---

29 *United Brands*, n 27, above, para 65.

30 *Hoffmann-La Roche & Co AG v Commission* Case 85/76 [1979] 3 CMLR 211, at para 39.

31 See, eg *United States v EI DuPont de Nemours & Co* 351 US 377, at 391 (1956).

> demand from those who would like to break away from the undertaking which has the largest market share—is by virtue of that share in a position of strength which makes it an unavoidable trading partner and which already because of this secures for it, at the very least during relatively long periods, that freedom of action which is the special feature of a dominant position.[32]

Market shares by themselves do not tell the whole story, and unless market shares are very high and have been sustained over a long period of time other evidence is likely to be required to establish jurisdiction. This evidence might include: the market shares of competitors; the duration of the market share held by the company; access to capital; access to distribution networks or sources of supplies; brand loyalty; the possession of intellectual property; and perhaps most importantly barriers to entry generally. The size of the market share which may trigger antitrust actions against monopoly firms in the EC and in the US is significantly different. In the EC a market share of 50 per cent is generally considered to be, without further evidence, itself evidence of the existence of a dominant position.[33] The lowest market share at which dominance has been found in the EC is the 39.7 per cent held by British Airways in the total airline sales in the UK.[34] It had previously been widely believed that the lower bound stood at 40 per cent, although this had never been formally stated. There were in this case substantial other indicia of dominance, with the Court on appeal making reference to 'the world rank [British Airways] occupies in terms of international scheduled passenger-kilometres flown, the extent of the range of its transport services and its hub network', along with its ability 'to offer a wider choice of routes and more frequent flights'.[35] In the US however a monopoly would not be found to exist for the purposes of s 2 of the Sherman Act at these low levels of market shares. It has therefore been noted that although there are frequent cases in which courts have found that market shares of 75 per cent are sufficient 'if the share is lower than 70 per cent courts become much more reluctant to find monopoly power'.[36] In a position which is directly contradictory with the one taken in the EC it has been held in the US in a number of cases that market shares of 50 per cent are, as a matter of law, insufficient to allow a case of monopolization to be established,[37] although there are some rare cases in which it has been suggested that a lower market share may suffice.[38]

---

32 *Hoffmann-La Roche*, n 30, above, para 41.

33 *AKZO Chemie BV v Commission* Case C-62/86 [1993] 5 CMLR 215.

34 *Virgin/British Airways*, Commission Decision 2000/74 [2000] OJ L30/1.

35 *British Airways plc v Commission* Case T-219/99 [2004] 4 CMLR 19.

36 Hovenkamp, H, *Federal Antitrust Policy: The Law of Competition and its Practice* (St Paul Minn: West Publishing Co, 3rd edn, 2005) at 6.2a.

37 See for example *Valley Liquors v Renfield Importers*, 822 F2d 656, 108 S Ct 488 (1987).

38 See *Broadway Delivery Corp v United Parcel Service of America Inc* 651 F2d 122 (2d Cir), 102 S Ct 512 (1981).

Condemned conduct

1-2.25 As noted above monopoly conduct may, for the purposes of establishing the reach of antitrust law, be classified as either exclusionary or exploitative, although these are not rigid classifications which define clear boundaries in each and every case. Price discrimination for example may be both exploitative *and* exclusionary. In the appropriate circumstances conduct falling within either category may be condemned in the EC, whereas in the US it is—save for the curious exception provided for by the Robinson Patman Act which outlaws certain forms of price discrimination—with exclusionary conduct that the concern lies. The most significant problem in the application of the law to monopoly conduct is to distinguish between that conduct which is pro-competitive, and that which is anti-competitive, and particular care must be taken to ensure that a monopolist is not condemned simply for being the better competitor than its smaller, and perhaps less efficient, rivals. Different approaches are taken in the US and the EC, with the latter being more ready to act against monopoly conduct. In the US the leading case in this respect is *Grinnell*, in which the Court held that:

> The offense of monopoly under s 2 of the Sherman Act has two elements: (1) the possession of monopoly power in the relevant market and (2) the wilful acquisition or maintenance of that power as distinguished from growth or development as a consequence of superior product, business acumen, or historical accident.[39]

1-2.26 A similar sentiment is expressed in *Spectrum Sports*:

> This court and other courts have been careful to avoid constructions of s 2 which might chill competition, rather than foster it. It is sometimes difficult to distinguish robust competition from conduct with long-term anti-competitive effects; moreover, single-firm activity is unlike concerted activity covered by s 1, which inherently is fraught with anti-competitive risk. For these reasons, s 2 makes the conduct of a single firm unlawful only when it actually monopolizes or dangerously threatens to do so.[40]

These and a great many other cases demonstrate a deep concern on the part of the US courts that the efficient monopoly must not be turned upon. In the EC in contrast, along with the lower level of market power at which a dominant position may be found to exist, the courts have indicated that once a firm is in a dominant position it will be held to a higher standard of conduct than its non-dominant competitors. The classic statement in this regard is that in *Michelin* where the Court stated:

> A finding that an undertaking is in a dominant position is not in itself a recrimination but simply means that irrespective of the reasons for which it has such a

[39] *United States v Grinnell Corp* 384 US 563 (1966).
[40] *Spectrum Sports Inc v McQuillan* 506 US 447 (1993) at 459.

> dominant position, the undertaking concerned has a *special responsibility* not to allow its conduct to impair genuine undistorted competition . . .[41]

It would be inappropriate, and impossible, here to provide a full survey of anti-trust law relating to monopoly conduct in the EC and US, and a short survey only of the more commonly encountered and discussed principles will be given, with the emphasis being on exclusionary conduct.

Predatory pricing

The most glaring example of exclusionary conduct is that of predatory pricing, which may be defined as a situation in which a monopolist sets a price below cost in the short term in order to eliminate a rival, giving the monopolist the ability to maintain a price above the competitive level in the future. In the US the leading case is *Brooke*[42] in which a two-fold test was set: first the alleged predatory price must be below a relevant cost measure; second there must exist a serious probability that the defendant would be able to recover the losses in the form of prices above the competitive level in the future. This would mean that the predatory monopolist would not only have to eliminate the targeted competitor, but would also have to be able to exclude future rivals who might be tempted to enter an apparently profitable market. That the courts in the US take a somewhat sceptical approach to claims of predation was made clear by the Supreme Court when it found that: 1-2.27

> the success of such schemes is inherently uncertain: the short-run loss is definite, but the long-run gain depends on successfully neutralising the competition . . . For this reason, there is a consensus among commentators that predatory pricing schemes are rarely tried, and even more rarely successful.[43]

Different cost measures may be appropriate in different cases, but the most widely commented on in the literature and case law is the Areeda-Turner rule which suggested that the average variable cost measure could, in many cases, be reliably used.[44] In industries with high fixed costs and very low variable costs it might be more appropriate to use a measure such as the long-run incremental cost, and the EC Commission published a draft paper relating to the application of 1-2.28

[41] *Nederlandsche Banden-Industrie Michelin NV v Commission* Case 322/81 [1985] 1 CMLR 282, para 57. Similarly in the *Hoffmann-La Roche* Case, n 30, above, the Court stated at para 91 that:

> The concept of abuse is an objective concept relating to the behaviour of an undertaking in a dominant position which is such as to influence the structure of a market where, as a result of the very presence of the undertaking in question, the degree of competition is weakened.

[42] *Brooke Group Ltd v Brown & Williamson Tobacco Corp* 113 S Ct 2578 (1993).

[43] *Matsushita Electric Industrial Co v Zenith Radio Corp* 475 US 574 (1986) at 589.

[44] Areeda, P and Turner, DF, 'Predatory Pricing and Related Practices Under Section 2 of the Sherman Act' (1975) 88 *Harvard Law Review* 697.

art 82 EC in which it made extensive reference to the average avoidable cost measure. In the EC the Court made it clear in the case of *Akzo* that there was no legal requirement in the EC to focus the test around any one cost-based approach, holding that:

> Article 82 does not prescribe any cost-based legal rule to define the precise stage at which price-cutting by a dominant firm may become abusive and indeed the broad application of the concept of abuse to different forms of exclusionary behaviour would argue against such a narrow test.[45]

1-2.29 The EC has shown itself to be more ready to make a finding of predation than are the US courts, and has not insisted that the enforcement authority or plaintiff show that the action will be profitable in the future, holding in one case that a price below average variable cost would be automatically held to be abusive, without the need to demonstrate any intent to eliminate a competitor, and without the need to show that recoupment of the losses would follow.[46] This difference in approach reflects in part the somewhat different emphasis of the law, and some US commentators have argued more generally that the EC is too quick to rely on antitrust law to protect competitors, particularly when these are small or medium-sized enterprises, rather than the process of competition itself.

Price discrimination

1-2.30 The application of discriminatory pricing by a monopolist is expressly condemned both in art 82, at para (c), and in the US, where it may fall to be condemned under either s 2 of the Sherman Act, or under the 1936 Robinson-Patman Act (s 2a of the Clayton Act), although it should be noted that this latter piece of legislation has been strongly criticized in the US, and that even the antitrust enforcers have shown themselves to be less than enthusiastic as to its terms. The Robinson-Patman Act has clearly been influential in the development of Korean antitrust law, and its terms are, to a significant extent, reproduced in the Korean Monopoly Regulation and Fair Trade Act. As noted above price discrimination may be both exploitative *and* exclusionary. In the former case discrimination may allow the monopolist to extract maximum prices from a range of different customers with different demands for the product. In the case of the latter lower prices may be targeted at sectors of a market subject to competitive pressures, with the monopolist being able to sustain these lower prices by virtue of the profit earned from the higher prices in sectors where the monopolist does not face competition. This is the aspect of art 82 EC which has most often resulted in action being taken against dominant companies, in part because the issue is so closely tied into single

---

[45] *AKZO Chemie BV v Commission* Case C-62/86 [1993] 5 CMLR 215 at para 75.
[46] *Tetra Pak v Commission (No 2)* Case C-333/94P [1997] 4 CMLR 662.

market considerations. In the leading case of *United Brands*[47] a banana producer was found to have infringed art 82 when it sold its bananas at the same time and place to wholesalers trading in different parts of the EC, and charged different prices for the bananas dependent on the demand conditions in each of the wholesalers' territories. The principle emerged that a monopolist could only charge different prices for equivalent transactions where the price difference was objectively justified, as might be the case for example if transport costs were different, or if a discount given for bulk purchase genuinely related to cost savings. Unfortunately even in situations in which price discrimination may be defended on the grounds that it is an economically efficient implementation of Ramsey pricing it is hard to justify this in EC antitrust law. Ramsey pricing suggests that it may be efficient for a monopolist to charge higher prices to those with a less elastic demand for the product, and lower prices to those with a more elastic demand. This might for example, permit the owner of an infrastructure or facility such as an airport to recover the high fixed costs from users with a strong demand, but to maximize usage by charging lower prices to cover variable costs from users with lower demand. In the application of the price discrimination provisions of art 82 EC it is not necessary to demonstrate that competition is harmed, as the wording of the prohibition itself states that on its face purchasers facing discrimination are axiomatically placed at 'a competitive disadvantage'. United States antitrust law is also hostile to discriminatory pricing: the Robinson-Patman Act outlaws price discrimination where the defendant has sold the same product at approximately the same time, to different purchasers at different prices, harming competition. As with the approach under art 82 EC, s 2(a) of the Act provides that: 'nothing herein contained shall prevent differentials which make only due allowance for differences in the cost of manufacture, sale, or delivery resulting from the differing methods or quantities in which such commodities are sold or delivered'. A seller is also allowed to discriminate in order to meet competition, if this is done in good faith.

Excessive pricing

It is axiomatic that a profit maximizing monopolist will raise prices above the competitive level by reducing output. Whether this conduct will, at the extreme, be subject to the strictures of antitrust law is, however, a matter of contention. In the jurisdictions subject to examination in this text it is not uncommon to find cases of monopolists being condemned for setting prices which are 'excessive'. While such an approach may be popular—at least with the monopolist's customers—it is difficult to apply with rigour in practice, and may be inefficient and anti-competitive in the long run. The US has eschewed controlling excessive **1-2.31**

[47] n 27, above.

prices as part of a general aspect of antitrust law, and US policy generally draws a distinction between price regulation, and the free interplay of market forces which may, where practices are exclusionary or monopolizing, be subject to antitrust intervention. In the recent Supreme Court case of *Verizon Communications Inc v Law Offices of Curtis V Trinko LLP*[48] the Court held that the charging of monopoly prices could be pro-competitive, and 'an important element of the free market system'.[49]

While the Supreme Court recognized the validity of the economic argument that high profits will, *ceteris paribus*, encourage entry into the market, the position taken in the EC, and in many other jurisdictions, contrasts strongly with that taken in the US. Article 82(a) EC makes reference to 'imposing unfair purchase or selling prices', and under this rubric the EC has developed a jurisprudence relating to the control of excessive pricing. The most recent case in which this difficult area has been developed is that of *Sundbusserne*[50] in which it was alleged that a port operator was charging excessive fees for its services. In the earlier case of *United Brands*[51] the ECJ had held that a price might be condemned as excessive where it was both unfair and bore no reasonable relation to the economic value of the product supplied. This begged the question of how to determine economic value, and what factors should be taken into account. In *Sundbusserne* the EC Commission explained the test it would apply with greater rigour, setting out a three-step analysis: (1) is the price excessive? (2) does the price exceed the economic value of the product? and (3) is the price unfair? In determining whether a price is excessive the Commission stated that a cost-plus formula would be employed where it was possible to determine costs. In determining economic value, regard would be had to both supply and, crucially, demand factors,[52] and fairness could be assessed by making comparisons with prices of equivalent products. The difficulties encountered in this analysis are significant, and may be insurmountable, and the approach has attracted much criticism from antitrust analysts. It is perhaps unfortunate that in jurisdictions which are emerging from a period of strong state intervention in the economy the temptation to employ antitrust law as a form of price regulation may at times prove to be irresistible.

[48] Judgment of 13 January 2004, 124 S Ct 872 (2004).

[49] Ibid, at para III(2).

[50] *Sundbusserne Sverige AB* Case COMP/A.36.568/D3 [2006] 4 CMLR 22. See Furse, M, 'Excessive Prices, Unfair Prices and Economic Value: The Law of Excessive Pricing under Article 82 EC and the Chapter II Prohibition' (2008) *European Competition Journal* 59.

[51] n 27, above.

[52] The argument can be made reasonably that where a consumer is prepared to pay a high price this is because they value the product that highly, and that factoring this demand-side valuation into the concept of 'economic value' fundamentally undermines any attempt to demonstrate that economic value is below the price set by the contracted transaction.

Refusals to supply and the essential facilities doctrine

The issue of whether a monopolist has an obligation to supply its goods or services to third parties when it does not wish to do so has exercised the courts in both the EC and the US. A general principle of the free market is that contracts should only be entered into willingly, and that trading relations should not be imposed on parties who are reluctant to enter into them. The EC has shown itself more willing to impose a requirement to supply on monopolists than is the case with the US authorities, where such a requirement may exist, but is strictly limited. Broadly in the EC a sliding scale of obligation exists depending on the relationship of the would-be customer and the nature of the item being available from the monopolist. In the case of an existing customer who is reliant on the monopolist and where the relationship has been freely entered into the monopolist must continue to supply where there is no objective justification for a refusal to supply.[53] Under this rubric a monopolist would be free to sever a relationship if proper notice was given of this intention, and the reason was a legitimate one. It would not be possible for example to refuse to supply, in the short term, an existing customer who had begun also to distribute a competitor's product. Where a new customer is seeking supplies the monopolist has an additional protection in that supply will only be required where the product is an essential one, and where it cannot reasonably be reproduced by the customer or reasonably acquired from another source.[54] Where a new customer is seeking access to intellectual property there is yet a further requirement that the refusal to supply must exclude effective competition, and prevent the emergence of a new product for which there would be consumer demand.[55] In the US the leading case to deal with the general principle of refusal to supply is *Colgate*[56] where the Supreme Court accepted the traditional view that in the absence of any otherwise unlawful purpose a monopolist could not be compelled to supply products to a person with whom they did not wish to deal. If, however, the purpose of the refusal to deal is 'to create or maintain a monopoly'[57] then the monopolist may be required to supply. Thus for example, in *Aspen Skiing*[58] a monopoly supplier of ski slopes which withdrew from a ski-pass arrangement with a smaller competitor was found to be in breach of s 2. This case was 1-2.32

[53] See, eg *United Brands*, n 27, above.

[54] *Oscar Bronner GmbH & Co KG v Mediaprint Zeitungs-und-Seitschriftenverlag GmbH & Co KG* Case C-7/97 [1999] 4 CMLR 112.

[55] *Radio Telefis Eireann and Independent Television Publications Ltd v Commission* Cases C-241–242/91P [1995] 4 CMLR 718, and *Microsoft Corporation v Commission* Case T-201/04 [2005] 4 CMLR 18. See also *IMS Health GmbH & Co OHG v NDC Health GmbH & Co KG* Case C-418/02 [2004] 4 CMLR 28.

[56] *United States v Colgate & Co* 39 S Ct 465 (1919).

[57] Ibid at 468.

[58] *Aspen Skiing Co v Aspen Highlands Skiing Corp* 105 S Ct 2847 (1985).

described by the Supreme Court in *Trinko*[59] as being 'at or near the outer boundary of s 2 liability'.[60] In *Trinko* the Court was overtly hostile to the 'essential facilities' doctrine, under which it was claimed that a monopolist supplier of an essential input, typically infrastructure, should be required to allow competitors to use its resource. The Court noted that:

> [c]ompelling such firms to share the source of their advantage is in some tension with the underlying purpose of antitrust law, since it may lessen the incentive for the monopolist, the rival, or both, to invest in those economically beneficial facilities.[61]

1-2.33 Hovenkamp states that requiring firms to deal on the basis of s 2 'must be regarded as a severe exception to the general, and quite competitive rule, that firms should develop their own inputs and expertise and conduct their own innovation'.[62]

Full line forcing, bundling, and tie-in sales

1-2.34 Three further examples only of abusive monopoly conduct will be dealt with here briefly: full line forcing, bundling, and tie-in sales. These arise when a monopolist compels, in various arrangements, the purchaser of product A to purchase also product B. Typically product A will be one in respect of which the monopolist holds market power (and in the extreme the monopolist may be the sole supplier), whereas in respect of product B there may be more effective competition. However, by using the power in the market for A the monopolist is able to reduce the effective competition that would otherwise be present in relation to B. Full line forcing arises where a producer requires a distributor to take the entire range of goods offered by the manufacturer. Bundling and tie-in sales are often confused in both the case law and in the legal literature, although not usually in the economic literature. In simple bundling cases the customer purchasing A must also purchase B. The most discussed cases in recent years to deal with this principle are those on both sides of the Atlantic arising in respect of Microsoft's incorporation of first Microsoft Internet Explorer, and then the Media Player, into various versions of the Windows operating system. A tie arises where the purchaser of A is required, over a time stream, to purchase B. This would be the case, for example, were a seller of a photocopier to require the purchaser to obtain their supplies of toner from them. In the EC art 82(d) may be applied to such arrangements if the view is taken that the two contractual elements are unconnected by 'nature' or 'according to commercial usage'. It may also be the case that the more general principles applicable to the operation of art 82 may be employed. In the US such practices may be condemned either as falling within s 2 of the Sherman Act where

[59] *Verizon Communications, Inc v Law Office of Curtis V Trinko, LLP* 124 S Ct 872 (2004).

[60] Ibid at 879.

[61] Ibid. A very similar point had been made by Advocate General Jacobs in *Oscar Bronner* (cited above, n 54).

[62] Hovenkamp, n 36, above, at 7.5b.

the imposer of the supplementary obligation is a monopolist, or as lying within s 1. The difficulty in applying this part of the law is to distinguish between linked purchases in which the link is legitimate, and those in which it is not. In the EC, for example, arguments relating to health and safety requirements have been rejected where the dominant seller of a liquids packaging system argued that its customers should be required to take the cardboard sheets used to form the cartons from the supplier. The EC Commission argued that there were in any event health and safety requirements imposed on the end packagers by other relevant legislation. Technical linkages may be particularly difficult to assess, as was demonstrated in the various Microsoft cases in which the company argued that it was offering a newer and better product which contained elements of two older separate products, rather than two separate products in the same bundle. The courts in the EC have asked whether the products are available separately, and whether separate demand exists for the two of them, and in the US the courts have asked whether the 'integrated' product is better than the two products sold separately and combined by the purchaser.

Merger Control

1-2.35 The third plank in most antitrust laws is that relating to merger control. While some jurisdictions have chosen not to incorporate merger control into their antitrust system this is an illogical position. The differences between the EC and US merger control regimes are significant, and this has on occasion given rise to tension between the two jurisdictions, with the EC for example, blocking a merger which had been cleared by the US authorities, when the two merging parties were US-based enterprises. There are two main antitrust concerns with mergers. The first is that horizontal mergers may give rise to substantial market power, creating 'unilateral' anti-competitive effects. As was noted above prohibiting monopolies or dominant companies from existing where these have arisen through a process of competition would not be an advisable policy, but prohibiting a monopoly arising through the acquisition of a competitor may be pro-competitive. The second major concern is that by reducing the number of competitors in a market a merger may, through coordinated effects, facilitate the attainment of a cooperative oligopolistic outcome. A less commonly encountered concern may relate to conglomerate mergers in which there is a possibility that 'portfolio effects' might enhance the market power in respect of merging parties who are not direct horizontal competitors.

1-2.36 The key questions to be asked of any merger regime are those of: (1) which mergers are subject to its jurisdiction; (2) what procedures apply when jurisdiction exists; (3) what is the substantive test by which mergers may be assessed; and

(4) what remedies may be imposed by the examining antitrust authorities. The approach taken in the US and EC to these questions will be addressed here only in short outline. There are many texts that deal at great length with the merger regimes in the two jurisdictions. In relation to the regimes dealt with in the rest of this book these questions are dealt with in as much detail as is possible.

1-2.37 Jurisdiction is usually established by a turnover threshold, although some regimes, including the UK's, may employ as an alternative a market share threshold, or a combination of the two tests. In the EC the required thresholds are exceptionally large, reflecting the balance drawn between centralized EC merger control, and the member states' individual regimes.[63] The EC thresholds are set in art 1(2) and (3) of the EC Merger Regulation ('ECMR').[64] Both thresholds require a very high worldwide turnover of the merging parties, with the lower threshold being set at €2,500 million. There is also a requirement that there be a specified spread of turnover across the EC member states. There is no reference in the legislation to a requirement that the parties be based in the EC, and the EC has regularly exercised extraterritorial jurisdiction in respect of its merger control regime. The same is true in the US, where jurisdiction is also determined by turnover, with the relevant thresholds being revised by the DOJ and Federal Trade Commission annually. In February 2008 the turnover thresholds were set at US$252.3m. The US also exercises jurisdiction over 'foreign' mergers on the basis of the application of the effects doctrine and the Foreign Trade Antitrust Improvements Act 1982. In both the EC and the US it is compulsory for parties to a merger which meets these turnover thresholds to notify their mergers to the relevant authorities, and mergers consummated without prior notification will be illegal. Although compulsory notification is now an accepted feature of merger control regimes this is not universally adopted, with the UK, for example, maintaining a system of voluntary notification.

1-2.38 For the first fifteen years of its life the substantive test set out in the ECMR was that of whether the merger would 'create or strengthen a dominant position as a result of which competition would be significantly impeded'.[65] The test in the US has been, since the enactment of the Clayton Act, that of whether a merger would 'substantially lessen competition'. Prior to the amendment of the ECMR in 2004 the EC Commission launched a consultation process in which it asked, inter alia, whether the EC test should be aligned to that of the US as this might 'facilitate

[63] There was initially reluctance on the part of some of the member states to grant the EC Commission the power to review mergers, and there remains resistance to the lowering of thresholds. Where the EC regime applies it precludes, save in defined and limited circumstances, the operation of the national regimes.

[64] Council Regulation (EC) 139/2004 on the control of concentrations between undertakings [2004] OJ L24/1.

[65] Regulation (EEC) 4064/89 on the control of concentrations between undertakings [1989] OJ L395/1, art 2(2).

merger parties' global assessment of possible competition issues arising from contemplated transactions, by obviating the need to argue their case according to differently formulated tests'.[66] While there was strength in this argument the majority of those who responded to the Green Paper were in favour of a compromise solution which would preserve the value of earlier case law while moving the EC position closer to that of the US. The result now is that the substantive test in the EC is that of whether a merger would 'significantly impede effective competition . . . in particular as a result of the creation or strengthening of a dominant position'.[67] In practice there may be little functional difference between the US and EC tests, although the US has argued in the past that the EC regime is overly concerned with protecting competitors, rather than with protecting the process of competition itself. It has also been pointed out that even were the tests to be identical on the face of the legislation there would remain differences in outcomes in particular cases.[68]

In both the EC and the US substantial guidance relating to the assessment of the **1-2.39**
competitive effects of mergers has been published. As noted above the major concerns arise in respect of horizontal mergers which, by definition, will increase the market power of the merging parties. Of key importance in this respect will be the market share of the merged party post-merger, the degree of market concentration, and the ease of entry into the market. The US places a significant degree of reliance on the application of the Herfindahl-Hirschmann index ('HHI') in analysing market concentrations, and this approach is reflected in many jurisdictions (Taiwan for example makes reference to HHI thresholds in a communication relating to mergers in the financial sector[69]). The EC Commission in its relevant guidance also places weight on HHIs. In neither regime are concentration ratios used to the exclusion of other relevant considerations, and each case will be analysed on its merits, but the fact that a merger may shift a market from being one of moderate concentration to one of high concentration (as defined in relevant guidance) may raise a presumption as to the existence of potential anti-competitive effects. In the EC it is generally the case, as with the application of the law relating

66 *Green Paper on the Review of Council Regulation (EEC) No 4064/89*, COM (2001) 745/6 final, 11 December 2001.

67 art 2(3), ECMR.

68 Thus, for example, in *General Electric/Honeywell* (2001) the EC and US reached different positions, with the US clearing the proposed merger and the EC blocking it. In response to criticism from the US the EC Commission argued that:

> It is unfortunate that, in the end, we reached different conclusions, but each authority has to perform its own assessment and the risk of dissenting views, although regrettable, can never be totally excluded. This does not mean that one authority is doing a technical analysis and the other pursuing a political goal, as some might pretend, but simply that we might interpret facts differently and forecast the effects of an operation in different ways (Press Release IP/01/939, 3 July 2001).

69 See further Chapter 4-4, below.

to monopoly conduct, that concerns arise at lower levels of market power and market concentration than is the case in the US. As noted above horizontal mergers may also produce anti-competitive effects by facilitating tacit coordination in a market as a result of a reduction in the number of competitors. It should be stressed that this does not require that the remaining firms in the market enter into an explicit cartel, but rather that individually each firm recognizes its dependence on the reactions of others, and that the circumstances are such as to facilitate coordination in the absence of express cooperation.[70] These cases are amongst the hardest of all merger cases to pursue. The EC Commission for example has lost two key appeals in relation to cases in which it has prohibited mergers on the basis that they would give rise to anti-competitive coordinated effects.[71]

1-2.40 It is rare that vertical mergers are challenged in either regime, and where they are this is likely to be the case only where the effect of the merger is to block access to an upstream input, or to a downstream distribution channel that would be of vital importance to competitors. There is no case in the EC in which a vertical merger has been blocked.

1-2.41 In both regimes a two-stage process is applied to merger control post-notification. In the EC these two phases are both internal to DG Competition, which is obliged to make a first decision within twenty-five working days. At the end of this Phase I process the Commission will make one of three decisions: the merger is not subject to EC jurisdiction; the merger is subject to EC jurisdiction but there are no serious doubts as to its legality; and finally that the merger is subject to EC jurisdiction and there are serious doubts as to its compatibility. It is only in this final circumstance that Phase II may be entered. Where this happens a great many mergers are likely to be abandoned. Under Phase II procedures the EC Commission has a further ninety days to take a final decision, which again may take one of three forms: the merger is compatible with the common market; the merger is compatible with the common market following the offering of commitments or

[70] In *BF Goodrich Co* 110 FTC 207 (1988) the US FTC explained the process by which coordinated effects arise in the following terms:

> The effective coordination of price and output strategies requires developing a consensus concerning price and output levels, and a means of enforcing its terms. The first step requires harmonizing the incentives of participating firms and mitigating firm uncertainty concerning rival firms, so that they can effectively coordinate their behaviour. The second step requires creating circumstances in which the prospective value to each participating firm of cheating on the consensus does not exceed the prospective loss from rival firm retaliation. In order to create and maintain these circumstances, participating firms must be able to monitor rival firm conduct; that is, they must be able to detect cheating on the consensus. They must also be able to retaliate effectively if and when cheating occurs.

[71] See Case T-342/99 *Airtours plc v Commission* [2002] ECR II-2585, [2002] 5 CMLR 7, and Case T-464/04 *Independent Music Publishers and Labels Association (Impala) v Commission* [2006] 5 CMLR 19.

the acceptance of undertakings as to remedies which will permit the merger to go forward; and the merger is not compatible with the common market, and is to be blocked. The EC Commission has blocked relatively few mergers since the entry into force of the ECMR in 1990.[72] An appeal against an adverse decision of the EC Commission may be made to the EC CFI. In the US the position is a little more complicated in that merger control powers are granted both to the US Department of Justice and to the US Fair Trade Commission, with case allocation being determined by an internal mechanism. As with the EC both may accept consent decrees to permit a merger to proceed with requirements as to remedies, or, at the end of this first review, an injunction may be sought to permanently block the merger in a relevant court. Again, as with the EC, many mergers in respect of which a permanent injunction may be sought are abandoned. In both regimes it is unlawful to implement a merger that falls to be notified before the approval of the relevant body has been granted.

There are virtually no private rights of action in respect of mergers within the EC **1-2.42** antitrust regime, but in theory private rights are more widely available in the US. In practice however private actions are limited by the existence of a requirement of 'antitrust injury'. Thus a competitor may not sue to block a merger, or to seek damages following its consummation unless the injury is of the nature that antitrust law is designed to prevent. Where a merger makes life harder for a competitor because the merged entity is better able to compete post-merger an antitrust injury has not occurred. More generally those most likely to complain of a merger's consummation are those least likely to have suffered an antitrust injury.[73]

Merger remedies take two main forms, structural and behavioural, and there is **1-2.43** clear preference in the agencies in both the EC and the US for structural remedies—typically divestiture.[74] The most obvious structural remedy is simply to block the merger in its entirety, or to require total divestiture where a merger has proceeded illegally. Structural remedies, if properly crafted, do not require the antitrust authority to take any further action in the market, and do not require it to monitor the merged entity in the future, although there may need to be some controls

[72] As at the end of 2008 only 20 mergers have been blocked.

[73] This statement may appear counter-intuitive, but where a merger increases market power leading to rising prices in the market smaller competitors may be able to shelter under this umbrella, benefiting from increased custom and the loss of competition. Competitors will suffer where a market is *more* competitive, but as stated this would not be actionable unless the form of competition was itself illegal, in which case s 2 of the Sherman Act might be applicable.

[74] In the EC for example the CFI has stated that structural remedies 'prevent once and for all, or at least for some time, the emergence or strengthening of the dominant position . . . and do not, moreover, require medium or long-term monitoring measures' (*Gencor Ltd v Commission* Case T-102/96 [1999] ECR II-753; [1999] 4 CMLR 971, at para 319).

over the divestiture process itself to ensure that the remedy is effective. Typically the requirement will be that the entity to be divested is commercially viable and attractive, and that it is sold to a party able properly to use its assets to compete with the merged entity. In some cases this will necessitate the divestiture of a branch or division of one or other of the merging parties. In others it might be a requirement to divest a brand, or to license or sell intellectual property. Behavioural remedies are less attractive to antitrust authorities, in part because of the issues of monitoring that arise, but also because they are often more difficult to assess *ex ante*. The most common form of behavioural remedy is usually a commitment to grant access to an input or service to a competitor.

1-2.44 There are two further aspects of merger control which merit brief discussion here, both relating to defences to the exercise of merger control that may be brought forward by merging parties: the failing firm defence, and the efficiencies defence. Both the EC and US recognize that these defences may be valid, but treat them with scepticism. The failing firm defence will apply where the party to be acquired is a failing firm and is likely to leave the industry in the event that it is not purchased by an entity able to employ its assets effectively. In such a case although the merger may lead to an increase in the market power of the acquiring firm the counterfactual is not that the competition provided by the failing firm would continue to have an impact on market behaviour. Antitrust authorities will require clear evidence that the firm would indeed exit the market in the absence of the merger. In Taiwan for example the TFTC, which publishes guidance relating to the failing firm defence,[75] requires evidence relating to the liquidity of the alleged failing firm. Reviewing authorities may also require evidence that there is no other realistic purchaser who would provide a less anti-competitive alternative to the purchaser seeking approval for the merger. The arguments in relation to the efficiencies defence are more controversial, and the debate is partly linked to the perceived role of antitrust law. It is common for firms merging to make arguments relating to the increased efficiency of the merged entity compared to the two separate entities. Indeed, if such arguments cannot be made then the only commercial case for the merger would be that it would increase the market power of the merged entity allowing it to levy higher prices, and few firms would attempt to justify a merger to antitrust authorities on this basis. In an influential article published in 1968 Williamson argued that mergers should be permitted where the efficiencies claimed for the merger outweighed the anticipated deadweight welfare loss.[76] It has been noted that if the objective of merger control is to protect consumers then the focus should be on price rises or other negative competitive

[75] See Chapter 4-4, below.

[76] Williamson, O, 'Economies as an Antitrust Defense: the Welfare Trade-Offs' (1968) 58 *American Economic Review* 18.

effects of the merger. If, however, the focus is on the total welfare of society (including the welfare of the owners of the merged entity) then mergers should indeed be permitted in the circumstances outlined by Williamson.[77] In practice neither the EC nor the US are likely to accept the efficiency defence where the harms to consumers or to competition are evident. In Taiwan there is substantial evidence of the willingness of the TFTC to approve mergers which might give rise to some competitive harm where the effect of the merger is to increase the efficiency of the enterprise, allowing it to contribute to economic development in Taiwan.

Application of Economic Principles and Evidence

Economics provides not only a justification for the existence of antitrust law, but also a framework and a set of tools by which the application of the law is informed. Some of these tools are highly sophisticated, requiring expert economic input into the antitrust process. The fact that monopoly cases cannot be reasonably pursued without a sensitive market analysis has been noted above. Whilst it may be the case that hard core horizontal infringements can be attacked on the basis of their form only, the same is not true of all agreements which contain restraints. The CFI held in *European Night Services v Commission*[78] that: **1-2.45**

> in assessing an agreement . . . account should be taken of the actual conditions in which it functions, in particular the economic context in which the undertakings operate, the products or services covered by the agreement and the actual structure of the market concerned unless it is an agreement containing obvious restrictions of competition such as price-fixing, market-sharing or the control of outlets. . . . It must be stressed that the examination of conditions of competition is based not only on existing competition between undertakings already present on the relevant market but also on potential competition, in order to ascertain whether, in the light of the structure of the market and the economic and legal context within which it functions, there are real concrete possibilities for the undertakings concerned to compete among themselves for a new competitor to penetrate the relevant market and compete with the undertakings already established in it.[79]

In EC antitrust law the definition of a relevant product market is one which 'comprises all those products and/or services which are regarded as interchangeable or substitutable by the consumer, by reason of the products' characteristics, their **1-2.46**

---

77 See, for example, Ilzkovitz, F and Meikeljohn, R (eds), *European Merger Control: Do we Need an Efficiency Defence?* (Cheltenham: Edward Elgar, 2006) at 50.

78 Joined Cases T-374/94 etc [1998] ECR II-3141.

79 Ibid at paras 136–7, references omitted.

prices and their intended use'.[80] As is explained further at para 13 of the Commission *Notice on market definition*:

> Firms are subject to three main sources of competitive constraints: demand substitutability, supply substitutability and potential competition. From an economic point of view, for the definition of the relevant market, demand substitution constitutes the most immediate and effective disciplinary force on the suppliers of a given product, in particular in relation to their pricing decisions. A firm or a group of firms cannot have a significant impact on the prevailing conditions of sale, such as prices, if its customers are in a position to switch easily to available substitute products or to suppliers located elsewhere. Basically, the exercise of market definition consists in identifying the effective alternative sources of supply for the customers of the undertakings involved, in terms both of products/services and of geographic location of suppliers.

1-2.47 The major conceptual framework for the evaluation of the extent to which any one supplier's products or services face competitive constraints imposed by available substitutes is the SSNIP test,[81] first enunciated by the US antitrust authorities for the purposes of merger control. In the EC the application of this test is explained at para 17 of the *Notice*:

> The question to be answered is whether the parties' customers would switch to readily available substitutes or to suppliers located elsewhere in response to a hypothetical small (in the range of 5%–10%) but permanent relative price increase in the products and areas being considered. If substitution were enough to make the price increase unprofitable because of the resulting loss of sales, additional substitutes and areas are included in the relevant market. This would be done until the set of products and geographical areas is such that small, permanent increases in relative prices would be profitable. The equivalent analysis is applicable in cases concerning the concentration of buying power, where the starting point would then be the supplier and the price test serves to identify the alternative distribution channels or outlets for the supplier's product.

1-2.48 The SSNIP approach may not work in every case, and a particular and now well-recognized problem may arise where the test is performed in respect of a product or service in which a monopoly is already held. If an existing monopolist is already pricing at the monopoly level any further price rise will show that substitutes are available. This false result is known as the 'cellophane fallacy' following the error made by the US Supreme Court in this respect in the case of *United States v EI DuPont*.[82] Given limitations in data, and the fact that in some cases the relevant market may be obvious (although this would always be a dangerous assumption),

---

[80] *Commission Notice on the definition of the relevant market for the purposes of Community competition law* [1997] OJ C372/5, para 7.

[81] SSNIP stands for 'small but significant non-transitory increase in price'.

[82] 351 US 377 (1956).

the EC antitrust authorities are not compelled to rely on the SSNIP test in every case. Thus, for example, in *Virgin/British Airways*[83] the Commission argued that other alternatives remained available to it. For supply side substitution to be taken into account in the definition of the relevant market, the requirement in the EC is that 'suppliers be able to switch production to the relevant products and market them in the short term without incurring significant additional costs or risks in response to small and permanent changes in relative prices'.[84] A wide range of evidence may be drawn on to assist with market definition, including information provided by the companies subject to investigation, competitors, upstream suppliers, customers, and consumers. In some cases authorities may rely to a significant degree on standard industrial classifications used for more general economic statistical purposes. This is the case for example in Korea, where such classifications have been relied upon in a number of antitrust cases. The EC Commission states that the specific evidence that may be relevant to the identification of the relevant product market, and in particular to the determination of whether products are demand substitutes, is the following: evidence of demand substitution in the recent past;[85] relevant quantitative tests;[86] views of customers and competitors;[87] consumer preferences;[88] barriers and costs associated with switching demand to potential substitutes;[89] and different categories of customers and price discrimination.[90]

The approach to the definition of a relevant geographic market is undertaken in a **1-2.49** similar way to that of the product market. For the purposes of EC antitrust law, the relevant geographic market is defined as comprising 'the area in which the undertakings concerned are involved in the supply and demand of products or services, in which the conditions of competition are sufficiently homogenous and which can be distinguished from neighbouring areas because the conditions of competition are appreciably different in those areas'.[91] The EC Commission lists the following as being the type of evidence that it considers relevant in defining the relevant geographic market: past evidence of diversion of orders to other

83 Commission Decision 2000/74 [2000] OJ L30/1.
84 n 80, above, para 20.
85 para 38.
86 para 39.
87 para 40.
88 para 41.
89 para 42.
90 para 43.
91 para 8.

areas;[92] basic demand characteristics;[93] views of customers and competitors;[94] current geographic pattern of purchases;[95] trade flows/pattern of shipments;[96] barriers and switching costs associated to divert orders to companies located in other areas.[97] Not all of this evidence will necessarily be examined in each and every case, as 'often in practice the evidence provided by a subset of these factors will be sufficient to reach a conclusion'.[98]

1-2.50 The relevant time period is less important to the definition of the relevant market, and analysis in this area is rarely a significant feature of case law. The issue may however be of relevance to particular markets which may be time sensitive. This might be the case for example in relation to seasonal markets (ice cream may constitute a relevant market in summer, but not in winter), or in relation to telecommunications or transport, where there may be different constraints depending on the time of day. The determination of market power once a relevant market has been identified is discussed above in relation to the application of the law to monopoly conduct.

1-2.51 Economic modelling of markets and market processes is increasingly complex. In the EC and US it is highly unlikely that any substantive antitrust case would proceed without the engagement of economists by the respondent, and in the agencies economists will be employed alongside lawyers and accountants. Some conduct may be condemned in the absence of sophisticated analysis purely on the basis of its form—this is the case for example with respect to 'hard core' cartel conduct in the UK which invites criminal sanctions[99]—but such examples are rare. In relation to merger control economic input will be fundamental to the development of the arguments on both sides of the case, and these may reach levels of sophistication and complexity that render making a final decision difficult.[100] The lack of developed expertise in this area in jurisdictions such as China and Vietnam, and the lack of experience of the judiciary in sophisticated economic matters may be of some concern to those seeking to rely on, or defend themselves from the application of, antitrust law in these regimes.

[92] para 45.
[93] para 46.
[94] para 47.
[95] para 48.
[96] para 49.
[97] para 50.
[98] para 52.
[99] See s 188 of the Enterprise Act 2002.
[100] There have been a number of cases in developed antitrust jurisdictions in which the judiciary have raised concerns about the complexity of the economic arguments being presented, and some in which judges have made it clear that they have had difficulty in following the expert evidence.

International Cooperation

There are a number of tiers at which cooperation in the application of antitrust law proceeds at the international level, ranging from informal bilateral contacts (there is for example a mechanism in place to facilitate dialogue between the EC and China in relation to antitrust law) to formal agreements and treaties (which may relate exclusively to antitrust law, or in which antitrust law may be a part of a wider arrangement).[101] Korea and Chile for example have concluded a trade agreement in which Chapter 14 relates to the application of antitrust law, with the parties undertaking to apply their antitrust laws 'so as to avoid that the benefits of the liberalization process in goods and services may be diminished or cancelled out by anti-competitive business conduct'.[102] Taiwan has concluded agreements with, inter alia, Australia and New Zealand, and a tripartite agreement between these States also operates in the area of antitrust policy. International organizations, such as the OECD and the WTO are also advocates of antitrust law, and provide fora in which antitrust policy and law is discussed and promoted.[103] Regional groupings are increasingly important in this area. At present there is no plurilateral agreement relating to the application of antitrust or the setting of antitrust standards, and States differ in their enthusiasm for the development of one. Antitrust has been raised as an issue to be discussed at the WTO, and there appears to be an emerging consensus that if such an agreement is to be concluded the WTO would be the appropriate forum. Korea and China are both, for example, strong proponents of multilateral solutions in this area,[104] while the US has been more reluctant to develop multilateral frameworks, preferring to rely on bilateral agreements. There are substantial barriers to the development of an international framework, and if agreement were to be reached it is most likely that this could be only on the most basic condemnation of hard core cartels. At present **1-2.52**

---

[101] See generally Noonan, C, *The Emerging Principles of International Competition Law* (Oxford: Oxford University Press, 2008).

[102] Chile/Korea Trade Agreement, Chapter 14, art 14:2(1).

[103] The OECD in particular takes an important role in antitrust policy. Its Competition Committee, in which a number of States which are not members of the OECD participate as observers, engages in peer review exercises of antitrust law regimes. The objective of the peer review process is to bring together the OECD member countries, relevant international organizations, and experts in antitrust law and policy to report thoroughly on antitrust law regimes of members and observers, and to make recommendations where it is appropriate to do so. Taiwan, for example, was subject to an OECD peer review in 2005–2006.

[104] See, eg, Noonan n 101, above, at 47. Under the terms of the Fair Trade Agreement between the Republic of Korea and the Republic of Chile (1 April 2004) the parties committed to 'apply their respective competition laws in a manner. . . so as to avoid that the benefits of the liberalization process in goods and series may be diminished or cancelled out by anti-competitive business conduct', and expressed a commitment to 'the importance of embracing principles on competition that would be accepted by both Parties in multilateral fora, including the WTO'.

the leading international body dealing with antitrust law is the International Competition Network, but this organization has no formal powers. The international positions of the jurisdictions covered in this book vis-à-vis antitrust matters are discussed as appropriate in the first chapter of each Part.

1-2.53 There have been calls within the Asian and East Asian antitrust communities for the development of competition fora at both the regional and global levels, and some tentative steps are being taken in this direction at the regional level.[105] There are also moves within the ASEAN grouping towards the development of common minimum standards in antitrust law.[106]

[105] See, eg, Lee, KJ, 'Towards a more comprehensive international competition forum in Asia and worldwide' Conference presentation, Asia International Competition Conference, 4 September 2008, Seoul; Wang, X, 'The need for a non-governmental, international competition forum in Asia' Conference presentation, Asia International Competition Conference, 4 September 2008, Seoul.

[106] The Association of Southeast Asian Nations includes as members Brunei Darussalam, Cambodia, Indonesia, Lao PDR, Malaysia, Myanmar, Philippines, Singapore, Thailand, and Vietnam.

Part 2

CHINA

2-1. The Chinese Antitrust Law Regime 67

2-2. China Agreements 79

2-3. China Monopoly and Abuse of Dominance 87

2-4. China Merger Control 97

2-5. China Procedure 111

2-1

THE CHINESE ANTITRUST LAW REGIME

Introduction	2-1.01	**Territorial Application**	2-1.19
The Anti-Monopoly Law	2-1.03	**International Cooperation and Agreements**	2-1.21
The Institutional Structure	2-1.08	**Pre-2007 Legislation**	2-1.22
Information sources	2-1.15		
General Exemptions	2-1.16		

Introduction

The new general competition law in China, 'the Anti-Monopoly Law', enacted in August 2007, entered into force on 1 August 2008.[1] The context in which this occurred has been discussed in Chapter 1, above. At the time of writing only a small number of decisions have been made by the administrative agencies, or cases brought by private parties, and much remains to be done to implement the law, and thus the picture remains in some aspects unclear. However, even the limited number of decisions taken to date are raising interesting, and important, issues, particularly in relation to merger control (see Chapter 2-5, below). As noted in Chapter 1, above, the Anti-Monopoly Law resembles, as do arts 81 and 82 EC and ss 1 and 2 of the Sherman Act, a general statement (albeit one more fleshed out than is the case with the EC or US primary legislation) of principles. Without further clarification this is unlikely to be an effective instrument. **2-1.01**

The purpose of this part of the book therefore is to introduce the legislation and the operative structure of the regime to the fullest extent possible given the **2-1.02**

[1] Anti-monopoly Law of the People's Republic of China, Order of the President of the People's Republic of China no 68, 30 August 2007. Laws are enacted by the National People's Congress and its Standing Committee. Administrative regulations are enacted by the State Council, to facilitate either the application of laws, or to fulfil general administrative responsibilities vested in the State Council. Government ministries and bodies vested with powers under the State Council may enact rules relating to the enforcement of laws within their responsibility.

information available. It was noted in the introductory chapter to this book that the new law is not the first competition law to have been enacted in China, and that while the earlier laws have been only sporadically enforced some conduct has been condemned, and some penalties imposed. The Anti-Monopoly Law has not repealed the earlier legislation,[2] and although it is generally believed that the older legislation will fall into disuse to the extent to which it purported to control anti-competitive conduct falling within the ambit of antitrust law (and it was never widely used), it does remain a possibility that cases will be brought under the earlier legislation. Indeed, an early draft of the Anti-Monopoly Law guidelines made explicit the fact that the relevant guidelines applied also to the Price Law of 1997. It is not possible to say with any certainty that practice under these earlier laws, which are not 'pure' competition laws, will be reflected in the application of the Anti-Monopoly Law, and it is to be hoped that this will not be the case, but some brief further mention of relevant cases is given in this Part as appropriate. In addition some attention will be paid to the arguments made to date, in both political debate and academic discussion of the likely prospects for the new legislation, about which significant comment has been somewhat pessimistic. Throughout this part of the book the relevant provisions of the Anti-Monopoly Law will be dealt with first, and where appropriate a short discussion of the 'old' law will follow or, more usually, will be dealt with in footnotes.

The Anti-Monopoly Law

2-1.03 The Anti-Monopoly Law ('AML', or 'the Law') consists of eight chapters: general provisions; monopoly agreement; abuse of market dominance; concentrations; abuse of administrative power; investigation; legal liabilities; and supplementary provisions.

2-1.04 It must be emphasized that although in many respects China is a vibrant economy in which private ownership of business plays a vital role, the State continues to have a considerable influence on most aspects of the economy, and is more interventionist than is the case in the EC or the US. China remains a '*socialist* market economy', although the most generally heard phrase is 'socialism with Chinese characteristics'. Article 4 of the AML states, therefore, that:

> [t]he State constitutes and carries out competition rules which accord with the socialist market economy, perfects macro control, and advances a unified, open, competitive, and orderly market system.

---

[2] It is, however, probably the case that certain 'provisional' laws relating to competitive conduct, including merger control (the Provisional Merger and Acquisition Rules, March 2003), have been implicitly, if not expressly, repealed, by the AML.

Article 1 of the AML states that: 2-1.05

> [t]his Law is enacted for the purpose of preventing and restraining monopolistic conducts, protecting fair competition in the market, enhancing economic efficiency,[3] safeguarding the interests of consumers and social public interest,[4] [and] promoting the healthy development of the socialist market economy.

It will be noted immediately, and there has been much comment addressing the issue, that art 1 presents a bewildering array of objectives, some of which may conflict ('enhancing economic efficiency' *and* 'promoting the healthy development of the socialist market economy'[5]). There is, unfortunately, no mechanism set out in the AML for reconciling any conflicts between the attainment of these different objectives, although it is the case that some of the more specific provisions hint at particular responses to be taken. Generally the Law applies to 'monopolistic conduct', which is defined in art 3 as extending to: (1) 'monopolistic agreements among business operators'; (2) 'abuse of dominant market positions by business operators'; and (3) concentrations that may have the effect of 'eliminating or restricting competition'. 2-1.06

'Business operators' are defined in art 12 of the Law as natural persons, legal persons, or any other organization engaged in the production or business of commodities, or which provides a service. Article 12 also provides a definition of 'relevant market', which 'refers to the commodity scope or territorial scope within which the business operators compete against each other during a certain period of time for specific commodities or services'. No further final guidance has yet been published on the assessment of relevant markets. Draft guidance was published in late January 2009, and at the time of writing this has not been finalized. It is clear from public statements made about the AML, and from the draft guidance that other antitrust regimes, and particularly the US and the EC, have been used as benchmarks at various points, and it is likely that the approach finally 2-1.07

[3] Wang Xiaoye notes that: 'In China, what is meant by "economic efficiency" includes both allocative efficiency and productive efficiency' (Wang, X, 'Highlight's of China's New Anti-Monopoly Law' (2008) 75 *Antitrust Law Journal* 133 at 142).

[4] '. . . the "public interests" provision in this article is a controversial concept. Some might consider the public interest as a consumer interest; others may consider it a national interest. In the literal meaning of the word "public", in my view, it should not include providing protection for certain businesses but, instead, for the universal good of the Chinese people. In any case, the "public interest" is not clearly defined and, therefore, is ambiguous in the context of this legislation. Yet it is a critical part of the law' (Wang, n 3, above, at 142). It has also been noted that 'officials more removed from the drafting efforts [of the AML . . .] tend to view competition policy as a complement or instrument of industrial policy' (Bush, N and Zhaofeng, Z 'Chinese Antitrust—Act II, Scene 1', *theantitrustsource* (<http://www.antitrustsource.com>) October 2008, 1 at 2).

[5] While no definition of the term 'socialist market economy' is given in Chinese law the term appears in a great many pieces of legislation. It does not appear to have any particularly significant impact. It remains the case however that some commentators have expressed concern that the inclusion of the term in the AML may lead to uncertainty as to the operation of the law.

taken to market definition will be influenced by the standard practices in these jurisdictions.

The Institutional Structure

2-1.08 The institutional structure within which the AML is to be applied is somewhat murky. Although two new organizations have been created these are under the control of more than one body, and it is likely that tensions will arise in balancing the various objectives of the Law within this structure.

2-1.09 The first new body created is the Anti-Monopoly Committee ('AMC'). Article 9 of the AML provides that this body was to be created by the State Council, and is to have responsibility for 'organizing, coordinating [and] guiding anti-monopoly work', thus taking the central role in organizing the application of the AML, rather than one related to direct enforcement. The AMC is an 'advisory and coordinating organ' under the control of the State Council. Such bodies do not normally have separate working groups such that the day-to-day tasks are fulfilled by officials in other relevant departments, responsible to the AMC.[6]

2-1.10 Five specific functions are given to the AMC: (1) studying and drafting competition policies; (2) assessing general situations of competition, and releasing assessment reports; (3) drafting and publishing anti-monopoly guidelines;[7] (4) coordinating enforcement of the AML; and (5) 'other functions as assigned by the State Council'. The State Council is responsible for the formulation of rules relating to the activities of the AMC, and for its composition. Although the AMC is created by, and controlled by, the State Council it has working relationships with four organizations, the State Council, the Ministry of Commerce

---

[6] Article 6 of the *Administrative Measures on Organizational Structure of Administrative Organs of the State Council* (1997) states that:

> An advisory and coordinating organ of the State Council organizes and coordinates the important tasks crossing different administrative organs of the State Council. The matters decided by a discussing and coordinating body of the State Council and agreed by the State Council will be carried out by the relevant administrative organs, in accordance with their respective responsibilities within their power. In exceptional or emergency circumstances, a discussing and coordinating body of the State Council can, with the approval of the State Council, issue temporary administrative measures.

Article 10 requires that the establishment of an advisory and coordinating organ should be strictly controlled. In particular an advisory and coordinating organ shall not be established where the matters can be handled by an existing administrative organ or through coordinating existing administrative organs. It also provides that an advisory and coordinating organ shall establish a working office to carry out its function.

[7] An official of MOFCOM indicated to me in Beijing in September 2008 for example that the AMC would have responsibility for drafting guidelines in areas that cut across the responsibilities of the administering bodies, such as market definition, or the analysis of competitive effects.

('MOFCOM') the National Development and Reform Commission ('NDRC'), and the State Administration for Industry and Commerce ('SAIC'), with attendant concerns being raised as to the possibility of tensions arising between these bodies.[8]

The AMC is headed by the Vice-Premier Wang Qishan, who also supervises China's trade and financial policy. The deputy directors of the AMC include the heads of MOFCOM (Chen Deming), the NDRC (Zhang Ping), and the SAIC (Zhou Bohua).[9] The working rules of the AMC were approved by the State Council on 13 September 2008. The AMC will set up a working office which will be headed by a vice minister of MOFCOM and will be located in MOFCOM. The deputy of the working office of the new Anti-Monopoly Law Enforcement Agency (see below) will be the director of the Anti-Monopoly Investigation Bureau in MOFCOM. It is apparent from these arrangements that, notwithstanding the split-institutional role in the application of the AML, MOFCOM is to play a dominant role. 2-1.11

At present MOFCOM is responsible for mergers and acquisitions and monopolistic practices relating to international trade;[10] the SAIC for anti-monopoly work relating to abuses of dominant positions and monopoly agreements, *except* those related to pricing, and the NDRC for breaches relating to pricing, whether monopolistic or multilateral. It need hardly be pointed out that this is a recipe for chaos: cases are often not clear-cut and anti-competitive conduct may consist in a bundle of behaviours relating to both price and non-price activity. 2-1.12

[8] Harris notes that this 'approach may cause interagency conflicts while creating inconsistencies and inefficiencies in policy development; administrative practices; and enforcement procedures, standards and decisions' (Harris, SH, 'The Making of an Antitrust Law: The Pending Anti-Monopoly Law of the People's Republic of China' (2006–2007) 7 *Chicago Journal of International Law* 169 at 171). See also Wang Xiaoye, 'Highlight's of China's New Anti-Monopoly Law' (2008) 75 *Antitrust Law Journal* 133 at 146: '. . . the Commission may become a coordinator among different organizations responsible for anti-monopoly enforcement but may not likely be as effective in determining or advocating competition policy'.

[9] The Commissioners, in order of seniority, are Zhang Mao (vice Chairman of NDRC), Ou Xinqian (vice Minister of Ministry of Industry and Information Technology), Yao Zhengke (vice Minister of Ministry of Supervision), Zhang Shaochun (vice Minister of Ministry of Finance), Gao Hongfeng (vice Minister of Ministry of Transport), Ma Xiuhong (vice Minister of Ministry of Commerce), Huang Shuhe (vice Chairman of State-owned Assets Supervision and Administration Commission of the State Council), Zhong Youping (deputy director of State Administration for Industry and Commerce), Zhang Qin (deputy director of State Intellectual Property Office), Zhang Qiong (deputy director of Legislative Affairs Office of the State Council), Cai Esheng (vice Chairman of China Banking Regulatory Commission), Gui Minjie (vice Chairman of China Securities Regulatory Commission), Wei Yingning (vice Chairman of China Insurance Regulatory Commission), and Wang Yumin (vice Chairman of State Electricity Regulatory Commission).

[10] It has been pointed out that MOFCOM's additional responsibility for assisting Chinese firms subject to antitrust actions in other jurisdictions may not sit well with a role in developing relations with other jurisdictions (see Bush, N and Zhaofeng, Z, 'Chinese Antitrust—Act II, Scene 1', *theantitrustsource* (<http://www.antitrustsource.com>) October 2008, 1 at 4).

2-1.13 A second body, the Anti-Monopoly Law Enforcement Agency ('AMEA') is responsible for the day-to-day activity of enforcing the AML.[11] Where necessary the AMEA may empower other bodies with responsibility for enforcing the law.[12] Although this provision has been criticized as giving rise to the possibility of a fragmented enforcement mechanism[13] it is a realistic one given China's immense size, and the lack of resources available to the AMEA. The AMEA is, in effect, an organization the staff and management of which is split between existing ministries and departments, such that at present it lacks internal coherence. The AMEA is split along the lines of responsibility set out in relation to the AMC, above.

2-1.14 The courts also have a role to play in the enforcement of the AML, and the early evidence suggests that there may be a significant amount of private litigation. The role of private litigation is discussed further in Chapter 2-5, below.

Information sources

2-1.15 It is difficult to obtain reliable and up-to-date information in English relating to Chinese law and particularly to its practice.[14] Even in Chinese some difficulties will be encountered. There is not, for example, a transparent and standard system of case reporting, although steps are being taken to redress this in the area of intellectual property law. Cases discussed in this text which were brought under the pre-anti-monopoly law legislation have been drawn from anthologized collections of case summaries published in Chinese. There are however some provisions within the Law which require the AMEA to publicize its decisions.[15] The Chinese government maintains a number of websites on which English language materials

---

[11] art 10, AML.

[12] art 10 specifies 'corresponding authorities in the people's governments of the provinces, autonomous regions and municipalities directly under the Central Government'.

[13] See, eg Deng, F and Leonard, GK, 'Incentives and China's New Antimonopoly Law' (2008) *Antitrust*, Spring, 73 at 74.

[14] The most comprehensive discussion of antitrust policy in China prior to the enactment of the Anti-Monopoly Law is Williams, M, *Competition Policy and Law in China, Hong Kong and Taiwan* (Cambridge: Cambridge University Press, 2005). Following the enactment of the law the *Antitrust Law Journal* published an issue containing a symposium on the new law (Volume 75:1 (2008)).

[15] Thus, for example, art 30 of the Law requires the AMEA, where it makes a decision prohibiting a concentration, or clearing a concentration with conditions, to 'timely publicize' the decision. There is no requirement as to the amount of detail which must be included in such an announcement. See further Chapter 2-4. It has also been noted that: 'Publication of decisions and the reasoning behind them, however, is a necessary but not sufficient condition for effective deterrence. It is also important to have a rule that serves the purpose, in a common law system, of "stare decisis", ie the enforcement authority must to some extent be bound by its prior decisions and reasoning' (Owen, BM, Sun, S, and Zheng, W, 'Antitrust in China: The Problem of Incentive Compatibility' (2005) 1 *Journal of Competition Law and Economics* 123 at 145). It is not clear that the AMEA will be so bound by its previous decisions, although it will be expected to operate within the guidelines published.

are hosted, but these are not reliable. The best source of information remains the alerts and newsletters published by the international law firms.

General Exemptions

There was substantial debate during the drafting of the AML as to the approach to be taken to State-owned enterprises ('SOEs') and to those enterprises in possession of monopolies granted by the State, but not owned by the State. Article 7 provides a general exemption in respect of these businesses, stating, in full, that: **2-1.16**

> With respect to the industries controlled by the State-owned economy and concerning the lifeline of national economy and national security or the industries implementing exclusive operation and sales according to law, the State protects the lawful business operations conducted by the business operators therein. The State also lawfully regulates and controls their business operations and the prices of their commodities and services so as to safeguard the interests of consumers and promote technical progress.[16]

This provision, however, and those which immediately follow, should be read alongside Chapter V of the AML, which relates to the 'abuse of administrative power to eliminate or restrict competition'. Although there is a difference between the operation of SOEs and the application of administrative monopoly, the latter is often used to protect the former such that the two issues are, to an extent,

---

[16] It is symptomatic of some of the difficulties that will be encountered in applying the law that the second paragraph of this article requires those falling within the first paragraph to 'operate according to the law, be honest, faithful and strictly self-disciplined, and accept public supervision, and not harm the consumer interests'. Huang, who participated in the drafting group for the new Law, is candid about the difficulties arising in relation to this provision:

> In the end, there was an ambiguous compromise on this issue: on one hand, the law respects the status quo of state monopoly, but, on the other hand, it also expresses that these business activities need to be limited and abuse of dominance should be prevented. . . . the provision does not say which law is going to be applied in these areas to limit or prevent anti-competitive practices. According to the pressure groups, all regulated industries and State-monopolized sectors have (or will have) their own tailored laws, with provisions related to competition, that empower the sector regulators to enforce [them]. The assertion by the pressure groups supporting the continued protection of the regulated and State-monopolized industries is that these industry-specific laws and regulations leave no role for the [AML] in these sectors, according to the rule of conflicts of laws[note]. Simply put, the issue remains unresolved and the fight is likely to continue at the level of rules implementation.
>
> Note: This conclusion is not shared by academics and other government agencies because, under the current Chinese legal framework, it is not uncommon that general laws take precedence over sector-specific laws. The only safe conclusion at this stage is that the hierarchy of relations between the [AML] and the sector laws is unclear.' (Huang, Y, 'Pursuing the Second Best: The History, Momentum, and Remaining Issues of China's Anti-Monopoly Law' (2008) 75 *Antitrust Law Journal* 117 at 127.)

interlinked. Article 51 of Chapter VII suggests that regulatory bodies that are subject to other laws will not be subject to the provisions of the AML.[17]

2-1.17 Article 55 of the AML states that the AML will not apply 'to the conduct of business operators to exercise their intellectual property rights under laws and relevant administrative regulations on intellectual property rights'. However, this right is proscribed to the extent that intellectual property rights are not to be used so as to allow holders to 'eliminate or restrict market competition by abusing their intellectual property rights' (see further Chapter 2-3, below).

2-1.18 Agricultural producers and rural economic organizations involved in agricultural activities are exempted from the strictures of the AML in that they may form alliances and may engage in concerted actions relating to 'activities such as production, processing, sales, transportation and storage of agricultural products'.[18]

Territorial Application

2-1.19 China accepts the effects doctrine, and art 2 of the AML states that the law is applicable both to conduct within China and to 'conducts outside the territory of the People's Republic of China if they eliminate or have restrictive effect on competition on the domestic market of the PRC'. There is no guidance provided for in the legislation as to how significant or direct the effect must be in order for jurisdiction under the AML to be asserted. This is in contrast to the approach taken in the US, where the Foreign Trade Antitrust Improvements Act introduced as a legislative requirement that, in order for the Sherman Act to apply, conduct would be required to have a 'direct, substantial and reasonably foreseeable effect' on commerce in the US. In the EC in contrast there is no such legislative requirement, although arts 81 and 82 EC can only be applied where there is an 'effect' on trade between member states, and the CFI and ECJ have embraced the requirement that a practice must be 'implemented' in the EC in order to be condemned under EC antitrust law.

2-1.20 It is unlikely however that China will take an expansionist approach to the assertion of antitrust jurisdiction. At present the institutions charged with enforcing the law do not have the resources to undertake substantial investigations, particularly in respect of conduct taking place outside the territory of China with an effect in China. The territorial provision may perhaps be better seen as a political

[17] Article 51 provides in its second paragraph that: 'Where it is otherwise provided in a law or administrative regulation for the handling [of an] organization empowered by law or administrative regulation to administer public affairs who abuses its administrative power to eliminate or restrict competition, such provisions shall prevail'.

[18] art 56, AML.

statement, alerting other States which do apply the effects doctrine in the area of antitrust that China has the power to do the same. It is also the case that China wishes to have a voice in discussions relating to the development of competition law principles at the international level, and again the territorial provision lends support to the seriousness of China's position.

International Cooperation and Agreements

The first formalized competition dialogue initiated by China with a third country took the form of an agreement on structured dialogue on competition entered into with the EU.[19] Under the Terms of Reference of the agreement a formal Competition Policy Dialogue has been opened within the context of 'a permanent forum of consultation and transparency'. Particular issues that will be the subject of dialogue include: (1) antitrust law and enforcement, including the exchange of views on new legislation, and on 'the fight against cartels'; (2) the role of merger control in the global economy; (3) liberalization in relation to public utilities, and state intervention in the market process; and (4) technical and capacity building assistance to China in relation to competition policy. It is intended that high level meetings take place at least once a year. It has also been reported that China signed a memorandum of understanding with Russia relating to cooperation in preventing unfair competition and implementing antitrust policies in 2005.[20] 2-1.21

Pre-2007 Legislation

Even before the enactment of the AML a bewildering range of Chinese legislation could be applied to conduct which would fall foul of 'standard' competition laws, although finding instances of the application of this law is difficult. Some examples are given in *Anti-Unfair Competition Law: Understanding, Application and Case Studies*[21] and *Anti-Unfair Competition Law Cases*.[22] In both of these works cases that would be recognizably classed as 'competition' cases within the western understanding of the word are interspersed with cases relating to unfair or inaccurate advertising, the defamation of the company bringing the case, the giving of discounts to encourage custom (by companies with no market power), and other similar matters. In the first work for example, only three cases would be 2-1.22

---

[19] EC Commission press release IP (04) 597, 6 May 2004; [2004] 5 CMLR 11.

[20] See Harris, SH, 'The Making of an Antitrust Law: The Pending Anti-Monopoly Law of the People's Republic of China' (2006–2007) 7 *Chicago Journal of International Law* 169 at 181, n 61.

[21] Gao, Y and Cao, D (eds) (Beijing: Peoples Court Publishing House, 2nd edn, 1997).

[22] Huang, Q, Cao, Q, and Tu, T (eds) (Hunan People Publishing House, 1998).

classed as antitrust cases in the US, or as breaches of competition law in the EC. All of these cases however could be classed in Chinese law as breaches of the Law Against Unfair Competition.[23]

2-1.23 The first of these cases for example related to the activities of a company with a monopoly supply of tap water in one city[24] which announced that all construction projects planning to supply its water in the future would be required to purchase pipes from a particular company, and would have to prove that they had done so. Another supplier of pipes, which claimed to have lost custom as a result of this action, approached the water supplier asking to be included as a recognized source of pipes but was told that this would only happen upon payment of RMB10,000 per month. The company sued on the basis of The Law of the People's Republic of China for Countering Unfair Competition (arts 6 and 23). The City Court declared the policy of the water supplier to be illegal, and it was ordered to provide water irrespective of the supplier of the pipelines used by construction companies.[25] The company was also ordered to pay a fine of RMB50,000. In a similar case a school building a new teaching block in Sichuan province in 1994 planned to install a telephone service with up to 1,000 extensions, and was told by the local telecommunications company that the school would be required to purchase its equipment from one of its related companies in order to be connected to the telephone network. Again this policy was declared to be illegal on the basis of the same provisions of the Law. The third case, again from 1994, related to a bid-rigging arrangement whereby three companies responding to a tender issued by a local government body in respect of a new residential development agreed that before the final deadline for the bid nobody would submit bids, and that on the last day one company only would bid. After that, if no other companies had come forward the successful company would pay RMB2,500,000 to each of the other two parties. Any of the parties breaking the arrangement by making a bid would be required to pay RMB1,000,000 to each of the other two. The nominated company was successful, but, after paying the first instalment agreed with the other two companies, refused to make further payments, whereupon it was sued. The case was arbitrated by the city construction institution, which held that the contract was in breach of art 15 of the Law Against Unfair Competition, and declared the bidding to have no legal effect, with the result that the project could

[23] The Law of the People's Republic of China for Countering Unfair Competition, discussed in more detail below, is the usual translation given to the relevant legislation by Chinese government sources published in English. However, a literal translation might be countering 'inappropriate' competition.

[24] The book is silent as to which city.

[25] A very similar case, relating to the supply of gas, arose in the city of Nantong when in 1994 the company required purchasers of gas to purchase ovens from a member of the same group. Again this was condemned under the same legislative basis (see *Anti-Unfair Competition Law Cases*, at 165).

be put out to tender again. The 'winning' company was penalized RMB3,180,000, and the other two RMB100,000 and RMB50,000. An arrangement to subvert a public auction constructed in a very similar way is referred to in *Anti-Unfair Competition Law Cases*. This latter text also makes reference to a number of cartel cases. For example in one city the five largest shopping malls concerted to raise the price of washing machines by 10 per cent, and in another instance the three largest film developers in a city called a meeting of the more than thirty other developers in the city and agreed a price rise of 50 per cent. Apart from tying cases there are only a small number relating to monopoly conduct which mirror the sorts of issues that would be dealt with under EC or US competition law. For example, a limited number of cases relate to situations in which products have been sold below cost, although these appear to be examples of loss leading incentives, rather than predation and it does not appear that the parties punished for infringing the law were able to exercise any market power. One case does mirror that of an issue which has arisen in relation to the application of the essential facilities doctrine in the EC. In 1994 Xian airport refused to allow taxis not operated by it to stop at the airport to pick up passengers. This act was declared to be in violation of the legislation, and the airport was required to open up access to other taxi companies. It should also be noted that a large number of reported cases relate to restrictions imposed by city or by regional government bodies. These few cases do little but to suggest both that anti-competitive activity exists in China, and that the way in which the law has been applied in the past does not typically mirror that of the application of competition law in a developed competition law regime.

As noted above the AML does not repeal this earlier legislation. Although it is now **2-1.24**
unlikely that the Law Against Unfair Competition will be applied by public authorities to cases that fall within the terms of the AML, there remains the possibility that private cases may be brought on the basis of the law, although these have had no substantial impact in the past.

2-2

CHINA AGREEMENTS

Introduction	2-2.01	Trade Associations	2-2.04
Horizontal Agreements	2-2.02	Exemptions	2-2.05
Vertical Agreements	2-2.03	Penalties	2-2.09

Introduction

Chapter II of the AML, which contains only four articles, relates to 'monopoly agreement', although the word monopoly has no particular significance here. The term 'monopoly agreement' is defined as referring to 'agreements, decisions or other concerted actions which eliminate or restrict competition'.[1] The Law first provides for proscriptions of certain categories of horizontal and vertical agreements, then sets out certain exemption criteria, and also contains a specific provision relating to the activities of trade associations. Chapter II is, however, very short, and further guidance is required to implement these provisions. The Chinese Contract Act provides, at art 52, that contracts are void if they infringe a legislative prohibition, with the consequence that contractual arrangements in breach of Chapter II of the law may not be relied on. **2-2.01**

Horizontal Agreements

Article 13 of the Law prohibits five specific categories of horizontal agreements. **2-2.02**

(1) Price-fixing.[2]
(2) Restricting the production quantities or sales volumes of commodities.

[1] art 13, AML.
[2] As noted in Chapter 1-1, the Price Law 1997, at art 14, prohibits business operators from colluding with each other in relation to setting prices, and allows for the confiscation of profits, and where there are no profits, penalties ranging from RMB30,000 to RMB300,000. In the event of serious breaches business operating licences may be revoked.

(3) Customer allocation in relation to downstream sales or dividing procurement markets in relation to the purchase of raw materials upstream.[3]
(4) 'Restricting the purchase of new technology or new facilities or the development of new technology or new products'. Although this provision is not inconsistent with international practice in antitrust law some concern has been expressed that this may act against the interests of foreign importers of technology who wish to license this to selected parties only, or who seek to impose exclusivity clauses in IP licences. It has already been held by the Chinese courts that it may be an illegal use of monopoly power to include restrictions on the use of competing technology in licences and the fear has been expressed that licensees may seek to rely on this provision to restrict the obligations which may be lawfully imposed on them.
(5) 'Making boycott transactions'.

A sixth sub-paragraph gives the AMEA the power to prohibit 'other monopoly agreements as determined by [it]'. Bid-rigging is not expressly condemned, although may be presumed to be caught under the rubric of price-fixing.[4]

---

[3] Although this provision is similar to art 81(1)(c) EC it is a peculiarity that it applies only to 'raw materials'. It has been suggested that 'there is nothing to indicate that this is a limitation and it is more likely that the division of the demand side market in its entirety is intended to be outlawed' (Lorenz, M, 'The New Chinese Competition Act' (2008) *European Competition Law Review* 257 at 258). It is not clear from the text of the AML that this interpretation is supported.

[4] Bid-rigging would have been expressly prohibited under an earlier draft text. The draft of 8 April 2005 prohibited bid-rigging at art 8(vii). It has been argued that it was a surprise that the draft should have contained such an explicit provision (Dabbah, MM, 'The Development of Sound Competition Law and Policy in China: An (Im)possible Dream?' (2007) 30:2 *World Competition* 341 at 357). However the evidence is that bid-rigging is prevalent in China. In the UK a disproportionately large number of cases brought under the Competition Act 1998 have related to bid-rigging. Indeed, the fact that bid-rigging cases are common generally is explicitly recognized by the OECD (see OECD, *Chinese Taipei—Peer Review of Competition Law and Policy 2006* (2006) at 17: 'Few [TFTC] actions have challenged construction industry bid-rigging, although this is a common setting for competition law enforcement elsewhere'). Existing laws, not repealed by the Anti-Monopoly Law, also deal with bid-rigging (see generally Jin, C and Luo, W, *Competition Law in China* (Buffalo NY: William S Hein & Co Inc, 2002) at 57–62).

Article 15 of the Law Against Unfair Competition states that:

> Bidding parties shall not submit bids in collusion with each other to force the bidding price up or down. A bidder shall not conspire with the party who invites bids in order to exclude competitors from fair competition.

Article 27 further provides that:

> Where bidding parties submit bids in collusion with each other to force the bidding price up or down, or where a bidding party conspires with the party inviting bids to prevent competitors from competing fairly, his successful bid is null and void. The supervision and inspection authority may, according to circumstances, impose on him a fine of more than RMB10,000 but not more than RMB200,000.

These provisions have been applied in a small number of cases, but were considered to be ineffective.

In 1998 the SAIC enacted the Interim Provision Concerning the Banning of Conspiracies in Bid Rigging, making it unlawful to engage in conspiracies between parties on both sides of the bidding process. The Interim Provision required that the parties must have intended to exclude

Note that in no case above does the legislation make reference to a term such as 'unless objectively justified', which did appear in earlier drafts of the legislation. This implies that all of the classes of agreements referred to may be capable of falling within the exemptions discussed below. It also suggests that *unless* the terms of the exemption criteria are met the agreements listed cannot otherwise be justified or in any other way relied upon.

Vertical Agreements

Vertical agreements are addressed in art 14, which sets out only two prohibitions, although, as with art 13, the AMEA is given the more general power to determine that other categories of agreements are illegal. The two categories of agreements prohibited at the time of writing are: (1) agreements which fix prices for resale to a third party; and (2) agreements which restrict the minimum price of resale to a third party. The difference between the two provisions lies in the use of the word 'fixing' in the first case, and 'restrict' in the second case, and the emphasis on 'minimum' prices in the second case. Thus although recommended resale prices would not be prohibited under art 14(1), unless it could be shown that these were backed up by some form of covert enforcement mechanism, minimum recommended prices might face condemnation under art 14(2) with a lesser standard of coercion applying than would be necessary for the application of art 14(1). Whether resale price maintenance should be condemned in a modern antitrust regime is a matter of some debate. It will be noted that art 14 does not prohibit the imposition of vertical territorial restraints, so does not apply to exclusive distribution agreements unless these contain price-fixing terms. Nor does it apply to selective distribution agreements. The article also does not apply to technology licensing agreements unless these contain price restrictions, but note that art 55 of **2-2.03**

competitors from the bidding processes, and that such a position could not be reached by negligence. The Bidding Law of the PRC was adopted on 30 August 1999 and became effective on 1 January 2000. This Law is 'applicable to the bidding activities within the territory of [the PRC]' (art 2). Article 5 of the Law provides that '[b]idding shall be carried out under the principles of openness, fairness, justice, honesty and creditworthiness'. Article 6 provides that there shall be 'no regional or departmental restrictions' on bidding processes subject to the strictures of the Act. Article 32 states in part that:

> [b]idders shall not collude with each other in setting bidding prices, nor shall they exclude other bidders from fair competition and harm the lawful rights and interests of the bid inviter and other bidders. Bidders shall not collude with the bid inviter in injuring the interests of the State, general public and other people.

In the event that the bid winner 'wins the bid by conspiring with other bidders or with the bid inviter or paying bribes to the bid inviter or members of the bid evaluation committee, the bid shall be invalid, and the bid winner shall be subject to a fine of not less than 0.5% but not more than 1% of the total value of the bidding project.' Illegal gains may be confiscated, and the person directly in charge of the bid may also face penalties.

the Law, discussed in the following chapter, may apply to the abusive use of intellectual property ('IP') and IP rights.

Trade Associations

2-2.04 Article 11 of the AML sets out a general statement as to the role of trade associations—the term itself is not defined in the legislation—stating that these are to 'intensify industrial self-discipline, guide business operators to lawfully compete [and] safeguard the competition order in the market'. Trade associations do not fall within the definition of 'business operator' in the AML and the general prohibitions of the AML do not therefore apply to their activities. It is generally the case that trade associations are viewed favourably within commercial circles within China and are seen as an important mechanism for industrial progress.[5] A formal recognition of trade associations flows from the fact that they may be registered with the Social Group Registration Authority. In the past trade associations' attempts to regulate industries, including setting prices, and encouraging export cartels, have been condoned by the authorities.[6] There was, however, considerable discussion during the review sessions enacting the AML of the Instant Noodle Trade Association which famously acted as a price-fixing body, until its actions were condemned under the Price Law by the NDRC. Article 16 of the AML provides simply that no trade association may act so as to organize or 'implement the monopolistic conduct as prohibited by this Chapter'. Article 16 therefore counterbalances art 11, but whether this will be an effective counterbalance remains to be seen. In cases in which trade associations effect a breach of the law by

---

[5] See, eg Fox: 'Trade associations in China are, to an extent, emanations of the state or work closely in tandem with the state. . . . Trade associations, like state monopolies and state blockage of trade, are often the biggest culprits in abusing power and harming consumers' (Fox, EM, 'An Anti-Monopoly Law for China—Scaling the Walls of Government Restraints' (2008) 75 *Antitrust Law Journal* 173 at 179).

[6] See Owen, BM, Sun, S, and Zheng, W, 'China's Competition Policy Reforms: The Anti-Monopoly Law and Beyond' (2008) 75 *Antitrust Law Journal* 231 at 248–9:

> . . . 'excessive competition' has become a major perceived problem in the Chinese economy. Some policy makers believe that most of China's industries, except those in which the government deliberately maintains monopolies by SOEs, are characterized by 'excessive competition'.
>
> Partly because of these perceptions the government has taken some measures to rein in 'excessive competition'. Most of those measures involve what is called 'industrial self-discipline', adopted under the direct supervision of the government. Under the practice of 'industrial self-discipline', the major companies in an industry reach price agreements or other agreements to limit competition, in an effort to stabilise the market. The trade associations that were converted from government ministries played important roles in the adoption of this 'industrial self-discipline'. (Internal footnotes omitted)

organizing an unlawful monopoly agreement they may be fined, and where the breach is serious they may face deregistration (see Chapter 2-5, below).

Exemptions

The Chinese Law more closely follows that of the EC than of the US in respect of the approach taken towards the legitimation of agreements which prima facie are in breach of the AML. An exemption mechanism is provided for in art 15 of the AML. In order for enterprises to benefit from an exemption they must, in the case of the first five categories of conduct set out below, '*prove*' that the agreement entered into falls within one of the specified categories, and, in language similar to that employed in the application of art 81(3) EC, that the agreement 'can enable consumers to share the interests derived from the agreement, and will not severely restrict the competition in relevant market (*sic*)'. As with the application of EC law, it may be presumed that where competition is *not* substantially restricted competitive forces themselves will ensure that the benefits of agreements are passed on to consumers. Although both the language and the approach here clearly flow from that of art 81(3) EC it has also been suggested that the burden facing those seeking to rely on the exemptions 'is similar to, but likely broader than, the "rule of reason" used by US courts',[7] although there is no clarification within the AML of the burden of proof or the evidence that will be required to satisfy the exemption provision. **2-2.05**

The provisions of arts 13 and 14 do not distinguish between those practices which may be able to claim the benefit of an exemption and those which may not (there is no concept of 'hard core' restrictions here), such that any practice falling within the prohibition may in fact benefit from an exemption in the appropriate circumstances. **2-2.06**

There are six specific circumstances in which exemptions may be allowed to agreements that would otherwise fall within arts 13 and 14, and a catch-all provision is also included: **2-2.07**

(1) Agreements which have the purpose of improving technologies, and researching and developing new products. Thus research and development agreements which do not substantially eliminate competition may benefit from the exemption. At the time of writing it is not possible to say with certainty how far such an agreement may extend, and whether, for example, the parties to a research and development agreement may also agree joint production

[7] Wang, X, 'Highlight's of China's New Anti-Monopoly Law' (2008) 75 *Antitrust Law Journal* 133 at 137.

and/or joint marketing of the fruits of the agreement. It is presumed that, as is the case with EC law, such arrangements may be exempted.

(2) Agreements which have as their purpose 'upgrading product quality, reducing costs, improving efficiency, unifying product specifications or standards, or carrying out professional labour division'.

(3) Agreements which have as their purpose the enhancing of operational efficiency and improving the competitiveness of small and medium-sized enterprises.[8]

(4) Agreements which match the objectives of public interests. Although the list of such interests is left open, the following are expressly referred to: (i) conserving energy;[9] (ii) environmental protection; and (iii) disaster relief.

(5) Crisis cartels. The language used in the legislation refers to 'mitigating the severe decrease of sales volume or obviously excessive production during economic recessions'. This provision should be a matter of some concern, and is out of line with more usual practice in antitrust law. As well as being objectionable on policy grounds the provision is also poorly drafted, and the meaning of 'economic recession' is uncertain.

(6) Agreements which have as their purpose 'safeguarding the justifiable interests in foreign trade or foreign economic cooperation'. It is noteworthy that an earlier draft of the legislation contained within it a much more express provision clearly directed at export cartels. This provision generated some hostile reaction from international commentators. The text as now written would however still permit export cartels, but only where these related to 'justifiable interests'.[10] It should also be emphasized to those counselling Chinese firms that an export cartel legitimated in China would still face potential condemnation under the laws of trading partners such as the US and the EC if it were found that s 1 of the Sherman Act or art 81 EC respectively were being breached. General principles of international law make a clear distinction between the authorization of an act in one State, and the State compelling the act. Only in the latter case would antitrust enforcement activity by a third State be excluded.

---

[8] There is no definition in the Law of 'small and medium sized business operators'. This provision has a counterpart in the German Act Against Restraints of Competition at s 3.

[9] Harris has pointed out that this provision should be otiose in modern antitrust law: '"Saving energy" should either be dealt with through the market mechanism, thereby ensuring that the most efficient producer will, *ceteris paribus*, be the most efficient user of energy and hence the winner in price competition, or by legislation distinct from the Anti-Monopoly Law' (Harris, SH, 'The Making of an Antitrust Law: The Pending Anti-Monopoly Law of the People's Republic of China' (2006–2007) 7 *Chicago Journal of International Law* 169 at 192).

[10] See, Draft of 8 April 2005, which contained at art 9(iv) the following exemption: 'Agreements to enhance the competitiveness of exports in global Market'.

(7) 'Other circumstances as stipulated by laws and the State Council.' Until acted upon this provision may be ignored. It does not allow the AMEA itself to create other grounds of exemption in the course of its day-to-day enforcement activity.

The AML does not itself specify the mechanism by which exemptions are to be granted, and separate rules are to be created in this regard. It may be the case that the provision is self-executing, with the parties assuming to benefit from the exemption unless the AMEA or another party acts so as to establish that they do not. **2-2.08**

Penalties

Provision is made in art 46 of the Law for the imposition of different levels of penalties in respect of breaches of these provisions, depending on whether an unlawful agreement is 'performed' or not (see Chapter 2-5, below). **2-2.09**

2-3

CHINA MONOPOLY AND ABUSE OF DOMINANCE

Introduction	2-3.01	**Abuse of Dominant Position**	2-3.06
The Assessment of Dominance	2-3.02	Intellectual property	2-3.09
		Abuse of Administrative Power	2-3.10

Introduction

Proscriptions on general monopoly conduct are set out in Chapter III of the AML, headed 'Abuse of dominant market status'.[1] The three articles set out in Chapter III relate to business operators, and not to administrative monopolies or administrative power, which are dealt with in Chapter V of the Law ('Abuse of administrative power to eliminate or restrict competition'). Chapter V marks a sea-change in the approach in China to the regulation of the economy, and given the structure of the Chinese economy may, if enforcement is rigorous, be significant in its impact. Two of the first four cases brought under the AML by private parties related to a (mis-)use of administrative power. Both of these sections of the Law are dealt with in this chapter. **2-3.01**

The Assessment of Dominance

Dominance is defined in art 17, para 2, as referring to: **2-3.02**

> a market position held by a business operator having the capacity to control the price, quantity or other trading conditions of commodities in [the] relevant market, or to hinder or affect any other business operator to enter the relevant market.

[1] For a strong analysis of this area of the AML see Emch, A, 'Abuse of dominance in China: a paradigmatic shift?' (2008) *European Competition Law Review* 615.

It should be noted that there is no reference here to the dominance existing within China.[2] A possible, but unwelcome, consequence of this lacuna is that, in conjunction with art 2 which delimits the territorial scope of the Law, a business operator could be found to be dominant globally, but *not* in China, and still be found to be subject to the jurisdiction of the Law. It is also clear from both art 17 and art 19 that the Law is intended to extend to situations of 'collective dominance', as is the case in the EC.

2-3.03 Article 12 of the Law defines a 'relevant market' as referring 'to the commodity scope or territorial scope within which the business operators compete against each other during a certain period of time for specific commodities or services'. No further guidance as to the assessment of the relevant market—a necessary precursor to the assessment of dominance—is given in the legislation. The AMEA will determine the methods and practices to be used in this respect, although it has been indicated that it is 'likely that [the authorities] will adopt the established methods and techniques used in the United States or in the European Union'.[3] It is likely that guidance may be prepared by the AMC as this is an area in which practice cuts across the boundaries of the responsibilities of the three managing ministries.

2-3.04 Article 18 of the Law sets out factors to be considered when determining whether a business operator holds a dominant market status. These are: (1) the market share and the 'competition situation of the relevant market'; (2) the extent to which the operator is able to control either the selling market, or the raw material procurement market; (3) financial and technical strength; (4) the extent to which other business operators rely on the possibly dominant operator; and (5) barriers to entry. Article 18(6) refers to 'other factors', such that the list in art 18 is an open one.

2-3.05 The Law sets out three presumptions under which a business operator may be assumed to be dominant, although it is made clear that these presumptions are rebuttable where the business operator 'can otherwise prove that they do not have a dominant market [position]'.[4] First, dominance may be presumed where the market share of the business operator is 50 per cent or greater. Secondly, dominance may be presumed where the concentration ratio ('CR') CR2 is two-thirds or more in the relevant market. Thirdly, dominance may be presumed

---

[2] The same is true in respect of the provisions relating to agreements, discussed in the previous chapter, and in relation to merger control, discussed in the following chapter, although the turnover thresholds required in the operation of the merger control regime do impose a Chinese nexus.

[3] Wu, Z, 'Perspectives on the Chinese Anti-Monopoly Law' (2008) 75 *Antitrust Law Journal* 73 at 83.

[4] art 19(3), AML. The article is silent as to how persuasive this evidence must be. The presumptive approach taken here is adapted from the German Act Against Restraints of Competition.

where the CR3 is three-quarters or more in the relevant market. In relation to the latter two presumptions, if any one of the relevant business operators has a market share of less than 10 per cent it will not be considered to be dominant.[5] Although it is clear on the face of the legislation that these presumptions are rebuttable, the fact that they exist, suggesting antipathy towards firms with high market shares, or a suspicion that oligopolistic markets may tend to collusion, may be a matter of some concern unless practice demonstrates that this is not the operating principle.

Abuse of Dominant Position

The language employed here immediately recalls that of art 82 EC, although the wording of the central provision, in art 17, is somewhat different.[6] Article 17 prohibits expressly six forms of abuse, and allows, at art 17(7), the AMEA to specify other forms of abuse if this is necessary. Six specific abuses are specified: **2-3.06**

(1) 'Selling commodities at unfairly high prices, or buying commodities at unfairly low prices'.

(2) Selling below cost, without justification.[7] An earlier version of the Law made explicit reference to the requirement that this be 'in order to eliminate

---

5 However, the effect of the third presumption may sometimes be anomalous. Consider for example a market with the following structure: A, 25%; B, 12%; C, 39%; D, 5%; E, 10%; F, 9%. The CR3 (A+B+C) would be 76%, meeting the threshold. B's market share is in excess of 10 per cent, and therefore B may be *presumed* to be dominant. Under US law no finding of monopoly status could be made in respect of any of these participants, and under EC law it is highly unlikely that even C, holding the largest single market share, would be found to be dominant (see Chapter 1-2, above). While a finding of dominance has been made in respect of British Airways having a 39.7% market share in the EC, this was an exceptional case. In this hypothetical case it is to be hoped that B, and even A and C, could readily rebut the presumption with the support of the evidence relating to market shares and, crucially, to the existence of a further three not-insignificant competitors. It may however be noted that the Korean antitrust system, discussed in Part 5 of this book, also makes use of concentration ratios in a way similar to that employed in the AML.

6 Harris argues that this article (in an earlier version but one substantially the same as the adopted version) 'contravenes accepted modern competition law norms in many respects' (Harris, SH, 'The Making of an Antitrust Law: The Pending Anti-Monopoly Law of the People's Republic of China' (2006–2007) 7 *Chicago Journal of International Law* 169 at 200). However with qualifications, all practices listed in the article could invite condemnation under the EC antitrust regime.

7 Below cost selling was already prohibited by the Law Against Unfair Competition 1993 and the Price Law 1997. The Price Law stipulated penalties to be applied in such cases. Article 11 of the Law Against Unfair Competition is in the following terms: 'A business operator shall not sell his products at a price that is below the cost for the purpose of excluding his competitors'. Below cost sales were allowed in relation to 'perishables or live products', disposal of items whose validity term was about to expire, or overstocks, seasonal sales, or sales made in the process of liquidations or for debt clearance. Article 14(2) of the Price Law provides that:

> Business operators shall not . . .
> Dump merchandise below cost in order to force out competitors or to monopolize the market, thereby disturbing the normal order of production and business and causing

competition'. It is unfortunate that this wording has been removed from the adopted provision, with the result that there is no apparent requirement to demonstrate harm to the competitive process or, indeed, to a specific competitor.

(3) Refusing to trade with other parties without justification. Although a general provision relating to the application of an 'essential facilities doctrine' was removed from the legislation in the face of intense criticism this paragraph admits its acceptance as part of the law of refusal to supply. It remains to be seen how onerous the obligation to trade (absent a 'justification' for not trading) is. In the EC and in the US the general position is taken that parties are free to choose their trading partners, and that obligations to trade will be imposed on monopolists only in exceptional circumstances (see Chapter 1-2, above).

(4) Compelling, without justification, other trading parties to trade exclusively with the monopolist or with other designated parties.

(5) Imposing, without justification, tie-in sales or 'other unreasonable trading conditions'.[8]

(6) Applying discrimination in relation to either prices or other trading conditions without justification.[9] This language very closely follows that of art 82(c) EC.

Finally, a seventh category is specified, consisting of 'other conducts determined as abuse of a dominant position by the [AMEA]'. It will be noted that this does not require that rules are introduced by the State Council in respect of the expansion of categories of abusive conduct, but that these can be determined on a case-by-case basis by the AMEA. The generality of this provision may make it hard to counsel effectively in relation to this area.

---

damages to the interests of the State or the legitimate rights and interests of other business operators, except for lawful disposal of merchandise such as fresh or live merchandise, seasonal merchandise and overstocked merchandise at reduced prices.

Penalties are provided for in the Provision Concerning the Administrative Punishment for Illegal Pricing Acts 1999, and are, in the case that illegal gains have occurred, a fine of between RMB30,000 and RMB300,000. Given that penalties may only be applied where gains have occurred, no sanctions are available under these laws in respect of failed attempts at exclusionary predation.

[8] Tie-ins have a long history in China. It is reported that in the 1980s 'if you wanted to buy a pack of good cigarettes you would have to buy a much cheaper pack of low-quality cigarettes'. While this position has changed, tie-in sales remain common in China (see generally Jin, C and Luo, W, *Competition Law in China* (Buffalo NY: William S Hein & Co Inc, 2002) at 40–4).

Tie-in sales are prohibited by the Law Against Unfair Competition 1993, art 12, which provides that: 'In selling his products, a business operator shall not make a tie-in sale against a buyer's wish or attach other unreasonable conditions'. However, no penalties were provided in respect of this practice, with the result that this legal provision is completely ineffective, and may be disregarded.

[9] Price discrimination is also prohibited by the Price Law 1997, art 14(5).

It should be noted at the outset that this article applies to *both* exclusionary abuses *and* to exploitative abuses, and that the article is therefore much closer to the spirit of EC law than it is to that of US law. In the US an exploitative price, as discussed in Chapter 1-2 above, cannot, in the absence of a special regulatory regime, invite condemnation. In the EC however antitrust law is not so clear in its goals, and exploitative pricing can be condemned under the operation of art 82, although many have pointed out the logical problems posed by such an approach.[10] **2-3.07**

There is no mechanism by which exemptions can be granted in relation to the abuse of a dominant position, but it will be noted that all the prohibitions except the first make reference to justifiability. It has been suggested by some commentators that the fact that art 17(1) does not do so means that this creates a *per se* abuse. However, the use of the word 'unfairly' applied in relation to both high and low pricing allows the exercise of some enforcement discretion and is tractable to justification. Further, it has been suggested that 'the principle of "rule of reason" analysis shall be adopted to determine if the practices listed above are abuses of dominant market positions'.[11] Guidelines are promised in relation to certain categories of conduct, including guidelines relating to pricing under the AML. It is believed that an early draft of the latter guidelines was somewhat formalistic in its terms, stating, inter alia, that a price would be excessive when it was 20 per cent above the maximum price of similar products or services, or, where there were no similar products to act as comparators, at a level such that the profit margin was greater than 20 per cent. It hardly needs to be said that those who have commented on the guidelines and who have experience of competition law and policy were quick to point out its flaws. **2-3.08**

Intellectual property

It was noted in the previous chapter that art 55 of the AML provides that the AML will not apply to the exercise of IP rights in accordance with relevant IP law, but that it shall apply to the conduct of business operators to 'eliminate or restrict market competition by abusing their intellectual property rights'. While some have called strongly for clarification of this principle[12] there are arguments **2-3.09**

[10] See, eg Furse, M, 'Excessive Prices, Unfair Prices and Economic Value: The Law of Excessive Pricing under Article 82 EC and the Chapter II Prohibition' (2008) *European Competition Journal* 59.

[11] Wu, n 3, above, at 85.

[12] See, for example, Harris, n 6, above, at 171, commenting on an earlier version of this article: Certain substantive provisions in the [Draft Law] appear to be inconsistent with international norms of competition law. Foremost among these is a vague article stating that an 'abuse' of intellectual property ('IP') rights resulting in the elimination or restriction of competition is subject to sanctions under the law. The absence of any definition of what conduct may constitute such an abuse of IP rights, and the possible imposition of

to support such a general proposition. It should be noted that the EC has developed a robust jurisprudence relating to the relationship between antitrust law and the exercise of IP rights, based not on precise legislative formulations, but on general principles of antitrust law. It is likely that guidelines will be issued in relation to the applicability of the AML to the exercise of IP rights. The fact that some commentators have been so hostile to the inclusion of this provision in the AML reflects concerns relating to China's past record in protecting IP rights, and to a fear that the AML provision may be used to require firms in possession of valuable IP rights to disclose these on compulsory terms.[13]

Abuse of Administrative Power

2-3.10 When placed in the context of the structure of the Chinese economy and the degree of state intervention at all levels the six articles of Chapter V of the AML are remarkable. These provisions are intended to address in particular local protectionism, and do not have their counterparts in US or EC antitrust law.[14] How effective these provisions are in practice remains, of course, to be seen.[15] It was noted in Chapter 1, above, that although administrative monopolies and SOEs

---

> compulsory licensing as a remedy, have engendered expressions of great concern, especially from foreign high technology companies with substantial operations or sales in China.

Ross notes that:

> Despite the efforts of legislators to insulate intellectual property rights from the reach of the AML, a tension inevitably arises as the core of a patent is the right to exclude, and the value of a trademark lies in its ability to brand a product that may otherwise be largely indistinguishable from the products of competitors. It remains unclear under what circumstances the exercise of intellectual property rights may be deemed to constitute an abuse of such rights when such rights include the right to deny licensees or otherwise to exclude competitors for the term of a patent or to restrict competition. Article 55 is therefore of major concern to foreign companies with advanced technology and globally recognized brands (Ross, L, 'China's Anti-Monopoly Law' (2008) *Antitrust*, Spring, 66 at 70).

It is not in fact clear that there was a legislative attempt to exclude IP rights from the scope of the Law. Had this been the intention it would have been relatively easy to achieve this. See also Harris, SH and Ganske, RJ, 'The Monopolization and IP Abuse Provisions of China's Anti-Monopoly Law: Concerns and a Proposal' (2008) 75 *Antitrust Law Journal* 213.

[13] It should also be noted that art 329 of the Contract Law of 1999 states that a 'technology contract which illegally monopolizes technology, restricts technological improvements or infringes on the technology of a third party is invalid'. See Emch, n 1, above, at 619.

[14] The closest analogy, particularly in respect of art 33, is to be found in arts 28–30 of the EC Treaty, which contain rules relating to the free movement of goods within the internal EC market.

[15] See Wu, n 3, above, at 94: '. . . even though *in theory* administrative monopoly is not a problem to be solved by the [Anti-Monopoly Law] and *in practice* it will indeed be very hard for the [Anti-Monopoly Law] to solve this problem, it is nonetheless necessary to have clear and specific regulations on administrative monopoly in the [Anti-Monopoly Law], which is a specific and fundamental law to protect competition.' (Emphasis in original)

are different, and may produce different anti-competitive effects, there is a relationship between the two, with administrative monopolies being used in some cases to support or protect SOEs. In some cases it may not be clear whether an entity is a commercial SOE or an administrative body.[16] Article 32 relates to the power of administrative bodies to designate certain suppliers of goods and services and to compel others to use those suppliers; art 33 relates specifically to measures which might prevent the free circulation of goods or services; art 34 to bidding procedures; art 35 deals with restrictions on investment; and arts 36 and 37 stipulate that administrative bodies may not frustrate the purposes of the AML.

Article 32 sets out a clear principle that: **2-3.11**

> Any administrative organ or organization empowered by a law or administrative regulation to administer public affairs may not abuse its administrative power, restrict, or restrict in a disguised form, entities and individuals to operate, purchase or use the commodities provided by business operators designated by it.

This provision formed the basis of the first private action brought in China on the basis of the AML. The action, which came before the No 1 People's Court, Beijing, was brought by eight companies producing anti-counterfeiting technologies. The defendant, the General Administration of Quality Supervision, Inspection and Quarantine of the PRC, created an Internet-based network providing a registration service to verify the legitimacy of products—the Product Identification, Authentication and Tracing system—and established a regulation in December 2007 to require 69 kinds of specific products (including food, makeup, wire, cable, agricultural material, etc) to register in that network, and to use the certified security number for each product on the package. If the products did not bear the security number they could not be lawfully sold. Those obliged to use the service were required to pay a fee for doing so. The 'service' was run by a company called ZhongXin National Inspection Information Technology Co Ltd, of which the administrative department was one of the three shareholders, although it did not contribute financially towards the development of the registration service. The plaintiffs' case was lodged on the first day on which the AML entered into force. The argument was made that the ongoing enforcement of the administrative regulations was in breach of the provisions of the AML relating to abuse of administrative monopoly, and was causing the plaintiffs harm by compulsorily diverting potential customers away from the services they offered. The case was

[16] See, eg Wen, X, 'Market Dominance by China's Public Utility Enterprises' (2008) 75 *Antitrust Law Journal* 151 at 156: 'Even the new [Anti-Monopoly Law] is not that clear as to what may fall within an administrative monopoly, where one typically finds [publicly owned-utilities].'

rejected by the Court on 4 September 2008 on the grounds that the limitations period for bringing the action had expired as the network had been set up more than two years previously. The plaintiffs announced that they intended to appeal to the High Court.

2-3.12 Article 33 is intended to address in part the well documented problems relating to the regional segmentation of the Chinese internal market. This regional segmentation is both the product of a poor transport infrastructure extending over a very large territory, and of a degree of regional protectionism, particularly in light of over-capacity in several industries as a result of now discredited industrial policies. Article 33 prohibits administrative bodies from engaging in any of five practices: (1) setting or implementing discriminatory charges or fixing discriminatory prices for non-local commodities; (2) imposing technical requirements or inspection standards that discriminate in favour of local commodities, or taking measures such as repeated inspections or certifications of non-local commodities so as to restrict the entry of non-local commodities into the local market; (3) adopting administrative licensing aimed at non-local commodities; (4) 'setting barriers or taking other measures so as to hamper commodities from outside the locality from entering the local market or local commodities from moving outside the local region'; and (5) taking any other steps to block the free circulation of commodities within China.

2-3.13 Article 34 makes it unlawful for administrative bodies to operate bidding procedures that favour local suppliers by setting differential qualification requirements, or by failing properly to publicize the tendering procedures in accordance with the requirements of relevant laws. Article 35 prevents administrative bodies from restricting direct inward investment within their jurisdiction, or from preventing companies from other parts of China from establishing local branches by imposing on them any treatment which is not equal to that applied to local participants.

2-3.14 Evidence of the scale of concern within the State Council of the degree of local resistance to the principle of fair competition across China, stripped of local favouritism and protectionism, is found in both arts 36 and 37. Article 36 makes it unlawful for administrative organs 'to force business operators to engage in the monopolistic conducts as prescribed by this law'. Article 37 is deceptive in its simplicity, stating in its entirety that '[a]ny administrative organ may not abuse its administrative power to set down such provisions in respect of eliminating or restricting competition'.

2-3.15 The penalties to be applied to administrative organs in breach of these provisions are specified in art 51 of the Law. Subject to the legal rules relating to the administration of such organizations, in the event that a breach occurs the superior authority of the offending organization 'shall order it to make correction and impose punishments on the directly liable person in charge and other directly liable persons'. This is to say that the AMEA itself has no direct control over these cases, and cannot stipulate the penalty to be applied in the event that a breach is uncovered.[17]

[17] Fox has described this enforcement mechanism as 'so weak that the prohibitory language may be mere aspiration' (Fox, EM, 'An Anti-Monopoly Law for China—Scaling the Walls of Government Restraints' (2008) 75 *Antitrust Law Journal* 173 at 177).

2-4

CHINA MERGER CONTROL

Introduction	2-4.01	Pre-notification review	2-4.17
Jurisdiction	2-4.05	**The Substantive Test**	2-4.18
'Foreign mergers'	2-4.10	**Efficiencies and the Failing Firm Defence**	2-4.21
Procedures	2-4.12	**Remedies and Penalties**	2-4.22
Notification requirements	2-4.12		
Expedited review	2-4.16		

Introduction

Given the global importance of Chinese trade and the level of business conducted in China it is possible that 'China has the potential, alongside the European Union and [the] United States, to develop into a key jurisdiction in deciding whether a transaction can be completed or not'.[1] Prior to the enactment of the AML the only laws which governed merger control in China were directed at foreign acquisitions of Chinese enterprises, or related to specific industries. This gave rise both to accusations of antitrust law being used to protect Chinese businesses and disadvantage foreign entrants into the market, and to inconsistencies and difficulties. A clear example of the latter may be seen in the approach taken by the Chinese authorities to the proposed acquisition by China Mobile Communications Corporation of Millicom International which, at US$3.5bn would have been one of the largest acquisitions by a Chinese firm of a foreign enterprise. In the event the bid collapsed, in part because China Mobile required the permission of no less than three ministries, giving rise to fatal uncertainties.[2] The AML brings into one place, with possible reservations in respect of certain **2-4.01**

[1] Lorenz, M, 'The New Chinese Competition Act' (2008) *European Competition Law Review* 257 at 263.

[2] See *Financial Times*, 4 July 2006 ('Millicom ends China Mobile's Bid').

regulated industries, an approach to merger control which does not discriminate between Chinese and foreign firms, and which offers a 'one-stop shop'.[3]

2-4.02 Article 5 of the AML states the basic principle that 'business operators may, through fair competition [and] voluntary alliance, concentrate themselves according to law, expand the scope of business operations and enhance market competitiveness'.[4] Chapter IV of the Law then sets out the provisions relating to 'concentrations', establishing a system of pre-merger review, with compulsory notification, for mergers which qualify under the terms of the Law. Article 28 states that where a concentration 'has or may have [the] effect of eliminating or restricting competition, the [AMEA] shall make a decision to prohibit the concentration'. At the time of writing only very limited guidance has been published in relation to the operation of the merger control regime and this is comprehensively discussed here. It may, however, be presumed that mergers between Chinese firms which can be demonstrated to lead to efficient industry consolidation are likely to be favourably treated. Officials of the State Council commented, when turnover thresholds were published in August 2008, that it was necessary for Chinese industrial policy for 'enterprises to be stronger and bigger' and that moves that facilitated this goal would be encouraged.[5]

2-4.03 The term used throughout the Law is 'concentration', which refers to three situations: (1) a merger of previously independent businesses; (2) the acquisition of control by one business of another through the acquisition of assets or equity; and (3) the acquisition of control or of the ability to exercise 'a decisive influence' 'by virtue of contract or by any other means'.[6] Article 21 makes notification of relevant mergers compulsory, and provides that such mergers must not be

---

[3] Although note a reservation in respect of mergers affecting national security which involve foreign parties (see further below).

[4] This article supports arguments made by pressure groups within China to the effect that the AML should not thwart mergers between SOEs designed to strengthen them in the face of foreign competition. See Huang, Y, 'Pursuing the Second Best: The History, Momentum, and Remaining Issues of China's Anti-Monopoly Law' (2008) 75 *Antitrust Law Journal* 117 at 128:

> It has been widely suspected among the local antitrust circles that the insertion [of art 5] was driven by the State-monopolies. Even though these enterprises have been huge conglomerates in the China market, due to State monopoly grants and favourable policy protection, they are still inefficient and their size is no match for the Fortune 500 companies. . . . [The SOEs] continue to press lawmakers, despite the rejection of the proposal of complete immunity for the State monopolies. At this time, they are raising an argument about concentration that the legislators cannot ignore: the AML should not prevent SOEs from growing stronger and competing more effectively with multinationals, and to that end concentration among domestic competitors should be encouraged. Hence art 5.

[5] Officials of the Legislation Office of State Council Answering Reporters' Questions Regarding *Rules of State Council on Notification Thresholds for Concentrations of Operators*, 4 August 2008 (<http://www.gov.cn/zwhd/2008-08/04/content_1063736.htm >).

[6] art 20, AML.

implemented without the approval of the Anti-Monopoly Law Enforcement Agency ('AMEA'). Concentrations need not be notified in the two circumstances specified in art 22, both of which relate to pre-existing relationships of control or ownership. Thus art 22(1) provides that notification is not required where 'one business operator who is a party to the concentration has the power to exercise more than half the voting rights of every other business operator, whether of the equity or the assets'. Article 22(2) is in similar terms, but applies where a business operator not involved in the concentration possesses 50 per cent or more of the voting shares or assets of all of those businesses which are involved in the concentration.[7]

Neither the terms 'control' nor 'decisive influence' are defined in the legislation.[8] **2-4.04** The fact however that a distinction is drawn between the two, as well as normal usage, suggest that 'control' involves a higher ability to direct the operations of the acquired entity than does the ability to exercise material influence. It is possible that guidance will be published in this respect, but more likely that the term will be gradually clarified through practice, as has been the case in the UK regime where very similar language is used. The general principle is likely to be that in order to determine whether control exists a full examination of the facts of the case, including the constitution documents of the relevant enterprises, and any particular voting patterns etc, may need to be carried out. Reference may also be made to the Company Law 2005, which defines both 'controlling shareholders' and 'actual controllers'. A 'controlling shareholder' is defined in art 217(2) as:

> . . . a shareholder whose capital contribution occupies 50 per cent or more in the total capital of a limited liability company or a shareholder whose stock occupies more than 50 per cent of the total equity stocks of a joint stock limited company or a shareholder whose capital contribution or proportion of stock is less than 50 per cent but who enjoys a voting right according to its capital contribution or the stock it holds is large enough to impose a large impact upon the resolution of the shareholders' meeting or the shareholders' assembly.

An 'actual controller' is defined in art 217(3) of the Company Law as:

> . . . anyone who is not a shareholder but is able to hold actual control of the acts of the company by means of investment relations, agreements or any other arrangements.[9]

---

[7] It may be questioned therefore whether it is intended that the merger control provisions relate to SOEs, all of whom ultimately have the same owner.

[8] Draft implementing regulations (Legislative Affairs Office of the State Council, 27 March 2007) stated that the ability to exercise a decisive influence would arise where a business operator was able to command a significant influence on the operational and manufacturing businesses of another.

[9] It has been suggested that 'these definitions from the Company Law should be applicable under the [AML]' (Wu, Z, 'Perspectives on the Chinese Anti-Monopoly Law' (2008) 75 *Antitrust Law Journal* 73 at 87).

If these definitions are read across into the AML it would be possible, for example, to find that 'control' existed over a company through purely contractual relationships or, in extreme circumstances, by virtue of the nature of the trading relationships between parties.

Jurisdiction

2-4.05 Article 21 of the AML provides that the State Council is to prescribe to the AMEA the thresholds to be applied to the control of concentrations. These rules were published on 1 August 2008 as State Decree No 529. The formulation of the thresholds is similar to that of the EC, in that both worldwide and Chinese turnover thresholds are specified.[10] Article 3 of the Decree is in the following terms:

> Where a concentration of undertakings meets any of the below thresholds, a premerger notification shall be filed with the competent commercial authority under the State Council, and no concentration shall be implemented without a notification:
> (1) The total worldwide turnover of all undertakings to the concentration in the previous fiscal year exceeds RMB10 billion, and the PRC turnover of at least each of two undertakings in the previous fiscal year exceeds RMB400 million; or
> (2) The total PRC turnover of all undertakings to the concentration in the previous fiscal year exceeds RMB2.0 billion, and the PRC turnover of at least each of two undertakings in the previous fiscal year exceeds RMB400 million.

2-4.06 Regard is to be had to the particular circumstances of sectors in which standard turnover assessments may not be appropriate to an assessment of power. Paragraph 2 of art 3 therefore provides that:

> Calculation of the turnover shall take into account the actual circumstances of such special industries and sectors as banking, insurance, securities, futures, etc. The detailed measures on calculation of the turnover shall be formulated by the competent commercial authority under the State Council together with relevant departments and institutions under the State Council.

2-4.07 Guidance on the calculation of turnover has, at the time of writing, still to be published.[11] Unfortunately art 4 of the Decree somewhat dilutes the clarity of

---

[10] The approach taken is also consistent with recommendations of the International Competition Network in relation to the exercise of control over anti-competitive mergers.

[11] Article 3 of the Decree further provides that:
Calculation of the turnover shall take into account the actual circumstances of such special industries and sectors as banking, insurance, securities, futures, etc. The detailed measures on calculation of the turnover shall be formulated by the competent commercial authority

art 3, providing that:

> With respect to a concentration which does not meet any of the notification thresholds prescribed under Article 3 but facts and evidence gathered pursuant to prescribed procedures indicate that such concentration has or may have the effect of foreclosing or restricting competition, investigations shall be carried out by competent commercial authority under the State Council in accordance with applicable laws.

It is clearly intended that this provision may be applied to prospective concentrations which the parties believe to be non-notifiable under the terms of art 3 of the Decree, but the means by which the AMEA may seize jurisdiction over a non-notifiable merger remain unclear. Officials of the State Council indicated that such jurisdiction might be asserted where the turnover thresholds were not met, but where market shares were very high. No further guidance in relation to this possibility has been given to date by officials of the State Council. It is also reasonable to suspect that given the lack of resources available to MOFCOM it is unlikely to be engaging in fishing trips looking for mergers to examine which have not been notified to it, although it may be susceptible to pressures from other ministries or organizations if complaints are made about these.

Turnover thresholds were adopted in preference to market share thresholds on the **2-4.08** grounds that they are 'objective, clear, easily judged' and are transparent.[12] It was also stated by Officials of the State Council that turnover is the 'key fact reflecting economic power'. It is, however, inevitable that turnover thresholds will lead to concentrations being notified that do not have significant anti-competitive impact. At the time of writing no mechanisms have been created to allow for abbreviated forms of notification and review in respect of concentrations to which the parties can readily demonstrate no anti-competitive impact. It was clearly the view of the State Council however that the turnover thresholds were sufficiently high and that concentrations with insignificant market impact would be unlikely to be caught within the thresholds.[13] It is likely that these notification criteria will be amended in the light of experience.[14]

---

under the State Council together with relevant departments and institutions under the State Council.

[12] Officials of the Legislation Office of State Council Answering Reporters' Questions Regarding *Rules of State Council on Notification Thresholds for Concentrations of Operators*, 4 August 2008 (<http://www.gov.cn/zwhd/2008-08/04/content_1063736.htm>).

[13] Studies conducted by the Quantitative and Technical Economics Institute of the Chinese Academy of Social Sciences compared turnover thresholds in a large number of other jurisdictions. Recommendations based on this study were then analysed in relation to the 2006 Annual Basic Unit Report of the National Bureau of Statistics. The majority of businesses in China would fall below the current thresholds. (Ibid)

[14] It was noted at the time of the announcement of the thresholds that

> . . . no country has a complete, reasonable and accurate method to determine the criteria for notification. They all provide general criteria first and then adjust them according to

2-4.09 There is no distinction drawn in the guidelines between horizontal and vertical mergers, such that notification will be required of mergers between non-competing firms where the thresholds are met. At the time of writing the State Council has not published further guidance relating to the operation of the merger control system although a draft of the jurisdiction guidelines included a provision establishing an abbreviated procedure for notifiable mergers which did not raise competition concerns.

'Foreign mergers'

2-4.10 As noted in Chapter 2-1, the AML expressly states that jurisdiction may be asserted over monopolistic conduct 'outside the territory of [China]' that has the effect of eliminating or restricting competition on the domestic market of China.[15] There is, therefore, no express provision in Chapter IV relating to mergers between parties none of whom are domiciled in China, but jurisdiction is implied from art 2. If further reinforcement of this principle were necessary it may be found in art 31, discussed below, which makes express reference to 'foreign investor[s]' participating in a relevant concentration. As discussed below in relation to the application of the substantive test, there is some concern that avenues may be open to Chinese domiciled companies to justify otherwise anti-competitive concentrations that may not be open to foreign companies. The test of whether a foreign merger will be subject to the jurisdiction of the Law is the same as that for a domestic merger, ie control is acquired, and this reaches the thresholds specified by the State Council in State Decree No 529, discussed above. It will be noted that the decree draws no distinction between foreign and Chinese companies. Like the EC and the US the sole test is that of turnover.

2-4.11 One of the first mergers to be notified under the terms of the AML was the proposed acquisition by Coca Cola Co of Huiyuan Juice Group Ltd, one of China's leading suppliers of fruit juices, and a very well-known brand in China. Technically, being listed on the Hong Kong stock exchange, Huiyuan is not a Chinese company, and its owners include Danone, but the announcement of the proposed purchase by Coca Cola was met with intense media comment in China, and Chinese competitors lobbied for the deal to be blocked.[16] The first merger decision made under the AML was that in *InBev NV/SA—Anheuser-Busch Companies*

actual situations. China's criteria for notification will be adjusted after a period of time of implementation, if they are not suitable. (Ibid)

[15] art 2, AML.

[16] See Bush, N and Zhaofeng, Z, 'Chinese Antitrust—Act II, Scene 1', *theantitrustsource* (<http://www.antitrustsource.com>), October 2008, 1 at 10. An existing provision under the 2006 merger regulations which protected 'famous brands' would have been inapplicable because Huiyuan had ceased to be Chinese. See further para 2-4.25 below.

Inc,[17] which was notified to MOFCOM on 10 September 2008. Supplementary notifications were made on 17 October and 23 October, with MOFCOM registering the notification on 27 October and the final decision being made on 18 November 2008.[18] According to MOFCOM's notice, in addition to reviewing the documents submitted with the notification, the views of relevant government departments were solicited, and evidence was heard or taken from 'related beer trade associations, major beer producers, raw beer material producers, as well as sellers of beer products'. The merger was cleared with conditions (see below).

Procedures

Notification requirements

At the time of writing the AMEA does not have the resources properly to conduct its own investigations of notified mergers, and it must be stressed that the notification materials submitted will themselves constitute the evidence, or the vast bulk of the evidence, that will be reviewed by the AMEA. Informal indications therefore suggest that the review will take the form of a review *of the notification*, rather than an independently conducted review of the competitive situation. **2-4.12**

Article 23 of the Law sets out the material that must be submitted when a merger notification is made to the AMEA. The following are required: (1) a declaration paper;[19] (2) an explanation of the competitive effects of the concentration on the relevant market(s) (a competitive impact statement); (3) the relevant concentration agreement; (4) financial and duly audited accounting reports for the previous fiscal year of those firms involved in the concentration; and (5) any other documents or materials as required by the AMEA. Although not expressly stated it may be implied from the terms of the article that notifications are to be made only when there is a genuine intent to enter into a concentration, and not speculatively. Where filings are not complete the parties must submit the relevant materials within the time period specified by the AMEA, or the filing shall be deemed to be not submitted.[20] In the past it has often been the case that when mergers were **2-4.13**

[17] Notice of the Ministry of Commerce of the PRC [2008] No 95.

[18] It appears to have been common practice under the earlier regime for the Chinese authorities to hesitate to accept notifications as being complete, such that deadlines were ostensibly complied with, but the total time from first notification to the resolution of the case could take somewhat longer than published deadlines would suggest.

[19] The declaration paper must include: the names of the business operators, their domiciles, statements as to the scope of the businesses, the date on which the concentration is intended to be implemented, and any other prescribed matters (art 23).

[20] art 24, AML.

required to be reviewed under earlier rules notifications were found to be incomplete, with further requests being made to notifying parties. It is quite possible that this practice may continue, such that the timetables specified in the legislation do not begin to run until relatively late in the notification process.

2-4.14 As is the case in the EC and the US a two-stage review procedure is provided for in Chapter IV, although the process is more similar to that of the EC in that both stages are conducted within the AMEA, and there is no need for the AMEA to seek a judicially sanctioned injunction against a merger. After notification the AMEA has 30 days in which to 'conduct a preliminary review' and 'make a decision on whether to conduct a further review, and notify the business operators in written form'.[21] It is unlawful to implement a notifiable concentration until the AMEA has taken a decision permitting that concentration to proceed. Where a decision is taken at the first stage that there are no objections to the concentration, the parties may proceed. Whereas art 26, discussed below, states that where the AMEA fails to make a decision at the second stage within the required time period the parties may consummate the concentration, no such provision is found in art 25. It may be presumed that the drafters of the legislation did not anticipate that there would be any circumstances in which the AMEA would fail to make either a clearance decision or a decision to move to the second stage of the proceedings within the allotted 30 days. It has also been suggested, although this is not clear on the face of the legislation, that 'if the [AMEA] makes no decision during the Phase I thirty-day period, the transaction can be deemed to be cleared'.[22] It is also the case that, unlike art 26, there is no provision by which this thirty-day period can be extended, although the clock will not start running until such time as the AMEA accepts that the filing is complete.

2-4.15 At the second stage proceedings the AMEA has a further ninety days in which to make a final determination. This period may be extended by up to a maximum of a further sixty days in three circumstances: (1) the parties themselves agree to the extension; this might be the case for example where the parties form the belief that they are able to persuade the AMEA of the merits of concentration but need more time to do so; (2) the documents submitted by the parties are either inaccurate or require further clarification; or (3) the relevant circumstances have changed 'significantly' since the concentration was notified. In the latter two cases the agreement of the parties to the extension period is not required.[23] As with stage one the parties may not consummate the concentration until it is cleared by the AMEA. If the AMEA fails to make a decision within the required time, including any

---

[21] art 25, AML.

[22] Wang X, 'Highlight's of China's New Anti-Monopoly Law' (2008) 75 *Antitrust Law Journal* 133 at 140.

[23] art 26, AML.

authorized extensions, the concentration is deemed to be cleared. Any decision made must again be notified to the parties in writing, with the added proviso that where the AMEA decides to prohibit the concentration it is required to 'explain the reasons'. At the time of writing no such decisions have been taken, and the detail of the reasoning to be disclosed is therefore not known. As discussed below the AMEA may also clear a concentration subject to conditions.[24] Article 30 of the Law requires the AMEA to publicize any prohibition decisions, or conditional clearance decisions, in a 'timely' manner, but does not specify the amount of detail which must be included in any such notice.

Expedited review

The draft Implementing Regulations[25] made clear that there would be a mechanism under which an expedited review could take place in the event that a merger subject to notification did not in fact raise competition concerns. This was omitted from the regulations published in August 2008. **2-4.16**

Pre-notification review

The circulated draft of the merger Implementing Regulations[26] made express provisions for a pre-notification discussion procedure, with an indication that the AMEA was obliged to provide guidance to the parties where this was requested. This was omitted from the regulations on jurisdiction published in August 2008. **2-4.17**

The Substantive Test

At the time of writing neither the AMEA nor the State Council have published guidance relating to the substantive assessment of mergers. The Law states, at art 27, that six factors are to be taken into account when a merger is being assessed: (1) the market shares of the parties to the concentration, and their degree of market power; (2) the extent of the market concentration; (3) the impact of the concentration on market entry, and on technological progress;[27] (4) the impact of the concentration on consumers and other businesses; (5) the impact on 'national economic development'; and (6) 'other elements that may have an effect **2-4.18**

[24] art 29, AML

[25] Legislative Affairs Office of the State Council, 27 March 2007.

[26] Ibid.

[27] It has been suggested by some commentators that this provision has the potential to operate so as to prejudice the interests of foreign companies, with the potential for the AMEA to find that superior technologies operate as barriers to entry, and perhaps to require licensing of, or access to, this technology as a condition in clearing mergers.

on [. . .] competition'. Although this list of criteria to be considered is a broad one, and one that is likely to lead to difficult balancing exercises, the wording of art 28 of the Law is based, at least in its first sentence, purely around a competition test. Thus art 28, as noted above, provides that concentrations will be prohibited where they will or may have the effect of 'eliminating or restricting competition'. The article at first blush appears to leave no discretion to the AMEA in this respect, as it states that the AMEA, in these circumstances, '*shall* make a decision to prohibit the concentration'.[28] This very clear statement of principle is, however, immediately qualified in two ways. The second sentence of art 28 states that if the parties to the concentration

> can prove that the concentration will bring more positive impact than negative impact on competition, or the concentration is pursuant to public interests, the [AMEA] may decide not to prohibit the concentration.

2-4.19 The first qualification appears to place a more rigorous burden on the notifying parties than the second. Where it is argued that the 'positive impact' of the concentration outweighs the harm to competition, the parties must 'prove' that this is the case. This test is therefore the one that applies to, inter alia, a failing firm defence or an efficiency justification, although the possibility remains that such situations may also arguably fall within the 'public interest' test given the breadth with which this is drawn. Where the argument is made that 'the concentration is in harmony with the public interests' no such high threshold is created. The Law is silent as to which public interests are to be taken into account, and if the list of objectives as set out in art 1 is to be taken as a guide, a very wide range of factors may be considered to be relevant. It may also be expected that it will be harder for parties to a purely 'foreign merger', with the requisite turnover and market impact in China, to argue that the second test is met than will be the case in respect of mergers between Chinese parties.[29] It is also possible that the reference to the impact of the merger on national development may be used to justify differential treatment, under which national mergers are treated more favourably than 'foreign' mergers. The Law also makes no reference to the procedures by which the

[28] Emphasis added.

[29] For example two merging Chinese companies may be able to argue that the concentration promotes technological progress within China, or protects jobs, or promotes exports, or is otherwise consistent with the objectives spelt out in art 1 of the Law. Two foreign companies without substantial facilities in China, but with substantial imports into the country, may meet the jurisdictional thresholds, but are unlikely to be able to build a case relating to the advantages of the merger to the 'public interest' in the same way. This conclusion is supported by Wang, n 22, above, at 143. It is also the case, as noted in Chapter 2-1, above, that the term 'public interest' is not defined in the Law, and that its application will raise difficulties. Wang has stated that: '. . . a transaction that benefits some public interest may not benefit competition. Thus it is not difficult to imagine that the goals to protect consumers and to protect the public interest could, thus, easily conflict with each other.' (Ibid)

parties are to demonstrate that the merger does create benefits, and it is to be hoped that guidance is produced in this respect.

Article 31 of the Law contains a provision which relates exclusively to foreign investors, stating that where any such investor is a party to a concentration involving 'domestic enterprises' and 'State security is involved, besides the examination [specified above] the examination on national security shall also be conducted in accordance with the relevant State provisions'. There is no definition of national security in the AML itself, and neither is one to be found in the general law of China. Even the Supreme Court has resisted defining the term. Regulations relating to merger control introduced in 2006 also included a provision relating to national security, although this is noticeably more widely drawn than is the case in respect of art 31 of the AML. Given that these earlier regulations were applied in relation to a merger between a French company and a Chinese company making cookware it is to be hoped that a more focused review is to apply under art 31 of the new Law.[30] It is not clear at the time of writing how the national security provision is to be applied, and how, if at all, this will be through a different procedure than the general competition review.[31] It is likely, however, that a special committee will be established to conduct national security reviews where the circumstances set out in art 31 apply. **2-4.20**

Efficiencies and the Failing Firm Defence

No express mention is made in the AML to either an efficiencies defence, or to a failing firm defence. However, as noted above, art 28 of the Law permits concentrations with adverse competitive effects to be cleared where the benefits of the concentration can be proved to outweigh the disadvantages. **2-4.21**

[30] See, Ross, L, 'China's Anti-Monopoly Law' (2008) *Antitrust*, Spring, 66 at n 16. Lorenz is not confident that standards will be more objective under the new law, noting that 'the existing foreign merger case law of [MOFCOM] shows that the "threat to national security" objection is raised where foreign investors have attempted to gain majority interests in well-known state enterprises. This policy is likely to be continued and institutionalised' (Lorenz, M, 'The New Chinese Competition Act' (2008) *European Competition Law Review*, 257 at 261). There will be little comfort in the comments of Xu Jialu, Vice-Chairman of the NPC who stated that:

> State security includes national defense security, information security, environmental security, and economic security. Western multinationals have now reached out to seize China's leading manufacturing enterprises. . . . These large state-owned enterprises have much proprietary intellectual property and represent China's leading-edge manufacturing technology. Control by foreign countries will pose a big obstacle to our future innovation. (See Bush and Zhaofeng, n 16, above at 9.)

[31] See generally Wu, n 9, above at 100–2.

Remedies and Penalties

2-4.22 Article 48 of the Law makes clear that it is illegal to implement a notifiable concentration until such time as the AMEA has made a clearance decision, or has failed to make a decision within the time allowed for. Article 29 of the Law provides that in addition to refusing to give permission for a notifiable concentration to proceed, the AMEA may also 'attach restrictive conditions' designed to reduce the adverse impact of a concentration on competition. It is not clear whether these conditions may be imposed at both the first and second stages of review, or at the second stage only. Although not expressly stated such conditions would have binding force on the parties. There is no express reference made to distinctions between behavioural remedies and structural remedies.[32] The previous practice of merger control in China has been to shy away from structural remedies short of a full blocking of the merger, although this is not consistent with international practice where the preference is very much for structural, rather than behavioural, remedies. In a legal and economic culture where state intervention is viewed more favourably than is the case in the US or the EC there may be less cultural resistance to the imposition of behavioural remedies.

2-4.23 Under the terms of art 48, wherever a business operator consummates a concentration in violation of the provisions of Chapter IV of the Law, the AMEA 'shall order it to cease doing so, to dispose of shares or assets, transfer the business or take other necessary measures to restore the market situation before the concentration' within a set time limit. In addition a relatively small penalty of up to RMB500,000 may be imposed on the parties.

2-4.24 In the first merger decision made under the AML, *InBev NV/SA—Anheuser-Busch Companies Inc* (see above),[33] the merger was cleared, but with the imposition of far-reaching and unusual conditions. Existing shareholdings in Tsingtao Brewery Co Ltd were not to be extended beyond the existing 27 per cent; MOFCOM was to be informed in a timely manner of changes in InBev's controlling shareholders; shares in the Pearl River Brewery Co Ltd were not to be increased beyond the existing 28.56 per cent; and the merged entity was not to purchase or hold shares in China Resources Snow Brewery (China) Co Ltd or Beijing Yanjing Brewery Co Ltd. If any breach of these conditions was contemplated post-merger a timely

[32] It has however been noted that: 'The scope of the restrictive requirements cannot be extended indefinitely. Among concentrations that have been approved by the United States and the European Union with conditions, the most common restrictive conditions include requesting the parties to allow competitors to use key equipment or intellectual property with consideration, taking measures to safeguard the independence of competition, and exiting certain activities' (Wu, n 9, above at 92).

[33] Notice of the Ministry of Commerce of the PRC [2008] No 95.

declaration would have to be made to MOFCOM, and implementation without the consent of MOFCOM would be unlawful. Thus it appears that MOFCOM has power to regulate future strategic acquisitions of a merged entity as a condition of allowing the notifying merger to proceed. The unusual approach taken here has raised concerns in the international business community, and if a precedent for such conditions has now been set it is clear that in future parties will have to assess with care strategic acquisitions in China.[34]

Following the response taken by the AMEA within MOFCOM to the *InBev NV/SA–Anheuser-Busch* merger there was speculation that the proposed, and notified, acquisition by Coca Cola of the Huiyuan Juice Group would be abandoned. This, however, was not the case. On 18 March 2009 this proposed merger was conferred the unenviable distinction of being the first merger to be blocked by MOFCOM.[35] The decision published by MOFCOM is so short as to render it impossible for someone outside the process to evaluate it properly. Reaction, however, was immediate, and media comment outside China was highly critical. Within China there was substantial comment on the merger before the decision was made, and it was clear that public opinion was against the merger: Huiyuan Juice is a household name in China, and notwithstanding the fact that the company was not Chinese—being listed on the Hong Kong stock exchange—there was widespread adverse comment as to the prospect of it being taken over by an American corporation. **2-4.25**

MOFCOM's decision states that the concentration was blocked on two grounds. First, the merger would create anti-competitive effects within the juice market in China, and would impact negatively, on the development of that market. Secondly, it was stated in the decision that the concentration would not 'comply with the public interest', although no clarification is given as to how this was assessed. It is clear from the terms of the decision that there was negotiation with the parties, and that remedies were offered, but that these were considered to be insufficient to deal with the harms identified by MOFCOM. The nature of those remedies is not explained. The analysis of competitive harms found by MOFCOM to flow from the proposed merger is reproduced here in its entirety, partly to demonstrate the extent to which decisions taken under the AML may be impervious to external analysis.

> After investigation, the Ministry of Commerce assesses this concentration thoroughly, and confirmed that the concentration would lead to negative effects as follows:
>
> 1. After the concentration, Coca-Cola Company would cause anticompetitive effects within the fruit juice beverage market. Because Coca-Cola company's

[34] See *Financial Times*, 30 November 2008, 'InBev ruling sparks fears for M&A in China'.

[35] *Coca Cola Corporation—Huiyuan Juice Group*, Notice 22 of 2009, 18 March 2009.

dominant position within carbonated drinks market would transmit into the fruit juice beverage market via this concentration, consumer welfare would be jeopardized as well.

2. Brand is the key feature of effective competition within beverage market. After the concentration, Coca-Cola Company's market power would be remarkably increased via its control of two well-known brands, i.e. 'Minute Maid' and 'Hui Yuan', together with its already existing dominant position within the carbonated drinks market and the transmission effect, the concentration will raise barriers of entry into the market to potential competitors.
3. The concentration would squeeze the 'living and developing space' of Chinese small and/or medium sized undertakings, and restrain the abilities of entering into competition and independent innovation within the fruit juice beverage market for domestic undertakings. It would also bring negative influences upon the structure of effective competition within the Chinese fruit juice beverage market. The concentration would go against a 'sustainable and healthy' development of the business of fruit juice in China.[36]

It is possible that the decision was correct on the facts, although it is not possible to determine this on the basis of publicly available information. The concern, however, is that the driving motivation behind the decision was one of industrial policy, rather than competition policy, and it has been suggested elsewhere that the decision was clearly protectionist.[37]

[36] Translation by Wang Zhining, PhD candidate, Glasgow University School of Law.

[37] See, for example, *The Economist*, 19 March 2009, 'Hard to Swallow':
'The most benign interpretation of the rejection being bandied about by lawyers and bankers is that it reflects a political response to critical comments by America's new administration. The more worrying interpretation is that, even as China publicly urges other countries to commit to opening their markets to Chinese investment and trade, it is imposing yet another barrier to outsiders.' (http://www.economist.com/business/PrinterFriendly.cfm?story_id=13331326)

2-5

CHINA PROCEDURE

Introduction	2-5.01	**Penalties**	2-5.10
Investigations by the AMEA	2-5.02	**Appeals**	2-5.15
Business secrecy	2-5.06	**Third Party Rights**	2-5.18
Complaints	2-5.07		
Final Decisions	2-5.08		
Commitments and undertakings	2-5.09		

Introduction

2-5.01 Chapters VI and VII of the AML set out the procedures relating to the investigation of monopolistic conduct and to the imposition of penalties and also create the basis on which the Law may be relied on in private actions. These provisions interact with general legal procedures in China, and particularly with administrative law. At the level of public enforcement the AMEA is the primary actor although, as noted in Chapter 2-1, it has the power to delegate authority to appropriate public bodies. It should be recognized at the outset that administrative bodies in China have far greater freedom of action and stronger powers than is the case in the EC or the US, and although judicial review mechanisms exist these are not strong (see below).

Investigations by the AMEA

2-5.02 The AMEA may act either on its own initiative or following a complaint. Article 38 specifies that the AMEA 'shall make investigations into suspicious monopolistic conducts in accordance with the law'. This does not create a requirement for the AMEA to carry out investigations into all suspicious conduct, but rather specifies that when it does act it is to follow the law. However, the final paragraph of art 38 states that the AMEA '*shall* make necessary investigations'[1] in cases in which the AMEA receives information that is in writing and is supported by 'relevant facts and evidence'. The AMEA is not required to make a definitive finding in every case which crosses this hurdle, and may abandon its investigations. The AMEA is not required to explain to the complainant the steps it has taken, or the reason for the abandoning of any investigation and no appeal is possible against a decision by the AMEA to abandon an investigation. Complaints, or 'tip-offs' may be made to the AMEA by any natural or legal person, and may be made by foreign parties. Article 38 requires the AMEA to keep the identity of the complainant or informer confidential.

2-5.03 Article 39 of the AML sets out the powers of investigation available to the AMEA, which are similar in some respects to those given to the EC Commission in Regulation 1/2003. In full the article is in the following terms:

> The [AMEA] may take any of the following measures in investigating suspicious monopolistic conducts:
> (1) Conducting the inspection by getting into the business premises of business operators under investigation or by getting into any other relevant place;
> (2) Inquiring of the business operators under investigation, interested parties, or other relevant entities or individuals, and requiring them to explain the relevant conditions;
> (3) Consulting and duplicating the relevant documents, agreements, account books, business correspondences and electronic data, etc. of the business operators under investigation, interested parties and other relevant entities or individuals;
> (4) Seizing and detaining relevant evidence; and
> (5) Inquiring about the business operators' bank accounts under investigation.

These powers may only be exercised following the approval of the Principal of the AMEA in response to a report submitted to him in writing. Investigations will be carried out by at least two enforcement officers, and they are required to present copies of their law enforcement certificates. The officers are required to make notes relating to the investigation, which are to be signed by the party or parties subject to investigation, and which are entered into the file. Investigations carried out under the power given in art 39 may result in on-site inspections that have previously been notified to the relevant parties, or that are carried out without prior warning. The AMEA does not have the power to compel the submission of documents or evidence held overseas, although it may take into account the extent of cooperation during an investigation when assessing any penalty in the event that a finding of a breach of the law is made. The AMEA has not yet entered into any agreements with foreign antitrust agencies relating to the investigation of

[1] Emphasis added.

suspected antitrust infringements. It is likely however that it will in future enter into such agreements as it gains maturity.

Where a business entity is under investigation both it and 'interested parties' are entitled to make statements to the AMEA.[2] The Law does not specify how 'interested parties' are to be determined. The AMEA is required to verify any facts and evidence presented to it by 'business operators and interested parties under investigation'. **2-5.04**

Article 42 creates a general obligation on 'business operators, interested parties and other relevant entities and individuals under investigation' to cooperate fully with the AMEA when it carries out its duties, and states specifically that it is unlawful to obstruct duly authorized investigations. Article 52 sets out penalties that may be applied to failures to comply with this obligation, with penalties applying both to offending individuals and to the business operators. Fines of up to RMB20,000 may be imposed on individuals, or up to RMB200,000 on entities in the event that they: refuse to submit materials requested; submit fraudulent materials or information; destroy or remove evidence; or obstruct an investigation. The AMEA may also order the parties to rectify the fault. Where the circumstances are 'serious' the penalties may be increased, rising to between RMB20,000 to RMB100,000 on individuals, and RMB200,000 to RMB1m on entities. **2-5.05**

Business secrecy

The AMEA and its officers are required to maintain the confidentiality of 'trade secrets' learned during the course of any investigation conducted by it.[3] It is not clear from the terms of the Law to what extent this obligation to secrecy is to be balanced with the rights of the defence if information that is classed as 'trade secrets' forms the basis for a finding of an infringement. An employee of the AMEA who discloses trade secrets learned during the course of his enforcement work may be subject to criminal liability if a crime is found to have been committed. If no crime has been committed he may be subject to 'a disciplinary sanction'.[4] **2-5.06**

Complaints

As noted above art 38 of the AML provides that any 'entity or individual may report suspicious monopolistic conducts to the [AMEA]'. The AMEA is required to conduct an investigation—although no requirement as to the rigour of the **2-5.07**

[2] art 43, AML.
[3] art 41, AML.
[4] art 54, AML.

investigation or the need to take a formal decision is set out—where the complaint is in the appropriate form and substantiated. It is inevitable that many complaints will be made, particularly by Chinese firms concerned at the activities of (more efficient) foreign competitors. One of the first complaints made related to the allegedly excessive prices charged by Microsoft. This complaint was submitted by a lawyer with one of China's largest law firms on 31 July 2008. The complaint has been acknowledged but, at the time of writing, no discernible action has been taken.[5]

Final Decisions

2-5.08 Article 44 of the AML gives the AMEA wide discretion in the final decisions it may take in the event that it finds that an infringement exists. The article states merely that where the AMEA 'deems that a monopolistic conduct is constituted . . . it shall make a decision on how to deal with the monopolistic conduct, and publicize it'. This leaves open to the AMEA a significant discretion in terms of the necessary remedies, which may presumably be both behavioural and structural, although this is not made clear on the face of the legislation. Under practice before the enactment of the AML where structural remedies were required to deal with monopolies these were effected through special regulation. Articles 46 and 47, which are part of Chapter VII (legal liabilities), also state that in the event that either a monopoly agreement is consummated in violation of the law, or a dominant position is abused, the AMEA shall order the parties to stop the violations.

Commitments and undertakings

2-5.09 Although the AML does not use the language of 'commitments' or 'undertakings', and does not create a mechanism similar to that under which consent decrees may be accepted in the US antitrust system, it does, at art 45, give the AMEA the power to terminate an investigation in cases in which an infringement appears to exist. The AMEA may accept such commitments where 'the business operators under investigation promise to eliminate the impact of the conduct by taking specific measures within the time limit prescribed by the [AMEA]'. Any such promise is to be supervised by the AMEA, which has the discretion whether to accept the promise and suspend the investigation or not. If a commitment is accepted the AMEA may resume its investigation where: (1) the commitment is not implemented; (2) there have been significant changes to the factual

[5] See 'China to investigate Microsoft under new anti-monopoly law', *Interfax China*, <http://www.interfax.cn/news/5134> (26 August 2008).

circumstances on the basis of which the commitment was made; or (3) the decision to suspend the investigation was taken on the basis of incomplete or inaccurate information provided by the parties making the commitments.

Penalties

The AML makes provision for the imposition of penalties in respect of breaches of the substantive law relating to monopoly agreements and to abuses of dominant position. Provision is also made for the imposition of penalties for procedural breaches during antitrust investigations (discussed above). At the time of writing the AMEA has not published further guidance relating to the calculation of penalties, and has not publicized a formal leniency programme, although as noted below some account is taken of the cooperation of business operators when penalties are assessed. Article 49 of the Law states, in language similar to that employed in Regulation 1/2003/EC, that in determining the specific amount of the penalty to be imposed under any of arts 46–48 the AMEA is to have regard to 'such factors as the nature, extent and duration of the violations'. **2-5.10**

Article 46 sets out the penalties to be applied in the event that a monopoly agreement is both entered into 'and performed'. In this case, as well as ordering the termination of the infringement (see above), the AMEA is to 'confiscate the illegal gains', *and* impose a penalty of between one per cent and ten per cent of the sales revenue in the previous year. In cases in which a monopoly agreement has been entered into but not been effected the fine is limited to less than RMB500,000. It is not clear in the use of the word 'performed' whether an agreement that the parties actively take steps to implement, but which is unsuccessful, will benefit from this lesser penalty. If, for example, a cartel arrangement is entered into, and adhered to by some but collapses because either cheating or market conditions conspire against it, it is arguable that the agreement has been performed, but has been unsuccessful. The two-pronged enforcement mechanism of requiring the AMEA to *both* confiscate the illegal gains *and* then to impose a penalty is a notable one. While this is arguably an economically efficient deterrence mechanism it is no easy task to calculate the ill-gotten gains from cartel activity.[6] In cases in which a party to the unlawful agreement 'voluntarily reports the conditions on reaching the monopoly agreement and provides important evidence to [the AMEA]' the **2-5.11**

[6] This point was well made by the UK Competition Commission Appeals Tribunal when it commented on the approach set out in the Office of Fair Trading guidance on the calculation of penalties. The OFT indicated that it would seek to at least recoup the profits made by illegal arrangements, but the CCAT was sceptical of the practicality of this approach (see *Napp Pharmaceutical Holdings Ltd v The Director General of Fair Trading* [2002] CompAR 13, at para 508).

fine may be reduced, or no fine at all may be imposed, with discretion left to the AMEA in this regard. At the time of writing it is not clear whether the report of the arrangement must be made before the AMEA has any other evidence as to its existence, but in any event the article leaves substantial discretion to the AMEA, such that even after the commencement of an investigation as long as the parties provide 'important evidence' during the course of an investigation penalties may be reduced. It is unfortunately the case that evidence suggests that the greater the discretion an antitrust authority has in relation to the operation of a leniency programme the less effective the programme will be. The provisions as written offer no guarantee of leniency, and make no differentiation between the order in which participants in an unlawful arrangement come forward, so as to reduce the incentive to be the first company to disclose the existence of the agreement.

2-5.12 Where a trade association is the facilitating mechanism whereby an unlawful agreement is reached the association may be fined up to RMB500,000, and in serious cases, may be deregistered by the social group registration authority.[7]

2-5.13 The penalties applicable in the event of a breach of the provisions relating to abuse of dominant position are set out in art 47. In this case the penalty is to be between one per cent and ten per cent of the previous year's total sales volume. As with art 46, the AMEA is also empowered to confiscate the illegal gains. There is no reference in this article to the 'performance' of the abuse. Thus, for example, a failed attempt at predation will still invite condemnation across the entire range of penalty. As with art 46 there is also an obligation on the AMEA to require the abusing party to terminate the infringement.

2-5.14 Article 48 sets out the penalties and powers applicable to parties who consummate concentrations in violation of the law. This provision is discussed in Chapter 2-4.

Appeals

2-5.15 Article 53 creates a right of appeal against decisions taken by the AMEA in the fulfilment of its duties under the Law. The procedure is slightly different in respect of decisions taken in relation to concentrations than it is in relation to other decisions. In both cases appeals may be made by 'any party concerned'. Where decisions are made under arts 28[8] and 29[9] the aggrieved party must first apply to the AMEA for an administrative reconsideration. If it is dissatisfied with the results of this reconsideration it may then launch an administrative lawsuit in

---

[7] art 46, AML.

[8] Prohibition or clearance of a concentration.

[9] Conditions attached to a clearance of a concentration.

accordance with the provisions of Chinese administrative law. Where other decisions are taken by the AMEA the aggrieved party has the option at the first instance of either applying for administrative reconsideration, or lodging an administrative lawsuit.

Administrative appeals generally are governed by the Administrative Litigation Law 1989 and the Administrative Review Law. These set out clear mechanisms for appeals against the actions or decisions of administrative bodies. There also exists in China a right under the Constitution to make complaints against actions taken by the State, and to seek compensation where these are found to be unlawful.[10] This right however is only available to Chinese citizens, and would not apply to a company not incorporated in China. Although these procedures are clear, judicial review of administrative actions in China is not generally perceived to be an effective redress against the misuse of administrative power. This in part reflects the position of the courts, which are not perceived as an entity independent of the State.[11] **2-5.16**

An official of the Supreme People's Court ('SPC') has stated that the AMC cannot be a defendant to an appeal relating to the application of the AML as it 'neither **2-5.17**

---

[10] See generally Hung, VM-Y, 'China's WTO Commitment on Independent Judicial Review: Impact on Legal and Political Reform' (2004) 52 *American Journal of Comparative Law* 77.

[11] See for example Owen, BM, Sun, S, and Zhen, W, 'Antitrust in China: The Problem of Incentive Compatibility' (2005) 1 *Journal of Competition Law and Economics* 123 at 137:

> Although the Chinese Constitution states that the People's Courts shall exercise their judicial power independently, in practice there is no institutional guarantee of judicial independence. First of all, in China the judiciary is not intended to be an institution that checks and balances the other branches of the government. Instead, the judiciary, along with everyone else, is expected to "follow the leadership" of the Communist Party and the governments at all levels.

Owen et al. also note that:

> Among the problems with the [Administrative Litigation Law] frequently cited by commentators are the narrow scope of the judicial review, the convoluted procedure for judicial review and the bias in favour of the government in judicial review of administrative actions (ibid).

See also Pate:

> It is not realistic for the international antitrust community to expect that Chinese antitrust can immediately implement nuanced analysis of complex concepts, such as market definition, ease of entry, and efficiencies. And the relationship between regulator and regulated cannot be expected to look as it does in the United States or Europe, where enforcers and private lawyers approach each other as equals who often have long working relationships. It is the ultimate requirement to justify enforcement decisions to a neutral, honest and independent judge that makes this possible. The different relationship between government and private enterprise, and particularly the absence of a history of judicial review, will make Chinese antitrust very different. (Pate, RH, 'What I Heard in the Great Hall of the People—Realistic Expectations of Chinese Antitrust' (2008) 75 *Antitrust Law Journal* 195 at 208.)

makes specific administrative acts nor enforces the law', and that only the AMEA's acts can be appealed.[12]

Third Party Rights

2-5.18 There was considerable debate during the drafting of the Law as to whether it should grant third party rights directly enforceable in the civil courts, with some commentators arguing that the judicial architecture did not have the necessary expertise to deal with such cases. In the event the choice was made to grant private rights clearly on the face of the legislation. Article 50 states that '[w]here any loss was caused by a business operator's monopolistic conducts to other entities and individuals, the business operator shall assume the civil liabilities.' The normal rules of civil procedure will apply to such actions.[13] It is not entirely clear at the time of writing whether in the longer term actions may be brought as stand-alone claims, or only following a finding of an infringement by the AMEA. A small number of cases have been accepted by the Courts to date, which may suggest that this practice will continue, with four cases being filed on the first day the AML entered into force.[14] In relation to the enforcement of securities laws the

[12] 'The discussion of the application of the Anti-Monopoly Law by the person in charge of the Administrative Court under the Supreme People's Court', <http://www.chinacourt.org/html/article/200811/03/328394.shtml>. The bulk of this interview is taken up with discussions of the application of the AML to administrative monopolies, perhaps suggesting that this is anticipated to be the area in which there will be most litigation.

[13] Article 123 of the Constitution provides that the People's Courts are to exercise the judicial power in the country. The court system in China is a centralized one, with a four-tier hierarchy. The Supreme People's Court is at the top of this hierarchy, below which sit Provincial High Courts (this category also includes the courts of certain cities, such as Shanghai, which in effect have provincial status), then Intermediate People's Courts, and finally Primary People's Courts. The law provides guidance as to which court a case may be brought in, taking into account factors such as the seriousness of the case. An appeal may only be made once up the hierarchy, such that only if a case originates in the Provincial High Courts can an appeal be made to the People's Supreme Court. There is, under China's civil law system, no systematic system of the reporting of judgments, which would be unnecessary in a system that does not recognize the principle of *stare decisis*. Judgments tend to be brief, with few reasons given for the decision taken. As a consequence it may be difficult, if not impossible, for prospective litigants to assess their likely success based on past cases. Although the problem is not unique to China it must also be recognized that few, if any, judges are likely to have the necessary background or training in industrial economic principles to apply the Anti-Monopoly Law effectively to substantive breaches.

[14] Two of these cases were filed against administrative monopolies (see Chapter 2-3, above), one against China Netcom relating to alleged discrimination, and the fourth against Chongqing Insurance Association alleging price-fixing and competition restrictions. Two months later an action was filed against Microsoft Corp in Beijing, with the complainant alleging that Microsoft was abusing its dominant position, and seeking damages of RMB1 (approximately 7 pence) (see Junfeng, L, 'Foreign-Invested Companies: More Risky Facing up to China's Anti-Monopoly Law' (2008), Symposium, Shanghai University/Liverpool John Moore's University). In late November it was reported that Baidu, the most prominent Internet search engine provider in China, was facing

SPC has held that private actions can only be instigated after an administrative finding of an infringement has been made. If this is the case in respect of the AML a potentially significant driver towards efficient and vigorous enforcement may be removed. It is frequent practice for the SPC to issue guidance in relation to the judicial approach to be taken to new laws and at the time of writing it remains a possibility that guidance may be published which will eliminate the possibility of an independent action without there first being a finding of an infringement by a relevant body. At the time of writing no such guidance has been published. However, a senior official in the Administrative Section of the SPC gave an interview in November 2008 in which it was indicated that the SPC was considering 'whether it is necessary to draft relevant judicial interpretation and judicial policy according to the needs of judicial practice'.[15] As noted above the fact that some cases have already been accepted, and ruled upon, may imply that the SPC is content for this practice to continue.

An earlier version of the article gave plaintiffs the right to multiple damages, but the assessment of damages is now left to the appropriate civil courts in accordance with the general principles of Chinese law. **2-5.19**

Based on scanty evidence it would appear to be the case that in recent years more cases are being brought by aggrieved consumers attempting to rely on earlier competition laws or business control regulations. Some of these are in respect of perceived 'overcharges' of as little as 50 US cents.[16] **2-5.20**

---

litigation from a large number of parties in relation to its search ranking practices, and the alleged blocking of sites whose owners did not pay for rankings (see *Financial Times*, 30 November 2008, 'Baidu faces wave of legal challenges').

15 'The discussion of the application of the Anti-Monopoly Law by the person in charge of the Administrative Court under the Supreme People's Court', <http://www.chinacourt.org/html/article/200811/03/328394.shtml>. Recognizing the difficulties facing the courts the official stated that:

> Currently, in regard to judicial application of the [AML], there are many issues that need to be studied. For example, how to determine the jurisdiction of anti-monopoly administrative cases in courts of first instance; how to identify the specific administrative conduct and abstract administrative conduct in a specific judicial action; how the court conducts a comprehensive review on the sued administrative conduct, particularly how to allocate the burden of proof; how to deal with simultaneous civil and administrative cases; the standard and content of the judicial application of the [AML] and so on.

In regard to the potential problems in the process of implementing the AML by the courts, the courts at all levels shall take precautions, make early preparations, carry out good investigations and studies, and sum up the experience of trials in time.

The official left open the possibility that the SPC might rule that private civil actions are only admissible following the taking of an administrative action by the AMEA, stating that 'it needs further study in practice regarding the issue of simultaneous civil and administrative lawsuits in order to ensure the unity of justice and the unity of law'.

16 See Wen, X, 'Market Dominance by China's Public Utility Enterprises' (2008) 75 *Antitrust Law Journal* 151, where details of some cases are given.

2-5.21 On 31 July 2008, the SPC issued a circular which urged all courts to familiarize themselves with the provisions of the AML, and to be prepared to deal with the complex issues of law and economics raised by these cases. The SPC has also assigned responsibility for cases to be heard by those courts that deal at present with claims arising in relation to intellectual property. In December 2008 the Shanghai No 2 Intermediate People's Court became the first court in the PRC to establish a dedicated panel to deal with cases, both private and administrative, brought under the AML.[17]

[17] See <http://news.xinhuanet.com/newscenter/2008-12/22/content_10543901.htm> (Chinese language).

PART 3

HONG KONG

3-1. Antitrust in Hong Kong 123

3-1

ANTITRUST IN HONG KONG

Introduction	3-1.01	Procedures	3-1.14
The *Proposals*	3-1.04	Institutional arrangements	3-1.15
Substantive provisions	3-1.06	Public enforcement	3-1.17
Agreements	3-1.08	Penalties, remedies, and leniency	3-1.20
Abuse of substantial market power	3-1.09	Private enforcement	3-1.25
Exclusions, exemptions, and *de minimis* provisions	3-1.10		
Merger control	3-1.13		

Introduction

As noted in Chapter 1-1, in March 2007, having robustly rejected calls for the introduction of a general law of competition for a number of years, the Hong Kong government took the decision to bring such a law forward. It is not entirely clear why this decision was made, although the fact that China introduced its Anti-Monopoly Law in 2007 did not go unnoticed in Hong Kong. At the time of writing a draft law has not yet been published. This single, short chapter is intended, based on a limited amount of preparatory material, to predict what shape the Hong Kong system might take, and how robustly this law will be applied. It is anticipated that a law will be introduced in 2009, but this is unlikely to take effect before 2010 at the earliest. The discussion here is based largely on the Commerce and Economic Development Bureau's ('CEDB') *Detailed Proposals for a Competition Law—A Public Consultation Paper*[1] (hereinafter '*Proposals*'). The proposed law is similar in many respects to that of the UK Competition Act regime, and there is also acknowledgement of international standards with reference made, for example, to ICN recommendations. **3-1.01**

[1] May 2008 <http://www.cedb.gov.hk>.

3-1.02 Until such time as the new law, if enacted, enters into force the system operating in Hong Kong in respect of the general law of competition[2] is that described in Chapter 1-1. In essence although the Competition Policy Advisory Group ('COMPAG') may receive complaints, and may chastise a company breaching the principles of the *Statement on Competition Policy*, it is powerless to take action against a company in wilful breach.

3-1.03 There remains opposition to the introduction of a general law of antitrust in Hong Kong, and it is perhaps surprising that one of the groups most vocal in this opposition is the small business community, which appears to fear that the law will be used against it in the form of vexatious litigation entered into by larger companies. It is further acknowledged in the *Proposals* that some fear that the law will create a regulatory burden.[3] There are a number of points in the *Proposals* where the concerns of the SME sector are addressed such as, for example, a commitment that one member of the proposed Competition Commission ('HKCC') 'should have experience in SME matters',[4] and Chapter V of the *Proposals* is dedicated to 'issues of concern' to SMEs. However, the Government has committed itself to bringing the new law forward, although the time-frame may slip from that first intended. Broadly, the consultation process carried out in 2006 showed support for the introduction of the law, although not in respect of a criminal sanction, and with reservations expressed in relation to merger control.

The *Proposals*

3-1.04 The foreword to the *Proposals* makes it clear that further consultation on the document is necessary, and that this is merely an early step in the preparation of a Bill. The discussion in this text therefore is fairly brief, and at the time of writing nothing can be taken for granted. Given Hong Kong's history and its legal system it is perhaps not surprising that in many respects the proposed law appears to be similar to the competition law operating in the UK, although as this in turn is substantially similar in many respects to that of the EC the new Hong Kong law will also appear familiar to those experienced with EC competition law.

3-1.05 Unlike the other regimes discussed in this text the stated aim of the proposal is admirably clear, in that 'the purpose of the legislation should be to enhance

[2] Special rules apply in relation to telecommunications and broadcasting at the time of writing. It is intended that these be repealed and that the new law apply equally to all sectors (see the *Proposals*, Chapter VI). However, responsibility for the application of competition law in these sectors will remain with the existing sector regulator, with the HKCC issuing guidance on the circumstances in which the sector-specific regulators would investigate cases in their sectors.

[3] n 1, above, Introduction, para 4.

[4] Ibid at I.II.4.

economic efficiency and thus the benefit of consumers through promoting sustainable competition'.[5] The subjects of the law would be, as is the case in the EC and in the UK, 'undertakings', carrying the definition of 'an individual, company or other entity that engages in economic activities'.[6]

Substantive provisions

The *Proposals* set out two core provisions, the first relating to agreements, in respect of which it is proposed that there be a 'general prohibition on agreements and concerted practices that have the purpose or effect of substantially lessening competition'.[7] The second core provision is concerned with 'abusing substantial market power with the purpose or effect[8] of substantially lessening competition'. The HKCC will be required to draw up guidelines relating to conduct, and the *Proposals* make clear that any list of 'hard-core' conduct deemed to be *per se* illegal is to be kept to a minimum.[9] **3-1.06**

It is noteworthy that in the *Proposals* there is at the time of writing no intention to introduce a prohibition of mergers which substantially lessen competition, the illogicality of which has been pointed out in Chapter 1-2, above (and see further below). **3-1.07**

Agreements

The new law will contain 'a general prohibition on agreements and concerted practices that have the purpose or effect of substantially lessening competition'.[10] The inclusion of 'concerted practices' is viewed as being of particular importance in light of the relatively small size of the Hong Kong economy, such that the reduced number of commercial actors in any given area may facilitate collusive practices. It is proposed that there be no list of prohibited agreements in the legislation itself, but that the HKCC be required to issue guidelines which would specify the sorts of conduct that would normally be considered to infringe the prohibition. The HKCC is to be 'required to have regard to the guidelines when **3-1.08**

---

5 Ibid at I.I.
6 Ibid I.I.2.
7 Ibid IV.23.
8 The meaning of 'purpose or effect' is discussed at paras III.15–18 of the *Proposals*. It is stated here that:

> Conduct that has an anti-competitive purpose inevitably has the potential to affect a market adversely, and is therefore undesirable—even if it does not have an immediate discernible effect. To focus only on the effect of conduct would mean that parties that intended to undermine competition but were unsuccessful would suffer no consequences. Noting that the current sector-specific competition laws in the telecommunications and broadcasting sectors in Hong Kong adopt a purpose or effect test, we propose that the new competition law follow a similar approach. (Internal footnote omitted)

9 Ibid at III.18.
10 Ibid, Proposal 24.

implementing the law'.[11] It is clear however that the concern will be primarily with horizontal, rather than vertical, agreements, with the *Proposals* stating that vertical agreements will 'only be addressed in the context of abuse of substantial market power'.[12] Although there has been discussion of removing vertical agreements from the scope of the law altogether, the approach appears to be that they will be included within the law, but that the HKCC will issue a block exemption regulation in respect of them, tailored to the Hong Kong circumstances.[13]

Abuse of substantial market power

3-1.09 The approach to abuses of dominant position, or what is currently termed abuses of a 'substantial degree of market power', will likely be very similar to that adopted in the EC and UK, although with a presumption that power exists at a lower threshold. The jurisdictional requirement will be that substantial market power is presumed to exist at a market share of around 40 per cent.[14] This approach is based on the view that in

> . . . a geographically concentrated economy, such as Hong Kong's, it is not unusual for a small number of firms to dominate certain markets. In such cases, the conduct of a firm with a significant market share, albeit short of the 50% presumption for 'dominance' could have a major effect on competition.[15]

There are to be no *per se* infringements, and in each case the HKCC will be required to demonstrate that the practice under investigation 'had the purpose or effect of substantially lessening competition' before an infringement decision could be made.

Exclusions, exemptions, and de minimis *provisions*

3-1.10 The new law generally is intended to apply equally to all sectors of the economy, although it will not be applied 'to the Government or statutory bodies', but there will be provisions relating to exclusions and exemptions, as well as *de minimis* provisions. A general exclusion will apply to undertakings performing 'services of general economic interest'. In line with the approach taken in the EC there is unlikely to be a precise definition of this term in the legislation, with the principles being determined on a case-by-case basis. A reserve power will be given to the

---

11 Ibid at III.8.

12 Ibid at IV.26.

13 The treatment of vertical agreements generally is discussed in Chapter 1-2. Note that there are substantial differences in the approach between the US and the EC, with the latter adopting a more intrusive regime. Given that the EC approach is significantly affected by non-efficiency considerations, and in particular single-market imperatives, it is probably right that Hong Kong should take a more relaxed approach to vertical agreements generally, in the absence of substantial market power, than is the case in the EC.

14 Ibid at III.12.

15 Ibid.

Chief Executive to exclude from the operation of the law conduct where 'there are sound public policy reasons for doing so'.[16] No further clarification as to what circumstances might generate such an intervention is set out in the *Proposals*, but in the UK such matters might relate to, for example, public and state security, plurality of the media, and certain arrangements in the financial sector.

The proposal in respect of exemptions is a hybrid of the approaches taken at different times in the EC, such that there will be three mechanisms by which parties may seek to benefit from exemptions. First, notifications to the HKCC for a formal exemption on an individual basis will be permitted. Secondly, block exemption regulations will be drawn up by the HKCC. Thirdly, parties may, on the basis of the legislative criteria and/or published guidance, make a self-determination as to whether the exemption criteria are satisfied, and may in the event of a dispute seek to rely on their interpretation before the Hong Kong Competition Tribunal ('HKCT'). The criteria will be that the agreements notified must yield efficiency gains that outweigh the harm, as long as, in line with EC and UK law, they only contain indispensable restrictions and do not permit the undertakings to eliminate competition. **3-1.11**

De minimis provisions are discussed in Chapter V of the *Proposals* which addresses 'issues of concern to [SMEs]'. It is proposed that, save in the case of hard-core conduct, the HKCC state in its guidelines 'that it would not pursue an agreement where the aggregate market share of the parties to the agreement did not exceed a certain level'.[17] Although the *Proposals* do not specify what this level will be, the figure of a combined market share of 20 per cent as employed in Singapore, is cited as an example. **3-1.12**

Merger control

It is noted in the *Proposals* that 'merger regulation is a feature of all major competition laws',[18] and there is recognition of the very obvious point that 'without merger regulation, undertakings may evade the prohibition on anti-competitive agreements simply by merging'.[19] Yet in the face of this undeniable truth the CPRC recommended that the new law should not incorporate a system of merger control on the grounds that in Hong Kong's relatively small economy a certain degree of market concentration is inevitable. There are traces too in this approach of the 'old' view that international competition exerts sufficient competitive pressure on Hong Kong to obviate the need for internal regulations. There is also a recognition however that international mergers may have significant impacts in **3-1.13**

[16] Ibid, Proposal 49.
[17] Ibid, Proposal 43.
[18] Ibid at III.19.
[19] Ibid.

Hong Kong, and that a merger control provision might permit Hong Kong to have a say in these (although crafting remedies, particularly if the merging entities have no presence in a territory, but merely sell their products into that territory, may be exceptionally difficult). The *Proposals* therefore set out the position as being one of reluctance at this stage to commit to a merger regime, although submissions were invited in respect of three options: (a) introducing merger provisions 'suitable to the Hong Kong context'; (b) introducing merger provisions into the law, but delaying their enforcement 'until after a review of the effect of the law';[20] and (c) not including merger provisions in the Bill.

Procedures

3-1.14 The Government proposes to create a new independent Competition Commission which would, in a manner similar to that of the EC Commission or the UK's OFT, have the power to investigate and take action against possible infringements of the substantive provisions of the law. The HKCC would have the power to act either in response to complaints, or whistle-blowing, or on its own initiative. A right of appeal against its decision would be available to a new Competition Tribunal ('HKCT'), a body whose functions and constitution, as set out in the *Proposals*, looks remarkably similar to the UK Competition Appeals Tribunal, although the HKCT may have an additional responsibility for setting penalties above the threshold limit on the HKCC's powers (see below). In addition full provision would be made for permitting private actions to proceed, albeit with some minor reservations, and for 'representative actions', which are also an important feature of UK competition law procedures since being introduced into the Competition Act 1998 by the Enterprise Act 2002.

Institutional arrangements

3-1.15 The HKCC will be an independent authority 'in the form of a body corporate', consisting of two tiers: an appointed Board of Commission members, and a full-time executive arm. The Chairman of the HKCC will be appointed by the Chief Executive. The need for the HKCC to be functionally independent of Government is seen as paramount. In the *Proposals* it is suggested that

> whilst the Policy Secretary with responsibility for economic development should be able to notify the [HKCC] of government economic policy, which the [HKCC] should be required to take into account when discharging its duties, he should have no power of direction over the [HKCC].[21]

The HKCC will assume both investigative and adjudicative roles in relation to the enforcement of the new competition law, with a split within the organization

20 Ibid at III.25(b).
21 Ibid at II.3.

between these functions, such that the investigative team is not the one making the decision as to whether an infringement has taken place or the penalty that any such infringement should attract. The HKCC would also have responsibility for: competition advocacy, both in the public and private sector; issuing guidance; and cooperation with other bodies, including those outside Hong Kong in relation to competition matters.

The HKCT will be established to hear applications for review of decisions of the HKCC, and also to be the forum where private actions are brought. This will be a 'separate and independent tribunal',[22] operating with judicial staff, and non-judicial staff with economic and commercial expertise, where procedures will be less formal than those of the standard court system. The HKCT will have the power to: give directions to parties concerning procedural matters; require any person to produce documents, or to appear to give evidence on oath; and to make costs awards. The Tribunal, which will not be bound by the normal rules of evidence, will primarily review the evidence relied on by the HKCC where the case is one of review, but will have the discretion to admit further material into the proceedings. **3-1.16**

Public enforcement

It is proposed that the HKCC be able to undertake investigations into potential anti-competitive practices both under its own initiative and following receipt of a complaint, although it is regarded as important that the HKCC should 'have the express power not to investigate complaints that it regards as vexatious or frivolous'.[23] Before commencing an investigation the HKCC will have to overcome the hurdle of having 'reasonable cause' to believe that an infringement of the law has occurred. The proposed Investigation Committee will undertake investigations, reporting its findings to the Board, with the party under investigation having the right to present its views and arguments before the taking of any final infringement decision. It is proposed that investigations may be carried out either with, or without, the knowledge of the party suspected of breaching the law. The general principle will be that confidential information will be kept confidential, unless there exist 'exceptional circumstances where disclosure of confidential information is necessary for the Commission to perform its duties'.[24] **3-1.17**

Express provision is likely to be made for the HKCC to enter into settlements as an alternative to proceeding to making a full infringement decision. This follows the approach of the US authorities in accepting 'consent decrees', and the practice of the EC Commission and the UK OFT in accepting 'commitments' in order to **3-1.18**

[22] Ibid at II.19.
[23] Ibid at II.9.
[24] Ibid at II.17.

speed up the enforcement processes, reducing burdens on both the enforcing agency, and the parties to the investigation.

3-1.19 Decisions of the HKCC may be appealed to the HKCT, which will have the power to substitute its own decision for that of the HKCC. It is anticipated in the *Proposals* that the only decisions of the HKCC which may be reviewed are those relating to a determination of whether or not a 'conduct rule' has been infringed, and those relating to penalties applied in respect of breaches of conduct rules.[25] It is intended that the HKCT has the power to suspend HKCC decisions during the course of an appeal, although this will not be an automatic process. Further appeals will be possible to the Court of Appeal and, in the last instance, to the Court of Final Appeal ('CFA'), with such appeals being limited to points of law and to remedies.

Penalties, remedies, and leniency

3-1.20 The proposed provisions relating to penalties are set out at paras III. 26–29 of the *Proposals*. These follow widespread international practice in setting penalties at a level of up to 10 per cent of turnover. There is to be no prospect, at least initially, of criminal sanctions being introduced. The HKCC will be required to publish guidance relating to the calculation of the penalty. More unusually it is proposed that the HKCC be able to impose penalties only up to a level of HK$10m (approximately US$1.25m), with any penalty higher than this being imposed by the HKCT on application by the HKCC. While such a provision may have some popular appeal in a community where many are uncertain about the value of competition law it is not entirely a logical one, particularly when SME concerns are so prevalent. The provision has the (presumably unintended) effect of giving greater protection to companies with large turnovers committing substantial abuses than it does to those with smaller turnovers or those perpetrating less serious breaches. However, the provision follows a judgment of the CFA under which certain procedural rights are accorded to those against whom high administrative penalties are imposed.

3-1.21 Following the UK example, the *Proposals* also suggest that individual directors and senior managers of undertakings found to have breached the law should 'face penalties that directly and significantly impact upon them'.[26] These are to take the form of director disqualification or prohibitions on 'participating at the senior

---

[25] 'Conduct rules' are defined in the *Proposals* as 'the prohibition on agreements and concerted practices that have the purpose or effect of substantially lessening competition and the prohibition on abuse of substantial market power' (I.2). This would exclude the HKCT from reviewing decisions to open an investigation or a decision to reject a complaint or close a file. It is not clear at the time of writing whether there is the intention to remove acts of the HKCC from the normal rules of judicial review operating in Hong Kong, which are similar to those in the UK.

[26] Ibid at III.28.

management level'. In both cases an application would be made to the HKCT by the HKCC.

The HKCC is also to be given the power to make 'directions' with the purpose of: (a) bringing the infringement to an end; (b) eliminating the harmful effects of infringements; and (c) preventing the reoccurrence of an infringement.[27] It is not clear at the time of writing whether this latter rubric would extend to the power to impose structural remedies, or whether such directions may only take the form of imposing behavioural remedies, such as orders to supply or to offer access, or to terminate anti-competitive arrangements, or alter prices and other terms and conditions of trade. **3-1.22**

On application to the HKCT only, interim orders may be sought.[28] While concerns might be raised about any additional delays that may be caused by the operation of this two-tier procedure, the view is set out in the *Proposals* that 'members of the judiciary are comparatively more experienced in assessing when it is appropriate to exercise injunctive powers'. **3-1.23**

The need for an effective leniency programme is stressed in the *Proposals*.[29] The HKCC will be required to issue guidance relating to the operation and terms of its leniency programme. A party who benefits from leniency granted by the HKCC will not be protected from private claims for damages.[30] **3-1.24**

Private enforcement

The proposed system for private actions is set out in Chapter IV of the *Proposals*. Importantly the decision has been taken, on the grounds that 'the [HKCC] would simply not be able to investigate all potential cases of anti-competitive conduct',[31] to permit both follow-on and stand-alone actions. Provision will be made for unrestricted standing such that those who have suffered *indirect* loss may bring actions in addition to those who have suffered *direct* loss. It is proposed that private actions which *only* involve competition disputes are heard by the HKCT, although of course the effect of the prohibitions is also likely to raise the possibility that other disputes, and in particular contractual disputes, may incorporate elements relating to the new competition law. In these latter 'composite' cases it is suggested in the *Proposals* that other courts have the discretion to separate the competition elements from the claim and to refer these to the HKCT, or themselves to hear the case in its entirety. **3-1.25**

[27] Ibid at III.29–30.
[28] Ibid at III.31–32.
[29] Ibid at III.33–34.
[30] Ibid at IV.29–31.
[31] Ibid at IV.5.

3-1.26 Concerns have been raised in the Hong Kong business community, and particularly by SMEs, that the introduction of the competition law might lead to excessive and vexatious litigation. These are addressed in part at paras 14–19 of the *Proposals*, in two primary recommendations. First it is suggested that the HKCT may strike out, of its own accord, or on an application by a third party or by the HKCC, 'any action which the Tribunal considers to be without merit or vexatious'. It is also intended that where a private action is brought at the same time as the HKCC is considering a matter the Tribunal has the power to suspend the case pending the resolution of the HKCC investigation. As noted above the *Proposals* suggest that the HKCT be given the power to impose interim orders on application by the HKCC, such that a delay in private actions is unlikely to result in permanent injury to the plaintiff. The HKCC is to be given the power to intervene in any privately brought competition case so as to give its views. This is a sensible procedure in an area which is highly specialized and in which the HKCC itself will be the body publishing the guidance on which much of the application of the law will be based.

3-1.27 Provision is likely to be made, if the *Proposals* are followed, for 'representative actions'. These have been adopted in the UK and are a response to the fact that although consumers are often the direct victims of anti-competitive activity each individual has only a small incentive to bring an action. Representative actions are those brought by designated bodies on behalf of a wider class, and are therefore similar to, but to be distinguished from, class actions. In the latter, members of the class are typically named individuals who have grouped together in a single action. In representative actions it is not required that individuals be named. Particular stress is placed in the *Proposals* on the fact that representative actions may benefit not just consumers, but also SMEs. Bodies will be able to bring representative actions where they have first obtained the permission of the HKCT to bring such an action.

3-1.28 There is no proposal to introduce a system of multiple damages, and the principles governing remedies will be those which apply under Hong Kong's general common law of remedies. The HKCT is to be given the power to apply injunctions, to award damages, to require the termination or variation of an agreement, or to provide such other relief as is deemed appropriate in the circumstances.

Part 4

TAIWAN

4-1.	The Taiwan Antitrust Law Regime	135
4-2.	Taiwan Agreements	145
4-3.	Taiwan Monopoly and Abuse of Dominance	169
4-4.	Taiwan Merger Control	177
4-5.	Taiwan Procedure	199

4-1

THE TAIWAN ANTITRUST LAW REGIME

Introduction	4-1.01	**Territorial Application**	4-1.11
The Fair Trade Commission	4-1.05	**International Cooperation and Agreements**	4-1.17
Information sources	4-1.08		
General Exemptions	4-1.09		

Introduction

The core legislation governing antitrust law in Taiwan is the Fair Trade Act ('TFTA'), which was first enacted on 4 February 1991, entering into force on 4 February 1992. The Act has since been amended generally on two occasions, in 1999 and most recently on 6 February 2002. The Enforcement Rules were also amended in June 2002. The body charged with the implementation of the Act is the Fair Trade Commission ('TFTC'), which came into existence on 27 January 1992, and whose function is discussed further below. There is also in some sectors additional legislation which contains antitrust provisions. This is the case, for example, in respect of the telecommunications industry liberalized in part in 1990.[1] There was debate during the enactment of the TFTA as to which legislative model to follow. In the final analysis the result was closer to that of the EC model than to the US, although there are US influences, and also some similarities with the law in Korea and Japan. **4-1.01**

Article 1 of the TFTA provides that the law has as its purpose 'maintaining trading order, protecting consumers' interests, ensuring fair competition, and promoting **4-1.02**

[1] See the Telecommunications Law, which inter alia contains provisions relating to the joint use of telecommunications conduits, network connectivity, equal access, and the prohibition of cross-subsidization.

economic stability and prosperity'.[2] It has been argued that '[t]he legislative history of the [TFTA] clearly suggests a strong emphasis on efficiency'.[3] The first part of the Act (arts 1–9) sets out general principles, including relevant definitions, which are dealt with as appropriate throughout this Part of the book. Chapter II (arts 10–17) deals with monopolies, mergers, and concerted practices, Chapter III (arts 18–24) with 'unfair competition',[4] Chapter IV (arts 25–29) with the powers and role of the Fair Trade Commission, Chapter V (arts 30–34) with damages, and Chapter VI (arts 35–44) with 'punishment'. The Act is relatively short, and should be read alongside Enforcement Rules, dealt with here as necessary, and guidelines published from time to time by the TFTC.

4-1.03 The law set out in the Act applies to 'enterprises', which are defined in art 2 as including companies, sole proprietorships and partnerships, trade associations,[5] and 'any other person or organization engaging in transactions through the

---

[2] Williams has noted that:

> The suggestion has been made that these policy goals create confusion on the part of the Commission as to its core rationale. Some [TFTC] decisions seem to use mercantilist logic, or protect employee welfare, or social customs, or attempt to maintain employment opportunities. These differing rationales constitute the justification, in the early decisions, made under the [TFTA] to approve or reject regulatory intervention without any apparent coherence, though on the whole the decision to appear to support market forces as opposed to non-market solutions. (Williams, M, *Competition Policy and Law in China, Hong Kong and Taiwan* (Cambridge: Cambridge University Press, 2005) at 384–5)

In the OECD *Peer Review*, it was noted that:

> Official statements about enforcement policies and legislative objectives generally repeat these same elements, without further explanation of their relationship or priority. For example, the objectives given for revising the merger control regime do not indicate a policy direction, other than enabling firms to remain competitive and efficient while preserving market competition. (OECD, *Chinese Taipei–Peer Review of Competition Law and Policy 2006*, OECD, 2006, p 12)

[3] Liu, LS, 'Fostering Competition Law and Policy: A Façade of Taiwan's Political Economy' (2002) *Washington University Global Studies Law Review*, vol 1, (1 & 2), 77 at 86. Liu cites an official statement of the Ministry of Economic Affairs as explaining that 'the [TFTA] should protect competition, not competitors, and certainly not inefficient competitors'. However, he also notes that 'after the lifting of the Martial Law Decree in mid-1987, Taiwan soon became preoccupied with fairness-related issues' (at 86). At 83 Liu states:

> Much of Taiwan's economic reform revolves around the issues of efficiency, fairness (or equality) and the trade-off between the two. . . . as the saying goes in imperial China, 'fear not insufficiency, but be concerned with inequality.' Traditionally, fairness has been more important than efficiency consideration.

[4] The provisions relating to unfair competition are dealt with in this book only in so far as they may be abuses of dominant positions, or agreements that would generally fall to be considered as part of the law of antitrust.

[5] See OECD, n 2, above, at 13:

> The specific mention of 'trade associations' ensures that these common occasions for misconduct do not escape coverage because of technicalities. It is noted further in the *Peer Review* at 34 that 'early [criminal law] prosecutions taught trade associations to eliminate the post of 'president', who would be an obvious target of criminal prosecution.

provision of goods or services'. The definition excludes therefore those purchasing goods or services as end consumers.

The term 'competition' is defined in art 4 as meaning 'any conduct of one enterprise to contest trading opportunities in the same market with one or more enterprises through offering more favourable price, quantity, quality, service or any other terms'. As the 2006 OECD *Peer Review* noted, it is unusual for such an explicit definition to appear on the face of the legislation.[6] **4-1.04**

The Fair Trade Commission

The TFTC is under the administration of the Executive Cabinet,[7] and is the central authority charged with the application and development of competition policy and fair trade law in Taiwan.[8] It has the main role in the drafting of relevant laws and regulations, and in investigating and determining cases in which competition may be being impeded. The TFTC also from time to time conducts industrial studies in particular markets or industries to facilitate its supervisory and enforcement roles.[9] In carrying out its functions the TFTC may consult with other relevant ministries and government departments, and may direct and supervise other public authorities at metropolitan and county level in relation to their administration of matters arising under the TFTA. Rules governing the constitution and allocation of powers within the TFTC are published from time to time as The Organic Statute of Fair Trade Commission, Executive Yuan'.[10] The Chair of the TFTC holds a rank of Cabinet status 'so as to be able to act as a more effective advocate of competition policy at the heart of government'.[11] **4-1.05**

The TFTC is divided into six departments: three numbered departments, and departments of planning and legal affairs, and a secretariat. Case allocation is to some extent determined on a departmental basis. The First Department for example is responsible for matters relating to monopolies, agreements, and mergers in relation to agriculture, commercial business, transportation and warehousing, **4-1.06**

[6] Ibid at 12.

[7] More properly referred to as the 'Executive Yuan'. Following principles established by Sun Yat Sen the Taiwan political machinery is divided into three: the Legislative Yuan, the Executive Yuan, and the Judicial Yuan. The judiciary is more independent of the Government than is the case in China.

[8] The OECD *Peer Review*, conducted in 2006, characterized the TFTC as 'a stable, experienced administrative agency'. (See, n 2, above, Foreword.)

[9] In 2007 for example the TFTC undertook a study on major chain convenience stores (*TFTC Competition Policy Newsletter*, 11:5, 31 October 2007).

[10] The current version was promulgated on 13 January 1992, and amended in 2000 and 2002.

[11] Williams, n 2, above, at 381.

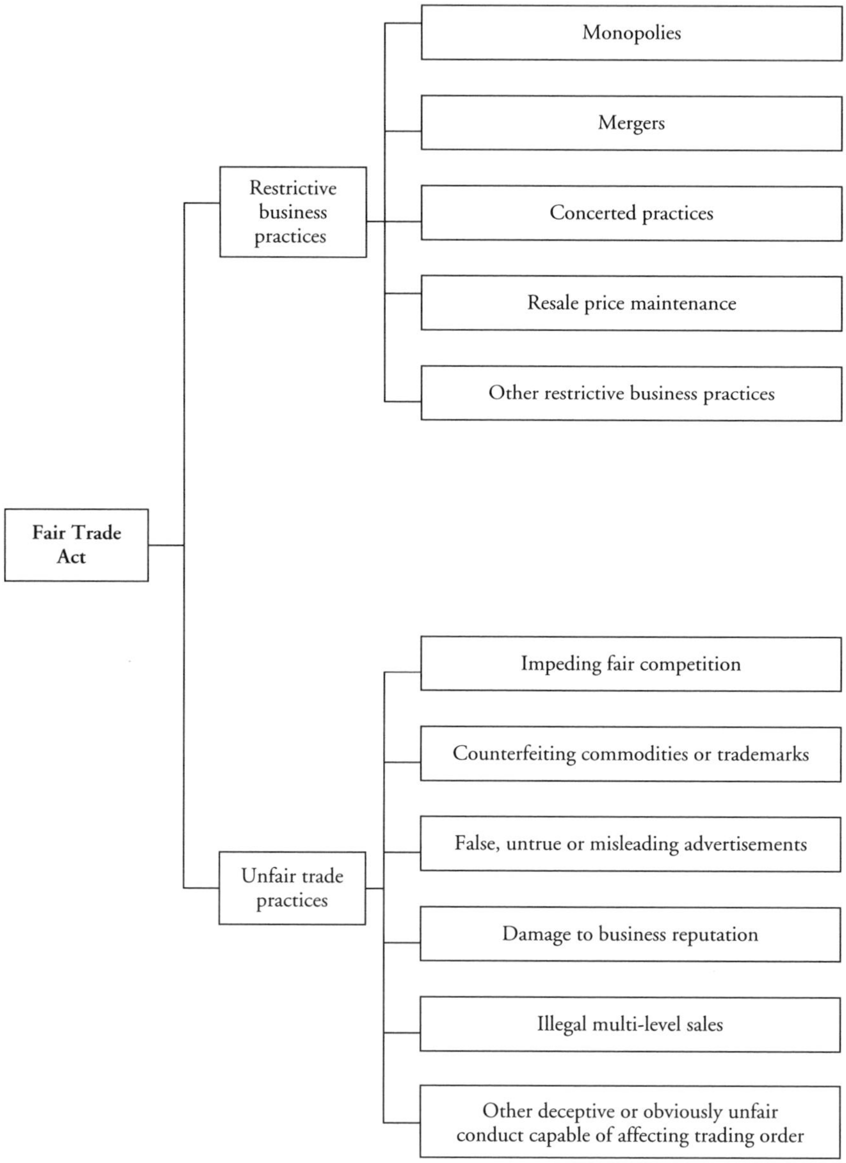

Figure 4-1.1 Regulatory framework of the Fair Trade Act.
Source: TFTC Website.

finance, insurance and real estate, and social and personal services. Other sectors are allocated to the Second and Third Departments.

The TFTC is headed by nine commissioners, each serving a three-year term. **4-1.07** Reappointment for one further term is possible. Of the nine Commissioners in office on 1 February 2007, five were experts in law, and four experts in economics. A Chairperson of the TFTC supervises all the affairs of the TFTC. All Commissioner appointments are made by the President on the recommendation of the Premier, and Commissioners must be 'well versed and experienced in law, economics, finance, tax, accounting or management'. They are also required to 'be beyond party affiliations' and to 'act independently in performing their duties under the law'. Meetings, which are not public, but of which public minutes are made, are held weekly. Article 14 of the Organic Statute sets out the following functions of the TFTC Commissioners' meetings: (1) review of fair trade policies; (2) deliberation and review of the administration of fair trade programs; (3) review of cases relating to public notice, approval, and disposition under the TFTA; (4) deliberation of matters arising under the TFTA and regulations; (5) review of proposals made by any of the commissioners; and (6) 'other matters requiring resolutions at the meeting of commissioners as prescribed by law'. Figure 4-1.2 sets out the workload for the TFTC from 2000 to June 2007. As at the end of June 2007 the TFTC had processed 29,580 cases out of the 29,905 it had received. There are no figures given for own-initiative actions.

Year	Complaints	Applications for concerted actions	Applications for mergers	Requests for interpretation
2000	1,372	12	1,187	126
2001	1,381	4	1,089	82
2002	1,186	8	132	61
2003	999	12	50	39
2004	1,058	2	33	55
2005	1,632	7	54	140
2006	1,304	9	79	47
2007 (to end June)	603	4	29	28

Figure 4-1.2 TFTC workload.
Source: *TFTC Competition Policy Newsletter*, 4:11, 31 August 2007.

Information sources

4-1.08 There is little secondary material published in English about antitrust law in Taiwan, although some is listed in the bibliography. The primary source for reference material is the website of the TFTC (<http://www.ftc.gov.tw>) which maintains an English language section including the core legislation, guidance, some case information, and a regularly published newsletter. The TFTC also publishes, since 2007, a quarterly journal dealing with aspects of antitrust law. Some of this material is duplicated on the APEC website, referred to in Chapter 1-1.

General Exemptions

4-1.09 Article 46 of the TFTA provides that: 'Where there is any other law governing the conducts of enterprises in respect of competition, such other law shall govern, provided it does not conflict with the legislative purposes of this law'. This does not create a general exemption from the TFTA, which has general application to all economic sectors, although the requirements at various parts of the TFTA to balance the public interest against any competitive harms may mean that various industries, such as those relating to sensitive national interests, are not constrained by the operation of the TFTA. Where there have been conflicts between the operation of the TFTA and specific measures taken by bodies other than the TFTC the conflicts have usually been resolved by advocacy undertaken by the TFTC.[12] The provisions of the TFTA also appear to apply to some, but not all, emanations of the State. The position in this regard does not always appear to be consistent. Thus, Williams reports that in one decision a government-owned printing unit was found not to be subject to the strictures of the TFTA, but that in another case the Law was partially applied to a bookstore which was also an emanation of the State.[13]

4-1.10 Article 45 of the TFTA provides that the Law shall not be applied to the legitimate exercise of intellectual property rights such as patents, trade marks, and copyrights. However, the Law may be applied to the exercise of these rights (see further Chapters 4-2 and 4-3 below).[14]

---

[12] See OECD, n 2, above, 40.

[13] See Williams, n 2, above, at 396; citing TFTC Interpretation No 034, 1 *Gazette of the TFTC*, September 1992, p 31, and TFTC Interpretation No 041, *Gazette of the TFTC*, December 1992, p 53. See also Liu, n 3, above, 99–102.

[14] Liu states that this provision 'should be characterized as a "rule of reason" approach to licensing and other antitrust issues related to intellectual property. In other words this provision does not contemplate a true exemption, which would presuppose a certain level of improper conduct'. (Liu, n 3, above, at 104–5.)

Territorial Application

There is nothing on the face of the TTFA which limits territorial jurisdiction, although art 47 sets out a limitation on the extent to which foreign companies may rely on Taiwanese antitrust law against Taiwanese companies, in providing in part that: 4-1.11

> . . . any national or organization of [Taiwan] in the country of such foreign juristic person or organization must be entitled to the right of the kind in accordance with any treaty, or any law, regulation or custom of such country, or through any agreement entered into by any organization(s) or institution(s) and approved by [the TFTC] for mutual protection.

It will be seen in Chapter 4-4, dealing with merger control, that the law in this area can be applied to 'foreign' mergers, and the applicable principles are set out there. The TFTC has published *Guidelines on Cases Involving Foreign Elements*[15] which deal with the handling of cases involving complaints made by foreign enterprises against Taiwanese enterprises, and those made against foreign enterprises, unless other laws, regulations, treaties and agreements, or customary international law apply. 'Foreign elements' is defined as applying to cases 'where the complainant, respondent, investigated party, applicant, party filing a report, or party requesting an official interpretation of the law is a foreign enterprise'.[16] 4-1.12

Where any complaint is filed relating to an alleged violation of the TFTA this is to be prepared in Chinese, and must be signed by the complainant.[17] The Guidelines refer back to art 47 of the TFTA, in specifying at para 5 of the Guidelines that in cases in which the complainant is a foreign enterprise 'the Commission may, when it considers necessary, specify a time period for the complainant to present the laws, regulations or customs under which a [Taiwanese] 4-1.13

[15] Approved on 21 February 1996; amended most recently on 13 December 2001; published by Fair Trade Commission Order 0910001327 of 8 February 2002.

[16] para 1(3).

[17] The complaint must specify: the name, age, nationality, occupation, and domicile of the complainant. If the complainant is a legal person or an organization, the complaint must also include details of the office or business place, and the administrator's details. The facts on the basis of which the breach of the law is alleged must be set out, along with evidence. Where the evidence is in the form of documents which are not in Chinese a translation of the documents must be provided. If the complainant is a foreign enterprise this must appoint an agent in Taiwan to handle matters on its behalf, and proof of the evidence of a power of attorney must be enclosed with the complaint. Where translations of documents are provided the Guidelines provide that in the case of foreign 'official documents' the authenticity may be determined by the TFTC, save that documents certified by a Taiwanese embassy, consulate, or official representative shall be presumed to be authentic. In the case of private documents the party presenting them must establish their authenticity, but 'those that have been notarized by a court of justice, a public notary, or certified by a representative office of [Taiwan] or those that are not contested by the opposing party shall be presumed to be authentic' (Guidelines, para 13).

citizen or organization is entitled to similar rights in the complainant's home country'. The complainant must also 'present facts and evidence to prove the extent of influence on Taiwan's market competition' resulting from the alleged unlawful act, whether this is engaged in 'within or outside the territory of [Taiwan]'. The complainant is further obliged to present an explanation as to the likelihood that the law of Taiwan is in fact being broken. Where a foreign enterprise makes a complaint relating to the conduct of a Taiwanese enterprise the TFTC shall decide on the basis of art 47 of the TFTA whether to accept the complaint or not. The Guidelines further provide that where there is no evidence of prior cases in which the authorities of the complainant's home country denied protection to a Taiwanese enterprise, the TFTC 'may decide ex officio whether or not to accept the case'.

4-1.14 Part III of the Guidelines sets out principles that apply in relation to the collecting of information outside of Taiwan, specifying five channels that may be used: (1) first the TFTC is to consider whether the information it requires can be obtained from a domestic source; (2) the TFTC may write to request the foreign parties to provide information; (3) the TFTC may request the information from representative offices of the Ministry of Foreign Affairs or the Ministry of Economic Affairs situated abroad; (4) the TFTC may conduct the investigation in accordance with art 27 of the TFTA,[18] but 'shall have an overall consideration of foreign sovereignty, the principle of reciprocity, and whether compulsorily demanding the concerned foreign enterprise to cooperate will achieve the goal of its investigation'; finally (5) the TFTC 'may collect the needed information or evidence through the help of private organizations, trade associations and others'. Paragraph 10 of the Guidelines is important, and provides that where a foreign enterprise does not cooperate with the investigation the TFTC 'may make a decision based on the readily available information and evidence'. Where hearings are held, or where evidence is to be presented before the TFTC this shall be in accordance with the procedural rules established in the TFTA, with the proviso that where persons making presentations are not Chinese-literate they may be 'accompanied by a person knowing the Chinese language who shall present his/her power of attorney'. Proceedings will be recorded in Chinese, and any documents must be provided in Chinese translation if the original language is not Chinese.

4-1.15 Part IV of the Guidelines relates to the service of documents outside the territory of Taiwan. In the event that extraterritorial service of official documents is necessary the TFTC may request the Ministry of Foreign Affairs to entrust the service to an agency of the relevant country with 'appropriate jurisdiction' or to a

[18] The operation of this article and the other provisions relating to procedures generally are discussed in Chapter 4-5.

Taiwan embassy or other official entity representing the Government in the country. Where it is impossible to effect service in this way or 'if it is foreseeable that following such provisions would be to no avail, service may be effected by publication' through the application of the provisions of the Code of Civil Procedure. The possibility is thus opened up, although this is an unlikely scenario, that a foreign enterprise could be notified of the need to provide documents only through a publication in Chinese in Taiwan. Where the TFTC is delivering other documents to parties located outside Taiwan it may, if the official methods set out above fail, be deemed to have served these 'following delivery through the postal system by return-receipt registered mail'. Official documents may be served without an English translation, but an English 'introduction' must be included to explain the 'nature and legal effects of the documents served'.

In the event that any fines are imposed on foreign enterprises the TFTC may file **4-1.16** a motion with the relevant Taiwan court seeking compulsory execution. Whether this can be enforced overseas will depend on relevant principles of international law, and may be influenced by any relevant treaty arrangements.

International Cooperation and Agreements

Paragraph 20 of the *Guidelines on Cases Involving Foreign Elements*, discussed above, **4-1.17** provides that: 'For the purpose of handling cases involving matters outside [Taiwan] the TFTC may proceed with the assistance of competent authorities of those countries entered into a bilateral agreement with [Taiwan]'. There are a number of cases in which the TFTC has, in the course of investigations, liaised with antitrust authorities in other jurisdictions. Perhaps in part because of the disputed legal nature of Taiwan's status in international law Taiwan has not entered into a great many bilateral treaties relating to antitrust law. At the time of writing the TFTC has entered into arrangements with Australia, New Zealand, and France.[19]

The most significant of these treaties is the agreement entered into with Australia **4-1.18** on 13 September 1996.[20] The purpose of this agreement is to:

> . . . promote co-operation and co-ordination between the agencies and lessen the possibility of differences between the agencies in the application of their competition and consumer laws where these differences are not the result of statutory provisions.

---

[19] There is also a trilateral agreement between Taiwan, Australia, and New Zealand, signed in 2002. The agreement with France was entered into in 2004.

[20] Cooperation and Coordination Arrangement between the Taipei Economic and Cultural Office and the Australian Commerce and Industry Office Regarding the Application of Competition and Fair Trading Laws.

The agreement makes provision for the exchange of information relating to enforcement activity, and is relatively 'hard' in the force of its terms.[21] The obligation to participate in the exchange of information is ameliorated by references to the need to avoid prejudice to the interests of the requested agency, and information exchanged cannot be passed on to any other authority without the explicit written permission of the supplying agency.

4-1.19 The TFTC has also entered into a Memorandum of Understanding with the Unfair Competition Regulatory Authority of Mongolia ('UCRAM'),[22] and provides technical support to Southeast Asian countries, including Thailand, Vietnam, and Indonesia.

4-1.20 Taiwan became one of the general observers in the Competition Committee of the OECD on 1 January 2002, and has been subject to a generally positive peer review appraisal of its competition law and policy.

[21] See Noonan, C, *The Emerging Principles of International Competition Law* (Oxford: Oxford University Press, 2007) 499–500.

[22] Signed on 15 March 2007. The emphasis of the MOU is on the provision of assistance and support by the TFTC to the UCRAM, but there are also provisions relating to the exchange of information.

4-2

TAIWAN AGREEMENTS

Introduction	4-2.01	Intellectual property licensing	4-2.25
Horizontal agreements	4-2.02	**Unfair Competition as it Relates to Horizontal and Vertical Agreements**	4-2.33
Approvals	4-2.08	**Penalties for Breach**	4-2.41
Trade associations	4-2.19		
Vertical agreements	4-2.20		
Multi-level sales	4-2.22		

Introduction

The primary legislation dealing with the law of anti-competitive agreements in the Taiwan antitrust system is brief, but goes further than that of s 1 of the Sherman Act in providing a set of criteria under which otherwise anti-competitive agreements may be exempted from the prohibition. The primary provisions dealing with anti-competitive agreements make formal and structural distinctions between horizontal agreements, which are dealt with in art 14 of the TFTA, and vertical agreements. The latter are dealt with in Chapter III of the TFTA, which contains general provisions relating to unfair competition, and also specific provisions relating to 'multi-level sales' arrangements, which are discussed below. There are also provisions in Chapter III, which relates to 'unfair competition' that may relate to both horizontal and vertical arrangements, and to unilateral conduct entered into by enterprises that do not have market power. Separate guidelines relate to intellectual property licensing arrangements, again based on the legislative principles of Chapter III of the Act (see below). **4-2.01**

Horizontal agreements

The first paragraph of art 14 of the TFTA provides simply that: **4-2.02**

> [n]o enterprise shall have any concerted action; unless the concerted action that meets one of the following requirements is beneficial to the economy as a whole and in the public interest, and the application with the central authority for such concerted action has been approved.

4-2.03 Article 7 defines 'concerted action' as meaning:

> . . . the conduct of any enterprise, by means of contract, agreement or any other form of mutual understanding,[1] with any other competing enterprise, to jointly determine the price of goods or services, or to limit the terms of quantity, technology, products, facilities, trading counterparts,[2] or trading territory with respect to such goods and services etc, and thereby to restrict each others' business activities.[3]

4-2.04 The broad rule with respect to horizontal anti-competitive agreements therefore is that they are illegal unless approval is granted by the TFTC. The TFTC has regularly condemned concerted actions with anti-competitive effects, requiring infringements to be brought to an end, and imposing penalties. The prohibition extends to the classic 'hard-core' restrictions, such as horizontal price-fixing, as well as to more complex restrictions, including, for example, the pooling of patent licences for the purposes of licensing.[4]

4-2.05 One of the most significant cases taken forward by the TFTC is that relating to a cement cartel with 21 members penalized a total of NT$210 million.[5] There had been a number of complaints against cement manufacturers extending back to at least 2001, with suspicions raised that companies were colluding in price rises. In 1997 an international cement cartel had been formed following the 1997 Asian financial crisis, against a market-specific background of over-supply and over-capacity and falling prices. Domestic prices fell dramatically in a number of Asian companies as international producers were accused of dumping supplies. The TFTC noted the difficulties that had been encountered by a number of competition authorities in investigating the market (a high degree of homogeneity and transparency fuelled a tendency towards converging sales terms) and undertook one of its most substantial investigations, lasting four years.[6] Statements were

---

[1] Footnote added. It is noted in OECD, *Chinese Taipei—Peer Review of Competition Law and Policy 2006*, OECD, 2006, p 14 that:

> The definition's reference to 'any other form of mutual understanding' is intended to be sure that the prohibition is not limited by contract law technicalities. It means a meeting of minds, whether legally binding or not, which would in effect lead to joint actions. . . . It is not supposed to cover pure oligopoly interdependence or conscious parallelism.

[2] 'Trading counterparts' is defined throughout the TFTA as meaning 'any supplier or purchaser that engages in or concludes transactions with an enterprise' (TFTA, art 3).

[3] There is no specific reference here to bid-rigging, a practice which appears to be common in Taiwan. However, bid-rigging may be attacked under the Government Procurement Act when the target is the Government or its emanations.

[4] See for example CD-R Patent Licensing Arrangements in Taiwan by Royal Philips Electronics, Sony Corporation (Japan) and Taiyo Yuden Co Ltd (Japan) (20 April 2006) discussed below.

[5] 15 December 2005, *TFTC Competition Policy Newsletter*, 1:10, 28 February 2006. NT$210 million approximated at the time to US$6.3 million.

[6] The OECD *Peer Review* commented on the enforcement activity of the TFTC generally in relation to international cartels that:

> . . . the [TFTC] has only a limited ability to undertake enforcement against international cartels. The [TFTC] has gotten some evidence in several cases about international collusion.

taken from a large number of relevant enterprises, with the final documentation held by the TFTC amounting to over 20,000 pages. The TFTC found at the end of its investigation that the cartel participants were guilty of a number of anti-competitive acts, including: (1) reaching an agreement to set up a joint venture to acquire harbour silos to prevent international cement groups from establishing domestic market channels; (2) negotiating the exit of some enterprises from the market in order to reduce price competition resulting from over-supply; (3) agreeing to allocate customers, staying out of each others' territories and agreeing to share silos so as to exclude foreign competitors; (4) agreeing to sell domestic cement to each other instead of importing from other countries at lower prices in order to restrict competition entering the market, and to facilitate the agreement of price rises amongst themselves; (5) reducing capacities and the quantities supplied, resulting in a price rise from NT$1,300 to NT$2,250; and (6) making an agreement with Japanese suppliers of slag (a key ingredient in cement production) to reduce the annual volumes of slag exported to Taiwan. As is clear from the price rises, the cartel was successful in reducing the quantity of cement imported into Taiwan, and in reducing the capacities of kilns in Taiwan.[7]

A recent example of the condemnation of a price-fixing arrangement is that in which the TFTC investigated an arrangement entered into by 12 liquid petroleum gas ('LPG') distributors.[8] Following a price rise by the producers a meeting of competitor distributors of LPG was arranged in a restaurant, at which an agreement was entered into to raise the price of LPG from NT$450 per barrel to NT$500 per barrel. Fines totalling NT$1,590,000 were imposed on the companies, and the TFTC ordered that the infringement be brought to an end. Price-fixing agreements have also been condemned where the arrangement took the form of a recommendation emanating from a trade association. In the case of *Taipei County Jewellers' Association* the association advised its 550 members that they should not sell gold at prices below the current international rate. The communications were made either by phone calls or by direct visits to members, which were backed up by a letter circulated to all members. There was no evidence of an enforcement mechanism, but the TFTC held that the communications would have a dampening effect on normal price competition, and had an anti-competitive effect. A penalty of NT$500,000 was imposed.[9] Not all price-fixing **4-2.06**

> But the [TFTC] concentrates on finding better proof of agreement about domestic sales, in the absence of realistic prospects of applying its law to non-resident international or foreign firms. (OECD, n 1, above, at 37)

[7] The TFTC also called on other competition authorities to tackle the international cement cartels, and offered to share its information with them.

[8] 6 September 2007.

[9] *TFTC Competition Policy Newsletter*, 3:11, 30 June 2007.

may be illegal however. In July 2007 the TFTC rejected a complaint as to price-fixing amongst stevedore enterprises in Taichung Harbour. The TFTC took the view that the agreement in question existed to resolve an issue concerning pay scales, and was also driven in part by 'substantial intervention of the business regulatory authorities'.[10]

4-2.07 Agreements to divide markets or to allocate customers will also invite condemnation unless they are able to claim the benefit of the approvals system. For example, in *King Cable TV and Everlasting Cable TV*[11] the two companies were condemned in relation to their practice of dividing subscribers between themselves. The action was taken following a complaint initiated by potential subscribers in a newly completed housing area. When the building administration committee requested that King Cable TV provide a service to the development it was told that King would not offer a service as the development lay in an area covered by Everlasting Cable TV. The TFTC carried out an investigation, in the course of which it surveyed potential customers and carried out interviews. In addition to a pattern of refusals to supply by the two companies it was noted by the TFTC that King's President held 25 per cent of the shares of Everlasting, which 'gave King the opportunity to take part in the board meetings of its competitor, which created a conduit between the two business strategies and thus resulted in concerted action'.

Approvals

4-2.08 Article 14 of the TFTA sets out criteria relating to exemptions. This article applies to horizontal arrangements, and not to vertical agreements, which fall to be considered under arts 18 and 19 of the TFTA. The specified requirements of art 14, for which exemptions from the general prohibition may be granted, are:

(1) unifying specifications 'for the purpose of reducing costs, improving quality, or increasing efficiency';[12]

---

[10] *TFTC Competition Policy Newsletter*, 5:11, 31 October 2007. See also *The Board of Directors of the Tourist Bus Association of Taiwan Province* (21 December 2006, *TFTC Competition Policy Newsletter* 2:11, 30 April 2007), in which the respondent was found to be in breach of art 14(1), TFTA by making a resolution requesting the association of each county/city to invite business operators and mobile licences' lessees to jointly raise transportation charges. A penalty of NT$500,000 was imposed. In *The Non-Life Assurance Association of the ROC* (25 January 2007, *TFTC Competition Policy Newsletter*, 2:11, 30 April 2007) an insurance trade association was penalized for acting to prevent its members from freely setting property insurance premiums at a time when the Government was promoting a liberalization in the market.

[11] 30 March 2006, *TFTC Competition Policy Newsletter*, 3:10, 30 June 2006.

[12] In two cases in 2006, for example, the TFTC approved joint ticketing arrangements in the transport sector (*Domestic Airlines*, 26 October 2006, and *Domestic Ferry Operators*, 16 November 2006). However the TFTC has also condemned an arrangement between four bus companies designed to result in uniform charges, the reduction of fare discounts and the number of bus trips (8 June 2006).

(2) joint research and development;
(3) specialization agreements;
(4) agreements entered into 'concerning solely the competition in foreign markets for the purpose of securing or promoting exports';
(5) 'joint acts in regards to the importation of foreign goods for the purposes of strengthening trade';
(6) agreements limiting production with the intention of dealing, in an orderly manner, with market downturns where 'the market price of products is lower than the average production costs so that the enterprises in a particular industry have difficulty' in maintaining their business;[13]
(7) 'joint acts for the purpose of improving operational efficiency or strengthening the competitiveness of small-medium enterprises'.[14]

This list is not on the whole a remarkable one: agreements falling within (1) would not generally invite condemnation in the EC or the US unless there were exceptional circumstances demonstrating that the agreement was in fact anti-competitive rather than pro-competitive. Research and development agreements and specialization agreements both benefit from block exemption regulations in the EC and fall under the rule of reason in the US. The provisions relating to export cartels follow those of the US Webb-Pomerene Export Act, and in the EC the general rule is that an agreement must have an effect and be implemented *within* the EC in order to be condemned. However, the reference to acts relating to imports for the purposes of strengthening trade is more idiosyncratic, and the acceptance of crisis cartels also remains a matter of some controversy amongst antitrust analysts, although the stringency of the information requirements in respect of applications for approval of such concerted actions suggests that the approval process would be a most rigorous one. **4-2.09**

Only the TFTC has the power to grant approval in relation to the exceptions set out in art 14, and any such decision shall be made within three months of an application being made,[15] although this period may be extended once.[16] Fuller procedures relating to the making of applications for approval of concerted actions under art 14 are set out in the Enforcement Rules to the Fair Trade Act at arts 13–25. The Enforcement Rules are prescriptive in the information that must be provided in order for an approval to be granted. In any case the parties are **4-2.10**

[13] Such arrangements, which are likely to be condemned in both the EC and the US are usually referred to as 'crisis cartels'.

[14] The definition of a small or medium-sized enterprise is that given in the Statute for the Development of Small and Medium-Sized Enterprises.

[15] The three-month period starts from the day after the TFTC receives the application, but if the application is incomplete or deficient the clock does not start running until it is completed in accordance with the requirements set by the TFTC (art 24, Enforcement Rules).

[16] art 14(2), TFTA.

required to complete an application for approval accompanied by documents specified in art 14(1) of the Enforcement Rules, which include: (1) a basic application form identifying the parties, the type of the concerted action, and its implementation period; (2) the contract or other documentary evidence of the concerted action; (3) details relating to the anticipated operation of the concerted action in practice; (4) basic data relating to the requesting enterprises; (5) quarterly reports for the previous two years setting out prices, production levels, and sales of the products or services to be affected by the action; (6) financial statements and operating reports for each of the enterprises; (7) information relating to the market structure at the horizontal, upstream, and downstream levels; (8) an assessment report of the impact of the concerted action;[17] and (9) any other documents specified by the TFTC.

4-2.11 The Enforcement Rules specify information that must be attached to the application in respect of each of the categories of concerted actions set out in art 14(1) of the TFTA. Generally, in relation to efficiency benefits claimed in respect of actions falling within unifying standards or specialization agreements the parties must include an assessment report 'that sets out in detail the anticipated concrete results in cost reduction, quality improvement, increased efficiency, or rationalization of operations'.[18] The remainder of the requirements are set out below.

4-2.12 *Research and development (art 14(1)(2))*: the difference between the funding required for individual R&D and that required for joint R&D; the anticipated concrete results in technological upgrading, quality improvements, cost reduction, or increased efficiency.[19]

4-2.13 *Export agreements (art 14(1)(4))*: the export value of each participating enterprise for the most recent one-year period, the percentage of the total export value of the same product for which it accounts, the enterprise's ratio of exports to domestic sales, and the anticipated concrete benefits in terms of the exporting of the goods.[20]

4-2.14 *Importation of foreign goods (art 14(1)(5))*: the export value of each participating enterprise for the most recent three years, a comparison of the costs required for

---

[17] This is required to contain the following information: (1) cost structure before and after the concerted action, and analytical data on the changes forecast; (2) the impact of the concerted action on enterprises affected by but not participating in the action; (3) the impact of the concerted action on the structure, supply and demand, and pricing of the relevant market; (4) the impact of the action on upstream and downstream enterprises; (5) an analysis of the concrete benefits and the detrimental effects of the action on the overall economy; and (6) any other required information.

[18] art 16, Enforcement Rules.

[19] art 17, Enforcement Rules.

[20] art 18, Enforcement Rules.

import by the individual enterprise versus those required for concerted imports, and the anticipated concrete results in strengthening trade.[21]

Crisis cartels (art 14(1)(6)): a monthly comparative breakdown for the preceding three years of the average fixed costs, average variable costs, and the pricing of the specified goods for each of the contributing enterprises; monthly breakdowns for each of the preceding three years of production capacities, equipment utilization rates, production and sales values, import/export values, and the inventory levels of each of the participating enterprises; changes in the numbers of businesses participating in the industry over the preceding three years; the market prospects for the industry; any methods adopted or contemplated apart from the concerted action to deal with the downturn; and the anticipated results of the concerted action.[22] **4-2.15**

Small and medium-sized businesses (art 14(1)(7)): demonstration that the relevant enterprises meet the requirements for being small and medium-sized enterprises, and the anticipated concrete results that would be achieved in improving operational efficiency or strengthened competitiveness.[23] The TFTC has published a *Guideline on Principles on Approving Exemptions for Concerted Pricing by Small or Medium-sized Enterprises*.[24] A presumption is set, which flows from the Act, that even in the case of SMEs, concerted pricing is anti-competitive, and the TFTC makes clear that enterprises may only apply for an exemption under this provision where the arrangement would be beneficial to the economy, and meets at least one of the conditions specified in the Guidelines. There are two such principles, the first of which is the principle of transaction stability, under which it may be accepted that in the case of sporadic transactions which are similar in nature and involve small amounts of money the transaction costs may be reduced, enhancing efficiency and competition based on service standards. The TFTC also recognizes in this respect that such agreements may prevent small and medium-sized enterprises being 'rushed into transactions and taken advantage of'. The second principle is that of information transparency, which applies where: (1) there is neither the purpose to affect, nor an effect on, supply or demand in international pricing; (2) there is an international market price which may be taken as a **4-2.16**

[21] art 19, Enforcement Rules.

[22] art 20, Enforcement Rules. It has been noted that:

Crisis cartel applications are rare. Joint action to limit output or stem price cuts in an economic downturn would be permitted only if conditions in the market have driven the market price below 'average production costs', and firms are threatened with exit or overproduction. . . . In any event, there have been few requests for exemption on this basis. The [TFTC] rejected an application for a capacity-reduction agreement among fibre manufacturers in 1998, on the grounds that conditions were not irretrievable and the market was likely to recover. (OECD, n 1, above, at 16)

[23] art 21, Enforcement Rules.

[24] Approved 2 November 1994, Amended 3 November 1999.

reference point; and (3) 'the disclosure of such information as valuation method, valuation base, and relevant parameters, can facilitate the acquisition of trading information, lessen the social costs of transactions, and help create trading opportunities'.[25] The Guidelines also set out the application requirements that apply when SMEs seek to rely on this provision.

4-2.17 Where an application is made for a grant of approval the TFTC may attach conditions to the approval, or may require undertakings to be complied with. Approvals may be granted for a maximum period of three years, but may then be extended following a written justification for such an extension being made by the appropriate enterprises.[26] In the event that any enterprise applying for approval under art 14(1) provides incomplete or 'deficient' materials the TFTC may require the enterprises to correct this within a specified period of time, and if such correction is not made the application will be rejected.[27] Article 16 of the TFTA provides that approvals may be revoked or their contents amended by the TFTC in situations in which either the cause for the approval no longer exists, the economic conditions change, or the enterprises engage in any conduct beyond the scope of the approval. The TFTC maintains a registry in which the details of approvals are recorded, and these are also published in the Government Gazette. In essence then the position is very similar to that which existed in the EC prior to the modernization of EC antitrust in 2004, under which only the central authority of the EC Commission had the power to grant exemptions from the application of art 81(1) EC, and the details of these were published. There are no more informal mechanisms by which approvals may be granted by the TFTC, and no formal block exemption regulations.

4-2.18 In practice approvals are not often requested in relation to horizontal cooperation agreements or arrangements, and the OECD peer review process found that the TFTC 'spends comparatively little time or resources processing applications for exemption',[28] although the statistics appear to indicate that there is a reasonable prospect of exemptions being granted if they are requested.

Trade associations

4-2.19 The TFTC has issued a Policy Statement on the application of the Act to the activities of trade associations.[29] A number of examples are given in this Statement

---

25 Guidelines, para 5(2).

26 art 15, TFTA. Extension applications must contain: (1) an application form; (2) a copy of the original approval; (3) the reasons for the request for an extension; and (4) any other materials required by the TFTC (art 25, Enforcement Rules).

27 art 23, Enforcement Rules.

28 OECD, n 1, above, at 16.

29 TFTC, 16 June 1993; amended 16 June 1999.

of Conduct which might breach the Act's proscriptions. These include: restricting entry and exit from specific markets; imposing restrictions on the types, specifications, or forms of goods or services; the conclusion of international agreements or contracts based on improper trading restrictions or unfair trading practices; causing members to treat others in a discriminatory manner or to commit other unfair acts; and 'any other improper joint actions that restrict business competition on specific markets'. Activities that do not fall within these headings, and which comply with the terms of the Business Organizations Law, or the Industrial Organizations Law are considered to be unlikely to breach the provisions of the TFTA. Such activities include the collection of information for members' reference, particularly where this is of a general nature,[30] or engaging in training and skills development for members of the association. In respect of some categories of conduct the TFTC advises that either clarification of the relevant rules, or its approval, should be sought. These include the setting of 'a non-compulsory set of specifications or standards with a view towards raising operational efficiency', and 'the formulation of a reasonable, non-compulsory code, in order to avoid unfair competition practices, such as exaggerated advertising and excessive distribution of free gifts'.

Vertical agreements

Article 14 of the TFTA, discussed above, applies only where the parties are 'competing enterprises', and does not therefore apply to vertical agreements, although it could apply to the actions of a number of distributors of the same producer, if these enter, through the distribution network, into an arrangement that would fall within the proscriptions of art 14. Some provisions of arts 19 and 20, which are discussed below, would also relate to vertical relationships. The TFTC has also published intellectual property licensing guidelines, which are discussed in full below. These guidelines are very similar in form to older style EC block exemption regulations, but similar guidelines have not been published in relation to other categories of vertical arrangements. **4-2.20**

The approach of the TFTA to vertical agreements is, in a manner which derives from the Japanese antitrust system, to classify them as part of the law of unfair competition found in Chapter III of the TFTA.[31] These provisions, which include a prohibition on resale price maintenance, are discussed below. **4-2.21**

[30] The Policy Statement makes reference in this category to 'information about overseas markets, and domestic and international economic trends'.

[31] See, eg Liu, LS, 'Fostering Competition Law and Policy: A Façade of Taiwan's Political Economy' (2002) *Washington University Global Studies Law Review*, vol 1, (1 & 2), 77 at 131.

Multi-level sales

4-2.22 Articles 23 to 23-4 of the TFTA relate to 'multi-level sales' arrangements, which are vertical in nature, but which take a slightly different form from standard exclusive or selective distribution systems operating in the EC or the US, and which respond to a particular form of business organization which has raised concern in Taiwan.[32]

The term 'multi-level sales' is defined in art 8 of the TFTA, and means:

> . . . the promotion or sales plan or organization pursuant to which the participants pay a certain consideration to obtain the right to promote or sell goods or services and the right to introduce other persons to participate in the plan or organization, thereby receiving a commission, bonus, or other economic benefit.

4-2.23 Article 23 prohibits the operation of any multi-level sales plan where the participants receive benefits mainly from inducing others to participate in the plan, rather than from the marketing or sales of goods 'at reasonable market prices'. Article 23-1 provides the right of any party to rescind its participation agreement within fourteen days of entering into it, and art 23-2 provides further that after this initial fourteen-day period, any party may terminate the agreement in writing and withdraw from the arrangement. In either case the multi-level sales enterprise may not claim damages or levy penalties.[33] Article 23-4 provides that the TFTC is to promulgate rules relating to records and procedures to be established by multi-level sales organizations. The most recent amendments to the Supervisory Regulations Governing Multi-Level Sales were made on 24 April 2002. These set out detailed reporting requirements for multi-level sales organizations to comply with. The TFTC is required to maintain a record of all the relevant organizations which have satisfied the filing requirements. Chapter 3 of the Regulations sets out the rights and obligations of participants in a multi-level sales organization. Before any participant enters such an organization he shall be fully informed of particulars set out in art 11 of the Regulations, including details of the capitalization of the organizing enterprise, the operational plans of the organization, and matters relating to the goods or services that the participant will be selling, and conditions relating to the terms under which the participant may withdraw from the organization. Chapter 4 of the Regulations relates to 'sales activities', setting

---

[32] The multi-level sales industry in Taiwan is the ninth largest in the world, and it has the highest population density of direct selling participants in the world (*TFTC Competition Policy Newsletter*, 3:11, 30 June 2007. From March to April 2007 the TFTC conducted a survey of multi-level sales enterprises. Over 700 responded to the TFTC's survey, and the total business volume in 2006 was NT$55.34 billion, with over 5,300,000 participants. In terms of products distributed through this route health food products dominated with 51.29% of the total sales, followed by cosmetic products (18.79%), clothing and accessories (6.58%), and cleaning products (6.04%) (*TFTC Competition Policy Newsletter*, 5:11, 31 October 2007).

[33] art 23-3, TFTA.

out eight activities that multi-level sales enterprises may not engage in: (1) requiring a participant to pay fees relating to training, seminars etc which are clearly incommensurate with the cost of those activities; (2) requiring participants to pay any unreasonable security deposits, breach penalties or other liabilities; (3) requiring participants to purchase more goods than could reasonably be sold in a short period, unless the price is paid only after the goods are resold; (4) unjustifiably withholding commissions or bonuses or other remunerations following the rescission of the agreement; (5) setting greater benefit levels that apply only where the participant pays unreasonable fees for training etc (note the link here with condition (1)); (6) giving some participants preferential treatment such that payments to others would be diminished; (7) hindering the return of goods following the rescission of the agreement or withdrawal from it on proper notice; (8) requiring the participant to undertake obviously unfair obligations. Chapter 5 creates a further supervisory mechanism in setting a regime for the inspection of multi-level sales enterprises by the TFTC. The TFTC has also issued *Guidelines on Investigations in Multi-level Sales Cases*.[34]

Special provisions relating to the penalties to be applied in the case of breaches of **4-2.24** the multi-level sales rules are set out in arts 35, 42, and 42-1 of the TFTA. Article 35 sets penalties of imprisonment and fines, or a combination thereof, and is discussed in Chapter 4-5 of this Part. Article 42 provides further that any enterprise in breach may also 'be subject to an order for dissolution, suspension or termination of the business operation if the violation is serious'. Any person in violation of art 23-1(2), 23-2(2), or 23-3(2) may be ordered to terminate his infringement or to take necessary corrective action within a time limit set out in the order, and a penalty ranging from NT$50,000 to NT$25m may be imposed. Failures to comply with the order may result in successive further orders being made, with penalties being increased to a maximum of NT$50m until the orders are complied with.[35]

Intellectual property licensing

Nowhere in the TFTA provisions relating to agreements is there any reference to **4-2.25** intellectual property licensing, although art 47 of the TFTA provides that: 'No provision of this Law shall apply to any proper conduct in connection with the exercise of rights pursuant to the provisions of the Copyright Law, Trademark Law, or Patent Law'. This has not, however, prevented the TFTC from publishing its *Guidelines on Technology Licensing Arrangements*[36] in the drafting of which the TFTC had regard, inter alia, to the relevant regulations in the US and the EC.

---

[34] First prescribed on 26 February 1997; most recent version circulated 1 June 2001.
[35] art 42, TFTA.
[36] 20 January 2001.

In common with the broad approach taken in those jurisdictions the TFTC recognizes that intellectual property licensing 'allows licensors to gain economic benefits', and allows licensees to 'acquire use of the technology to develop new goods markets'. At the same time the use of restrictions in licences 'may lead to monopolization of the licensed technology, or further, lead to restraint of competition or to unfair competition in a manner inconsistent with the [TFTA]'. The Guidelines are very similar in form to the pre-modernization style of the EC block exemption regulations, containing first definitions, then a list of 'white' clauses that are presumed not to infringe the prohibitions of the TFTA, a list of 'black' clauses whose inclusion does infringe the TFTA, and a list of 'grey' clauses that 'may' violate the law. These are all set out below.

4-2.26 A technology licensing arrangement is defined in the Guidelines as an arrangement 'that involves the licensing of patents, know-how or a combination of the two'.[37] The 'fundamental principle' guiding the approach of the TFTC is that it will not, in reviewing technology licensing cases, presume that the owner of the intellectual property holds market power within a relevant market. In accordance with the requirement of art 47 of the TFTA any arrangement which is 'in form a proper conduct in connection with the exercise of rights' under relevant intellectual property laws cannot be subject to review and condemnation under the terms of the TFTA. Where, however, conduct takes this proper form, but 'in substance oversteps the scope of proper exercise of rights . . . and contravenes their legislative purpose of protecting invention and innovation' a full review under the standards set by the TFTA may be undertaken by the TFTC. In its assessment of the competitive effects of licensing arrangements the TFTC will have regard to competition in 'goods markets', 'technology markets', and 'innovation markets'. A technology market is defined by substitutable technology, and an innovation market as being one 'in which research and development of relevant goods may take place'.[38] Within these markets the TFTC will consider the following factors:

(1) The market power of the licensor with regards to the licensed technology.
(2) The market position of the parties in the relevant market and the status of that market.

[37] para 2(1). Patents are defined as 'invention or new utility model patents which have been obtained in accordance with the Patent Law of Taiwan' (para 2(2)). Know-how means 'methods, technologies, manufacturing processes, formulas, computer programs, designs, or other types of information that may be used in production, marketing or management which meet the following criteria: (1) The information is not generally known by those are familiar with the given area. (2) The information has actual or potential economic value because of its secret nature. (3) The owner has adopted reasonable protective measures.'

[38] para 4(2)(ii) and (iii).

(3) The degree to which the arrangement will increase opportunities for the utilization of the technology, or to which it will exclude competition.
(4) The ease of entry into the relevant market.
(5) The length of the term of the licensing arrangement, and the duration of the restrictions it contains.
(6) Any international or industry precedents applicable to the relevant market for the licensed technology.

Paragraph (5) of the Guidelines sets out a list of types of clauses in licensing arrangements which are not presumed to be anti-competitive. These are: **4-2.27**

(1) Limitations restricting the scope of use by the licensee to manufacture, use, or sell the fruits of the technology subject to the licence.
(2) Restrictions relating to the validity of the intellectual property. These may also be accepted where, through no fault of the licensor, the content of any know-how has been publicly disclosed, such that the know-how has lost its status as a trade secret. It may be presumed that this would apply only where the know-how was secret at the time of the creation of the arrangement as, if the know-how was at that point public, there would be no reason for the licensee to enter into a fee-paying, restrictive arrangement.
(3) Clauses relating to the calculation of royalty payments where, for ease of calculation, the fees are calculated on the basis of the finished quantities of the goods that are produced or sold that employ the licensed technology, or are based on the number of times that such materials or parts are used in the manufacturing process.
(4) Requirements that the licensee continue to pay royalties after the agreement has ended for any use already made of the patent. As with (2) this applies also to payments in respect of publicly disclosed know-how for the duration of the agreement.
(5) Requirements imposed on the licensee to grant non-exclusive licences to the licensor with respect to any improvements made by the licensee to the technology, or new uses developed by the licensee for that technology.
(6) Requirements that the licensee shall, to the best of its ability, manufacture and sell goods using the licensed technology.
(7) Obligations imposed on the licensee to maintain the secrecy of any intellectual property or know-how licensed.
(8) Minimum production, usage, or sale requirements imposed on the licensee.
(9) Requirements that the licensee maintain quality in terms of the goods produced, raw materials used, or component parts of the goods that employ the licensed technology.
(10) Restrictions on transferring or sub-licensing the technology.

(11) Restrictions on the continued usage of the technology or know-how post-termination of the agreement. This only applies to the extent that the technology continues to be covered by relevant intellectual property protection, or that know-how has continued to be secret.

4-2.28 Paragraph (6) sets out the 'black' clauses which are considered prima facie to be in violation of the TFTA. In particular some of these clauses are considered to be in breach of art 19 of the TFTA which relates to certain matters falling under the heading of 'unfair competition' (see below). These are:

(1) 'Arrangements between parties . . . who are in a competitive relationship, in which through contract, agreement, or other form of mutual understanding they jointly determine the price of the goods employing the licensed technology, or restrict the quantities of goods, trading partners, trading regions, or areas of research and development, thus mutually restricting each other's business activities in a manner sufficient to influence the functions of the relevant market in violation of article 14 of the [TFTA]'.

(2) Arrangements containing any of the following terms are deemed to fall within the prohibition of art 19(1)(vi) of the TFTA (see below):

- (i) Restrictions on competing activities of the parties with respect to R&D, manufacture, use, or sale of competing goods.
- (ii) Restrictions relating to marketing methods or the scope of use of the licensed technology which have as their goal market segmentation.
- (iii) Mandatory requirements imposed on the licensee to take other patents or know-how which are not needed.
- (iv) Mandatory requirements on the licensee to assign back exclusively to the licensor any improvements to the licensed patent or know-how.
- (v) Restrictions on the free use of the technology, or the imposition of royalty payments, after the patent has been extinguished, or the know-how has been publicly disclosed where this has been imputable to the licensor.
- (vi) Restrictions on the licensee's manufacture, use, or sale of competing goods, or the utilization of competing technology after the termination of the agreement.
- (vii) Restrictions on the price at which the licensee may sell the fruits of the licence.
- (viii) Restrictions on the ability of the licensee to challenge the validity of the intellectual property which forms the subject of the licence.
- (ix) Refusals by the licensor to provide the licensee with information relating to the scope, content, or valid term of a patent.

Finally, para (6) provides that where either the licensor or licensee is a monopolistic enterprise the analysis of whether any of the clauses falling on the above list shall be determined on a case-by-case basis.

The grey list is set out at para (7) of the Guidelines, and sets out conditions in the agreement which '*may* violate the law'. Paragraph 7(1) lists content that may be in violation of art 19(1)(iv) of the TFTA.[39] Five examples of such conditions are set out: 4-2.29

(1) Restrictions containing distinctions between regions in which the licensing is applicable within the territory of Taiwan during the term of the patent or the time for which the know-how remains secret.
(2) Restrictions on either the scope of sales of the trading counterparts which are unrelated to the application of the licensed technology, and restrictions on the areas or scope of the applications in which the licensee may practise the licensed technology.
(3) Upper limits on the quantities of the goods that may be produced or sold by the licensee, or on the number of times the know-how or patented technology may be used.
(4) Requirements that the licensee must sell the fruits of the licence through either the licensor or a person designated by the licensor.
(5) Royalty fees based on the quantity of a particular type of good manufactured or sold, irrespective of whether the licensed technology was used in that particular production.

Article 19 of the TFTA may also be violated where the licensee is required to purchase inputs required in the production flowing from the licensed technology where the requirement is likely to restrain or impede fair competition unless the requirement is related 'to reasonable and necessary efforts to assure effective utilization of the licensed technology, to maintain the reputation of a trademark associated with the licensed technology or to maintain the secrecy of the know-how involved'.[40] Discrimination between the conditions imposed on different licensees may also be in breach of art 19 of the TFTA. 4-2.30

Where a technology licensing arrangement contains provisions that are not listed in the Guidelines the application of the competition rules shall be considered on the basis of the context of the particular agreement in accordance with the terms of the TFTA. 4-2.31

[39] art 19(1)(iv), which is discussed below, provides, inter alia, that it is an offence to cause 'another enterprise to refrain from competing in price . . .'.
[40] para 7(2).

4-2.32 The compatibility of a licensing arrangement with art 14 of the TFTA was considered in the case of *CD-R Patent Licensing Arrangements in Taiwan by Royal Philips Electronics, Sony Corporation (Japan) and Taiyo Yuden Co Ltd (Japan)*.[41] Philips, Sony, and Taiyo Yuden each owned a number of patents relating to CD-R technology. A licensing arrangement was entered into under which the latter two companies first licensed their rights to Philips, which in turn bundled the rights together for onward licensing. A complaint was filed with the TFTC alleging a number of unlawful licensing practices in Taiwan, and the TFTC stated that the following practices were called into question: (1) joint licensing and package licensing by the respondents; (2) the method by which the respondents set royalties;[42] (3) blanket licensing under which the terms of some of the patents were shorter than the contractual period; (4) alleged improper tie-in sales of various patents under the blanket licensing; (5) refusal to disclose important trading information such as details of the licensing arrangement. The TFTC found that the system of joint licensing of the relevant patents was a concerted arrangement within the terms of art 14. The three participants in the joint scheme would not individually license the technologies, and all applicants for licences were referred to Philips which offered only the bundled licence. The parties had also agreed on the royalties to be charged for the bundled licence. Thus the TFTC held that 'by giving up their separate licensing rights under the arrangement [the respondents] left prospective licensees in the position of being able to turn only to Philips for licensing, and deprived them of the opportunity to freely select their trading counterparts'. The agreement on royalty payments 'furthermore thwarted prospective licensees' opportunities to pursue more favourable terms' such that 'the arrangement . . . thereby adversely affected the market function of supply and demand with respect to the patented CD-R technology at issue'. Noting that the prohibition of art 14 against concerted actions was 'relatively strict', and that the parties had failed to apply for an exemption as set out in the article, the TFTC found that the joint licensing arrangement constituted a breach of the art 14 prohibition. A breach of art 10 was also established, with the TFTC finding that Philips had used its dominant position to unfairly dictate contract terms, and had failed to provide information to the licensees that should properly have been disclosed.[43] The companies were ordered 'to immediately cease the illegal practices', and penalties totalling NT$14 million were imposed.

41 20 April 2006.

42 The issue of the licence fee levels required was considered under art 10, TFTA, and is discussed in Chapter 4-3, below.

43 See Chapter 4-3, below.

Unfair Competition as it Relates to Horizontal and Vertical Agreements

Chapter III of the TFTA deals with 'unfair competition', and contains within it a wide range of proscriptions, relating to both terms of trade and to unilateral business activities such as passing-off and intellectual property infringements, and in particular, with the control of some aspects of vertical agreements. Although some of the substantive rules of this part of the Act do not fall within a definition of 'antitrust' that would be recognized in the EC or US, and are not therefore discussed here, some matters are relevant to antitrust analysis (as has been discussed above in relation to, for example, technology licensing). In particular arts 18 and 19 of the TFTA are 'antitrust' provisions, and are discussed here.[44] **4-2.33**

All provisions of Chapter III of the Act are addressed to all enterprises, whatever their size. The article itself does not on its face create a system of efficiency justification or review, or set procedures by which to determine that the conduct specified is, in each individual case, anti-competitive. There is, however, provision in the Enforcement Rules to the Fair Trade Act that makes it clear that it is not necessarily the case that all conduct falling within the examples given will be automatically illegal. However, breach of some of the provisions will be treated as a *per se* infringement, with no procedures set by which an efficiency defence could be mounted. **4-2.34**

Article 18 provides for the illegality of agreements under which a purchaser of goods for resale may not enter into an agreement with the supplier which fixes the prices of those goods. This applies both to 'trading counterparts', and to other third parties who in turn purchase from the trading counterparts. It is notable that this provision applies to *all* forms of price setting at the vertical level, whether maximum or minimum pricing terms are applied. Quite simply, art 18 states that '*any* agreement contrary to this provision shall be void'.[45] An example of the application of art 18 may be found in the case of *Bristol-Myers Squibb Australia Pty*[46] in which the TFTC found that a violation of art 18 had occurred as a result of the restrictions on the resale price of milk powder imposed on distributors by Bristol-Myers and Nestlé. The companies had set resale prices to be charged by pharmacies for the powdered milk, and had then refused to supply those who breached **4-2.35**

---

[44] Articles 20–22 relate to what would more normally be referred to as fair trading matters, covering such practices as the use of trade names, trade marks, branding or packaging, false or misleading misrepresentations or false statements about other businesses.

[45] Emphasis added.

[46] *Restrictions on the Resale Price of Milk Powder by Bristol-Myers Squibb Australia Pty Ltd (Taiwan Branch) and Nestlé Ltd (Taiwan Branch)*, *TFTC Competition Policy Newsletter*, 4:11, 31 August 2007.

those set prices. The TFTC carried out on-site inquiries at more than ten counties and cities, and interviewed both resellers and pharmacies. Penalties of NT$6,500,000 were imposed on the two companies.[47] A breach of this provision may be found where the restriction is in the form of a 'request' rather than a contractual obligation. Thus in *Taiwan Salt Industrial Co Ltd*[48] the enterprise was condemned for issuing letters to franchisees and distributors requesting them to follow resale price restraints. In practice, whether a requested, suggested, or recommended resale price would be a violation of the TFTA is subject to a review of its potential 'binding effect'. The TFTC will therefore review whether the trading counterparties would be treated disadvantageously if they decided not to follow the suggestion or recommendation.

4-2.36 Article 19 contains within it six prohibitions:

(1) Causing an enterprise to cease supplies to, purchases from, or trading with another enterprise in order to harm the latter. This would extend therefore both to actions such as collective boycotts in the enforcement of cartels, or refusals of supply to A by a company with market power in order to persuade A not to take supplies from B in order to exclude B from the market. Although the provision applies to all enterprises, it is most likely to be applied to enterprises with market power, as in the absence of market power it is less likely that the enterprise would be in a position to coerce a trading partner to its strategy.

(2) 'Treating another enterprise discriminatively without justification'. This would apply equally to discriminatory terms accepted by trading partners as part of an agreement or system of agreements, or to terms imposed unilaterally by enterprises with market power. There is no limitation set in the provision in terms of the nature of the discrimination, such that the article makes it unlawful to discriminate on, for example, price, delivery terms, quantities supplied, the quality of the goods or services, and of the service offered to the

[47] See also *Champion Building Material Co Ltd and Sanyo Pottery & Porcelain Co Ltd*, (21 December 2006, *TFTC Competition Policy Newsletter*, 2:11, 30 April 2007). Here the two enterprises required their downstream distributors to sell products according to list prices. The report of the Decision states that:

> . . . an enterprise shall allow its trading counterparts to decide on sales prices freely. Thus, if an enterprise sets limitations on the resale prices of its products and takes measures to request trading counterparts to follow them, such an act of restraining downstream business operators' trading activities has already deprived the downstream business operators of their freedom to decide on prices according to their own cost structure and market competition and has therefore weakened the price competition among different sales operators within the same brand. This type of act is expressly prohibited in the Fair Trade Law.

In this case the enterprises were ordered to cease their illegal activity and were each fined NT$720,000.

[48] 18 January 2007, *TFTC Competition Policy Newsletter*, 2:11, 30 April 2007.

trading partner. While there is no clarification provided for within the article, justifications would exist on terms similar to those in the EC and the US, and would extend therefore to any objectively justifiable factor, such as differences in cost savings due to economies of scale in delivery if size orders varied, or differences in credit terms based on the creditworthiness of the customer. Article 26 of the Enforcement Rules to the Fair Trade Act specifies that, along with 'other reasonable grounds', the following factors shall be considered when determining whether there is just cause for the imposition of discriminatory terms: (1) supply and demand conditions on the market; (2) cost differences; (3) transaction amounts; and (4) credit risks.

(3) 'Causing the trading counterpart(s) or its competitors to do business with itself by coercion, inducement with interest, or other improper means'. In the EC and US such conduct might be caught within abuse of dominance or monopolization provisions, but the range of conduct that might fall to be condemned in the Taiwanese system is greater than that in the EC and US. Along with paragraph (4) breach of this provision could also constitute breach of the Taiwan Criminal Code, art 304 of which makes coercion a criminal offence.

(4) Causing another party to refrain from price competition, or to take part in a merger, by coercion, inducement with interest, or other improper means. It is surprising that this general prohibition, which in effect condemns the use of improper means to achieve an anti-competitive end is limited only to price competition and to mergers. It would be equally harmful to coerce another enterprise to a market sharing arrangement, but this would not be caught by art 19(4). The limitation on price competition proscribed by this provision would also be illegal under art 14 TFTA, which does not exempt arrangements from the prohibition based on the degree of pressure on an enterprise to participate in the arrangement.

(5) Paragraph 5 prohibits the acquisition of trade secrets, such as information relating to sales and production, or technology, by improper means. This is the only express prohibition on information exchange within the TFTA, although there may be situations in which art 14 would apply to the exchange of information which supported concerted actions. It is unclear whether the term 'improper means' in art 19(5) would extend to information exchanged freely for the purposes of an anti-competitive end, but such a reading of the article would appear to be too wide. It is also a breach of art 317 of the Criminal Code of Taiwan to disclose industrial or commercial secrets obtained in the course of employment, such that any company officer or employee disclosing such information could also be open to prosecution. Article 19(5) is better viewed as part of the law of unfair competition, and is aimed at preventing an enterprise from competing with another by unfair, or

indeed illegal, means, such as by infringing a competitor's trade secrets. Information sharing among competitors is subject to the law of art 7 (above).

(6) 'Limiting its trading counterparts' business activity improperly by means of the requirements of business engagement'. This paragraph would apply, inter alia, to vertical arrangements in which the contracts imposed unacceptable limitations on, for example, territorial activity, or terms of resale. This is made clear in art 27 of the Enforcement Rules to the Fair Trade Act, which states that 'restrictions . . . refers to the circumstances under which an enterprise engages in restrictive activity in regards to tie-ins, exclusive dealing, territory, customers, use or otherwise'. In making an assessment of the reasonableness of any restriction falling within art 19(6) the TFTC will have regard to 'the totality of such factors as the intent, purposes, and market position of the parties, the structure of the market to which they belong, the characteristics of the goods, and the impact that carrying out such restrictions would have on market competition'.[49] Article 19(6) has been employed to condemn bundling of products by the Taiwan Tobacco and Liquor Corp when the company implemented a measure under which distributors were required to purchase five new brands of cigarettes before they were allowed supplies of the best-selling Long Life Gentle (*sic*) brand. At the time of the action there was a disruption in the market due to an anticipated tax increase, which resulted in panic buying. The TFTC held that the relative importance of the Long Life Gentle brand was such that customers would be 'forced to buy the new cigarette brands so as to avail themselves of preferential endorsements for buying the old cigarette brand, and not because conditions such as the quality and price of the new cigarette brands were used as factors for making the trade decision'.[50]

In practice however there have been few cases in which art 19 has been applied so as to condemn either vertical agreements in their entirety, or clauses within vertical agreements.[51]

4-2.37 The TFTC has published very short guidelines, '*Consideration of the Likelihood of Impeding Fair Competition*', which relate to the application of art 19. This guidance distinguishes between acts which may be automatically assumed to be illegal,

[49] art 27, Enforcement Rules.

[50] 21 September 2006, *TFTC Competition Policy Newsletter*, 6:10, 21 December 2006. A NT$3.01 million penalty was set in this case.

[51] As well as the cases mentioned above, the OECD *Peer Review* cites two decisions in which suppliers to large department stores were precluded under the sales contract from supplying products to defined competing outlets (see OECD, n 1, above, at 19).

such as those falling within paras (3), (4), and (5), which as noted above may in some cases also constitute breaches of the Taiwan Criminal Code, and those acts in respect of which 'the unfairness . . . is not obvious', and which are therefore to be subject to a more sensitive competitive scrutiny. The aim of any scrutiny is to determine 'whether or not the results increase or decrease competition in the marketplace'. The TFTC states that it is not necessary in order to condemn such an action for it to show that there has already been harm to competition, but rather that such harm is likely. First it has to be determined whether the action may impair competition, and secondly, economic analysis will proceed by the 'reasonableness principle' in order to determine whether in fact fair competition has been or would be impeded.

Article 24 of the TFTA is the last substantive provision of the TFTA, and provides **4-2.38** that in addition to any other proscriptions of the Act, 'no enterprise shall otherwise have any deceptive or obviously unfair conduct that is liable to affect the trading order'. The TFTC has published Guidelines dealing with this provision, which clarifies the relationship between art 24 and other rules dealing with consumer protection.[52] The TFTC states in the Guidelines that the key element of this provision is the requirement that the conduct be 'sufficient to affect the trading order'. The TFTC has also stated that where any other provision of the TFTA is sufficient to establish the illegality of an act then art 24 will not be applied, but that 'if those specific provisions fail to evaluate the alleged unlawful act in its entirety [there will] be room for the supplementary application of art 24'.[53] Generally it is clear from the wording of the Guidelines that art 24 only applies to matters falling within the 'fair trade' rubric of the TFTA, rather than within the antitrust provisions. However, the final part of the Guidelines makes reference to 'abusing an advantageous market position to engage in unfair trade'. This final paragraph calls attention to situations in which as a result of holding an 'information asymmetry or other relative trading disadvantage' the enterprise engages in unfair trade. Examples given are those in which the enterprise

> provides imperfect substitutes for basic necessities or services or does business in a matter contrary to business ethics or public order and good morals during a time when market mechanisms failed and market supply and demand are not in equilibrium.

A second example is that where conduct is 'obviously unfair . . . resulting from **4-2.39** non-transparency of information'. The TFTC has been criticized for overreliance

[52] *Principles Governing the Application of Article 24 of the Fair Trade Act*, circulated by Order 0910000252, 9 January 2002.
[53] para 2.

on the use of art 24 in cases in which it has not had sufficient evidence to proceed on the basis of the more conventional antitrust elements of the TFTA.[54]

4-2.40 An example of the operation of art 24 may be found in a decision taken by the TFTC when it condemned three milk producers for simultaneously raising prices. The language used by the TFTC is not always that of standard antitrust analysis. A statement by the TFTC in its report of the Decision to the effect that 'each enterprise in each industry shall on their own initiative consider each operating cost and condition in relation to its business and reflect on the changes in the prices of products . . . for the purpose of mutual competition' is an approach that is not unusual. However, more idiosyncratically the TFTC noted that 'in terms of the spirit of the [TFTA] the enterprises had the obligation to prevent the increase in prices from happening. Nevertheless they did not prevent the phenomenon from happening: instead, they went against the essence and spirit of free competition.' Penalties totalling NT$11,500,000 were imposed. There is no evidence in the report of the Decision to suggest that the parties concerted in raising prices, and in fact price rises were announced after the Council of Agriculture raised the price it paid for the purchase of milk.[55] In another case the TFTC found that six sand and gravel companies were in breach of art 24 when they had hoarded their products in response to an announcement by China that it was to cease exports. This 'malicious' hoarding enabled the companies to benefit from price rises as a result of the imbalance between supply and demand of sand and gravel in Taiwan. There was no evidence reported by the TFTC of a concerted action amongst the suppliers, and none of them individually held market power. However, the fact that the conduct 'seriously affected the trading order and was ethically reprehensible' resulted in condemnation and the imposition of penalties.[56]

Penalties for Breach

4-2.41 The system of penalties established under the TFTA is discussed in Chapter 4-5. In brief, the TFTC may order that any breach of the substantive provisions of the TFTA be brought to an end, and may impose penalties of up

[54] The OECD *Peer Review*, for example, found that:

> The catch-all general provision, art 24, has been used extensively, often with a consumer-protection emphasis. The [TFTC] relies upon this article where the evidence is not sufficient to demonstrate a violation of more specific statutory prohibitions. . . . Courts are challenging excessive reliance on art 24 on the grounds that it is too vague and thus leaves too much to the [TFTC]'s discretion. (OECD, n 1, above, at 25).

[55] *Uni-President Enterprises Corporation, Wei Chuan Corp and Kuang Chuan Dairy Co Ltd, TFTC Competition Policy Newsletter*, 5:11, 31 October 2007.

[56] 29 May 2006, *TFTC Competition Policy Newsletter*, 4:10, 31 August 2006. Another 11 companies in the same market had been condemned for precisely the same actions in May 2006.

to NT$25 million on infringing parties.[57] Where any order to amend conduct is not complied with further penalties may be successively imposed. In some cases breaches of art 14 may result in the imposition of penalties of up to NT$100 million, or terms of imprisonment of up to three years.[58]

[57] art 40, TFTA.
[58] art 35, TFTA.

4-3

TAIWAN MONOPOLY AND ABUSE OF DOMINANCE

Introduction	4-3.01	Remedies and penalties	4-3.12
Assessing dominance	4-3.03	Case examples	4-3.13
Abusive conduct	4-3.07		

Introduction

The law relating to monopoly conduct in Taiwan is set out in art 10 of the TFTA, which provides that: **4-3.01**

> No monopolistic enterprises shall:
> (1) directly or indirectly prevent any other enterprises from competing by unfair means;
> (2) improperly set, maintain or change the price for goods or the remuneration for services;
> (3) make a trading counterpart give preferential treatment without justification; or
> (4) otherwise abuse its market power.

There are no further provisions in the legislation which clarify the conduct proscribed by this article, and no guidelines have been published in relation to monopoly conduct generally, although some further guidance may be obtained from case law which is discussed below. Further rules relating to the determination of whether an enterprise is monopolistic are set out in arts 5 and 5-1 of the TFTA, and in the Enforcement Rules to the Fair Trade Act of 2002, and are discussed below. **4-3.02**

Assessing dominance

Articles 5 and 5-1 of the TFTA give guidance as to the meaning of the term 'monopolistic enterprise', although there is no further guidance published relating to the assessment of relevant markets or the determination of market power within a market. Article 5 provides that a monopolistic enterprise is one which **4-3.03** 'faces no competition or has a dominant position to enable it to exclude competition in a relevant market'. Although it is not specified on the face of the legislation the exclusion of competition need not be absolute for the monopoly status to be determined. The second paragraph of art 5 extends this definition to situations of collective dominance, providing that: '[t]wo or more enterprises shall be deemed monopolistic enterprises if they do not in fact engage in price competition with each other', and where as a whole they have the same status as is required for the satisfaction of the first paragraph.[1] The term 'relevant market' is defined in the third paragraph of art 5 as being 'a geographic area or a coverage wherein enterprises compete in respect of particular goods or services'. The more normal practice in relation to geographic markets is for the TFTC to find that markets are national in scope, but there are examples of narrower regional markets being established.[2]

4-3.04 Article 5-1 expands on art 5, incorporating both concentration ratio and *de minimis* limitations on the operation of art 5. It states that:

> An enterprise shall not be deemed a monopolistic enterprise as defined in [art 5] if none of the following circumstances exist:
> (1) the market share of the enterprise in a relevant market reaches one-half of the market;
> (2) the combined market share of two enterprises in a relevant market reaches two-thirds of the market; and
> (3) the combined market share of three enterprises in a relevant market reaches three-fourths of the market.
> Under any of the circumstances set forth in the preceding paragraph, where the market share of any individual enterprise does not reach one-tenth of the relevant market or where its total sales in the preceding fiscal year are less than one billion New Taiwan Dollars, such enterprise shall not be deemed as a monopolistic enterprise.

4-3.05 However, the final paragraph of art 5-1 gives the TFTC the power to revoke this exception in any particular case if either it, or the goods or services it provides, is 'subject to legal or technological restraints, or there exists any other circumstance under which the supply and demand of the market are affected and the ability of others to compete is impeded'.

4-3.06 Articles 3 and 4 of the Enforcement Rules to the Fair Trade Act of 2002 set out in brief further considerations relating to the assessment of whether an enterprise is a monopoly. Article 3 sets out factors which 'shall' be taken into consideration,

---

[1] It has been reported that although the TFTA appears to apply to situations of 'oligopoly coordination and interdependence', the TFTC has not, in practice, 'applied this law to such a situation' (OECD, *Chinese Taipei—Peer Review of Competition Law and Policy 2006*, OECD, 2006, p 20).

[2] See for example *The Great Taipei Gas Corp* (9 May 2000), discussed below, in which the relevant geographic market was that of Greater Taipei.

but does not eliminate the possibility that, in relevant circumstances, other factors too may be considered. The factors set out in art 3 are: (1) the market share; (2) the possibility of demand side or supply side substitution to the goods or services 'giving regard to considerations of time and place'; (3) 'the ability of the enterprise to influence prices in a particular market'; (4) the existence of 'formidable difficulties' in relation to entry into the market by competitors; and (5) the role of imports and exports. In calculating the market share of the enterprise alleged to be a monopolist art 4 provides that:

> Production, sales, inventory, and import/export value (volume) data for the enterprise and the particular market shall be taken into account when calculating the market share of an enterprise.

Such data may either be that obtained by the TFTC during the course of its investigations, or may be obtained from other government departments.

Abusive conduct

The wording of art 10 of the TFTA is more specific than that of s 2 of the Sherman Act in that it does provide some indication of the nature of the condemned conduct, but is less specific than that of art 82 EC, and the examples given are of a general nature. Aside from the catch-all rubric of art 10(4) the provisions relate to (1) exclusionary conduct; (2) pricing, which is drafted so broadly as to extend to any form of monopoly pricing, both exclusionary and exploitative;[3] and (3) extracting unreasonably beneficial discriminatory terms from trading counterparts. While the language and structure of this provision may be unfamiliar, the range of conduct the various parts of the article may extend to includes most, if not all, of the abusive practices that may be caught by art 82 EC. **4-3.07**

Exclusionary conduct has been condemned where refusals to supply, or to quote prices for, products were intended to deprive a competitor of customers. In requiring dominant suppliers to supply new customers, or at least to quote a price at which they would be prepared to supply, the TFTC has taken an approach very similar to that under the controversial essential facilities doctrine to which reference is made in Chapter 1-2.[4] Refusals to supply may also be condemned under art 10(4).[5] **4-3.08**

---

[3] TFTC press release 0307, 27 February 2003, discussed below. Having put Microsoft under pressure to lower prices in this case the TFTC stated in the press release that it 'fully respected the mechanism of the market economy', and that the modification to prices was 'in line with the legislative purposes of the [TFTA]'.

[4] See *Wen Chiu Inc/China Petroleum Corporation*, 12 October 2000, discussed below.

[5] This was the case in *Chinese Petroleum Corporation*, 7 March 2002, where a refusal to consider a request to renew a supply contract on its expiration by the dominant supplier was condemned.

4-3.09 Exploitative pricing has been condemned by the TFTC in a number of cases, including *The Great Taipei Gas Corp*[6] and it is clear from these and from the approach of the TFTC in the Microsoft Corp settlement that the approach to excessive pricing is similar to that in the EC, as opposed to that in the US where there is no relevant antitrust law in this area (see Chapter 1-2). This approach has also been applied in relation to intellectual property licensing in *CD-R Patent Licensing Arrangements*[7] and it appears that the TFTC may be more interventionist in regulating pricing than is the EC Commission in the application of art 82 EC. In this case, which was a complex one involving several heads of jurisdiction, the TFTC established that the respondents were in a monopoly position in respect of CD-R technology, and that their profits would 'far exceed their initial forecasts'. The TFTC held that 'by maintaining their royalty prices and failing to allow efficacious adjustments in response to changing market demand, the respondents violated the prohibition'.[8]

4-3.10 Discriminatory treatment may also be condemned, but is permitted if it is justifiable. In *Chinese Petroleum Corp* for example the dominant supplier operating a franchise system in respect of gas stations provided different kinds of service to different franchisees, and also varied the amounts of the performance bonds which were collected as a surety from the stations. A complaint alleging a breach of art 10 was rejected, with the TFTC in part stating that this was standard business practice in the retail sector, and did not constitute unlawful preferential treatment. The same company however was found to have engaged in discriminatory

---

6 9 May 2000 (see below).

7 *CD-R Patent Licensing Arrangements in Taiwan by Royal Philips Electronics, Sony Corporation (Japan) and Taiyo Yuden Co Ltd (Japan)* (2002). See Williams, M, *Competition Policy and Law in China, Hong Kong and Taiwan* (Cambridge: Cambridge University Press, 2005) at 402:

> The [TFTC] has been criticised in relation to its decision in [the 2002] case, in that one of the main bases of the decision appears to be an idea that the price demanded by the intellectual property owners for the relevant licenses was excessive. Not only is the interface between competition law and intellectual property rights an extremely contentious one but the [TFTC] appears to have adopted a very narrow definition of the relevant market, excluding potentially close substitute storage media. Consequently, a finding of dominance in relation to this narrowly defined market was relatively easy. The decision has also been criticised on the basis that it clearly favoured domestic hardware manufacturers over the interests of foreign intellectual property owners, a suspicion being that the [TFTC] may often have unduly favoured domestic business interests over those of foreign intellectual property owners.

See also Shieh, M-Y, 'A discussion of the relationship between the patent law and the Fair Trade Law in Taiwan with a review of the *Phillips CD-R* decisions', in Hwang, T-L and Chen, C (eds), *The Future Development of Competition Framework*, (The Hague: Kluwer Law International, 2004).

Note that similar concerns have been expressed in relation to the potential operation of art 55 of the Chinese Anti-Monopoly Law (see Chapter 2-3, above).

8 It is highly unlikely that a price set by a patent holder would be challenged in the EC, although there has been some discussion in case law as to the reasonableness of licence terms generally.

pricing in breach of art 10(2) when it imposed discriminatory prices against distributors in Southern Taiwan in respect of products in which it had market power, where it determined that these had purchased other products from its competitors.[9]

As is to be anticipated, the approach taken to refusals to supply in the application of art 10(4) is a wide one. In *CD-R Patent Licensing*[10] the TFTC considered in some detail licensing terms imposed by Philips which as a result of a concerted action held control over key patents in relation to CD-R technology, and found that Philips exploited a dominant position on the market by refusing to disclose important trading information. In full the TFTC stated that: 4-3.11

> . . . Philips, taking advantage of its dominant position in the market for CD-R technology, withheld key trading information including detailed information regarding the content of the patents, their scope, and their duration, demanded that licensees execute the disputed licensing contract, and began seeking back royalties. The disputed licensing agreement also required that licensees withdraw their negotiating patent licensing matters with CD-R manufacturers, offered blanket licensing of nearly 100 patents without offering any licensing on a patent-by-patent basis, and specified only the numbers and names of the patents at issue as registered in the United States and Japan. It utterly failed to disclose whether any corresponding patents existed in other countries and the terms of the foreign patents, and also failed to state concretely the patents that individual firms might be able to use in specific products and the scopes of such patents. It demanded that local firms sign licensing agreements under this blanket offer and pay enormous royalties.
>
> In the CD-R technology patent licensing market, Philips, Sony, and Taiyo Yuden constitute a monopoly as defined in the Fair Trade Act. Under the three firms' joint licensing arrangement . . . Philips took advantage of its dominant position in the CD-R technology patent licensing market and of Sony's and Taiyo's names. It demanded that licensees sign the contexts licensing agreement and sought payment of royalties outright while at the same time refusing to provide the licensees with important trading information . . . Philips also demanded that the licensees withdraw any invalidation actions against the patents at issue before signing the licensing agreement. Philips was obviously relying on its advantageous market position to compel the licensees to accept the licensing agreement.

This pattern of behaviour was found to be in breach of art 10(4).

Remedies and penalties

The approach to remedies and penalties in the enforcement of the TFTA is discussed in Chapter 4-5. In brief, art 41 of the TFTA gives the TFTC broad powers to require those in breach of the law to bring the infringement to an end, and to 4-3.12

[9] 7 March 2002.

[10] Above. In August 2005 the High Administrative Court overturned the decision taken by the TFTC.

impose penalties of up to NT$25 million. Breaches of obligations imposed under art 41 may give rise to imprisonment or to fines of up to NT$100 million. As is clear from the Microsoft case discussed below the TFTC may also enter into administrative settlements as an alternative to pursuing a case to a formal infringement decision.

Case examples

4-3.13 There are few cases falling under art 10 of which details are available in English, in part perhaps because some cases that might be dealt with as breaches of art 10 may also be dealt with as breaches of the fair competition provisions of the Act, which are discussed at Chapter 4-2, and it is not always clear from the material which is available which of the possibly applicable provisions are being applied in those cases about which comment is available.

4-3.14 In *Wen Chui Inc/China Petroleum Corporation*[11] the complainant had requested price quotations relating to the supply of aviation fuel from China Petroleum which at the time was the only company licensed, in the context of a liberalization process, to sell aviation fuel. The complainant intended to provide refuelling services to aircraft, but was unable to do so. The TFTC found that the approach of China Petroleum was 'plainly a delaying tactic that it employed to force a competitor's trading counterpart to trade with itself'. Although China Petroleum had by the time the TFTC considered the complaint entered into agreements to provide fuelling services to all of the domestic airlines, the TFTC noted that 'any airline could have concluded a refuelling agreement with another company if that airline had terminated its agreement with China Petroleum'. The TFTC found that China Petroleum was in breach of art 10(1) of the TFTA, ordered it to terminate the infringement, and imposed a penalty of NT$5 million. The circumstances under which the US or EC antitrust authorities are prepared to compel a monopolist to supply a new customer are greatly limited, but it is noteworthy that one area where such obligations have been imposed in the EC is in the context of newly liberalized industries, where monopolies may be an historical legacy of regulation, rather than the result of private investment in a competitive environment.

4-3.15 One case to receive wide coverage is that of the administrative settlement agreement entered into between the TFTC and Microsoft and its affiliates.[12] The main concern in this case at the outset was that Microsoft was engaged in 'monopoly pricing', under its unified worldwide pricing policy. The scope of concern widened however, and the final settlement included sections on: (1) pricing of

---

[11] 12 October 2000.

[12] TFTC press release 0307, 27 February 2003.

Microsoft software products for consumers and academic users; (2) promoting consumer interests; (3) facilitating intra-brand competition; (4) after-sale services for Microsoft products; (5) reasonable sharing of software code; and (6) implementation of the US consent decree in Taiwan. The agreement also contained a dispute resolution mechanism. In response to the pricing concerns Microsoft committed to reduce its prices by an average of 26.7 per cent, with the largest cut being one of 54.5 per cent. The settlement also addressed bundling, with Microsoft agreeing to supply sufficient quantities of the individual software applications making up the Office XP suite so as to allow consumers to purchase the components separately if they wished, and to make English language supplies available if there were insufficient Chinese versions to meet demand. Microsoft also undertook to negotiate with the Government regarding the sharing of its source code, and to 'positively and actively consider accepting applications from local IT companies to participate in Microsoft's Enterprise Shared Source Program'.

Exploitative pricing was also condemned in the first monopoly case to be dealt **4-3.16**
with by the TFTC on the basis of art 10. This was the case of *The Great Taipei Gas Corp*[13] in which Taipei Gas was investigated following concerns relating to the nature of the gas meters it installed at customers' premises. Gas meters were supplied in two grades each of which had basic set monthly usage. If a customer's usage was below that set, they would still be obliged to pay a fee set at the usage level. The larger grade meters were supplied even where it was clear that usage would not meet the level set on the billing system, with the effect that many customers paid more than was necessary. The proportion of the larger flow meters installed by gas providers ranged from 1.77 per cent to 13.99 per cent, but for Great Taipei the proportion was nearly 70 per cent. The TFTC found that the company had 'used its distinctive market position as a monopolistic enterprise to install the higher flow rate . . . meters in order to increase the quantity of customers paying the higher basic monthly fee and thereby to obtain improper gains over a long period of time'. A breach of art 10(2) of the TFTA was found to have occurred, with the company being fined NT$5m. The company was also ordered to set the monthly basic fee for customers with the larger flow meters at the level of the lower flow meter where the lower flow meter would have been adequate for the customer's needs.

[13] Sometimes translated as the '*Taipei Metropolitan Gas Company Case*' (see, eg Liu, LS, 'Fostering Competition Law and Policy: A Façade of Taiwan's Political Economy' (2002) *Washington University Global Studies Law Review*, vol 1, (1 & 2), 77 at 114).

4-4

TAIWAN MERGER CONTROL

Introduction	4-4.01
Jurisdiction	4-4.06
'Foreign mergers'	4-4.11
Procedures	4-4.13
Pre-merger contacts and review	4-4.13
Notification	4-4.14
Application of the Substantive Test	4-4.20
General review	4-4.21
Market definition	4-4.24
Market power assessment	4-4.25
Horizontal mergers	4-4.26
Vertical mergers	4-4.30
Conglomerate mergers	4-4.31
Efficiencies and the failing firm defence	4-4.32
The case record	4-4.34
Remedies and Penalties	4-4.38

Introduction

Taiwan has a well-developed system of merger control, the primary rules for which are set out in the TFTA at arts 11–13, which are supplemented by provisions in the Enforcement Rules to the Fair Trade Act of 2002, and are clarified in a number of guidelines, cited here as appropriate.[1] The terms of the Act may apply to joint-ventures as well as to full structural mergers. The term 'merger' itself, which is the one used in the legislation, is defined at art 6 of the TFTA, and refers to any situation: **4-4.01**

(1) where an enterprise and another enterprise are merged into one;
(2) where an enterprise holds or acquires the shares or capital contributions of another enterprise to an extent of more than one-third of the total voting shares or total capital of such other enterprise;[2]

[1] For alternative coverage of the Taiwan merger regime see Franck, SM and Hwang, C, in Dabbah, MM and Lasok, P, *Merger Control Worldwide* (Cambridge: Cambridge University Press, 2005) vol 2, 1212–25, and Liu, LS-L, in Rowley, JW and Baker, DI, *International Mergers: The Antitrust Process*, Looseleaf (Sweet & Maxwell) Chapter 58.

[2] It is further provided in this respect that: 'In computing the shares or capital contributions [referred to here], the shares or capital contributions of another enterprise held or acquired by an enterprise(s) controlled by, controlling, or affiliated with the acquiring enterprise under

(3) where an enterprise is assigned by or leases from another enterprise the whole or the major part of the business or properties of such other enterprise;
(4) where an enterprise operates jointly with another enterprise on a regular basis or is entrusted by another enterprise to operate the latter's business;[3] or
(5) where an enterprise directly or indirectly controls the business operation or the appointment or discharge of personnel of another enterprise.[4]

4-4.02 The term 'enterprise' is a wide one, extending to any company form, partnership, sole-trader/proprietor, and trade associations, although the latter are unlikely to be involved in situations giving rise to a merger within the meaning of the Act.[5]

4-4.03 The TFTC has substantial powers of review over mergers falling within its jurisdiction, and a significant arsenal of remedies may be employed if it deems it necessary to do so.

---

subparagraph 2 shall be included'. In response to a request for clarification of the methods of determining whether the circumstances set out in art 6(2) pertain, the TFTC held that the proper method was 'to divide the sum of voting shares (or capital) of the company to be merged by the sum of shares (or capital) controlled (or to be controlled) respectively by the companies (and their parents and affiliates) entering into the combination'. The TFTC pointed out that different approaches might be taken under company law and under the TFTA as the purposes of the two regimes were different (11 November 1998). Changes in the amount of a share holding may lead to this provision being invoked. Thus where a company holds a 19.5% stake in another, and then plans the purchase of a further block of shares taking its holding to over one-third of the total voting shares approval of the TFTC must be sought (see, eg *Uni-President Enterprises Corporation/The Tait Group of Companies* (18 October 2007)).

[3] Under this rubric it is not necessary that there be an actual exchange of assets or a formal acquisition of Party A by Party B. In *Sin Tai Bei Cable System Co Ltd/Li Guan Cable System Co Ltd/Da An Wen Shan Cable System Co Ltd/Wan Hsiang Cable System Co Ltd* (1 April 2004) the TFTC condemned and imposed administrative fines in the amount of NT$500,000 on each of four telecommunications companies which were found to have engaged in frequent business transactions which 'were not in the nature of normal business transactions among enterprises in the same industry', and instead met the criteria for the application of art 6(1)(4), TFTA. The effect of the actions undertaken by the companies was therefore in part to have implemented a merger without the required prior approval of the TFTC in violation of art 11(1), TFTA (see below). In *National Petroleum Corporation* (13 September 2007) the TFTC found that a merger had taken place without the proper notification having been made when the National Petroleum Corporation had taken a role as managing director of the Formosa Petroleum Corporation. National was ordered to file a merger report or adopt corrections within three months, and a penalty of NT$1,000,000 was imposed.

[4] The TFTC may make a distinction between control *de jure* and control *de facto*. In *Far Eastern Department Stores* (21 December 2006) the TFTC dealt with a merger situation in which Far Eastern and its subsidiary acquired 54.45 per cent of the shares of Pacific Circulation Investment, which in turn owned more than half of the shares in Pacific SOGO Department Stores Co Ltd. The TFTC found that Far Eastern therefore had 'control of possession' and 'legal control' over Pacific Circulation, such that it could control shareholders' meetings and the board of directors, and could also indirectly control the business operations and personnel appointments of Pacific SOGO through the parent/subsidiary relationship between Pacific Circulation and Pacific SOGO.

[5] art 2, TFTA.

The merger provisions of the TFTA are general ones, and there are no special regimes extending to particular sectors. There are some limitations on the acquisition of Taiwan enterprises in certain sectors by foreign companies, and a general prohibition on investment from China into Taiwan.[6] **4-4.04**

The merger provisions have been substantially amended in terms of jurisdictional scope since first enacted, at which time far too many innocuous mergers were brought under the notification requirements. In particular franchise arrangements often fell to be notified as mergers depending on the size of the franchisor, such that the figures for the earlier years of merger control in Taiwan show a level of activism that would not properly reflect the degree of control exercised.[7] **4-4.05**

Jurisdiction

The core rules relating to jurisdiction are setout in art 11 of the TFTA, which contains both market share and turnover thresholds, the latter being determined from time to time by the TFTC. A division is made between non-financial and financial enterprises in the turnover threshold.[8] Where any merger meets the thresholds set notification is compulsory. The market share thresholds are that: (1) as a result of the merger the enterprise(s) will have a market share of at least one-third of the relevant market; or (2) one of the enterprises involved in the merger has a market share of at least one-quarter. The second requirement does not stipulate that the enterprise with at least a 25 per cent market share must be merging with a competitor, so the situation can arise where a merger is notifiable even when it leads to no increase in any market share of the parties. In such a case however **4-4.06**

[6] The limitations on foreign acquisitions of or investment in Taiwan industry sectors are set out in a Negative List for Investment by Overseas Chinese and Foreign Nationals, issued under the authority of the Statute for Investment by Foreign Nationals and Statute for Investment by Overseas Chinese.

[7] In 2002 Liu wrote that:

> In Taiwan's merger control regime, concerns with fairness seem to occupy a prominent position as concerns the anti-competitive effects of mergers. This occurs because merger control reflects a populist attitude towards regulating the convergence of economic resources among business firms as well as concerns with irregular corporate activities, such as related party transactions at other than arm's length and the threat that larger businesses present to smaller ones. (Liu, LS, 'Fostering Competition Law and Policy: A Façade of Taiwan's Political Economy' (2002) *Washington University Global Studies Law Review*, vol 1, (1 & 2), 77 at 119)

The fact remains however that the TFTC has blocked only a very small number of mergers in the exercise of its merger control powers.

[8] The term 'financial enterprise' is defined in art 10 of the Enforcement Rules as being referring to 'financial institutions under article 4 of the Financial Institution Merger Law and financial holding companies under article 4 of the Financial Holding Company Law'.

approval is likely to be readily granted.[9] These thresholds do not apply however in four circumstances specified in art 11-1. The first three circumstances arise:

(1) Where any of the enterprises participating in a merger already holds no less than 50 per cent of the voting shares or capital contribution of another enterprise in the merger and merges with such other enterprise;

(2) Where enterprises of which 50 per cent or more of the voting shares or capital contribution are held by the same enterprise merge;

(3) Where an enterprise assigns all or a principal part of its business or assets, or all or part of any part of its business that could be separately operated, to another enterprise newly established by the former enterprise solely.

The fourth situation relates to provisions in the Company Law[10] and the Securities and Exchange Law,[11] covering certain share redemptions.

4-4.07 The TFTC's approach to calculating market shares is flexible, and will depend on the particular circumstances of the case. In *Yahoo! Taiwan Inc/Wretch*[12] the TFTC considered the determination of market shares in a merger of Internet information providers, where Wretch was a community website. The TFTC considered the number of visits to websites, but decided that market shares would be calculated on the basis of the income from online advertisements.[13]

4-4.08 Where the TFTC sets a turnover threshold this is to be in accordance with the principle set out in art 11(1)(3) of the TFTA which makes reference to 'sales for the preceding fiscal year of one of the enterprises in the merger'. The Enforcement Rules state at art 6 that the reference to sales 'means the total sale or operating revenue of an enterprise'. The turnover thresholds were most recently set on 25 February 2002,[14] and are as follows:

(a) where an enterprise in a merger is a non-financial enterprise, its sales for the preceding fiscal year exceed NT$10bn, and the enterprise it merges has a sales amount exceeding NT$1bn in the preceding fiscal year;

[9] This was the case for example in *Tyco International Ltd/CIT Group Inc* (31 May 2001) where the TFTC cleared a merger in part on the grounds that the 'types of business [the parties] each operates are entirely different' such that 'the combination. . . . has no adverse effect on Taiwan's overall economic interests and on the competition of the relevant markets'.

[10] art 167(1).

[11] art 28-2.

[12] 29 March 2007.

[13] There was no statistical information available for the TFTC to rely on in this respect, and it relied on figures provided by a magazine, and the Internet Advertising and Media Association of Taipei.

[14] Public Notice Ref: Kun Chi Tzu, No 0910001699.

(b) where an enterprise in a merger is a financial enterprise, its sales for the preceding fiscal year exceed NT$20bn, and the enterprise with which it merges has a sales amount exceeding NT$1bn in the preceding fiscal year.

In relation to mergers involving only foreign parties the TFTC takes the position that it is only the level of sales in Taiwan that is to be taken into account. This includes export sales into Taiwan, and sales by subsidiaries active in Taiwan if these exist. This is a more generous rule than that applying in respect of Taiwan national parties merging, where all sales, including exports outside of Taiwan, will be taken into account in establishing the jurisdictional threshold. **4-4.09**

It is possible that jurisdiction will exist in cases in which mergers take place between members of the same corporate group. This was the case for example in *Yahoo! Group/Kimo.com*[15] where the TFTC recognized that both of the companies participating in the merger belonged to the same group, such that the merger constituted 'an internal reorganization among Yahoo! affiliates and a redeployment of existing market power rather than a consolidation of market power with a separate business'. The merger was approved, and it would be unusual indeed were a merger between companies that were already part of the same group not to be cleared. Similarly in *United Daily News*[16] the TFTC approved a merger which 'was purely an act of internal reorganization among affiliated companies'. Mergers that take this form may be able to benefit from the procedures for simplified review discussed below. **4-4.10**

'Foreign mergers'

The Act applies equally to foreign mergers which reach the jurisdiction thresholds set out in art 11, although some of the implementing rules and guidelines make specific modifications in respect of the obligations faced by foreign parties. The TFTC has published *Guidelines on Extraterritorial Mergers*,[17] which apply to 'a merger of two or more foreign enterprises outside the territorial domain of Taiwan', with 'merger' having the meaning given by art 6(1) of the TFTA. The Guidelines provide that it is a requirement that the merger must have 'a direct, substantial, and reasonably foreseeable effect on the domestic market'.[18] It will be noted that this wording is in essence the same as is found in the US Foreign Trade Antitrust Improvements Act, which has codified the US approach to the assertion of extra-territorial jurisdiction, and in the context of merger control this is not, or **4-4.11**

---

[15] 21 December 2000.

[16] *United Daily News/Economic Daily News/Min Sheng News/United Evening News/Star News* (19 May 2005).

[17] First passed on 3 August 2000, and most recently promulgated by letter dated 24 February 2005.

[18] para 2.

at least should not be, controversial. The Guidelines set out eight considerations to be taken into account in determining whether jurisdiction should be asserted in extraterritorial cases: (1) the relative weight of the merger's effects on the relevant domestic and foreign markets; (2) the nationalities, residence, and main place of business of the parties; (3) the degree of intent underlying any effect on competition in the Taiwan market, and the directness of such an effect; (4) the principle of comity, which in the wording here is set out as 'the likelihood of creating conflicts with the laws or policies of the home countries of the combining enterprises'; (5) whether remedies could be enforced; (6) the effect on the foreign companies of any enforcement; (7) any relevant international law set out in conventions, treaties, and regulations of international organizations; and (8) 'other factors deemed important' by the TFTC. Finally in this part of the Guidelines it is stated that jurisdiction will *not* be asserted in any case in which none of the merging parties have 'production or service facilities, distributors, agents or other substantive sales channels within the territorial domain of Taiwan'. This additional rubric brings the position closer to that in the EC, where a degree of *active* trading into the EC is necessary in order for jurisdiction under the EC merger regime to be asserted. When it is necessary to determine the sales volume of either of the foreign parties the Guidelines provide that this 'shall be assessed by the monetary amount of . . . sales within the territorial domain of Taiwan and the monetary amount of products or services imported from that foreign enterprise by domestic enterprises'.[19]

4-4.12 There have been a number of cases in which 'foreign' mergers have been approved by the TFTC, and none in which wholly foreign mergers have been blocked. In *Lockheed Martin Corporation/Northrop Grumman Corp*[20] the TFTC considered the combination between the two US aviation companies, both of which had subsidiaries in Taiwan. The TFTC noted that as Taiwan had no capability to manufacture products supplied by the two companies, there was no impact on industries in Taiwan. The Ministry of National Defence had also indicated that the combination would not affect military procurement in Taiwan. It is not uncommon for mergers between foreign parties to be subject to the TFTC review and approval process where there are Taiwan subsidiaries involved. In *Intel Corp/ TXC Corp*[21] the TFTC approved a merger between two US companies, one of which had a subsidiary in Taiwan. Opinions were taken from the Industrial

[19] para 4. Although for the purposes of this calculation it will not necessarily be the case that the foreign company is actively selling in Taiwan through a local distributor or agent, or other form of sales channel, the fact that the relevant turnover threshold stipulated under art 11 is reached does not necessarily mean that jurisdiction will be asserted, as noted above.

[20] 5 November 1997.

[21] 11 March 1998.

Development Bureau and the Institute for Information Industry, both of whom argued that the merger would have no negative impacts on competition in Taiwan. In the same month in the case of *Nestlé Corp/Borden Corp*[22] the merger was again between foreign parties, but would also see the transfer of a Taiwan subsidiary of Borden Corp to Nestlé's Taiwan subsidiary, Nestlé Taiwan. The two subsidiaries' products were not in competition with each other, and the merger was cleared.

Procedures

Pre-merger contacts and review

There are no formal provisions relating to pre-merger contacts with the TFTC. **4-4.13**
However, there is evidence to suggest that in some cases the TFTC may be prepared to offer informal and non-binding advisory opinions. Anecdotal evidence suggests that effective communication with the TFTC at an early stage in the merger process may resolve many potential problems.

Notification

As noted above, art 11 of the TFTA requires that any merger falling within **4-4.14**
the terms of art 11 'shall be filed with the [TFTC] in advance'. This 'report of a merger'[23] shall be filed by the relevant enterprise as specified in art 7 of the Enforcement Rules, which imposes the obligation on:

(1) the enterprises in the merger, where an enterprise is merged into another, assigned by or leases from another enterprise(s) the operations or assets of another, regularly runs operations jointly with another, or is commissioned by another enterprise to run an operation;
(2) the holding or acquiring enterprise, where an enterprise holds or acquires shares or capital contribution of another enterprise; and
(3) the controlling enterprise, where an enterprise directly or indirectly controls the business operations or the appointment or discharge of personnel of another enterprise.

Where the enterprise that would be required to file the report has not yet been established, the obligation to report falls jointly on the existing enterprise(s).

[22] 18 March 1998. There are many other examples of jurisdiction being asserted in similar cases, but the pattern of approval is consistent.
[23] art 7, Enforcement Rules to the Fair Trade Act of 2002.

In the event that a financial holding company participates in a merger either by itself or through any subsidiary the report must be filed by the financial holding company. All forms and attachments shall be submitted in duplicate.[24]

4-4.15 Article 8 specifies the material and information that must be included in the filed report, and the TFTC from time to time sets out the form in which all of this data should be submitted. The current instructions may be found in the Directions for Enterprises Filing for Merger.[25] First there must be a 'report form' setting out the following information: (1) the 'type and substance of the merger'; (2) the basic legal details of the participating enterprises, including the names and place of business; (3) the proposed date of the merger; (4) details of the relevant legal representation; and (5) 'other required information', which may be specified by the TFTC. This report must be signed and sealed by each of the parties participating in the merger, and their representative(s).[26] The parties must then provide certain basic information, including: (1) the name and residence of the responsible administrator for each enterprise; (2) each enterprise's capital and business assets; (3) each party's turnover in the preceding fiscal year, along with the turnover of any enterprise which is a subsidiary of or is controlled by the parties; (4) the number of employees of each party; and (5) relevant certificates of incorporation. There is then a requirement for a further seven sets of information: (1) financial statements and operating reports for each of the relevant parties in the preceding year; (2) data relating to production and operating costs, sales prices, and production and sales values of the goods or services produced by the relevant parties; (3) 'an explanation of the benefits of the merger for the overall economy and any disadvantages due to restraints on competition'; (4) information relating to future major plans of the parties; (5) an overview of long-term investments held by the parties in other enterprises; (6) the most recent prospectus or annual report where the stocks of either party are listed on the stock exchange; and (7) information relating to market structure, as regards competitors and the upstream and downstream activities of the participating parties. Finally para (10) of this article permits the TFTC to require any other documents it specifies.

[24] Other requirements are that the submission must be on A4 pages, numbered on the lower left corner, and bound with a table of contents.

[25] First passed on 12 April 1995, amended most recently on 8 August 2002, and circulated by letter (93) on 11 February 2004.

[26] Directions for Enterprises Filing for Merger, para 2. It is further provided that, in respect of extraterritorial mergers, 'if difficulties do exist for obtaining the signing/sealing of the participating enterprise(s), please submit other documents sufficient to prove the agreement to merge'. Where material is submitted which contains foreign language content a Chinese summary of that must be included.

The material submitted will be directed within the TFTC to the relevant department dealing with merger review, which will first determine whether the merger meets the relevant thresholds for jurisdiction to be established. If the jurisdiction thresholds are not met the TFTC will issue a letter to that effect, and the parties may proceed with the merger. If jurisdiction is established the Department will prepare a case to be put before the Commissioners, who are to make a final decision as to whether the merger should be cleared, blocked, or cleared with conditions. As discussed in Chapter 4-5 of this Part the Commission has extensive powers to request information, to require parties to make statements to it, and may in some cases hold public hearings. **4-4.16**

Article 11(3) of the TFTA states that the parties to a notifiable merger may not consummate the merger until a period of thirty days has elapsed from the filing of the material required.[27] If the TFTC does not extend this thirty-day standstill period, or does not make a decision within the thirty-day period the parties may proceed to merge, unless they themselves consent to an extension, or the filing itself 'contains any false or misleading' items.[28] The thirty-day period however does not start running until such time as the notification report has been filed in conformity with art 8 of the Enforcement Rules, and is complete.[29] Article 9 of the Enforcement Rules gives the TFTC the power to issue a notice requiring that there be a supplement to the filed material, or that corrections be made where the materials filed fail to comply with the art 8 requirements. Any such notice must state the reasons for the belief that the filing is in error or incomplete, and a time limit must be set within which the supplementary material should be filed, or the correction made. If the notice is not complied with within the time limit set the TFTC may reject the filing in its entirety. Figure 4-4.1 sets out the procedures in relation to merger pre-notifications. **4-4.17**

Decisions made by the TFTC in relation to its merger control powers may be published in the Government Gazette, although there is no formal requirement for compulsory publication.[30] **4-4.18**

There are no filing fees applicable in the Taiwan system. **4-4.19**

[27] In particular cases the TFTC 'may shorten or extend the period as it deems necessary'. Where it does so it must notify the parties in writing. Any extension of the period may not exceed a further 30 days, such that the total period of suspension of the merger must not exceed 60 days.

[28] art 11(5), TFTA.

[29] art 11, Enforcement Rules.

[30] art 12, Enforcement Rules.

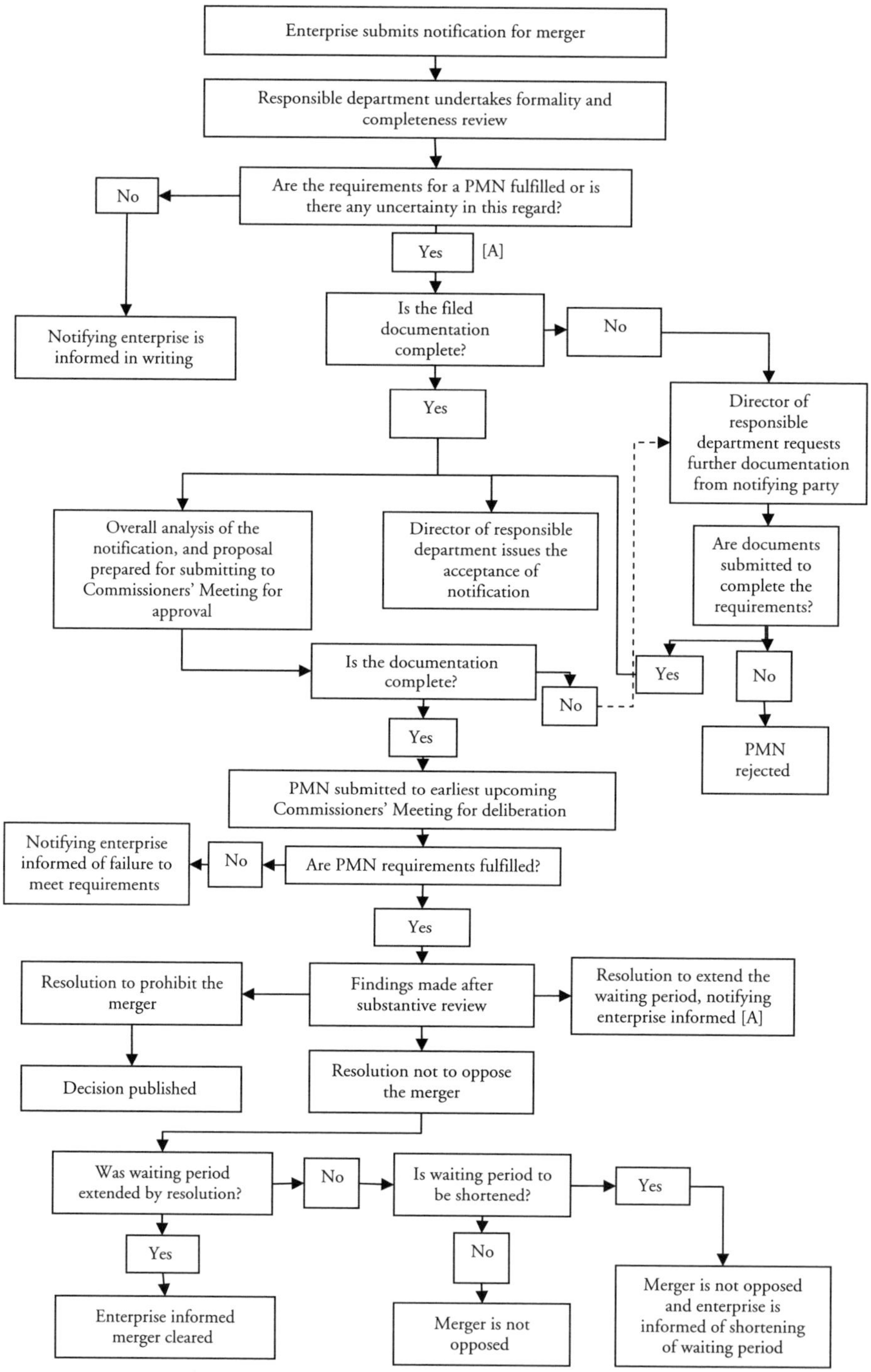

Figure 4-4.1 Pre-merger notification ('PMN') procedures.

Application of the Substantive Test

The TFTA does not set out a 'competition' test on the basis of which a merger is to be judged. Rather the approach on the face of the legislation is to require mergers falling within the specified thresholds to be notified, with the TFTC having the power then to block these mergers, or to permit them subject to the acceptance of appropriate undertakings. As discussed below, art 12 of the TFTA does contain an express 'efficiencies' defence. **4-4.20**

General review

The TFTC has not published substantial guidelines relating to the assessment of the competitive effects of a merger, but some guidance may be found both in the *Guidelines on Handling Merger Filings*,[31] and in previous decisions.[32] The Guidelines apply to all mergers falling within the terms of the TFTA unless the TFTC has issued industry-specific guidance. Two standards of review, simplified or general, may be adopted depending on the circumstances of the merger. **4-4.21**

Paragraph VII of the Guidelines specifies the mergers in respect of which the simplified review is available. In the case of a horizontal merger[33] this is the case where the combined market shares of the parties post-merger would be less than 15 per cent. This will not apply where the market is already concentrated, such that the CR2 is 66 per cent, or the CR3 is 75 per cent post-merger. In the case of a vertical merger the simplified review will apply where the post-merger share in each relevant market would be no greater than 25 per cent. There are no concentration ratio exceptions in this latter case. The situation is somewhat different in respect of a conglomerate merger as market shares will not be increased directly as a result of the merger, and the TFTC instead will consider whether, taking into **4-4.22**

[31] Passed on 15 June 2006, promulgated by letter No 090005804 of 6 July 2006.

[32] The TFTC also set up a special group to respond to competition policy challenges arising from reforms taking place in the financial sector in 2005 and 2006. The TFTC was particularly concerned to monitor mergers arising as a result of the reforms, and pointed to experience in the US, the EC, and Japan as providing useful benchmarks for the approach to be taken in Taiwan. Thus, for example, it made reference to the use of the Herfindahl-Hirschman Index (HHI) as a proxy means for the assessment of changes in market concentration and hence in market power. As part of this exercise the TFTC stated that where concentration levels were below HHI 1,000 there would be no competitive concerns raised by mergers. The use of the HHI is not otherwise referred to expressly in guidance published by the TFTC, but there is evidence to show that this is one of the factors considered by the TFTC in its assessment of the potential competitive effects of horizontal mergers (see *TFTC Competition Policy Newsletter*, 2:10, 30 April 2006).

[33] Horizontal, vertical, and conglomerate mergers are defined in the Guidelines (see below).

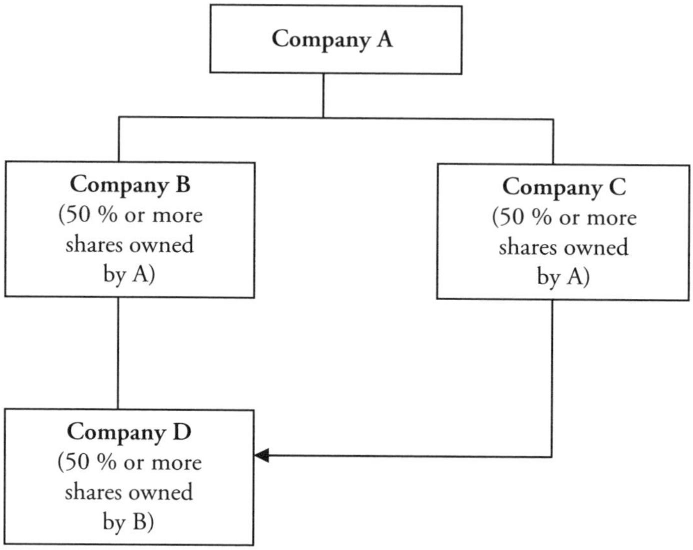

Figure 4-4.2 Subsidiary mergers—simplified procedure applies.

account the factors discussed below in relation to the assessment of conglomerate mergers, the parties 'do not have any major potential competition possibility between each other'. Mergers between controlling and 'subordinate' enterprises that have the effect of changing the relationship between them may also be subject to the simplified procedure where either there is a direct merger between a parent and an already existing subsidiary in which at least a 50 per cent holding exists, or where one of the parties already owned more than one-third of the voting shares or paid-up capital of the other. The simplified procedure will also apply where a company merges with a subsidiary of another company, both having the same parent. The example in Figure 4-4.2 is given in the Guidelines.

4-4.23 Even where the simplified procedure would otherwise apply exceptions exist, with the general procedure being applicable where: (1) the merger involves a major public interest;[34] (2) 'one of the merging parties is a holding company as defined in the Taiwan Stock Exchange Corporation Regulations'; (3) there is difficulty in defining the scope of the relevant market, or in calculating the market shares of those engaged in the merger; or (4) the relevant market is subject to high entry barriers, concentration, 'or other unfavourable and questionable circumstances that severely limit competition'.[35]

[34] 'Public interests' are not specified in the Guidelines.
[35] Guidelines, para VIII.

Market definition

The TFTC does not provide detailed guidance in relation to market definition or the assessment of market power. The definition of a relevant market provided in the Guidelines is a standard one of 'a geographic area or a coverage wherein enterprises compete in respect of particular goods or services'.[36] The Guidelines further recognize the existence of both product and geographic aspects to market definition. The definition of a product market is similar to that adopted in early case law in the EC, and does not incorporate directly the rigour of, for example, an SSNIP test. Paragraph III(1) of the Guidelines states that a product market 'means the scope of goods or services that in terms of functionality, characteristics, purposes of prices, have a high degree of demand or supply substitution'.[37] A geographic market 'means a region or scope in which the merging parties supply particular goods or services, and the trading counterpart can select or switch easily to other suppliers'. In relation to the enforcement of antitrust law generally the TFTC has usually taken Taiwan as a whole to be the relevant geographic market, but there are some cases in which narrower regional markets have been found to exist.[38] The temporal aspects to market definition are dealt with only in a passing reference, in the part of the Guidelines dealing with market definition, to the fact that the TFTC may examine 'the duration of a merger's effects'. **4-4.24**

Market power assessment

The Guidelines make reference to market share assessment rather than an assessment of market power, reflecting the emphasis in the primary legislation on market share presumptions. Paragraph IV of the Guidelines provides that in calculating the market share of the relevant enterprises account shall be taken of 'production, sales, inventory, and import/export value (by volume) data for the enterprise and for the relevant market'. The preference is for the sales value to be the determining factor in the calculation of the market share, but where this is not appropriate another basis may be selected according to the characteristics of the relevant market. There is no indication in the Guidelines as to when it might not be appropriate to rely on sales values. The data relied on may be that collated by the TFTC in **4-4.25**

[36] para II(1).

[37] Demand substitution is separately defined as the ability of customers to switch to other sellers or to substitute the goods or services supplied in the face of a price rise. Supply substitution is separately defined in standard terms, making reference to the ability of a competitor, either existing or potential, to offer goods or services in response to a change in price imposed by the current seller. There is no reference in the Guidelines to the time within which either demand or supply substitution has to occur in order to impact on the definition of the relevant market (paras II(2), (3)).

[38] This was the case for example in *Taiwan Broadband Communication Consultant Co* (18 August 1999) where the TFTC recognized the existence of narrower than national geographic markets operating in the broadband cable market. See also *Holiday Entertainment Co Ltd/Cashbox Partyworld Co Ltd* (8 March 2007) in which the relevant geographic market was Taipei City/County.

the course of its investigation into the merger, or that obtained from other government agencies. Even where market power is enhanced by a merger, approval might be granted where the effect is to increase the ability of the merged entity to compete with a substantial competitor. This was the case in *Taiwan Mobile Co/Taiwan Fixed Network/Tai-Hsin International Telecommunications Co Ltd*[39] in which a merger in the telephony market came at a time when there was a trend towards integration in fixed and mobile telephony. Although the merger increased the market power of the merged entity the presence of a powerful competitor was recognized, and the TFTC held that 'the result of the competition between the enterprises involved in this merger and Chunghwa Telecom might even benefit the consumer with more preferential services'.[40]

Horizontal mergers

4-4.26 A horizontal merger is defined in the Guidelines as being one in which the enterprises participating in the merger have the relationship of being horizontal competitors.[41] Paragraph IX of the Guidelines sets out the factors to be considered in determining the competitive effects of horizontal mergers. Four main considerations are set out along with a general reference to 'other factors'. The four core factors are: (1) unilateral effects; (2) coordinated effects; (3) entry; and (4) countervailing power. There is also a presumption that certain horizontal mergers raise 'obvious suspicion'. This will be the case where certain market share thresholds are reached. These are: (1) that the post-merger market share of the merged entity would be 50 per cent or greater; (2) the CR2 is two-thirds or greater and the post-merger market share of the merging parties is at least 15 per cent; and (3) the CR3 is 75 per cent or greater and the post-merger market share of the merging parties is at least 15 per cent.

4-4.27 The approach taken to unilateral and coordinated effects of mergers has been discussed in Chapter 1-2, above, and the approach set out in the TFTC Guidelines, although short, is compatible with the treatment of these matters in the EC and the US. In assessing unilateral effects the TFTC will consider the extent to which the merging parties 'are not restrained' by competition, and have the ability to raise prices post-merger. Relevant factors may be 'the market shares of the merging enterprises, homogeneity of goods or services, production capacity and import competition'. The TFTC's explanation of coordinated action is that this may be a factor where, post-merger, the merged entity and its competitors 'restrict business activities among themselves or, even though they are not mutually restricting one

[39] 12 April 2007.

[40] It was also a factor that the pricing plans of telecommunications operators had to be reported to the relevant regulatory agency for approval prior to their implementation.

[41] para II(4).

another from competition . . . they have taken concerted actions to remove market competition in practice'. In an approach very similar to that adopted by the EC, the TFTC will take into account 'whether the market condition is conducive for the enterprises to form concerted actions, the ease of monitoring violated acts and the effectiveness of punishments'.

The approaches to entry and to countervailing power (both at supplier and customer level) are again standard. In relation to entry the Guidelines state simply that the TFTC will consider 'the likelihood and timeliness of entry by potential competitors and whether such entry would exert competitive pressures on the existing enterprises in the market'. For countervailing power effects to be considered it will be necessary to demonstrate that this is sufficient to restrict the parties, post-merger, from raising prices. **4-4.28**

It is clear from the case record that mergers are likely to be approved where they are implemented at the horizontal level, and do not have significant impacts on market shares.[42] **4-4.29**

Vertical mergers

A vertical merger is defined in the Guidelines as being one in which the participating enterprises have either upstream or downstream relations.[43] As would be expected less attention is paid to vertical mergers in the Guidelines, and the TFTC indicates only that it will consider: (1) the way in which other competitors will select their suppliers and customers after the merger; (2) barriers to entry raised by the merger; (3) the possibility of post-merger market abuse; and (4) 'other factors that may result in market foreclosure'.[44] **4-4.30**

Conglomerate mergers

A conglomerate merger is defined in the Guidelines as being one in which the merging parties have neither horizontal nor vertical relations.[45] The assessment of the effects of conglomerate mergers can be extremely complex, particularly where 'portfolio effects' are identified. The TFTC Guidelines note that where a conglomerate merger has horizontal or vertical effects these will be analysed in accordance with the methodologies set out above, with the TFTC also taking into **4-4.31**

[42] See for example *Citi Group Inc/Bank of Overseas Chinese* (24 May 2007) in which it was noted simply that the merger would result in a change in market share which 'was not big' given the fractured nature of the industry. In *Family Mart Co Ltd/Niko Mart* (23 August 2007) the post-merger market share would have been 21.48 per cent, and the TFTC found that 'the market concentration showed no serious deterioration'. The mergers in both cases were approved.

[43] para II(5).

[44] para XI.

[45] para II(6).

account: (1) the impact of regulation and other controls on the parties' cross-industry operations; (2) the impact of technology on future cross-industry operation; (3) the plans, if any, of the parties for other cross-industry operations outside the merger; and (4) 'other factors'.

Efficiencies and the failing firm defence

4-4.32 Article 12 of the TFTA makes explicit an efficiency defence, providing that the TFTC may not prohibit a merger where 'the overall economic benefit of the merger outweighs the disadvantages' flowing from the competitive harm. The TFTC may, however, attach conditions or require undertakings in respect of any decision taken so as to ensure that the claimed benefits do in fact exceed the harms flowing. Some further clarification is supplied in the *Guidelines on Handling Merger Filings*. Where a filing is made in respect of a merger that raises a suspicion of 'obvious competition restraints' the parties are required to submit evidence relating to certain 'economic benefits' of the merger. The benefits specified are: (1) consumer interests; (2) the weak position of the parties; (3) the fact that one of the parties is a failing firm; and (4) 'other concrete results related to overall economic benefits'. The evidence suggests that the TFTC may be sympathetic to efficiency claims, and it is rare for a merger to be blocked where, notwithstanding anti-competitive effects, positive benefits flow from the merger (see further below). Even where competitive concerns are not raised by a merger the TFTC often emphasizes efficiency claims for the merger in its approval statements.[46]

4-4.33 In the event that the merging parties wish to rely on the failing firm defence they must demonstrate that: (1) if in debt, the failing firm is unable to repay the debt within a short period; (2) there are no less restrictive competitive strategies than the merger which would allow the firm to survive; and (3) the failing firm will 'inevitably' withdraw from the market if it cannot merge.

The case record

4-4.34 Taiwan has blocked very few mergers. A very significant number of cases dealt with by the TFTC in the early years of the regime related to franchise operations,

[46] See for example *Lite-On Technology Corporation/Lite-On Enclosure Inc* (16 October 2003) in which the merger was a vertical combination in the personal computer manufacturing industry. The TFTC noted without criticism the claims of the parties to the effect that the merger would 'reduce internal cost by sharing resourced, increase the technology exchange, integrate marketing, explore new markets, and increase operational efficiency and international competition'. In 2003 the TFTC cleared a substantial merger in the telecommunications industry (*Far Eastern Telecommunications Co Ltd/Yuan Her Telecommunications Co Ltd/KG Telecommunication Co Ltd* (4 December 2003)) finding that although the cellular phone service market exhibited high barriers to entry, the merger would 'assist the participating companies to expand their business scale, lower operation cost, provide a higher quality service, and a better development of the telecommunications environment'.

which fell to be considered because of the turnover or market share of the franchisor. Not surprisingly these cases have not given rise to competition concerns. Between the entry into force of the TFTA and 2002 only three mergers were blocked, with all of these having taken place in the cable TV sector in 2000.[47] Thus, for example, a merger between Eastern Multimedia Co Ltd and four cable television stations was blocked on 19 April 2000. The parties had argued that by combining they could offer consolidated, inter-industry cable television, telecommunications, and Internet services and 'contribute to the overall economic interest of developing broadband transmission'. The TFTC however took the view that such development could happen irrespective of the merger on other platforms, and that therefore the claimed benefit could be achieved without the anti-competitive effects anticipated of the merger were it to be approved. These were significant, as it was anticipated that the merged entity would have a significant advantage over rivals including the ability to negotiate lower prices for content and higher prices for service provision, and there was the prospect that its power would be such as 'to scare off potential competitors'. More recently the TFTC has approved mergers in this sector. In *Estar Cable TV Corporation*[48] for example the TFTC approved a merger between Estar and ten cable TV companies on the grounds that the merger would give rise to substantial efficiencies and technological developments in the cable TV industry.[49]

Other mergers have, rarely, been blocked in the six years since 2002, but these are very much exceptional cases. In *Sin Tai Bei Cable System Co Ltd/Li Guan Cable System Co Ltd*[50] the TFTC blocked a merger between two cellular telecommunications companies finding that the competitive disadvantages of the merger were substantial and were not outweighed by any efficiencies claimed by the parties. A merger between two participants in the Karaoke industry was blocked in 2007 on the grounds that the post-merger market share would exceed 90 per cent and that there would be no effective competition to the merged entity.[51] **4-4.35**

In September 2008 the TFTC moved to block a proposed acquisition of more than 30 per cent of the shares of Wei Lih Food Industrial Co Ltd by Cayman President Holdings Limited, which was in turn a wholly owned subsidiary of Uni-President Enterprises Corp. Both Wei Lih and Uni-President were producers of instant noodles products, and Uni-President had already acquired 31.84 per cent **4-4.36**

---

47 Although Liu reports that the TFTC did, in effect, block a number of potential mergers in the market for gas stations by way of an administrative letter sent to the China Petroleum Corporation in November 1997 (Liu, n 7, above, at 125).

48 14 June 2001.

49 See also *Crown Ltd* (25 January 2007) in which a merger involving 13 parties in the cable TV business was approved on the grounds that no competitive concerns were raised.

50 8 August 2002.

51 *Holiday Entertainment Co Ltd/Cashbox Partyworld Co Ltd* (8 March 2007).

of the shares of Wei Lih in 2007. The TFTC found that the proposed merger would lead to a substantial reduction of competition in the light of the parties' high combined market share in the relevant market, that the company would, post-merger, have the power to raise prices, and that the merger would create significant entry barriers.

4-4.37 There is little in the available merger reports of the TFTC that provides useful insights as to future practice. It is, however, clear from the materials available that the TFTC places some weight on the balancing factor of the public interest, and in particular of the development of industrial policy, when clearing mergers that might give rise to some potential anti-competitive harm. An example of such an approach may be found in the case of the merger between Taiwan Semiconductor Manufacturing Co Ltd ('TSMC'), and ACER Semiconductor Manufacturing Co, approved by the TFTC on 14 July 1999. It was clear that the merger increased horizontal concentration in the manufacture of integrated circuits, although not dramatically. TSMC would increase its market share in the integrated circuit manufacturing market from 36 per cent to 40 per cent, and its foundry market shares were also going to rise from 54 per cent pre-merger to 58 per cent post-merger. The TFTC recognized that although this increase in share was relatively small, it would allow TSMC to expand its capacity, raising higher entry barriers. There was also a prospect that small-sized integrated circuit manufacturers could be driven out of the market in the face of TSMC's dominance, and its lower operating costs. Having noted the competitive concerns arising from the merger however, the TFTC stated that 'the combination is expected to benefit the nation's overall economic development'. The merger could make it easier for TSMC to fulfil orders at a time when the industry was operating at maximum capacity, and efficiencies would be obtained from a plan to move ACER's assets to foundry production. As a result, the TFTC held that:

> . . . the entire integrated circuit manufacturing industry in Taiwan can expand its production to reach profits through operations under economic scale, reduce production costs, and elevate the industry's competitiveness in the world market. At the same time, TSMC's top quality manufacturing capability can be introduced into ACER Semiconductor, which not only helps to upgrade ACER's, but also the entire local industry's production knowhow, further improving the operating structure of local industry.

In consequence the TFTC cleared the merger on the grounds that 'the advantage from the combination to the overall economy outweighs the disadvantage of restricting competition in the particular market'.[52]

[52] An almost identical approach was taken in relation to a merger between United Microelectronics Corp and four other companies also active in the integrated circuit industry on 28 July 1999.

Remedies and Penalties

Article 13 of the TFTA provides that where any merger falling within the terms of art 11 is consummated without notification being given, or where the TFTC has taken a decision prohibiting the merger, or where undertakings or conditions are not complied with, the TFTC may prohibit the merger, and may 'prescribe a period for such enterprise(s) to split, to dispose of all or a part of the shares, to transfer a part of the operations, or to remove certain persons from positions, or make any other necessary dispositions'. There is some evidence to suggest that a merger falling within the Act's jurisdiction thresholds that has been consummated without the approval of the TFTC is void without any further action to that effect being necessary. However, the position is a little unclear, and it may be the case that the TFTC has first to declare the merger illegal. **4-4.38**

Where enterprises are in breach of any order made under art 13 the TFTC may 'order the dissolution of such enterprise(s), or the suspension or termination of their operations'. The TFTC also has the power to impose penalties as provided for in art 40 of the TFTA. This provides that where any enterprise proceeds with a merger in contravention of art 11(1) or (3) of the Act, or where the TFTC has prohibited the merger, or fails to comply with undertakings imposed by the TFTC, an administrative penalty of up to NT$50m, but not less than NT$100,000 may be imposed. Where a merger is consummated in breach of art 11(5)(2)[53] the penalty will be between NT$50,000 and NT$500,000. There have been a number of cases in which such penalties have been imposed. A penalty of NT$800,000 was imposed in respect of each of four mergers entered into without approval by Eastern Multimedia Co on 7 January 1998, with the parties being required to take corrective measures, unless they chose to notify the mergers to the TFTC and seek approval in accordance with the established procedures. In *Holiday Group Co/ Young Sound Multimedia Co*[54] the TFTC had examined a notification for merger made on 9 May 2003. The documents submitted by the parties however did not disclose the fact that Holiday Group had already loaned Young Sound, or otherwise provided it with financial assistance of, an amount exceeding its total capital. Thereafter Holiday Group personnel had accompanied Young Sound when business was being promoted. In these circumstances the TFTC found that a merger had already taken place, in contravention of art 11(5)(2) of the TFTA, and a penalty in the amount of NT$400,000 was imposed. **4-4.39**

53 This is the proviso that relates to filings containing false or misleading information.
54 29 July 2004.

4-4.40 Article 13 of the TFTA also authorizes the TFTC to require that an enterprise in breach of art 11(1) or (3) is 'to remove certain persons from positions'. Such actions are rare, but in the case of *Fuyang Media Co Ltd*[55] the TFTC ordered Fuyang to move staff, including directors and supervisors of the company, to other positions after they continued to act in breach of the TFTA. Administrative penalties of NT$8,000,000 were also imposed in this case.

4-4.41 There is limited guidance available from the TFTC as to the crafting of undertakings or conditions where these are necessary to ensure the approval of the merger. Franck and Hwang note that, in relation to partial divestitures the TFTC has, 'unofficially . . . indicated a willingness to consider a "carve out" of Taiwan assets or business activities on a case-by-case basis and will look at the level of activity in Taiwan and the degree of impact the combination will have in Taiwan'.[56] However, they also note that the lack of precedent in this area makes it 'difficult' to be certain as to whether partial divestiture will be possible in any particular case.

4-4.42 There are few cases reported in English in which approval has been given to a merger subject to conditions. One such is that of *Holiday Limited Co/Cashbox Party World Karaoke Parlours*[57] in which a number of conditions were set. The first was that in the event of 'any further vertical merger between the applicants and [specified businesses] all participants in the merger must submit an application of merger to the [TFTC]'. This condition is not simply restating the impact of the TFTA, as it applies even were jurisdiction not normally to arise. Four further behavioural conditions were also set on the merged entity, which was required: (1) not to use its market power post-merger to demand exclusive trading; (2) not to prohibit trading counterparts to trade with others; (3) not to demand preferential treatment or engage in undue price-fixing, price maintenance, or price changes; and (4) not to 'engage in acts that would restrain competition or abuse the market position'. It will be noted that these are in part significantly interventionist conditions. Given that the TFTC had earlier in its brief report of the case stated that the Karaoke market would remain competitive and that 'the merger would not create restraints on competition in relevant markets after the merger' it appears here to have created an obligation for the merged entity to comply with standards of antitrust behaviour that might not otherwise apply to it. It is unclear what limits the merged entity had left to it to price independently in light of the condition that it was not to put into effect undue price changes. Similar conditions

[55] 19 July 2007. The action taken at this time followed a TFTC Disposition of 26 March 2004 (No 0903034) due to the fact that Fuyang took part in an illegal merger.

[56] n 1, above, vol 2, 1212 at 1217.

[57] 3 July 2003. Note that on 8 March 2007, the TFTC refused approval to a merger between Holiday Entertainment Co and Cashbox Partyworld Co Ltd (the merger approved subject to conditions on 3 July 2003 was not consummated).

were set in *Yahoo! Taiwan Inc/Wretch*[58] where the merged company was required not to 'improperly decide on, maintain or alter prices', but also to 'not improperly obstruct other competitors' website links, email receipt and transmittal or other services'. In *Uni-President Enterprises Corporation/The Tait Group of Companies*[59] the TFTC required the applicant to refrain from 'restraining sellers or channel businesses to trade with it', and 'business transactions between itself and specific drink suppliers were prohibited on the basis of its market status'.

Private parties have rights in relation to the merger control provisions of the TFTA, and the Act generally provides that any party injured by breaches of the TFTA may bring an action for damages.[60] It is also possible for a private party to seek an injunction to restrain unlawful anti-competitive conduct.[61] In practice there is little prospect of successful actions being brought in relation to unlawful merger activity. The extent of private rights in the application of Taiwan's antitrust law is discussed at Chapter 4-5. **4-4.43**

58 29 March 2007.
59 18 October 2007.
60 art 31, TFTA.
61 art 30, TFTA.

4-5

TAIWAN PROCEDURE

Introduction	4-5.01	**Corrective Measures and Penalties**	4-5.21
Investigations	4-5.03	Leniency	4-5.30
Complaints	4-5.11	**Appeals**	4-5.31
Hearings and Access to File	4-5.12	**Third Party Rights and Damages**	4-5.32

Introduction

In essence the Fair Trade Act ('TFTA') is a form of administrative law, with the Fair Trade Commission ('TFTC') being placed at the heart of the enforcement mechanisms relating to the TFTA's application.[1] Chapter IV of the TFTA sets out the primary rules applicable to the role of the TFTC. Article 25 provides that in addition to having a role in the development of competition policy and law the TFTC is to review fair trade matters relating to the TFTA, investigate activities of enterprises and economic conditions, and investigate and dispose of any case violating the TFTA.[2] Throughout the application of this part of the TFTA the **4-5.01**

[1] See, eg Liu, LS, 'Fostering Competition Law and Policy: A Façade of Taiwan's Political Economy' (2002) *Washington University Global Studies Law Review*, vol 1, (1 & 2) 77 at 81: '... after its first decade, the [TFTA] has become a form of administrative law. This phenomenon has important ramifications on the TFTC as an institution, and it affects the case load and case selection, enforcement position, and ultimate effectiveness of the [TFTA].'

[2] Liu states that:

> [The TFTA], art 25(3) authorizes the TFTC to review the economic conditions and commercial activities of enterprises. Unfortunately the vague language of art 25(3) leaves unclear whether the TFTC possesses the power to compel the release of information when it engages in general 'investigations' when no allegation of illegal conduct exists, or whether it merely possesses the power to conduct 'surveys', in which case it could not compel enterprises to furnish sensitive, proprietary information such as lists of their most important customers. Although this issue remains unsettled, the TFTC's current inclination is to assert the former argument.

Ibid at 145.

TFTC is required to 'carry out its duties independently in accordance with the law'.[3]

4-5.02 Chapter V makes provision for compensation by way of damages to those harmed by breaches of the TFTA, which in part mirror the right to obtain treble damages that exists under US antitrust law, and Chapter VI provides for various punishments, which vary depending on the provision within the TFTA which is being breached. The procedures relating to the imposition of penalties are discussed in this chapter, and the penalties themselves have been referred to as appropriate in the chapters above dealing with monopoly conduct, agreements, and mergers.

Investigations

4-5.03 Article 26 of the TFTA gives the TFTC the power to 'investigate and handle, upon complaints or ex officio,[4] any violation of the provisions of this Act that harms the public interest'. In making its investigations the TFTC may require the parties and any related third party to make statements,[5] or 'notify relevant agencies, organizations, enterprises, or individuals to submit books and records, documents, and any other necessary materials or exhibits',[6] and may 'despatch personnel for any necessary on-site inspections of the office, place of business or other locations of the relevant organizations or enterprises'.[7]

4-5.04 Figures 4-5.1(a) and (b) set out the TFTC approach to investigations.

4-5.05 An official notice must be given in respect of persons required to make statements, and the notice is to be served at least 48 hours prior to the date when the

---

3 art 28, TFTA.

4 The evidence suggests that most TFTC enforcement actions are carried out in response to complaints. In 2006 the TFTC received 1,304 complaints. There is some doubt as to whether the TFTC is permitted to decide whether to accept or reject complaints based around its administrative priorities, and the better view appears to be that it does not have this discretion. Unless a complaint is rejected as being one which is not related to the powers of the TFTC under the terms of the TFTA it appears that the TFTC is obliged to consider all complaints made to it. Where *ex officio* investigations are carried out these are sometimes in response to general concerns, rather than to suspicions of specific infringements. Thus, for example, in 2007 the TFTC carried out an investigation on its own initiative into reported price rises in relation to several key commodities. The purpose of the investigation was stated as being to 'understand the market status . . ., maintain market trading order and protect the consumers' interests by preventing businesses from jointly driving up or manipulating prices'. In reporting the fact that the investigation was being carried out the TFTC warned companies of its intention to punish 'any act to artificially manipulate or jointly raise prices' (*TFTC Competition Policy Newsletter*, 3:11, 30 June 2007).

5 art 27(1), TFTA.

6 art 27(1)(2), TFTA.

7 art 27(1)(3), TFTA.

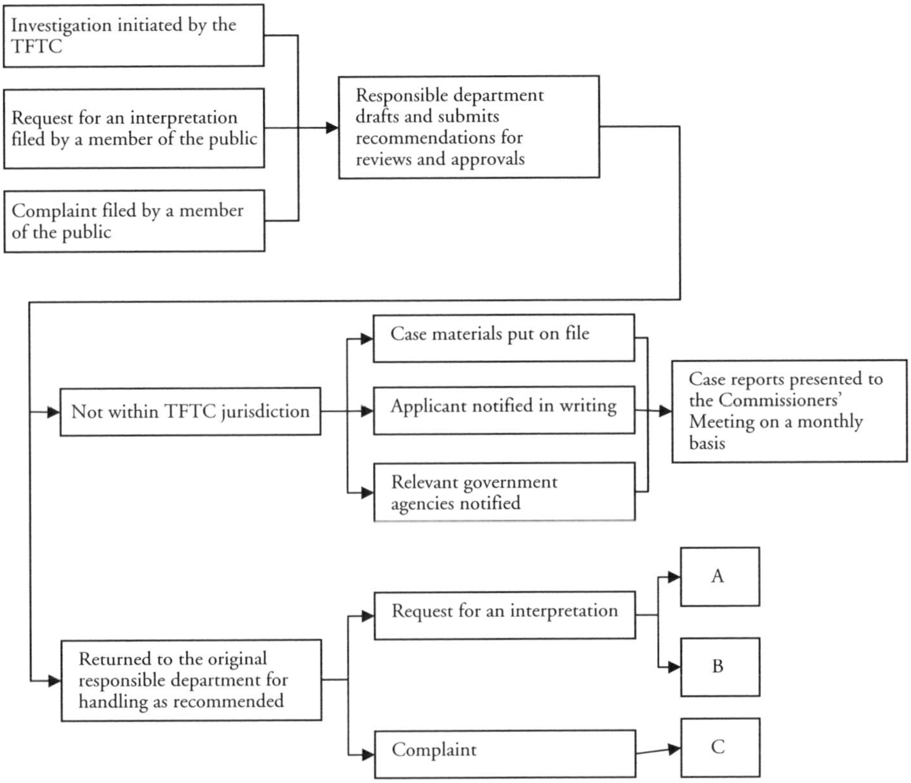

Figure 4-5.1(a) TFTC investigations.

appearance is required, unless there are 'cases where urgent circumstances exist'.[8] The notice is to specify: (1) the details of the recipient; (2) the matter under investigation and explanations of materials that the notified party is to provide; (3) the date, time, and place of any required appearance; and (4) the penalties that may be applied if the required person(s) fails to appear without justification. Any person attending the TFTC in response to such a notice may retain a lawyer to appear on their behalf, although the TFTC may, if circumstances warrant, require that the person appear themselves.[9] Where a person has made a statement in accordance with art 27(1) of the TFTA the TFTC is required to produce a written record of the statement, which is to be signed by the 'notified person'.[10]

[8] art 31(2), Enforcement Rules.
[9] art 32, Enforcement Rules.
[10] art 33, Enforcement Rules. If the notified person refuses to sign the record, that fact shall be recorded.

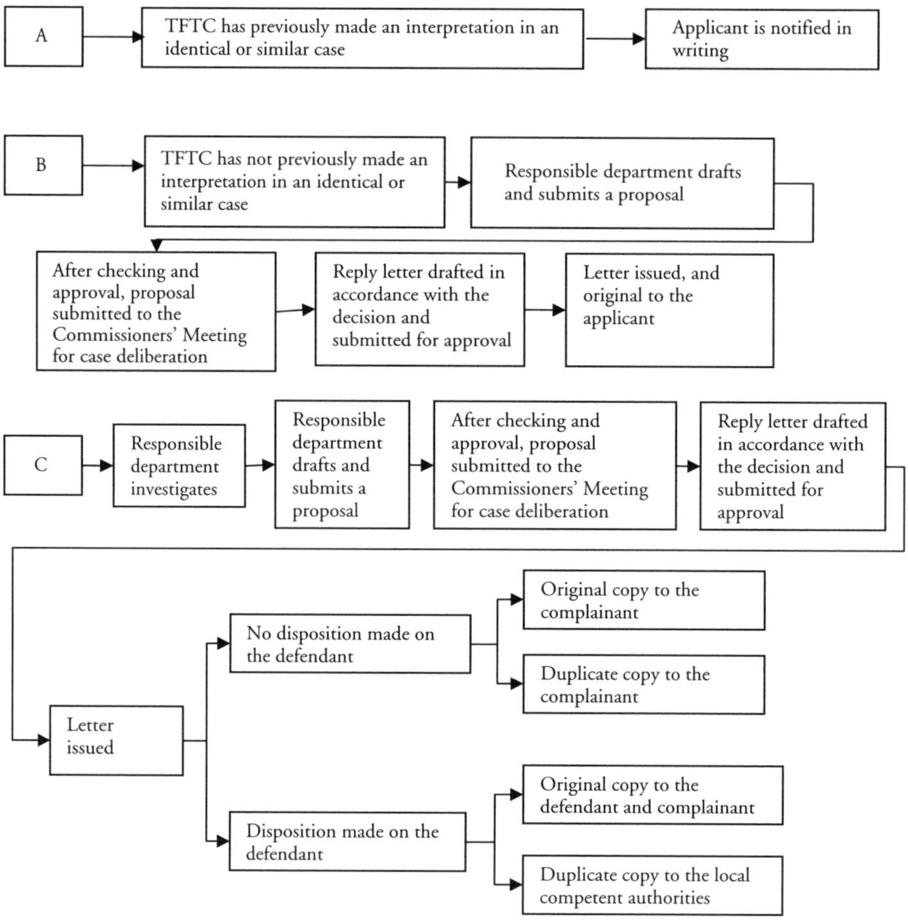

Figure 4-5.1(b) TFTC investigations.

4-5.06 When the TFTC requests persons listed in art 27(2) to submit the materials there referred to, it will issue a notice similar to that required in respect of statements. It is thus required to set out the details of the person of whom the material is being requested, the matter to be investigated, an explanation of the material that is to be submitted, a time limit for compliance, and the provisions concerning punishment for failures to comply without proper justification.[11] Once materials have been received by the TFTC it is required, if asked, to issue a receipt.[12]

4-5.07 If on-site investigations are carried out the investigator is required to present necessary official documents which establish his right to carry out the investigation,

[11] art 34, Enforcement Rules.
[12] art 35, Enforcement Rules.

and if he fails to do so the enterprise or person being investigated may refuse entry.[13] On-site investigations may either be notified to the enterprise in advance, or may be carried out without notice being given. As is discussed below access to the files of the TFTC is a right accorded to certain persons, including those under investigation. However, both art 27 of the TFTA and other laws guarantee that business secrets will not be disclosed. Parties may indicate when information is surrendered to the TFTC that this contains business secrets which are not to be disclosed. Parties may, however, be notified of access to file requests, and their permission may be sought to disclose information. Permission may be refused when the relevant material relates to business secrets.

Where any person subject to a lawful investigation under the TFTA does not comply with the requirements of the TFTC without justification, or refuses to submit materials requested within the time limits set out, or refuses to appear to make statements, the TFTC may set an administrative penalty of NT$20,000 to NT$250,000.[14] Continued refusal to comply may result in penalties being imposed up to the levels of NT$50,000 to NT$500,000 until such time as the person or enterprise complies with the obligations set. **4-5.08**

The TFTC has produced guidance relating to situations in which an enterprise has ceased its infringing conduct.[15] This provides that: **4-5.09**

> [w]here an enterprise has voluntarily ceased or corrected the violating act prior to the Commission's investigation on its own initiative or based on a complaint, the Commission may stop the investigation or decide not to make any disposition, unless the violating act seriously affects the trading order or is a concerted action that has been implemented.[16]

However, where the voluntary cessation arises after the Commission has begun an investigation the Commission shall, 'as a matter of principle', dispose of the matter in accordance with the TFTA.

In addition to the formal collection of information by mechanisms set out above the TFTC may also undertake wider information gathering exercises, and has, amongst other approaches, surveyed customers of enterprises against which complaints have been made,[17] made reference to trade publications,[18] and reviewed statistical data maintained by government departments or agencies. **4-5.10**

---

[13] art 27(2), TFTA.

[14] art 43, TFTA.

[15] *Guidelines for Reviewing Cases Involving Enterprise's Voluntary Cessation or Correction of Violating Acts*, first prescribed on 27 March 1996, most recent version circulated on 25 August 1998.

[16] para 2.

[17] See, eg *The Great Taipei Gas Corp* (9 May 2000).

[18] *Yahoo! Taiwan Inc/Wretch* (29 March 2007).

Complaints

4-5.11 The right of foreign parties to file complaints, set out in art 47 of the TFTA, and the treatment of these complaints has been referred to in Chapter 4-1 of this Part. In relation to complaints generally art 30 of the Enforcement Rules to the Fair Trade Act permits the TFTC to 'refuse to process complaints that lack substantive content or have no genuine name or address affixed thereto'. It appears to be the case however that the TFTC responds to the vast majority, if not all, of the complaints that it receives.

Hearings and Access to File

4-5.12 The TFTC may hear oral arguments in cases under its consideration and in some cases may also hold public hearings. The TFTC has published Guidelines in respect of both procedures. Parties may also have access to file, subject to restrictions where material is confidential. The procedure relating to public hearings and access to file is discussed below.

4-5.13 The Guidelines relating to oral argument,[19] specify at para 1 that:

> [o]ral arguments may be held in important and complex or controversial cases, which are under deliberation by the [TFTC] and the evidence thereof remains insufficient after investigations pursuant to the provisions of art 27 of the Fair Trade Act.

It is for the TFTC to determine whether oral arguments may be made, although the parties to the case may themselves request this.[20] Where such a request is made it may be rejected by the TFTC if it 'does not consider oral arguments necessary'. Where the TFTC does reject a request for an oral argument it shall notify the requesting party in writing, and shall state its reasons for the rejection.[21] All oral arguments are to be conducted in Chinese, with foreign language speakers providing their own interpreters.[22]

4-5.14 Where the TFTC decides to hear oral arguments written notifications will be sent to concerned parties, witnesses, and related persons ten days prior to the date for the oral argument. A longer notice period may be given in respect of persons who do not have a domestic domicile, place of business, or appointed representative.[23] The notice will set out, inter alia, the time and place of the meeting, whether the

---

[19] *Guidelines for Oral Arguments in Cases Before the Fair Trade Commission*, passed on 6 November 1996, most recent version promulgated by Order 0910001325, 8 February 2002.

[20] Parties who may apply for oral arguments to be heard are: (1) filers of mergers; (2) an applicant for approval of a concerted action; (3) complainants and respondents of complaints (para 3).

[21] *Guidelines for Oral Arguments*, para 2.

[22] Ibid at para 4.

[23] Ibid at para 5.

party should personally attend or whether an agent may be appointed to represent them, and a summary of opinions provided by the respondent in the case (typically the TFTC). Oral arguments will be held before at least half of the members of the TFTC, and the proceedings shall be chaired by the Chairperson of the Commission, the Vice Chairperson, or a member of the Commission. The Chairperson is required to conduct the proceedings 'in a fair and impartial manner'.[24] The proceedings will take the following order: presentation of an abstract of the case; the complainant will present a statement of the facts and legal arguments; the respondent will present a defence based on the facts and legal arguments; the parties may be asked questions on which clarification is needed; and the parties will be asked if they wish to present any further arguments. A record shall be prepared of the proceedings, which is to be supplemented by a video or audio recording. Parties are to sign the record.

Public hearings may be held in some cases, although there is not a general requirement that such hearings be held.[25] General rules relating to such hearings are set out in the Administrative Procedure Law, Chapter 1, s 10. Such hearings are designed to provide 'the concerned party and other interested parties of the case an opportunity to state their opinions and present evidence'. The emphasis of the hearing is on the disclosure of facts, and no judgment or decision on the case is made at the hearing itself. Participants at such hearings are exhorted to 'do their utmost to provide detailed explanations and information, enabling the Commission to discover facts from written documents, filed investigations and hearings, and hence conclude a correct and proper decision for the case'.[26] Hearings may be held in cases falling within the following categories: (1) important matters involving fair trade policies; (2) important matters seriously affecting the interests of enterprises and consumers; (3) matters that will have a significant impact on industry; (4) matters that fall within the competence of the authorities of several governmental agencies. In relation to specific antitrust cases hearings may be held in relation to the following cases: monopoly cases falling under art 10 TFTA; merger cases falling under art 11(1) or (3) TFTA or cases in which the merging parties have failed to comply with requirements imposed by the TFTC, cases where mergers are prohibited pursuant to art 12 TFTA, or 'major or complicated cases'; concerted actions falling under art 14 TFTA including cases where applications for approval of concerted actions are denied. In addition hearings will be heard in respect of cases which would exert 'across-the-board influence in their **4-5.15**

[24] Ibid at para 10.

[25] See Fair Trade Commission *Guidelines on the Procedure of Public Hearings*, passed on 30 November 2000, amended on several occasions, most recent version promulgated by Order 0940005985, 22 July 2005. Hearings were first employed in the investigation of the cement cartel (15 December 2005, *TFTC Competition Policy Newsletter*, 1:10, 28 February 2006).

[26] *Guidelines on Public Hearings*, art 2.

respective markets, or have substantial influence on the interests of upstream and downstream industries and the public'.[27]

4-5.16 Hearings may not be demanded by the parties, and shall be initiated only by the Commissioners and after a Commissioners' meeting makes such a decision. Parties may however file a written application to the Commission explaining why a hearing should be held, but the TFTC may reject such an application by written notice if it deems that a hearing is unnecessary.[28] The general principle is that all such hearings are conducted orally and are held in public. However the TFTC may decide not to make the entire or part of the hearing open to the public either on its own initiative, or in response to an application by a party that a public hearing would be against the public interest or would cause 'major harm to the interests of the party concerned'.[29]

4-5.17 When the decision to hold a hearing is made the TFTC shall give written notice of this to the parties concerned, which must include details of the rights of the parties attending, and a deadline by which they must indicate whether they will appear. The hearing will be publicized in relevant Gazettes, and may also be published on the TFTC website and its other publications.[30] Any party may indicate to the TFTC its desire to attend a hearing, but the Regulations stress that space is limited and that for those parties not invited by the TFTC to participate, attendance cannot be guaranteed. Where parties attend written comments should be submitted by them at least ten days before the hearing. A party may request confidentiality in respect of such submissions where this is necessary, but if doing so should also submit an abstract which is suitable for public disclosure.[31]

4-5.18 Where cases are complex preliminary hearings may be held to facilitate the main hearing, and to determine and clarify the matters to be dealt with at the hearing.[32] Hearings are managed by a moderator who is required to 'preside over the hearing in an impartial manner',[33] and presided over by the Chairperson of the Commission or a person designated by him, and all Commissioners are to attend hearings, unless they have a special reason not to. All hearings are conducted in Chinese, and foreign participants are required to bring their own interpreters.[34]

---

[27] Ibid at art 4.
[28] Ibid at art 5.
[29] Ibid.
[30] Ibid at art 6.
[31] Ibid at art 12.
[32] Ibid at art 17.
[33] Ibid at art 19. The moderator is given, in art 19, a number of specific powers in relation to the conduct of the hearing, including forbidding presentations in order to avoid prolonging proceedings. Any party 'may immediately raise objections to what he/she considers to be any illegal or improper disposition rendered by the moderator' (art 20).
[34] Ibid at art 16.

The proceeding requirements are set out at art 18 of the *Guidelines on Public Hearings*. The moderator is to introduce the proceedings, and will explain the nature of the case under discussion. The TFTC will present a summary of its case, and will be followed by the party or parties concerned, other interested parties, witnesses and expert witnesses, and then other third parties. Questions may be put to those making presentations by the moderator, the Chairperson, or members of the TFTC, as long as these relate directly to the case in question.

A full record of the proceedings is required to be prepared by the administrative **4-5.19** staff of the TFTC. Records are to be signed by those who made presentations or asked questions at the hearing.

The rights of those subject to investigation are set out in part at art 27 of the **4-5.20** TFTA, which permits those claiming or defending their legal rights to 'apply to read, transcribe, photocopy, or photograph relevant materials or files' held by the TFTC.[35] The TFTC has published further rules and guidance relating to the rights of defendants. In 2002 a Regulation was passed relating to access to files and materials held by the TFTC.[36] The Regulation governs access to material 'during the course of an investigation', which means the period from the acceptance of a formal case filing by the Commission through to either the submission of the proposal put to the Commissioners', or where cases are subject to simplified procedures to the submission of the drafted decision to the Commissioner in charge of the review. As stated in art 27 of the TFTA, there are some materials, including those containing business secrets, which are not available to applicants for disclosure. Where materials or files are restricted these should be sealed or removed such that remaining materials are still available for access.[37] Access may be granted following the completion of an application form, and the applicant may appoint any employee or lawyer to review the material by way of an appointment letter submitted to the TFTC. Access will be granted within fifteen days of the receipt of the application, unless the provider of the information is contacted by the TFTC to ascertain whether the information is that to which access can be granted. Access is granted only at the offices of the TFTC, and a fee must be paid, although this is

[35] There are five exceptions to this general rule, in that parties may not make copies of, or read: (1) drafts of administrative documents, or working documents prepared for a case; (2) materials related to national defence, military affairs, diplomatic affairs, and any other official secrets; (3) materials relating to personal privacy, professional secrets, or business secrets that are required to be kept secret by the TFTC by virtue of provisions in other laws or regulations; (4) material the disclosure of which is likely to infringe the rights and interests of other third parties; and (5) where the disclosure is likely to 'seriously obstruct the performance of the official duties in maintaining social order, public security, or any other public interests'.

[36] Regulation Governing Access to Materials and Files of the Fair Trade Commission, Executive Yuan, circulated by Order 0910003769, 1 May 2002.

[37] Regulation, art 3.

not high.[38] Applicants may photocopy, print, or transcribe information, although art 9 of the Regulation provides that they may not in any way tamper with the materials, and may not take bound files apart. In each case the Regulation specifies that the applicant 'shall be granted one-time access only', although where the applicant can give a justifiable reason for further access this may be granted.[39] This might be the case for example where the TFTC subsequently gathered more information which it intended to rely on in formulating the decision relating to the applicant's conduct. Finally the Regulation states that those granted access to files may not use the information contained therein for any purpose other than that of the antitrust case itself.[40]

Corrective Measures and Penalties

4-5.21 Articles 35–37 of the TFTA set out specific penalties that may be levied in respect of breaches of articles 10 (monopoly conduct), 14 (concerted actions), 19 (unfair competition), or 23 (multi-level sales) of the TFTA. Before these penalties can be applied the TFTC must first have ordered the relevant enterprise or person to terminate the infringement, to rectify its conduct, or to take corrective measures in accordance with art 41 of the TFTA, which confers an ability on the TFTC to impose an administrative penalty independently of the operation of arts 35–37.

4-5.22 Article 41, which lies at the heart of the TFTC's enforcement powers, provides in part that the TFTC may:

> . . . order any enterprise that violates any of the provisions of this Law to cease therefrom, rectify its conduct or take necessary corrective action within the time prescribed in the order; in addition it may assess upon such enterprise an administrative penalty of not less than [NT$50,000 nor more than NT$25m].

Where the enterprise(s) subject to the order does not take the necessary corrective measures within the time limit set in the order the TFTC may continue to assert the order, and each time it does so may impose an administrative penalty of not less than NT$100,000 nor more than NT$50m, in effect therefore applying a system similar to that of the daily penalty rates operated by the EC Commission in the enforcement of EC antitrust law.

4-5.23 Article 40 sets out the sanctions that are applicable in the event of breaches of the provisions of the TFTA relating to merger control, and has been discussed in Chapter 4-4 of this Part.

[38] The fee levels are set in the current version of the Regulation Fee Standards for Disclosing or Providing Information by the Fair Trade Commission, Executive Yuan.
[39] Regulation, art 8.
[40] Ibid at art 10.

Where any person refuses to pay a penalty set under arts 40, 41, 42, or 43 the matter 'shall be referred to the court for compulsory execution'.[41] **4-5.24**

Having employed the procedure referred to in art 41, the provisions of arts 35 and 36 of the TFTA may also be applied. In respect of violations of the monopoly provisions of art 10 the 'actor' shall be punished by 'imprisonment for not more than three years or detention, or by a fine of not more than [NT$100m], or by both'.[42] This penalty may be applied where the enterprise has refused to comply with an order made under art 41, or has complied with the order, but has committed the same or a similar violation again. There is no time period specified in the article within which this recidivism must have occurred for the enterprise to be punished without the reapplication of art 41. The same is true for breaches of the concerted actions provisions of art 14 of the TFTA. In respect of breaches of the unfair competition provisions of art 19 a failure to comply with an order made under art 41 may be punished by imprisonment for a term of not more than two years, or by a fine of not more than NT$50m, or both. As with arts 10 and 14 recidivism will also activate this provision. Breaches of the rules of art 23 relating to multi-level sales organizations shall be punished by imprisonment for not more than three years, or detention, or a fine of not more than NT$100m, or both.[43] **4-5.25**

In arts 35 and 36 provision is made for the punishment of both legal and natural persons. Article 38 specifies, in slightly awkward language, that in any case in which a legal person is convicted of an offence both the natural person and the legal person shall be punished as appropriate. **4-5.26**

There are no guidelines as to the amount of the penalty that is to be set, but art 36 of the Enforcement Rules specifies that 'all circumstances shall be taken into account', and also sets out eight factors to which the TFTC may have regard in particular: **4-5.27**

(1) the motivation, purpose, and expected improper benefit of the actions;
(2) the degree of harm caused by the act to the market;
(3) the duration of the harm caused by the act;
(4) the benefits derived from the improper act;
(5) the scale, operating condition, and market position of the infringing enterprise;
(6) whether or not the type of act found to constitute the infringement has in the past been the subject of corrections or warnings by the TFTC;

[41] art 44, TFTA.
[42] art 35, TFTA.
[43] art 35, TFTA.

(7) the past conduct of the enterprise, including the types of violations it may have committed, the number of violations, the time between each violation, and the punishment, if any, previously meted out; and
(8) any remorse shown and the degree of cooperation during the course of the investigation.

4-5.28 In some cases the TFTC has issued warnings to companies rather than imposing penalties or making final behavioural orders. Thus, for example, in relation to an investigation into the distribution and pricing of school textbooks the TFTC issued a warning applicable to qualified publishers 'to correct the trading order in the textbook market'.[44]

4-5.29 In addition to the formal steps set out above the TFTC may also enter into Administrative Settlement Agreements as an alternative to proceeding to a final infringement decision. This was the case, for example, in relation to Microsoft Corp when in 2003 the TFTC and the company entered into a settlement agreement of wide scope, which is discussed in more detail in Chapter 4-3. One of the notable features of the agreement was its adoption in Taiwan of the terms of the Consent Decree entered into by Microsoft in the US. In relation to this case the TFTC stated that there were both factual and legal issues which were uncertain, and that by adopting an administrative settlement 'both parties can avert lengthy legal proceedings and seek to build consensus . . . [achieving] efficient dispute resolution'.[45]

Leniency

4-5.30 The TFTC does not operate a formal leniency programme.

Appeals

4-5.31 The Administrative Appeal Law and the Administrative Litigation Law[46] provide that appeals from decisions of the TFTC may be made in the first instance to the Appeals Committee of the Executive Yuan. Further appeals may be made to the High Administrative Court, and thence to the Supreme Administrative Court. Appeals may be brought by any party that can demonstrate that its legal rights

---

[44] *Nanyi Bookstore*, 25 September 1999.

[45] TFTC press release 0307, 27 February 2003. The procedure followed by the TFTC in developing the settlement is explained in the press release. A task force was set up in order to conduct the comprehensive review needed in the case. This met 28 times from May 2002 until the conclusion of the process. Negotiations with Microsoft commenced on 2 December 2002. Twelve meetings were held, and 'the final round of negotiation even lasted non-stop for more than 27 hours'.

[46] Sometimes translated as the Administrative Procedure Law.

have been prejudiced by any decision taken by the TFTC. Any administrative appeal to the Executive Yuan must be made within thirty days after the receipt of the relevant decision taken by the TFTC. The TFTC then has a period of twenty days within which to respond. Hearings are not normally held, and there are no formal procedures for obtaining documents through a discovery process. The Executive Yuan can review both the facts and the law in appeals, and although it may substitute its own decision for that of the relevant agency, it is more likely to remit the case back to the TFTC for reconsideration in light of the Executive Yuan's comments. In the High Administrative Court the approach is one of judicial review. There is also no right of discovery and very little prospect of making oral arguments, with the judges working instead from filed briefs only, save in exceptional cases.

Third Party Rights and Damages

Although third party civil rights are clearly set out on the face of the legislation, **4-5.32** the rights of third parties in practice are limited. Liu has stated that 'compared with the courts, the TFTC monopolizes [TFTA] enforcement. . . . the TFTA is not and never will become judge-made common law. Very few [TFTA] cases even exist, and none of them constitute meaningful precedent.'[47]

The rights of third parties to sue for damages and other forms of relief are set out **4-5.33** in arts 30–34 of the TFTA. Article 30 provides that, in the event of any violation of the TFTA which harms the rights or interests of a third party, that party may 'demand the removal of such infringement'. Such relief may also be sought where there is the likelihood that the TFTA will be infringed.

Article 31 establishes the right to seek damages, in the event that any harm flows **4-5.34** to a third party as a result of a breach of the provisions of the TFTA. Where the relevant court finds that the infringement is intentional art 32 of the TFTA permits the court to award punitive damages up to a maximum of three times the actual damages suffered. In making such an award the court must take into account 'the nature of the infringement'. Whether to award treble damages is at the discretion of the court, and it appears that in practice significant damages

---

[47] Liu, n 1, above, at 94. See also ibid at 140: '. . . Taiwan's competition law provides for apparently strong but practically weak civil relief.' However, there have been developments in Taiwan's civil procedure rules which might assist the bringing of actions by private parties, although the record to date is poor in this respect. In particular following changes to the Consumer Protection Law of 1994 *parens patriae* actions may now be brought on behalf of consumers by recognized consumer groups, and class actions may also be brought. Although the TFTA expressly allows for injunctive relief to be sought Liu notes that 'no party to a major case has ever sought injunctive relief' (ibid at 141).

awards have not been made. The second paragraph of art 32 gives the claimant the right to seek damages based solely on the amount of the gain to the defendant. The TFTA does not set out rules relating to standing and causation, and it will be noted that this text leaves several questions unanswered, in particular that of how direct the harm has to be for the right to be established. The reference to the unlawful gain as a basis for action is also problematic, and it has been pointed out in the UK that making such assessments can be very complex.

4-5.35 There is a limitation period of two years within which damages may be sought, the period running from such time as the claimant was aware of both the act and the person liable for the damage alleged. In any event no claim may be brought after ten years has lapsed from the time of the infringing conduct.[48]

4-5.36 There is one further twist in this Chapter of the Act, in that the claimant may request the Court, if an infringement is found, to have the content of the judgment published in a newspaper at the expense of the defendant.[49]

4-5.37 Private litigation is before the district courts in the first instance, and procedures are set out in the Code of Civil Procedure. Appeals are to the High Courts and the Supreme Court.

[48] art 33, TFTA.
[49] art 34, TFTA.

PART 5

KOREA

5-1.	The Korean Antitrust Law Regime	215
5-2.	Korea Agreements	225
5-3.	Korea Monopoly and Abuse of Dominance	245
5-4.	Korea Merger Control	263
5-5.	Korea Procedure	289

5-1

THE KOREAN ANTITRUST LAW REGIME

Introduction	5-1.01	**Territorial Application**	5-1.10
The Fair Trade Commission	5-1.06	**International Cooperation and Agreements**	5-1.13
Information sources	5-1.08		
General Exemptions	5-1.09		

Introduction

The Constitution of Korea sets out, in art 119(2), the power of the State to regulate economic affairs within the framework of a free and fair market.[1] This constitutional power makes reference to the desirability of maintaining balanced growth and stability. Korea enacted the Monopoly Regulation and Fair Trade Act ('MRFTA') on 31 December 1980.[2] The Act entered into force on 1 April 1981, and has since been amended on over ten occasions. More recently proposals have been brought forward for further amendments, but at the time of writing these have not been put into effect, and relate to holding company arrangements, which are not dealt with in this text. The Act contains within it provisions relating to monopolization, agreements, and mergers, all of which are dealt with in more detail in the following chapters of this Part. The MRFTA contains fifteen chapters and a number of addenda, although none of the latter have significant substantive effect on the operation of the Act as at 1 February 2009. The Act contains within it both substantive and procedural rules. Article 1 of the MRFTA states that the **5-1.01**

[1] Article 119(1) of the Constitution states that: 'The economic order of the Republic of Korea is based on a respect for the freedom and creative initiative of enterprises and individuals in economic affairs'.

[2] Law No 3320.

purpose of the Act is, inter alia, to promote fair and free competition.[3] This is to be achieved by 'preventing the abuse of market dominance by enterprisers and the excessive concentration of economic power, and by regulating improper cartels and unfair business practices'.[4]

5-1.02 Chapter 1 of the Act sets out the basic definitions employed throughout the Act; Chapter 2 relates to the prohibition of abuse of 'market-dominating positions'; Chapter 3, which has been heavily amended in recent years, to merger control and combinations of enterprises;[5] Chapter 4 applies to 'improper cartels'; Chapter 5 to 'unfair business practices'; Chapter 6 to 'enterprisers' organization', or, in other words, to the activities of trade associations; Chapter 7 to restrictions on resale price maintenance; Chapter 8 to 'restrictions on the conclusion of international contracts'; and the remaining chapters provide for the institutional structure, including the establishment and constitution of the Korean Fair Trade Commission ('KFTC'), and enforcement powers. Chapter 11 of the Act, discussed in Chapter 5-5, expressly grants third parties the right to seek damages in cases where an 'enterpriser or enterprisers' organization [violates] the provisions of this Act and consequently causing damage to a person'. More recently a specialist organization, the Korean Fair Trade Mediation Committee was created under Chapter 9-2 of the MRFTA, whose role and function is discussed further in this Part below.

5-1.03 The MRFTA is supplemented by the Enforcement Decree of the Monopoly Regulation and Fair Trade Act, and a number of specific guidelines have also been

[3] In November 2007 the Supreme Court of Korea held that the primary purpose of the Act, at least in relation to the control of monopoly conduct, should be to protect the process of competition, rather than (inefficient) competitors:

> . . . if any strategic business activity with no or obscure anti-competitive intent or purpose is treated as a violation of the law which regulates restrictions on competition, solely on account of a certain degree of disadvantage to another enterpriser, it may create a concern of making such regulation for the sake of protection of competitors rather than of competition, and it may also bring about a risk of impeding the intrinsic efficiency of the market economy that would otherwise reorganize the market with competitive enterprisers, by virtue of unreasonably shrinking business activity of enterprisers. (*POSCO v The Korea Fair Trade Commission*, Supreme Court of Korea, Case 2002*Du*8626, 22 November 2007)

[4] All translations of legislation and guidance are those given on the KFTC website, unless otherwise specified. In the summer of 2008 the KFTC updated its website, in the process providing a consolidated version of the MRFTA. The translation of this is in parts significantly different from that provided on the KFTC website earlier, and is in places idiosyncratic. However, for the sake of consistency it is this translation which is relied on in this Part of the book. The full text of the MRFTA is set out in Appendix 3.

[5] Chapter 3 is also addressed to the relationships within groups of companies, targeted at the *Chaebols*. These provisions are unlikely to be applicable to non-Korean enterprises and are not dealt with further in this text. For a comment on these powers see Lee, HY, 'Regulation of Undue Internal Dealings under the Monopoly Regulation and Fair Trade Act' (2005) 4:2 *Journal of Korean Competition Law* 83.

published, most of which are of a general nature. These are discussed as appropriate in the remainder of this Part.[6]

The MRFTA applies, for the most part, to the actions of 'enterprisers' (although individual officers and other relevant persons may be subject to its jurisdiction).[7] The term 'enterpriser' is defined at art 2(1), and means: **5-1.04**

> . . . a person who operates a manufacturing business, a service business, or any other business. Any officer, employee, agent or other person acting in the interest of the enterpriser shall be considered an enterpriser in relation to the application of provisions pertaining to the enterprisers organization.

While the MRFTA is the major instrument relating to competition law in Korea it is not the only one. There are various sector-specific instruments, and in 2002 the Fair Franchise Transactions Act was enacted.[8] This Act applies exclusively to franchises, its purpose being to institute 'a fair and rational transaction system for franchises' by 'ensuring mutually complementary and balanced development of the franchiser/franchisee relationship on an equal footing'.[9] The terms of this Act are further considered in the following chapter. **5-1.05**

The Fair Trade Commission

The KFTC was established on the basis of the authority provided for by art 35 of the MRFTA. It has the status of a central administrative organization under art 2 of the Government Organization Act. It has jurisdiction over the matters set out in the MRFTA, and is also charged with engaging in 'competition-encouragement policies'.[10] It has described its role as being 'to nurture growth potential by enhancing efficiency in resource allocation through transparent business management and fair competition'.[11] It consists of nine Commissioners, led by a Chairman, **5-1.06**

[6] Some guidelines are very specific. See for example the *Notification on the Types and Criteria for Unfair Business Practices and Abuse of Market-Dominant Position Relating to Newspaper Business.*

[7] It also in Chapter 6, noted above and discussed in Chapter 5-2 below, regulates the activities of 'enterprisers' organizations'.

[8] The Act entered into force on 1 November 2002. It has since been amended, most recently by Law 8630, of 3 August 2007.

[9] art 1, FFTA.

[10] art 36(6), MRFTA. This role extends to consultation and coordination activities in respect of legislation and secondary legislation and administrative measures which may affect competition. Between 2005 and 2007, for example, the KFTC recommended revisions of 79 regulations that it argued had anti-competitive effects (KFTC Newsletter, 1 May 2008). In the OECD *Annual Report on Competition Policy Developments in Korea 2003* attention is drawn to the role of the KFTC in 'pre-consultation and regulatory reform on any anti-competitive laws' (para 4). The KFTC also places focus on encouraging companies to develop antitrust compliance programmes.

[11] KFTC, *Direction of Competition Policy in 2004*, part II.

whose term of appointment is three years, with one renewal of term possible. The Chairman and Vice-Chairmen are Presidential appointments based on recommendations made by the Prime Minister, and the remaining members are appointed on recommendation by the Chairman. It is expressly stated in the legislation that the offices of the Chairman and Vice-Chairman are considered to be 'political appointees'.[12] Members may be either public officials of the appropriate grade with experience in monopoly regulation and fair trade, lawyers (including judges), academics, or business managers all of whom must have at least fifteen years' experience. Members may not be dismissed from the KFTC unless they have been sentenced to imprisonment, or are incapable of performing their duties through prolonged illness. Meetings are either plenary or chamber. Plenary meetings consist of all the members, and may be held where the matters specified in art 37-3(1) are under consideration. These include: interpretation and application of the relevant legislation and notices; appeals made under art 53;[13] and matters relating to reform of regulations or public notices, or those 'having substantial economic impact'. The head office of the KFTC is in Seoul, but there are regional offices in other major metropolitan cities. In December 2005 the KFTC undertook an internal reorganization, and the current structure is set out at Figure 5-1.1.

5-1.07 In addition to its specific role of enforcing Korean antitrust law as specified in the MRFTA and other relevant legislation the KFTC has a more general role to promote competition in Korea. It has the power, for example, to bring forward proposals to deal with structural problems in markets which have for a long time been characterized by oligopolistic or monopoly dominance. Since 2001 the KFTC has operated a 'clean market project', under which it selects industries each year for particular examination which are believed to lack competition and to have significant impact on consumers. The examination of such industries may focus on 'any identified anti-competitive elements in the overall process, including production, distribution, marketing and consumption'.[14] The KFTC must also be consulted by the heads of administrative departments when it is proposed by that department to bring forward legislation or regulations that contain within them provisions that are anti-competitive.[15] While the KFTC *must* be consulted in such cases it does not have the power to prevent such legislation being enacted, but may make recommendations for changes. Anecdotal evidence suggests that the KFTC has had a notable record of successes in this aspect of its work.

---

[12] art 37(3), MRFTA. However, art 35(1) provides that the KFTC is established 'for the purpose of *independently* promoting the objectives of this Act' (emphasis added).

[13] Article 53 provides a right of appeal in respect of measures taken by the KFTC. The application of this provision is discussed further in Chapter 5-5, below.

[14] OECD *Annual Report on Competition Policy Developments in Korea 2003*, para 17.

[15] art 63, MRFTA.

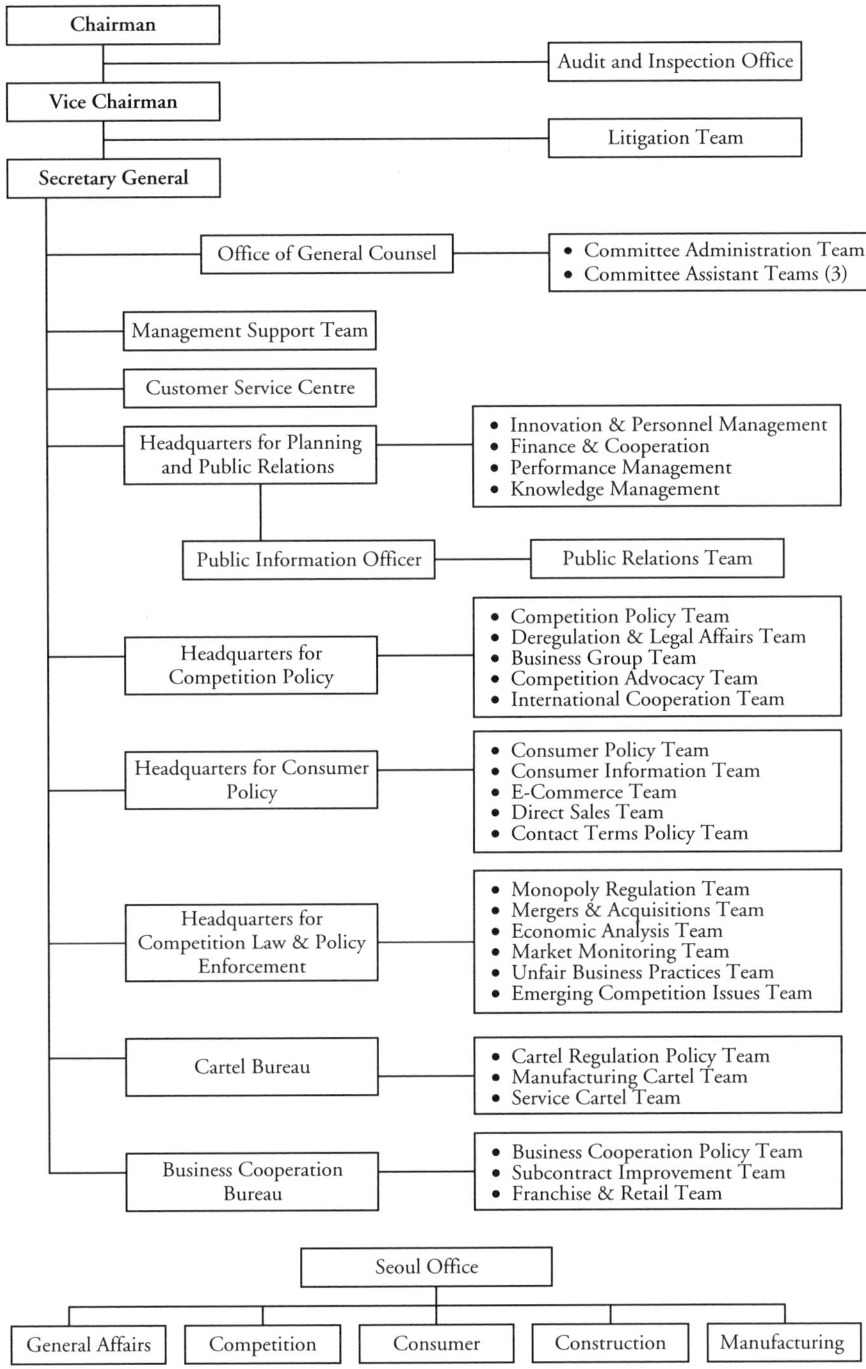

There are other regional offices in Pusan, Kwangju, Daejon, and Daegu

Figure 5-1.1 Organizational structure of the KFTC.

Information sources

5-1.08 The operation of the Korean competition law regime is generally transparent. The KFTC, for example, published its important decisions in full text in a quarterly series (annually between 1981 and 1995), and publicizes its enforcement activity regularly in English. Compared to some other East Asian jurisdictions there is a substantial amount of material publicly available in English relating to the Korean competition law regime, and its operation, most of which is to be found on the KFTC website. In particular this website contains the full translated text of the majority of the relevant legislation, although it is not comprehensive as regards secondary materials. The KFTC also publishes a regular newsletter relating to enforcement activities and other recent developments in English (although this publication has at times been interrupted). In 2008 the KFTC for the second time published its Annual Report in English, and noted that it intended to continue this practice in the future. Both English language Annual Reports available at the time of writing are referenced in this Part of the book as appropriate. The website also includes the texts of various speeches by officials, and some policy documents. Some of the decisions taken by the KFTC are available in English on the APEC website.[16] There has been little substantial international publication on this regime, and the most significant articles available in English are referred to here, or are referenced in the bibliography.[17]

General Exemptions

5-1.09 The general principle operating in Korea is that all sectors, including government entities acting in commercial areas, are subject to competition law. Where administrative guidance exists in relation to particular industrial sectors this too may operate to remove the behaviour from the scope of the operation of the MRFTA. However, such guidance must be firmly grounded in legislation, and if it is not, its existence may not serve to protect those following it from the application of the MRFTA.[18] Specific exemptions relating to categories of otherwise condemned conduct are dealt with as appropriate in relation to that conduct in this text. There are some general exemptions from the application of the law set out at Chapter 12 of the MRFTA. There are three such general exemptions. The first is that the MRFTA does not make unlawful any act which is carried out in accordance with

---

16 <http://www.apecc.org>.

17 For a very useful entry point into the resources available see Kim, Y-H, 'A Guide to Korean Antitrust Law' (2002) 2 *Journal of Korean Law* 161.

18 See Supreme Court of Korea, case 92*Nu*8040, 13 November 1992.

any other Act, or any decree made under any other Act. The second is that it does not apply to any act 'deemed to be an exercise of rights under the Copyright Act, Patent Act, Utility Models Act, Design Act, or Trademark Act'.[19] The final general exemption is that the prohibitions do not apply to any legitimate acts of associations established in accordance with the specified requirements. The requirements are that: (1) the aim of the association shall be to promote mutual aid among small-scale enterprisers,[20] or consumers; (2) membership of the association must be voluntary, with free withdrawal; (3) all members of any such association shall have equal voting rights; and (4) in the case of any association which makes profits, the distribution of profits to members shall be determined by the articles of incorporation of the association. There are also some specific exemptions, such as for liner conferences—in respect of which Korea takes the view that it is international practice to recognize and permit the existence of such structures—producer cooperatives in agriculture and forestry, and, as discussed in Chapter 5-2, minimum resale price maintenance is still permitted in respect of literary works.

Territorial Application

The MRFTA may be applied extraterritorially.[21] It is thus expressly stated in **5-1.10**
art 2-2 that even though activities take place overseas they may be subject to the application of the MRFTA where 'they have any influence on the domestic market'. The first case in which the KFTC applied the Act in this way was in the graphite electrodes cartel case[22] (also subject to enforcement action undertaken by the EC and US authorities) and on 20 March 2002 fines totalling US$8,532,000 (Won8,812m) were imposed on six manufacturers from the US, Japan, and Germany. The KFTC noted in its decision that the parties:

> . . . held several meetings in London, Tokyo and other cities from May 1992 to February 1998; later reaching agreements on price-fixing and market allocation targeting the world market, including the Korean market, consequently implementing their agreements.

---

19 art 59, MRFTA.

20 In effect, 'small and medium-sized enterprises'. The Act does not provide a definition of 'small-scale'.

21 See Jung, Y, 'Korean Competition Law: First Step Towards Globalisation' (2005) 4:2 *Journal of Korean Competition Law* 177 and Kim, W-K, 'The Extraterritorial Application of US Antitrust Law and its Adoption in Korea' (2003) 7 *Singapore Journal of International & Comparative Law* 386.

22 KFTC Decision 2002-07 (4 April 2002).

In taking this decision the KFTC drew a clear link between the existence of the cartel, and its impact in Korea. The KFTC further noted in the Decision that:

> [t]hey imported graphite electrodes amounting to US$553m from the six companies from May 1992 to February 1998, and during the period the import price increased from an average of US$2,255 per ton in 1992 to an average of US$3,356 in 1997 (about 48.9% price increase). The damage incurred by the companies importing graphite electrodes is estimated at approximately US$139m. Korea's major industries (such as automobile and shipbuilding which necessitate much steel) were also influenced by this international cartel.

5-1.11 An appeal was launched by Showa Denko KK against the decision taken against it by the KFTC, and ultimately the case was heard by the Supreme Court of Korea, which upheld the right of the KFTC to take action against international participants in such practices where there was an effect on the market in Korea.[23] The Court held, in part, that:

> . . . the fact that the business operator who conducts unfair collective activities is stipulated [in art 2 of the MRFTA] to be the 'operator of manufacturing business, service business and other businesses', and is not limited to domestic business operators, and the fact that there is a need to include foreign business operators in the scope of the application of the [MRFTA] in the case where an unfair collective activity in a foreign country affects the domestic market, the [MRFTA] shall be applied within the limit of the effect on the domestic market of a consensus, if a foreign business operator reaches a consensus jointly with another business operator to limit competition and that such consensus includes the domestic market and affected the domestic market.[24]

5-1.12 A similar approach was taken in the *Vitamins* case,[25] prosecuted also in the EC and the US. In a decision similar to that taken in these regimes, the KFTC found that multinational companies had engaged in a cartel relating to raw vitamins extending from 1989 through to 1999, both fixing prices and setting sales volumes in the Korean market.[26] In April 2003 penalties of Won4bn were imposed on six companies from Switzerland, France, Germany, Japan, and the Netherlands. Although the size of the penalties, approximately US$3.5m, pales into insignificance when compared with those imposed in the US and the EC, the cumulative effect of such penalties imposed across numbers of regimes, and the burdens of cooperating with investigative procedures, must be presumed to have a dampening effect on international cartel activity.

---

[23] The judgment of the Seoul High Court is discussed at Jung, n 21, above.

[24] *Showa Denko KK v The Korea Fair Trade Commission*, Supreme Court of Korea, case 2004*Du*11275, 24 March 2006. An appeal from the judgment of the Seoul High Court, 2002*Nu*6127, 26 August 2003.

[25] KFTC Decision 2003-098, 29 April 2003.

[26] See judgment of the Seoul High Court, 2003*Nu*9000.

International Cooperation and Agreements

Article 36-2 of the MRFTA sets out principles to be applied in relation to the KFTC's cooperation with other jurisdictions and the approach to be taken to international cooperation in the application of antitrust law. Article 36-2(1) permits the Government to enter into agreements with third parties which relate to competition and allows such agreements to extend to conduct not directly violating Korean antitrust law. The KFTC is required to support law enforcement by foreign governments falling under any agreement signed pursuant to art 36-2(1).[27] Korea is an active member of the OECD and the ICN. The OECD-Korea Regional Centre for Competition was established in Seoul in 2004, and in April 2004 Korea hosted the ICN Annual Conference. **5-1.13**

Korea has entered into a number of bilateral arrangements with other States in relation to the application of competition law. With the EU for example, a bilateral EU/Korea Competition Dialogue was announced on 28 October 2004.[28] The cooperation is based on three key principles: (1) improvement of the legal framework relating to competition law; (2) exchanges of experience in relation to cases and to views on substantive competition policy issues; and (3) the holding of high-level meetings between Korea and the EU on at least an annual basis. The KFTC has also entered into a more formal agreement with Australia in September 2002,[29] under which the respective competition authorities will 'share information, cooperate with and provide assistance to each other in their enforcement activities to the extent compatible with their essential interests', and has a cooperation arrangement with Mexico (April 2004). A Memorandum of Understanding between the KFTC and Turkey covers exchange of information, rendering of expert assistance, and exchanges of studies, consultations, and materials. A Memorandum of Understanding regarding cooperation in competition policy has also been signed between Korea, the Interstate Council for Antimonopoly Policy of the CIS countries, the Competition Council of Latvia, **5-1.14**

---

[27] art 36-2(2), MRFTA. The effect of the first two paragraphs of art 36-2 is to introduce a system similar to that of the positive comity found in the EC–US cooperation agreement referred to in Chapter 1-2 above. Article 36-2(3) further provides that even in the absence of a formal agreement entered into under art 36-2(1) the KFTC may still assist a foreign government in its enforcement activity 'if there is any guarantee from the requesting country that it will also support the same or similar cases requested by the [Korean] Government in the future'. The cooperation provided by the KFTC may not go outside the scope of its powers under the MRFTA, such that, for example, documents subject to confidentiality requirements may not be disclosed to foreign governments or enforcement agencies.

[28] EC Commission press release IP (04) 1325, 28 October 2004; [2005] 5 CMLR 1457.

[29] Cooperation arrangement between the Fair Trade Commission of the Republic of Korea and the Australian Competition and Consumer Commission regarding the application of their competition and consumer protection laws, 29 September 2002.

and the Competition Council of Romania.[30] In 2005 Korea concluded an agreement with Singapore in respect of competition enforcement and cooperation. There are also competition-related provisions in the Korea–Chile Free Trade Agreement, and in the Korea–EFTA Free Trade Agreement of 2003. Agreements have also been entered into with, inter alia, Singapore (2005), the EFTA (2005) and as part of a free trade agreement entered into with the US in 2007 which at the time of writing is under legislative review in the US. This latter agreement incorporates the principle of positive comity, which is not contained in the other agreements.[31]

30 17 September 2003.

31 See Shin, HY, *Korean Competition Law* (Seoul: Bubmunsa, 2007) 428 ff.

5-2

KOREA AGREEMENTS

Introduction 5-2.01
Chapter 4, MRFTA—'Improper Cartels' (Horizontal Agreements) 5-2.02
Horizontal agreements 5-2.17
Enforcement examples 5-2.17
Chapter 6, MRFTA—Enterprisers' Organizations (Trade Associations) 5-2.22
Enforcement examples 5-2.25
Chapter 7, MRFTA—Resale Price Maintenance 5-2.26
Enforcement examples 5-2.27
Chapter 8, MRFTA—International Contracts 5-2.28
Vertical Agreements 5-2.29
Penalties for Breach 5-2.31
Franchise Agreements 5-2.34

Introduction

There are a number of different areas of the MRFTA which relate to what may be classed as multilateral anti-competitive conduct, or the law of anti-competitive agreements. The part of the law which bears the closest relationship in terms of subject matter to the standard prohibitions of the Sherman Act s 1, or art 81 EC is set out in Chapter 4 of the MRFTA, although this is applied exclusively in relation to horizontal agreements. Chapter 5 of the MRFTA prohibits 'unfair business practices', and its terms extend to the control of vertical agreements, and, in some cases, to horizontal practices (such as, for example, collective refusals to deal). There are in addition prohibitions on resale price maintenance in Chapter 7, and certain activities of 'enterprisers' organizations' in Chapter 6. Certain other provisions relate to agreements made by *chaebols*. All of these different provisions are grouped here, although those relating to *chaebol* structures are not dealt with. There is also entirely separate legislation which deals with franchise agreements, and while this is concerned for the most part with standards of 'fairness' there are also provisions within this legislation which relate to competitive conduct. This law is discussed at the end of this chapter. **5-2.01**

Chapter 4, MRFTA—'Improper Cartels' (Horizontal Agreements)

5-2.02 The core of the law relating to anti-competitive agreements is set out at Chapter 4 of the MRFTA which controls 'improper cartels'.[1] The KFTC has also published a set of guidelines relating to the notification of concerted acts, and there is the possibility of the grant of an exemption, although this power is the exclusive prerogative of the KFTC. Article 19(1) of the MRFTA provides that:

> [n]o enterpriser shall agree with other enterprisers by contract, agreement, resolution, or any other means to engage jointly in any of the following acts or let others engage in such kinds of activities that unfairly restrict competition . . .

5-2.03 There then follows a list of nine practices that are prima facie condemned. These are as follows: (1) fixing, maintaining, or changing prices;[2] (2) determining the terms and conditions for transactions or payments; (3) restricting production, delivery, transportation, or transactions in goods or services; (4) limiting the territory of trade or customers; (5) preventing or restricting the establishment or extension of facilities or the installation of equipment necessary for the production of goods or services; (6) restrictions on the types or specifications in the production or trade of goods; (7) the establishment of a venture jointly to carry out or manage the main parts of a business; (8) bid-rigging (any act of 'deciding matters [such as] bidding price, auctioning price, auctioneer, or bidder in bids or auctions'); (9) 'any practice that substantially minimizes competition in a particular business area by means [that] interferes with or restricts the activities or contents of the business'. It is not necessary for any agreement entered into falling under art 19(1) to be put into practice, and the illegality lies in the act of the illegal meeting of the minds.[3]

5-2.04 There exists the possibility of exemption from any of the above practices when the requirements set by Presidential Decree are met and where the purpose of the practice relates to any of the criteria specified in art 19(2). Exemptions may be granted, only on individual authorization by the KFTC, therefore where the

---

[1] An older translation on the KFTC website used the term 'unfair collaborative acts', which is perhaps a more accurate summary of the contents of Chapter 4. See generally Lee, MH, 'Recent Developments in the Treatment of Collusion by the Korean Courts' (2005) 4:2 *Journal of Korean Law* 155.

[2] This prohibition extends to the setting of standard prices against which discounts to individual purchasers were subsequently negotiated (See *General successor of Park Hwa-sam, supervisor for the reorganizing stock company Mona Lisa v Fair Trade Commission*, Supreme Court of Korea, Decision 2000*Du*1386, 28 May 2002), and to delivered pricing and based-point pricing schemes (Supreme Court of Korea, Decision 2000*Du*7872, 8 May 2001).

[3] See, eg Supreme Court of Korea, Decision 98*Du*15849, 23 February 1999.

purpose of the practice is to achieve: (1) industry rationalization; (2) research and development; (3) addressing problems raised by economic depression; (4) industrial restructuring; (5) rationalization of trade terms and conditions; (6) enhancement of the competitiveness of small and medium-sized enterprises. Although guidelines exist there are an exceptionally small number of cases in which exemptions have been granted. It will be noted that on the face of the legislation there is no need, as is the case with the application of art 81 EC for example, to demonstrate that the benefits accrued from such practices will be passed on to consumers, and the Act is silent as to any mechanism for balancing the benefits of such conduct with the harm that may flow. Anti-competitive acts undertaken in order to comply with legal dictates are not subject to proscription under the MRFTA, although those undertaken in response to 'administrative guidance' may be proscribed, and penalized, where that administrative guidance has no basis in law (see further below). It is worthy of note that the fact that such cases still arise demonstrates that tensions continue to exist between the demands of competition law, and the cultures of particular ministries or industries. The KFTC has held that an agreement which had as its purpose to 'improve the working environment', and to address problems caused by a labour shortage, was not exempt from the application of art 19 of the MRFTA, stating that although such measures would be legal where they were undertaken by individual operators, they would not be legal where a common position in an industry was reached by way of an agreement. In the same case the KFTC held that a determination to cooperate with an energy conservation initiative sponsored by a government ministry could not justify concertation.[4]

The KFTC has stated that, 'in competition law enforcement [it] pays most attention to horizontal collusion', and that it 'has tried to establish a *per se* rule against price fixing'.[5] The *Concerted Acts Review Guidelines*[6] adhere to the principle that certain hard-core conduct is prima facie illegal, and is unlikely to be exempted. This is in conformity with case law emanating from the courts, in which it has been consistently held that price-fixing, market sharing, and bid-rigging may be condemned without there being the need to establish the existence of competitive harm.[7] Conduct considered to be hard-core includes price setting, output restrictions, allocation of territories, and bid-rigging. Non-hard-core restrictions, which **5-2.05**

[4] *Korea Oil Station Association ('KOSA')*, KFTC News, 2005-10. If such measures were to be lawful they would have to be based on a clear legal provision.

[5] OECD *Korea—Report on Competition Law and Institutions (2004)*, DAF/COMP(2005)9, para 4. Two recent cases provide evidence of the attack on this form of conduct. *The Korea Herald* reported on 17 October 2008, p 7, that the KFTC had fined dealers of BMW and Lexus respectively a total of Won21.7bn. The dealers had, at the horizontal level, drawn up agreements relating inter alia to limits on discounts.

[6] KFTC Notification no 49, 21 December 2007.

[7] See Lee, n 1, above at 159.

include typically research and development or specialization joint-ventures, are to be assessed on a balancing exercise of their anti- and pro-competitive effects. In undertaking this exercise regard is to be had to the relevant market, market shares, and market power. There is a presumption that where the combined market shares of the relevant enterprises are 20 per cent or below non-hard-core restrictions will be permitted. Where market shares exceed 20 per cent, other relevant indicators of market power, and the nature of the market will be considered. This analysis may include changes to market shares over time, the possibility of competition from abroad, and the possibility of successful entry into the market. The nature of the restrictions contained in the agreement will also be considered, with particular attention being paid to the duration of the restrictions, the usage and control of assets, the nature of any financial relationships, the remaining extent of competition between the parties, and the extent of any information exchanges between the parties relating to prices or outputs. The efficiency claims for the agreement will be considered, and in the final stage a balance between the pro- and anti-competitive effects will be made. It should be noted that absent these guidelines and the possibility of obtaining an exemption on a case-by-case basis there are no generalized block exemptions of the type that are so important to the EC system for the control of anti-competitive agreements.

5-2.06 Any contract entered into which relates to any of the unfair collaborative acts set out in art 1(1) is null and void, and may not therefore be relied upon.

5-2.07 The KFTC has taken determined efforts in recent years to improve its ability to detect and punish anti-competitive agreements, and cartel conduct in particular.[8] The reorganization of the KFTC in December 2005 led to the creation of a dedicated cartels unit, with three teams working on such cases under the leadership of a Director General-level Bureau Head. In 2007 a change was made in the approach to cartels under which parties would be presumed to be in a cartel where there is a coincidence in behaviour, and where there is only 'a probability of an agreement in the light of circumstantial conditions such as features of the trade, goods and services in question, economic reasons for the specific behaviour' and the appearance of contact between the parties.[9]

5-2.08 The Supreme Court of Korea has held that in the case of a long-running cartel or concerted practice which consists of ongoing anti-competitive arrangements each

[8] The fact that the Korean economy has been subject in the past to extensive cartelization has been widely acknowledged. See, eg Suh, DW, 'Enforcement Direction of Competition Law' (2005) 4:2 *Journal of Korean Law* 29 at 39: 'As Korea traditionally has a strong deep sense of mutual cooperation, Korean businesses tend to be less aware of seriousness of cartel. Therefore, cartel has been prevalent in almost every sector of the market.'

[9] See KFTC *2008 Annual Report*, p 5. See also the approach taken in relation to the presumption of concerted action set out in art 19(5), discussed below.

meeting or concerted action between the parties is to be treated as a part of a continuous infringement and that participation in such an arrangement ceases only when the anti-competitive action itself is terminated.[10]

Article 19(5) of the MRFTA addresses in part the difficulties of proving the existence of concerted actions. It provides that: **5-2.09**

> [i]f two or more enterprisers commit any of the acts listed in Clause (1) and practically restrict competition in a particular business area, they shall be presumed to have committed an unfair collaborative act despite the existence of an explicit agreement to engage in such act.[11]

In effect this suggests that parallel conduct may be prima facie evidence of the existence of an unlawful arrangement, although it falls short of outlawing truly independent parallel conduct. The effect of the provision however, as interpreted by the Supreme Court, is that the KFTC is required to establish the existence of 'plus' factors in determining the unreasonableness of any alleged collusion.[12] This presumption has been considered by the Supreme Court of Korea in cases relating to oligopolistic industries, in particular to toilet paper and instant coffee. In the former case it considered the difficulties of applying art 19 to oligopolistic industries in which uniform prices were alleged, by the KFTC, to be the result of illegal concertation under art 19, but where the parties themselves argued that the uniform prices were merely the result of individually taken decisions based in part upon a strategy of following the prices set by the market leader.[13] The KFTC had found that the appellant, together with a number of other companies, had restricted competition by agreeing on prices in the production of toilet paper. The market was oligopolistic, and one firm possessed the lion's share of the market. The Supreme Court first held that, were factory prices for the products to be determined by coordinated action, this would axiomatically fall within the category of conduct prohibited by art 19. The Seoul High Court had held that where identical factory prices had been maintained for a period of time it could be presumed that a breach of art 19 had occurred, and at one part of its judgment the

[10] See *Showa Denko KK v The Korea Fair Trade Commission*, Supreme Court of Korea, case 2004*Du*11275, 24 March 2006. An appeal from the judgment of the Seoul High Court, 2002*Nu*6110, 19 August 2004.

[11] It has been noted that:

> This provision is unique to the MRFTA. The purpose of this stipulation is to reduce the KFTC's burden of proof in response to the difficulty of finding direct proof of collusion such as a written agreement. . . . the Supreme Court has consistently followed its own highly controversial interpretation of art 19(5) since 2002. (Lee, n 1, above at 160)

[12] It also appears to be the case that criminal sanctions cannot be imposed in respect of a breach of art 19(5), although the Supreme Court has not definitively ruled that this is the case (see Supreme Court Decision 2002*Du*7456, 28 October 2004.

[13] See *General successor of Park Hwa-sam, supervisor for the reorganizing stock company Mona Lisa v The Korea Fair Trade Commission*, Supreme Court of Korea, Decision 2000*Du*1386, 28 May 2002. An appeal from the judgment of the Seoul High Court, Decision 98*Nu*10822, 20 January 2000.

Supreme Court follows this reasoning. The appellant argued that the presumption of unlawful concerted action could be rebutted on the basis that the identical prices were in fact merely the result of one firm unilaterally setting its prices, and the other market participants simply following its price leadership without there being any express or implicit communication between the parties. The Seoul High Court had rejected this argument in the present case, holding that:

> . . . in spite of the fact that the manufacturing costs of the four toilet paper companies are respectively different, and the fact that the influence of fluctuations in response to the price for raw materials is different depending on the difference in circumstances of managing, distribution structure, sales strategy and costs of the companies, the four companies lowered or raised the price at or close to the same time by the same amount. In particular the companies' establishment of an identical price on June 1, 1996 and afterwards maintenance of that price for a period of one year and eight months without prior collusion is practically impossible.

5-2.10 It was further noted by the Seoul High Court that as soon as the KFTC began an investigation the factory prices changed for each company to different extents. The Supreme Court held that notwithstanding the uniformity of prices in the market the presumption that these were reached by coordinated action could be rebutted, holding in part that:

> [i]n situations where within an oligopolistic market structure, following businesses engage in unilateral copying of the price set by the advance business in setting their own prices after the business possessing the high market share, the following businesses set prices based on an independent assessment.

5-2.11 On an analysis of the chain of events, which began with a drastic reduction in the price of the raw materials for toilet paper (pulp and recycled paper) and a subsequent order issued to the toilet paper companies by the Government to reduce prices, the Supreme Court held that:

> . . . considering the characteristics and circumstances of the toilet paper distribution market, the distribution structure and price decision structure, the position the [companies] possess in the market, past records of price copying and the political economic background . . . the first price reduction and first price increase seem to be nothing more than a simply copying activity.

Even though two companies acted in an identical manner in following the market leader the Court held that this was not itself, in the light of the present facts, proof that concerted action in breach of art 19 had been undertaken.[14] However the

[14] The judgment is not always entirely clear in its terms, and at one point the Supreme Court states that 'the price matching activity for which they engaged in cannot be viewed as activity that will bring about the restriction of competition in substance considering the market share [possessed], it cannot be presumed that they agreed to engage in collaborative acts'. There should not, however, be any relationship between the market shares of the participants and presumptions of concertation, unless the market shares are in some way evidence of a tendency to converge

Court also found that concertation *had* occurred in relation to a second price increase in July 1997 and a third in December 1997. In these cases the price movements were much more closely aligned in time, and the Court found that this was the result of a market structure in which information was able to flow between the companies.[15]

In a later case related to sales of instant coffee[16] two producers (Dongsu and Nestlé Korean) *increased* their market shares by raising the prices of their coffee in response to consumer preferences for perceived premium brands. They ended up with exactly the same price. The Court held that any assessment of whether there was a restriction on competition would have to be determined, without there being the assumption of an agreement, on the basis of whether the alleged practice would produce anti-competitive effects. In the present case the Court held that given the unusual nature of the market there was no anti-competitive outcome. **5-2.12**

The effect of the Supreme Court's decisions in these and other cases is that the presumption of the existence of an anti-competitive 'agreement' may be rebutted if the parties are able to prove either that there is no agreement, or, as was the case in *Wood Pulp* in the EC, that there are legitimate reasons to explain the consistency of the parties' conduct other than illicit coordination. **5-2.13**

---

or to differ on pricing. The Court here appears to be blurring the distinction between the *form* of the conduct and the *impact* of the conduct under examination. See also Lee, n 1, above, at 163:

> The plain language of the provision extends the presumption to the existence of the unreasonable collaborative practice itself. Nevertheless, the provision has subsequently been interpreted so as to presume only the existence of an agreement, while eliminating the presumption of unreasonableness of the corresponding collusion. (Internal footnotes omitted)

[15] Thus the Court held that:

> . . . the phenomenon of price alignment intensified as the date of internal consultations for the decision [relating to] the price increase occurred at the same time while the real price increase occurred on the same day, and this kind of phenomenon is attributable to the characteristic of the distribution structure in which toilet paper manufacturers notify the distributions of price changes in advance. In light of such circumstances, even considering the characteristic of the toilet paper market and the factors of change in each stage of price change . . . it is difficult to find that [the following corporations] unilaterally copied the price of an advance corporation.

The similarity of this case to that of the *Wood Pulp* case in the EC is striking. In this case the EC Commission had condemned a number of producers of wood pulp for concerting on prices on the basis that price alignments could not be explained by any means other than that concertation was taking place. In part the EC Commission relied on the fact that prices were announced in advance, holding that this was a practice intended to reinforce the concertation. On appeal the ECJ found that there was at least one other plausible explanation for the price alignments, and that the advance announcements served a legitimate aim in the light of the characteristics of the relevant market (*Wood Pulp* Case 85/202 [1985] OJ L85/1; on appeal *Re Wood Pulp Cartel: A. Ahlström Oy v Commission* Cases C-89, 104, 114, 116, 117, and 125–129/85 [1993] 4 CMLR 407).

[16] Supreme Court Decision 99*Du*6514, 99*Du*6521, 15 March 2002; an appeal from Seoul High Court Decision 98*Nu*11214, 28 April 1999.

5-2.14 In relation to bid-rigging, a practice believed to be endemic in Korea, the KFTC began operating the Bid Rigging Indicator Analysis System in December 2005. This is addressed only to the public procurement system, but is designed to detect suspicious bidding behaviour in respect of such bids. This approach was reinforced in an amendment to the MRFTA with the addition of art 19-2 which expressly applies to 'improper cartels in public bids'. Under this provision the KFTC may request information from public authorities and bodies that have established or held bidding processes in order to facilitate the detection of concerted bidding practices. Article 19(1)(8) of the MRFTA prohibits bid-rigging in other (private) sectors of the economy. The KFTC has made clear in recent statements its intent to act aggressively towards bid-rigging arrangements. In April 2008 for example penalties of Won5.1bn were imposed on construction companies which entered into a bid-rigging arrangement in relation to contracts to extend a subway line. Prices were agreed in advance in respect of a number of bidding procedures, with certain companies agreeing to submit higher bids in order to create an illusory competitive process, and the larger companies mapped out between them who was to be awarded each contract. All participants, including those who had no intention of bidding other than as 'foils', were punished.[17]

5-2.15 Companies or organizations may request that the KFTC conduct a 'business review' to determine whether a particular agreement or practice is unlawful, although such requests are not common.[18]

5-2.16 As noted above, Chapter 5 of the MRFTA, which prohibits unfair business practices, may in limited circumstances also be applied to concerted horizontal action. This is most notably the case in respect of collective refusals to deal, which are discussed at para III.1.A of the *Notification on Unfair Business Practices Review Guidelines*.[19] Collective refusals to deal are presumed on their face to be illegal, but may be accepted in situations in which there is a market shortage, or where a potential customer faces bankruptcy. Efficiency justifications for such refusals may be accepted, but only where these are significant, and outweigh any consumer detriment. Where the market share of the parties imposing the collective boycott is less than ten per cent, or the combined turnover is less than Won2bn, a safe harbour exists. The same part of the Act may also be applied to collective price discrimination.

---

[17] Decision of 30 April 2008, KFTC Newsletter, 4 July 2008.

[18] In 2005, for example, the KFTC reviewed an agreement at the request of the Korea Oil Station Association under which it had been decided to close member gas stations on every other Sunday. A request was made by the Association to the relevant government agency to issue administrative guidance to support the decision. The KFTC held that 'to uniformly close gas stations based on a resolution of an enterprisers organization or an agreement among competitors is to unreasonably restrict business activities and thus violates [the MRFTA]' (KFTC News, 2005-10).

[19] Enacted 27 December 2004; most recently amended 11 May 2005.

Horizontal agreements

Enforcement examples

Enforcement action is regularly undertaken by the KFTC in the application of Chapter 4 of the MRFTA, and there is significant evidence that cartel activity in Korea remains widespread notwithstanding an increasingly rigorous enforcement regime.[20] Some examples are dealt with here, but the following does not represent a comprehensive overview of cases dealt with. It is clear from the more recent cases to have resulted in infringement decisions that the level of penalties is being increased in line with the raising of the maximum penalty to ten per cent of turnover and with the determination of the KFTC to move against hard-core cartels in particular. **5-2.17**

Price-fixing agreements are regularly condemned by the KFTC. A typical example of such a case is that of the action taken against four manufacturers operating a cartel in the construction machinery business: Daewoo Heavy Industries, Hyundai Heavy Industries Co, Volvo Construction Equipment Korea Ltd, and Clark Material Handling Asia Ltd.[21] The first three companies participated in an agreement in relation to excavators and wheel-loaders for four years from May 2001 to November 2004. Prices and the timings of price increases were fixed, and on three occasions in 2002 the companies met to determine the bidding prices and the winners of a government procurement process. As a result of these arrangements the KFTC found that the companies had won no less than 337 government procurement bids. A second cartel, which did not involve Volvo, related to forklifts and again set the extent and timing of price rises, and bid-rigging arrangements were also in place. A total fine of some Won71.46bn was imposed. More recently in 2008 the KFTC imposed penalties totalling Won9.593bn on eight domestic banks who entered into a collusive agreement relating to the rates of commission applied to withdrawal fees.[22] The cartel ran from at least April 2002 at which point the participants responded to a change in the regulations relating to the calculation of interest charges which was expected to result in a reduction of profits. In its report of the case the KFTC pointed out that the banks had collected commissions and fees under the arrangement totalling Won195.8bn.[23] **5-2.18**

[20] In the KFTC newsletters it is rare for cartel enforcement activity not to be reported. In the issue of 27 February 2008, for example, the KFTC reports infringement decisions relating to cartels in the market for car servicing and bus operators.

[21] KFTC Decision 2005-080, 24 June 2005.

[22] KFTC Decision 2008-079, 5 March 2008.

[23] In the same issue of the KFTC Newsletter as this case is reported (1 May 2008), the KFTC also reports on another cartel in the banking sector under which 17 domestic banks and the Korea Financial Telecommunications & Clearings Institute agreed to raise the prices for giro service fees by between 15 and 28%, leading to the imposition of penalties of Won45,330,000.

5-2.19 Late in 2005 the KFTC imposed penalties of Won6.5bn on five companies involved in the caustic soda market. Sales of caustic soda in Korea accounted for some Won152.9bn in 2004, and with five companies accounting for 95 per cent of the market: Hanwha Chemical, LG Petrochemical, Samsung Fine Chemicals, DC Chemical, and Paik Kwang Industrial.[24] The companies were found to have agreed on the level and timings of price increases, and to have met at least three times in 2004 for the purposes of facilitating the agreement. The companies also coordinated on export policy, diverting into exports any domestic surplus so as to prevent price cutting in Korea, and in September 2002 the companies allocated export quotas determined for 2003 based on their production capacities. The largest single penalty of Won3.3bn was imposed on Hanwha Chemical (the company also being compelled to publish the fact of being subject to a corrective order in the newspapers[25]). A further complaint was filed with the public prosecutor's office against Hanwha, LG Petrochemical, and Samsung Fine Chemicals for taking the lead in the export cartel.[26]

5-2.20 In September 2005 a number of telecommunications operators were found to have taken steps to 'avoid' price competition in the long distance call market.[27] The practice had the further effect of restricting the development of differentiated products, and in particular of lower priced fixed-rate products. Three operators were found to have agreed in June 2004 on rates for long distance calls, the allocation of subscribers, and restrictions on the bundling of products. Fines of some Won20bn were imposed. Two of the companies involved in that practice were found in the same month to have set international call rates for calls to the US, Japan, and China in 2002. In 2003 this agreement was expanded to all IDD calls, and discount hours and rates were cut. A further penalty of Won5.4bn was imposed. Yet another agreement was found to exist in relation to charges for high-speed Internet access, with six providers agreeing not to provide free services, to set a ceiling for network fees, and to operate a 'joint supervisory team and a council of high-speed internet service providers', in order to implement and monitor the agreement. The companies argued before the KFTC that they were obliged by administrative dictate to make such an agreement in accordance with rules laid down by the Ministry of Information and Communication. However, the KFTC found both that no direct guidance on the level of rates had been given, and also relied upon an earlier Supreme Court ruling to the effect that where a cartel was implemented in accordance with administrative guidance which itself had no

[24] KFTC Decision 2005-232, 22 November 2005.

[25] The power to require companies to published details of their condemned acts has since been removed from the MRFTA.

[26] The cartel came to light in part through information disclosed to the KFTC by informants, and rewards were paid (see further Chapter 5-5, below).

[27] KFTC Decision 2005-331, 15 December 2005.

basis in law, the cartel arrangement would invite condemnation. The KFTC pointed out that:

> Administrative guidance such as guidance, directives and recommendations might cause improper concerted acts, even though it is issued by administrative agencies out of good will to achieve their specific goals. Such cases include administrative guidance demanding price increases or decreases, allocating the amount of supply or sales and designating business territories for each company.
>
> However, it is the KFTC's position, and the Court's position, that concerted acts occurring as a result of administrative guidance not based on provisions in laws or regulations are illegal under competition laws. Concerted acts following administrative guidance with legal grounds in law are not governed by the competition law under the condition that (i) they have an explicit and direct basis in the law, (ii) the purpose, means, content and method of such acts are in accord with the law, and (iii) the concerted act occurs as a result of the administrative guidance.[28]

As noted above bid-rigging has in recent years become a matter of enforcement priority to the KFTC. In March 2008 it took action against members of a bid-rigging cartel managed by Motorola Korea in relation to the supply of trunked radio systems supplied under bidding terms to public authorities.[29] Prior to entering into bidding in respect of fifteen bids the cartel participants agreed who was to offer the lowest price, and the price which that would be. The companies were required to cease their unlawful arrangement, and fines totalling Won978m ($978,000) were imposed on the participants, with Motorola Korea being fined Won696m.

The KFTC has applied the MRFTA to international cartels that have had an impact in Korea in two notable cases: the graphite electrodes cartel, and the vitamins cartel,[30] both of which have invited condemnation around the world. In the graphite electrodes cartel case the KFTC found that a concerted practice existed between a number of international suppliers. The parties concerted from at least 21 May 1992 to around the end of 1997. Fines were imposed on the parties, although some companies had their penalties reduced as a result of their cooperation during the course of the investigation (see further Chapter 5-5, below). The Supreme Court of Korea, as noted in Chapter 5-1, upheld the right of the KFTC to apply the MRFTA to conduct concluded outside Korea to the extent that this produced an 'effect' on the domestic market.[31] **5-2.21**

[28] KFTC News, 2005-10.

[29] KFTC Decision 2008-137, 2 May 2008.

[30] Both actions are referred to in Chapter 5-1, above.

[31] *Showa Denko KK v The Korea Fair Trade Commission*, Supreme Court of Korea, Case 2004*Du*11275, 24 March 2006. An appeal from the judgment of the Seoul High Court, 2002*Nu*6110, 19 August 2004.

Chapter 6, MRFTA—Enterprisers' Organizations (Trade Associations)

5-2.22 An enterprisers' organization is defined in art 2(4) of the MRFTA, as 'a juristic person or federation organized by two or more enterprisers for the purpose of promoting their common interests, regardless of the organization's form' (in other words, a 'trade organization'). Such bodies are not *per se* prohibited under Korean antitrust law, but their activities may, as is the case elsewhere, be subject to stricture. The Supreme Court of Korea has held that whether an organization is a trade association is to be determined by examination of its articles of incorporation and its activities as a whole.[32]

5-2.23 Such organizations are prohibited in art 26 of the MRFTA from engaging in any acts in breach of art 19(1) (see above), any acts restricting the number of enterprises in any business area,[33] any act unreasonably restricting the activities of its members,[34] and any act which induces or assists any person from engaging in the unfair trade practices prohibited in art 23(1) or resale price maintenance as prohibited in art 29. The provisions of art 19(2) (setting conditions or prices for trade in goods) and (3) (acts restricting production etc) also apply to the activities of enterprisers' organizations. The Supreme Court of Korea has held that:

> . . . the purpose of an enterprisers organization is to augment the combined profit of the member enterprisers, and therefore a certain amount of restriction on the member enterprisers' activities as a result of the organization's decision making for the accomplishment of that purpose is foreseen to a certain extent; however, if the contents of such a decision excessively limit the business contents or activities of the member enterprisers to the extent that it impedes fair and free competition among the member enterprisers, it will not be allowed.[35]

---

[32] *Korean Medical Association Inc v The Fair Trade Commission*, Case 2001*Du*5347, 20 February 2003. An appeal from the judgment of the Seoul High Court, 2000*Nu*3278, 17 May 2001. In this case the Court defined an 'enterprisers' organisation' as 'an association or affiliation of more than two persons in the manufacturing, service and other businesses established for the promotion of common interests'. The Court found that the doctors' association established under the Medical Service Act for the improvement of public health and social welfare, development and supply of medicine and as an advocate of medical personnel's rights was an association falling within the terms of art 2(4).

[33] art 26(2), MRFTA.

[34] art 26(3), MRFTA.

[35] *Korea Customs Brokers Association v The Fair Trade Commission*, 2001*Du*175, 15 June 2001. An appeal from Seoul High Court, Decision 99*Nu*13538, 5 December 2000. In that case the KFTC had found that a restraint of trade clause contained in a Regulation promulgated by the association was in breach of art 26. The Supreme Court held that the restraint of trade clause served a legitimate purpose, and that

> . . . banning the actions of enticing and attracting business from the previous business clients in such a manner actually promotes fair and free competition between the customs

In a case in which the profession or membership of the association is restricted in its activity by laws or regulations, restrictions on the members imposed by the association in respect of activities in which freedom of action is permitted under the laws or regulations may invite condemnation.[36] This was the case in the action taken against the Korean Medical Association where the Association acted in such a way as to prevent members from opening clinics against the will of the members. This activity was not subject to legislative restrictions and was condemned.[37] The KFTC may impose corrective measures where breaches of art 26 occur,[38] or may publish guidance to be observed by the association.[39] Penalties may also be imposed either on the association, of up to Won500m, or on individual member enterprises, of up to five per cent of turnover.[40] **5-2.24**

Enforcement examples

There are a relatively small number of reported actions taken against enterprisers' organizations. An example is that of the case involving the Gangdonggu Taekwondo Association,[41] in which the association articles provided that the Dan grading tests could be carried out only with the permission of the association, and that it could take disciplinary action against any member which violated this principle. The KFTC found that testing was an important part of the business of Taekwondo gyms, and that to prevent any independent testing constituted an unreasonable restriction on business. Gyms were also not allowed to engage in independent marketing, and new gyms would not be able to open within a 300-metre radius of existing gyms without the consent of those gyms. All of these restrictions were found to be in breach of art 26 of the MRFTA. Practices of the Korean Medical Association, as discussed above, were also condemned when these led to restrictions on the competitive activity of doctors in opening clinics. **5-2.25**

> offices as the customs clearance work will have to be received by the abilities or the activities of the customs broker himself or herself . . . [the] Regulation should be regarded positively, as it establishes a sound order in customs clearance and prevents absurdities, thereby preventing unfair trade.

[36] For a discussion of the issue of legislative pre-emption, see Lee, n 1, above, at 170–3.

[37] See *Korean Medical Association Inc v The Fair Trade Commission*, Case 2001*Du*5347, 20 February 2003. It did not matter in this case that the restrictions were imposed in order to protest against planned changes to the regulation of the medical profession in Korea, and were not entered into as part of a profit-raising scheme.

[38] art 27, MRFTA.

[39] art 26(3), MRFTA.

[40] art 28, MRFTA.

[41] KFTC Decision 2005-161, 18 August 2005. KFTC News, 2005-9.

Chapter 7, MRFTA—Resale Price Maintenance

5-2.26 As is the case in the US where the Robinson Patman Act sets out special rules relating to resale price maintenance ('RPM') a separate Chapter 7 of the MRFTA makes provision for the condemnation of this practice, and guidelines were published in August 2006.[42] Resale price maintenance is defined as 'an act of trading goods or services wherein an enterpriser compels a counterpart enterpriser or another enterpriser by the next stage of transaction to sell or provide them only at a price fixed in advance at each stage of distribution or executes transactions under any agreement or binding condition for such purpose'.[43] The core principle is set out at art 29(1) which states that 'no enterpriser shall engage in resale price maintenance'. Minimum RPM is *per se* illegal.[44] Maximum RPM may, however, be acceptable where 'there are justifiable reasons [for] preventing the transactions of commodities or services in excess of the specified prices', and the Guidelines iterate this principle, stating that maximum RPM is not, *per se*, illegal, and that the legality of the practice is to be assessed by reference to the market power of the party imposing it.[45] The possibility that maximum RPM may be a tool employed to further concertation at the horizontal level may also be taken into account. Further exemptions apply in respect of literary works,[46] and in respect of goods that have met the conditions specified at art 29(2)(1)–(3), and have been designated *in advance* by the KFTC. The conditions specified are that: (1) uniformity in the quality of the good must be easily identifiable; (2) the good must be used 'daily by ordinary customers'; and (3) free competition must exist with respect to the good concerned. Applications for such exceptions must be made to the KFTC and any such decision taken shall be made public. Where an exception is granted the KFTC may nevertheless require that amendments are made to

42 Notification of resale price maintenance review guidelines, Notification No 34, 30 August 2006.

43 art 2(6), MRFTA.

44 In October 2008 the KFTC drew attention to this fact when it sanctioned, but did not fine, Audi Korea which had attempted to impose RPM. Fines were not, in this case, imposed as the KFTC found that individual dealers had continued to offer discounts, and that there was no evidence that the company took enforcement action against dealers (*The Korea Herald*, 17 October 2008, p 7).

45 It is clear however that the presumption is that maximum RPM is harmful, and that it can be only 'exceptionally deemed as legitimate under the rule of reason analysis' (Suh, n 8, above, at 40).

46 Guidelines have been published relating to the notification of RPM in respect of literary works. The application of RPM to books was for many years exempted from the general illegality of RPM arrangements in the UK (see *Re Net Book Agreement, 1957* [1962] 3 All ER 751), but was eventually also outlawed (see *Re Net Book Agreement 1957 (M and N)* [1997] 16 LS Gaz R 29), and has also been condemned in the application of art 81 EC (see *Publishers' Association—Net Book Agreements* 89/44 [1989] OJ L22/12).

relevant contracts where the arrangement 'threatens to cause serious harm to the interests of consumers or contradicts public interest'.[47] The Guidelines apply to all forms of RPM (maximum, minimum, and recommended). A number of examples are given of practices that may be considered to amount to coercive RPM, including: notification of prices by the manufacturer, and a refusal to supply those who discount below these prices; enforcing contracts which specify RPM, or requesting guarantees in respect of the prices to be set; and refusals to support sales promotions unless recommended prices are to be adhered to. Recommending resale prices is not illegal unless the recommendations are backed up with some form of coercive measures.

Enforcement examples

In August 2005 penalties were imposed against Hewlett-Packard Korea Ltd ('HP'), and Epson Korea Co Ltd ('Epson'), and a warning was issued to Samsung Electronics ('Samsung') for setting the prices with respect to a number of printer supplies, including toner, and compelling their distributors to abide by the prices.[48] The three companies held a combined market share in the Korean market for inkjet printer supplies of approximately 90 per cent. Where distributors refused to follow the prices set by HP and Epson they would be punished by a variety of means, including the imposition of rebate cuts, the suspension of shipments, or simple refusals to supply. In the cases of HP and Epson cease and desist orders were issued, and the companies were obliged to publish the fact of the violation in the newspapers, and to each of their business partners. Samsung faced a lower penalty, as although it set prices, it did nothing to enforce them.[49] **5-2.27**

Chapter 8, MRFTA—International Contracts

Special provisions are set out in art 32 of the MRFTA in respect of 'international contracts'. There is no definition of 'international contract' provided in the legislation, but some explanation has been given in the KFTC *Guidelines on International Contracts*. The prohibition applies to international contracts 'concerning improper cartels, unfair business practices, and resale price maintenance'.[50] The prohibition will not apply where the KFTC determines that the effect of the agreement in any particular area of business is 'negligible' or finds that 'there are other unavoidable reasons to validate such contract'. Whenever any international **5-2.28**

47 art 30, MRFTA.
48 KFTC Decision 2005-163, 31 October 2005.
49 KFTC News, 2005-9.
50 art 32(1), MRFTA.

contract is entered into the parties may request that the KFTC examine the contract and make a determination whether it is in violation of art 32(1).[51]

Vertical Agreements

5-2.29 Vertical agreements may be subject to control under a number of provisions of the MRFTA. Although on the face of it art 19, discussed above, may apply both to horizontal and vertical agreements the article has never been applied to vertical agreements.[52] There is no clear rule determining this approach, but nevertheless it seems now to be settled law that this is the case.[53] Where market power is substantial art 3-2 (abuse of monopoly power, see Chapter 5-3 below) may be applicable.[54] Article 23 which restricts unfair business practices may also be applicable to vertical agreements even in the absence of market power. For example art 23(1)(5) provides that it is illegal to engage in an 'act of trading under terms and conditions that unfairly restrict or disrupt business activities'. This provision has, for example, been applied to acts restricting parallel imports into Korea of trademark-protected items marketed in Korea through a Korean distributor.[55] The approach taken to vertical agreements in Korean antitrust law is somewhat stricter than is the case in either the EC or the US, particularly where the imposer of a vertical restraint is able to exercise market power. Article 23 does not make reference to the power of the enterprises whose actions may be subject to control or sanction, and although the same is true of the US Federal Trade Commission Act ('FTCA'), s 5, there is no doubt that the MRFTA is applied more stringently to vertical agreements than is the case in the US.

5-2.30 The leading decision in relation to territorial protection imposed via vertical restraint is that of *DPK International*.[56] DPK held the Domino Pizza franchise for Korea, a market share of only ten per cent, which was substantially lower than Pizza Hut's market share of 50 per cent, and imposed territorial restrictions on its franchisees. The arrangement was condemned by the KFTC. The awarding of exclusive dealing rebates, which, dependent on the market power of the awarding enterprise, may be viewed as a matter of the law of anti-competitive agreements or

---

51 art 33, MRFTA.

52 See, eg Lee, n 1, at 159:

> Many scholars have argued that art 19, like its US and EU counterparts, may be applicable to vertical as well as horizontal restraints. However, the KFTC has, in practice, dealt with vertical restraints by means of art 23 of the MRFTA. . . Thus, in practice, art 19 has been applied only to horizontal restraints.

53 In this respect the position appears to follow closely that of Japanese antitrust law.

54 This was the case for example in the *Microsoft* case, discussed extensively in Chapter 5-3, and in the *Intel* case reported at KFTC Newsletter, 4 July 2008.

55 See, for example, *Han-Song Motors Corporation v Fair Trade Commission*, Supreme Court of Korea, Decision 2000*Du*3184, 2 May 2002.

56 Decision 2000-163, 15 November 2000.

the law relating to monopoly, was dealt with by the KFTC in respect of Intel Corporation under the latter rubric.[57] There is however nothing in principle to prevent the application of art 23 to such practices.

Penalties for Breach

The fact that contracts which breach art 19(1) of the MRFTA cannot be relied upon and are unenforceable has been noted above. While this may be an issue of import in relation to, for example, distribution agreements, this is less relevant to hard-core restraints in respect of which parties are unlikely to be anticipating that their arrangements will have legal force, and are more likely to be implementing any such arrangement covertly in the hope of avoiding detection. Article 21 provides that the KFTC may order any enterpriser engaged in a breach of art 19 'to discontinue the act, announce the receipt of [the] corrective order, or take other corrective measures'. Article 22 provides for penalties in the event of a breach of up to an amount not exceeding ten per cent of turnover. Where turnover cannot be calculated a fine may be imposed of up to Won2bn. It will be noted that penalties therefore may be higher in respect of unlawful multilateral conduct than in the case of individual abuses of a dominant position. The reference to turnover does not specify that this is turnover in the products or services which are the subject of the unlawful restriction, but is rather on the face of the legislation the turnover of the enterprises in total. Penalties may be reduced in respect of parties who have notified the KFTC of their restrictive practices or who have cooperated with any investigation.[58] In effect this provision incorporates a leniency regime onto the face of the legislation. Although the legislation itself does not set a clear leniency schedule it does provide in art 22 that 'companies that have reported improper cartels' may have penalties imposed under art 22 reduced either in part or in full.[59] The same is true of those who cooperate during the course of any investigation. No guidance is given in the legislation as to whether reporting the existence of an unlawful arrangement will merit a greater leniency tariff than subsequent cooperation during the course of any investigation. It is further provided in art 22-2(2) that unless it is necessary in order to protect the rights of the defence in subsequent legal proceedings, information relating to whistle-blowers and to those who have cooperated with investigations shall not be released.[60] 5-2.31

57 Decision of 4 June 2008 (KFTC Newsletter, 4 July 2008). See Chapter 5-3, below.
58 art 22-2, MRFTA.
59 The KFTC has also published leniency guidelines, no 2007-13 (27 December 2007).
60 The KFTC leniency programme is discussed in Chapter 5-5.

5-2.32 In relation to the RPM outlawed by art 29 standard corrective measures may be imposed under art 31, and art 31-2 provides for a penalty of up to two per cent of the enterpriser's turnover, or, where turnover cannot be calculated, of up to Won500m.

5-2.33 If any international agreement is found to be in breach of art 32(1) the KFTC may order corrective measures,[61] or may impose a penalty. In the case of an 'enterprisers organization' the penalty is limited to Won500m, and in the case of an enterpriser the penalty may not exceed two per cent of turnover or, where this cannot be determined, an amount not in excess of Won500m.

Franchise Agreements

5-2.34 A separate piece of legislation, the Fair Franchise Transactions Act ('FFTA')[62] applies to franchise agreements. The legislation has characteristics of both standard competition law, but also of trade protection and is concerned with 'fairness' and good dealing between the parties, as well as with competitive aspects of franchise transactions.

5-2.35 A franchise is defined in the legislation as:

> . . . a continuous business relationship in which franchiser allows franchisee to sell goods . . . or services under certain quality standards using its trademarks, service marks, trade name, signs and other business marks . . . and supports, educates and controls franchisee as regards relevant management and operating activities, and in which franchisee pays franchise fees to franchiser in return for the use of business marks and the support and education concerning the management and operating activities.[63]

5-2.36 Chapter 2 of the FFTA sets out 'basic principles' that are to apply to franchise transactions. The first principle is that both parties are to 'perform their respective duties in good faith'.[64] Articles 5 and 6 set out obligations on both parties which relate mainly to the maintenance of quality standards protecting the franchise reputation. There are some elements however within these criteria which directly relate to competition. For example, art 5(6) prohibits the franchisor from competing with the franchisee by 'opening [a] directly managed shop . . . or a franchise

[61] art 34, MRFTA.

[62] Law no 6704, enacted on 13 May 2002, as amended. The Act entered into force in November 2002.

[63] art 2(1), FFTA. 'Franchiser means a business entity that grants franchise management rights to franchisee in connection with a franchise'; 'Franchisee means a business entity to whom franchise management rights are granted by franchiser in connection with a franchise' (art 2(2) and 2(3), FFTA).

[64] art 4, FFTA.

business engaging in a similar line of business to that of the franchisee within the business area of [the] franchisee during the period of the franchise agreement'. Article 6(11) prohibits the franchisee from engaging in the same line of business as the franchisor during the franchise period. Article 12 of the FFTA sets out a number of prohibitions of 'unfair transactions', which do relate to competition obligations. The article thus makes it unlawful for the franchisor to: (1) unfairly discontinue or refuse the supply of goods or services to, or the support for operating activities of [the] franchisee, or to significantly restrict the contents thereof; or (2) unfairly restrict or limit the price of goods or services dealt with by [the] franchisee, its counterparties, area of transactions, or business activities. It should be noted however that to the extent to which the provisions of the MRFTA also may apply to franchise arrangements, art 29(1) of the MRFTA, which prohibits RPM, is not to apply in respect of franchise arrangements.[65] Other provisions of art 23 of the MRFTA are also disapplied.[66]

Franchises may not be terminated without correct procedures, as set out in the Act, being complied with. The Act established a 'Franchise Transaction Dispute Conciliation Council', the role of which is to intercede in disputes between franchisors and franchisees under the terms of the legislation, and to ensure compliance with it, and much of the Act is taken up with the constitution of the Council and its powers. The KFTC has some powers to enforce the legislation. A breach of art 12(1) for example may be remedied with the KFTC requiring the franchisor to cease the infringement, or to take any measures required to remedy such a violation.[67] Where the KFTC does act under the FFTA many of the procedural rules of the MRFTA (discussed in Chapter 5-5 of this text) are applicable. **5-2.37**

Breaches of the FFTA may be punished by, inter alia, terms of imprisonment of up to five years, or penalties up to Won150m. **5-2.38**

65 art 38, FFTA.

66 art 38, FFTA. Article 23, MRFTA is not applicable to the following extent. Inapplicability limited to: art 23(1)(1), acts unfairly refusing transactions; art 23(1)(3), acts unfairly enticing customers of competitor to engage in transactions; art 23(1)(4) and (5), acts making transactions on the condition of unfairly restricting the business interests of the counter-party.

67 art 33, FFTA.

5-3

KOREA MONOPOLY AND ABUSE OF DOMINANCE

Introduction	5-3.01	Remedies and penalties	5-3.19
Abuse of Dominant Position	5-3.04	Case examples	5-3.20
Assessing dominance	5-3.05	**Unfair Trade Practices**	5-3.24
Abusive conduct	5-3.08		

Introduction

In November 2007 the Supreme Court of Korea handed down a significant judgment relating to a part of the monopoly provisions of the MRFTA (*POSCO v The Korea Fair Trade Commission*, Supreme Court of Korea, case 2002*Du*8626, 22 November 2007, discussed in detail below). Not only did the Court comment on the tensions raised between the principles applying to the control of monopoly conduct, the principles applying to free markets, the private enjoyment of property, and the right to contract freely, but it also clarified some of the general principles to be applied in this area of law, including those relating to market assessment, and to the place of the law generally. Discussing the general purpose of the law of dominance in Korea the Court held that: **5-3.01**

> In light of the economic circumstances of this country where adverse effects of monopoly or oligopoly are feared due to the influence of the developing-economy of the past, regulation on abusive acts of market-dominating positions is crucial in order to preserve the competitive function as a prerequisite to a proper orientation of the principle of market economy. On the other hand, given the recent trend of economic modernization and globalization, it is also necessary to carefully manoeuvre such regulation so that it could enhance enterprisers' competitiveness based on their creativeness and eventually contribute to consumers' welfare and economic development. Moreover, such regulation should not be unreasonable or excessive as to become an obstacle to enterprisers' exercise of their abilities.

There are two main mechanisms within the MRFTA by which unilateral, abusive anti-competitive conduct may be condemned, and a number of special provisions **5-3.02** relating to corporate activity in the *chaebol* groups, which are not dealt with in this text. Provisions of Chapter 2 of the MRFTA dealing with abusive conduct, and Chapter 5 dealing with the prohibition of unfair trade practices are covered in more detail, although some of the enforcement activity in relation to unfair trade activity does not extend to practices that would be considered as falling within an 'antitrust' remit in the EC or US. The key difference between the provisions is that while both may relate to unilateral conduct, Chapter 2 is restricted to the activities of those in possession of market power, and Chapter 5 has a wider application, relating to all firms. There is also in Chapter 6 of the Act a prohibition of various acts of 'enterprisers' organizations'. This provision is dealt with in Chapter 5-2, above.

5-3.03 More generally art 3 of the MRFTA provides that the KFTC is to have a role in promoting competition in markets in which oligopolies or monopolies (or monopsonies) have been in existence 'for an extended period of time'. To further competition in such markets the KFTC may give opinions to the heads of relevant administrative authorities as to measures necessary to improve market structures. It may, to this end, conduct research in relation to market structures, and has the power to obtain from any enterprise data necessary for the purposes of such research.[1]

Abuse of Dominant Position

5-3.04 Chapter 2 of the MRFTA deals with the 'prohibition on the abuse of market dominance', and is very short, consisting of only five articles. The central provision of this Chapter of the Act is that of art 3-2, which prohibits 'market-dominating enterprisers' from engaging in the abuses specified therein.[2] Five specific examples of abuse are set out, and the wording of the legislation is such as to indicate that this is a closed set, although the categories are themselves so wide that this should not lead to anti-competitive conduct not contemplated at the time the legislation was written from going unsanctioned. Article 4 sets out the presumptive thresholds to apply in the assessment of dominance.[3] Articles 5

[1] art 3, MRFTA.

[2] In common with other jurisdictions there have not been a large number of monopoly cases leading to infringement decisions in Korea, such that there remains 'uncertainty regarding the nature of the abuse concept' (Lee, BE 'Prohibition of Abuse of Market-Dominating Undertakings under the Monopoly Regulation and Fair Trade Act' (2005) 4:2 *Journal of Korean Law* 61 at 67).

[3] These are first that one enterprise has a market share in excess of 50 per cent; and second that the CR3 is at least 75 per cent (and in the determination of this figure any firm with a market share of less than 10 per cent is to be excluded from the calculation).

and 6 relate respectively to corrective measures that may be imposed by the KFTC, and to penalties. The Supreme Court of Korea has held that:

> . . . in order to determine whether a particular enterpriser has a market-dominating position, a market by relevant product which is the subject of the transaction (the 'relevant product market') and a market by relevant geographic area which is the geographical scope of the transaction (the 'relevant geographic market') should specifically be determined with respect to the business area of which competition issues are to be examined, and then the likelihood of dominance in such market should be recognized.[4]

Assessing dominance

Article 2(7) provides that: **5-3.05**

> the term 'market-dominating enterpriser' refers to any enterpriser enjoying market dominance and possibly determining, maintaining, or changing the prices, quantity or quality of commodities or services or other terms and conditions of business as a supplier or customer in a particular business area individually or jointly with other enterprisers.[5]

---

[4] *POSCO v The Korea Fair Trade Commission*, Supreme Court of Korea, Case 2002*Du*8626, 22 November 2007.

[5] 'Particular business area' is further defined as meaning 'an area wherein any competitive relation exists by subject, stage, or geographical area of such trade, or there is a possibility of such' (MRFTA, art 2(8)). There is no specific guidance relating expressly to the determination of the relevant product and geographic markets under Korean antitrust law, but the judgment of the Supreme Court of Korea in *POSCO* is instructive as to the approach to be taken. The Supreme Court held that:

> [t]he scope of [the product] market should be determined by taking into account the totality of the circumstances such as prices of the products related to the transaction, similarity in function and efficiency, recognition of purchasers as to the possibility of substitutability and associated purchasing behaviours, recognition of sellers as to the substitutability and relevant types of business decision-making, homogeneity and similarity of business area as recognized in terms of social and economic perspective etc. In addition, the speed of technology advancement, market situation as to other products that are necessary in manufacturing the product and other new products that are manufactured using the product, easiness of substitution in terms of time, economic and legal perspective etc should also be considered. . . .
>
> The scope of [the relevant geographic] market should be determined by taking into account the totality of the circumstances such as prices and characteristics of the products related to the transaction, production volume, business capacity and shipping costs, recognition of purchasers as to the possibility of shift of purchase area and associated behaviours of shifting the purchase area by purchasers, recognition of sellers as to the possibility of shift of purchase area and relevant types of business decision-making, easiness of shifting the purchase area in terms of time, economic and legal perspective etc. In addition the speed of technological advancement, market situation as to other products that are necessary in manufacturing the said relevant product and other new products that are manufactured using the said relevant product, etc should also be considered.
>
> As the trend of globalization and free trade enables free import and export, the relevant products that are traded in domestic market include products that are imported from overseas, as well as those manufactured in Korea. In case such import can be made without difficulty, the likelihood of import of relevant product should also be taken into account in

Such a position may be exercised either unilaterally, or 'jointly with other enterprisers'.[6] Article 4 of the MRFTA sets out the presumptions that are to apply in determining whether a particular enterprise is dominant and subject to the rules set out in Chapter 2. This article has been subject to amendment in recent years. The article first contains a *de minimis* provision under which no enterprise with an annual turnover of less than Won4bn shall be found to be market dominating. It should be noted that this provision applies to the *total* sales or purchases of the enterprise, and not to those in relation to the product or service in respect of which concerns are raised. Under the terms of art 4 clear presumptions are set out, although these are no more than that, such that an enterprise that did not meet the presumptive thresholds could, in appropriate circumstances, be found to be dominant. The article contains two presumptions, the first of which is that dominance is to be presumed where the market share of the enterprise is 50 per cent or greater. The second presumption is that dominance exists where 'the total market share of at least three enterprisers is [75 per cent] or more; excluding those whose market share is less than [10 per cent]'.[7]

5-3.06 The KFTC has published guidance on abusive conduct, which deals in part with the assessment of dominance.[8] Even where market share thresholds or concentration ratios required to meet the presumption are satisfied the KFTC may still draw attention to other features of the market which support this finding of dominance. Thus, for example, in *Hyundai Motor Co*[9] as well as the near 50 per cent market share held by Hyundai in the market for car sales, and the 70 per cent plus share held in conjunction with its associate Kia Motors, the KFTC pointed to the capital requirements for entry into the market, and the significant economies of scale enjoyed by Hyundai. The Guidelines set out the approach to determining

determining the likelihood of market dominance by an enterpriser. Since it is appropriate to regard the enterprisers overseas as being in competitive relation and to include them in determining the market dominance as long as the said relevant product is likely imported at present or in the future, the following factors should be taken into account in such a case as well as such many factors to be considered in determining the relevant geographical market as reviewed above: the composition of the relevant product market by domestic and overseas enterprisers, the ratio of import in Korea out of an overseas enterpriser's manufacturing volume or that of export to the outside of Korea out of a domestic enterpriser's manufacturing volume, easiness, stability and continuity of such import and export, import and export barriers with or without form, difference in domestic and overseas prices, and co-relation between domestic and overseas prices etc. (*POSCO v The Korea Fair Trade Commission*, Supreme Court of Korea, case 2002*Du*8626, 22 November 2007)

[6] As is discussed below the analysis of market dominance held by more than one party may be somewhat terse.

[7] In other words, the application of a CR3 test of 75 per cent or greater, excluding small and medium-sized enterprises from the calculations.

[8] *Notification on abuse of dominant position review guidelines*, enacted 8 September 2000; last amended May 2002.

[9] KFTC Decision 2007-281, 18 May 2007; KFTC *2008 Annual Report*, p 48.

the existence of dominant enterprises at para III, drawing attention first to the market share thresholds set out as presumptively leading to dominance under the terms of the MRFTA. It then discusses: entry barriers; the relative size of any competitors to the alleged dominant enterprise; collective dominance;[10] 'substitutable and interchangeable goods and markets'; countervailing buyer power ('purchasing power'); and the financial strength of the enterprise. This is a standard set of criteria, applied by many competition authorities, and there is nothing in the content of the Guidelines in this respect which is peculiarly distinctive. In assessing entry barriers the KFTC will consider: legal and institutional restrictions; minimum capital requirements; intellectual property rights and technological barriers; location conditions; the availability of raw materials; the presence of rival distribution networks, and the cost of establishing such a network; product differentiation; the ratio of imports and the ease of substitutability in their respect; and any tariff and non-tariff trade barriers. To ensure that this exercise is not merely a theoretical one, the KFTC will also have regard to whether there has been a recent history of successful entry into the market (recent in this case meaning within the last three years), whether there are any enterprises that have expressed a desire to enter the market, and appear to have the capacity to do so, and whether there exist enterprises who would, in the face of a price rise in the market, be induced to enter. At para III.3 the KFTC notes that 'where the scale of the competitors is relatively large, the investigated enterprise can be possibly regarded as [non dominant]'. It has been recognized elsewhere, and is intuitive, that a company with a market share of 40 per cent, facing 60 competitors each with a 1 per cent market share is 'more' dominant than one facing two competitors each with a 30 per cent market share. In assessing relative strengths the KFTC may have regard to market shares, manufacturing capacities, purchase and selling ratios, and financial strengths. The discussion of collective dominance is not as sophisticated as the language in the merger guidance discussed in Chapter 5-4. As is the case elsewhere reference is made to the extent to which products are homogeneous, and the stability and transparency of the market, but there is no reference either to the number of competitors, or to the possibility of detecting and punishing deviance from an 'agreed' norm.

Part IV of the Guidelines focuses on factors relating to the determination of abusive conduct, and is discussed as appropriate below. **5-3.07**

[10] This language is not used in the Guidelines, which refer instead to the 'possibility of collusion' (para III.4).

Abusive conduct

5-3.08 Five categories of 'abusive acts' are specified in art 3-2 of the MRFTA.[11] The following acts may be abusive: (1) unreasonably determining, maintaining, or changing prices; (2) controlling the sale of commodities or services; (3) interfering with the business activities of other enterprisers; (4) impeding the participation of new competitors; (5) unfairly excluding competitive enterprisers, or acts which 'may considerably harm the interest of consumers'. Clearly these are broad categories.[12] Article 3-2(1)(1) for example could be applied to predatory prices, excessive prices, and discriminatory prices. The Guidelines focus on increases or decreases in the prices of the products, and discriminatory prices which are exclusionary and which may be condemned under art 3-2(1)(3). The price to be used as a reference point in analysing the legitimacy of the pricing is the recommended resale price, or when this is not available, a 'common commercial price'. The KFTC may take into account changes in demand that have affected the price, changes in the costs, substitutable products in the same relevant market, and the conduct of *other* companies in the relevant market. It may also consider whether, in the case of price rises, the enterprise in question is able to act as a price leader. There have been no cases at the time of writing in which an excessive price has been condemned *simpliciter*, and it remains unclear whether the KFTC would have the power to specify a price at which the product or service must be sold, or whether it would simply have the power to order that the excessive price not be charged, without specifying the size of reduction required.

5-3.09 Article 3-2(1)(2) is further clarified at para IV.2 of the Guidelines. The concern here is clearly with output reductions that may facilitate price rises, a relevant factor in the assessment being that of whether there has been any price increase after the output restriction.

5-3.10 Article 3-2(1)(3) relates to 'unreasonably interfering with the business activities of other enterprisers' and extends to a wide range of conduct, including interfering with the purchase of raw materials, and recruiting certain key personnel of the competitor.[13] In *Hyundai Motor Co*[14] for example the KFTC found an

---

11 In practice there have not been a great many cases brought under art 3-2 which have proceeded to final infringement decisions, with only 51 cases being brought in the ten years since 1998. See generally Lee, n 2, above.

12 It is further provided at art 3-2(2) that 'categories or standards for abusive acts shall be specified by Presidential Decree' (see art 5 of the MRFTA Enforcement Decree).

13 The Guidelines refer to, inter alia, 'long-term employed engineers', and employees 'who have important business information' (para IV.3.B(1), (4)). Other conduct which may be prohibited under this provision includes: unreasonable prices which are discriminatory; forcing enterprises to accept business activities which are disadvantageous to them; unreasonably withdrawing investment capital; and unreasonably interfering with patent applications.

14 17 January 2007; KFTC *2008 Annual Report*, p 48.

infringement in Hyundai's practice of obstructing its sales agencies from relocating their businesses without objective justification by way of entering into an agreement with the trade union representing its own staff at sales outlets controlled by Hyundai. Hyundai also restricted recruitment of salespersons in independent agencies, again under an agreement with its own trade union. A further breach under this provision lay in Hyundai's practice of unilaterally allocating and coercing sales quotas and imposing penalties on agencies whose sales results were below expectations.[15] Article 3-2(1)(3) was also found to be breached by Microsoft in the infringement decision taken by the KFTC in 2007, discussed below.

Article 3-2(1)(3) is also interpreted by the KFTC in the Guidelines as encompassing conduct which 'unreasonably refuses, stops or restricts the supply of relevant goods or services which are essential for production, supply or distribution'.[16] Thus, although not formally enunciated on the face of the legislation, an essential facilities doctrine applies in Korea,[17] and its application may be extended to subject matter otherwise protected by intellectual property.[18] The criteria for determining whether a particular supply is considered to be essential are set out in the Guidelines. These are: whether it is impossible for the customer to produce, distribute, or sell their product without the input, or whether the refusal to supply places it at a '*very* anti-competitive disadvantage';[19] when the supplier holds monopoly power; and, in a sentence reminiscent of the formula used in the EC *Oscar Bronner* case, 'when it is legally and economically impossible for the enterprise [to] reproduce or substitute the element'.[20] Refusals to supply an essential input may be found in both an outright refusal, but also in the setting of prices which are 'unreasonable', or in setting unfair conditions, such as those which are discriminatory or which impose unreasonable ties. A defence lies in the right of **5-3.11**

[15] A penalty of Won21.58bn was imposed in this case.

[16] The concept was introduced by the Enforcement Decree of 2001, art 5(3) and (4), under which a dominant firm was prohibited from refusing, discontinuing, or limiting, without justifiable reason, the use of or access to essential facilities.

[17] See for example the *POSCO* case discussed below (*POSCO v The Korea Fair Trade Commission*, Supreme Court of Korea, Case 2002*Du*8626, 22 November 2007).

[18] See for example a decision issued by the KFTC on 31 August 2005 against Insung Industry Co Ltd which had 'unfairly' refused to provide new technologies in the construction industry to the winner of a successful bidder for a public construction project. The KFTC pointed out at the time that these 'measures have a great importance since they made it clear that even intellectual property rights . . . if they were abused to the detriment of transacting partners, could be subject to the regulation of the Korean competition law' (KFTC News, 2005-9).

[19] para IV.3.C(1)(a), emphasis added.

[20] This lacks the better part of the *Oscar Bronner* criteria, under which the reproduction of the sought-after input would be impossible even by an enterprise of the same size and resources as the monopoly supplier. Without this qualifying rubric the possibility remains open that the essential facilities doctrine could be overused, and relied on by those who *are* unable to duplicate the resource due to their own limitations resulting in a distortion in investment incentives.

the monopoly holder of the resource to recoup their investment cost, the impossibility of separating out elements of the input and supplying some but not others to the would-be customer, shortages, and safety factors.

5-3.12 The leading case to deal with the application of art 3-2(1)(3) at the time of writing is *POSCO*, decided by the Supreme Court of Korea in November 2007.[21] This case sets a clear limit on the principle of refusal to deal in holding that, to be prohibited, any such refusal must be accompanied by clear evidence of either anti-competitive injury or the intent to cause such injury.

5-3.13 The KFTC had ordered corrective measures against POSCO, a supplier of 'hot rolled coil for cold-rolled steel plates for automotives', following a refusal by POSCO on five separate occasions to supply orders submitted by Hyundai Hysco. The Court defined a refusal to deal that would fall within the proscription of art 3-2(1)(3) as being a refusal that made 'it difficult for another enterpriser to carry out its business activities' as a result of the 'unreasonable refusal to deal'. The Court recognized the tension that exists in antitrust law between the application of a rule that requires monopolists to supply third parties with the 'general principles of freedom of contract and private autonomy', noting that 'a question arises as to what the "unreasonable" means as an element required to constitute an abusive act by a market-dominating enterprise'.[22] The Court noted that the MRFTA may prohibit refusals to deal under two separate provisions, art 3-2(1(3) and art 23(1)(1) (see below), and that a different approach had to be taken when determining whether a refusal to deal was a breach of the monopoly provisions, as in the present case. In light of the purpose of art 3, as defined by the Supreme Court, the Court held that:

> . . . the unreasonableness under the context cannot be recognized only based on the fact that a market-dominating enterpriser refuses to deal with unfair intent or purpose against a particular enterpriser who is a transacting partner or the fact that a

---

[21] *POSCO v The Korea Fair Trade Commission*, Supreme Court of Korea, Case 2002*Du*8626, 22 November 2007.

[22] The Court held in this respect, after citing art 23 of the Constitution, which recognizes the right to private property, and art 119 which gives the State the power to coordinate economic affairs, that:

> . . . this country is based upon the market economy order which is established upon the private property system and the principle of private autonomy in economic activities. Although enterprisers are basically endowed with freedom of contract which generally encompasses freedom in their decision to contract, selection of trading counterparts, determination of terms and conditions of transactions etc, such freedom of contract can be restricted in the event that market dominance and abuse of economic power are feared. Although such restriction or regulation is a modification to the civil law principle of freedom of contract, it does not negate the civil law principle itself, but rather it is understood as purporting to restore its original function by rectifying defects in such civil law principle. (*POSCO v The Korea Fair Trade Commission*, Supreme Court of Korea, Case 2002*Du*8626, 22 November 2007)

> particular enterpriser receives detriment such as in a case where a particular enterpriser experiences or is likely to experience difficulties in its business activities due to such act of refusal to deal. Rather, the unreasonableness can be recognized when there is an act of refusal to deal which can be considered as an act which is likely to create an anti-competitive effect from an objective point of view, and is accompanied by intent or purpose of maintaining or enhancing monopoly in the market, such as intent or purpose of artificially influencing market order by restricting free competition in the market.[23]

In the present case it was found by the Seoul High Court[24] that POSCO had argued that were it to continue to supply hot-rolled coil it would have to abandon its sale of cold-rolled steel plates, which were a product with a higher value. It was also found however that POSCO did supply the requested product to other third parties and that Hyundai Hysco had also entered the market for cold-rolled coil in direct competition with POSCO, such that there was an appearance that the refusal to supply was a disciplining measure designed to eliminate or frustrate a competitor. The refusal to supply had caused Hyundai Hysco considerable difficulties. Although it had managed to find another source of supplies these had to be imported at substantially higher prices. The Seoul High Court found that this refusal to supply was in breach of art 3-2(1)(3), and upheld the decision taken by the KFTC. The Supreme Court however was unconvinced by this litany of harm, finding instead that: **5-3.14**

> . . . the circumstances relied on by the original court judgment are nothing but a list of specified disadvantages that [Hyundai Hysco] in the present case experienced due to the act of a refusal to deal and are not sufficient in reaching a conclusion that there

---

[23] The Court further held that:

> . . . the Defendant who claims that an act of refusing to deal by a market-dominating enterpriser falls under the abusive acts must prove that such refusal to deal is a behaviour which is likely to create an anti-competitive effect, such as increase in price, reduction in production, impediment to innovation, reduction in the number of efficient competitors, decrease in diversity etc, and is accompanied with the intent and purpose to create such effects. In case it is shown that the said effects have actually occurred as a result of the act of refusing to deal, it is possible to presume that the restriction on competition was likely to occur at the time of such act and that there has been intent and purpose to the same effect. Otherwise, however, it should be determined whether the act of refusing to deal was an act which was likely to create an anti-competitive effect and whether there has been any intent or purpose to such effect, by taking into account the totality of the circumstances such as background and motive of refusal to deal, detailed facts of the refusal, characteristics of the relevant market, degree of disadvantages occurred to the transacting partner as a result of the refusal, any change in price or production in the relevant market, impediment to innovation, decrease in diversity etc. The relevant market shall include not only a market where the market-dominating enterpriser and its competitors belong, but also a market which supplies raw materials, components or semi-products that are necessary in manufacturing the product of the said market, or a market where new products are manufactured using the product that is produced in the said relevant market.

[24] *POSCO v Korea Fair Trade Commission* Seoul High Court, Case 2001*Nu*5370, Judgment of 27 August 2002.

> has actually been an anti-competitive effect. . . . despite the Plaintiff's act of refusing to deal, (i) [Hyundai Hysco] has been importing hot-rolled coils from Japan as necessary and manufacturing and selling cold-rolled steel plates, has been carrying out a normal course of business activities as a manufacturer and seller of cold-rolled steel plates by enjoying net profits continuously since 2001 when the cold-rolled steel plant was established and started manufacturing and (ii) no data is suggesting that competition was restricted.

The Court also drew attention to the fact that POSCO had, after entering the market for cold-rolled coil, continued to supply existing customers who were also its downstream competitors with hot-rolled coil, but that the refusal to supply Hyundai Hysco was a refusal to supply a new customer who also happened to be in direct competition with POSCO.[25]

5-3.15 Article 3-2(1)(4) is similar in its terms to art 3-2(1)(5), the former prohibiting acts which unreasonably impede the participation of *new* competitors, and the latter covering *existing* competition. Impeding market entry may be condemned where it is direct or indirect. 'New competitors' is intended to cover potential entrants who have not yet established themselves with any presence in the market, or an entrant who has not yet started business. Illegal conduct includes unreasonable exclusive contracts entered into with distributors, unreasonable acquisition of any rights held by the entrant which are necessary for it to do business, and unreasonable refusals to deal with new competitors, or with other enterprises which are prepared to deal with the entrant.

5-3.16 Article 3-2(1)(5) which prohibits an 'act of unfairly excluding competitive enterprisers, or act that may considerably harm the interest of consumers' is in effect two separate prohibitions, which may be applied severably. Thus, for example, in *Microsoft*,[26] a breach of the second condition of the article was found in respect of its bundling and tying practices (see further below). A breach of this part of the article was also found in respect of a practice entered into by fifteen systems operators which were affiliates of Tbroad, a company with a strong position in local broadcasting markets. The companies packaged channels for broadcasting into building developments and apartment complexes, and refused to renew collective contracts under which their services were offered. Further, in April 2005, a number

[25] Three members of the Court dissented from this majority judgment. The result of the case is very similar, if not identical, to that which would exist in the EC antitrust jurisprudence where, absent the application of a (highly restricted) essential facilities doctrine, a dominant supplier is not required to supply a new customer, but may be prevented, in the short term, from ceasing supplies to an existing customer, even where that customer enters into direct competition with the supplier (see, eg *BBI/Boosey & Hawkes*, Commission Decision 87/500 [1987] OJ L286/36 and *United Brands Co v Commission* Case 27/76 [1978] 1 CMLR 429).

[26] KFTC Decision 2006-042, 24 February 2006.

of large multiple systems operators unilaterally adjusted their packages of channels moving popular low-end channels into higher-fee packages. The KFTC found in part that the systems operators:

> took advantage of the limited scope of consumers' options in a monopolized market by deliberately deteriorating product quality through unilateral rearrangement of channels after they first attracted consumers to subscribe to their service with discounted long-term contracts and burdened them with heavy penalties for breach of the contracts.

There have been a number of cases in which a breach of the first part of art 3-2(1)(5) has been found to exist. The Guidelines make reference to only two practices which fall to be condemned: supplying goods at unreasonably high prices, or selling goods at unreasonably low prices with the intent of eliminating competition; and entering into conditional contracts which restrict the ability of the competitor to trade with other enterprises. The most recent reported case at the time of writing relates to conduct entered into by Interpark Gmarket Inc, which ran an e-market site, and took steps to prevent those selling through its platform from doing business with a rival.[27] The company was found to have compelled sellers using its site to raise prices on the rival's site, and to lower prices on its site, or to suspend business with the rival. Pressure was also put on sellers to restrict supplies to the rival. Seven sellers were thus persuaded to withdraw from selling on the rival site. Gmarket was found to be dominant by virtue of its market share of 39.5 per cent, and the combined market share of the largest two parties in the market stood at 91.4 per cent, satisfying the CR3 75 per cent market presumption set out in art 4 of the MRFTA. Further entry barriers were found to exist in that barriers, such as 'know-how, set-up cost of infrastructure . . . and operational programs, recognition and credibility' made new entrants' access to the market difficult. There was clear competitive harm to the rival in the loss of custom from the seven identified sellers, and correctional measures and penalties were imposed on Gmarket.[28] **5-3.17**

Recently the KFTC has again followed the position taken in the EC (and in this case in Japan) and initiated action against Intel. In September 2007 the KFTC sent allegations to Intel relating to an alleged illegal use of its dominant position in the market for computer chips. The concerns of the KFTC, which are similar to those expressed in Japan and the EC are that in its battle with competitor Advanced Micro Devices ('AMD') in the central processing unit ('CPU') market, Intel both offered inducements to customers in the form of predatory pricing, and pressured customers to take Intel chips rather than those produced by its **5-3.18**

---

[27] KFTC Decision 2008-215, 25 July 2008.
[28] KFTC, *2008 Annual Report*, p 54.

competitor.[29] A decision was taken in respect of Intel Corporation on 4 June 2008.[30] In essence the KFTC found that Intel had provided rebates to two customers, Samsung Electronics and Sambo Computer, respectively ranked 1st and 2nd in the Korean PC market, on the condition that they not purchase CPUs manufactured by AMD. The KFTC found that it would have been impossible for AMD to compete with the terms offered by Intel, even if it had offered its CPUs to manufacturers at no cost. In markets where the rebates were not offered AMD's market share was rising, in some cases to as high as 30 per cent, but in the markets in which Intel was able directly to affect purchasing decisions Intel was able to respond to AMD's growth, offering new rebates, such that the market share in those sectors was generally no higher than ten per cent.[31]

Remedies and penalties

5-3.19 Where a breach of art 3-2 of the MRFTA is found to have been perpetrated the KFTC may order the infringer 'to reduce prices, discontinue the violation, announce its receipt of a corrective order to the public, and take other measures required for correction'.[32] This too is a very widely drafted provision, and permits the KFTC to craft any necessary conduct remedy to alleviate the abuse identified.[33] The specific reference to price reductions is unnecessary given the wide scope of the provision, but is a legacy of the pre-history of the legislation, under which the Act's antecedents were directed significantly towards price controls. A failure to comply with any corrective measure ordered may lead to imprisonment for a period of up to two years or a fine of up to Won150m.[34] Article 6 further provides that a penalty ('surcharge') may be imposed of up to three per cent of the turnover of the enterprise. Where there is no turnover, or where it is difficult to compute the turnover, fines may not exceed Won1bn.

Case examples

5-3.20 The case to attract the most publicity in recent years was that brought against Microsoft Corp and Microsoft Korea in December 2005, which took a very similar pattern to that in the EC, although it addressed only issues of the bundling

[29] See *Financial Times*, 12 September 2007.

[30] The addressees of the Decision were Intel Corporation, Intel Semi-Conductor, and Intel Korea (hereinafter 'Intel').

[31] See KFTC Newsletter, 4 July 2008. The KFTC commented on the difficulty of the investigation, noting that 'it took three years of thorough investigation and discussions with domestic and foreign economists and jurists before a final decision was made'.

[32] art 5, MRFTA.

[33] Note however criticisms of the lack of flexibility shown by the KFTC in this regard discussed in Chapter 5-5, below.

[34] art 67(6), MRFTA.

of software. Specifically the KFTC found that Microsoft, in breach of art 3-2, and art 23 (which inter alia bans tie-in sales)[35] was in violation by:

(a) First, tying Windows Media Server Program to the Windows PC Server Operating System, where Microsoft has market dominance.
(b) Second, tying Windows Media Player to the Windows PC Operating System, where Microsoft has monopoly power.
(c) Third, tying the instant messaging program to the Windows PC Operating System, where Microsoft has monopoly power.[36]

The argument advanced by the KFTC was that these practices reduced or stopped competition in the tied markets of media servers, media players, and messengers, and raised entry barriers in the tying product markets of the PC server operating systems, and PC operating systems. Remedies were imposed that required Microsoft to unbundled Windows Media Server from the Windows server operating system within 180 days of the decision being taken. In relation to the Media Player and Messenger tying Microsoft was required to offer a new version of Windows in which the products were separated from the operating system (a 'stripped version'). The company was also required to 'do its best to confer with domestic messenger service providers to make Microsoft Messenger and its competing programs "talk" to each other'.[37] The remedies were to remain in force for ten years, with Microsoft having the opportunity to request the KFTC to review the remedies every year after a five-year period had elapsed. A penalty of Won32.5bn was also imposed.[38] The report of the decision gives some indication of the approach that will be taken by the KFTC in relation to the infringements under examination. **5-3.21**

In relation to tying, the approach taken by the KFTC is virtually identical to that adopted in the EC, with the test being that of 'whether the tying product and the tied product are separate products, which are traded separately and recognized and perceived separately by consumers, and whether there is a sufficient demand **5-3.22**

---

35 This was the first case in which both of these articles were applied simultaneously.

36 The terminology here is slightly awkward. In the standard economic literature a tie-in occurs when the purchase of an ongoing stream of a product—for example, printer toner—is tied to the purchase of a single product at a specific time—for example a printer. The practice whereby two products, for which there exists separate demand, are sold only in a single transaction is better referred to as 'bundling', although there is a significant degree of inconsistency in the use of this terminology in case law.

37 See KFTC, *Annual Report on Competition Policy Development in Korea*, September 2006, p 15.

38 See KFTC *2008 Annual Report*, pp 42 ff. The investigation was the largest conducted by the KFTC, having been initiated by a complaint made on 5 September 2001.

for separate purchase of the tied product'. For Microsoft the Windows operating system and the three tied products—Windows Media Server ('WMS'), Windows Media Player ('WMP') and Messenger—were distinguished from each other in terms of function and usage. All were traded separately and were found by the KFTC to be severable from the tied product, and were 'generally not sold together as a unit'. The second test for tying put forward by the KFTC was that of whether there was coercion in that the customers were not given the option of buying the tying product without the tied product. Microsoft's practice of bundling the products was, the KFTC found, coercive in that the consumer did not have the choice when purchasing from Microsoft, and given Microsoft's market share of 99 per cent for PC operating systems consumers did not have a viable alternative. The final criterion was that of whether the practice was in fact anti-competitive. In the media server market the KFTC reported that the number of companies adopting WMS 'skyrocketed' with, as of August 2004, some 93 per cent of Internet broadcasters adopting WMS. The market share of Real Media in the media server market fell from 90 per cent in 1999, to 19 per cent in 2000, to zero per cent in 2004. In the media player market Microsoft's market share stood at 60.5 per cent in 2004, compared to 39.4 per cent in 2000, and in the messenger market Microsoft's Messenger 'had its market share soar while competitors' messengers declined in the same market'.[39] These figures, coupled to the approach taken by Microsoft in relation to the bundling of the products, convinced the KFTC that 'the radical market concentration . . . was not a result of fair competition driven by their quality or functions but a result of Microsoft's unfair bundling'.[40]

5-3.23 In January 2008 the KFTC took action against four multiplex cinema chains for abusing their market dominance in respect of screening practices and the payments made to film distributors.[41] The exhibitors ignored a standard trade practice under which films would be screened for at least two weeks, terminating exhibition runs within six days 'thus decreasing profits of distributors'. The report of the decision in the KFTC newsletter does not provide a full analysis of *why* this practice should be found to be abusive, nor indeed of how the law was applied to four cinema chains without an express finding of joint dominance.[42] In its analysis of the market power of the cinemas the KFTC reported that the top four multiplex cinemas were affiliated with large conglomerates, and had 'strengthened their market dominance by forming a hierarchy in the movie-related markets including production, distribution and filmed entertainment market', as a result of which

---

[39] KFTC, *2008 Annual Report*, pp 45–6.

[40] See also the *Intel* case, discussed above.

[41] KFTC Decision 2008-57, 21 February 2008.

[42] KFTC Newsletter, 27 February 2008.

the number of small and medium-sized cinemas in Korea dropped from 233 in 2004 to 188 in 2006.

Unfair Trade Practices

The provisions of Chapter 5 of the MRFTA are unusual in modern antitrust law, although there are influences of both Japanese and US law here. They identify 'unfair' practices, but do not require that there be any market power on the part of the party committing the wrongdoing, which invites a number of concerns. Without market power one may question the extent to which any of the identified practices may be a cause for concern, or indeed the extent to which they would be viable. The provision however is widely used, and Korean commentators argue that it may be viewed as an equivalent—although not an exact one—of s 5 of the US FTCA. Article 23 of the MRFTA is in this light to be seen as an *ex ante* provision and should be regarded as the general position, more likely to be used (in part because less rigour may be attached to its application) than art 3-2. The fact that the analysis may be less rigorous was confirmed by the Supreme Court of Korea in *POSCO*.[43] **5-3.24**

Six specific practices are condemned, and a 'catch-all' provision is included at art 23(1)(8) which prohibits 'any act that threatens to impede fair trade other than those listed [above]'. The practices condemned are: (1) refusals to supply[44] and discrimination; (2) any act 'designed to exclude competitors unfairly'; (3) any act unfairly inducing customers to deal with the perpetrator; (4) acts 'of engaging in a trade with a transacting partner by unfairly taking advantage of its position in the business area'; (5) the imposition of terms or conditions which 'unfairly restrict or disrupt business activities'; (6) an 'act of assisting a person with special interest or other companies by providing advanced payment, loans, manpower, immovable assets, stocks and bonds, or intellectual properties or by transacting under substantially favourable terms'.[45] **5-3.25**

---

[43] *POSCO v The Korea Fair Trade Commission*, Supreme Court of Korea, Case 2002*Du*8626, 22 November 2007.

[44] In *Pasteur Dairy Industry Co v The Fair Trade Commission*, 97*Nu*19427, 9 June 2000 the Supreme Court of Korea ruled that the Seoul High Court (96*Gu*25137, 4 November 1997) had been wrong to overturn a KFTC decision which found that a refusal by a supplier to renew an agent's contract was not an infringement of art 23. The supplier had argued that the contract renewal was based on the failure of the agent to attend meetings, and that the agent had failed to deliver supplies to a number of customers. The Supreme Court held that the High Court had failed to consider properly whether these reasons were just 'factors to be considered as secondary matters' or whether 'they constitute so serious a transactional breach' that the refusal was justified.

[45] art 23(1)(7), MRFTA. The Supreme Court of Korea has considered the standards for determining whether an act of assistance is improper in the case of *Daewoo Co Ltd et al v Fair Trade Commission*, Decision 2001*Du*2935, 14 October 2004. It held in part that the issue 'shall be

5-3.26 The relevant categories or standards for unfair trade practices are determined by Presidential Decree, and the KFTC has published *Notification on Unfair Business Practices Review Guidelines*.[46] It is also provided that businesses may produce fair trading codes voluntarily, and have these examined by the KFTC.[47]

5-3.27 The stance taken in the Guidelines towards collective refusals to deal has been discussed in Chapter 5-2, above. Paragraph III.1.B sets out, in brief, the approach taken to unilateral refusals to deal, stating that in determining whether such a refusal is unfair the KFTC will take into account: whether the refusal relates to an essential facility; whether there are alternative sources of supply available to the putative customer; whether competition at any level is being substantially lessened by the refusal; ease of entry into the market; and whether the refusal is linked to the maintenance of resale price maintenance, or to a horizontal concerted practice. Where there are market shortages or the refusal to deal is the result of a bankruptcy, or there are efficiency gains from the refusal, the KFTC may not move to condemnation. Refusals to deal under this Part of the Act will also not be condemned where the market share of the refusing party is ten per cent or less.[48] The Guidelines also deal with discrimination, exclusion (including predatory pricing), and coercive practices including tie-ins. Discriminatory pricing and discriminatory conditions of trade without objective justification are likely to be condemned, although not where the party imposing the discrimination has a

decided specifically and individually under the holistic approach of considering diverse factors such as the size of the assisting transactions, economic benefits, the duration, frequency and timing of assistance, the financial situation of the assisted entity at the time of the assistance, not to mention the disparity between the payment and its return payment in its return', and that the following factors shall be considered: 'the relation between an assisting entity and an assisted entity; the purpose or intention of an act of assistance; the structure and nature of the market to which an entity to be assisted belongs, the size of the assisting transaction, and the financial benefit from assistance and the duration of the assistance; the restraint on competition in the market to which an assisted entity belongs and the effect of economic concentration; the degree of change in competitive capacity and competition conditions of [SMEs]; the change in the market share of an assisted entity before and after an act of assistance; the degree of openness of the market, etc.'

[46] Enacted 27 December 2004. Most recently amended 11 May 2005.

[47] art 23(4) and (5), MRFTA.

[48] In *POSCO* the Supreme Court of Korea held that:

> . . . with respect to a refusal to deal as a type of unfair trade practice as regulated by [art 23(1)(1)], there is no limit in the subject of the act. Moreover, in a case of a refusal to deal as a type of unfair trade practices, by focusing on whether a certain refusal to deal impedes fair trade, when it is found that a particular enterpriser's business activities are made difficult or are likely to be made difficult by excluding an opportunity to trade, the unreasonableness should be appreciated based upon whether a particular enterpriser who is a transacting partner is disadvantaged by the concerned refusal to deal, rather than by considering the effect on the market by said refusal deal, such as in the case in which a refusal to deal is used for the purpose of securing a means to accomplish the goal of improper regulation of the transacting partner, etc. (*POSCO v The Korea Fair Trade Commission*, Supreme Court of Korea, Case 2002*Du*8626, 22 November 2007)

market share below ten per cent, or a turnover of less than Won2bn. The rubric on predatory pricing extends to both short-term and long-term behaviour, but again a market share of less than ten per cent by the predator excludes condemnation. Predatory conduct might fall to be condemned under art 23(1)(2), which prohibits acts 'designed to exclude competitors unfairly'. However, the Supreme Court of Korea has held that in a case where a bid to run an information service was made at an offer that did not even cover labour costs there was no breach of art 23(1)(2). The bidder argued that a low price had been offered in order to 'accumulate skill and experience by stepping into a new market', and the Court accepted this. It appears to have been important that the Court found that the successful bidder would not be able to exclude competition by offering such low prices repeatedly in relation to other bids. The Court held in part that:

> supply of products or service at a low price is hardly considered an impediment to fair trade in itself. As a result, supply of products or service at a low price is an act impeding fair trade only when it is done 'unjustly'. Whether there is unfairness should be decided according to the possibility of impeding fair trade after overall review of various factors in a given situation, such as intention and objective of each unfair bargain, the extent of the low price, the possibility of repetition, the characteristics of products or services in unfair bargain and its market situation, the behaviour's position in the market, the effect on competitors etc.[49]

In the event of any breach of art 23(1) the KFTC may order corrective measures or the deletion of any offending clause from a contract, publish details of the violation, and take any other appropriate corrective measures.[50] Penalties of up to two per cent of turnover may be imposed in the event of breaches of art 23(1)(1)–(5), and of up to five per cent in the event of a breach of art 23(1)(7). **5-3.28**

In February 2008 the KFTC established the Korean Fair Trade Mediation Committee ('KFTMC'),[51] provision for which was made under art 48-2 of the MRFTA. It was the hope of the KFTC that the KFTMC would reduce the need for public enforcement of the MRFTA provisions relating to fair trade. Formally the KFTMC was established in order to arbitrate disputes related to unfair business practices under art 23(1) of the MRFTA, and the arbitration of disputes related to franchising under the Fair Franchising Act. The role of the KFTMC is considered in outline in Chapter 5-5, below. **5-3.29**

---

[49] *Hyundai Information Technology Corporation v The Fair Trade Commission*, Supreme Court of Korea, Decision 99*Du*4686, 12 June 2001.

[50] art 24, MRFTA.

[51] Different translations of the agency name are given in Korean materials translated into English. The agency is known either as the Korea Fair Trade Arbitration Agency or, in the version which will be used here, the Institute of Korean Fair Trade Arbitration.

5-4

KOREA MERGER CONTROL

Introduction	5-4.01
Jurisdiction	5-4.08
'Foreign mergers'	5-4.08
Procedures	5-4.09
Pre-merger contacts and review	5-4.09
Notification	5-4.10
Foreign mergers	5-4.19
Powers of the KFTC	5-4.21
Application of the Substantive Test	5-4.22
General Review	5-4.23
Market definition	5-4.24
Market power assessment and the competitive effects of the merger	5-4.30
Competitive assessment	5-4.31
Horizontal mergers	5-4.32
Vertical mergers	5-4.40
Conglomerate mergers	5-4.42
Efficiencies and the failing firm defence	5-4.46
Remedies	5-4.50

Introduction

The core legislation relating to merger control in Korea is the Monopoly Regulation and Fair Trade Act ('MRFTA'), the relevant provisions of which should be read alongside the Enforcement Decree of the Monopoly Regulation and Fair Trade Act ('the Enforcement Decree'), and the M&A Notification Guidelines.[1] Some sector-specific rules also apply. The Telecommunications Business Act of Korea provides that a transfer of all or a part of, or a merger with, a telecommunications business requires the approval of the Ministry of Information and Communication ('MIC'). The Banking Act of Korea applies to business transfers or mergers between financial institutions, which requires the approval of the Korean Financial Supervisory Commission ('KFSC'). In both of these special **5-4.01**

[1] For another analysis of the Korean merger regime, see Jung, K-T and Hyun, J-W in Dabbah, MM and Lasok, P, *Merger Control Worldwide: First Supplement to the First Edition* (Cambridge: Cambridge University Press, 2006) at 48–63. There have however been amendments to the merger control provisions of the MRFTA since the publication of this supplement. See also Yun, SR and Hong, DS, 'Merger Regulations under the Korean Competition Law—Based on M&A *Review Guidelines* and KFTC's Decisions' (2005) 4:2 *Journal of Korean Law* 103.

cases the parties involved in the transaction do not need to notify their transaction to the KFTC, even if the transaction falls within the notifying thresholds discussed below, if the MIC or KFSC have consulted in advance with the KFTC. Generally the KFTC has been active in the area of merger control, and in 2008 it recognized the need to focus its attention more on notified mergers that raised concerns by raising the thresholds at which notification was required.[2]

5-4.02 Article 7 of the MRFTA is the central provision that establishes the merger control regime. Article 7(1) provides in part that: '[n]o one shall . . . substantially minimize competition in a particular business area . . . by committing any of the acts described below (hereinafter referred to as "combination of enterprises")'. Five categories of transactions are identified in art 7(1): (1) stock acquisitions;[3] (2) the concurrent holding of officers' positions (interlocking directorships), although this provision also applies to persons who are not officers, but 'who continue to be engaged in the affairs of the company'; (3) mergers with other companies; (4) the acquisition or transfer of the whole or part of a business of another company, or the acquisition or transfer of the whole or main part of fixed assets used by another company; and (5) participation in the establishment of a new company. Article 7(2) expressly provides that art 7(1) shall not apply where the KFTC finds that efficiencies gained through the combination outweigh any harms flowing from any restriction on competition, or where the failing firm defence applies.[4]

5-4.03 In order for art 7 to apply a combination of enterprises must have occurred such that 'a controlling relation between the parties engaging in the business combination shall exist'.[5] The criteria for determining whether a controlling relationship exists are set out in the *M&A Review Guidelines* ('*Review Guidelines*'). The *Review Guidelines* define criteria in relation to: (1) share ownership; (2) interlocking directorates; and (3) participation in the incorporation of a new company.

[2] See generally KFTC Newsletter, 1 May 2008.

[3] Article 7-2 provides that: 'The acquisition or ownership of shares under this Act shall be determined by the genuine ownership of shares, regardless of the names listed on the register'.

[4] Article 7(2)(2) provides precisely that art 7(1) may not apply where 'such combination is made with a nonviable company . . . [such as] a company whose total capital as indicated in a balance sheet is less than its paid-in capital for a reasonable period of time'. Art 12-4 of the Enforcement Decree clarifies this provision further, stating that art 7(2)(2) applies to 'cases where—1. the continued use of the company's production facilities etc in the relevant market is difficult without a combination of enterprises; 2. it is difficult to achieve a combination of enterprises that is less anti-competitive than the combination of enterprises concerned'.

[5] Para IV, *Notification on M&A Review Guidelines*, enacted by the KFTC, Notification no 1998-6, 15 June 1998 (as amended).

These criteria are fundamental to the determination of whether a relevant merger situation exists, and are therefore given here in full. In relation to the acquisition or ownership of shares a controlling relation will be found to exist where:

A. The Acquiring Party and others' shareholding ratio of the Acquired Party is 50 per cent or more.
B. Despite the shareholding ratio of the Acquiring Party and others is less than 50 per cent, in the case of the following:
   (1) the Acquiring Party and others have the largest shareholding ratio and, considering the distribution of shares, are able to control the company by exercising shareholders' rights; or
   (2) the Acquired Party receives most of the primary raw materials from the Acquiring Party, and the Acquiring Party is in a market-dominant position with respect to the production of the primary raw materials.

In relation to interlocking directorates control will be found to exist where: **5-4.04**

A. The number of directors of the Acquiring Party and others who have interlocking directorate of the Acquired Party (hereinafter 'interlocking director') exceeds one-third of all directors at the Acquired Party, thus enabling the Acquiring Party and others to exercise substantial influence on the overall management of the Acquired Party.
B. The interlocking director concurrently holds such position as the chairman of the board of directors at the Acquired Party that grants the power to exercise substantial influence on the overall management of the company.

In relation to participation in the incorporation of a new company the existence of a controlling relationship is to be determined as for the case of share ownership. **5-4.05**

Article 7(4) of the MRFTA establishes that competition may be presumed to be 'practically suppressed' in two particular cases. The relevant text is as follows: **5-4.06**

> If a combination of enterprises falls under any of the following cases, competition is presumed to be suppressed in any particular business area:
> 1. The aggregate of the market share of a company taking part in a combination of enterprises (referring to the aggregate of market shares of the affiliated companies; the same shall apply herein) falls under any of the following categories:
>   A. The aggregate market share of the company concerned satisfies the presumptive requirements for a market-dominating enterprise.
>   B. The aggregate market share of the company concerned is the largest in the relevant business area.
>   C. The aggregate market share of the company concerned exceeds the market share of the company with the second largest market share (referring to a company with the largest market share besides the company concerned) by not less than 25 percent of the aggregate market share.

2. A large company[6] combines enterprises directly or through a person with special interest in accordance with the following requirements:
   A. A combination of enterprises in a particular business area where small or medium-sized companies covered by the Framework Act on Small and Medium Enterprises account for not less than two-thirds of the entire market share.
   B. A combination of enterprises wherein the combined company has a market share of not less than 5 percent.

5-4.07 The KFTC is relatively active in relation to the number of merger cases it deals with each year. Like most authorities the number of decisions taken condemning mergers is very small. The following table of activity is drawn from the Annual Report for 2008:[7]

	2001	2002	2003	2004	2005	2006	2007
Cases reviewed	644	602	589	749	658	744	857
Mergers found to be anti-competitive	1	2	7	6	1	7	3
Notification guidelines violations	44	44	36	29	16		

The fall in the number of cases reviewed from 2004 to 2005 was in part a result of a relaxation of certain reporting requirements by the KFTC in an attempt to focus its resources more effectively.

Jurisdiction

'Foreign mergers'

5-4.08 The merger provisions of the MRFTA apply to 'foreign mergers' where the relevant thresholds are established. The *M&A Reporting Guidelines* for overseas mergers and acquisitions was amended with effect from 1 July 2003, in part in recognition of the increasing globalization of merger control. The KFTC noted the fact that 'M&As abroad have had increasing influence on competition in the domestic market', and the fact that an increasing number of regimes impose obligatory notifications on mergers taking place outside their own markets. In amending the *Reporting Guidelines* the KFTC argued that the new approach

6 Large companies are defined in art 12-2 of the Enforcement Decree as being 'a company whose total assets or sales revenues exceed two trillion Won'. Sales revenues are further defined as being 'the sales revenues in the income statement of the year immediately prior to the year of the [merger]' (art 12(3), Enforcement Decree). Reference may also be had to arts 2(1)(7) and 4 of the MRFTA, which define market dominating enterprises, and which are discussed in Chapter 5-3.

7 KFTC, *2008 Annual Report*, p 110.

would 'lay the foundation to prevent anti-competitive effects of overseas M&As on domestic market and consumers'.[8] Notification procedures, which are less burdensome in respect of mergers in which both the acquiring and the acquired company are foreign than they are for Korean companies, are dealt with below.

Procedures

Pre-merger contacts and review

Article 12(8) of the MRFTA expressly permits parties contemplating a transaction which falls under art 7(1) to 'request the [FTC] to determine whether such combination may be categorized as one that substantially minimizes competition' before the compulsory notification period provided for in art 12(6) (discussed below). Part V of the Notification Guidelines (discussed generally below) provides simply that where parties request a pre-merger review they are to file the relevant forms and documents set out in the Guidelines. Where an art 12(8) request is made the KFTC has thirty days within which to make its decision, although where necessary the KFTC may extend this period by a further ninety days.[9] **5-4.09**

Notification

Article 12 of the MRFTA provides that notification of certain transactions is compulsory, although notification may be made *after* the merger has been implemented. Whether notification is required is determined largely by thresholds set out from time to time in Presidential Decrees. The relevant thresholds are set out in art 18 of the Enforcement Decree, and are that the enterprises concerned have total assets, which are defined in art 12(2) MRFTA as being 'the sum of total assets or revenues of a company maintaining the status of affiliate from the day before the combination of enterprises to the day after the combination of enterprises',[10] or turnover of at least Won100bn. Five circumstances are set out in art 12(1)(1)–(5) in which notification is to be made: (1) where at least 20 per cent of the stocks issued by a company are held;[11] (2) in the event A becomes the largest **5-4.10**

---

[8] KFTC, *Regarding Notification on Overseas M&A* <http://www.ftc.go.kr>.

[9] art 12(9), MRFTA. It is not uncommon for preliminary reviews to be requested. This was the case, for example, in respect of *POSCO/POSTEEL/Korea Core* (KFTC, *2008 Annual Report*, pp 68 ff).

[10] Article 12 of the Enforcement Decree further provides that total assets 'means the total assets in the balance sheet as of the closing date of the fiscal year immediately prior to the year of the combination of enterprises'. Special provision is made in respect of financial or insurance companies.

[11] This figure is 15 per cent in the case of a stock-listed corporation or association-registered corporation under the Securities and Exchange Act. The effect of this provision is that where A owns 18 per cent of the stock of B, and then acquires a further three per cent, a notifiable merger situation has been created.

shareholder in B, following the acquisition of at least 20 per cent of shares and a notification under art 12(1)(1); (3) in the case of the creation of interlocking directorates; (4) where activities fall within art 7(1)(3) (merger) or (4) (acquisition of assets) of the MRFTA (see above); and (5) in the event of A becoming the largest investor in a newly-established B. Article 12-2 sets out a special regime for notifying mergers in the cable-broadcasting sector, specifying that these are to be reported to the relevant government administrative department where the merger would fall under the terms of art 12(1).

5-4.11 Further provision in respect of notification is made in the Enforcement Decree, art 18. Article 18(3) of the Enforcement Decree provides that the relevant parties are to:

> submit to the [KFTC] a notification form stating the names, sales, total assets, line of business of both the enterprise subject to notification and its counterpart enterprise, the nature of the said Combination of Enterprises, and the status of the relevant markets along with documents necessary to substantiate anything asserted in the notification.

5-4.12 Figure 5-4.1 sets out the notification time-frames in respect of various categories of mergers.

5-4.13 Where notifications are deemed to be insufficient the KFTC may order revisions to be made within a set period. Any relevant deadlines are suspended during this period. Notifications are to be made within thirty days of the date of the relevant merger.[12] Notifications are not required in the circumstances set out in art 12(3).[13]

5-4.14 Standard notification forms are available on the KFTC website, as is the most recent version of the M&A Notification Guidelines, last updated on 20 December 2007. Article 69-2 of the MRFTA sets out the penalties ('fine for negligence') that may be applied in the event that a required notification is not made, or is made falsely. Enterprises may be fined up to Won100m, and persons may be fined up to Won10m. The procedures with respect to art 69-2 fines are further clarified in art 65 of the Enforcement Decree. Notification of the penalty must be made in writing, 'clearly specifying the violation, method of appeal, duration of appeal, and the amount of the administrative fine'. The person subject to the fines must

---

[12] art 12(6), MRFTA.

[13] Article 12(3)(1) exempts certain mergers involving small and medium enterprise start-up investment companies established under the terms of the Support for Small and medium Enterprise Establishment Act. Article 12(3)(2) exempts combinations between certain businesses regulated respectively by the Specialized Credit Financial Business Act and the Korea Technology Credit Guarantee Fund Act. Article 12(3)(3) exempts acquisitions of investment companies regulated by the Indirect Investment Act, the Private Investment for Infrastructure Act, real estate companies falling under the Real Estate Investment Act, and investment companies established for the purposes of the Legal Person Tax Act.

	Category of merger	Types of M&A	Notification Period
Pre-merger notification	Large enterprisers	Acquisition or ownership of shares	Private transactions: 30 days after the agreement of acquisition * In the event of an open transaction under stock-exchange rules post-merger notification is required
		Merger	30 days after merger agreement
		Transfer of business	30 days after the transaction agreement
		Acquisition of shares of newly established company	30 days after the decision of the establishment of the new company
Post-merger notification	Non-large enterprisers	Acquisition or ownership of shares	30 days after any one of the following, whichever falls first: transfer of the ownership and payment; the day after payment is due; the effective day of the transfer; the confirmed date of the acquisition of stock or shares
		Merger	30 days after the registration of the merger
		Transfer of business	30 days after full payment* * If full payment is made within 90 days, then 30 days after this date
		Acquisition of shares of newly established company	30 days after the due date of the payment of the acquisition price
	Large enterprisers	Interlocking directorships of large-scale companies	30 days after the decision of the board to the directorial appointment

Figure 5-4.1 Merger notification time-frames.
Source: Shin, HY, *Korean Competition Law* (Seoul: Bubmunsa, 2007) 176–7.

be given the opportunity to provide his/her opinion within a set period, and art 65(3) of the Enforcement Decree provides that in determining the amount of the fine the KFTC 'shall take into consideration the motives, results etc of the concerned violation'.

5-4.15 The Guidelines provide for two different notification procedures: 'general notification' and 'simplified notification'.

5-4.16 Simplified notifications may be made in the case of mergers falling into one of five categories as defined in para II.1.1 of the M&A Notification Guidelines:

(1) If the combining entities are Specially Related Parties . . .;[14]
(2) In the event of an M&A, a controlling relationship as referred to in Article 5 of the Notification, is not created between the companies concerned (referring to the acquiring party[[15]]) and the acquired party[[16]]as described in Article 11-4 and 11-5 of the Notification . . .;
(3) Entities other than Large-Scale Corporation[s] . . . [are] involved in a conglomerate M&A.
(4) Where any of the following subparagraphs apply and the combination 'is certainly not for controlling enterprises but investment purpose':
    (a) Joining personal effect floater companies under the terms of the Indirect Investment Act;
    (b) An M&A with an asset securitization company under art 5(2) of the Asset Securitization Act;
    (c) An M&A with a company established for the purposes of investment, and which will be dissolved after the completion of the investment purpose.
(5) Where post-merger concentration levels or market shares fall under any of the following subparagraphs:
    (a) In the case of a horizontal merger either:
        (i) The post-merger HHI is less than 1,200;
        (ii) The post-merger HHI is between 1,200 and 2,500 and the incremental change is less than 250; or

[14] The term 'specially related parties' is defined in art 11 of the Enforcement Decree.

[15] 'Acquiring party' is defined in para II.1.4 in the following terms: '"Acquiring party" includes a corporation acquiring or owning the shares concerned; a large-scale corporation whose officers or employees (hereinafter, "officers and staffs") concurrently assume the position of officers in the acquired corporation; an investing corporation which takes part in the incorporation of a new corporate entity (excluding participation in such incorporations as defined in [art 7(1)(5)(a) and (b) of the MRFTA]); in case of a merger, the remaining corporation after the merger; and in case of business transfer, the transferee of a business: *provided*, however, that Specially Related Parties other than corporations acquiring or owning shares or participating in the incorporation of a new corporate entity shall be considered as the "Acquiring Party".'

[16] 'Acquired party' is defined in para II.1.5 in the following terms: '"Acquired party" includes the corporate entity which issued the shares concerned, in case of the acquisition or ownership of shares; a corporation which appointed officers from the officers and staffs of a large-scale enterprise, in the case of interlocking directorate; a new established corporation, in the case of the incorporation of a new corporation; a corporate entity which ceases to exist as a result of consolidation, in the case of a merger; and the transferee of the business, in the case of a business transfer'.

(iii) The post-merger HHI is greater than 2,500, and the incremental change is less than 150.

(b) In the case of a vertical or conglomerate merger either:

(i) The HHI in the relevant market is less than 2,500 and the company's market share[17] post-merger is less than 25 per cent; or

(ii) The merged entity ranks fourth or less in the market.

Simplified notification may be made online at the KFTC website. The general principle, set out in the Guidelines, is that mergers subject to the simplified review shall be presumed not to be anti-competitive,[18] and that in principle the results of any review will be notified within fifteen days of the notification being accepted.[19] **5-4.17**

Where notification is made under art 12(6) it is an offence to 'register the fact of a merger, execute the contracts for the takeover of business, or acquire stocks' within thirty days of the date of notification. This period may be shortened, or extended up to a maximum of a further ninety days by the KFTC.[20] The approach taken to mergers subject to 'general' or 'ordinary' review is set out more fully below. **5-4.18**

Foreign mergers

Unlike earlier versions of the notification guidelines there are no specific provisions in the most recent version in relation to 'foreign mergers', such that the Guidelines are to be applied in their entirety to foreign mergers, and market assessments become of the utmost importance in determining whether a foreign merger would be potentially subject to the Korean merger regime. In practice, because of their limited impact on Korean HHIs, many foreign mergers with an impact in Korea are likely to fall within the simplified review requirements set out above. **5-4.19**

At the time of writing there is no case in which the KFTC has blocked a merger in which both parties were enterprises based outside Korea. The KFTC has, however, imposed penalties on foreign corporations who have failed to comply with the MRFTA reporting requirements.[21] It has also imposed remedies on foreign **5-4.20**

[17] For the purposes of the Guidelines, market shares are defined by reference to the percentage of the sales amount of the relevant company in a relevant product nationally. Where the total sales amount is difficult to calculate, or is considered to be inappropriate, the production quantity, or capacities, may be relied on in the alternative (para II.1.10).

[18] A 'competition-restrictive M&A', or an M&A which substantially restrains competition, is defined in para II.1.6 as referring 'to a merger which results in reduced competition in a given area of trade so as to create or consolidate a state in which a certain company or a certain business group freely influences or is expected to freely influence the price, output and quality of a product, terms of trade etc'.

[19] para III.

[20] art 12(7), MRFTA.

[21] In December 2003 for example the KFTC reported that it had imposed a penalty of Won5m (US$4,167) on Globespan Virata Inc, a US-based corporation which had failed to comply with the

parties in respect of assets held in Korea. This was the case for example in *Owens Corning/Saint-Gobain Vetrotex.*[22] In this case the US enterprise Owens Corning acquired the entirety of the fibreglass reinforced business of Saint-Gobain Vetrotex, a French enterprise. Both companies held subsidiaries in Korea, giving rise to a horizontal merger situation. The relevant geographic market was found to be that of Korea (notwithstanding the fact that exports accounted for nearly 20 per cent of sales), and the merger would have substantially lessened competition, with the number of the players reduced from four to three post-merger, and the share of the post-merged entity would have been approximately 54 per cent. Entry barriers were substantial, and the post-merged entity would have a significant capacity over rivals already in the market. The KFTC also raised the concern of post-merger coordination between the parties with the possibility that this would take the form of a cartel. The remedy imposed required one or other of the merging parties to divest their relevant assets in Korea.

Powers of the KFTC

5-4.21 In the event that a merger is found to fall within art 7(1) of the MRFTA the KFTC has substantial powers under art 16 to impose corrective measures. It may, in particular: (1) require the cessation of the practice concerned; (2) require the disposal of all or part of the stocks acquired; (3) compel the resignation of officers; (4) require the transfer of a business; (5) require the cancellation of debt guarantees; (6) require publication of the fact that a corrective order has been made; (7) impose restrictions on methods of business so as to 'prevent the negative effects of restricted competition'. If these powers are not sufficient art 16(1)(8) provides that the KFTC may take any other measures necessary 'to reprimand such violation'. Where a company has been created as a result of a merger which violates the MRFTA the KFTC may 'file a lawsuit to nullify said establishment of a company or said merger of companies'.[23]

Application of the Substantive Test

5-4.22 As noted above the standard of review of a merger is whether it may 'substantially lessen competition in a particular business area'. This is standard language familiar to anyone with experience of the operation of the US merger regime. The KFTC published *M&A Review Guidelines* in April 1999. These have since been amended, most recently in December 2007.

requirements of art 12, MRFTA when it engaged in a transaction with another US company (KFTC News, 2004-1).

[22] KFTC, *2008 Annual Report*, pp 72 ff.

[23] art 16(2), MRFTA.

General Review

Mergers subject to general review are scrutinized in accordance with the methodology set out in the *Review Guidelines*, which employ principles similar to those utilized in the EC and US, although the language is a little different, and the level of detail is less. A general review may be undertaken when the merger does not satisfy the requirements of the simplified review, set out above, and when a controlling relationship is established by the acquiring party with regard to the acquired party. Prima facie a controlling relationship is established when the acquiring party holds 50 per cent or more of the shareholding of the acquired party.[24] Where the shareholding does not reach 50 per cent four factors may be considered to determine whether a controlling relationship exists: (1) the level of shares held by each shareholder and their distribution; (2) whether the acquired party receives most of its raw materials from the acquiring party; (3) interlocking directorates; and (4) transaction, capital, and coordinating relationships between the parties. In the event that two or more acquiring parties exist the KFTC will consider: (1) 'the shareholding ratio, gap, and relations of each acquiring party'; and (2) the purpose of the acquisition, and any contractual relationships between the acquiring parties following the acquisition. Interlocking directorates may also result in a controlling relationship where the result is to allow the exercise of 'substantial influence' on the management of the acquired party. This is considered to arise where the number of directors appointed by the acquiring party exceeds one-third of all directors, or where a director holds a position such as to confer substantial influence, such as that of the Chairman of the Board. **5-4.23**

Market definition

The *Review Guidelines* do not use the term 'market definition', but refer instead to the 'criteria for a given area of trade', which 'may be defined according to the object of transaction, transaction territory, stage of transaction and party to transaction'.[25] The 'object of transaction' equates to the 'product market', and the given area of trade 'refers to the aggregate of products to which major buyers of a specific product can switch, in response to a significant and non-transitory increase in the price of such product'.[26] The language here is drawn from the SSNIP test, although the formulation of this in the *Review Guidelines* is not precisely the same as in the case of the US and EC. Paragraph VI.1.B of the *Review Guidelines* states that whether specific products belong to the same area of trade is to be determined by reference to: (1) similarities in the function and usage of products; (2) similarities in the price of products; (3) buyers' and sellers' perceptions of substitutability **5-4.24**

24 para V.1.A, *Notification on M&A Review Guidelines.*
25 para VI, *Notification on M&A Review Guidelines.*
26 para VI.1.A, *Notification on M&A Review Guidelines.*

and related purchase patterns; (4) Korean standard industry classifications;[27] (5) the stages of transaction; and (6) the parties to the transaction. If it is noted that in practice the emphasis is on consumer preferences and demand substitution this is not to suggest that the KFTC analysis is unsophisticated. The use of the SSNIP test is common, and the KFTC may take some effort to apply this with rigour. In *Hite Beer Co/Jinro Distilling Co*[28] there was argument as to whether Soju (a Korean spirit) and beer were in the same, or different, markets. The KFTC took the view that the 'two liquors are different from each other in many respects such as taste, alcoholicity, and demand'. More rigorously it relied on the application of a critical sales decline analysis (used for the first time in Korea in this case) to determine the SSNIP boundary.

5-4.25 The 'transaction territory' equates to the geographic market, in which a given area of trade is again framed in SSNIP terms. In determining the bounds of the geographic market reference is to be made to:

(1) Characteristics of the product (perishability, changeability, breakage, etc of the product) and the seller's business capabilities (production capacity, the scope of sales network, etc)

(2) Buyers' perception of the possibility to shift to other geographic areas for sources of the product and their related behavioural patterns in shifting purchase areas.

(3) Sellers' perception of the possibility of their buyers shifting to other geographic areas for sources of the product and their related managerial decision-making patterns.

(4) Ease of shifting purchase areas from the time, economic, and legal aspects.[29]

5-4.26 It has been noted however that 'what is provided in the [legislation] and the *Review Guidelines* is insufficient for the task of market delineation; nor have the case law and KFTC rulings treated the matter in depth'.[30] In particular the criticism has been made that:

> ... in most cases only insufficient explanations are given for the delineation of markets. For instance, in the Haitai case, the KFTC distinguished between the market for fruit drinks and that for carbonated drinks citing merely that there are differences in the raw materials and the production method, without giving any concrete account of such differences.[31]

27 As determined by the National Statistical Office, pursuant to the Statistics Act, art 17(2).

28 KFTC Decision 2006-9; see also *Annual Report on Competition Policy Development in Korea*, September 2006, p 17.

29 para VI.2.B, *Notification on M&A Review Guidelines*.

30 Yun, S-R, 'Regulation of Business Combination under the Antimonopoly Regulation and Fair Trade Act with Emphasis on the Case Law' (2002) 2 *Journal of Korean Korean Law* 1 at 10.

31 Ibid at 13.

Notwithstanding this criticism the practice of the KFTC provides the most reliable guidance to the approaches likely to be taken in future cases, and examples of the relevant case law are given here. **5-4.27**

A number of examples may demonstrate the approaches taken by the KFTC in market definition. In *Kolon Industries Inc/Kohap Co Nylon Film*[32] Kolon argued that the relevant product market was that for all film products used for food-packaging, including PET film, OPP film, CPP film, and nylon film. The KFTC rejected this broad approach on the grounds that the physical and material characteristics, as well as the usage, of nylon film was different from that of other film products. The fact that the price of nylon film was significantly higher than that of other film products supported this stance. In *SK Inc/DOPCO*[33] the KFTC found that the carriage of oil by pipeline was in a different market than the carriage of oil by ship or other means of transport. In the present case the cost and price of oil transfer by pipeline was significantly more than for alternative methods.[34] However, in *Gillette Co/Rocket Korea Co*[35] the KFTC found that disposable and rechargeable batteries were in the same market, notwithstanding the significant price differences between them, given the fact that the characteristics and usage of the products were the same. The lack of demand and supply-side substitutability were relied upon in *INI Steel Co/Hyundai Hysco Co/Hanbo Steel Co*[36] in which the KFTC found that iron reinforcing bars were not in the same market as steel bars. In *Samick Musical Instruments Co/Youngchang Piano Co*[37] the Seoul High Court upheld the finding of the KFTC that upright pianos (normally used in domestic circumstances), grand pianos (normally used for teaching or performance), and digital pianos constituted separate product markets based on lack of demand substitutability.[38] Supply-side substitutability was found to be a key factor in determining that the many different types and sizes of stainless steel foil or paper fell within the same relevant market.[39] Although sold in different grades and sizes all such products could be produced on the same production line, giving rise to significant ease of supply-side substitution. **5-4.28**

As with other jurisdictions geographic markets may be defined as being wider than that of Korea (extending to global, although there is at present no case in which this position has been taken), as extending to all of Korea, or as being a part **5-4.29**

32 KFTC Decision 2003-018.

33 KFTC Decision 2001-090.

34 This decision has been criticized by a number of Korean commentators on the grounds that it is an example of the reverse cellophane fallacy.

35 KFTC Decision 98-282.

36 KFTC Decision 2004-285.

37 KFTC Decision 2004-271.

38 Ruling of Seoul High Court, Case 2005/3174, Decision of March 2006.

39 *Incheon Steel Co/Sammi Steel Co*, KFTC Decision 2000-151.

of Korea. In *Muhak Co/Daesun Distilling Co*[40] the relevant product was Soju. Muhak argued that the relevant geographic market was the whole of Korea, but the KFTC found that south-eastern Korea (Pusan and Kyungnam) constituted a separate market due to the strong preference expressed by consumers for locally produced spirits. The preference was such that it would be difficult for rival producers to enter these markets in the face of local brand loyalty. The effect of this decision was to find that Muhak was dominant in these narrow markets. Following a challenge to the decision the KFTC applied the SSNIP test, and reached the same conclusion, in which it was later supported by the Seoul High Court. A similar decision was taken in *Hite Beer Co/Jinro Distilling Co*[41] in which the KFTC confirmed that the geographic market for Soju consisted of two distinct areas within Korea: Pusan and surrounding districts, and the rest of Korea. The decision in this case rested on three main factors: (1) where prices were increased outside of Pusan by the parties market shares decreased; (2) in that area hometown brand preference was not particularly strong; and (3) the application of the Elzinga-Hogarty test.[42]

Market power assessment and the competitive effects of the merger

5-4.30 As discussed below the KFTC's determination of the competitive effects of a merger is based significantly, as would be expected, on an analysis of post-merger market share. The relevant guidelines suggest market shares that may be indicative of power and of competitive detriment. The principles applied may be demonstrated by reference to a number of cases, some of which are dealt with here. A leading case is that of *Incheon Steel Co/Sammi Steel Co.*[43] Here the parties were active in the market for stainless steel foil, with the share of the merging parties being 41.2 per cent. The share of the next biggest firm (POSCO) was 23.4 per cent, and POSCO had a powerful position in relation to the supply of the raw material for the manufacture of stainless steel. Incheon argued that the upstream power of POSCO would act as a constraint on the merging parties. The KFTC however considered that the combined post-merger market share of the two entities would give rise to a position of collective dominance, arguing that POSCO would raise its raw material prices if Incheon were to raise its prices for the finished product, and that there was further a prospect of both parties aligning

[40] KFTC Decision 2003-28.

[41] KFTC Decision 2006-9.

[42] It is worth noting that in this case too the KFTC found that separate markets existed for beer and Soju, in part based on an analysis of consumer preferences, but also by reference to the practice of other competition authorities in determining relevant markets in the case of alcoholic beverages.

[43] KFTC Decision 2000-151.

prices in the foil market.[44] In the case of *Beckton Dickinson Korea Holding Inc/ Shindongbang Medical Co*[45] the relevant market was that for intravascular catheters, and the effect of the merger would be to give rise to a post-merger market share of 79.2 per cent. The high market share alone gave rise to a finding that the merger would be anti-competitive, even though there was significant evidence of ease of entry, and evidence of successful entry in the past.

Competitive assessment

The *Review Guidelines* deal with both horizontal and vertical mergers when setting out the approach to be taken to the assessment of competition. As with the US and the EC the focus is on horizontal mergers, which are presumed to give rise to greater competitive concerns than are vertical mergers. It is worth noting however that the presence of the *chaebol* structure raises vertical concerns that are not often present in other jurisdictions. There are elements throughout this part of the *Review Guidelines* that are distinctive, although the basic structure is a standard one. Thus in discussing the approach to be taken to horizontal mergers the *Review Guidelines* deal with: market concentration, foreign competition in the market and international competition, the threat of entry, the possibility of collusion by competitors (coordinated effects), and the existence of similar goods and adjacent markets. These are dealt with here in turn. **5-4.31**

Horizontal mergers

The approach to market concentration is set out at para VII.1.A of the *Review Guidelines*. The KFTC states that: **5-4.32**

> [w]hether a horizontal combination substantially restricts competition is judged by the comprehensive consideration of market concentration before and after the business combination, the degree of foreign competition introduced and the international competition situation, the possibility of entry, the possibility of collusion between competing businesses, and the existence of similar goods and adjacent markets.[46]

HHIs are referred to only in so far as it is made clear that mergers that fall outside the HHI thresholds for the application of the simplified review procedure (discussed above) 'can substantially lessen competition in the relevant market'. It is, however, made clear that further analysis may be necessary to determine whether in fact this is the case.

---

[44] The case was further complicated with the KFTC anticipating the possibility of vertical foreclosure by POSCO, and by the fact that a significant proportion of output was for export.

[45] KFTC Decision 2000-38.

[46] Guidelines, para VII.1.

5-4.33 In analysing the changes in market concentration the *Review Guidelines* do not make reference to changes in concentration ratios, but rather opt for a generalized statement of practice:

> Trend of changes in the degree of market concentration during the last few years shall be considered when evaluating the degree of market concentration. In the case of a trend towards a considerable increase in market concentration during the last few years, business combinations by businesses with high market shares may increase the possibility of substantially restricting competition. In such case, factors including development of new technology, patent rights and others that may cause changes henceforth shall be considered.[47]

5-4.34 The treatment accorded to unilateral anti-competitive effects of a merger is short in the Guidelines.[48] However, some presumptions are set out in art 7(4) of the MRFTA. Thus it may be presumed that competition is 'suppressed' where, post-merger, the market share of the enterprise satisfies the presumptive requirements to be found a 'market dominating enterprise',[49] where the merged entity has the largest market share,[50] or where the market share exceeds that of the next largest enterprise by at least 25 per cent.[51] It is stated that where the post-merged entity may be able to raise prices, and, perhaps superfluously, where it may be difficult for customers to source substitutes, the merger may be found to give rise to a substantial lessening in competition. Four criteria are referred to as being relevant to making such a determination: (1) the post-merger market share of the merged entity, the incremental change as a result of the merger, and the gap between the merged entity and its competitors;[52] (2) the level of product substitutability and the ease with which customers may switch between suppliers; (3) any gaps in the production capability of the merged entity and its competitors;[53] and (4) the existence of bulk purchasers.[54] The treatment of product substitutability is given further clarification at para VII.1.F of the Guidelines in which reference is made to products which may be 'deemed similar to the product [affected by the merger]

---

47 Guidelines, para VII.A(2).

48 See, Guidelines, para VII.B.

49 art 7(4)(1)(1)(a), MRFTA. The market dominating presumption is set out at art 4, MRFTA.

50 art 7(4)(1)(1)(b), MRFTA.

51 art 7(4)(1)(1)(c), MRFTA.

52 In earlier versions of the Guidelines it was made clear that where there was only a minimal increase in the market share, even at high levels of concentration, the merger might not be presumed to give rise to anti-competitive effects. Note that the simplified review may apply at HHI levels above 2,500 where the incremental change in the market share is less than 250 (Guidelines, para II.1(5)(a)(iii)).

53 This factor was relevant in, for example, *Owens Corning/Saint-Gobain Vetrotex* (KFTC, *2008 Annual Report*, pp 72 ff).

54 There is now no definition of bulk purchaser in the Guidelines. A definition was included in the earlier version, and was related to the market share of the merged entity. It may be presumed now that the approach will be close to that of the analysis of buyer power in the EC and US merger regimes.

in function and use but constitutes a different product market'. Where such products may nevertheless exercise some competitive constraint on the merged entity, substitution across these closely related product markets is to be taken into account. The same is true in the case of proximate geographic markets, with the KFTC considering 'the geographical proximity among the markets and means of transportation and the possibility of development of transport technology'.

The presence of international competition may mitigate against findings of a restriction of competition. For this to be the case it must be evident that an increase in imports would be possible in the short term in response to a rise in prices in the domestic market as a result of the merger. A number of factors are set out in the *Review Guidelines* as being relevant to assessing the 'potential foreign competition pressure': **5-4.35**

(a) changes in the proportions of imported goods;
(b) international price and the status of supply and demand of the product;
(c) the extent of domestic market opening and the current status of foreign investment;
(d) the existence of a formidable international competitor;
(e) customs tariffs and plans to lower customs tariffs;
(f) price differences between the domestic market and the international market; and relative changes in exchange rates; and
(g) other non-tariff barriers.[55]

It is stated by the KFTC that where exports take up a 'considerably large portion of sales', and where substantial competition exists in the international market, any merger in the Korean market is unlikely to substantially restrict competition.[56] The reasoning in this respect is that exports can be readily diverted to domestic consumption in response to price increases. The same reasoning is used even in the case that it is the merged entity itself which contributes significantly to exports. **5-4.36**

Entry into the market as a competitive constraint counteracting the adverse effects of a merger is dealt with at para VII.1.E, with the basic position being that: **5-4.37**

> [i]f new entries in the concerned market can be made easily in the near future, the number of competitors reduced by a business combination is likely to rise and therefore the merger is less likely to substantially restrict competition.

The KFTC indicates that the following factors will be relevant to an assessment of entry conditions: legal and institutional barriers; the size of minimum capital **5-4.38**

---

55 Guidelines, para VII.1.D(1).
56 Guidelines, para VII.1.D(2).

required; technology requirements, including any intellectual property barriers; location conditions; raw material availability; the viability of establishing distribution networks, and the extent of competing networks; and the level of product differentiation. In particular entry will be considered to be easy if there exists:

(a) A company which has publicly announced its intent, plans, etc to invest and participate in the market.
(b) A company which is deemed likely to participate in the market in the near future without a significant burden of cost of entry or exit in response to a meaningful and non-transitory increase in price in the market, such as being able to enter the concerned market without a significant modification to its existing production facilities.[57]

5-4.39 The possibility of a merger giving rise to coordinated effects[58] is one which gives rise to complex analytical problems in any regime. The concern in essence is that a reduction in the number of competitors may facilitate either express or tacit collusion in a market (the latter falling short of any formal arrangement but arising as a result of the mutual recognition of competitor interdependence). This is an area with which even well developed merger regimes have struggled. In the EC for example it has been made clear through a succession of cases that the basic criteria for determining whether such a situation may arise is that the market be transparent, stable, and that a 'punishment mechanism' exists to sanction those who depart from the cooperative strategy. In a market characterized by a structure in which large conglomerates play an important role these concerns may be exacerbated. In the case of Korea the KFTC states that whether such collusion is facilitated will be assessed by reference to a number of factors including:

(1) whether rival companies can easily share information on the market situation, trading in the market, and the activities of individual companies;
(2) the degree of product homogeneity;
(3) the degree of transparency in the market relating to prices and marketing methods;
(4) the extent of past concertation in the market or related markets;
(5) whether competitors would be able easily to reach an 'agreement' as to coordinated activity;
(6) whether compliance with such an agreement could be monitored, which in turn will be affected by:
    (i) whether information relating to transactions can be easily and accurately shared amongst rival enterprises;

---

57 Guidelines, para VII.1.E(3).

58 This language is not used in the Guidelines, which instead refer simply to the 'possibility of collusion between competitors'.

(ii) the existence of large-scale customers tied into long-term contracts; and
(iii) whether there exists spare production capacity in the market.[59]

Vertical mergers

The assessment of vertical mergers, a matter which may be presumed to raise less concern than horizontal mergers, but where harmful competitive effects may still be identified—particularly in relation to market foreclosure—is set out at para VII.2 of the *Review Guidelines*. The central role played by market foreclosure ('market blocking') is stressed at the outset, although the KFTC will also examine the possibility that a vertical merger may facilitate coordinated effects. The KFTC indicates that the following factors may be taken into account in assessing whether foreclosure is likely to arise: **5-4.40**

(1) The market share ratio of a raw material supplier and the ratio of the total amount of purchase by the buyer of raw materials to the total domestic supply amount.
(2) The market share of a raw material buyer.
(3) The purpose of the merger.
(4) The possibility of securing substituting channels for supply and sales including those for import and export by competitors.
(5) The extent of vertical integration of competitors.
(6) The growth prospect of the relevant market and the concerned company's business plans such as plans for facility expansion.
(7) The possibility of excluding competitors.
(8) Situation of and effect on the product market in raw material-dependent relations with the concerned product and the market which produces the end product.
(9) Foreclosure effects arising from vertical chains across large-scale corporations, particularly where these increase the size of capital needed to enter the market.

The KFTC will also consider the extent to which vertical mergers may give rise to coordinated effects through mechanisms such as facilitating collection of information on rivals' pricing and business activities.

Although vertical mergers are not generally considered to raise competition concerns unless the effect of the merger is to foreclose entry, and as a result are not usually closely scrutinized by competition authorities the KFTC did pay careful attention to the merger between POSCO, POSTEEL, and Korea Core in 2007, **5-4.41**

[59] Guidelines, para VII.1.C.

in which a vertical merger took place between an electrical steel sheet supplier and a core[60] manufacturer.[61] On 2 April 2007 POSTEEL contracted to acquire 51 per cent of the shares of Korea Core, which was a purchaser of the electrical steel sheet produced by POSCO and sold through its affiliate POSTEEL. POSCO requested a preliminary review under art 12(8) of the MRFTA, leading to requests for information from the KFTC and on-site investigations. By entering into the merger POSCO hoped in part to reduce imports of electrical steel sheet, and to manage customer churn. POSCO also feared that buyer power would be increased were other supplies to become readily available to its customers. The KFTC found that the merger substantially lessened competition by foreclosing the market relating to the supply and demand of electrical steel sheet. POSCO was a near-monopolist in the market for the supply of electrical steel sheet, with a market share of approximately 93 per cent, and a share of supply to the core market of some 98 per cent. The market share of Korea Core was nearly 30 per cent, and the CR3 in that market was just under 70 per cent. It was also a concern of the KFTC that POSCO was, through the merger, trying to restructure the core market, placing Korea Core at the centre of the market, and it would be 'difficult for Korea Core's competitors to secure a stable supply from other alternative electrical steel sheet sources, thus making it harder for other electrical steel sheet makers to secure customers'. Although the KFTC recognized the possibility of foreclosure it also found that one effect of the merger would be to enable Korea Core to secure a stable supply and to allow it to produce each core product at full capacity. In light of the story told in relation to competitive harm it is perhaps surprising that the KFTC nevertheless approved the merger, although it did require a range of behavioural undertakings to be put in place. In particular POSCO was prohibited from reducing supplies 'for no fair reason', and from favouring Korea Core in making supplies available. POSCO was required to support this undertaking by setting up a compliance monitoring consultation group, and reporting the results regularly to the KFTC.

Conglomerate mergers

5-4.42 The approach to conglomerate mergers is set out in the *Review Guidelines* at para VII.3, and the treatment is brief. Conglomerate mergers are those which are neither horizontal nor vertical,[62] the main concern being that companies with power in one market might move into a new market through acquisition, and be able to

[60] The downstream market was defined as being that for 'domestic core product', including motor core, motor assembly, EWI core, strip, and other silicon steel plate products.

[61] KFTC Decision 2007-351, 3 July 2007. See KFTC, *2008 Annual Report*, pp 68ff.

[62] Guidelines, para II.9.

restrict competition in that new market. Thus the approach of the KFTC is to consider whether any of the following factors are present that may give rise to concern:

(1) Whether there exists a special condition for market entry.
(2) The acquiring party is a potential entrant to the market and meets one of the following criteria:
    (a) It is judged that had it not been for the concerned combination, because of producing products with similar production technology, distribution channels and stages of purchase, etc, the acquiring company would have entered into the given area of trade using other means with less competition-restrictive effects.
    (b) It is deemed that the existence of the acquiring party and others, which have the possibility to enter the given area of trade, is deterring the enterprises in the given area of trade from exercising market dominance.
(3) The degree of market share of the acquired party and the market concentration in the relevant market.
(4) Whether there are strong potential entrants other than the merging company.

Two further considerations are noted in respect of conglomerate mergers. The first is that a merger is: **5-4.43**

> … likely to substantially restrict competition if it results in a significant enhancement of the overall business capabilities of the firms concerned such as technology, sales power and the ability to mobilize capital and procure raw materials, to the point of eliminating competitors based on factors other than price and quality.[63]

The second is that a conglomerate merger will be deemed to be likely to substantially restrict competition where it has the effect of raising the barriers to entry. In its discussion of the SK Telecom/Hanaro Telecom merger[64] the KFTC noted that 'when it comes to conglomerate mergers, anti-competitive concerns are relevant including potential anti-competitiveness, the possibility of exclusion of competitors and the expansion of entry barriers'. In that case the fact that the parties post-merger would be able to bundle their products was considered likely to lead to a reduction in potential competition, strengthening the position of SK Telecom in the mobile phone market. **5-4.44**

The first decision in which the KFTC expressed concerns relating to a conglomerate merger was that taken in *Hite Beer Co/Jinro Distilling Co*[65] in which a number of remedies were imposed, with the KFTC taking the view that it should 'impose **5-4.45**

[63] Guidelines, para VII.3.B.
[64] KFTC Decision 2008-105, 13 March 2008; KFTC Newsletter, 27 February 2008.
[65] KFTC Decision 2006-9.

ex-ante and ex-post monitoring measures at the same time so that the adverse effect of [the] competition restrictions can be appropriately corrected while the positive effect of enhanced efficiency can be maximized'. Elsewhere, when it has been clear that there has been little reduction in concentration as a result of a conglomerate merger the KFTC has fast-tracked clearances. This was the case, for example, in relation to Woori Financial Group/LIG Life Insurance in which the KFTC found that there was no overlapping activity of any significance, with the market share of LIG in the domestic life insurance market being only 0.6 per cent prior to the acquisition.

Efficiencies and the failing firm defence

5-4.46 The treatment of efficiencies claimed for mergers is a matter of some controversy in competition law. Typically scepticism will be shown towards claims of efficiencies that outweigh competitive harms, and authorities will be concerned about information asymmetries between them, and those claiming the efficiencies. It has been noted above that art 7(2) of the MRFTA expressly provides for an efficiency defence, stating, at art 7(2)(1), that a merger which substantially restricts competition shall not be prohibited where 'the promotion of efficiency attainable through the combination of enterprises is greater than the negative effect produced by the restricted competition'. The onus is placed on the parties claiming these efficiencies to '*prove* that they meet such requirements'.[66] Relevant efficiencies are those arising 'in the areas of production, sales and R&D or the effect of enhanced efficiency on the economy as a whole'. The *Review Guidelines* deal separately with the two rubrics. In respect of the first category of efficiencies the KFTC states that the following will be taken into consideration:

(a) Whether the production cost can be cut through the economy of scales, integration of production facilities, rationalization of production process, etc.
(b) Whether the sales cost can be lowered or sales or exports can be boosted by integrating or sharing sales network.
(c) Whether sales or exports can be boosted by sharing market information.
(d) Whether logistics costs can be cut by sharing transportation and storage facilities.
(e) Whether production-related technology and research abilities can be improved by complementing each other's technology, or sharing or effectively utilizing skilful workforce, organization and capital.
(f) Whether other expenses can be significantly reduced.

66 art 7(2), MRFTA, emphasis added.

In relation to efficiencies claimed for the economy as a whole the following factors may be taken into account: 5-4.47

(a) Whether it makes a significant contribution to job creation.
(b) Whether it makes a significant contribution to the development of regional economies.
(c) Whether it makes a significant contribution to the development of forward- and backward-related markets.
(d) Whether it makes a significant contribution to the stabilization of the nation's economy by means of a stable supply of energy, etc.
(e) Whether it makes a significant contribution to the improvement of environmental pollution.

As with other regimes which incorporate an efficiency defence the KFTC requires in addition that the efficiencies claimed must be 'difficult' to obtain through means other than the merger.[67] Any cost reductions claimed are not to be achieved through 'competition-restrictive methods' such as restricting output, or lowering the quality of service.[68] It must also be the case that the efficiencies will arise 'in the near future', and that this shall be demonstrated such that it is not a 'mere expectation' that efficiencies will be generated.[69] No indication is given as to what length of time counts as the 'near' future, and as this rubric has only recently been inserted into the Guidelines, there is no practice guidance in this respect. Two final requirements for the application of the defence are the restatement that the merger must be the only means by which the efficiencies may be generated[70] (this is in somewhat more forceful language than that at the start of this section of the Guidelines, which refers merely to the 'difficulty' of generating the efficiencies by other means), and that in order for a merger to be cleared on efficiency grounds the efficiencies must outweigh the detrimental effects of the merger.[71] There is no discussion as to the precise standard by which this is to be judged—whether the total welfare standard, or the consumer welfare standard are to be employed remains a matter of conjecture. 5-4.48

The 'failing firm defence' is expressly recognized in art 7(2)(2) of the MRFTA. If the acquired entity is 'nonviable' an otherwise anti-competitive merger will be permitted. The *Review Guidelines* also recognize the defence in relation to failing business units. The definition of a non-viable company is given in the *Review Guidelines* as being one that is 'in default due to exacerbated financial position' or 5-4.49

[67] Guidelines, para VIII.1.B.
[68] Guidelines, para VIII.1.B(1).
[69] Guidelines, para VIII.1.B(2).
[70] Guidelines, para VII.1.B(3).
[71] Guidelines, para VIII.1.C.

is deemed likely to default 'in the near future'.[72] Whether this position has been reached may be judged by a number of criteria, including the fact that the target has filed for bankruptcy, or liquidation, and whether the total shareholder equity is less than the paid-in capital for 'a considerable period of time'. Two additional restrictions are imposed on the reliance on the failing firm defence. These are that without a merger it would not be possible, without difficulty, to use the assets of the failing firm on a continuous basis, and the second is that there is no reasonably available less restrictive merger than the one in question. In the case of *POSCO/POSTEEL/Korea Core*,[73] for example, it was established that the target company was a failing firm, but the KFTC also argued that the merger was not essential to the maintenance of Korea Core's assets in the market, and that other less anti-competitive merger options were available.

Remedies

5-4.50 The KFTC has wide discretion as to remedies that may be required in merger situations, and may approve mergers subject to conditions. Article 16 of the MRFTA sets out the broad basis for 'corrective measures', and provides that where there has been any violation of the relevant rules the KFTC 'may order such a company ... or violator required to take any of the following corrective measures'. Specific examples of remedies are set out in art 16(1), including: cessation of the practice concerned; disposition of all or part of the stocks; resignation of officers; 'transfer of business'; 'restrictions on the business method or business scope to prevent the negative effects of restricted competition pursuant to the combination of enterprises'; and 'other necessary corrective measures'. In addition art 16(2) makes specific provision in respect of merger situations, stating that:

> [i]f a company has been established, or in case companies have been merged in violation of the provisions of [the MRFTA], the [KFTC] may file a lawsuit to nullify said establishment of a company or said merger of companies.

5-4.51 As with other jurisdictions structural remedies are likely to be preferred to behavioural remedies given the fact that these do not give rise to problems of monitoring. Structural remedies may take various forms, and have been employed in a number of cases.

5-4.52 Disposition of stocks was required in *Songwon Co/Daehan Special Chemicals Co*[74] in which disposition of a part of the stock holdings was required, and in *Muhak Co/Daesun Distilling Co*,[75] a total disposition was required.

---

[72] Guidelines, para VIII.2.A.
[73] See KFTC, *2008 Annual Report*, pp 68ff.
[74] KFTC Decision 82-24.
[75] KFTC Decision 2003-28.

Transfers of business have been required in several cases, of which the most noted are *P&G/Ssangyong Papers Co*,[76] in which the KFTC ordered the merging parties to divest four businesses relating to sanitary towels and nappies, and *Beckton Dickinson Korea Holding Inc/Shindongbang Medical Co*,[77] in which divestitures were required related to medical equipment businesses. A recent example of divestiture remedies being required arose in the *Eland Retail Co and KDF Ltd Distribution Co Ltd/Carrefour Korea* merger assessed in September 2006.[78] In this case, which related to retail stores, concerns were raised in relation to restrictions of competition in regional markets.[79] The acquiring companies were ordered to sell one store in each of three regions: in one region this resulted in a requirement to sell one store from five, in another one from two. A six-month time limit for divestiture was set, although the KFTC indicated that, with permission, this could be extended by up to a year. Restrictions were set on permissible purchasers, who could not be a 'specially related party',[80] and could not rank among the top three companies in terms of turnover in 2005. Further, the stores had to remain in the relevant market such that they continued to provide competition to the merged entity. On occasion the KFTC has been somewhat prescriptive in its imposition of divestiture remedies. In the case of *Kolon Industries Inc/Kohap Co Nylon Film*[81] the domestic market was dominated by three companies with market shares of 45.9 per cent (Kolon), 29.1 per cent (Hyosung), and 13.1 per cent (Kohap). The KFTC attempted to achieve a degree of balance in the market by requiring a post-merger disposal of production lines to Hyosung. **5-4.53**

Unusually the KFTC resorted during the mid-1990s' financial crisis to imposing restrictions on market shares. This was the case for example in *Delphinium Enterprise PTE Ltd/Hansol Co/Shinho Paper Co*[82] and *SK Telecom Co/Shinsegi Telecom Co*[83] in which limitations of 50 per cent were imposed. These measures have been subject to criticism from commentators within Korea, and it is anticipated that they will not be employed in the future, being limited to the very specific problems arising during the financial crisis. **5-4.54**

In relation to behavioural remedies the main tool employed by the KFTC is restrictions on price levels. In the case of *Gillette Co/Rocket Korea Co*[84] the KFTC restricted price increases in respect of the Duracell Alca battery of no greater than **5-4.55**

[76] KFTC Decision 98-84.
[77] KFTC Decision 2000-38.
[78] KFTC Decision 2006-261, 6 November 2006.
[79] KFTC Press Release, 18 September 2006. This was the first case in which the KFTC considered regional restrictions of competition.
[80] As defined in art 11 of the Enforcement Decree.
[81] KFTC Decision 2003-18.
[82] KFTC Decision 98-269.
[83] KFTC Decision 2000-79.
[84] KFTC Decision 98-282.

27.5 per cent over a five-year period, unless the market share of the post-merger entity fell below 50 per cent. Similarly in *Kia Motors/Asia Motors*[85] price increases for vehicle trucks in the one to five ton category were based on an export price measure, the restrictions being inapplicable if market shares of competitors rose above 5 per cent. At a pre-merger review of the *Hite Beer Co/Jinro Distilling Co* merger[86] the KFTC determined that prices should not be raised beyond the consumer price index for five years following the merger.

5-4.56 The KFTC has also imposed other forms of behavioural remedies, and imposed a package of six measures on SK Telecom when it approved its acquisition of Hanaro Telecom in 2008.[87] Inter alia, SKT was required: to restrict the bundling of its services, and to not compel distributors to promote exclusively its bundled service; to not disadvantage operators other than Hanaro when reselling wireless communications services to them; and to not refuse access to its 800Mhz frequency band in which it held a monopoly.

5-4.57 It is not uncommon for the KFTC to impose reporting requirements on companies post-merger.[88]

---

85 KFTC Decision 99-43.

86 KFTC Decision 2006-9; see also *Annual Report on Competition Policy Development in Korea*, September 2006, p 17.

87 KFTC Newsletter, 27 February 2008.

88 See, eg *POSCO/POSTEEL/Korea Core*, KFTC, *2008 Annual Report*, pp 68 ff.

5-5

KOREA PROCEDURE

Introduction	5-5.01	**Corrective Measures and Penalties**	5-5.13
Investigations	5-5.04	Leniency	5-5.21
Hearings, Access to File, and Secrecy	5-5.09	**Appeals**	5-5.24
Complaints	5-5.11	**Damages**	5-5.28
		Arbitration	5-5.29

Introduction

The outline of the institutional regime relevant to the application of competition law in Korea has been dealt with earlier in this Part. The procedures relating to the merger control regime have been covered in Part 5-4, and are not further dealt with here. In November 2005 the KFTC amended its case handling process, adopting a new 'deliberation preparation process'. Under this system case examiners and respondent enterprises 'exchange and refute each other's evidence and arguments in writing sufficiently to get facts, contested issues, and arguments straight before going to the KFTC's court for official deliberations'.[1] The KFTC argues that not only are cases handled more effectively under this system, but that the rights of respondents too are enhanced. The longest case in the application of Korean antitrust law is that leading to the infringement decision taken in respect of Microsoft on 24 February 2006. A complaint was made by Daum Communication Corp on 5 September 2001, following which the KFTC conducted extensive research. In April 2004 a taskforce was launched with responsibility for handling the case effectively, and the KFTC opened investigations into further aspects of Microsoft's conduct, both under its own initiative and following further complaints. The full committee of the KFTC deliberated the case on seven **5-5.01**

[1] See KFTC, *Annual Report on Competition Policy Development in Korea*, September 2006, p 8. The investigation that concluded in an infringement decision being taken in respect of Intel Corporation (4 June 2008) was also a lengthy one, lasting in excess of three years.

occasions, during which 'the examiners and Microsoft representatives engaged in heated debates'.[2]

5-5.02 In 2007 the KFTC amended its Regulation on Case Handling Procedures, providing in some respects clearer rights to the defence, and greater support for the investigation of cartels.

5-5.03 When documents are required under the law to be delivered to foreign parties who do not reside in Korea the postal system may be used.[3]

Investigations

5-5.04 The KFTC may launch an investigation into suspected unlawful conduct on its own initiative, or may respond to complaints made to it.[4] Wherever an investigation is taken forward the KFTC is obliged to give notice in writing to the persons concerned, setting out the results of its investigation and stating whether any corrective measures have been imposed.[5] It may not impose any corrective measures or impose any penalties in respect of conduct which has been terminated more than five years previously.[6] Article 50 sets out the powers of the KFTC to investigate infringements. These powers are substantial, and are similar to those available to the EC Commission, or to officials of the DOJ or FTC in the US. It is expressly stated in art 50-2 of the MRFTA that all investigations carried out under this Part of the Act should be undertaken 'within the minimum scope as necessary to enforce the law without abusing the investigation right for other purpose'.

5-5.05 The KFTC has the power to: (1) summon the parties concerned, other interested parties, or witnesses, to attend a hearing and to give testimony;[7] (2) appoint expert witnesses if this is necessary;[8] (3) issue orders to any enterpriser, organization of enterprisers, or an office or employee of any enterpriser or organization, to report on the business situation, or to present necessary information or materials, or to 'report on the maintaining custody of the presented materials or information'.[9] The power to ask questions of parties, or to require that information and evidence

[2] KFTC *2008 Annual Report*, p 43.

[3] See *Showa Denko KK v The Korea Fair Trade Commission*, Supreme Court of Korea, Case 2004*Du*11275, 24 March 2006. An appeal from the judgment of the Seoul High Court, 2002*Nu*6110, 19 August 2004.

[4] art 49(1) and (2), MRFTA.

[5] art 49(3), MRFTA.

[6] art 49(4), MRFTA.

[7] art 50(1)(1), MRFTA.

[8] art 50(1)(2), MRFTA.

[9] art 50(1)(3), MRFTA.

be submitted to the authority is supplemented by a power, in situations in which it is deemed necessary, to conduct on-site investigations and to enter:

> the office or business place of an enterpriser or an enterprisers' organization to examine the business and management situation, records, documents, electronic materials, voice-recording materials, video materials, and other materials or matters prescribed by the Presidential Decree as necessary to enforce this Act as well as get the statements of the parties concerned, interested parties and witnesses at a designated place under the conditions prescribed by the Presidential Decree.[10]

Such inspections shall be carried out by a 'public official' under the control of the KFTC. Any official conducting such an investigation has the power to order any enterpriser, enterprisers' organization, officer, or employee to present necessary materials for examination, and to take copies of these into their possession.[11] Officials conducting such investigations are required to present evidence of their status to an appropriate person during the course of the investigation.[12]

Penalties may be imposed by the KFTC in the event that those subject to investigation obstruct that investigation. In July 2005 for example the KFTC imposed penalties on executives and employees of a company subject to a cartel investigation who, during the course of an on-site investigation, removed and destroyed evidence from the company's sales department. At the same time the KFTC announced that it was going to amend its guidance on penalties so as to exclude as a beneficiary of a reduction in penalty any company that obstructed an investigation, and to make companies liable for the acts of any employees obstructing an investigation such that any such conduct would incur an uplift in the penalties imposed.[13] **5-5.06**

In one special case, relating to the investigation of potential breaches of art 23(1)(7) which prohibits certain financial arrangements, the KFTC may obtain evidence from the head of any financial institution, including personal financial data.[14] More generally the KFTC may 'solicit the opinions of the heads of the relevant **5-5.07**

[10] art 50(2), MRFTA.

[11] art 50(3), MRFTA.

[12] art 50(4), MRFTA.

[13] See KFTC News, 2005-8. The Guidance on penalties was first published in April 1994. The most recent amendment is that of 31 December 2007. However, this Guidance does not provide guidance relating directly to the calculating of the penalty.

[14] art 50(5), MRFTA. It is an offence to disclose the information provided under this provision for any other purpose than the enforcement of the Act. Unlawful disclosure carries a maximum possible penalty of up to five years' imprisonment, or a fine of up to Won30m (art 69(1), MRFTA). Article 50(6), MRFTA provides that the information requested under art 50(5) 'shall be confined to the minimum level only for the investigation'. However, anecdotal evidence suggests that some professional advisers take the view that the KFTC is somewhat over-inclusive in its information gathering.

administrative authorities, other authorities or associations'.[15] It may also delegate to the heads of relevant authorities or other public bodies any necessary investigations or may request from them relevant materials.[16]

5-5.08 Although generally those subject to investigation are required to comply fully with the lawful demands of the KFTC they may, in cases where *force majeure* prevents them from doing so, request extensions to time limits set either under the law or by the KFTC. However the circumstances in which this right may be invoked are highly limited, with the MRFTA referring only to natural disasters.[17]

Hearings, Access to File, and Secrecy

5-5.09 Before taking any final decision ordering corrective measures, or imposing a penalty, the KFTC shall give the enterprise concerned and other interested parties—including complainants—the right to state their opinions.[18] A hearing may be held at the KFTC for this purpose, although there is not on the face of the legislation an absolute right to such a hearing.[19]

5-5.10 Those whose acts are being subjected to a formal examination by the KFTC are to be sent an examination report when this has been completed, together with the necessary attachments which relate to the facts found in the examination report. Any party to the proceedings, or other interested party, may request access to the information held by the KFTC or to data held relating to any measures taken under the MRFTA. Access will be granted if the party providing the data consents, or where access is necessary to the public interest.[20] Otherwise there are protections accorded to information obtained during the course of the application of the Act. Article 62 provides that no official who has obtained information during the course of their duties under the Act may 'use it for a purpose other than to enforce this Act', and there is a duty not to divulge any confidential information or secrets disclosed to officials during the course of any investigation. Any breach of art 62 may result in imprisonment for a maximum of two years, or a fine not exceeding Won200m.[21] There is a general requirement set out at art 43(1) of the MRFTA to the effect that all decisions of the KFTC shall be disclosed, 'provided that this shall not apply where the [KFTC] deems it necessary to protect trade

15 art 64(1), MRFTA.
16 art 64(2), MRFTA.
17 art 50-3, MRFTA. The KFTC is required to consider any such request, and to delay the investigation if this is deemed to be appropriate after reviewing the circumstances.
18 art 52, MRFTA.
19 Article 52(2), MRFTA states that the parties 'may' attend a hearing.
20 art 52-2, MRFTA.
21 art 69(2), MRFTA.

secrets of an enterpriser or enterprisers' organization'. It is noted below that leniency applicants may not have their status disclosed, save where this is necessary to ensure fairness in relevant legal proceedings.

Complaints

Article 49(2) of the MRFTA provides that 'any person discovering a violation of the provisions of this Act may report the occurrence of such to the [KFTC]'. The KFTC is required where it launches an investigation following a complaint to give notice in writing to the complainant of the outcome of the investigation, including any corrective measures ordered.[22] It is neither obliged to respond to every complaint it receives, nor to launch an investigation in all cases.[23] **5-5.11**

Korea is unusual in offering rewards for those who inform of infringements. The principles are set out in *Notification on Reward for Informants*, published on 1 April 2005, and a legislative basis is provided in art 64-2 of the MRFTA. Rewards may be offered to those reporting a range of competition law violations to the KFTC, including: collusion, certain notification violations, and prohibited activities of business associations. Rewards will be paid only where evidence is supplied and when the case is found to be legitimate. In the event that there are multiple reports of the same case only the first person to come forward will be rewarded. Those who come forward with such information are offered confidentiality protection. The KFTC has argued that the policy is successful, and in April 2005 the ceiling on awards was significantly increased to Won1bn. In 2005 the record amount of Won66.87m was awarded in one case.[24] The size of any reward paid is determined by the penalty levied on the infringing parties and the strength of the evidence submitted by the informant. **5-5.12**

Corrective Measures and Penalties

It has been noted above that where the KFTC finds a violation of the MRFTA it may order corrective action to be taken.[25] The KFTC may in addition make a recommendation to any enterpriser or enterprisers' organization recommending **5-5.13**

---

[22] art 49(3), MRFTA.

[23] Article 53, MRFTA provides that those dissatisfied with measures taken by the KFTC under the Act may appeal. The failure to open an investigation does not constitute a measure taken, and hence the failure to respond to a complaint by opening an investigation, or the closure of a file is not an appealable measure.

[24] See KFTC, *Annual Report on Competition Policy Development in Korea*, September 2006, p 13. The evidence in this case given to the KFTC included the names of executives of the six cartel member companies, meeting places, and details of arrangements put into place by the cartel members.

[25] For a discussion of the remedial powers of the KFTC, and the rights of private parties to remedies under the MRFTA see Park, S-E, 'Korean Competition Statute: Its Limits and Measures for

that corrective action be taken in order to comply with the standards of conduct laid down in the Act. Any person receiving such a recommendation is required to notify the KFTC within ten days whether it intends to comply with the recommendation. If it does so the recommendation will be treated as if it were a corrective measure.[26] Wherever it is necessary to ensure compliance with corrective measures the KFTC may request cooperation from other relevant public bodies or associations.[27] It may be presumed that such recommendations, if accepted, are then less likely to be subsequently challenged by those subject to their strictures, such that the approach is similar to, but not the same as, the commitment decisions that may be made by the EC Commission, and the consent decrees that may be applied in the US.

5-5.14 In November 2005 the KFTC published *Guidelines on Operating Corrective Measures* that set out the authority of the KFTC to issue specific performance orders and other necessary related orders, as well as simply to require infringements to cease. This move was in part a deliberate policy to introduce more diverse corrective measures, in response to a recognition that 'it was difficult to take an appropriate action against law violations which are getting more diverse and complicated'.[28] Under the terms of the Guidelines specific performance orders can include: (1) orders forcing addressees to provide third parties with access to essential facilities; (2) orders to withdraw unfair refusals to deal, and to reinitiate transactions; (3) orders to nullify cartel agreements (although note that such agreements cannot be formally relied upon as they are null and void under the terms of the MRFTA); (4) orders to unbundle sales where bundling or tie-in practices are found to exist. Other related orders that may be made (so-called 'complementary orders') include strong duties on addressees to notify others that they have been made subject to corrective measures by the KFTC.[29] The KFTC takes the view that a positive duty to bring such action to the attention of affected competitors or customers has the effect of preventing repetition of such conduct. Respondents may also be obliged to notify the KFTC as to the implementation of the corrective measures ordered, and in the case of uncovered cartels for example, to report on how prices of the products involved in the cartel are changing over time following the termination of the cartel arrangements. Respondent enterprises may also be *required* to implement antitrust education and compliance programmes, and to report the results of these programmes to the KFTC.

Improvements' (2005) 4:2 *Journal of Korean Law* 139, although note that some of the provisions discussed here have since been amended.

[26] art 51, MRFTA.

[27] art 64(3), MRFTA.

[28] KFTC News, 2005-11.

[29] As mentioned in Chapters 5-2, 5-3, and 5-4 there are a number of provisions under which parties subject to corrective orders may be required to publicize this fact.

The Supreme Court of Korea has held that corrective measures orders need not be overly specific in their terms. In *Korean Medical Association Inc v The Korea Fair Trade Commission*[30] the Court stated that: **5-5.15**

> [i]f an order of corrective measures . . . is too specific, an Order would be meaningless as inapplicable to numerous everyday transactions with different details. Therefore, an Order cannot avoid being inclusive or abstract due to its essential nature. Further, the purport of the system for order of corrective measures justifies an interpretation that an Order may not only suspend past acts of violations but also prohibit similarly patterned acts that may repeat themselves in the near future.[31]

In cases which are considered not to be serious the KFTC may issue 'warnings' to parties or recommendations to undo the wrongful practice (see above). **5-5.16**

The term used in the legislation in respect of penalties is 'surcharge', and the relevant levels, which vary according to the provisions of the Act that are being breached, have been referred to as relevant in the preceding chapters. The general provisions relating to the imposition and collecting of penalties are set out in Chapter 10-2 of the MRFTA. When assessing the level of the penalty the KFTC is to have regard to: (1) the nature and degree of the practice; (2) the duration and frequency of the practice; and (3) the benefits accruing to the parties from the practice.[32] The relevant standards for the imposition of penalties are to be determined by Presidential Decree, but, as noted above, the KFTC has not published guidance relating to the calculation of the penalty. It is made clear that liability may be imposed on any subsequent owner of the company if the company has merged or been acquired after the breach of the law, but before the imposition of the penalty.[33] The calculation of the penalty proceeds in four steps: (1) the determination of the basic amount; (2) mandatory adjustments; (3) case-specific discretionary adjustments; and (4) the resulting calculation of the final penalty. **5-5.17**

[30] Case 2001*Du*5347, 20 February 2003.

[31] It has also been noted however, that:

Another factor that limits the [KFTC's] efforts is the general perception that legal commentators have with regard to corrective orders; that is, they are overly intrusive. Based on the fact that corrective orders issued by the [KFTC], in essence, either limit one's action or impose a certain obligation against one's own free will, legal commentators view that any and all corrective orders that the [KFTC] issue must have a firm legal basis. Due to such scrutiny imposed by the commentators, the [KFTC] has a tendency not to issue any corrective order other than those expressly prescribed in the Statute, despite the fact that the Statute clearly affords it with authority to exercise its discretionary judgment to enforce a corrective order other than the ones the Statute prescribes. Specifically, the Statute stipulates a catch-all clause which, in its essential parts, provides that the [KFTC] 'may render any other corrective measure which it deems necessary to cure the violation.' Despite such clear language which affords the [KFTC] with a legal basis to issue other types of corrective orders as it deems necessary, the [KFTC] often resorts to taking a passive approach in rendering orders due to potential legal challenge. (Park, n 25, above, at 147)

[32] art 55-3, MRFTA.

[33] art 55-3(2), MRFTA.

5-5.18 Penalties are to be paid by the date specified by the KFTC, subject to the fact that in circumstances where the infringer has difficulty paying the penalty, it may be possible for payment in instalments to be arranged, and the period within which the penalty has to be paid may be extended.[34] Where payment is not made by the due date the KFTC may impose further penalties. The KFTC may delegate to the National Tax Office the collection of the penalty, and has extensive powers to obtain documents from other administrative agencies to assist in the collection of such penalties.[35]

5-5.19 The KFTC will take into account, in setting the level of the penalty following the finding of an infringement, the fact that a company has implemented a compliance programme. A reduction of between 50 and 30 per cent may be given depending on the results of an evaluation of the compliance programme and the record of its implementation. Reductions in penalties will also be given to companies who have voluntarily terminated their infringements before the taking of a final infringement decision. In this latter case a reduction of 20 per cent in penalty will be made. In *Showa Denko KK v The Korea Fair Trade Commission*, the Supreme Court of Korea held that the KFTC had failed to take appropriate account of a degree of cooperation by the appellant during the course of the KFTC's investigation into the graphite electrodes cartel when the penalty for the appellant was set. The Court noted that 'the plaintiff cooperated in the investigation by responding to the defendant's request to submit data, which is not too different in the degree of cooperation when compared with other companies'.[36]

5-5.20 A number of penal provisions are set out in relation to both substantive and procedural breaches of the Act. Different levels of penalties addressed to individuals are set out in Chapter 14 of the Act. A jail term of up to three years, and/or a fine of up to Won200m may be imposed on individuals who, inter alia: (1) commit an abuse under art 3-2; (2) unlawfully merge companies in breach of art 7(1); (3) breach the provisions on holding companies set out in arts 8-2(2), (3), and (5); (4) violate the conditions on cross-shareholdings in arts 9 and 10(1); (5) guarantee debts in violation of art 10-2(1); (6) engage in collaborative practices in breach of art 19(1).[37] Jail terms of up to two years are also provided in respect of a second list of breaches, with the financial penalty being reduced to a maximum of

---

[34] art 55-4, MRFTA. Examples of factors which may justify delayed payment, or the acceptance of an instalment system include those where substantial damage has been caused to a business by, eg fire, or where the business 'is at considerable risk because of unfavourable business conditions' (art 55-4(1)(2), MRFTA).

[35] art 55-6, MRFTA.

[36] Case 2004*Du*11275, 24 March 2006 (an appeal from the judgment of the Seoul High Court, 2002*Nu*6110, 19 August 2004).

[37] art 66, MRFTA. The concern here with the creation, or extension of, monopoly power is noteworthy.

Won150m. Breaches falling into this category include: (1) committing unfair trade practices in breach of art 23(1); (2) violation of the provisions relating to enterprisers' organizations; (3) maintaining resale price maintenance in violation of art 29(1); (4) conclusion of international contracts in violation of art 32(1); and (5) failure to comply with corrective measures or prohibition orders.[38] Where any offence falling under these provisions is prosecuted a complaint must first be filed by the KFTC with the Prosecutor General where 'the violation is deemed gross and considerable' such that it 'may substantially suppress competition'.[39] The Attorney General may request that the KFTC file such a complaint where it has not done so already in order to allow a criminal prosecution to proceed. The failure to comply with certain reporting requirements or to submit data, as specified in art 68, may be punished by the imposition of financial penalties of up to Won100m.

Leniency

A leniency programme[40] was first introduced into the MRFTA in 1996 and applied from 1997. However, the programme was, in the words of the KFTC, 'underutilized', and was substantially overhauled in 2005. It now finds expression in *The Enforcement Decree of the Monopoly Regulation and Fair Trade Act.* The programme was amended in July 2006 and again in 2007 in an attempt to simplify the procedures for those making voluntary reports of participation in cartel activity to the KFTC. Leniency applications may be made orally (in which case the application shall be recorded by audio or video tape), by fax, or by email to leniency@ftc.go.kr to the Cartel Regulation Policy Team of the KFTC. Following from the experience gained in the US the programme's structure now offers the familiar clarity as to the penalty reductions available in the case of notification, and 'amnesty plus' under which confessors will be awarded with additional leniency in respect of the case currently under investigation if they provide evidence of participation in other cartels. In essence where the relevant criteria are satisfied confessors are automatically eligible for a reduction in penalty. The first applicant for leniency will be granted a 100 per cent reduction in penalty where the appropriate criteria are met, the second a reduction of up to 50 per cent,[41] and the third no reduction at all. Where a third party not engaged in the cartel has alerted the KFTC to the cartel's existence the first undertaking in the cartel to come 5-5.21

[38] art 67, MRFTA.

[39] art 71, MRFTA.

[40] 'Notification on Implementation of Leniency Program for Corrective Measures against Confessors' (hereinafter, 'Leniency Program Notification').

[41] The upper limit for leniency for the second applicant was previously 30 per cent, but the evidence suggested that this figure was too low, with parties preferring to seek to downplay their involvement in the hope of a lower penalty, rather than to confess their involvement.

forward with evidence of its existence may be eligible for a 100 per cent reduction in penalty, unless the evidence provided by the third party was sufficient to prove the case in question, in which case no further leniency will be granted. A company which has coerced others into cartel participation will not be eligible for leniency.[42]

5-5.22 Applicants for leniency are required to cooperate with any investigation that proceeds, and art 5 of the Leniency Program Notification requires parties to: (1) state every fact they know about the cartel without hesitation; (2) 'promptly submit all materials, which they have or can obtain, related to the concerned cartel'; (3) answer questions and cooperate with the KFTC's fact-finding exercises; and (4) ensure that their staff, including where possible former employees, show 'sincere and continued cooperation'. Leniency will also be withdrawn where applicants 'deliberately destroy, manipulate, damage or hide evidence and information related to the concerned cartel'. Finally, leniency applicants are not to disclose to third parties either the fact of their participation in a cartel, or their cooperation with the KFTC in its investigation, without the permission of the KFTC. The KFTC in turn has the duty to protect the identity of leniency applicants.

5-5.23 It also appears to be the case that a grant of leniency by the KFTC will protect the holder from the imposition of criminal sanctions should the public prosecutors decide to pursue this route. In July 2007 the KFTC imposed penalties against a sugar cartel, with one participant receiving total immunity under the leniency programme. The Seoul Prosecutor's Office sought to bring prosecutions against all three participants based on the KFTC decision, but failed in respect of the leniency applicant.[43]

Appeals

5-5.24 Appeals against decisions of the KFTC taken under the MRFTA may be made in the first instance to the KFTC within thirty days of the notification of the contested decision. This time period may not be extended.[44] Article 53 provides

[42] art 35(1)(5), Enforcement Decree. Coercion extends to situations in which the applicant 'physically abused or threatened other enterprisers to make them participate in the concerned cartel or to dissuade them from quitting it', or to situations in which 'the enterpriser in question pressured or sanctioned other enterprisers to make them participate in the concerned cartel or to dissuade them from quitting it to the extent that their normal business activities in the concerned market are disturbed' (art 6(2) of the Leniency Program Notification).

[43] See Spratling, GR and Arp, DJ, 'Making the Decision: What to do when Faced with International Cartel Exposure—Developments Impacting the Decision in 2008', Conference Presentation, Asia International Competition Conference, Seoul, 4 September 2008.

[44] art 53, MRFTA.

that an appeal may be made by 'any party' dissatisfied with the measures taken. The KFTC is to make a decision in respect of any appeal within sixty days, although where this is not possible there may be a further extension of up to thirty days.[45]

Where an appeal has been made to the KFTC by a person against whom corrective measures have been ordered, the effect of that order may be suspended where the KFTC deems this necessary in order to 'prevent irrevocable damage or harm caused by the enforcement of such orders or continuance of procedures'.[46] Such a suspension may be made either on request of the appellant, or on the initiative of the KFTC. Any decision taken suspending enforcement may itself be revoked where the circumstances change.[47] **5-5.25**

Where any person is dissatisfied with the outcome of an appeal to the KFTC a further appeal may be made (a 'lawsuit') to the Seoul High Court, which has exclusive jurisdiction in this aspect, within thirty days of the receipt of the decision taken by the KFTC in response to the initial appeal.[48] There are no circumstances under which the time limit for this final appeal may be extended. In any case in which the outcome of an appeal is to reduce a penalty imposed by the KFTC, either in whole or in part, the KFTC is required to repay any monies collected, and may also be required to pay interest.[49] **5-5.26**

Final appeals to the Supreme Court may be made, but are not common, and in recent years there has been a decline in the number of appeals at all levels (in 2005 for example there were only seventeen instances in which appeals were filed with the High Court, down from sixty cases the previous year). The KFTC attributes this reduction to improved case management, and to an increased acceptance of KFTC decisions by respondents recognizing that their rights have been respected during enhanced KFTC procedures. In addition the amount of litigation in the Seoul High Court over previous years provided the KFTC with substantial guidance, which was incorporated and followed in later cases, thus reducing the scope for future appeal. In the appeals determined conclusively by the Court in 2005 the KFTC won in twenty-six of the forty-five cases, and had partial success in a further eleven cases (over 81 per cent of all cases).[50] **5-5.27**

45 art 53(2), MRFTA.
46 art 53-2, MRFTA.
47 art 53-2(2), MRFTA.
48 art 54, MRFTA.
49 art 55-7, MRFTA.
50 See KFTC, *Annual Report on Competition Policy Development in Korea*, September 2006, p 12.

Damages

5-5.28 Breaches of the MRFTA give rise to a right to damages, but not to the right to seek injunctive relief. Article 56(1) provides that:

> [a]ny enterpriser or enterprisers' organization violating the provisions of this Act and consequently causing damage to a person shall be liable for compensating such person for damage. If the enterpriser himself/herself or the enterprisers' organization itself proves that he/she/it did not intend to commit any fault, and no error is found on his/her/its part, however, this provision shall not apply.

The liability that arises is strict, although an amendment to the MRFTA removed an express provision to the effect that it was *not* a defence to such an action for the defendant to prove that he acted neither intentionally nor negligently.[51] The court hearing the action shall have access to the relevant records of the KFTC if these will facilitate its deliberations, and may request that the KFTC transmit to it 'the records of the particular case (including protocols and stenographic records of examination of persons concerned, references and expert witnesses, and all judicial evidence)'.[52] Actions for damages were originally strictly 'follow on', and could only be brought following an order of the KFTC against the defendant to take corrective measures, and not until such orders had 'become final and conclusive'.[53] However, following changes made in 2005 claims can now be brought at any time, without the need for the KFTC to have first taken action. The courts however may be reluctant to act where the KFTC is simultaneously investigating the alleged breach. Steps have also been taken to reduce the difficulties claimants face in assessing or proving the amount of damage, with courts being able to assess the amount of damage based on the 'result of evidentiary investigation and intent of [the] overall pleading'.[54] Following amendments to the MRFTA an earlier provision which time-barred claims being advanced more than three years after the date the claim first arose has been repealed. The damages provisions of the MRFTA are without prejudice to the more general law in relation to damages under the Civil Act, art 750.[55] Damages under the general rules of tortious liability are limited to the damage actually suffered, such that

---

51 art 56(2), MRFTA, now repealed.

52 art 56-2, MRFTA.

53 art 57(1), MRFTA, now replaced.

54 art 57, MRFTA.

55 See Park, n 25, above, at 145:

> In general, injured parties in [MRFTA] violation cases may raise civil claims for damages under general tort theory . . . the claimant bears the burden of proof in showing the existence of four requisite elements. . . . (i) there has been an illegal act, (ii) such act has been committed intentionally or negligently, (iii) such act caused damage, and (iv) actual damage has been sustained by the claimant.

there is no right equivalent to the US Clayton Act treble-damages remedy. The evidence suggests, however, that private actions for damages under the MRFTA remain the exception rather than the rule. There is, in particular, no right to launch a class action in Korean law, and generally Korean society is not one in which the law is used as a regular means of dispute resolution.

Arbitration

In 2007 the KFTC established a new organization, the Korean Fair Trade Mediation Committee ('KFTMC'). The KFTMC exists, inter alia, to arbitrate disputes arising out of the application of the law relating to unfair business practices and the Fair Franchising Act.[56] The KFTMC also exercises jurisdiction over disputes arising under art 23(1).[57] Any party who alleges they have suffered loss as a result of a breach of art 23(1) may request that a dispute resolution proceeding be opened, unless the KFTC considers that it would be more appropriate for it to take action under arts 24 or 51 of the MRFTA. Requests which fulfil the criteria for the application of art 48-6 will be forwarded to the KFTMC which may provide arbitration, and which may also undertake its own necessary investigations into the alleged conduct by requesting documents. Resolution proceedings, which do not preclude the possibility of the bringing of a lawsuit under art 56(1), must be resolved within sixty days, and will be abandoned if they are not so concluded, or if either of the parties unilaterally withdraws, or if a lawsuit is brought. If the parties to the dispute accept the resolution they are then obliged to comply with its terms, and to report that they have done so.[58] **5-5.29**

[56] art 48-2, MRFTA.
[57] art 48-3, MRFTA.
[58] art 48-8, MRFTA.

Part 6

VIETNAM

6-1.	The Vietnamese Antitrust Law Regime	305
6-2.	Vietnam Agreements	313
6-3.	Vietnam Monopoly and Abuse of Dominance	321
6-4.	Vietnam Merger Control	329
6-5.	Vietnam Procedure	337

6-1

THE VIETNAMESE ANTITRUST LAW REGIME

Introduction	6-1.01	**Acts of the State**	6-1.17
Institutional Arrangements	6-1.08	**Territorial Application**	6-1.18
Vietnam Competition-Administration Department ('VCAD')	6-1.10	**International Cooperation and Agreements**	6-1.20
Vietnam Competition Council	6-1.14	**Intellectual Property**	6-1.21
General Exemptions	6-1.15		

Introduction

On 3 December 2004 the National Assembly of the Socialist Republic of Vietnam enacted the Law on Competition (hereinafter 'VLOC'),[1] and other provisions relevant to the application of this law have been brought forward. The commitment to competition as a dominant mode of economic activity is evident from the words of art 4(1), which states that 'enterprises enjoy freedom to competition within the legal framework'. This is, however, somewhat mitigated by art 4(2), which provides that this competition: **6-1.01**

> must be implemented on the principles of honesty, non-infringement upon the interests of the State, public interests, legitimate rights and interests of enterprises, consumers and compliance with the provisions of this Law.

The VLOC is more invasive and in particular creates more specific rules relating to matters such as dominant firm pricing, than is the case in antitrust regimes in the West. At the same time the degree of specificity of some of the prohibitions is such that avoidance is a relatively straightforward matter.

The VLOC entered into force on 1 July 2005, but it was not until 22 October 2008 that it was reported that the first investigation to be carried out under the **6-1.02**

[1] Law No 27/2004, 3 December 2004.

Law took place (see further Chapter 6-2, below). Unlike a number of other antitrust laws (although in common with the US and EC law), the VLOC makes no reference to its broader objectives or economic context. The preamble simply states that 'this Law provides for competition', and art 1, which sets out the 'scope of regulation' specifies only that the law 'provides for competition-restricting acts, unfair competition acts'[2] and procedures relating thereto. The effect of art 4(2), however (quoted above) should be noted. A distinction is made in the VLOC between conduct in restraint of competition, which encompasses the standard antitrust heads of restrictive agreements, dominance/monopoly, and merger control, and conduct which is deemed to be unfair competition.

6-1.03 The VLOC is a relatively long statute (and is reproduced as Appendix 4). It contains 123 articles in six chapters. Chapter 1 (arts 1–7) sets out general provisions (including provisions relating to the use of administrative power by state management agencies), chapter 2 (arts 8–38) sets out antitrust provisions, dealing with restrictive agreements, abuse of dominant position, mergers ('economic concentration'), and procedures relating to exemptions. Restrictive agreements may also be condemned under certain provisions of chapter 3 (arts 39–48) which deals with unfair competition acts.[3] Chapter 4 (arts 49–55) provides for the creation of two specialist agencies, the Competition Administration Department ('VCAD')[4] and the Competition Council ('VCC'). The powers of investigation and procedures to be applied in relation to the handling of competition cases are specified in chapter 5 (arts 56–121), and the final two arts set out in chapter 6 relate to the implementation of the VLOC, stating in part that 'the Government and the Supreme People's Court shall detail and guide the implementation of this Law'.[5]

[2] Article 4, VLOC, draws a clear distinction between 'competition-restricting acts' and 'unfair competition acts'. The former are defined in art 3(3) as meaning 'acts performed by enterprises to reduce, distort and prevent competition on the market'; the latter are defined in art 3(4) as meaning 'competition acts performed by enterprises in the process of doing business, which run counter to common standards of business ethics and cause damage or can cause damage to the State's interests, legitimate rights and interests of other enterprises or consumers'. It is clear then that the scope of 'unfair competition acts' is drawn more widely than is the scope of 'competition-restricting acts', and that the provisions relating to unfair acts may apply to conduct that would not fall to be condemned in the application of 'standard' antitrust provisions.

[3] This chapter deals with: (1) misleading indications; (2) infringing business secrets; (3) constraints in business; (4) 'discrediting other enterprises'; (5) disturbing the activities of other businesses; (6) misleading advertising; and (7) sales promotions. Only (3) and (5) are considered, in part, in this book.

[4] In the VLOC this department is called the 'Competition Managing Agency'. However, when constituted it was given the title of Competition Administration Department (see the Decree on functions, duties, powers and organizational structure of the Vietnam Competition Administration Department, 9 January 2006). Throughout this book the current title will be used.

[5] art 123, VLOC.

The antitrust provisions of the VLOC are more similar to those of the EC than to those of the US, with some provisions using language very similar to that employed in the EC, and in particular with the creation of an exemption process to be applied on application only, rather than the operation of a 'rule of reason' approach. Overall however, whatever international comparisons were made in the drafting of the Law, the Law remains a distinctive product of the Vietnamese political economy, and is idiosyncratic. **6-1.04**

The provisions of the VLOC should be read alongside three further decrees enacted to give fuller effect to the VLOC: the Decree on Competition;[6] the Decree on Dealing with Breaches in the Competition Sector (hereinafter 'DDB');[7] the Decree on functions, duties, powers and organizational structure of the Vietnam Competition Administration Department;[8] and the Decree on the establishment, functions, duties, powers and organizational structure of the Vietnam Competition Council.[9] Relevant provisions of these three decrees are dealt with in this text as appropriate. Although this book deals comprehensively with the legislation and decrees that have been published to date, there has been no significant enforcement activity at the time of writing, although there have been calls within Vietnam for the Law to be applied effectively. The lack of case law, and in particular the lack of judicial interpretation of the terms of the legislation, limits the extent to which substantive guidance can be provided as to the way in which the law will operate in practice. **6-1.05**

The provisions of the VLOC apply to the parties specified in art 2 of the Law, namely 'business organizations and individuals', including 'enterprises operating in the State-monopolized sectors', and 'foreign enterprises operating in Vietnam', as well as to professional associations. The latter term is drawn widely, encompassing 'commodity line associations and trade associations'.[10] The VLOC applies even to the 'public-utility services', although not to the extent that the activities of these are regulated by laws which are not competition laws, and it is made clear at art 15 of the VLOC that the State retains control over such vital decisions as pricing and production quantities (see further Chapter 6-3, below). **6-1.06**

To date enforcement activity has been severely limited, although in 2008 three cases were opened in relation to restraints of competition, one in relation to an **6-1.07**

---

[6] Decree on Competition: Providing detailed regulations for implementation of a number of articles of the Law on Competition, 15 September 2005.

[7] 30 September 2005. Also relevant in respect of the enforcement of the VLOC is the Ordinance on Dealing with Administrative Offences, 2 July 2002.

[8] 9 January 2006.

[9] Ibid.

[10] art 3(2), VLOC.

alleged price-fixing cartel in steel, one relating to insurance premiums, and one in relation to an abuse of dominance case.[11]

Institutional Arrangements

6-1.08 Article 7 of the VLOC reserves to the Government the function of performing 'uniform State management over competition', and the lead role is given to the Ministry of Industry and Trade ('MIT').[12] Other state bodies, including 'ministerial-level agencies' and provincial and municipal government bodies, are subordinate to the MIT in the regulation of competition, being required 'to coordinate with the [MIT] in performing the State management over competition'.[13] Although two specialist organizations have been created under the authority of the VLOC it is clear that there remains a political influence on the management of competition policy, with certain decisions, including those related to exemptions, being reserved to the Minister of Industry and Trade or to the Prime Minister.

6-1.09 The VCAD and the VCC are established on the basis of the provisions of arts 49–52 and 53–55 respectively of the VLOC.

Vietnam Competition-Administration Department ('VCAD')

6-1.10 The VCAD's roles in relation to the management of the VLOC are spelt out in art 49(2) of the VLOC. These are: (a) to operate the merger control system established by the VLOC; (b) to consider exemption applications, and to put forward to the Minister of Industry and Trade, or the Prime Minister, recommendations in respect of these; (c) to investigate competition cases falling within the competition-restricting acts and unfair competition acts provisions of the VLOC; (d) 'handling and sanctioning unfair competition acts'; and (e) any other tasks assigned by laws to it. The Decree relating to the VCAD in fact gives it far wider responsibilities in relation to the management of competition in the Vietnamese economy, including responsibilities for combating dumping, subsidies, international trade disputes, and consumer protection. In practice the effect of this appears to be to reduce the capacity of the VCAD to act in competition cases.

---

[11] This detail was provided directly to the author by the VCAD and no further details, save for those referred to in the following chapters, are available in respect of these cases at the time of writing.

[12] The VLOC specifies the Trade Ministry (see, eg art 7), but following a government reorganization this is now the Ministry of Industry and Trade.

[13] art 7(3), VLOC.

In respect of the VLOC the Decree gives the VCAD the following responsibilities: (1) to draw up and submit to the Minister legal documents relating to competition; (2) to organize the implementation of legal measures as these are introduced; (3) to oversee legal measures falling within the competence of other agencies which are competition-related and, where necessary, to 'request' that the agencies address these where they do not conform with the VLOC; (4) to organize the investigation of competition-restricting acts and unfair competition and any other acts that violate the VLOC (although note that the VCAD initiates investigations, but that final infringement decisions can be taken only by the VCC); (5) to evaluate exemption requests (see Chapter 6-2, below) and to submit these along with recommendations to the Minister of Industry and Trade or the Prime Minister as appropriate; (6) 'to supervise the process of economic centralization'; (7) to collate information relating to dominant and monopoly enterprises and the application of the law to trade associations, and exemption cases; (8) the development of international cooperation in respect of competition law; (9) to request individuals or organizations to provide information necessary for the performance of its functions; (10) to take enforcement action in the form of the application of 'administrative prevention measures' and administrative sanctions (see Chapter 6-5, below); (11) to advocate on behalf of competition law, including the provision of training to officials; and (12) to perform any other duties given to it by the Minister of Industry and Trade. **6-1.11**

The Head of the VCAD is appointed by the Prime Minister at the recommendation of the Minister of Industry and Trade.[14] To further the investigation of competition cases special investigators assigned to the VCAD are to be appointed by the Minister of Industry and Trade. These investigators have the role of investigating specific cases where the head of the VCAD has made a decision to the effect that an investigation should take place.[15] A number of committees exist within the VCAD to support and develop its work, including committees responsible for competition investigations, competition supervision and management, and international cooperation. Like the Head, department Directors are also appointed by the Minister, and all staff of the VCAD are drawn from the MIT, subject to their having the requisite qualifications as specified in the VLOC. Few staff in the VCAD are specialists in competition law or policy. **6-1.12**

In addition to its role in enforcement the VCAD is attempting to support advocacy issues in Vietnam. A business survey conducted in 2008 showed that while **6-1.13**

[14] art 50, VLOC.

[15] art 51, VLOC. The qualifications that investigators must possess are spelt out in art 52. Investigators must: (a) be ethical; (b) hold at least a bachelor's degree in either law, economics, or finance; (c) have worked for at least five years in one of those areas; and (d) have been trained in professional investigation skills.

business generally was aware of the existence of the law, there was less knowledge of the technical requirements of the Law.

Vietnam Competition Council

6-1.14 The Decree on the establishment, functions, duties, powers and organizational structure of the VCC provides only scant further detail as to the role and procedures to be applied by this agency, largely reproducing the terms of arts 53–55 of the VLOC. The VCC is a state law enforcement agency[16] 'composed of between 11 and 15 members', who are appointed by the Prime Minister on the recommendation of the Minister of Industry and Trade.[17] Appointments are for five-year terms, and are renewable. There is no statutory limitation on the number of consecutive appointments that any one member may hold. The primary role of the VCC is to address complaints relating to breaches of the VLOC. The VCC does not have the power to initiate actions. The VCC is headed by a Chairman, who is also an appointee of, and who may be dismissed by, the Prime Minister. The Chairman has the responsibility of organizing the operation of the VCC, and in particular it is he who is to decide on the constitution of a subsidiary body, the Competition Case-Handling Council ('CCHC'), which is to be comprised of at least five members. The CCHC is to deal with individual cases, and to make determinations in respect of these. The VCC is assisted in the performance of its functions by a secretariat, whose functions and duties are determined by the MIT. The relationship between the VCAD and the VCC in respect of competition cases is illustrated at Figure 6-5.1.

General Exemptions

6-1.15 As noted above the VLOC purports to apply to all enterprises in Vietnam, irrespective of ownership, and it is expressly provided at art 5(1) that 'where there is any disparity between the provision of this Law and those of other laws on competition-restriction acts or unfair competition acts, the provisions of this Law shall apply'.

6-1.16 If there exist international agreements entered into by Vietnam (including the WTO agreements) which conflict with the provisions of the VLOC the former are to have precedence.[18]

[16] The Decree further specifies that the agency is 'independent'.

[17] art 53, VLOC. In order to be eligible for appointment to the VCC persons must: (a) be ethical, honest and 'impartial', but must also have 'the sense of protecting socialist legality'; (b) hold at least a bachelor's degree in either law, economics, or finance; (c) have worked for at least nine years in one of those areas; and (d) be capable of fulfilling the tasks set for the VCC (art 55(1), VLOC).

[18] art 5(2), VLOC.

Acts of the State

Article 6 of the VLOC is addressed to 'State management agencies', and is potentially of great significance in the context of the operation of the Vietnamese economy. It sets out four prohibitions binding on the agencies, which may not: (1) compel any person to purchase, or sell, goods or services from or to enterprises designated by the agency, unless that enterprise is a designated state monopoly, or there has been emergency legislation to permit the otherwise prohibited action; (2) discriminate between enterprises; (3) compel professional associations or any other enterprises to enter into agreements or alliances which restrict competition; and (4) engage in any 'other acts that prevent lawful business activity of enterprises'. 6-1.17

Territorial Application

Chapter 1 of the VLOC is silent on the issue of extraterritorial application of the Law, although art 2, which specifies the subjects of the Law, states that the Law is applicable to 'foreign enterprises operating in Vietnam'. Likewise, art 2 of the Decree on Competition states that the Decree applies to those 'conducting business ... in Vietnam'. This would appear to exclude the operation of the effects doctrine, such that the Law could not be applied to, for example, a merger between two foreign parties selling to Vietnamese customers in their own territories, but could apply to the extent that the foreign companies were directly present in the Vietnamese market.[19] 6-1.18

It is anticipated at art 57 of the VLOC, which sets language requirements, that foreign parties may be involved in proceedings, with the Law stating that these 'may use their native language and script', and that in this case interpretation will be required. 6-1.19

[19] It has been suggested that:

The phrase 'overseas enterprises operating in Vietnam' . . . is understood to encompass foreign commercial presences in Vietnam, such as: foreign branch offices; foreign contractors with an office in Vietnam and/or directly supplying services in Vietnam, such as foreign construction contracts. . . .The phrase . . . may also encompass offshore foreign entities investing in onshore foreign invested enterprises or in onshore foreign commercial presences. . . . However, this has yet to be confirmed by Vietnam's competition authorities, so the exact range of foreign entities which are subject to the [VLOC] remains uncertain (Phillips Fox, *Competition Law Update*, July 2006).

International Cooperation and Agreements

6-1.20 Given the relatively underdeveloped state of the Vietnamese antitrust system it has not entered into substantive international agreements relating to the application of antitrust law. The VCAD is assigned the responsibility of developing international cooperation.[20] Vietnam participates in APEC, and was involved in the setting up of the Association of Southeast Asian Nations ('ASEAN') working group on competition policy. An economic partnership agreement entered into with Japan makes some provision for cooperation between the parties in respect of competition policy.[21]

Intellectual Property

6-1.21 There is only one reference to intellectual property rights in the VLOC. This arises at art 119(3) buried away towards the end of the chapter related to enforcement. This provision states that 'other agencies with sanctioning competence shall sanction intellectual property-related unfair competition acts according to law provisions on handling administrative violations'.

6-1.22 The most important law relating to intellectual property in Vietnam is the Law on Intellectual Property Rights of 29 November 2005. This states at art 7(2) that the exercise of intellectual property rights 'shall not violate the interests of the State and the public interests, the legitimate rights and interests of other organizations and individuals' legitimate rights and interests, and shall not violate related laws and regulations'. There are also provisions in this legislation relating to compulsory licensing where the owner of an IP right engages in anti-competitive activity,[22] and a prohibition in art 130 of 'unfair competition acts'. There is no link between this provision and the VLOC. Exactly one year after the enactment of this legislation the Law on Technology Transfer was passed, which contains within it specific provisions relating to competition aspects of technology transfer, although the system developed is not as full as that, for example, set out in the relevant EC legislation in this area

[20] Decree on functions, duties, powers and organizational structure of the Vietnam Competition Administration Department, 9 January 2006, art 2(8).

[21] Agreement between Japan and the Socialist Republic of Vietnam for an Economic Partnership, 25 December 2008. See in Particular Chapter 10 of the Agreement.

[22] art 145, Law on Intellectual Property Rights. At the time of writing there have been no cases in which this provision has been applied.

6-2

VIETNAM AGREEMENTS

Introduction	6-2.01	Exemptions	6-2.06
Horizontal Agreements	6-2.02	**Vertical Agreements**	6-2.10
Trade associations	6-2.04	Multi-level sales	6-2.11

Introduction

The primary prohibition on restrictive agreements is found in art 8 of the VLOC, although certain restraints may also be prohibited under art 42 which falls within the chapter dealing with 'unfair' competitive acts. This provision is more likely to be applied to vertical restraints in an approach similar to that adopted in Korea (see Chapter 5-2) where horizontal restraints exclusively are dealt with under the primary provision. An exemption system, which operates on the basis of individually-granted exemptions, which must be applied for, is set out in arts 25–39. The granting of exemptions is in part a politicized process, such that exemptions can be granted only by the Trade Minister or the Prime Minister. **6-2.01**

Horizontal Agreements

Article 8 of the VLOC prohibits eight categories of multilateral anti-competitive arrangements, although it does not stipulate that such agreements be between parties operating at the same industrial level: **6-2.02**

(1) Price-fixing agreements. The Decree on Competition makes it clear that such agreements may be either explicit or implicit. The following practices are referred to in art 14 of the Decree as falling within art 8(1): (1) to apply uniform prices; (2) to increase prices by a specific amount;[1] (3) to apply a uniform

[1] The wording here is unfortunate, and appears to imply that an agreement simply to increase prices by an unspecified amount would not be caught.

pricing formula; (4) to maintain a fixed ratio for the price of related goods; (5) not to grant discounts, or to apply discounts at a uniform rate; (6) to restrict customers' credit; (7) not to reduce prices without notification to the other parties to the agreement; and (8) to use a uniform price at the commencement of negotiations on prices. In October 2008 the *Global Competition Review* reported that, for the first time, a price-fixing agreement was under investigation by the VCAD. In this case the Vietnam Steel Association agreed to act in concert in the face of falling prices on the grounds that firms would exit the market if prices continued to fall.[2] A second investigation was opened in 2008 in relation to an alleged price-fixing of insurance premiums.

(2) and (3) 'Agreements on distributing outlets, sources of supply of goods, provision of services' (market sharing agreements) and agreements relating to output restrictions. The Decree on Competition states that such agreements include those which set quantities, locations, or under which parties agree to purchase goods or services from only one or more specified suppliers.[3]

(4) Agreements restricting technical or economic progress or restricting investments. The definition of the first clause of this provision in the Decree on Competition is a very restrictive one, as it prohibits only 'reaching an agreement to purchase a patent, utility solution or industrial design in order to destroy it or keep it from being used'.[4] Not only is this limited definition flawed on its own terms (for example, an agreement between A and B not to use respectively held patents would not be outlawed) it also is flawed in taking an exceptionally narrow approach to agreements not to compete on technology. An agreement to restrict investment is defined as one 'not to provide any more capital for expanding production, for improving the quality of goods and services, or for other developmental research'.[5]

(5) Agreements which impose on parties obligations or conditions 'which have no direct connection with the subject of such contracts'. Article 18 of the Decree on Competition provides further detail in respect of this provision. Four conditions precedent to signing contracts are prohibited: (1) restrictions on production or distribution of other goods or the purchase and provision of other services, unless this is in accordance with the laws on agency; (2) territorial restrictions on resale, unless these relate to goods whose trading is restricted by other laws; (3) restrictions on customers purchasing goods for

[2] The Association Chairman was quoted as saying: 'We know we will violate the competition law . . . if we join hands to hurt consumers, and we are not allowed to do so. But that is not the case here'.

[3] art 15, Decree on Competition.

[4] art 16(1), Decree on Competition.

[5] art 17(2), Decree on Competition.

resale; and (4) restrictions on the 'forms and quantity' of goods provided. Thus this provision appears to attack terms commonly used in distribution agreements, such as exclusive purchasing requirements, and the imposition of territorial exclusivity. Such practices are more likely to be efficiency-enhancing than detrimental.[6] To outlaw restrictions on the 'forms' and 'quantities' of goods provided under the agreement is, to say the least, an idiosyncratic provision the reason for whose inclusion in the prohibition is not readily apparent.

(6) Agreements designed to foreclose markets. The Decree on Competition, art 19, distinguishes between agreements designed to preclude 'participation' in a market and those designed to preclude other businesses from 'developing'. In both cases the prohibitions apply where an agreement is entered into which operates against those not party to the agreement. In the first case there are two prohibitions: (1) 'requesting, appealing or enticing' customers not to enter into relations with those not party to the agreement; and (2) 'selling or purchasing goods or providing services at a price which is sufficient to ensure that enterprises not being party to the agreement will not be able to participate in the relevant market'. The first of these prohibitions is drawn widely, and the use of 'entice' in particular is open to wide interpretation. The second prohibition is not exceptional in banning multilateral attempts at predation, although the 'test' is not as strict as that for predation. It should be noted in particular that a prohibition on prices which are set so low as to preclude competition does not draw a distinction between an 'equally efficient' competitor, such that prices would, in the proper sense, be predatory, and a competitor who lacks the ability to compete effectively on price. The latter may find a protection in this prohibition although this would not be an efficient application of antitrust. In the case of agreements which have as their object preventing other businesses from developing there are also two prohibitions: (1) 'requiring, appealing or enticing' distributors or retailers trading with those party to the agreement to be discriminatory when trading with others; (2) selling goods or offering services at prices which do not permit those not party to the agreement to expand the scale of their activities.

(7) Agreements designed to eject market participants, other than those party to the agreement. The prohibitions specified in the Decree on Competition are the same as for those of art 19 (above).

(8) Bid-rigging agreements. A number of forms of bid-rigging are specified as being unlawful in the Decree on Competition: (1) withdrawing from a tender

[6] The condemnation of absolute territorial protection within the EC system may be seen as a peculiarity arising from single-market imperatives, and unrelated to competitive efficiency arguments.

process in order for one or more other agreed parties to win; (2) hindering the bidding of those not party to the agreement by, for example, refusing to supply necessary materials; (3) offering uncompetitive prices, or terms with which the party inviting the tender would not agree in order to pre-determine the winning bid; and (4) agreeing on the numbers of times when each party will win a bid in a specified period. Anecdotal evidence suggests that bid-rigging is prevalent in Vietnam.[7]

6-2.03 The final three of these categories of agreements are prohibited *per se*, irrespective of the market power held by those participating in the agreement,[8] and may not benefit from exemptions,[9] whereas those in the first five categories are prohibited only in the event that the parties pass a *de minimis* threshold of a combined market share of 30 per cent,[10] and may benefit from an exemption if certain criteria are met (see below). The term 'combined market share' is defined in art 3(6) as meaning the 'aggregate market share on the relevant market[11] of enterprises participating in the competition-restriction agreement'. Market share is in turn defined as the percentage of sales turnover of the relevant enterprise of the aggregate turnover of all the enterprises 'dealing in such kind of goods or service on the relevant market'.[12]

Trade associations[13]

6-2.04 It was noted in Chapter 6-1 that the VLOC expressly applies to the activities of trade associations,[14] and there is no general exemption applying to the activities of these bodies. Further, public authorities ('state management agencies') are expressly prohibited from encouraging such associations to act restrictively.[15]

---

[7] See, eg CUTS International, 'A guide to competition issues in Vietnam', pp 20–1. Note too that the Law on Bidding of 2005 also contains rules relating to bid-rigging. This specifically states that it applies to foreign contractors.

[8] art 9(1), VLOC.

[9] art 10, VLOC.

[10] art 9(2), VLOC. In other words, horizontal price-fixing is permitted where the combined market share of the participating enterprises is less than 30 per cent. Anecdotal evidence suggests that in a number of cases in which concerns were raised the parties were able to argue, successfully, that they fell below the requisite market share thresholds, and that proceedings were therefore abandoned at an early stage.

[11] The definition of the relevant market is dealt with in Chapter 6-3, below.

[12] art 3(5), VLOC. In the case that the relevant market is that for the purchase of goods or services a similar definition applies, with the market share being the percentage of the purchases of the relevant goods or services by the enterprise in question of the aggregate purchases.

[13] Although the VLOC uses the term 'professional association', this is defined in such a way that the term 'trade association', which is expressly encompassed within the definition of professional association is employed here as being more widely used and understood.

[14] art 2(2), VLOC.

[15] art 6(3), VLOC.

Article 47 of the VLOC, which falls within the chapter prohibiting unfair competition, prohibits trade associations from engaging in discrimination, consisting in: (a) refusals to admit eligible enterprises to the association or in a discriminatory way refusing to allow enterprises to withdraw from them; and (b) 'irrationally restricting the business activities or other business-related activities of member enterprises'.[16] There are six grounds on which exemptions may be granted. The Law states, at art 10(1), that exemptions will be available where the parties meet one of the specified conditions 'in order to reduce costs to benefit consumers'. It is not clear that the parties are required to demonstrate that consumers will benefit, or if it is axiomatically presumed that prices to consumers *will* fall, where the agreement meets one of the specified purposes. In one of the specified instances it is hard to understand how the agreements in question could lead, at least directly, to a fall in prices for consumers (item (f) below). The six categories of conduct are given here in full. **6-2.05**

(a) Rationalizing the organizational structure, business model, raising business efficiency.
(b) Promoting technical and technological advances, raising goods and service quality.
(c) Promoting the uniform application of quality standards and technical norms of products of different kinds.
(d) Harmonizing business, goods delivery, and payment conditions, which have no connection with prices and price factors.
(e) Enhancing the competitiveness of small and medium-sized enterprises.
(f) Enhancing the competitiveness of Vietnamese enterprises on the international market.

Articles 25–38 set out the procedures to be applied in the exemption process.

Exemptions

Article 10 of the VLOC creates a broad system of exemption from the prohibitions established in art 8(1)–(5), but not in respect of agreements designed to foreclose markets, collectively exclude existing participants from the market, or bid-rigging arrangements. It will be noted immediately that exemptions *may* be granted in respect of two categories of conduct which are considered in many regimes to be hard-core to the extent that they may even invite criminal sanction, **6-2.06**

[16] The penalties for breach of this provision are spelt out at art 37, Decree on Dealing with Breaches in the Competition Sector. A fine of from Dong15m to Dong25m may be imposed. Where there are a number of offences relating to one enterprise, or an offence in relation to a number of enterprises simultaneously, or where a member enterprise is forced to withdraw from the association as a result of restrictive activities the fine may range from Dong30m to Dong50m.

viz price-fixing and market-sharing agreements. Procedures relating to the exemption process are set out in section 4 of Chapter 2 of the VLOC. It is unlawful to put into place an agreement in restraint of competition even where an exemption has been applied for on good grounds until such time as a final decision is made. The penalties that may be imposed are discussed in Chapter 6-5, below. Article 85(2) of the Decree on Competition however states that when penalties are calculated it may be an extenuating circumstance if 'the conduct in breach has a positive impact on the development of the economy'. In principle this provision could mitigate, perhaps entirely, penalties in the case that an agreement has been entered into prior to the granting of an exemption, but where an exemption is subsequently forthcoming.

6-2.07 Exemptions are to be decided, in respect of agreements, by the Minister of Industry and Trade,[17] in response to applications submitted by relevant parties, who must be the parties who are intending to participate in the restrictive agreement.[18] Article 28 of the VLOC specifies the contents of the 'dossier' that must be submitted when an application for an exemption is made, which include: (a) the application in the form prescribed by the VCAD; (b) valid copies of the business registration certificates of each enterprise which is a party to the agreement, or the trade association charter as appropriate; (c) the last two years' financial statements, duly audited, of each enterprise involved; (d) reports from each of the participating enterprises of their market shares over the last two years; (e) a report explaining how the criteria of exemption specified in art 10 are satisfied;[19] and (f) written confirmation that the person making the submission is duly authorized to do so by the notifying parties. The dossier must be truthful, and the parties are liable for any errors or misrepresentations.[20] Once the dossier is submitted the VCAD must, within seven working days, notify the parties as to whether their application is complete, or specify what further material is required for the submission to be accepted.[21] A fee must be paid at the time the dossier is submitted. The parties are free to withdraw their application at any time, but if they do so the fee is not refundable.[22] Even where a dossier is accepted as complete the VCAD may subsequently require that the parties submit further 'necessary' documents and information relating to the proposed agreements, or provide explanations of matters dealt with in the dossier. Apart from the use of the word 'necessary' there is no

[17] art 25(1), VLOC.

[18] The parties may appoint a 'lawful representative' to carry out the procedures relating to the exemption process (art 27, VLOC).

[19] The Decree on Competition requires that any such application be accompanied by an explanatory report 'in the form of a feasibility study either formulated or evaluated by a science and technology organization or a research and development organization established pursuant to the Law on Science and Technology' (art 40).

[20] art 28(2), VLOC.

[21] art 30(2), VLOC.

[22] art 33, VLOC.

limitation set in the VLOC on the nature of the information that may be required by the VCAD. The VCAD also has the power to request information from 'related' parties.[23] The term 'related' extends to any organization or individual who may be in a position to comment in an informed way on the proposed arrangement, including competitors, customers, other government agencies, etc. Any such request must be complied with within fifteen days.[24]

A formal decision in response to an application for exemption must be made within sixty working days of the receipt of the complete dossier,[25] although this period may be extended by up to a further sixty days in the event that the case involves 'many complicated circumstances'.[26] By the end of this period the Minister of Industry and Trade must make one of two decisions: (a) approval of the exemption; or (b) rejection of the exemption. Although this article does not specify that the decision to grant the exemption may be conditional on obligations being accepted by the parties, or modifications made to the agreement(s), art 35(c) of the VLOC appears to imply that these may be imposed. Article 35(c) specifies that a decision relating to the grant of an exemption must set out any 'conditions and obligations of the parties'. It is possible that this clause is intended to apply to merger proceedings but if this is the case this is not made clear on the face of the legislation.[27] If granted an exemption will be time-limited, although there is no statutory limit on this period. The VCAD is required to publicize the existence of exemptions granted. Third parties who object to the grant of an exemption may lodge a complaint according to the relevant administrative legal principles. **6-2.08**

Exemptions may be cancelled in the following circumstances: (1) the application was fraudulent; (2) the enterprises benefiting from the exemption fail to comply with obligations or conditions imposed on them within the specified time limit; or (3) the conditions which justified the grant of the exemption no longer exist.[28] **6-2.09**

Vertical Agreements

Although the provisions of art 8 could be applied, in some cases, to the operation of vertical restraints (as is the case for example in relation to art 8(5) which extends, inter alia, to tying agreements), it is more likely that these would be subject to **6-2.10**

[23] art 32, VLOC.
[24] art 32(2), VLOC.
[25] art 34(1), VLOC.
[26] art 34(2), VLOC. Two separate extensions may be made, each of a maximum of 30 days. In each event the VCAD must notify the applicant parties in writing no later than three days before the expiration of the original deadline.
[27] Article 37(2) (discussed in brief below) further suggests that obligations and conditions may be imposed in respect of exemptions relating to competition-restricting agreements.
[28] art 37, VLOC.

control under art 42 of the VLOC, which makes it unlawful for enterprises 'to constrain customers, business partners of other enterprises by performing acts of threatening or forcing them not to enter into transactions or to stop transactions with such enterprises'. The inclusion of restrictive clauses, such as an exclusive dealing clause, in contracts could be interpreted as a measure which 'forces' the trading counterparty not to do business with other enterprises. The question of whether such a contract amounts to the application of 'force' might depend on the market power of the enterprise in whose favour the clause operates. Article 44 could also be applied to vertical agreements. This specifies that it is unlawful for enterprises to 'disturb lawful business activities of other enterprises by performing acts of directly or indirectly preventing, or disrupting the latter's business activities'.

Multi-level sales

6-2.11 The VLOC contains provisions relating to multi-level sales,[29] which are a form of vertical distribution arrangement defined in the Law as existing where: (a) the marketing of retail goods is conducted through a multi-level and multi-branch network of participants; (b) goods are marketed directly to customers' homes; and (c) participants enjoy bonuses based on sales levels, and the participation of sellers lower in the hierarchy than themselves who have been recruited into the network by them.[30] Article 48 of the VLOC prohibits four specific practices: (1) requiring those who participate to pay a deposit, buy an initial volume of goods, or otherwise pay money to operate in the network; (2) not buying back at at least 90 per cent of the purchase price of goods sold to participants for resale; (3) providing bonuses or commissions based mostly on the enticement of others into the resale network; and (4) supplying false information as to the benefits of participating in the network, or as to the nature of the goods supplied through the network. The penalties to be applied in respect of breaches of these provisions are set out in the Decree on Dealing with Breaches in the Competition Sector, art 38, and range from Dong50m to Dong100m depending on the circumstances of the case.

---

29 Similar provisions exist in the Taiwan Fair Trade Act (see Chapter 4-2, above).

30 art 3(11), VLOC.

6-3

VIETNAM MONOPOLY AND ABUSE OF DOMINANCE

Introduction	6-3.01	The assessment of dominance	6-3.05
The Assessment of Dominance and Monopoly	6-3.02	**Conduct Prohibited**	6-3.10
The determination of the relevant market	6-3.02	State-monopolized domains	6-3.15

Introduction

The law relating to abuse of dominant position is set out at s 2 of Chapter 2 of the Vietnam Law on Competition ('VLOC'). The law is unusual in creating two different sets of presumptions relating to market power, one applying to firms in a dominant position, and the other to monopolists, with different conduct proscriptions applying in both cases. As noted in Chapter 6-1, above, the law applies to State-owned enterprises ('SOEs'), although not to the extent that non-competition laws set them specific objectives or operating principles which are not compatible with the competition provisions of the VLOC. Further, art 15 (see below) makes it clear that while the VLOC expressly applies to enterprises in the 'State-monopolized domains', to a significant extent their activities are regulated by the State and not subject to VLOC prohibitions. **6-3.01**

The Assessment of Dominance and Monopoly

The determination of the relevant market

Article 3(1) of the VLOC states that: **6-3.02**

> Relevant market means the relevant market of products and the relevant geographic market.

> Relevant market of products means a market of goods, services which are interchangeable in terms of characteristics,[1] use, purposes and prices.
>
> Relevant geographic market means a specific geographical area in which exist goods, services which are interchangeable under similar conditions of competition, and which is considerably differentiated from neighbouring arcas.

It will be noted that the temporal aspect of market definition appears to be excluded from consideration in the application of the VLOC.[2]

6-3.03 Further guidance is given in the Decree on Competition, Chapter II, section I of which is headed, 'determining what is [the] relevant market', and which applies to any procedure falling within the VLOC which calls for a market to be defined. While this part of the Decree incorporates a version of the SSNIP test (discussed in Chapter 1-2, above), there are some peculiarities to the way in which a relevant market is to be established in the application of antitrust law in Vietnam. Under the terms of the Decree goods or services are deemed to be capable of being substituted for each other if they have the same characteristics, or the same usage, or:

> . . . if above 50% of a random sample quantity taken from one thousand consumers living in the relevant geographical area change to purchasing or intend to purchase other goods or services with the same characteristics and use purpose as the goods they are currently using or intend to use where the price of such goods or services increases more than 10% and remains stable for six consecutive months.[3]

It need hardly be pointed out that this is a very distinctive approach to the application of an SSNIP test, that reliance on such a survey is unlikely to produce robust results, and that a circularity enters the process with a requirement that a geographic market be determined within which the survey is to be conducted before a product market has been determined. Only where the approach outlined here is deemed to produce 'results insufficient to make a conclusion' is the VCAD or VCC to consider either cross-elasticities of demand, entry into the market, the durability of the good or service, and supply-side substitution.[4] Article 5 of the Decree deals with the special case of 'lock-ins' or 'consumables' (products whose purchase flows from that of a primary product, such as toner cartridges used

[1] Characteristics are defined in art 4(2) of the Decree on Competition as being 'determined on one or more of the following bases: (a) physical features; (b) chemical features; (c) technical features; (d) side effects on the user; (e) ability to assimilate'.

[2] The Decree on Competition also does not refer to temporal market aspects. Although it does make reference to 'durations of supply' and the 'use duration' of goods (see art 6) this is not in a context which suggests that a rigorous analysis of temporal market factors is to be undertaken.

[3] Decree on Competition, art 4(5)(c).

[4] Supply-side substitution is defined as meaning 'the capability of an enterprise which is currently producing or distributing any one product or service to change to the production or distribution of another product or service within a short period without any significant increase in expenses in a context where there are price increases for such products or services' (Decree on Competition, art 6).

with printers). In this case the approach in the Decree is not dissimilar to that under EC competition law, such that products will 'be deemed to be a product auxiliary to the relevant product if when its price increases or decreases the demand for the relevant product also undergoes an equivalent increase or decrease'. In other words, where prices in the consumable market determine demand in the primary market, the consumable shall be deemed not to constitute a relevant product market.

The concept of the relevant geographic market is dealt with in art 7 of the Decree. Regard is to be had to the ease with which competitors in contiguous areas may be able to operate in the area in which the enterprise under investigation is located, transportation costs, durability of the product or service, and any relevant barriers to market access. In order for goods from outside the locality of the enterprise to be considered as being in the same geographic market the price of such products, taking into account transport costs, should not be more than 10 per cent of those supplied by the enterprise under investigation. The Decree is further unusual in that it defines barriers to entry (although a reference to 'other barriers' makes the definition an open one). Barriers are stated to consist in: (1) intellectual property rights; (2) financial barriers; (3) administrative decisions by state bodies; (4) regulations; (5) import duties and quotas; and (6) 'practices of consumers'.[5] **6-3.04**

The assessment of dominance

The presumptions under which a dominant position is to be presumed are based in the first instance on market shares and concentration ratios, and are set at remarkably low thresholds. However, other factors may, in some circumstances, be taken into account as set out in the Decree on Competition. **6-3.05**

Article 11(1) of the VLOC states enterprises shall be considered to be in a dominant position where their market share is 30 per cent or greater,[6] *or* if they 'are capable of restricting competition considerably'. It is perhaps unfortunate that the language here uses 'or' rather than 'and'. There may be many cases in which a market share of 30 per cent does not confer on the enterprise holding it the ability to restrict competition, let alone to do so 'considerably', and this threshold is significantly lower than would generally be considered by industrial economists to be one at which significant market power is confirmed. There is no case in the history of EC or US antitrust jurisprudence in which a firm with such a low **6-3.06**

[5] Decree on Competition, art 8.

[6] Market share 'means the percentage between sale turnover of this enterprise and aggregate turnover of all enterprises dealing in such kind of goods or service on the relevant market or the percentage between purchase turnover of this enterprise and aggregate purchase turnover of all enterprises dealing in such kind of goods or service on the relevant market on a monthly, quarterly or yearly basis' (VLOC, art 3(5)). Turnover is defined in the Decree on Competition, arts 9–12.

market share has been found to be subject to the strictures of the law on dominant position or monopolization.

6-3.07 Article 11(2) creates a hybrid threshold in that it sets out presumptions relating to 'groups of enterprises', but these assumptions are to apply only in situations in which the members of the 'group' 'take concerted action to restrict competition'. Three alternative concentration ratios are specified as conferring on the members of each 'group' a dominant position: a CR2 of 50% or greater; a CR3 of 65% or greater; and a CR4 of 75% or greater. Unlike some other jurisdictions that employ concentration ratio presumptions, such as the Korean, the system here does not allow for the exclusion from these calculations of enterprises holding small market shares. Thus, for example, where a CR3 exists of, say, 70%, with firm A holding 40%, firm B holding 25%, and firm C holding 5%, firm C will be considered, under the art 11(2) presumption, to be jointly holding a dominant position, and may therefore be subject to the strictures of art 13 (below). It appears to be the case however that where the CR thresholds are met, an *individual* act by one of the relevant enterprises will not be found to be in breach of the provisions relating to dominance unless it is individually dominant. Only if all the relevant enterprises act in the same manner will a collective infringement be found.

6-3.08 Article 11 does not contain within it any measure which permits an enterprise, on the basis of objective evidence, to rebut the presumption of dominance, and is therefore insensitive to market realities, and in particular to the existence of countervailing power, or the absence of barriers to entry. However, the wording of the Decree on Competition appears to suggest that such a rebuttal can be made, and that the analysis may not be as formalistic as implied in art 11. Section 4 of the Decree on Competition sets out, at art 22, 'bases for determining the capability of enterprises to substantially restrain competition in a relevant market', although it does not specify on which provision of the VLOC this rests. Article 22 sets out a number of factors, of which the one given most emphasis is the financial resource of the enterprise, its founders, and parents. Reference is also made to its technological capacity, its intellectual property portfolio, and the scale of its distribution network. There is no reference to the relative size of other enterprises in the relevant market.

6-3.09 The definition of a monopoly, found in art 12, is a 'pure' economic one, in that it applies only where 'there is no enterprise competing . . . on the relevant market'. As with art 11 it does not appear that the enterprise holding the 100% market share is able to rebut the presumption that it is a monopoly. While this is perhaps more reasonable than is the case in the operation of the low thresholds provided for in art 11, it is nevertheless trite to point out that even an enterprise holding a 100 per cent market share may not, in all cases, hold significant market power.

Conduct Prohibited

Prohibitions are established in arts 13 and 14 of the VLOC. The first set of prohibitions applies to enterprises in a dominant position and to those holding monopolies. The second set is a further restriction on monopolies, but does not apply to dominant positions. In art 13 the focus is on exclusionary abuses, although art 13(2) could also be applied to control exploitative pricing where this is 'irrational', whereas in art 14 a prohibition on exploitative conduct is set out more expressly. **6-3.10**

Article 13 prohibits the following conduct. **6-3.11**

(1) Selling goods or services at prices lower than the aggregate costs in order to eliminate competitors. The VLOC does not provide a definition of 'aggregate costs',[7] but there is substantial detail set out in the Decree on Competition at arts 23–26, which includes provisions relating to the assessment of 'prime costs', distribution costs, and overheads. It is not an offence for a company in a dominant or monopoly position to sell goods below cost where: (a) these are fresh foods; (b) the goods are no longer in fashion; (c) the goods are out of season; (d) a lawful promotional campaign is under way; (e) the enterprise faces bankruptcy etc; and (f) the price is set in order to comply with state policy on price stabilization.[8]

(2) Imposing irrational buying or selling prices or fixing minimum re-selling prices causing damage to customers. The word 'irrational' here is not a helpful one. It is, of course, entirely rational for a firm in possession of market power to profit-maximize and to set prices above the competitive level. 'Irrational purchase prices' are defined in art 27 of the Decree on Competition as arising where the purchasing price falls below the cost of production. Although it is clear that art 13(2) is intended to curtail exploitative dominant firm pricing it is, as discussed in Chapter 1-2, almost impossible to define with rigour an 'excessive price'. The Vietnamese approach is set out in the Decree on Competition at art 27(2), and is no more satisfactory than attempts made elsewhere. This states in full that:

> [t]he practice of fixing a selling price of goods or services shall be deemed unreasonable thereby causing loss to customers if demand does not suddenly increase to a level exceeding the designed output of the production capacity of the enterprise and the following two conditions are satisfied:
>
> (a) The average retail price set in the same relevant market for a minimum period of sixty consecutive days increases once at more than 5%, or increases

[7] Article 3(7) defines 'total cost' as meaning: '(a) cost of production of products or services; purchasing price of goods; (b) cost of circulation to bring goods, services to consumers'.

[8] art 23(2), Decree on Competition.

a number of times at a total level of more than 5% of the selling price prior to such minimum period;

(b) There are no extraordinary fluctuations resulting in an increase in the prime cost of producing such products or providing services of more than 5% for a minimum period of sixty consecutive days prior to the commencement of the price increase.

In effect this rubric appears to introduce as part of the Vietnamese antitrust law a price-control mechanism operating in respect of all enterprises which are either dominant or are monopolists. The inflexible nature of this provision is, in practice, likely to render it unworkable.

No gloss is given to the rubric in art 13(2), relating to minimum resale price maintenance ('RPM'), in the Decree other than to restate that this is unlawful.

(3) Restricting production, distribution of goods, services, limiting markets, preventing technical development, causing damage to customers. This clause would extend to refusals to supply and would possibly, even absent express language, support the application of an essential facilities doctrine.[9] The Decree on Competition differentiates between 'restraining production etc', 'limiting the market', and 'impeding technical development'. Under the first rubric three practices are prohibited: (a) reducing supply where there are no large fluctuations in the supply and demand conditions; (b) 'fixing the amount of goods or services to be supplied at a level sufficient to create a market shortage'; and (c) hoarding goods in order to create instability.[10] It need hardly be stated that these provisions are severely interventionist. The second rubric sees the prohibition of restrictions of supply to specific geographical areas, and 'purchasing goods or services from only one or a number of specified sources'.[11] Again this provision, which appears to create an obligation to purchase on a dominant or monopoly enterprise, is remarkable. Although there is an exception where 'other sources fail to satisfy the conditions set by the purchaser'—which arguably is so widely drafted as to render the prohibition an irrelevance—the article is, if applied literally, overly invasive on normal commercial relations, and in particular does not take into account the efficiencies that may flow from a stable contractual relationship. The final rubric relating to impeding technical development prohibits the acquisition of intellectual property in order to prevent its use, or threatening a person engaged in technical research to abandon that research.[12]

[9] Some sector-specific regulation in Vietnam, such as the Telecommunications Law of 2002 and the Electricity Law of 2004 makes reference to requirements to provide access to facilities.

[10] art 28(1), Decree on Competition.

[11] art 28(2), Decree on Competition.

[12] art 28(3), Decree on Competition.

(4) Imposing discrimination 'in order to create inequality in competition'. The explanation of this rubric in the Decree on Competition is robust to criticism. It is stated in art 29 of the Decree that it is unlawful to discriminate 'in order to place one or a number of enterprises in a better competitive position than other enterprises'. Discrimination may be found to exist in relation to prices, payment terms, and volumes. However, the limitation of this principle would appear to permit, for example, Ramsey pricing (see Chapter 1-2, above).

(5) Imposing obligations in sales contracts which 'have no direct connection with the subject of such contracts' (ie practices such as full-line forcing, tie-in sales, or exclusive dealing commitments). Five practices are expressly prohibited under this rubric: (a) restrictions relating to other goods and services; (b) imposing geographical restrictions on sales; (c) imposing restrictions on sales to customers who are purchasing to resell; (d) restrictions on the forms and quantities of goods to be supplied (although in practice of course any contract is likely to stipulate both the form of the good to be supplied and the quantity to be supplied—there is no definition of the term 'restriction'); and (e) tying.[13]

(6) 'Preventing new competition from entering the market'. It is unlawful for a dominant or a monopoly enterprise to: (a) request customers not to trade with a new competitor; (b) threaten or compel distributors not to handle the goods of a new competitor; and (c) sell goods at prices such that a new competitor is not able to access the market.[14] In the latter case it should be noted that this is not a rigorous application of a predatory pricing rule, as there is no requirement here that the sale should be below cost, and an inefficient entrant may find themselves shielded by this rule if it is applied literally.

At the time of writing there have been no cases in which this article has been applied, and notwithstanding the terms of the Decree on Competition guidance is limited, such that it is not possible with any certainty to predict the circumstances in which the article will be invoked, the degree of competitive harm that must be demonstrated for the prohibitions to take force, and the extent to which conduct may be justified on objective efficiency-enhancing grounds. **6-3.12**

Article 14 creates two further strictures that apply to monopolies: (1) 'imposing unfavourable conditions on customers';[15] and (2) using the monopoly power held **6-3.13**

[13] art 30, Decree on Competition. Tying is defined as 'tying the purchase or sale of goods and services which are the subject matter of the contract to the purchase of other goods and services from a pre-nominated supplier or other entity'.

[14] art 31, Decree on Competition. Goods may be sold at low prices in the circumstances specified in art 23 of the Decree (see above).

[15] These are conditions which can 'cause difficulty to the customer during the process of performance of the contract' (art 32, Decree on Competition).

'to unilaterally modify or cancel the contracts already signed without plausible reasons'.[16]

6-3.14 The provisions of the VLOC relating to unfair competition acts may be applied to all enterprises, including those holding dominant or monopoly positions. Two of these provisions may be considered to be 'antitrust'-related: (1) constraining customers or business partners of other enterprises from transacting with those enterprises;[17] and (2) disturbing the lawful business activities of other enterprises.[18]

State-monopolized domains

6-3.15 State monopolies, including those in the utilities sectors, are subject, as stated above, to the VLOC, but art 15 severely limits the application of the general proscriptions to them. The article makes clear that it is the role of the State to control these enterprises, and that this control extends to: setting prices, setting production quantities, determining the scope of conduct, ordering goods or services, planning, and bidding. In the event that such enterprises engage in 'activities outside the State-monopolized domains' they are subject only then to the general provisions of the VLOC.

---

16 It is unlawful for the monopolist to change or cancel 'unilaterally a signed contract without prior notice to the customer where there is no liability to bear any sanction', or 'based on one or more reasons not directly related to essential conditions in order to continue to implement fully the contract where there is no liability to bear any sanction' (art 33, Decree on Competition).

17 art 42, VLOC.

18 art 44, VLOC. The penalties for breach of this provision are spelt out at arts 32 and 34 of the Decree on Dealing with Breaches in the Competition Sector ('DDB'). A fine of from Dong5m to Dong10m may be imposed. Where a disruption of business is directed at the largest customer or business partner of a competitor, or where the disruption results in the disrupted enterprise being unable to conduct normal business, the penalty may be Dong10m to Dong20m (art 32(2), DDB).

6-4

VIETNAM MERGER CONTROL

Introduction	6-4.01	**Remedies**	6-4.13
Concentrations	6-4.02	Other investigations	6-4.14
Exemption	6-4.05	**Territorial Application**	6-4.15
Notification and Procedure	6 4.08		

Introduction

Vietnam's merger control regime is given effect in s 3 of Chapter 2 of the VLOC **6-4.01** (arts 16–24). This is the first law in Vietnam which regulates mergers in a comprehensive manner. The provisions apply to 'economic concentrations', which may take a number of forms: mergers, consolidations, acquisitions, joint ventures, and 'other acts of economic concentration prescribed by law'.[1] Concentrations which give rise to the creation of specified market share thresholds are prohibited unless an exemption is granted under art 19. The granting of exemptions is somewhat politicized given the vagueness of some of the exemption criteria and by virtue of the fact that in certain cases the power to grant an exemption is vested exclusively in the Prime Minister. The law specifically recognizes the 'failing firm defence', and also acknowledges an 'efficiency defence', although this term is not used. Mergers may also be cleared where they give rise to any of a wide range of benefits, some of which are only unclearly defined. Notification is compulsory, unless mergers fall under certain defined thresholds (see below). Generally the Company Law of 1990 recognizes that members of limited liability companies have the right to take decisions relating to the merger of the company of which they are members, and that they have the right to transfer their shares. The Law

[1] art 16, VLOC.

on State-Owned Enterprises of 1995 specifically recognizes that mergers may be a legitimate means of restructuring.[2]

Concentrations

6-4.02 As noted above, art 16 of the VLOC specifies a number of different arrangements as giving rise to concentrations falling within the Law. These are defined as follows.

(1) A merger 'means an act whereby one or several enterprises transfer all of its/their property, rights, obligations and legitimate interests to another enterprise, and at the same time terminate the existence of the merged enterprise(s)'.[3]

(2) A consolidation refers to a situation in which two or more existing enterprises transfer their property, rights and obligations to a new enterprise and at the same time terminate their existence.[4]

(3) The term 'acquisition' refers to any situation in which one enterprise acquires either the whole of another enterprise, or a part of it 'sufficient to control or dominate all or one of the trades' of the acquired party.[5] There is no definition of 'control' set out in the VLOC, but the Decree on Competition states, at art 34, that this situation arises where an enterprise gains 50 per cent of the voting rights at the general meeting, or 'at a level which according to law or the charter of the controlled enterprise is sufficient to enable the controlling enterprise to govern the financial policies and operations of the controlled enterprise'. An acquisition is not deemed to have occurred where a financial institution acquires an enterprise with the intention of selling it within a year, as long as it does not exercise its right to control or govern the enterprise.[6]

(4) A joint venture ('JV') may be classed as giving rise to a concentration where 'two or more enterprises jointly contribute part of their property, rights, obligations and legitimate interests to the establishment of a new enterprise'.[7] This is a somewhat loose definition, and leaves open the question of the extent to which the parties to the JV allocate control over the JV between them.

---

[2] In addition, art 44 of the Law on Cooperatives of 1997 states that cooperatives may merge. Articles 94 and 95 of the Civil Code of 2005 also provide for mergers and consolidations of legal persons. Under these provisions legal persons may merge with other legal persons of the same type following an agreement to do so or following a decision by a competent state agency.

[3] art 17(1), VLOC.

[4] art 17(2), VLOC.

[5] art 17(3), VLOC.

[6] art 35, Decree on Competition.

[7] art 17(4), VLOC.

6-4.03 Article 18 prohibits all such concentrations where 'the combined market shares of enterprises participating in [the] economic concentration account for over 50% on the relevant market', unless cases fall within the provisions of art 19, or where, even after the implementation of the concentration, the parties remain small or medium-sized enterprises, as prescribed in the law. Market shares are determined in accordance with the procedures discussed in Chapter 6-3, above, unless the relevant enterprise is a newly established one. In this case the Decree on Competition sets out two relevant provisions under which market shares may be determined on the basis of as low as one month's figures.[8] There is no competition test set out in art 18, such that the analysis of the merger may, unless the parties seek to rely on the art 19 exemption, be devoid of any economic reasoning, save for a formalistic market-share calculation exercise.

6-4.04 Recent statements from the Competition Administration Department ('VCAD') suggest that it will pay particular attention to mergers in which the parties have combined market shares in excess of 30 per cent, and that it has decided to increase its activity and profile in the area of merger control. However, there is, at the time of writing, no evidence of an increased vigilance.

Exemption

6-4.05 Under the terms of art 19 exemptions to mergers that would otherwise prima facie be prohibited may be granted in two circumstances. The first of these, specified in art 19(1) is that the failing firm defence applies, such that 'one or more of the participants . . . is/are in danger of dissolution or bankrputcy'.[9] There are no further criteria specified in the VLOC as to the determination of the immediacy of the failure, or as to the consideration of whether other, less restrictive, arrangements might exist which would mitigate against the failure. Decisions in relation to this clause may be made by the Minister of Industry and Trade. The second, more general, exemption of art 19(2) allows for mergers to be cleared where the concentration 'has an effect of expanding exports or contributing to socio-economic

[8] art 13(2), (3). The Decree is silent as to how market shares are to be ascertained in the case that there is a proposal to initiate a new enterprise which falls within the concentration provisions, but where there is, as at the time of notification or request for an exemption, no turnover.

[9] art 19(1), VLOC. The Decree on Competition states that: '[a]n enterprise which is currently at risk of being dissolved means an enterprise in the category of enterprises for which the law or its charter prescribes that it be dissolved but it has not yet conducted dissolution procedures or it is currently conducting dissolution procedures but there is not yet a dissolution decision from the competent body pursuant to law'. An enterprise currently at risk of becoming bankrupt 'means an enterprise as stipulated by the Law on Bankruptcy' (art 36). If an application for an exemption is made under art 19(1) (see below) that relies on this criterion, a report must be included that '*proves* that one or more of the parties participating in the [concentration] is currently at risk of being dissolved or becoming bankrupt' (art 40(2), Decree on Competition).

development, technical and technological advance'. The second part of this latter rubric is so general as to extend, without further guidance, to a wide range of claimed benefits, including, inter alia, efficiencies, saving jobs, industrial restructuring, the creation of national champions (also expressly recognized in the first clause), and environmental considerations. The Decree on Competition requires that any such application be accompanied by an explanatory report 'in the form of a feasibility study either formulated or evaluated by a science and technology organization or a research and development organization established pursuant to the Law on Science and Technology'.[10] Only the Prime Minister has the right to make final decisions in relation to the application of art 19(2). The exemption procedures that apply are similar to, and in parts identical to, those which apply in respect of exemption applications made in respect of agreements (see Chapter 6-2, above).

6-4.06 In the event that merging parties wish to rely on art 19 they are required to submit a dossier setting out their arguments as to why this provision should apply, as an alternative to making the otherwise requisite notification.[11] Dossiers must be submitted by the parties, or by a duly appointed lawful representative.[12] Exemption dossiers must contain: (1) the application in a specified form; (2) business registration details of those parties engaging in the concentration; (3) duly audited financial statements of the relevant enterprises for the last two years; (4) reports for the last two years on market shares of the participating enterprises; (5) 'a report elaborating the satisfaction of the cases eligible for exemption';[13] and (6) written authorization of the representative appointed by the parties to submit the dossier.[14] A fee must be paid in respect of any exemption dossier submitted. This is not refundable should the parties decide to abandon the application.[15] Exemption dossiers are to be submitted to the VCAD, which must within seven days acknowledge their receipt, or specify that the dossier is incomplete, and detail the contents that remain to be submitted.[16] The VCAD may request further information from the parties even after it has acknowledged that the dossier is complete if such information is necessary, and may require the parties to provide explanations as to the

---

[10] art 40.

[11] art 20(2), VLOC.

[12] arts 26 and 27, VLOC.

[13] The Decree on Competition requires that any such application be accompanied by an explanatory report 'in the form of a feasibility study either formulated or evaluated by a science and technology organization or a research and development organization established pursuant to the Law on Science and Technology' (art 40).

[14] art 26, VLOC.

[15] art 30, VLOC.

[16] art 30, VLOC.

material submitted.[17] Information may also be requested from any relevant third parties, including suppliers, customers, competitors, and government agencies.[18]

The Minister of Industry and Trade, in the case of the application of art 19(1), shall either approve or disapprove the exemption within a period of sixty days. This time period may be twice extended by up to a maximum of thirty days in the event that the case 'involves many complicated circumstances'.[19] The total period that may elapse therefore between the making of the complete submission and the taking of a final decision is 127 (7 + 60 + 30 + 30) working days, which is longer than that in relation to notifications which fall to be dealt with solely in terms of whether art 18 is to be applied or not (see below). In the case of decisions in relation to art 19(2) to be made by the Prime Minister the period allowed is ninety days from the receipt of the completed dossier, or in the case of complex cases, an extremely long period of 180 days. No extensions may be made.[20] **6-4.07**

Notification and Procedure

Notification of concentrations falling within the terms of art 17 is compulsory prior to the consummation of the merger where the merging parties hold a combined market share, pre-merger, of 30 per cent or greater, leaving it to the parties to make their own market share assessment. Notifications are not required where the market shares fall below these levels or where, post-merger, the parties would still be small or medium-sized enterprises.[21] As noted above, where a party seeks to claim the benefit of an exemption in relation to a notifiable concentration, an alternative procedure under which a different dossier is required is stipulated. The VCAD has issued notification forms.[22] **6-4.08**

The notification dossier is required to contain the material set out in art 21 of the Law: (1) a written notification in a form to be set by the VCAD; (2) valid copies of business registration certificates of all notifying parties; (3) duly audited financial statements of all parties for the most recent two years; (4) a list of 'dependent units' (subsidiaries) of each of the parties; (5) details of the goods and services dealt in by the parties and their subsidiaries; and (6) reports detailing market shares **6-4.09**

---

[17] art 31, VLOC.

[18] art 32, VLOC. Article 41 of the Decree on Competition makes further provision in respect of the obligations of the VCAD to seek information from relevant state organizations, and the responsibility of those organizations to provide it.

[19] art 34, VLOC.

[20] art 34(3), VLOC.

[21] art 20(1), VLOC.

[22] These forms are published under the authority conferred by Decision 17/QD-QLCT, 4 July 2006 (see Form MD–4).

of each of the participating enterprises for the last two years. The parties are responsible for ensuring the truthfulness of the information submitted. Notification is to be made to the VCAD which is to acknowledge its receipt within seven working days.[23] Where the VCAD finds that the dossier is incomplete it is to notify the parties of this, and 'to clearly point out the contents that have to be supplemented'.

6-4.10 Once a complete notification dossier has been accepted by the VCAD it has 45 working days within which to make one of two decisions: (a) that the concentration does not fall within one of the prohibitions; or (b) that the concentration is prohibited under art 18 of the VLOC. In the latter case the VCAD is required to 'clearly state' its reasons for applying the prohibition in writing. However, as the prohibition is a presumptive one which makes no reference to a competition test, but only to the meeting of market share thresholds it may be presumed that such 'clearly stated' reasons may be limited to a statement of the finding that the market share thresholds that invoke the prohibition are satisfied. The forty-five working-day period may be extended by a maximum of thirty working days, up to two times, in the event that the concentration 'involves many complicated circumstances'.[24] This is to say that in complicated cases there may be a period of review which extends up to a maximum of 112 working days (7 + 45 + 30 + 30).

6-4.11 In 2007 only one merger notification was submitted to the VCAD,[25] which suggests that many merging parties choose simply to ignore the merger procedures, or to resolve matters by informal contacts prior to any formal mechanism being invoked. More significantly perhaps, as at mid-2008 there had been some twenty instances of consultations taking place between the VCAD and parties contemplating mergers.

6-4.12 It remains the case that the application of a merger regime based purely on market share thresholds raises difficulties. The definition of a relevant market, and the determination of shares within that market are both matters which may be contested. The VCAD appears to be in favour of revising the law to incorporate a notification requirement based on turnover.

---

[23] art 22, VLOC.

[24] art 23(2), VLOC. Where an extension is made the parties must be notified in writing no later than three days before the end of the originally set time limit. Although the law does not state this it may be presumed that the parties may themselves ask the VCAD to extend the time limit if they have reason to believe that a longer period is more likely to lead to a favourable outcome, this would be at the discretion of the VCAD. There is no right to appeal against the extension of the time limit.

[25] This involved the acquisition by a Thai company of a subsidiary of the Vietnam National Oil and Gas Group. The merger was abandoned for reasons other than the regulatory hurdle set by Vietnam.

Remedies

Remedies and procedures generally are dealt with in Chapter 6-5. In respect of concentrations which have been unlawfully entered into the DDB states that, in addition to the imposition of penalties, 'the merging enterprises may be subject to compulsory demerger from the merged enterprise and the merged enterprise may be subject to compulsory split in order to restore the former status quo'.[26] Similarly, where assets have been acquired such that an illegal concentration has occurred 'the acquiring enterprise may be compulsorily required to re-sell the assets it acquired'.[27] The DDB is silent on the procedures to be applied, and on the approach to be taken in circumstances where it is difficult or impossible to force a divestiture. **6-4.13**

Other investigations

In the event that parties do not notify a merger that falls within the ambit of the VLOC the merger cannot lawfully be consummated. However, where a merger does proceed the VCAD, in conjunction with the Competition Council ('VCC'), has the power to conduct investigations into suspected breaches of the VLOC either on receipt of a complaint or on its own initiative (see Chapter 6-5, below). Article 89 anticipates that such investigations may relate to concentration situations, stating that in the event an official investigation takes place it shall determine (a) the relevant market, (b) the party's market share, and (c) evidence relating to violations. The time limit for such an investigation is 180 days after the decision to launch it is taken. Investigations cannot be opened more than two years after the date of the alleged infringement. In the case of a consummated merger that would be two years from the date of the transaction to which the VLOC applied. **6-4.14**

Territorial Application

It is the case in Vietnam, as mentioned in Chapter 1-1, that most large-scale mergers involve foreign parties in some way. As stated in Chapter 6-1, the VLOC applies to 'foreign enterprises operating in Vietnam'.[28] There is no limiting language here, such as the requirements for the application of the effects doctrine under US antitrust law, so the question is one of whether the enterprises are **6-4.15**

---

[26] See, eg art 25, DDB.
[27] art 27, DDB.
[28] art 2(1), VLOC.

'operating' in Vietnam. It is certainly the case that where a 'foreign' enterprise has a subsidiary in Vietnam the latter may be subject to the merger control provisions of the VLOC. It may be presumed to be the case that where a foreign company purchases a Vietnamese company, the merger too may fall within the jurisdiction of the VLOC, although if the foreign company was not previously doing business in Vietnam there will be no impact on market shares. The question of what may be the case where two foreign companies selling into Vietnam merge is less clear. Whether jurisdiction may be asserted will depend on the extent to which selling into Vietnam constitutes 'operating' in Vietnam. If the companies are selling directly into Vietnam it may be the case that they are considered to be operating there. Whether jurisdiction could *effectively* be asserted in such a case however is uncertain.

6-5

VIETNAM PROCEDURE

Introduction	6-5.01	**Rights of the Parties**	6-5.25
Investigations and Evidence	6-5.06	**Remedies and Penalties**	6-5.27
Hearings	6-5.19	Leniency	6-5.34
Complaints	6-5.21	**Third Party Rights**	6-5.35
Other third parties	6-5.24	**Appeals**	6-5.36

Introduction

Chapter 5 of the Vietnam Law on Competition ('VLOC') which deals with the investigation and handling of competition cases[1] is the longest chapter of the Law, containing details relating to investigative procedures, the participants in them including those in the responsible agencies, hearings, the effect of decisions taken, complaints about decisions, and the treatment accorded to violations of the legislation. The VLOC is supplemented by the Decree on Competition, which deals primarily with substantive provisions, but which does contain procedural provisions, and the Decree on Dealing with Breaches in the Competition Sector (hereinafter 'DDB'), which provides substantial further detail to the procedural provisions of the VLOC. **6-5.01**

Cases which are competition cases are to be determined in accordance with the VLOC. Cases which are unfair competition cases, which as has been noted above is of only limited application to antitrust, are to be dealt with under the terms of the VLOC *and* administrative law requirements.[2] Actions may be brought by the agencies on the basis of either complaints—although as discussed below **6-5.02**

[1] 'Competition cases' are defined in art 3(8) of the VLOC as meaning 'a case showing signs of violation of the provisions of this Law, which is investigated and handled by a competent state agency according to law provisions'.

[2] art 56, VLOC.

complainants may not have strong incentives to complain given that they face liabilities and expenses—or on the own initiative of the Competition Administration Department ('VCAD'). The VCAD has a general power in the enforcement of the VLOC, but cases which are deemed to fall within the 'competition-restricting' provisions of the Law are to be investigated in most cases by the Competition Council ('VCC'), after the case has been passed to it by the VCAD, with the VCC making final decisions following a hearing. A general principle in the operation of the VLOC is that:

> [a]ny offence must be identified promptly and dealt with expeditiously, justly and thoroughly; and the consequences arising from the offence must be rectified correctly as stipulated by law.[3]

6-5.03 A particular characteristic of the Vietnamese regime is the extent of fees that are applied in its administration. It was noted in Chapters 6-2 and 6-4 that fees are levied when parties apply for exemptions. Fees are also imposed in respect of case-handling procedures, and any party found to have violated the VLOC is to pay an administrative fee related to the procedure, irrespective of any corrective orders made. No fees are payable in the event that the investigated parties are found not to have violated the VLOC.[4] The following fees are applicable: unfair competition case, Dong10m; competition case, Dong100m.[5]

6-5.04 An appeals procedure is available, but in the first instance the adjudicating body is that which has made the contested decision (see below).

6-5.05 The procedures to be applied in the operation of the Vietnamese antitrust regime are not the most straightforward ones. Figure 6-5.1 provides a simplified schema of the system.

Investigations and Evidence

6-5.06 Investigations into parties who are suspected of breaching the VLOC may be commenced either at the initiative of the VCAD or on receipt of a complaint dossier from a complainant (see further below).[6] In both cases a limitation period of two years applies, timed from the date of the alleged infringement, after which a complaint cannot lawfully be made, or an own-initiative investigation

[3] art 3(a), DDB.

[4] arts 62 and 63, VLOC.

[5] art 53, Decree on Competition. A significant part of the Decree deals with fees and the collection thereof.

[6] art 65, VLOC. See also art 86, VLOC.

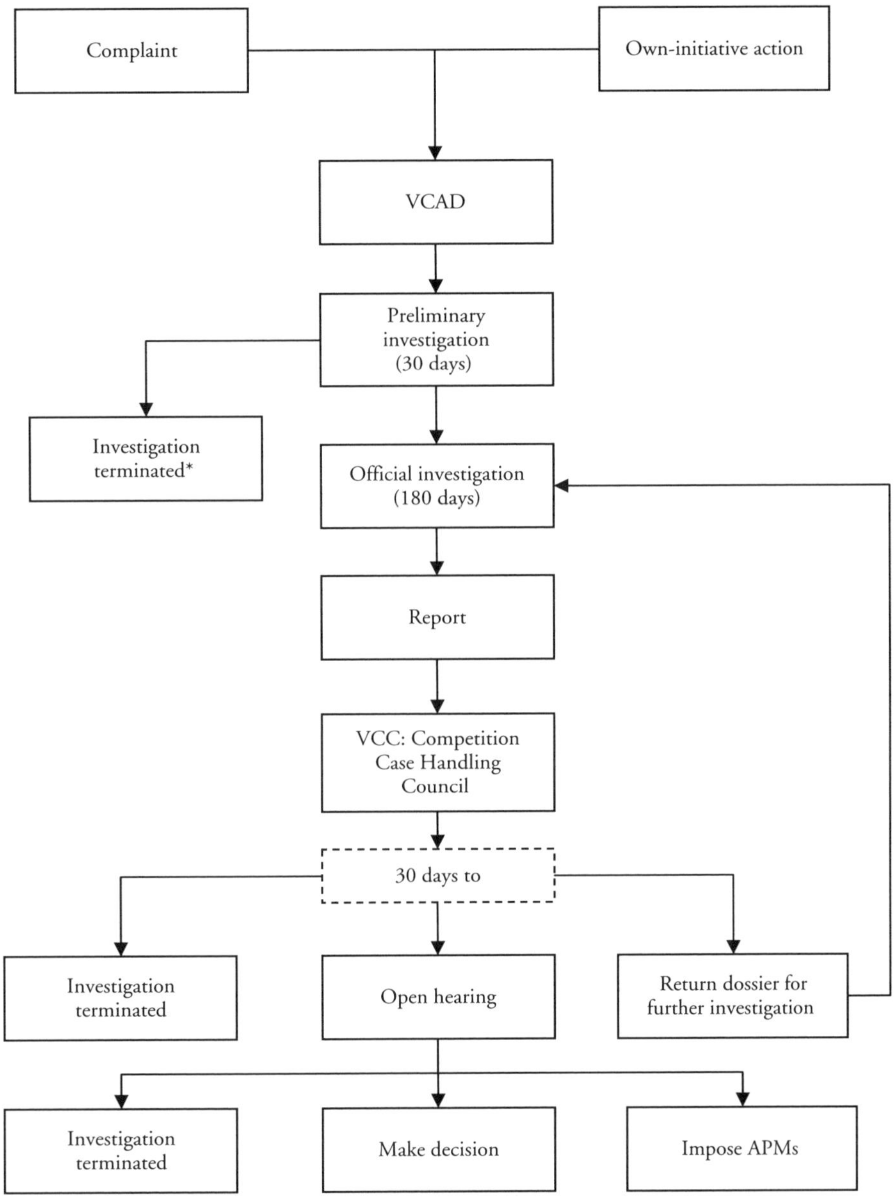

Figure 6-5.1 Competition enforcement procedures in Vietnam.
* In all cases to date this has been the outcome

commenced.[7] Investigations may not be initiated by the VCC, which becomes involved in competition cases only when a case is passed to it by the VCAD. The VLOC sets out at different places the powers of the VCAD and the VCC in relation to competition cases.

6-5.07 Although the rules relating to the collation of evidence during an investigation are exhaustive some matters are not required to be proven. These are specified in art 75 of the Decree on Competition, which states that three 'elements and events shall not be required to be proven': (a) 'clear elements and events which everyone knows and which are recognized' by the relevant body; (b) relevant matters which have been determined in legally effective decisions and judgments of courts or administrative bodies; and (c) those matters which are recorded in legally authenticated notarized documents.

6-5.08 The VLOC distinguishes two different types of investigation: preliminary investigations,[8] and 'official investigations'.[9] The preliminary investigation, the content of which is not specified, must be concluded within (a somewhat rapid) 30 days of the issuance of a decision to conduct the investigation.[10] By the end of this period the investigation must either be terminated or an official investigation must be opened. The content of official investigations relating to restrictive agreements, abuse of dominant position or monopoly, and concentrations is limited to: (a) identifying the relevant markets; (b) verifying the market share of the investigated party; and (c) collecting and analysing evidence relating to acts that violate the VLOC.[11] The time limit for an official investigation is 180 days from the date of the issuance of the decision to commence the investigation, although this may, 'in case of necessity', be extended by up to sixty days on no more than two occasions, leading to a possible total of 300 days.

---

[7] art 9(2), DDB however states that:

> If during the [limitation period] an organization or individual commits a new breach of the laws on competition, or deliberately evades or prevents the breach being dealt with by the competent body, the limitation period. . . shall be re-calculated from the date on which the new breach is committed or from the date of termination of the conduct to evade dealing with the breach or to prevent the breach being dealt with.

[8] arts 86–88, VLOC.

[9] arts 88–90, VLOC.

[10] art 87(1), VLOC. Where decisions or documents are required to be served on parties, art 68 of the Decree on Competition states that three methods are acceptable: (1) personal delivery, or delivery via the post office or authorized third party; (2) public display; (3) notification via the mass media. Further rules are set out in arts 69–73 of the Decree.

[11] art 89, VLOC. On the face of it the contents of this investigation do not permit sensitive analyses of markets. For example, although it is the task of the investigation to determine the market share of the party under investigation there is no reference to determining the wider competitive picture as might be determined by an analysis of the market shares of other parties under investigation, or the ease of entry into the market. In the case of investigations into breaches of the provisions on unfair competition the 'investigators must identify the grounds to deem that the investigated parties have performed or are performing unfair competition acts' (art 89(2), VLOC).

The Head of the VCAD is given the power: (1) to assign investigators to a particular case; (2) to monitor their actions; (3) to modify or cancel 'groundless and illegal decisions' made by them; (4) to change the investigators; (5) to request expertise (see below); (6) to apply, modify, or cancel APMs (see below); (7) to initiate preliminary investigations, terminate investigations, or conduct official investigations falling under the competence of the VCAD; (8) to invite witnesses; (9) to sign written conclusions on the case; (10) to transfer cases to the VCC where these relate to 'competition-restricting acts'; and (11) to 'settle complaints and denunciations' falling under the VCAD's competence.[12] **6-5.09**

'Investigators' have substantial power in the decision-making process in Vietnam, and their role is not limited merely to the collection of relevant evidence.[13] Once investigators are appointed these have the power to request that 'necessary' information and documents be supplied by relevant organizations and individuals, including those under investigation.[14] Parties may be required to give 'explanations' relating to the case. Investigators may not take testimony from complainants or other persons unless they have not produced an explanation of the relevant matters in written form.[15] Where testimony is taken this can happen only at the headquarters of the VCAD or the VCC.[16] **6-5.10**

It is also the function of investigators to propose the application of administrative preventive measures ('APMs'), where they conclude that this is necessary.[17] APMs may be applied by the Head of the VCAD and by the Chairman of the VCC at the instigation of complainants (see above), investigators, or presidents of hearings held by the VCC. Article 76(6) gives the Head of the VCAD the power to apply, alter, or cancel APMs pending the transfer of case dossiers to the VCC, and the Chairman of the VCC has a corresponding power when receiving competition case dossiers.[18] Parties subject to APMs may lodge complaints (appeals) about the decisions taken in accordance with the provisions of the VLOC (see below).[19] Those subject to APMs may claim compensation from complainants where it is **6-5.11**

---

[12] art 76, VLOC.

[13] The law specifies the evidence that may be used in the course of VCAD and VCC investigations, although this is of such a general description as to be very inclusive, including, 'exhibits' ('. . . things used as tools or means for commissioning of violations, money and other things having the effect of proving acts of violating the provisions of this Law' (art 60(2)(a), VLOC)), testimonies of witnesses, and explanations offered by organizations and individuals, original documents or duly notarized copies of documents, and expert opinions.

[14] art 77, VLOC. See also art 3, Enforcement Decree, which requires those providing information, including state bodies, financial, credit and accounting or auditing organizations to 'promptly provide necessary information which is complete, truthful and accurate'.

[15] art 78(1), Decree on Competition.

[16] art 78(2), Decree on Competition.

[17] art 77(4), VLOC.

[18] art 79(4), VLOC.

[19] art 61(5), VLOC.

found that the complaint wrongly led to the imposition of an APM (see below), and in cases where APMs are applied that are in variance of the requests of investigators or hearing presidents, causing damage. In the latter cases the VCAD or VCC and the harmed parties are to attempt to reach an agreement as to the level of compensation. If no agreement can be reached the wronged parties may bring lawsuits under the appropriate civil procedures.[20] Article 88 of the Decree on Competition sets out five such measures that may be taken during the course of an investigation: (1) temporary detention of a person; (2) temporary detention of material evidence; (3) the carrying out of body searches; (4) the carrying out of searches of vehicles and 'other objects'; and (5) searches of places.[21] Article 88(4) thus opens up the possibility of 'dawn raids' being conducted where the investigators consider this necessary.[22] Such searches for evidence may be conducted both at business premises and at private residences, although in the case of the latter it is necessary to obtain further administrative approvals.

6-5.12 Article 78(1) provides that investigators must notify the parties of the fact that a duly authorized investigation is under way, which appears to preclude the possibility of an investigation being conducted without the parties' knowledge, which may seriously undermine enforcement efforts in relation to hard-core anti-competitive activity. Investigators are required to preserve the business secrets of enterprises,[23] to preserve the relevant documents,[24] and to make 'minutes' of their investigations.[25] At the end of either a preliminary or an official investigation they are required to deliver a report on the investigation, which must contain: (a) a brief account of the case; (b) 'verified circumstances and evidence'; and (c) proposals as to the measures to be taken.[26] At the termination of an investigation the Head of the VCAD is required to pass on the investigation reports, together with the entire case dossier, to the VCC where the cases relate to competition-restricting acts.[27] Investigations may be supported by a number of other bodies, including the police, at the request of the VCAD.[28]

6-5.13 When an investigation is underway both those subject to investigation and complainants have similar obligations, in that they must, whichever agency is

---

[20] art 61(4), VLOC. The Law further provides that in such cases disciplinary action should be brought against those responsible, and that they may be forced to indemnify the VCAD or VCC against the damages.

[21] See further arts 89–95, Decree on Competition.

[22] See art 94, Decree on Competition.

[23] art 78(2), VLOC.

[24] art 78(3), VLOC.

[25] art 91, VLOC. The contents of these minutes is specified in art 91. Minutes must be signed by the parties, unless they refuse to do so, in which case a record will be made of this by the investigators.

[26] art 93(2), VLOC.

[27] art 93(1), VLOC.

[28] art 97, VLOC.

conducting the investigation: (a) 'supply full, truthful, accurate evidence in a timely manner related to their proposals or requests'; (b) 'appear in response to the summonses of the [VCAD] or the [VCC]'; and (c) 'abide by decisions' of the relevant organizations.[29] Both the parties under investigation and complainants on whose request cases are being brought may be represented by lawyers during the course of proceedings in order 'to protect the legitimate rights and interests of the parties they represent'.[30]

Witnesses may be called during the course of the investigation either at the initiative of the case-handling team, or at the request of the parties to the case.[31] These may be required to supply documents or 'things' related to the case, to give testimony[32] and to participate in hearings. Experts may also be called where these have 'necessary knowledge about the matters'.[33] They may be given access to, and asked to comment on, materials held by the investigating agency and may raise questions in relation to the case, and may also 'write their opinions on the written general conclusions if disagreeing with the general conclusions'.[34] The agency is not bound to allow experts to participate in proceedings, but if it refuses to do so is to give reasons in writing.[35] Experts and witnesses may also be summonsed to appear at hearings held by the Competition Case Handling Council. **6-5.14**

Some of the procedures to be applied in the VCC are similar to those which apply to investigations conducted by the VCAD, although where the VCC requires that further investigation be undertaken this falls within the purview of the investigators assigned to the VCAD.[36] The Chairman of the VCC is required to establish a 'Competition Case Handling Council' ('CCHC'),[37] which is to 'work independently',[38] when he receives a competition case dossier from the VCAD.[39] **6-5.15**

[29] art 66(3), VLOC.

[30] art 67, VLOC. Lawyers must 'fully meet the procedure-participating conditions prescribed by legislation on lawyers' (art 67(1)). The full rights, and importantly, the obligations, of the lawyers participating in proceedings are set out in the article.

[31] art 68, VLOC. See also art 92 which sets out the rules under which involved parties may request that witnesses be invited.

[32] Testimony may not be compelled where it would relate to state or professional secrets, or where it would 'disadvantageously affect' parties who are 'close relatives' (art 68(2)(e), VLOC).

[33] art 69, VLOC. Experts may be appointed on the initiative of the head of the VCAD or the VCC (art 80, Decree on Competition).

[34] art 69(2)(g), VLOC.

[35] art 72, VLOC.

[36] art 96, VLOC. In the event that such further investigations are required the time limit for their completion is 60 days after the making of the request.

[37] Article 54(3) states that this is to be 'composed of at least five members of the [VCC], one of whom shall chair hearings to deal with a specific competition case'.

[38] art 80(1), VLOC.

[39] art 99, VLOC.

6-5.16 Within thirty days of the receipt of the case dossier the CCHC is to: (a) open a hearing; (b) return the dossier for additional investigation where it finds that the evidence presented is not sufficient to determine whether a violation of the VLOC has taken place;[40] or (c) terminate the case.[41] Cases may be terminated in one of three circumstances: (1) the Head of the VCAD proposes this and the CCHC agrees;[42] (2) the party under investigation has voluntarily terminated the infringement and the complainant withdraws its complaint; and (3) in the case of own-initiative investigations, where the party terminates the alleged infringement, and the Head of the VCAD proposes the termination of the investigation.[43] Decisions of the CCHC are cast by majority vote.[44]

6-5.17 A president for a hearing (see below) shall be appointed from within the members of the CCHC. The president has the following powers: (1) to organize the study of competition case dossiers; (2) on the basis of decisions made by the CCHC, to propose to the VCC Chairman the imposition of APMs, their modification or cancellation, request additional investigations, or the termination of the investigation; (3) sign the decision to open a hearing; (4) summon participants to the hearing; and (5) sign and announce the decision on the handling of the case, and other decisions of the CCHC.[45]

6-5.18 Following a hearing the CCHC is required to make a decision which is to contain a brief account of the case, an analysis, and conclusions.[46] Decisions come into force thirty days after they have been signed, unless there is an appeal ('complaint') under art 107 of the VLOC (see below).

Hearings[47]

6-5.19 Hearings must be held in relation to all competition cases falling to be determined by the VCC.[48] Article 101 of the Decree on Competition states that:

> [a] council dealing with a competition case must directly determine the elements of a competition case by questioning and by hearing explanations from complainants,

[40] See also art 100, VLOC.
[41] art 99(2), VLOC.
[42] This may be the case where there is insufficient evidence of breaches of the law.
[43] art 101, VLOC.
[44] art 80(2), VLOC. Where the vote is tied, the president of the hearing in question has the casting vote.
[45] art 81, VLOC. For each hearing constituted within the VCC a clerk is appointed, whose duties are determined by art 82, VLOC. It is his/her job to prepare the groundwork for the hearing, to announce its rules, and to prepare minutes. The clerk is not in any sense a 'hearing officer' in the context of EC proceedings. It is not the role of the clerk to ensure that, for example, the proceedings are conducted fairly and impartially.
[46] art 105, VLOC.
[47] See generally arts 101–130, Decree on Competition.
[48] art 98, VLOC.

> from parties subject to investigation, from persons with related interests and obligations and from other participants; by considering and checking collated data and evidence; and by hearing the investigator who previously investigated the competition case summarise his conclusions on the investigation. A decision dealing with a competition case shall only be based on the results of questioning during the investigative hearing, on open debate and on evidence which has been considered and checked during the investigative hearing.

Where the CCHC decides to proceed to a hearing it must open this within fifteen days of making such a decision.[49] Decisions to open hearings must be communicated to the parties at least ten days before the date of the opening of the hearing.[50] Persons to attend will also be sent summonses, again with at least a (short) ten days' notice.[51] The general presumption is that hearings are to be held in public, save for circumstances in which the contents relate to national or business secrets.[52] Following a hearing the CCHC is to make its decision by secret vote. **6-5.20**

Complaints

Those who believe that their rights and/or interests have been infringed by parties in breach of the terms of the VLOC may lodge a complaint with the VCAD, taking the form of a complaint dossier.[53] The limitations period for complaints to be brought is two years from the date of the alleged infringement. Article 58 requires complaint dossiers to contain a written complaint in the form required by the VCAD, and evidence of the alleged violation. Unusually parties submitting a complaint are required to pay a fee in advance of the complaint being considered.[54] Parties submitting complaints 'must provide evidence proving that such complaint . . . is legitimate and based on valid grounds'.[55] Similarly those complained of are entitled to provide evidence to the effect that their opposition to the complaint is valid. **6-5.21**

The VCAD is compelled to accept such complaints—as long as the required fee is paid—and must acknowledge their receipt within seven working days of the submission. Articles 58 and 59 are silent, however, on the extent of the obligations of the VCAD once a complaint has been accepted. However, art 61(2)(a) gives **6-5.22**

---

[49] art 99(3), VLOC.

[50] art 102(1), VLOC.

[51] art 103, VLOC.

[52] art 104(1), VLOC.

[53] art 58, VLOC. The content of this dossier is spelt out at art 45 of the Decree on Competition.

[54] art 59, VLOC. Those making complaints are 'accountable' for the veracity of the information contained in the complaint. The right to request APMs is iterated in art 66(2)(b).

[55] article 74(1), Decree on Competition.

complainants the right to propose that administrative preventive measures be taken against those whose acts are the subject of the complaint, although when they do so they must 'pay a guarantee money',[56] and where preventive measures are applied wrongly following such an application the complainant must pay compensation to the wronged parties.[57] Likewise in the event that a party is investigated and is found not to have breached the VLOC the complainant is required to pay an administrative charge.[58]

6-5.23 Complainants have the same rights in relation to the conduct of proceedings as do the parties under investigation (art 66(2), VLOC, see below).

Other third parties

6-5.24 Article 71 of the VLOC makes provision in respect of 'persons with interests and obligations related to competition cases', who may file independent claims or participate in competition cases on the side of either complainants or those under investigation. These persons have the same rights in the proceedings as those persons on whose 'side' they enter the case.

Rights of the Parties

6-5.25 Along with the general right to have cases handled in a way which complies with the Law,[59] and the right to appeal certain decisions, various specific rights are given to those subject to investigation by the VCAD and VCC. In particular art 66 of the VLOC spells out certain rights, and obligations, of 'involved parties'. Rights are specified in art 66(1), and include the right to: (1) produce evidence, and be informed of the contents of evidence produced against them; (2) participate in hearings (see above); (3) request a change in the investigators in the event

[56] art 61(3), VLOC.

[57] Article 61 provides that the parties shall first attempt to agree the level of compensation between themselves, but if they are unable to do so the wronged party may bring a claim for damages under the appropriate civil law procedures.

[58] art 63(3), VLOC.

[59] art 56(1), VLOC. Article 56(3) further requires those charged with operating the procedures to 'respect legitimate rights and interests of the related organizations and individuals'. Related individuals are defined as:

> . . . a person who does not lodge a complaint file about a competition case and who is not the party subject to investigation, but resolution of the competition case does involve such person's interests and obligations; and such person himself, or the complainant, or the party subject to investigation proposes that such person participate in the legal proceedings in his capacity as a person with related interests and obligations and the administrative body for competition and/or the council dealing with the competition case agree to such participation' (art 48(1), Decree on Competition).

that one of the circumstances of art 83, VLOC, arises,[60] or to request that those conducting the procedures or other participants in the procedures be changed; (4) have legal representation; (5) request witnesses; and (6) request that expert opinion be sought by the VCAD or the VCC.

Business secrets are protected by virtue of art 56(3) of the VLOC, which requires 'investigators, the head of [the VCAD] and Competition Council members' to 'within the scope of their respective tasks and powers, keep confidential business secrets of enterprises'. Article 3(10) of the VLOC defines business secrets as information which meets all of three conditions; (1) the information must not be common knowledge; (2) it must be 'applicable to business and, once used, placing the holder of such information at an advantage' over those who do not hold the information; and (3) it must be kept confidential by the owner through measures which keep the information from disclosure and easy access. 6-5.26

Remedies and Penalties

There are two sets of provisions in the VLOC relating to remedies. The first is that relating to APMs, which may be applied during the course of an investigation (see above).[61] The second forms part of the subject matter of art 117, which sets out the means by which breaches of the law may be sanctioned, and the remedies that may be required to redress with the consequences of breaches. 6-5.27

The two primary forms of sanction are 'warnings' and fines, and art 4 of the DDB states that one or the other of these '*must*' be imposed in respect of each breach of the Law that is identified in a formal decision taken at the end of the appropriate procedure. Two further penalties are provided for in art 117(2): (1) revocation of business certificates; and (2) confiscation of materials used for the commission of violations.[62] 6-5.28

Fines may be imposed by the CCHC and the VCC in the case of breaches of the provisions on restrictive agreements, abuses of dominant positions or monopoly, and concentrations up to a limit of 10 per cent of the turnover of the breaching parties in the fiscal year preceding that of the violation. The DDB sets out rules 6-5.29

[60] Article 83 specifies that investigators, and other relevant agency staff, may not be assigned to a case where certain conflicts of interest could arise.

[61] See art 61, VLOC.

[62] This provision is without precedent in competition laws in western regimes, and it is difficult, in relation to competition cases (rather than unfair competition cases) to contemplate that there are such things that can be confiscated. Article 4(3) of the DDB states that these penalties *may* be imposed, 'depending on the nature and seriousness of a breach'.

relating to the determination of the penalty. Article 7 of the DDB provides that the following factors are to be considered in determining the level of the penalty: (1) the level of restraint of competition; (2) the amount of loss caused; (3) the power of the breaching enterprise to restrain competition; (4) the duration of the breach; (5) the profits gained; and (6) attenuating or aggravating circumstances.[63] Chapter II of the DDB specifies the maximum levels of penalties that may be applied in relation to particular categories of breaches of the VLOC. The penalties set out are as follows.

- In respect of agreements to fix prices,[64] to share consumer markets or sources of supplies of goods and services,[65] to limit or control the quantities of goods produced or services supplied,[66] to limit technological development or to restrain investment,[67] to impose on other enterprises supplementary obligations not directly related to the subject matter of the contract,[68] which prevent or otherwise hinder other enterprises from participating in the market,[69] which exclude from the market existing competitors,[70] or which are bid-rigging agreements,[71] where the market share of the participants to the agreement is at least 30%: ≤ 5% of turnover.
- Any agreement falling into the above categories which operate in respect of 'foodstuffs, food products, medical apparatus', medicines, fertilizer, animal feed, seeds or domestic animals, medical or healthcare services: 5–10%.[72]
- Breaches of dominant positions taking the form of: selling goods below cost in order to exclude competitors;[73] fixing unreasonable selling or purchase prices or fixing minimum resale prices;[74] restraining the production or distribution of

[63] art 118(1), VLOC. A number of circumstances are stated in the Decree on Competition to be either extenuating or aggravating circumstances to be taken into account when penalties are determined. Extenuating circumstances include: the giving of voluntary testimony of the unlawful conduct prior to its discovery by the VCAD; measures taken to prevent or mitigate the adverse impact of this conduct; the provision of evidence voluntarily whose existence was unknown to the VCAD or the VCC; and that the unlawful conduct 'has a positive impact on the development of the economy' (see discussion of this point in Chapter 6-3, above). Aggravating circumstances exist where: there have been a number of breaches in the same sector or a second offence in the same sector; deliberate breaches arising after a rejection of a request for an exemption; continued unlawful conduct after an authorized person has requested that the conduct be terminated; and actions taken to conceal the fact of the breach or to avoid its detection (art 85).

[64] art 10(1), DDB.

[65] art 11(1), DDB.

[66] art 12(1), DDB.

[67] art 13(1), DDB.

[68] art 14(1), DDB.

[69] art 15(1), DDB.

[70] art 16(1), DDB.

[71] art 17(1), DDB.

[72] arts 10(2), 11(2), 12(2), 13(2), 14(2), 15(2), 16(2), and 17(2), DDB.

[73] art 18(1), DDB.

[74] art 19(1), DDB.

goods or services, or impeding technical or technological development;[75] discrimination;[76] imposing conditions or enforcing obligations not directly related to the subject matter of the contract;[77] preventing market entry by new competitors:[78] ≤ 5%.

- In any of the cases above relating to dominant position or monopoly in which either the relevant markets is that for 'foodstuffs, food products, medical apparatus', medicines, fertilizer, animal feed, seeds or domestic animals, medical or healthcare services; *or* in which the market share of the enterprise is ≥ 50%;[79] *or* where the enterprise has the largest market share, *or* where the enterprise 'took the role of organizing or inducing other enterprisers in a dominant market position to act together in the practice of the breach':[80] 5–10%.
- In respect of conduct constituting an abuse of a monopoly position consisting in any of the practices set out above relating to dominant positions, or which impose disadvantageous conditions on customers, or change or unilaterally cancel contracts: ≤ 10%.[81]
- In relation to the consummation of an unlawful merger;[82] a prohibited consolidation of enterprises;[83] a prohibited acquisition of an enterprise;[84] or a prohibited joint venture:[85] ≤ 5%.
- In relation to a merger where the 'merged enterprise coerced directly or indirectly the merging enterprises to carry out the merger';[86] or similarly commissioned an acquisition:[87] 5–10%.
- In relation to prohibited consolidations,[88] or joint ventures,[89] the effect of which is to result 'in a significant increase in the price of goods and services on the relevant market': 5–10%.
- For failure to notify a concentration: 1–3%.[90]

---

[75] art 20(1), DDB.
[76] art 21(1), DDB.
[77] art 22(1), DDB.
[78] art 23(2), DDB.
[79] arts 18(2), 19(2), 20(2), 21(2), 22(2), and 23(2), DDB
[80] arts 18(3), 19(3), 20(3) 21(3) 22(3), and 23(3), DDB.
[81] art 24, DDB.
[82] art 25(1), DDB.
[83] art 26(1), DDB.
[84] art 27(1), DDB.
[85] art 28(1), DDB.
[86] art 25(2), DDB.
[87] art 27(2), DDB.
[88] art 26(2), DDB.
[89] art 28(2), DDB.
[90] art 29, DDB.

- In respect of restrictive agreements or concentrations entered into where an application for an exemption has been made but not yet determined: Dong30m–Dong50m.[91]

6-5.30 The DDB also makes some provision in respect of penalties relating to procedural infringements. A warning or a penalty ranging from Dong500,000 to Dong1m may be imposed in cases of: (1) failure to supply information, or the supply of incomplete information or data when a legitimate request has been made by the VCAD or VCC; (2) failure to supply information within the time limit set; (3) deliberately supplying false or misleading information; (4) coercing others to supply false information; and (5) concealing or destroying information.[92] Where the information is 'of particular importance for a proper resolution' of the case, the penalty may be increased to a fine of Dong1m to Dong3m.[93] Other penalties (including those related to breaches of the procedural rules) will be assessed and imposed on the basis of the legal provisions of relevant administrative or other relevant laws.[94]

6-5.31 Parties may also agree to voluntarily terminate alleged infringements. Where they do so the presumption appears to be that proceedings will be terminated at that point as long as the Head of the VCAD agrees in the case that the investigation was opened on the initiative of the VCAD, or where the complainant withdraws their complaint (see above). In both cases the VLOC states that the party under investigation is also expected to remedy the consequences of the alleged infringement.[95]

6-5.32 Other remedies are specified in art 117(3), although these are described there as 'sanctions'. These include: (1) the imposition of structural remedies in the case of abuses of dominant positions and monopolies; (2) the imposition of structural remedies in the case of unlawfully consummated concentrations; (3) 'public corrections'; (4) the amendment of contracts or transacting terms where these contain illegal provisions; and (5) 'other necessary measures'.[96] Thus at a number of points in the DDB it is noted that particular remedies may be applicable. These include: restructuring of an enterprise engaged in breaching a dominant position,[97] compulsory resale or use of intellectual property,[98] and compulsory amendment of contractual terms.[99] The CHCC and the VCC have the power to impose

[91] art 41, DDB.
[92] art 39(1), DDB.
[93] art 39(2), DDB.
[94] art 118(2), VLOC.
[95] art 101, VLOC.
[96] See also art 4(4), DBB.
[97] arts 18–23, DDB.
[98] art 20(4), DDB.
[99] art 24(2)(b), DDB.

remedies, although in certain cases they may need to request that action be taken by other relevant public authorities (such as is the case for example in relation to the revocation of business registration certificates). The VCAD has somewhat reduced powers, and cannot, for example, impose fines under art 117(1)(b), or require the revocation of business registrations.

Where parties do not themselves undertake any corrective actions imposed within thirty days of the making of such a decision the relevant agencies may themselves organize the execution of the orders.[100] **6-5.33**

Leniency

There is no formal leniency programme in operation in Vietnam. However, art 85 of the Decree on Competition sets out a list of aggravating and extenuating circumstances to be taken into account when penalties are assessed. As noted above it is an extenuating circumstance to notify an infringement to the VCAD or to the VCC prior to its discovery by that body. There is however no formal schedule determining penalty reductions, such that potential whistle-blowers have no means of determining *ex ante* the rewards of coming forward. **6-5.34**

Third Party Rights

There is no general right to bring a stand-alone action in respect of breaches of the VLOC. Actions can be brought only following the making of an infringement decision by the enforcement authorities. The VCC cannot itself order compensation, such that an injured third party has only distant prospects of recovering damages. Article 117(3) contains within it a provision which requires those who have caused 'damage to the interests of the State, [or the] legitimate rights and interests of other organizations or individuals' to pay compensation according to the provisions of the Law. Article 6 of the DDB reinforces this rule, stating at art 6(1) that: **6-5.35**

> [a]ny organization or individual breaching the laws on competition, thereby causing loss to the interests of the State or to the lawful rights and interests of other organizations and individuals, must pay compensation for such loss.

The procedures under which actions for compensation may be brought are those applying to the general civil law in Vietnam.

[100] art 121, VLOC. See also arts 55 and 56, DDB.

Appeals

6-5.36 Section 7 of Chapter 5 of the VLOC contains provisions relating to 'complaints about [CCHC] decisions which have not yet come into force'—or, in simpler language, appeals. Any involved party who disagrees with the whole or part of a decision taken by the CCHC may lodge a complaint with the CCHC. Where the decision complained of is made by the Head of the VCAD the appeal is addressed to the Minister of Industry and Trade. There is no provision in the VLOC for appealing decisions made by the Prime Minister (in the case of merger exemptions based on enhancing exports or 'contributing to socio-economic development, technical and technological advance'[101]). Appeals are to be made in writing, and have their validity checked within five days of submission.

6-5.37 Where an appeal is made the effect of the parts of the decision which have been appealed shall be stayed. The agency receiving the appeal is to transfer the appeal, along with its comments and the entire case dossier, to the VCC or the Minister within fifteen days. A final decision must be taken in a further thirty days, with the possibility of one extension of thirteen days in 'specially complicated cases'.[102]

6-5.38 The VCC may make three decisions in response to appeals: (1) to uphold the contested decision; (2) to amend part or the whole of the decision if it is deemed to be 'illegal'; and (3) to cancel the decision and to remit the case dossier to the CCHC for reconsideration where either the evidence has not been fully obtained and verified, or the CCHC composition was in breach of the law or serious procedural violations occurred.[103] The powers of the Minister are identical, save for the latter rubric which does not apply in relation to the VCAD.[104]

6-5.39 A further appeal may be made to the competent provincial or municipal court if the appellant remains unsatisfied with the administrative disposal of the appeal.[105]

101 art 19(2), VLOC.
102 arts 110 and 111, VLOC.
103 art 112, VLOC.
104 art 113, VLOC.
105 art 115, VLOC.

Appendices

1. China: Anti-Monopoly Law	355
2. Taiwan: Fair Trade Act of 2002	365
3. Korea: Monopoly Regulation and Fair Trade Act	377
4. Vietnam: Law on Competition	419

APPENDIX 1

China: Anti-Monopoly Law[1]

Adopted at the 29th meeting of the Standing Committee of the 10th National People's Congress of the People's Republic of China on August 30, 2007)

CONTENTS

Chapter I General Provisions
Chapter II Monopoly Agreement
Chapter III Abuse of Market Dominance
Chapter IV Concentration of Business operators
Chapter V Abuse of Administrative Power to Eliminate or Restrict Competition
Chapter VI Investigation into the Suspicious Monopolistic Conducts
Chapter VII Legal Liabilities
Chapter VIII Supplementary Provisions

Chapter I General Provisions

Article 1 This Law is enacted for the purpose of preventing and restraining monopolistic conducts, protecting fair competition in the market, enhancing economic efficiency, safeguarding the interests of consumers and social public interest, promoting the healthy development of the socialist market economy.

Article 2 This Law shall be applicable to monopolistic conducts in economic activities within the People's Republic of China.

This Law shall apply to the conducts outside the territory of the People's Republic of China if they eliminate or have restrictive effect on competition on the domestic market of the PRC.

Article 3 For the purposes of this Law, 'monopolistic conducts' are defined as the following:

(1) monopolistic agreements among business operators;
(2) abuse of dominant market positions by business operators; and
(3) concentration of business operators that eliminates or restricts competition or might be eliminating or restricting competition.

Article 4 The State constitutes and carries out competition rules which accord with the socialist market economy, perfects macro-control, and advances a unified, open, competitive and orderly market system.

[1] This version is of the AML is taken from the 'China Trade in Services' website (< http://tradeinservices.mofcom.gov.cn/en/b/2007-08-30/9043.shtml>), which is hosted by MOFCOM and therefore this is considered to be the 'official' translation of the law. It is unfortunate therefore that the translation given here is riddled with grammatical errors. However, the decision has been taken not to correct these.

Article 5 Business operators may, through fair competition, voluntary alliance, concentrate themselves according to law, expand the scope of business operations, and enhance competitiveness.

Article 6 Any business with a dominant position may not abuse that dominant position to eliminate, or restrict competition.

Article 7 With respect to the industries controlled by the State-owned economy and concerning the lifeline of national economy and national security or the industries implementing exclusive operation and sales according to law, the state protects the lawful business operations conducted by the business operators therein. The state also lawfully regulates and controls their business operations and the prices of their commodities and services so as to safeguard the interests of consumers and promote technical progresses.

The business operators as mentioned above shall lawfully operate, be honest and faithful, be strictly self-disciplined, accept social supervision, shall not damage the interests of consumers by virtue of their dominant or exclusive positions.

Article 8 No administrative organ or organization empowered by a law or administrative regulation to administer public affairs may abuse its administrative powers to eliminate or restrict competition.

Article 9 The State Council shall establish the Anti-monopoly Commission, which is in charge of organizing, coordinating, guiding anti-monopoly work, performs the following functions:

(1) studying and drafting related competition policies;
(2) organizing the investigation and assessment of overall competition situations in the market, and issuing assessment reports;
(3) constituting and issuing anti-monopoly guidelines;
(4) coordinating anti-monopoly administrative law enforcement; and
(5) other functions as assigned by the State Council.

The State Council shall stipulate composition and working rules of the Anti-monopoly Commission.

Article 10 The anti-monopoly authority designated by the State Council (hereinafter referred to as the Anti-monopoly Authority under the State Council) shall be in charge of anti-monopoly law enforcement in accordance with this Law.

The Anti-monopoly Authority under the State Council may, when needed, authorize the corresponding authorities in the people's governments of the provinces, autonomous regions and municipalities directly under the Central Government to take charge of anti-monopoly law enforcement in accordance with this Law.

Article 11 A trade association shall intensify industrial self-discipline, guide business operators to lawfully compete, safeguard the competition order in the market.

Article 12 For the purposes of this Law,

'business operator' refers to a natural person, legal person, or any other organization that is in the engagement of commodities production or operation or service provision, and

'relevant market' refers to the commodity scope or territorial scope within which the business operators compete against each other during a certain period of time for specific commodities or services (hereinafter generally referred to as 'commodities').

Chapter II Monopoly Agreement

Article 13 Any of the following monopoly agreements among the competing business operators shall be prohibited:

(1) fixing or changing prices of commodities;
(2) limiting the output or sales of commodities;

(3) dividing the sales market or the raw material procurement market;
(4) restricting the purchase of new technology or new facilities or the development of new technology or new products;
(5) making boycott transactions; or
(6) other monopoly agreements as determined by the Anti-monopoly Authority under the State Council. For the purposes of this Law, 'monopoly agreements' refer to agreements, decisions or other concerted actions which eliminate or restrict competition.

Article 14 Any of the following agreements among business operators and their trading parties are prohibited:

(1) fixing the price of commodities for resale to a third party;
(2) restricting the minimum price of commodities for resale to a third party; or
(3) other monopoly agreements as determined by the Anti-monopoly Authority under the State Council.

Article 15 An agreement among business operators shall be exempted from application of articles 13 and 14 if it can be proven to be in any of the following circumstances:

(1) for the purpose of improving technologies, researching and developing new products;
(2) for the purpose of upgrading product quality, reducing cost, improving efficiency, unifying product specifications or standards, or carrying out professional labor division;
(3) for the purpose of enhancing operational efficiency and reinforcing the competitiveness of small and medium-sized business operators;
(4) for the purpose of achieving public interests such as conserving energy, protecting the environment and relieving the victims of a disaster and so on;
(5) for the purpose of mitigating serious decrease in sales volume or obviously excessive production during economic recessions;
(6) for the purpose of safeguarding the justifiable interests in the foreign trade or foreign economic cooperation; or
(7) other circumstances as stipulated by laws and the State Council.

Where a monopoly agreement is in any of the circumstances stipulated in Items 1 through 5 and is exempt from Articles 13 and 14 of this Law, the business operators must additionally prove that the agreement can enable consumers to share the interests derived from the agreement, and will not severely restrict the competition in relevant market.

Article 16 Any trade association may not organize the business operators in its own industry to implement the monopolistic conduct as prohibited by this Chapter.

Chapter III Abuse of Market Dominance

Article 17 A business operator with a dominant market position shall not abuse its dominant market position to conduct following acts:

(1) selling commodities at unfairly high prices or buying commodities at unfairly low prices;
(2) selling products at prices below cost without any justifiable cause;
(3) refusing to trade with a trading party without any justifiable cause;
(4) requiring a trading party to trade exclusively with itself or trade exclusively with a designated business operator(s) without any justifiable cause;
(5) tying products or imposing unreasonable trading conditions at the time of trading without any justifiable cause;
(6) applying dissimilar prices or other transaction terms to counterparties with equal standing;
(7) other conducts determined as abuse of a dominant position by the Anti-monopoly Authority under the State Council.

For the purposes of this Law, 'dominant market position' refers to a market position held by a business operator having the capacity to control the price, quantity or other trading conditions of commodities in relevant market, or to hinder or affect any other business operator to enter the relevant market.

Article 18 The dominant market status shall be determined according to the following factors:

(1) the market share of a business operator in relevant market, and the competition situation of the relevant market;
(2) the capacity of a business operator to control the sales markets or the raw material procurement market;
(3) the financial and technical conditions of the business operator;
(4) the degree of dependence of other business operators upon the business operator in transactions;
(5) the degree of difficulty for other business operators to enter the relevant market; and
(6) other factors related to determine a dominant market position of the said business operator.

Article 19 Where a business operator is under any of the following circumstances, it may be assumed to have a dominant market position:

(1) the relevant market share of a business operator accounts for 1/2 or above in the relevant market;
(2) the joint relevant market share of two business operators accounts for 2/3 or above; or
(3) the joint relevant market share of three business operators accounts for 3/4 or above.

A business operator with a market share of less than 1/10 shall not be presumed as having a dominant market position even if they fall within the scope of second or third item.

Where a business operator who has been presumed to have a dominant market position can otherwise prove that they do not have a dominant market, it shall not be determined as having a dominant market position.

Chapter IV Concentration of Business Operators

Article 20 A concentration refers to the following circumstances:

(1) the merger of business operators;
(2) acquiring control over other business operators by virtue of acquiring their equities or assets; or
(3) acquiring control over other business operators or possibility of exercising decisive influence on other business operators by virtue of contact[2] or any other means.

Article 21 Where a concentration reaches the threshold of declaration stipulated by the State Council, a declaration must be lodged in advance with the Anti-monopoly Authority under the State Council, or otherwise the concentration shall not be implemented.

Article 22 Where a concentration is under any of the following circumstances, it may not be declared to the Anti-monopoly Authority under the State Council:

(1) one business operator who is a party to the concentration has the power to exercise more than half the voting rights of every other business operator, whether of the equity or the assets; or
(2) one business operator who is not a party to the concentration has the power to exercise more than half the voting rights of every business operator concerned, whether of the equity or the assets.

Article 23 A business operator shall, when lodge a concentration declaration with the Anti-monopoly Authority under the State Council, submit the following documents and materials:

(1) a declaration paper;
(2) explanations on the effect of the concentration on the relevant market competition;

[2] This should read 'contract'.

(3) the agreement of concentration;
(4) the financial reports and accounting reports of the proceeding[3] accounting year of the business operator; and
(5) other documents and materials as stipulated by the Anti-monopoly Authority under the State Council.

Such items shall be embodied in the declaration paper as the name, domicile and business scopes of the business operators involved in the concentration as well as the date of the scheduled concentration and other items as stipulated by the Anti-monopoly Authority under the State Council.

Article 24 Where the documents or materials submitted by a business operator are incomplete, it shall submit the rest of the documents and materials within the time limit stipulated by the Anti-monopoly Authority under the State Council; otherwise, the declaration shall be deemed as not filed.

Article 25 The Anti-monopoly Authority under the State Council shall conduct a preliminary review of the declared concentration of business operators, make a decision whether to conduct further review and notify the business operators in written form within 30 days upon receipt of the documents and materials submitted by the business operators pursuant to Article 23 of this Law. Before such a decision made by the Anti-monopoly Authority under the State Council, the concentration may be not implemented.

Where the Anti-monopoly Authority under the State Council decides not to conduct further review or fails to make a decision at expiry of the stipulated period, the concentration may be implemented.

Article 26 Where the Anti-monopoly Authority under the State Council decides to conduct further review, they shall, within 90 days from the date of decision, complete the review, make a decision on whether to prohibit the concentration, and notify the business operators concerned of the decision in written form. A decision of prohibition shall be attached with reasons therefor. Within the review period the concentration may not be implemented.

Under any of the following circumstances, the Anti-monopoly Authority under the State Council may notify the business operators in written form that the time limit as stipulated in the preceding paragraph may be extended to no more than 60 days:

(1) the business operators concerned agree to extend the time limit;
(2) the documents or materials submitted are inaccurate and need further verification;
(3) things have significantly changed after declaration.

If the Anti-monopoly Authority under the State Council fails to make a decision at expiry of the period, the concentration may be implemented.

Article 27 In the case of the examination on the concentration of business operators, it shall consider the relevant elements as follows:

(1) the market share of the business operators involved in the relevant market and the controlling power thereof over that market,
(2) the degree of market concentration in the relevant market,
(3) the influence of the concentration of business operators on the market access and technological progress,
(4) the influence of the concentration of business operators on the consumers and other business operators,
(5) the influence of the concentration of business operators on the national economic development, and

[3] This should read 'preceding'.

(6) other elements that may have an effect on the market competition and shall be taken into account as regarded by the Anti-monopoly Authority under the State Council.

Article 28 Where a concentration has or may have effect of eliminating or restricting competition, the Anti-monopoly Authority under the State Council shall make a decision to prohibit the concentration.

However, if the business operators concerned can prove that the concentration will bring more positive impact than negative impact on competition, or the concentration is pursuant to public interests, the Anti-monopoly Authority under the State Council may decide not to prohibit the concentration.

Article 29 Where the concentration is not prohibited, the Anti-monopoly Authority under the State Council may decide to attach restrictive conditions for reducing the negative impact of such concentration on competition.

Article 30 Where the Anti-monopoly Authority under the State Council decides to prohibit a concentration or attaches restrictive conditions on concentration, it shall publicize such decisions to the general public in a timely manner.

Article 31 Where a foreign investor merges and acquires a domestic enterprise or participate in concentration by other means, if state security is involved, besides the examination on the concentration in accordance with this Law, the examination on national security shall also be conducted in accordance with the relevant State provisions.

Chapter V Abuse of Administrative Power to Eliminate or Restrict Competition

Article 32 Any administrative organ or organization empowered by a law or administrative regulation to administer public affairs may not abuse its administrative power, restrict or restrict in a disguised form entities and individuals to operate, purchase or use the commodities provided by business operators designated by it.

Article 33 Any administrative organ or organization empowered by a law or an administrative regulation to administer public affairs may not have any of the following conducts by abusing its administrative power to block free circulation of commodities between regions:

(1) imposing discriminative charge items, discriminative charge standards or discriminative prices upon commodities from outside the locality,

(2) imposing such technical requirements and inspection standards upon commodities from outside the locality as different from those upon local commodities of the same classification, or taking such discriminative technical measures as repeated inspections or repeated certifications to commodities from outside the locality, so as to restrict them to enter local market,

(3) exerting administrative licensing specially on commodities from outside the locality so as to restrict them to enter local market,

(4) setting barriers or taking other measures so as to hamper commodities from outside the locality from entering the local market or local commodities from moving outside the local region, or

(5) other conducts for the purpose of hampering commodities from free circulation between regions.

Article 34 Any administrative organ or organization empowered by a law or administrative regulation to administer public affairs may not abuse its administrative power to reject or restrict business operators from outside the locality to participate in local tendering and bidding activities by such means as imposing discriminative qualification requirements or assessment standards or releasing information in an unlawful manner.

Article 35 Any administrative organ or organization empowered by a law or administrative regulation to administer public affairs may not abuse its administrative power to reject or restrict business operators from outside the locality to invest or set up branches in the locality by imposing unequal treatment thereupon compared to that upon local business operators.

Article 36 Any administrative organ or organization empowered by a law or administrative regulation to administer public affairs may not abuse its administrative power to force business operators to engage in the monopolistic conducts as prescribed in this Law.

Article 37 Any administrative organ may not abuse its administrative power to set down such provisions in respect of eliminating or restricting competition.

Chapter VI Investigation into the Suspicious Monopolistic Conducts

Article 38 The anti-monopoly authority shall make investigations into suspicious monopolistic conducts in accordance with law.

Any entity or individual may report suspicious monopolistic conducts to the anti-monopoly authority. The anti-monopoly authority shall keep the informer confidential.

Where an informer makes the reporting in written form and provides relevant facts and evidences, the anti-monopoly authority shall make necessary investigation.

Article 39 The anti-monopoly authority may take any of the following measures in investigating suspicious monopolistic conducts:

(1) conducting the inspection by getting into the business premises of business operators under investigation or by getting into any other relevant place,
(2) inquiring of the business operators under investigation, interested parties, or other relevant entities or individuals, and requiring them to explain the relevant conditions,
(3) consulting and duplicating the relevant documents, agreements, account books, business correspondences and electronic data, etc. of the business operators under investigation, interested parties and other relevant entities or individuals,
(4) seizing and detaining relevant evidence, and
(5) inquiring about the business operators' bank accounts under investigation.

Before the measures as prescribed in the preceding paragraph are approved, a written report shall be submitted to the chief person(s)-in-charge of the anti-monopoly authority.

Article 40 When inspecting suspicious monopolistic conducts, there shall be at least two law enforcers, and they shall show their law enforcement certificates.

When inquiring about and investigating suspicious monopolistic conducts, law enforcers shall make notes thereon, which shall bear the signatures of the persons under inquiry or investigation.

Article 41 The anti-monopoly authority and functionaries thereof shall be obliged to keep confidential the trade secrets they have access to during the course of the law enforcement.

Article 42 Business operators, interested parties and other relevant entities and individuals under investigation shall show cooperation with the anti-monopoly authority in performing its functions, and may not reject or hamper the investigation by the anti-monopoly authority.

Article 43 Business operators, interested parties under investigation have the right to voice their opinions. The anti-monopoly authority shall verify the facts, reasons and evidences provided by the business operators, interested parties under investigation.

Article 44 Where the anti-monopoly authority deems that a monopolistic conduct is constituted after investigating and verifying a suspicious monopolistic conduct, it shall make a decision on how to deal with the monopolistic conduct, and publicize it.

Article 45 As regards a suspicious monopolistic conduct that the anti-monopoly authority is investigating, if the business operators under investigation promise to eliminate the impact of the conduct by taking specific measures within the time limit prescribed by the anti-monopoly authority, the anti-monopoly authority may decide to suspend the investigation. The decision on suspending the investigation shall specify the specific measures as promised by the business operators under investigation.

Where the anti-monopoly authority decides to suspend the investigation, it shall supervise the implementation of the promise by the relevant business operators. If the business operators keep their promise, the anti-monopoly authority may decide to terminate the investigation.

However, the anti-monopoly authority shall resume the investigation, where

(1) the business operators fail to implement the promise,
(2) significant changes have taken place to the facts based on which the decision on suspending the investigation was made; or
(3) the decision on suspending the investigation was made based on incomplete or inaccurate information provided by the business operators.

Chapter VII Legal Liabilities

Article 46 Where business operators reach an monopoly agreement and perform it in violation of this Law, the anti-monopoly authority shall order them to cease doing so, and shall confiscate the illegal gains and impose a fine of 1% up to 10% of the sales revenue in the previous year. Where the reached monopoly agreement has not been performed, a fine of less than 500,000 yuan shall be imposed.

Where any business operator voluntarily reports the conditions on reaching the monopoly agreement and provides important evidences to the anti-monopoly authority, it may be imposed a mitigated punishment or exemption from punishment as the case may be.

Where a guild help the achievement of a monopoly agreement by business operators in its own industry in violation of this Law, a fine of less than 500,000 yuan shall be imposed thereupon by the anti-monopoly authority; in case of serious circumstances, the social group registration authority may deregister the guild.

Article 47 Where any business operator abuses its dominant market status in violation of this Law, it shall be ordered to cease doing so. The anti-monopoly authority shall confiscate its illegal gains and impose thereupon a fine of 1% up to 10% of the sales revenue in the previous year.

Article 48 Where any business operator implements concentration in violation of this Law, the anti-monopoly authority shall order it to cease doing so, to dispose of shares or assets, transfer the business or take other necessary measures to restore the market situation before the concentration within a time limit, and may impose a fine of less than 500,000 yuan.

Article 49 The specific amount of the fines as prescribed in Articles 46 through 48 shall be determined in consideration of such factors as the nature, extent and duration of the violations.

Article 50 Where any loss was caused by a business operator's monopolistic conducts to other entities and individuals, the business operator shall assume the civil liabilities.

Article 51 Where any administrative organ or an organization empowered by a law or administrative regulation to administer public affairs abuses its administrative power to eliminate or restrict competition, the superior authority thereof shall order it to make correction and impose punishments on the directly liable person(s)-in-charge and other directly liable persons. The anti-monopoly authority may put forward suggestions on handling according to law to the relevant superior authority.

Where it is otherwise provided in a law or administrative regulation for the handling the organization empowered by a law or administrative regulation to administer public affairs who abuses its administrative power to eliminate or restrict competition, such provisions shall prevail.

Article 52 As regards the inspection and investigation by the anti-monopoly authority, if business operators refuse to provide related materials and information, provide fraudulent materials or information, conceal, destroy or remove evidence, or refuse or obstruct investigation in other ways, the anti-monopoly authority shall order them to make rectification, impose a fine of less than 20,000 yuan on individuals, and a fine of less than 200,000 yuan on entities; and in case of serious circumstances, the anti-monopoly authority may impose a fine of 20,000 yuan up to 100,000 yuan on individuals, and a fine of 200,000 yuan up to one million yuan on entities; where a crime is constituted, the relevant business operators shall assume criminal liabilities.

Article 53 Where any party concerned objects to the decision made by the anti-monopoly authority in accordance with Articles 28 and 29 of this Law, it may first apply for an administrative reconsideration; if it objects to the reconsideration decision, it may lodge an administrative lawsuit in accordance with law.

Where any party concerned is dissatisfied with any decision made by the anti-monopoly authority other than the decisions prescribed in the preceding paragraph, it may lodge an application for administrative reconsideration or initiate an administrative lawsuit in accordance with law.

Article 54 Where any functionary of the anti-monopoly authority abuses his/her power, neglects his/her duty, seeks private benefits, or discloses trade secrets he/she has access to during the process of law enforcement, and a crime is constituted, he/she shall be subject to the criminal liability; where no crime is constituted, he/she shall be imposed upon a disciplinary sanction.

Chapter VIII Supplementary Provisions

Article 55 This Law does not govern the conduct of business operators to exercise their intellectual property rights under laws and relevant administrative regulations on intellectual property rights; however, business operators' conduct to eliminate or restrict market competition by abusing their intellectual property rights shall be governed by this Law.

Article 56 This Law does not govern the ally or concerted actions of agricultural producers and rural economic organizations in the economic activities such as production, processing, sales, transportation and storage of agricultural products.

Article 57 This Law shall enter into force as of August 1, 2008.

The Standing Committee of the National People's Congress 2007-08-30

APPENDIX 2

Taiwan: Fair Trade Act of 2002

Chapter I: General Principles

Article 1

This Law is enacted for the purposes of maintaining trading order, protecting consumers' interests, ensuring fair competition, and promoting economic stability and prosperity. Unless otherwise provided in this Law the provisions of other relevant laws shall apply.

Article 2

The term 'enterprise' as used in this Law shall include,

1. a company,
2. a sole proprietorship or partnership,
3. a trade association, and
4. any other person or organization engaging in transactions through the provision of goods or services.

Article 3

The term 'trading counterpart' as used in this Law means any supplier or purchaser that engages in or concludes transactions with an enterprise.

Article 4

The term 'competition' as used in this Law means any conduct of one enterprise to contest trading opportunities in the same market with one or more enterprises through offering more favourable price, quantity, quality, service or any other terms.

Article 5

The term 'monopolistic enterprise' as used in this Law means any enterprise that faces no competition or has a dominant position to enable it to exclude competition in a relevant market.

Two or more enterprises shall be deemed monopolistic enterprises if they do not in fact engage in price competition with each other and they as a whole have the same status as the enterprise defined in the provisions of the preceding paragraph.

The term 'relevant market' as used in the first paragraph means a geographic area or a coverage wherein enterprises compete in respect of particular goods or services.

Article 5-1

An enterprise shall not be deemed a monopolistic enterprise as defined in the preceding article if none of the following circumstances exists:

1. the market share of the enterprise in a relevant market reaches one-half of the market;
2. the combined market share of two enterprises in a relevant market reaches two-thirds of the market; and

3. the combined market share of three enterprises in a relevant market reaches three-fourths of the market.

Under any of the circumstances set forth in the preceding paragraph, where the market share of any individual enterprise does not reach one-tenth of the relevant market or where its total sales in the preceding fiscal year are less than one billion New Taiwan Dollars, such enterprise shall not be deemed as a monopolistic enterprise.

An enterprise exempted from being deemed as a monopolistic enterprise by any of the preceding two paragraphs may still be deemed a monopolistic enterprise by the Central Competent Authority if the establishment of such enterprise or any of the goods or services supplied by such enterprise to a relevant market is subject to legal or technological restraints, or there exists any other circumstance under which the supply and demand of the market are affected and the ability of others to compete is impeded.

Article 6

The term 'merger' as used in this Law means a situation:

1. where an enterprise and another enterprise are merged into one;
2. where an enterprise holds or acquires the shares or capital contributions of another enterprise to an extent of more than one-third of the total voting shares or total capital of such other enterprise;
3. where an enterprise is assigned by or leases from another enterprise the whole or the major part of the business or properties of such other enterprise;
4. where an enterprise operates jointly with another enterprise on a regular basis or is entrusted by another enterprise to operate the latter's business; or
5. where an enterprise directly or indirectly controls the business operation or the appointment or discharge of personnel of another enterprise.

In computing the shares or capital contributions referred to in subparagraph 2 of the preceding paragraph, the shares or capital contributions of another enterprise held or acquired by an enterprise(s) controlled by, controlling, or affiliated with the acquiring enterprise under subparagraph 2 shall be included.

Article 7

The term 'concerted action' as used in this Law means the conduct of any enterprise, by means of contract, agreement or any other form of mutual understanding, with any other competing enterprise, to jointly determine the price of goods or services, or to limit the terms of quantity, technology, products, facilities, trading counterparts, or trading territory with respect to such goods and services, etc., and thereby to restrict each other's business activities.

The term 'concerted action' as used in the preceding paragraph is limited to horizontal concerted action at the same production and/or marketing stage which would affect the market function of production, trade in goods, or supply and demand of services.

The term 'any other form of mutual understanding' as used in Paragraph 1 means other than contract or agreement, a meeting of minds whether legally binding or not which would in effect lead to joint actions.

By means of its charter, a resolution of a general meeting of members or a board meeting of directors or supervisors, or any other means, to restrict activities of enterprises is also deemed as horizontal concerted action as used in Paragraph 2.

Article 8

The term 'multi-level sales' as used in this Law means the promotion or sales plan or organization pursuant to which the participants pay a certain consideration to obtain the right to promote or sell goods or services and the right to introduce other persons to participate in the plan or organization, thereby receiving a commission, bonus, or other economic benefit.

'To pay a certain consideration' as used in the preceding paragraph means the payment of money, the purchase of goods, the provision of services, or the undertaking of an obligation. The term 'multi-level sales enterprise' as used in this Law means an enterprise that adopts a multi-level sales operations plan or organization and conducts overall planning of multi-level sales activity. A participant of a foreign enterprise or a third party that introduces the multi-level sales plans or organizations of such enterprise shall be deemed a 'multi-level sales enterprise' as referred to in the preceding paragraph.

The term 'participant' as used in this Law means the following:

1. a person who takes part in the organization or plans of a multi-level sales enterprise and promotes or sells goods or services, and may introduce other persons to participate;
2. a person who, by agreement with a multi-level sales enterprise, obtains the right to promote or sell goods or services and introduce other persons to participate only after cumulatively paying a certain amount of consideration.

Article 9

The term 'competent authority' as used in this Law means the Fair Trade Commission, Executive Yuan, at the central government level; the metropolitan government at the metropolitan level; and the county (or city) government at the county (or city) level.

For any matter provided for in this Law that concerns the authorities of any other ministries or commissions, the Fair Trade Commission, Executive Yuan may consult with such other ministries or commissions to deal therewith.

Chapter II: Monopolies, Mergers and Concerted Actions

Article 10

No monopolistic enterprises shall:

1. directly or indirectly prevent any other enterprises from competing by unfair means;
2. improperly set, maintain or change the price for goods or the remuneration for services;
3. make a trading counterpart give preferential treatment without justification; or
4. otherwise abuse its market power.

Article 11

Any merger that falls within any of the following circumstances shall be filed with the central competent authority in advance:

1. as a result of the merger the enterprise(s) will have one third of the market share;
2. one of the enterprises in the merger has one fourth of the market share; or
3. sales for the preceding fiscal year of one of the enterprises in the merger exceeds the threshold amount publicly announced by the central competent authority.

The threshold amount of the sales referred to in Subparagraph 3 of the preceding paragraph may be announced separately for financial enterprises and non-financial enterprises by the Central Competent Authority.

Enterprises shall not proceed to merge within a period of 30 days from the date the Central Competent Authority accepts the complete filing materials, provided that the Central Competent Authority may shorten or extend the period as it deems necessary and notifies the filing enterprise of such change in writing.

Where the Central Competent Authority extends the period in accordance with the proviso of the preceding paragraph, such extension may not exceed 30 days; for cases of extension, decisions on the filing shall be made in accordance with the provisions of Article 12.

Where the Central Competent Authority fails to notify of the extension as referred to in the proviso of Paragraph 3 or makes any decision as referred to in the preceding paragraph when the period is going to expire, the enterprises may proceed to merge provided that the merger may not proceed under any of the following circumstances:

1. Where the filing enterprises consent to a further extension of the period.
2. Where the filing contains any false or misleading item.

Article 11-1

The provisions of Paragraph 1 of the preceding Article shall not apply to any of the following circumstances:

1. Where any of the enterprises participating in a merger already holds no less than 50% of the voting shares or capital contribution of another enterprise in the merger and merges such other enterprise.
2. Where enterprises of which 50% or more of the voting shares or capital contribution are held by the same enterprise merge.
3. Where an enterprise assigns all or a principal part of its business or assets, or all or part of any part of its business that could be separately operated, to another enterprise newly established by the former enterprise solely.
4. Where an enterprise, pursuant to the proviso of Article 167, Paragraph 1 of the Company Law or Article 28-2 of the Securities and Exchange Law, redeems its shares held by shareholders so that its original shareholders' shareholding falls within the circumstances provided for in Article 6, Paragraph 1, Subparagraph 2 herein.

Article 12

The central competent authority may approve an application for merger filed pursuant to the preceding article if the overall economic benefit of the merger outweighs the disadvantages resulted from competition restraint.

Article 13

Where any enterprise(s) fail to file an application for any merger that is required for approval, or proceed with the merger despite that the application is not approved, the central competent authority may prohibit such merger, prescribe a period for such enterprise(s) to split, to dispose of all or a part of the shares, to transfer a part of the operations, or to remove certain persons from positions, or make any other necessary dispositions.

For enterprise(s) violating the disposition made by the central competent authority pursuant to the preceding paragraph, the central competent authority may order the dissolution of such enterprise(s), or the suspension or termination of their operations.

Article 14

No enterprise shall have any concerted action; unless the concerted action that meets one of the following requirements is beneficial to the economy as a whole and in the public interest, and the application with the central competent authority for such concerted action has been approved:

1. unifying the specifications or models of goods for the purpose of reducing costs, improving quality, or increasing efficiency;
2. joint research and development on goods or markets for the purpose of upgrading technology, improving quality, reducing costs, or increasing efficiency;

3. each developing a separate and specialized area for the purpose of rationalizing operations;
4. entering into agreements concerning solely the competition in foreign markets for the purpose of securing or promoting exports;
5. joint acts in regards to the importation of foreign goods for the purpose of strengthening trade;
6. joint acts limiting the quantity of production and sales, equipment, or prices for the purpose of meeting the demand orderly, while in economic downturn, the market price of products is lower than the average production costs so that the enterprises in a particular industry have difficulty to maintain their business or encounter a situation of overproduction; or
7. joint acts for the purpose of improving operational efficiency or strengthening the competitiveness of small-medium enterprises.

After receipt of the application referred to in the preceding Article, the Central Competent Authority shall make a decision of approval or rejection within three months, the period of which may be extended once if necessary.

Article 15

The central competent authority may attach conditions or require undertakings in the approval it grants pursuant to the provisions of the preceding article.

The approval shall specify a time limit not exceeding three years. The enterprises involved may, with justification, file a written application for an extension thereof with the Central Competent Authority within three months prior to the expiration of such period; provided, however, that the term of each extension shall not exceed three years.

Article 16

After a concerted action is approved, the Central Competent Authority may revoke the approval, alter the contents of the approval, or order the enterprises involved to cease from continuing the conduct or rectify its conduct, or to take necessary corrective actions if the cause for approval no longer exists, the economic condition changes, or the enterprises involved engage in any conduct beyond the scope of approval.

Article 17

The Central Competent Authority shall establish a specific registry to record the approvals, conditions, undertakings, time limits, and relevant dispositions referred to in the preceding three articles and publish these matters in the government gazette.

Chapter III: Unfair Competition

Article 18

Where an enterprise supplies goods to its trading counterpart for resale to a third party or such third party makes further resale, the trading counterpart and the third party shall be allowed to decide their resale prices freely; any agreement contrary to this provision shall be void.

Article 19

No enterprise shall have any of the following acts which is likely to lessen competition or to impede fair competition:

1. causing another enterprise to discontinue supply, purchase or other business transactions with a particular enterprise for the purpose of injuring such particular enterprise;
2. treating another enterprise discriminatively without justification;
3. causing the trading counterpart(s) of its competitors to do business with itself by coercion, inducement with interest, or other improper means;

4. causing another enterprise to refrain from competing in price, or to take part in a merger or a concerted action by coercion, inducement with interest, or other improper means;
5. acquiring the secret of production and sales, information concerning trading counterparts or other technology related secret of any other enterprise by coercion, inducement with interest, or other improper means; or
6. limiting its trading counterparts' business activity improperly by means of the requirements of business engagement.

Article 20

No enterprise shall have any of the following acts with respect to the goods or services it supplies:

1. using in the same or similar manner, the personal name, business or corporate name, or trademark of another, or container, packaging, or appearance of another's goods, or any other symbol that represents such person's goods, commonly known to relevant enterprises or consumers, so as to cause confusion with such person's goods; or selling, transporting, exporting, or importing goods bearing such representation;
2. using in the same or similar manner, the personal name, business or corporate name, or service mark of another, or any other symbol that represents such person's business or service, commonly known to relevant enterprises or consumers, so as to cause confusion with the facilities or activities of the business or service of such person; or
3. using on the same or similar goods the mark that is identical or similar to a well-known foreign trademark that has not been registered in this country; or selling, transporting, exporting, or importing goods bearing such trademark.

The preceding paragraph shall not apply to any one of the following:

1. using in an ordinary manner the generic name customarily associated with the goods or the representation customarily used in the trade of the same category of goods; or selling, transporting, exporting or importing goods bearing such name or representation;
2. using in an ordinary manner the name or representation that is customarily used in the trade of the same type of business or service;
3. using in good faith one's own name, or selling, transporting, exporting or importing goods bearing such name; or
4. using, with good faith, in the same or similar manner the representation referred to in the first or second subparagraph of the preceding paragraph before such representation having become commonly known to the relevant enterprises or consumers, or using such representation by any successor that acquires such representation together with the business from a bone fide user; or selling, transporting, exporting or importing goods bearing such representation.

Where any enterprise has any of the acts set forth in the third and fourth subparagraphs of the preceding paragraph which is likely to damage or cause confusion with the business, goods, facilities, or activities of another enterprise, the latter enterprise may request the former to add appropriate representation unless the former only transports such goods.

Article 21

No enterprise shall make or use false or misleading representations or symbol as to price, quantity, quality, content, production process, production date, valid period, method of use, purpose of use, place of origin, manufacturer, place of manufacturing, processor, or place of processing on goods or in advertisements, or in any other way making known to the public.

No enterprise shall sell, transport, export or import goods bearing false or misleading representations referred to in the preceding paragraph.

The two preceding paragraphs shall apply mutatis mutandis to the services of an enterprise.

Where any advertising agency makes or designs any advertisement that it knows or is able to know is misleading, it shall be jointly and severally liable with the principal of such advertisement for damages arising therefrom. Where any advertising medium communicates or publishes any advertisement that it knows or is able to know is likely to mislead the public, it shall be jointly and severally liable with the principal of such advertisement for the damages arising therefrom.

Article 22

No enterprise shall, for the purpose of competition, make or disseminate any false statement that is able to damage the business reputation of another.

Article 23

No multi-level sale shall be conducted if the participants thereof receive commissions, bonuses, or other economic benefit mainly from introducing others to participate, rather than from the marketing or sale of the goods or services at reasonable market prices.

Article 23-1

Any participant in multi-level sales may rescind the participation agreement by giving the multi-level enterprise written notice within fourteen days after entering into such agreement.

Within a period of thirty days after rescission of the agreement takes effect, the multi-level sales enterprise shall accept the application from the participant for returning of goods, collect or accept goods returned by the participant, and return to the participant all the payment for goods made upon purchase and any other fees paid upon participation, accumulated until the time of rescission.

In returning the payments made by the participant according to the preceding paragraph, the multi-level sales enterprise may deduct upon the time of returning of the goods the value decreased due to the damage or loss attributable to the participant, and any bonus or remuneration already paid to the participant for purchase of such goods.

If the returned goods as referred to in the preceding paragraph are collected by the enterprise, the enterprise may deduct the shipping costs required for such collection.

Article 23-2

After the lapse of the period for entitlement to rescind the agreement as referred to in the first paragraph of the preceding article, the participant may still terminate the agreement by writing and withdraw itself from the multi-level sales.

Within thirty days from the termination of the agreement in accordance with the preceding paragraph, the multi-level sales enterprise shall buy back all goods possessed by the participant at ninety percent (90%) of the original purchase price; provided that it may be deducted the bonuses or remuneration paid to the participant for the purchase as well as the amount of the decreased value of the goods.

Article 23-3

When the participant exercises the right to rescind or terminate the agreement in accordance with the two preceding articles, the multi-level sales enterprise may not claim damages or levy penalties against the participant for such rescission or termination.

The provisions of the two preceding articles that relate to goods shall apply mutatis mutandis to the supply of services.

Article 23-4

Regulations concerning any multi-level sales enterprise's filing for record, inspection of activities, Certified Public Accountant (CPA) certification and public disclosure of financial statements, the matters that participants should be informed, the content of participation agreements, the protection of participants' interest, conduct prohibited as materially affecting the rights and interests of participants, and management obligations toward participants are to be promulgated by the Central Competent Authority.

Article 24

In addition to what is provided for in this Law, no enterprise shall otherwise have any deceptive or obviously unfair conduct that is able to affect trading order.

Chapter IV: Fair Trade Commission

Article 25

In order to manage matters in respect of fair trade as set forth in this Law, the Executive Yuan shall establish the Fair Trade Commission, which shall be in charge of the following matters:

1. preparation and formulation of fair trade policy, laws and regulations;
2. review of any fair trade matters related to this Law;
3. investigation of activities of enterprises and economic conditions;
4. investigation and disposition of any case violating this Law; and
5. any other matters related to fair trade.

Article 26

The Fair Trade Commission may investigate and handle, upon complaints or ex officio, any violation of the provisions of this Law that harms the public interest.

Article 27

In conducting investigations under this Law, the Fair Trade Commission may proceed in accordance with the following procedures:

1. to notify the parties and any related third party to appear to make statements;
2. to notify relevant agencies, organizations, enterprises, or individuals to submit books and records, documents, and any other necessary materials or exhibits, and
3. to dispatch personnel for any necessary on-site inspection of the office, place of business, or other locations of the relevant organizations or enterprises.

An investigator carrying out its duties under this Law shall present the documents supporting its duties; the person to be investigated may refuse the investigation where the investigator fails to present such documents.

Article 27-1

During the course of an investigation conducted pursuant to the preceding Article, a party or a related person, for the need of claiming or defending its legal rights and interests, may apply to read, transcribe, photocopy, or photograph relevant materials or files except the following:

1. Drafts of an administrative decision or any other working document prepared for a case.
2. Materials related to national defence, military affairs, diplomatic affairs, and any other official secrets that are required to be kept confidential by laws or regulations.
3. Materials relating to personal privacy, professional secrets, or business secrets that are required to be kept confidential by laws or regulations.
4. Where it is likely to infringe the rights and interests of a third party.

5. Where it is likely to seriously obstruct the performance of the official duties in maintaining social order, public security, or any other public interests.

Procedural matters and restrictions relating to the qualifications of applicants, the application period, the scope of materials or files available for access, and the way to proceed as referred to in the preceding paragraph shall be prescribed by the Central Competent Authority.

Article 28

The Fair Trade Commission shall carry out its duties independently in accordance with the law and may dispose of the cases in respect of fair trade in the name of the Commission.

Article 29

There shall be a separate law enacted to govern the organizational structure of the Fair Trade Commission.

Chapter V: Compensation for Damages

Article 30

If any enterprise violates any of the provisions of this Law and thereby infringes upon the rights and interests of another, the injured may demand the removal of such infringement; if there is a likelihood of infringement, prevention may also be claimed.

Article 31

Any enterprise that violates any of the provisions of this Law and thereby infringes upon the rights and interests of another shall be liable the damages arising therefrom.

Article 32

In response to the request of the person being injured as referred to in the preceding article, a court may, taking into consideration of the nature of the infringement, award damages more than actual damages if the violation is intentional; provided that no award shall exceed three times of the amount of damages that is proven.

Where the infringing person gains from its act of infringement, the injured may request to assess the damages exclusively based on the monetary gain to such infringing person.

Article 33

No claim for damages as prescribed in this Chapter shall be allowed unless the right is exercised within two years after the claimant knows the act and the person liable for the damages; nor shall the claim be allowed after lapse of ten years from the time of infringing conduct.

Article 34

In filing a suit with a court in accordance with this Law, the injured may request the content of the judgment to be published in a newspaper at the expenses of the infringing party.

Chapter VI: Punishment

Article 35

If any enterprise violating the provisions of Articles 10, 14, or paragraph 1 of Article 20 is ordered by the central competent authority pursuant to Article 41 to cease therefrom, rectify its conduct, or take necessary corrective action within the time prescribed in the order, and after the lapse of such period, shall such enterprise fail to cease therefrom, rectify such conduct, or take any necessary corrective action, or after its ceasing therefrom, shall such enterprise have the same or similar violation again, the actor shall be punished by imprisonment for not more than three years or detention, or by a fine of not more than one hundred million New Taiwan Dollars, or by both.

Any person violating any of the provisions of Article 23 shall be punished by imprisonment for not more than three years or detention, or by a fine of not more than one hundred million New Taiwan Dollars, or by both.

Article 36

If any enterprise violating the provisions of Article 19 is ordered by the central competent authority pursuant to Article 41 to cease therefrom, rectify its conduct, or take necessary corrective action within the time prescribed in the order, and after the lapse of such period, shall such enterprise fail to cease therefrom, rectify such conduct, or take necessary corrective action, or after its ceasing therefrom, shall such enterprise have the same or similar violation again, the actor shall be punished by imprisonment for not more than two years or detention, or by a fine of not more than fifty million New Taiwan Dollars, or by both.

Article 37

Shall any enterprise violate the provisions of Article 22, the actor shall be punished by imprisonment for not more than two years or detention, or by a fine of not more than fifty million New Taiwan Dollars, or by both.

No action shall be brought against the violation referred to in the preceding paragraph unless there is a complaint filed.

Article 38

Shall any juristic person be convicted of the violation referred to in any of the three preceding articles, not only the actor shall be punished in accordance with the provisions of the three preceding articles, the juristic person shall also be fined as prescribed in each of the respective articles.

Article 39

Where any other laws provide for more severe punishment than those prescribed in the preceding four articles, the provisions of such other laws shall apply.

Article 40

1. Where any enterprise(s) proceeds with a merger in violation of Paragraph 1 or 3 of Article 11 herein, or proceeds with a merger despite that the Central Competent Authority decides upon the filing to prohibit such merger, or fails to perform the undertakings required as pursuant to Paragraph 2 of Article 12, in addition to the disposition pursuant to the provisions of Article 13, an administrative penalty of not less than one hundred thousand nor more than fifty million New Taiwan Dollars shall be assessed upon such enterprise(s).
2. Where any enterprise(s) proceeds with a merger under the circumstance set forth in Subparagraph 2 of the proviso of Article 11, Paragraph 5, an administrative penalty of not less than fifty thousand nor more than five hundred thousand New Taiwan Dollars shall be assessed upon such enterprise(s).

Article 41

The Fair Trade Commission may order any enterprise that violates any of the provisions of this Law to cease therefrom, rectify its conduct or take necessary corrective action within the time prescribed in the order; in addition, it may assess upon such enterprise an administrative penalty of not less than fifty thousand nor more than twenty-five million New Taiwan Dollars. Shall such enterprise fails to cease therefrom, rectify the conduct or take any necessary corrective action after the lapse of the prescribed period, the Fair Trade Commission may continue to order such enterprise to cease therefrom, rectify the conduct or take any necessary corrective action within the time prescribed in the order, and each time may successively assess thereupon an administrative penalty of not less than one hundred thousand nor more than fifty million New Taiwan Dollars until its ceasing therefrom, rectifying its conduct or taking the necessary corrective action.

Article 42

Any person violating the provisions of Article 23, in addition to being subject to the disposition pursuant to the provisions of Article 41, may be subject to an order for dissolution, suspension or termination of business operation if the violation is serious.

Any person violating any of the provisions of paragraph 2 of Article 23-1, paragraph 2 of Article 23-2, or Article 23-3, may be ordered to cease therefrom, rectify its conduct, or take necessary corrective action within the time prescribed in the order; in addition, an administrative penalty of not less than fifty thousand nor more than twenty-five million New Taiwan Dollars may be assessed upon it. After the lapse of the prescribed period, shall it fail to cease therefrom, rectify its conduct or take any necessary corrective action within the time prescribed, it may be ordered continuously to cease therefrom, rectify its conduct or take necessary corrective action within the time prescribed, and in addition, an administrative penalty of not less than fifty thousand nor more than fifty million New Taiwan Dollars may be assessed successively thereupon each time until it ceases therefrom, rectifies its conduct, or takes necessary corrective action. Shall the violation be serious, an order for dissolution of the enterprise or suspension or termination of its operations may be made.

Any enterprise violating the regulations which is promulgated by the Central Competent Authority pursuant to the provisions of Article 23-4 shall be subject to the disposition prescribed in Article 41.

Article 42-1

The periods for suspension of business operation ordered pursuant to this Law shall be limited to six months each.

Article 43

Shall any person subject to any investigation conducted by the Fair Trade Commission pursuant to the provisions of Article 27 refuse the investigation without justification, or refuse to appear to respond or to render relevant materials such as books and records, documents, or exhibits by the set time limit, an administrative penalty of not less than twenty thousand nor more than two hundred fifty thousand New Taiwan Dollars shall be assessed upon it. Shall such person continue to refuse without justification upon another notice, the Fair Trade Commission may continue to issue notices of investigations, and may assess successively thereupon an administrative penalty of not less than fifty thousand nor more than five hundred thousand New Taiwan Dollars each time until it accepts the investigation, appears to respond, or surrenders relevant materials like books and records, documents, or exhibits.

Article 44

Shall any person upon which an administrative penalty is assessed pursuant to the preceding four articles refuse to pay such penalty, the matter shall be referred to the court for compulsory execution.

Chapter VII: Supplementary Provisions

Article 45

No provision of this Law shall apply to any proper conduct in connection with the exercise of rights pursuant to the provisions of the Copyright Law, Trademark Law, or Patent Law.

Article 46

Where there is any other law governing the conducts of enterprises in respect of competition, such other law shall govern; provided that it does not conflict with the legislative purposes of this Law.

Article 47

Any unrecognized foreign juristic person or organization may file a complaint for public prosecution, private prosecution, or civil action pursuant to the provisions of this Law; provided, however that any national or organization of the Republic of China in the country of such foreign juristic person or organization must be entitled to the right of the kind in accordance with any treaty, or any law, regulation, or custom of such country; or through any agreement entered into by any organization(s) or institution(s) and approved by the Central Competent Authority, for mutual protection.

Article 48

The enforcement rules of this Law shall be made and promulgated by the Central Competent Authority.

Article 49

This Law shall take effect one year from promulgation. Amendments to this Law shall take effect from the date of promulgation.

APPENDIX 3

Korea: Monopoly Regulation and Fair Trade Act[1]

Chapter 1 General Provisions

Article 1 (Purpose)

This Act seeks to promote fair and free competition such that creative enterprising activities are fostered, to protect consumers, and to strive for the balanced development of the national economy by preventing the abuse of market dominance by enterprisers and excessive concentration of economic power and by regulating improper cartels and unfair business practices.

Article 2 (Definitions)

For the purpose of this Act, the terms used herein shall have the following definitions:

1. The term 'enterpriser' refers to a person who operates a manufacturing business, a service business, or any other business. Any officer, employee, agent, or other person acting in the interest of the enterpriser shall be considered an enterpriser in relation to the application of provisions pertaining to the enterprisers' organization.

1-2. The term 'holding company' pertains to a company that makes its primary business the control of any domestic company's business through the ownership of stocks (including equities; the same shall apply hereinafter) and whose total assets are above the amount set by the Presidential Decree. In this case, the standards for primary business shall be prescribed by the Presidential Decree.

1-3. The term 'subsidiary' refers to a domestic company whose business is controlled by the holding company under the criteria prescribed by the Presidential Decree.

1-4. The term 'business-related sub-subsidiary' pertains to a domestic company whose business is controlled by subsidiaries. A business-related sub-subsidiary is closely related to the subsidiaries concerned as per the Presidential Decree.

2. The term 'Business Group' pertains to a group of companies whose businesses are substantially controlled by the same person according to the following pursuant to the standards prescribed by the Presidential Decree:
   A. The 'same person' is a company or a group composed of such person and one or more companies he/she controls.
   B. The 'same person' is not a company or a group composed of two or more companies he/she controls.
3. The term 'affiliated company' refers to the case wherein two or more companies belong to the same Business Group; each company is an 'affiliated company' of the others.
4. The term 'enterprisers' organization' pertains to a juristic person or federation organized by two or more enterprisers for the purpose of promoting their common interests regardless of the organization's form.
5. The term 'officer' refers to a director, a representative director, a managing partner with unlimited liability, an auditor, or a person in a similar position or a commercial employer

[1] As amended, text up to date as at 15 January 2009.

who is capable of carrying out general business for the main office or a branch office, e.g., manager, etc.

6. The term 'resale price maintenance' pertains to an act of trading goods or services wherein an enterpriser compels a counterpart enterpriser or another enterpriser by the next stage of transaction to sell or provide them only at a price fixed in advance at each stage of distribution or executes transactions under any agreement or binding condition for such purpose.
7. The term 'market-dominating enterpriser' refers to any enterpriser enjoying Market Dominance and possibly determining, maintaining, or changing the prices, quantity, or quality of commodities or services or other terms and conditions of business as a supplier or a customer in a particular business area individually or jointly with other enterprisers.
8. The term 'particular business area' pertains to an area wherein any competitive relation exists by subject, stage, or geographical area of such trade, or there is a possibility of such.

8-2. The term 'practices practically suppressing competition' refers to any of the practices that affect or threaten to affect the setting of price, quantity, quality, or other terms or conditions of trading in accordance with the intent of a certain enterpriser or an enterprisers' organization owing to reduced competition in a particular business area.

9. The term 'credit' pertains to any loan and guarantee or acceptance of company obligations by domestic financial institutions.
10. The term 'financial industry or insurance industry' refers to any of the financial and insurance businesses under the Korea Standard Industrial Classification as notified by the Commissioner of the Korea National Statistical Office pursuant to the provision of Clause 1, Article 22 (Standard Classification) of the Statistical Act.

Article 2-2 (Application to Extra-Territorial Activities)

The Act shall apply even to activities carried out overseas when they are deemed to have influence on the domestic market.

Chapter 2 Prohibition on the Abuse of Market Dominance

Article 3 (Improvement, Etc., of Monopoly or Oligopoly in Market Structures)

1 The Fair Trade Commission shall establish and implement action plans to promote competition in markets where monopolies or oligopolies have existed for an extended period of time in relation to the supply or demand of goods or services.

2 In case of a need for the Fair Trade Commission to carry out action plans formulated under Clause (1), it may give opinions to the chief officers of the appropriate administrative authorities in relation to the introduction of competition or other measures as necessary to improve the market structures.

3 The Fair Trade Commission shall conduct research on the market structures and announce the results to establish and promote the action plans referred to in Clause (1).

4 The Fair Trade Commission may request an enterpriser to submit the necessary data for the research and announcement related to the market structure as referred to in Clause (3).

5 The Fair Trade Commission may entrust the affairs referred to in Clauses (3) and (4) to other agencies under the conditions prescribed by the Presidential Decree.

Article 3-2 (Prohibition on the Abuse of Market Dominance)

1 No market-dominating enterpriser shall commit any of the following acts (hereinafter referred to as 'abusive acts'):

1. Act of determining, maintaining, or changing the price of commodities or services unreasonably (hereinafter referred to as 'price').

2. Act of unreasonably controlling the sale of commodities or provision of services.
3. Act of unreasonably interfering with the business activities of other enterprisers.
4. Act of unreasonably impeding the participation of new competitors.
5. Act of unfairly excluding competitive enterprisers or act that may considerably harm the interest of consumers.

2 The categories or standards for abusive acts shall be specified by the Presidential Decree.

Article 4 (Presumption of Market-Dominating Enterpriser)

An enterpriser with any of the following market shares in a particular business area (excluding an enterpriser whose annual sales and/or purchases in a regular field of trade amount to less than Won4 billion) shall be presumed to be a market-dominating enterpriser as referred to in Clause 7, Article 2 (Definitions):

1. The market share of one enterpriser is 50/100 or more.
2. The total market share of at least three enterprisers is 75/100 or more, excluding those whose market share is less than 10/100.

Article 5 (Corrective Measures)

In case of any act violating the provisions of Article 3-2 (Prohibition on the Abuse of Market Dominance), the Fair Trade Commission may order the market-dominating enterpriser involved to reduce prices, discontinue the violation, announce its receipt of a corrective order to the public, and take other measures required for correction.

Article 6 (Surcharge)

In case of abusive acts by a market-dominating enterpriser, the Fair Trade Commission may slap such enterpriser with surcharges equal to not more than 3 percent of the turnover specified by the Presidential Decree (referring to the profits of the business particularly for the person designated by the Presidential Decree; the same shall apply hereinafter). In the absence of a turnover, or in case of difficulty in computing the turnover under the Presidential Decree (hereinafter referred to as 'in the absence of turnover, etc.'), however, surcharges of not more than Won1 billion may be imposed.

Chapter 3 Restriction on the Combination of Enterprises and Suppression of Economic Power Concentration

Article 7 (Restriction on the Combination of Enterprises)

1 No one shall substantially minimize competition in a particular business area directly or through a person deemed by the Presidential Decree to have special interest (hereinafter referred to as 'person with special interest') by committing any of the acts described below (hereinafter referred to as 'combination of enterprises'); note, however, that this provision shall not apply to cases wherein a person other than a company whose total asset or turnover (referring to the sum of total assets or turnover of affiliated companies) meets the amount specified by the Presidential Decree (hereinafter referred to as 'large company') and commits any of the acts described in Item 2.

1. Acquisition or ownership of stocks of other companies.
2. Concurrent holding of an officer's position in another company (hereinafter referred to as 'concurrent holding of an officer's position') by an officer or an employee (referring to a person who continues to be engaged in the affairs of the company although he/she is not an officer; the same shall apply hereinafter).
3. Merger with other companies.

4. Acquisition through transfer, lease, or acceptance by the mandate of the entire or main part of the business of another company or acquisition through the transfer of the whole or main part of the fixed assets used for the business of another company (hereinafter referred to as 'acquisition through the transfer of business').
5. Participation in the establishment of a new company; note, however, that this shall not apply to the following cases:
   A. A person other than those with special interests (excluding those specified by the Presidential Decree) does not participate in the establishment of a new company.
   B. A person participates in the establishment of a company via division as per Article 530-2 (Division and Merger Through the Division of Company) (1) of the Commercial Act.

2 The provisions of Clause (1) shall not apply if the Fair Trade Commission deems that a combination of enterprises meets the requirements described below. In this case, the parties concerned shall prove that they meet such requirements.

1. The promotion of efficiency attainable through the combination of enterprises is greater than the negative effect produced by the restricted competition.
2. Such combination is made with a nonviable company meeting the requirements prescribed by the Presidential Decree, e.g., a company whose total capital as indicated in a balance sheet is less than its paid-in capital for a reasonable period of time.
3. [Deleted]
4. If a combination of enterprises falls under any of the following cases, competition is presumed to be suppressed in any particular business area:
   1. The aggregate of the market share of a company taking part in a combination of enterprises (referring to the aggregate of market shares of the affiliated companies; the same shall apply herein) falls under any of the following categories:
      A. The aggregate market share of the company concerned satisfies the presumptive requirements for a market-dominating enterprise.
      B. The aggregate market share of the company concerned is the largest in the relevant business area.
      C. The aggregate market share of the company concerned exceeds the market share of the company with the second largest market share (referring to a company with the largest market share besides the company concerned) by not less than 25 percent of the aggregate market share.
   2. A large company combines enterprises directly or through a person with special interest in accordance with the following requirements:
      A. A combination of enterprises in a particular business area where small or medium-sized companies covered by the Framework Act on Small and Medium Enterprises account for not less than two-thirds of the entire market share.
      B. A combination of enterprises wherein the combined company has a market share of not less than 5 percent.
5. The Fair Trade Commission may establish and announce policies in relation to the standards for the combination of enterprises that practically suppress competition in a particular business area under Clause (1) to which the provisions of Clause (1) do not apply as per Clause (2).

Article 7-2 (Standards for the Acquisition or Ownership of Shares)

The acquisition or ownership of shares under this Act shall be determined by the genuine ownership of shares regardless of the names listed on the register.

Article 8 (Report on the Establishment of and Conversion into a Holding Company)

Any person who has established a holding company or has converted a company into a holding company shall make a report to the Fair Trade Commission under the conditions prescribed by the Presidential Decree.

Article 8-2 (Restrictions, Etc., on the Holding Company)

1 The terms used herein have the following definitions:

1. The term 'joint venture' pertains to the enterprise (except that invested in by the person among specially related persons other than those specified by the Presidential Decree) where changes in shareholdings among shareholders are difficult since more than two persons as shareholders (among the shareholders having relations with specially related persons, those except the one specified by the Presidential Decree shall be regarded as one person) owning a substantial amount of shares and possibly having influence on business management severely restrict the ceiling of shareholdings with any contract or other similar measures.
2. The term 'venture holding company' refers to the holding company having venture companies (hereinafter referred to as 'venture company') as subsidiaries pursuant to Clause 1, Article 2 (Definition) of the Act on Special Measures for the Promotion of Venture Business in accordance with the criteria prescribed by the Presidential Decree.

2 No holding company shall commit any of the following acts:

1. Act of having obligations exceeding twice the total capital (referring to an amount obtained by deducting the obligations from the total assets indicated in the balance sheet; the same shall apply hereinafter); if the debts of companies surpass twice the total amount of capital at the time of establishing/transforming into a holding company, however, they may have debts surpassing twice the total amount of capital for two years following the establishment/transformation into a holding company.
   A. [Deleted]
   B. [Deleted]
   C. [Deleted]
2. Act of owning less than 40/100 of the total number of its subsidiary's issued stocks [20/100 in case the relevant subsidiary is a subsidiary of a venture business holding company, a jointly invested corporation, or a stock-listed corporation (hereinafter referred to as 'foreign listed company'); referred to as 'the standard for holding the shares of subsidiaries' herein]; under any of the following cases, however, this provision shall not apply if they fall under the standard for holding shares of subsidiaries:
   A. At a time when the company establishes or transforms into a holding company, if it holds subsidiaries' shares falling short of the standard in less than two years from the date of establishment of/transformation into a holding company.
   B. If the company is listed on the stock market or registered with the Association pursuant to the provisions of the Securities and Exchange Act, or the shareholdings of subsidiaries under a joint venture amount to less than that specified in the standards in less than a year.
   C. When a company that had been a venture holding company has fallen short of the standards for holding shares of affiliates, and it no longer falls under the category of holding company in less than a year.
   D. When the subsidiary first allocates shares to the Employee Share Ownership Program as per the provisions of Article 191-7 (prior allocation of the member of the Employee Share Ownership Program) of the Securities and Exchange Act and falls short of the

shareholding standards for affiliates by exercising new stock preemptive rights or requesting for the conversion of bond of warrant or convertible bond issued as per the provisions of Article 513 (Issuance of Convertible Bonds) or Article 516-2 (Issuance of Bond with Warrant) of the Commercial Act in less than a year.

E. When a company other than a subsidiary has become a subsidiary in less than a year, thereby falling short of the share ownership standards.

F. When a subsidiary falls short of the standard for shareholdings in subsidiaries in less than a year in the process of upgrading its status (limited to the situation wherein it no longer falls under the category of subsidiary within a year).

G. When a subsidiary falls short of the standard for shareholdings in subsidiaries in less than a year in the process of merging with the company.

3. Act of owning stocks of a domestic company (excluding a company that operates a private investment business as per Clauses 1-4, Article 4 (Method of Promoting a Private Investment Business) of the Act on Private Participation in Infrastructure; the same shall apply hereinafter) other than a subsidiary owning more than 5% of the total amount of issued shares (for a holding company whose sum of share prices in domestic companies other than subsidiaries is less than 15% of the sum of share prices of subsidiaries, however, this provision does not apply) or act of owning stocks of domestic affiliates other than subsidiaries, excluding domestic companies or domestic affiliates other than subsidiaries holding shares for any of the following reasons:

A. A company is converted into a holding company or involved in activities stipulated herein at the time of establishment in less than two years following the conversion into/establishment of a holding company.

B. In the process of letting the company other than affiliates fall under the category of affiliate in less than a year (limited to the case of becoming a subsidiary within the same period).

C. In the process of letting domestic affiliates that do not have shares become affiliated companies in less than a year after having shares in the affiliates concerned (limited to the case wherein a company became an affiliated company during the same period).

D. In the process of preventing the affiliate from falling under the category of affiliate in less than a year.

4. Act of owning stocks of a domestic company other than those of a company operating a financial or an insurance business (including a company meeting the standards prescribed by the Presidential Decree such as companies closely connected with the financial business or insurance business) for a holding company that owns stocks of its subsidiary operating a financial or an insurance business (hereinafter referred to as 'financial holding company'); if it holds shares in domestic companies other than those operating a financial or an insurance business at the time of conversion into/establishment of a financial holding company, however, it may hold shares of domestic companies for two years.

5. Act of owning stocks of a domestic company operating a financial or an insurance business for a holding company that is not a financial holding company (hereinafter referred to as 'general holding company'); if it holds shares in domestic companies operating a financial or an insurance business at the time of conversion into/establishment of a holding company, however, it may hold shares of domestic companies for two years following the conversion into/establishment of a holding company.

3 A subsidiary under a holding company shall not commit any of the following acts:

1. Act of holding shares equal to less than 40% of the total amount of issued shares of business-related sub-subsidiaries (or 20% if the sub-subsidiaries are listed companies in the stock market, a registered company in the trade association, or a joint venture as per the regulations of the Securities and Exchange Act; 'standards for holding shares of business-related sub-subsidiaries' shall apply hereinafter); note, however, that this provision shall not apply to

business-related sub-subsidiaries falling short of the standards for holding shares of business-related sub-subsidiaries under the following cases:

A. The company concerned holds shares of business-related sub-subsidiaries, but they fall short of the standard at the time they became subsidiaries in less than two years.

B. The company is listed on the stock market and registered in the trade association pursuant to the provisions of the Securities and Exchange Act, or the business-related sub-subsidiaries no longer fall under the category of business-related sub-subsidiary in less than a year; thus falling short of the standards for holding shares in business-related sub-subsidiaries.

C. For the new issuance or sale of shares by a business-related sub-subsidiary pursuant to the provisions of Article 191-7 (prior allocation of the member of the Employee Share Ownership Program) of the Securities and Exchange Act or allocation of shares in the Employee Share Ownership Program, there is a need for convertible bonds or to convert into bond with warrant pursuant to the provisions of Article 513 (Issuance of Convertible Bonds) or Article 516-2 (Issuance of Bond with Warrant) under the Commercial Act. Otherwise, the time for holding a business-related sub-subsidiary's shares is limited through the exercise of pre-emptive rights in less than a year.

D. Companies other than business-related sub-subsidiaries become business-related sub-subsidiaries, but they fall short of the standard for holding shares of business-related sub-subsidiaries in less than a year.

E. Business-related sub-subsidiaries have not fallen under the category of business-related sub-subsidiary, and they fall short of the standards for holding shares of business-related sub-subsidiaries in less than a year (limited to cases wherein the provision on the business-related sub-subsidiary no longer applies during the same period).

F. Business-related sub-subsidiaries merge with another company, and they fall short of the standards for holding shares of business-related sub-subsidiaries in less than a year.

2. Any activity of holding shares in domestic affiliates other than business-related sub-subsidiaries excluding domestic affiliates holding shares for any of the following reasons:

   A. Domestic affiliates holding shares at the time of becoming a subsidiary in less than two years.

   B. In letting companies other than affiliates become business-related sub-subsidiary in less than a year (limited to cases wherein a company became a business-related sub-subsidiary during the same period).

   C. In the process of letting domestic affiliates that do not have shares become business-related sub-subsidiaries in less than a year after having shares in the affiliates concerned.

   D. In the process of preventing a business-related sub-subsidiary from becoming a business-related sub-subsidiary in less than a year (limited to the situation wherein the company concerned has not become an affiliate during the same period).

   E. In the process of the business-related sub-subsidiary's merger with another company and holding of shares of another affiliate in less than a year after acquiring shares.

   F. An affiliate having its own shares holding shares of other domestic affiliates in less than a year due to a company division.

3. Any activity of controlling companies operating a financial or an insurance business as a business-related sub-subsidiary; in the case of a controlling company operating a financial or an insurance business as a business-related sub-subsidiary when a general holding company has become an affiliate, however, the business-related sub-subsidiary may be controlled for two years starting from the date it became an affiliate.

4. The business-related sub-subsidiary of a non-financial holding company shall not own shares in domestic affiliates excluding domestic affiliates holding shares for any of the following reasons:

   1. Domestic affiliates holding shares at the time of becoming a business-related sub-subsidiary in less than two years.

2. If a domestic company that is not an affiliate but holds shares becomes an affiliate in less than a year.
3. When the business-related sub-subsidiary with its own shares holds shares of other domestic affiliates due to a company division in less than a year after acquiring shares.
4. When the business-related sub-subsidiary holds all issued stocks of the domestic affiliate (excluding a company operating a financial or an insurance business).
5. A company with a business-related sub-subsidiary holding shares as described in Item 4, Clause 4 (hereinafter referred to as 'great sub-subsidiary') may not hold shares of domestic affiliates excluding domestic affiliates holding shares for any of the following reasons:
   1. Domestic affiliates holding shares at the time of becoming a business-related great sub-subsidiary in less than two years.
   2. If a domestic company that is not an affiliate but holds shares becomes an affiliate in less than a year.
6. The grace period for the regulation for applying Clause 2, Article 1, Items 2-A, 3-A, 4, and 5, Clause 2, Items 1-A, 2-A, and 3, Clause 3, Item 1, Clause 4, and Item 1, Clause 5 may be extended by two years after obtaining approval from the Free Trade Commission based on the changes in economic conditions, e.g., sudden changes in the price of stock, stock disposal prohibition agreement, and considerable losses in business.
7. A holding company shall submit a report on its business contents and those of its subsidiaries, business-related sub-subsidiaries, and great sub-subsidiaries (hereinafter referred to as 'holding companies') to the Fair Trade Commission particularly the status of stockholding and financial standing under the conditions prescribed by the Presidential Decree.

Article 8-3 (Limitation on the Establishment of a Holding Company by Large Business Groups Subject to the Limitation on Debt Guarantees)

If the same person controlling a company belonging to a Business Group subject to the limitations on debt guarantees as designated in accordance with Article 14 (Designation, Etc., of Business Group, Etc., Subject to the Limitations on Cross-Shareholding) (1) or person with special interests in the same person intends to establish a holding company or convert the company into a holding company, he/she shall have the existing debt guarantees under Article 10-2 (Prohibition on Debt Guarantees for Affiliated Company) and falling under the following cases nullified:

1. Debt guarantees between a holding company and its subsidiary.
2. Debt guarantees between a holding company and other domestic affiliated companies (excluding a subsidiary controlled by the holding company).
3. Debt guarantees between subsidiaries.
4. Debt guarantees between a subsidiary and other domestic affiliated companies (excluding a holding company controlling the subsidiary and other subsidiary controlled by the holding company).

Article 9 (Prohibition, Etc., on Cross-Shareholding)

1 Any company belonging to a Business Group whose total assets, etc., fall under the criteria prescribed by the Presidential Decree and consequently receiving the designation specified in Article 14 (Designation, Etc., of Business Group, Etc., Subject to the Limitations on Cross-Shareholding) (1) (hereinafter referred to as 'Business Group Subject to the Limitations on Cross-Shareholding') shall not acquire or own stocks of an affiliated company acquiring or owning its stocks; note, however, that this shall not apply under any of the following cases:
   1. Merger of companies or acquisition via the transfer of an entire business.
   2. Enforcement of security rights or receipt of accord and satisfaction.

2 Any company with cross-shareholding under the proviso of Clause (1) shall dispose of stocks within six months of acquiring or holding them. Note, however, that this provision shall not apply to cases wherein an affiliated company acquiring or holding its own stocks disposes of them.

3 Any company belonging to a Business Group subject to the limitations on cross-shareholding and serving as an investment company for the establishment of small and medium-sized enterprises in accordance with the Support for Small and Medium Enterprise Establishment Act shall not acquire or hold stocks of a domestic affiliated company.

Article 10 (Ceiling on the Total Amount of Shareholding)

1 Any company belonging to the same Business Group with total assets of Won10 trillion (hereinafter referred to as 'Business Group Subject to the Ceiling on the Total Amount of Shareholding') shall be prohibited from acquiring or owning stocks of another domestic company in excess of the amount derived by multiplying its net asset amount by 40/100 (hereinafter referred to as 'shareholding ceiling amount'); note, however, that this provision shall not apply under any of the following cases:

1. The company acquires or owns new stocks of another domestic company within the ratio of acquired or owned stocks to the gross number of stocks issued by said company. In this case, the same shall be limited to within two years of the date of acquisition or ownership.
2. The company acquires or owns stocks of another domestic company through the execution of a collateral right or receipt of accord and satisfaction. Note, however, that the same shall be limited to within 6 months of the date of acquisition or ownership.
3. Among foreign invested companies pursuant to the Foreign Investment Promotion Act, the company subject to the ceiling on the total amount of shareholding in other domestic companies acquires or owns shares of a company wherein at least 10% of its shares are held by a foreign investor (foreign investors having relations based on capital equity investment in accordance with the provisions of Item 4 (b), Clause 1, Article 2 of the Foreign Investment Promotion Act and specially related persons pursuant to the provision of Article 6 of the Foreign Investment Promotion Act of companies having relations based on capital equity investment as per Item 4 (b), Clause 1, Article 2 of the Foreign Investment Promotion Act). In this case, the exemption period shall not be more than six months when the foreign investor's shareholding ratio is less than 10% of the total issued shares.
4. Companies acquire or own shares for technical cooperation with small and medium-sized companies, corporate restructuring to pursue technological cooperation with small and medium-sized companies, and enhancement of corporate competitiveness and international competitiveness of the industry as specified in the Presidential Decree, e.g., new industry pursuant to the provision of Article 7 of the Industrial Development Act, and they meet the conditions set by the Presidential Decree.
5. The company acquires or owns stocks in excess of the ceiling on the total amount of shareholdings in other domestic companies for the purpose of converting into a holding company or preventing its transformation into a holding company by acquiring, owning, or disposing of stocks or by decreasing or increasing its assets, and such acts satisfy the requisites prescribed by the Presidential Decree. Note, however, that the period when the company may acquire or own stocks shall be from the date of acquisition or ownership to the end of the relevant business year; if such conversion into a holding company or into a company other than a holding company takes considerable time, and reasonable reasons are established, the Fair Trade Commission may extend such period until the next business year.
6. The company owns stocks of any of the following companies (in this case, when the procedures for each of the following items have been completed, the same shall be limited to within 6 months of the date of completion):
   A. Company that is currently undergoing the procedure for company restoration as initiated in accordance with the Integrated Insolvency Act.

B. [Deleted]

C. Company that is currently undergoing the necessary procedure after having been declared bankrupt as per the Integrated Insolvency Act.

D. Company that is currently undergoing the procedure for management as initiated in accordance with Article 7 (Management of Companies Showing Signs of Insolvency) (1) 1-1-3 of the Corporate Restructuring Promotion Act.

2 The net asset amount as per the provisions of Clause (1) excluding each item shall be equal to the amount derived according to the following methods:

1. Total assets.

A. Total assets indicated in the balance sheet for the designated previous fiscal year as per Article 14-1.

B. In the case of a company operating a financial or an insurance business, the bigger of the total assets and capital.

C. In case a newly established company does not have a balance sheet for the previous fiscal year, the paid capital for the designated current date.

2. Net assets.

A. The amount derived by subtracting the invested money (the amount derived by multiplying the par value of 1 share by the number of shares owned; the same shall apply hereinafter) as of the end of the previous fiscal year from the amount of total assets or capital – whichever is bigger – as indicated in the balance sheet for the previous fiscal year.

B. In case a newly established company does not have a balance sheet for the previous fiscal year, the amount derived by subtracting the invested amount of the affiliate in the company from the paid capital at the time of establishment.

C. In the case of Items A and B, the amount derived by subtracting the invested money of the affiliate from the increased total capital as a result of the total capital increase following the issuance of new stock, merger, or convertible bond after the establishment of the company or in the previous fiscal year.

3 The value of stocks acquired or owned as per the provisions of Clause (1) except each item shall be computed according to prices at the time of acquisition of such stocks; in case the price at the time of acquisition reflects the contribution to be paid to the Government, however, the value shall be computed based on the amount derived by subtracting such contribution from the prices at the time of acquisition.

4 In applying the provisions of Clause (1), if the prescribed investment limit amount is exceeded due to a decrease in the net asset value of a company (excluding cases wherein the net asset value of the company decreases following the acquisition of treasury stocks; the same shall apply hereinafter), or in case the already excessive amount increases, the smaller amount from among the following shall be deemed the investment limit amount for two years starting from the date of decrease of the net asset value (the same shall apply to cases wherein the net asset value of the company decreases again after the prescribed period elapses):

1. Amount of investment made in another domestic company as of the date of decrease of the net asset value.
2. Investment limit amount derived in case the net asset value does not decrease.

5 If the investment limit amount increases in excess of the amount deemed the investment limit amount in Clause (4) following an increase in the net asset value as per the provisions of Clause (2) 3, the provisions of Clause (4) shall not apply.

6 If the stocks acquired or owned by a company belonging to a Business Group subject to the limitations on the total investment amount fall under any of the following, such stocks shall not be regarded as the stocks of another domestic company as per Clause (1) except each item:

1. Acquiring or owning stocks of a company operating a private investment project under the conditions described in Item 1 or 4, Article 4 (Method of Operating a Private Investment

Project) of the Act on Private Participation in Infrastructure; in this case, the same shall be limited to within 20 years of the date of acquisition or ownership may be extended by not more than 10 years as deemed necessary by the Fair Trade Commission, e.g., the period including the construction period of the said private investment project and free-use period exceeds 20 years.

2. Acquiring or owning stocks of any of the following companies to take over such company:
   A. Government-invested institution as per Article 2 (Application Scope) of the Framework Act on the Management of Government-Invested Institutions (hereinafter referred to as 'Government-Invested Institutions').
   B. Corporation as per Article 2 (Applicable Companies) of the Act on the Improvement of Managerial Structure and Privatization of Public Enterprises.
   C. Government-contributed organization as prescribed by the Presidential Decree.
   D. Affiliated company of the companies in Items (a)–(c).
3. Acquiring or owning the stocks of a company falling under the standard as prescribed by the Presidential Decree, e.g., carrying out a business identical to that of the company under the provisions of portions other than each item or having close relation with the business contents of such company.
4. Acquiring or owning the stocks of company wherein the State or local government acquires or owns at least 30/100 of the gross number of issued stocks; in this case, if the share ratio of the State or local government in the said company falls short of 30/100, it shall be limited to within 6 months of the said date.
5. Acquiring or owning the stocks of a company falling under the standard as prescribed by the Presidential Decree, e.g., sales amount, as a company approved as affiliate based on Article 16 (Affiliate) of the Act on North-South Cooperation.

7 The provisions of Clause (1) shall not apply to any of the following companies:

1. Company operating a financial business or an insurance business.
2. Holding company, etc.
3. Company that is currently undergoing the initiated procedure for turnaround under the Integrated Insolvency Act or initiated procedure for management under Article 7 (Management of Company Showing Symptoms of Business Failure) (1) 1 or 3 of the Corporate Restructuring Promotion Act; in this case, once each procedure has been completed, it shall be limited to within one year of the date of completion.
4. Company equipped with the monitoring and controlling mechanism specified by the Presidential Decree for the directors' meeting, board of directors' meeting, and shareholders' meeting to ensure the smooth implementation of management activities and transparent decision making.
5. Company whose total capital for the previous year is less than that specified by the Presidential Decree.

8 Business group whose financial structure, number of affiliates, and ownership control structure conform to the Presidential Decree but is excluded from the Business Group subject to the ceiling on the total amount of shareholding.

Article 10-2 (Prohibition on Debt Guarantees for Affiliated Company)

1 Any company (excluding a company operating a financial business or an insurance business; the same shall apply hereinafter) belonging to a Business Group falling under the criteria set forth in the Presidential Decree, e.g., total amount of assets in excess of a specific scale, and consequently receiving the designation as per Article 14 (1) (hereinafter referred to as 'Business Group Subject to the Limitations on Debt Guarantees'), shall not give debt guarantees to its domestic affiliated

companies; note, however, that this shall not apply to a debt guarantee under any of the following cases:

1. Guarantee made in connection with any debt of a company taken over according to the plan or criteria for rationalization under the Restriction of Special Taxation Act.
2. [Deleted]
3. Guarantee with respect to debts as deemed necessary to enhance the international competitiveness of enterprises or as set forth by the Presidential Decree.

2 For the purpose of Clause (1), the term 'debt guarantee' refers to any guarantee to be made to a domestic affiliated company by a company belonging to a Business Group subject to the limitations on debt guarantees in connection with the credit of a domestic financial institution under any of the following cases:

1. Financial institutions prescribed by the Banking Act, Korea Development Bank, Export-Import Bank of Korea, Long-Term Credit Bank, and Industrial Bank of Korea.
2. [Deleted]
3. Insurance companies as prescribed by the Insurance Business Act.
4. Investment and sales companies, investment agencies, and financial institutions as prescribed by the Act on Capital Market and Financial Investment Business.
5. [Deleted]
6. Other financial institutions as prescribed by the Presidential Decree.

3 [Deleted]

4 [Deleted]

Article 10-3 [Deleted]

Article 11 (Limitation on the Voting Rights of Financial or Insurance Companies)

No financial or insurance company belonging to a Business Group subject to the limitations on cross-shareholding shall exercise voting rights for acquired or owned stocks of domestic affiliated companies. Note, however, that this provision shall not apply to any of the following cases:

1. Acquiring or owning stocks to operate a financial business or an insurance business.
2. Acquiring or owning stocks by obtaining approval, etc., pursuant to the Insurance Business Act, etc., to operate and manage insurance properties efficiently.
3. Passing of a resolution for any of the following matters during the general meeting of stockholders of a relevant domestic affiliated company (limited to stock-listed corporation; in this case, the number of voting stocks from among those of the financial or insurance company shall not exceed 15/100 of the gross number of stocks issued by said affiliated company including the number of stocks to be exercised by persons other than those stipulated by the Presidential Decree among specially related persons with the said affiliated company):
   A. Appointment or dismissal of officers.
   B. Amendment of the articles of incorporation.
   C. Merger of said affiliated company with another company or transfer of all or part of the business to another company.

Article 11-2 (Resolution of the Board of Directors and Publication on Large-Scale Intra-Group Transaction)

1 Any company belonging to a Business Group falling under the criteria set forth in the Presidential Decree, e.g., total amount of assets in excess of a specific scale, (hereinafter referred to as 'company subject to the publication of internal trading') and intending to carry out trading under any of the following cases (hereinafter referred to as 'large-scale intra-group transaction') with

specially related persons or for such specially related persons beyond the business scale prescribed by the Presidential Decree shall publish such intention in advance following a resolution of the board of directors (the same shall apply to cases wherein such company intends to change major contents as prescribed in Clause (2)):

1. Act of channelling or trading funds, e.g., suspense payments and loans, etc.
2. Act of offering or trading securities, e.g., stocks and company bonds, etc.
3. Act of offering or trading assets, e.g., real estate or intangible property rights, etc.
4. Act of offering or trading goods or services for the same affiliate or to the affiliate as prescribed by the Presidential Decree considering the stockholder constituent.

2 Any company subject to the publication of internal trading in making the publication pursuant to the provisions of Clause (1) shall include the objective of the trading, partners, scale, and terms of such trading in its publication as prescribed by the Presidential Decree.

3 The Fair Trade Commission may entrust the business related to the publication as prescribed in the provisions of Clause (1) to institutions in charge of receiving reports as established pursuant to the provisions of Article 161 (Submitting Report) of the Act on Capital Market and Financial Investment Business. In this case, the Fair Trade Commission shall determine the methods, procedures, and other necessary matters relevant to the publication following consultations with such entrusted institutions.

4 A company operating a financial or an insurance business but subject to the publication of internal trading may engage in trading without obtaining a resolution of the board of directors if it intends to carry out fixed trading according to the abovementioned provision and shows consistency with the standards prescribed by the Presidential Decree, notwithstanding the provisions of Clause (1); note, however, that such company shall publish the contents of such trading.

5 In accordance with Clause 1, a listed company is in the committee only when the committee includes more than 3 external directors, and the number of external directors is more than 2/3 of all committee members as prescribed by Clause 19, Article 2 (Definitions) of the Securities Exchange Act) according to Article 393-2 (Committees in the Board of Directors) of the Commercial Act shall be considered a resolution of the board of directors.

Article 11-3 (Disclosure of Important Contents of Non-listed Companies, Etc.)

1 Companies falling under business conglomerates meeting the standards, e.g., total amount of assets above a certain level as stipulated by the Presidential Decree (except companies operating a financial or an insurance business) and those except listed companies in the stock market and registered in the association shall disclose the following (note, however, that those disclosed in accordance with Article 11-2 shall be excluded):

1. Important issues related to corporate ownership and governance structure, e.g., status of share ownership, changes in the largest shareholders and major shareholders (meaning those under the provision of Clause 1 (2), Article 9 of the Capital Market and Financial Investment Business Act), and changes in business executives as stipulated by the Presidential Decree.
2. Activities causing important changes to the corporate financial structure, e.g., acquisition of assets and shares, transfer, security offer, waiving or undertaking of debt as stipulated by the Presidential Decree.
3. Activities causing important changes to business activities, e.g., management transfer, acquisition by transfer, merger and acquisition, share swap, etc., as stipulated by the Presidential Decree.

2 The provisions under Clauses 2 and 3, Article 11-2 (Resolution of the Board of Directors and Publication on Large-Scale, Intra-Group Transaction) shall apply to the disclosure under Clause 1.

Article 12 (Notification on the Combination of Enterprises)

1 A company having a certain total value of assets or turnover as determined by the Presidential Decree (limited to large companies if the combination of enterprises falling under Item 3 is made; referred to as 'company subject to notifying the combination of enterprises' herein) or a person with special interests in a company subject to notifying the combination of enterprises participating in a combination of enterprises falling under Items 1-5 for the counterpart enterprise whose total amount of assets and turnover is set by the Presidential Decree (referred to as 'counterpart company' herein) shall issue a notification to the Fair Trade Commission as set by the Presidential Decree as a company other than that subject to notifying the combination of enterprises. If the company falling under the category of counterpart company engages in a combination of enterprises under any of the following cases, the same shall apply:

1. In case the company holds at least 20 percent (15 percent for a stock-listed corporation or Association-registered corporation under the Securities and Exchange Act) of the total number of stocks issued by other companies (excluding non-voting stocks pursuant to Article 370 (Non-voting Shares) of the Commercial Act; the same shall apply hereinafter).
2. In case the company becomes the largest shareholder by additionally acquiring shares of another company after notifying the combination of enterprises in accordance with the provision of Clause 1.
3. In the case of interlocking directorate (except for the case of interlocking business executive in affiliates).
4. When carrying out the activities in Item 3 or 4, Clause 1, Article 7 (Restriction on the Combination of Enterprises).
5. When acquiring the largest stocks of a new company to be established.

2 The total amount of assets or revenues of a company subject to notifying the combination of enterprises and its counterpart company as stipulated in Clause 1 is the sum of total assets or revenues of a company maintaining the status of affiliate from the day before the combination of enterprises to the day after the combination of enterprises; in case of business transfer pursuant to the provision in Item 4, Clause 1, Article 7 (Restriction on the Combination of Enterprises), the total assets and turnover of companies transferring their business (including the lease of business operation, entrustment of business management, and transfer of fixed assets used for business operation) exclude the total amount of assets or revenues of affiliates.

3 Notwithstanding the provisions of Clause (1), any of the following companies shall not be subject to notifying the combination of enterprises:

1. If the small/medium enterprise startup investment company or small/medium enterprise startup investment association under Items 4 and 5, Article 2 of the Support for Small and Medium Enterprise Establishment Act combines with the founder (hereinafter referred to as 'founder') under Item 2, Article 2 or a venture business.
2. If the venture capitalist or venture business investment association under Article 41 (Application Scope) (1) and (3) of the Specialized Credit Financial Business Act combines with the new technology enterprise under Clause 1, Article 2 (Definitions) of the Korea Technology Credit Guarantee Fund Act.
3. If the company subject to notifying the combination of enterprises owns the stocks of the following companies in excess of the rate in Item 1, Clause 1 or makes the largest investment by jointly participating in the establishment of the following companies:
   A. Investment company (excluding corporate takeover securities company in Article 142-1) under the Indirect Investment Asset Management Act.
   B. Company designated as a private investment business enforcer in infrastructure based on the Act on Private Participation in Infrastructure.
   C. Investment company established to invest in the company specified in Item C (company in Item 1, Clause 1, Article 51-2 of the Corporate Tax Act).

4 The provisions of Clause (1) shall not apply if the head of the central administrative agency concerned has consulted in advance with the Fair Trade Commission regarding the combination of enterprises under the relevant Acts.

5 In computing the rate of holding or acquisition pursuant to Clause (1) 1, 2, or 5, the stocks owned by a person with special interest in the company concerned shall be included.

6 Notifications on the combination of enterprises under Clause (1) shall be issued within thirty days of the date of such combination. If one or more companies involved in a combination of enterprises falling under Clause (1) 1, 2, 4 or 5 are larger companies, notifications on the combination of enterprises shall be issued within thirty days as set by the Presidential Decree, e.g., date of conclusion of contracts for merger.

7 No one who has issued a notification under the proviso of Clause (6) shall register the fact of a merger, execute the contracts for the takeover of business, or acquire stocks within thirty days of issuing such notification. If necessary, however, the Fair Trade Commission may shorten or extend the period to not more than 90 days from the date following the expiry date.

8 Any person intending to combine enterprises under Article 7 (Restriction on the Combination of Enterprises) (1) may request the Fair Trade Commission to determine whether such combination may be categorized as one that substantially minimizes competition even before the period requiring a report under Clause (6).

9 Upon the request for an evaluation under Clause (8), the Fair Trade Commission shall notify the company concerned of its decision within thirty days. If necessary, however, the Fair Trade Commission may extend such period to not more than 90 days from the date following the expiry date.

10 When the duty to file a report pursuant to Clause (1) falls on two or more companies, such companies shall file the report jointly. Note, however, that this provision shall not apply if the Fair Trade Commission has designated one of the companies belonging to a Business Group consisting of the company obligated to file a report as the representative responsible for filing the report (referred to as 'representative' herein) under the conditions prescribed by the Presidential Decree.

Article 12-2 (Exception in the Notification Procedure for the Combination of Enterprises).

1 If the company applying for recommendation for approval, change, and permit (hereinafter referred to as 'approval, etc.') for change in the largest investor or establishment or merger of the following corporations (hereinafter referred to as 'corporate establishment, etc.') falls under the company subject to notifying the combination of enterprises as per Clause 1, Article 12 (Notification on the Combination of Enterprises), the notification document on the combination of enterprises must be submitted as well when applying for approval, etc., to the competent authorities issuing approval, etc. (including the Korean Broadcasting Commission; the same shall apply hereinafter):

1. Establishment of company under Clause 2, Article 13 (Takeover and Merger of Business) of the Telecommunications Business Act.
2. Merger of corporations (only for a corporation that is a general wired broadcaster under Item B, Clause 3, Article 2 (Definitions of Terms; hereinafter referred to as 'general wired broadcaster') according to Item 1, Clause 1, Article 15 (Approval, Etc.) of the Broadcasting Act.
3. To control the management rights of the general wired broadcaster or to become the largest investor of the general wired broadcaster under Clause 1, Article 15-2 (Change and Approval of the Largest Investor) of the Broadcasting Act.

2 If the applicant for approval, etc., submits the notification document on the combination of enterprises to the competent authorities as per Clause 1, the date the document has been received shall be the notification date as per Clause 2, Article 12.

3 Upon receiving the notification document on the combination of enterprises, the competent authorities must forward it to the Fair Trade Commission immediately.

4 Those needing to issue notification on the combination of enterprises under Clause 6, Article 12 must submit to the Fair Trade Commission the document on the approval, etc., of corporate establishment when issuing notification on the combination of enterprises.

5 Upon receiving the document on the approval, etc., of corporate establishment under Clause 4, the Fair Trade Commission must forward it to the competent authorities immediately.

Article 13 (Report on the Status of Shareholding)

1 All companies belonging to a Business Group subject to limitations on cross-shareholding, a Business Group subject to the restriction on the total amount of shareholding in other domestic companies, or a Business Group subject to the limitations on debt guarantees shall submit to the Fair Trade Commission a report on the status of ownership of their stockholders, financial standing, and status of their ownership of other domestic companies' stocks under the conditions prescribed by the Presidential Decree.

2 All companies belonging to the Business Group subject to the limitations on debt guarantees shall submit to the Fair Trade Commission a report on the status of debt guarantees issued in favor of domestic affiliated companies after obtaining confirmation from a domestic financial institution pursuant to the Presidential Decree.

3 The provision of Article 12 (10) shall apply mutatis mutandis to reports referred to in Clauses (1) and (2).

4 [Deleted]

Article 14 (Designation, Etc., of Business Group, Etc., Subject to the Limitations on Cross-Shareholding)

1 The Fair Trade Commission shall designate a Business Group subject to the ceiling on the total amount of cross-shareholding, a Business Group subject to the restrictions on the total amount of shareholding in other domestic companies, and a Business Group subject to the limitations on debt guarantees (hereinafter referred to as 'Business Group, Etc., Subject to the Limitations on Cross-Shareholding') under the conditions prescribed in the Presidential Decree and shall notify companies belonging to such groups accordingly.

2 The provisions of Articles 9-11 and 13 shall apply from the date of receipt of notification referred to in Clause (1).

3 Notwithstanding Clause (2), if a company notified as a company belonging to a Business Group subject to the limitation on cross-shareholding and designated as a Business Group, etc., subject to the limitations on shareholdings pursuant to the provision of Clause 1 or a company incorporated as an affiliated company into a Business Group, etc., subject to the limitations on cross-shareholding pursuant to the provisions of Article 14-2 (1) and notified as a company belonging to a Business Group, etc., subject to the limitations on cross-shareholding is in violation of the provisions of Article 9 (1) or (3), 10 (1), or 10 (1) or 10-2 at the time of receiving such notice, such violation shall be dealt with as follows:

1. If the company violates the provisions of Article 9 (1) or (3) [including cases wherein the company issuing the stocks acquired or owned is newly incorporated as an affiliated company and deemed to violate Article 9 (3)], the same provisions shall not apply for one year from the date of designation or affiliation.
2. If the company violates the provisions of Article 10 (1), the total amount of shareholdings on the date of designation or affiliation shall be deemed to be the investment limit amount for one year from the date of such designation or affiliation. Note, however, that the same shall not apply to cases wherein the investment limit amount exceeds the amount deemed to be the investment limit amount following an increase of the net asset value.

3. If the company is in violation of the provisions of Article 10-2 (1) (including the case wherein the company receiving debt guarantees is newly incorporated as an affiliated company and deemed to commit a violation), the same shall not apply for two years from the date of designation or incorporation; when the turnover procedure is initiated based on the Integrated Insolvency Act on the company under regulations other than those in the items, the item shall not apply until the date the turnover procedure has ended. When a company covered by regulations other than those in the items has debt guarantee on the company subjected to the initiated turnover procedure, the item shall not apply until the date the turnover procedure has ended for the company receiving debt guarantee.

4 The Fair Trade Commission may request a company or a person with special interest in a company to provide the documents necessary for evaluating the possible designation of a Business Group as referred to in Clause (1).

5 A company (except the company in liquidation or whose business is suspended for more than one year and whose total amount of assets at the end of the previous year is less than that specified by the Presidential Decree) belonging to a Business Group, etc., subject to the limitations on cross-shareholding shall undergo audit by a certified public accountant, and the Fair Trade Commission shall use the balance sheet revised according to the opinions on the audit of the certified public accountant.

Article 14-2 (Incorporation into and Exclusion from Affiliated Companies)

1 When a corporation needs to be incorporated into or excluded from a Large Business Group, the Fair Trade Commission shall determine whether said corporation meets the criteria for an Affiliated Corporation and decide whether to incorporate such corporation into or exclude it from Affiliated Corporations at the request of the said corporation (including Specially Related Persons of the corporation) or on the Fair Trade Commission's own initiative.

2 The Fair Trade Commission may request the company concerned to submit data on the composition of stockholders and directors, status of debt guarantees, financial standing, transactions, and other related matters as deemed necessary for the evaluation referred to in Clause (1).

3 Upon receiving a request for evaluation as referred to in Clause (1), the Fair Trade Commission shall notify the requesting person of the results of the evaluation within thirty days. Note, however, that the Fair Trade Commission may extend such period to not more than sixty days as deemed necessary.

Article 14-3 (Presumption of Incorporation into Affiliated Company and Notification Date)

If a company receiving a request under Article 14 (4) or 14-2 (2) refuses to submit data without justifiable reason or submits false data, and it is consequently not incorporated into a Business Group, etc., subject to the limitations on cross-shareholdings even if it should be incorporated, the Fair Trade Commission considers the company to have been incorporated into a Business Group, etc., subject to the limitations on cross-shareholding and notifies the company in question accordingly on the date specified by the Presidential Decree.

Article 14-4 (Requests for the Confirmation of Documents with Competent Authorities)

The Fair Trade Commission may request any of the following authorities to confirm or investigate data related to the status of ownership of stockholders of domestic affiliated companies belonging to a Business Group, etc., subject to the limitations on cross-shareholding, data related to debt guarantees, data related to advanced payments, loans, or securities, data related to transactions or provision of immovable assets, and other matters as necessary for enforcing Articles 9-11 and 13-14-2:

1. Financial Supervisory Service pursuant to the Act on the Establishment, etc., of a Financial Supervisory Organization.
2. [Deleted]
3. Domestic financial institutions pursuant to any item of Article 10-2 (2).
4. Other institutions set forth by the Presidential Decree vis-à-vis financial transactions and exchange of stocks.

Article 14-5 (Opening of Information on the Status of Cross-Shareholding)

1 The Fair Trade Commission may open the following information on a Business Group, etc., subject to the limitations on cross-shareholding to enhance the transparency of the business group and prevent excessive concentration of economic power:
   1. Information set by the Presidential Decree, e.g., general status and control structure status of companies under the Business Group, etc., subject to the limitations on cross-shareholding.
   2. Information set by the Presidential Decree, e.g., investment, debt guarantee, and trading relation between a company under a Business Group, etc., subject to the limitations on cross-shareholding and Specially Related Person of the corporation or companies under a Business Group, etc., subject to the limitations on cross-shareholding.

2 The Fair Trade Commission may establish and manage an information system to process and open the information specified in Clause 1 effectively.

3 Matters on the opening of information other than those included in Clauses 1 and 2 shall be governed by the Act on Information Disclosure of Public Institutions.

Article 15 (Prohibition on Evasion of Law)

1 No one shall commit any act of evading the application of the provisions of Articles 7 (1) and (3), 8-2 (2)-(5), 8-3, 9, 10 (1), 10-2 (1), or 11.

2 The categories and standards for acts of evasion of law under Clause (1) shall be determined by the Presidential Decree.

Article 16 (Corrective Measures)

1 If any company has violated (or is likely to violate) the provisions of Articles 7 (1) and (3), 8-2 (2)-(5), 8-3, 9, 10 (1), 10-2 (1), 11, or 15, the Fair Trade Commission may order such company (referring to the company involved in the combination of enterprises in violation of Article 7 (1)) or violator required to take any of the following corrective measures upon receiving the report under the proviso of Article 12 (6), the Fair Trade Commission shall order the company or violator to take corrective measures within the period prescribed in Article 12 (7):
   1. Cessation of the practice concerned.
   2. Disposition of all or part of the stocks.
   3. Resignation of officers.
   4. Transfer of business.
   5. Cancellation of debt guarantees.
   6. Publication of receipt of corrective order.
   7. Restrictions on the business method or business scope to prevent the negative effects of restricted competition pursuant to the combination of enterprises.
   8. Other necessary corrective measures to reprimand such violation.

2 If a company has been established, or in case companies have been merged in violation of the provisions of Articles 7 (1) and (3), 8-3, or 12 (7), the Fair Trade Commission may file a lawsuit to nullify said establishment of a company or said merger of companies.

3 The Fair Trade Commission may decide and announce the criteria for imposing the correctives measures in each clause for violating Article 7 (1).

Article 17 (Surcharge)

1 The Fair Trade Commission may impose on a company that has acquired (or owns) stocks in violation of Article 9 or 10 (1) a surcharge of not more than ten percent of the purchase price of stocks acquired or owned.
2 The Fair Trade Commission may impose on a company that has guaranteed debt in violation of the provisions of Article 10-2 (1) a surcharge of not more than ten percent of the value of the debt guarantee in question.
3 [Deleted]
4 The Fair Trade Commission may impose a surcharge of not more than ten percent of the following amounts on a company violating the provisions of Article 8-2 (2) or (5):
   1. In case the provisions of Article 8-2 (2)-1 are violated, the surcharge shall be the debt exceeding twice the amount of total capital indicated in the balance sheet (referred to as 'standard balance sheet' herein) as prescribed by the Presidential Decree.
   2. In case the provision under Item 2, Clause 2, Article 8-2 is violated, the amount derived by multiplying the total amount of the book value in the balance sheet of the subsidiary to the amount derived by subtracting the percentage of owned stocks of the subsidiary from the following percentage, and then dividing the amount by the percentage of owned stocks of the subsidiary:
      A. Said subsidiary is a stock-listed corporation, an association-registered corporation, or a joint venture company as per the Securities and Exchange Act: 30/100.
      B. [Deleted]
      C. [Deleted]
      D. Not falling under item (a): 40/100.
   3. In case the provisions under Item 3 or 5, Clause 2, Item 2, Clause 3, and Clause 4 or Clause 5, Article 8-2 are violated, the amount shall be the total amount of book value indicated in the balance sheet of shares owned as a result of the violation.
   4. In case the provisions of Item 1, Clause 3, Article 8-2 are violated, the amount derived by multiplying the total amount of the book value in the balance sheet of the sub-subsidiary to the amount derived by subtracting the percentage of owned stocks of the sub-subsidiary from the following percentage, and then dividing the amount by the percentage of owned stocks of the sub-subsidiary:
      A. If said business-related sub-subsidiary is a stock-listed company, an association-registered corporation, or a joint venture company as per the provisions of the Securities and Exchange Act, the amount shall be 20/100.
      B. In case of a business-related sub-subsidiary not falling under Item (a), the amount shall be 40/100.

Article 17-2 (Special Case of Corrective Measures, Etc.)

1 If an affiliate of a Business Group designated as the Business Group subject to the limitations on the total amount of shareholdings in other domestic companies or a company incorporated as an affiliate into the Business Group subject to the limitations on the total amount of shareholdings in other domestic companies has violated Clause 1, Article 10 by continually owning – even after the one-year period allowing for exception in limitations on the total amount of shareholdings in other domestic companies in accordance with the provision in Clause 1, Article 10 has elapsed – shares continually owned, designated, or held at the time of incorporation, the Fair Trade Commission may order a prohibition on exercising its voting right in lieu of the provisions of Articles 16 (Corrective Measures) and 17 (Surcharge).

2 The company subjected to an order to prohibit any exercise of the voting right under Clause (1) (hereinafter referred to as 'subject company') shall notify the Fair Trade Commission of the details of stocks subjected to an order to prohibit any exercise of the voting right within the period prescribed by the Presidential Decree for not more than one month starting from the date of receiving such order of prohibition.

3 If the subject company fails to report the details of stocks subjected to an order to prohibit any exercise of the voting right within the period in Clause (2), the Fair Trade Commission may make a decision ex officio regarding the stocks whose voting right cannot be exercised under the conditions prescribed by the Presidential Decree.

4 The subject company shall make a public notification under the conditions prescribed by the Presidential Decree of the details of stocks to be notified to the Fair Trade Commission under Clause (2) or to be subjected to an ex officio order of prohibition by the Fair Trade Commission under Clause (3).

5 If a company has exercised the voting right in violation of an order to prohibit any exercise of the voting right under Clause (1), the Fair Trade Commission may impose on the company a penalty surcharge of not more than the amount obtained by multiplying the acquisition price of stocks whose voting rights have been exercised by 10/100.

Article 17-3 (Compulsory Performance Money)

1 The Fair Trade Commission may impose compulsory performance money (fine) of not more than the amount derived by multiplying 3/10000 by the following amount per day on a violator who fails to take corrective measures within the specified period pursuant to Article 16 (Corrective Measures) and in violation of Article 7 (1) (note, however, that the Fair Trade Commission may impose a fine of not more than Won2 million per day on a person who makes a combination of enterprises in violation of Article 7(1)2):

1. Total amount of the book value of stocks acquired or owned and obligations accepted for the combination of enterprises listed in Article 7(1)1 or 5.
2. Sum of the book value of stocks granted in compensation for a merger and obligations accepted for the combination of enterprises listed in Article 7(1)3.
3. Amount of business taken over from another company for a combination of enterprises listed in Article 7(1)4.

2 Policies relevant to the imposition, payment, collection, and refund of compulsory performance money shall be specified by the Presidential Decree; note, however, that compulsory performance money in arrears shall be collected in accordance with the policies on the disposition of national taxes in arrears.

3 The Fair Trade Commission may entrust to the Commissioner of the National Tax Administration matters relevant to the collection or disposition of violators defaulting in the payment of compulsory performance money under Clauses (1) and (2).

Article 18 (Enforcing Compliance with Corrective Measures)

1 No company that has been ordered to dispose of stocks pursuant to Article 16 (Corrective Measures) (1) shall exercise voting rights with respect to such stocks from the date of receiving such order.

2 No company that has engaged in cross-shareholding in violation of the provisions of Article 9 shall exercise voting rights with respect to such stocks from the date of receiving a corrective order until the violation has been corrected.

3 In giving an order to a company that has violated the provisions of Article 10 (1) to dispose of its stocks in accordance with the provisions of Article 16 (Corrective Measures) (1) 2, if the Fair Trade Commission does not affirm the stocks subject to such disposal, the company issued such

order shall notify the Fair Trade Commission of the details of stocks for which no voting rights are exercised within 10 days of receiving such order. In this case, the company shall be prohibited from exercising its voting rights for the stocks notified to the Fair Trade Commission 10 days after receiving such order, notwithstanding the provision in Clause 1.

4 If it is not notified within the period specified in Clause (3), the Fair Trade Commission may designate stocks for which the company may not exercise its voting rights as prescribed by the Presidential Decree.

Chapter 4 Prohibitions on Improper Cartels

Article 19 (Prohibition on Improper Cartels)

1 No enterpriser shall agree with other enterprisers by contract, agreement, resolution, or any other means to engage jointly in any of the following acts or let others engage in such kinds of activities that unfairly restrict competition (hereinafter referred to as 'improper cartels'):

1. Act of fixing, maintaining, or changing prices.
2. Act of determining the terms and conditions for the transactions of goods or services or payment of prices thereof.
3. Act of restricting production, delivery, transportation, or transaction of goods or services.
4. Act of limiting the territory of trade or customers.
5. Act of preventing or restricting the establishment or extension of facilities or installation of equipment required for the production of goods or rendering of services.
6. Act of restricting the types or specifications of goods or services in producing or transacting goods or services.
7. Act of jointly carrying out and managing the main parts of a business or establishing a company, etc., to carry out and manage the main parts of a business jointly.
8. Act of deciding matters prescribed by the Presidential Decree, e.g., bidding price, auctioning price, auctioneer, or bidder in bids or auctions.
9. Any practice that substantially minimizes competition in a particular business area by means other than those under Items 1-8 or interferes with or restricts the activities or contents of the business.

2 The provision of Clause (1) shall not apply if unfair collaborative acts are deemed by the Fair Trade Commission to meet the requirements specified in the Presidential Decree in case they are committed for any of the following purposes:

1. Industry rationalization.
2. Research and technology development.
3. Overcoming economic depression.
4. Industrial restructuring.
5. Rationalization of trade terms and conditions.
6. Enhancement of competitiveness of small and medium enterprises.

3 Any and all relevant policies with respect to the standards, methods, and procedures for authorization under Clause (2) and modification of authorized matters shall be specified by the Presidential Decree.

4 Any contract, etc., stipulating the improper cartels listed in Clause (1) between enterprisers shall be null and void.

5 If two or more enterprisers commit any of the acts listed in Clause (1) and practically restrict competition in a particular business area, they shall be presumed to have committed an unfair collaborative act despite the absence of an explicit agreement to engage in such act.

6 The Fair Trade Commission may establish and announce the criteria for examining improper cartels.

Article 19-2 (Measures for Preventing Improper Cartels in Public Bids)

1 The Fair Trade Commission may request for cooperation and submission of bidding materials from the heads of the government investment institution or central administrative institution of the local government institution (hereinafter referred to as 'head of public institution') to disclose or prevent improper cartels on bidding as ordered by the government investment institution or national or local government institutions.
2 The head of a public institution as decided by the Presidential Decree must submit the information on bidding to the Fair Trade Commission when the bidding price has been decided or if the bidding notice has been served.
3 The scope of information on bidding under Clause 2 and submission procedure are decided by the Presidential Decree.

Article 20 [Deleted]

Article 21 (Corrective Measures)

Where an enterpriser commits any act in violation of the provisions of Clause 1, Article 19, the Fair Trade Commission may order the enterpriser to discontinue the act, announce the receipt of corrective order, or take other corrective measures.

Article 22 (Surcharge)

The Fair Trade Commission may impose on those demonstrating any behavior violating the provision of Clause 1, Article 19 a surcharge of not more than 10 percent of the turnover as prescribed by the Presidential Decree. In the absence of turnover, etc., however, a surcharge of not more than Won2 billion may be imposed.

Article 22-2 (Mitigations or Waiving of Corrective Measures or Surcharges for Whistleblowers, Etc)

1 For any of the following companies, the corrective measures under Article 21 (Corrective Measures) or surcharge under Article 22 (Surcharge) may be mitigated or waived:
   1. Companies that have reported improper cartels.
   2. Companies that have cooperated in the investigations by providing evidence, etc.
2 The Fair Trade Commission or those working in the commission shall neither provide nor disclose the identity and reported information of the person who cooperated in the research or whistleblowers excluding the cases specified in the Presidential Decree, e.g., when necessary for lawsuits.
3 Matters required for the scope of companies subject to mitigation or waiving of corrective measures or surcharges under Clause (1) and standard for or extent, etc., of mitigation or waiving, prohibition on providing and disclosing information, and materials under Clause 2 shall be prescribed by the Presidential Decree.

Chapter 5 Prohibition on Unfair Business Practices

Article 23 (Prohibition on Unfair Business Practices)

1 No enterpriser shall commit any of the following acts that are likely to impede fair trade (hereinafter referred to as 'unfair business practices') or make an affiliated company or other enterprisers perform such acts:
   1. Act that unfairly rejects any transaction or discriminates against a certain transacting partner.

2. Act designed to exclude competitors unfairly.
3. Act of unfairly coercing or inducing customers of competitors to deal with the enterpriser in question.
4. Act of engaging in a trade with a transacting partner by unfairly taking advantage of its position in the business area.
5. Act of trading under terms and conditions that unfairly restrict or disrupt business activities.
6. [Deleted]
7. Act of assisting a person with special interest or other companies by providing advanced payment, loans, manpower, immovable assets, stocks and bonds, or intellectual properties or by transacting under substantially favorable terms.
8. Any act that threatens to impair fair trade other than those listed in Items 1–7.

2 The categories or standards for unfair business practices shall be prescribed by the Presidential Decree.

3 If necessary for the prevention of acts violating the provisions of Clause (1), the Fair Trade Commission may establish and announce the guidelines to be observed by enterprisers.

4 To prevent the unreasonable inducement of customers, enterprisers or enterprisers' organization may voluntarily write a code (hereinafter referred to as 'fair competition code').

5 The enterprisers or an enterprisers' organization may request that the Fair Trade Commission examine whether or not the fair competition code as referred to in Clause (4) violates the provisions of Clause (1)3 or 6.

Article 24 (Corrective Measures)

When an act in violation of the provisions of Article 23 (1) is committed, the Fair Trade Commission may order the enterpriser concerned to discontinue such unfair business practices, to delete any pertinent provision from a contract, to announce the receipt of corrective order to the public, or to take other necessary corrective measures against such act.

Article 24-2 (Surcharge)

In case of practices in violation of the provisions of Clause 1, Article 23, the Fair Trade Commission may impose on the person concerned a surcharge of not more than two percent (five percent in case the provisions of Item 7 are violated) of the turnover prescribed by the Presidential Decree. In the absence of turnover, however, a surcharge of not more than Won500 million may be imposed.

Chapter 6 Enterprisers' Organization

Article 25 [Deleted]

Article 26 (Prohibited Activities of Enterprisers' Organization)

1 No enterprise organization shall commit any of the following acts:

1. Any act of unfairly restricting competition including acts falling under the items in Article 19.
2. Any act of restricting the present or future number of enterprisers in any business area.
3. Any act of unreasonably restricting the business matters or activities of member enterprisers (referring to an enterpriser as a member of the enterprisers' organization; the same shall apply hereinafter).
4. Any act of inducing a person to engage in unfair business practices under each item of Article 23 (1) or to engage in practices of resale price setting under Article 29 or assist a person in committing such act.
5. [Deleted]

2 The provisions of Article 19 (2) and (3) shall apply mutatis mutandis to cases referred to in Clause (1) 1. In this case, the term 'enterpriser' shall be taken to mean 'enterprisers' organization'.
3 In case of a need to prevent any act violating the provisions of Clause (1), the Fair Trade Commission may establish and announce any and all guidelines to be observed by the enterprisers' organization.
4 If it wishes to establish such guidelines as referred to in Clause (3), the Fair Trade Commission shall consider opinions from the heads of related administrative agencies.

Article 27 (Corrective Measures)

When an act violates the provisions of Article 26, the Fair Trade Commission may order the enterprisers' organization concerned (if necessary, including the member enterprises concerned) to discontinue such act, to announce the receipt of corrective order to the public, or to take other necessary corrective measures.

Article 28 (Surcharge)

1 With regard to the violations of each item of Article 26 (1), the Fair Trade Commission may impose on the enterprisers' organization concerned a surcharge of not more than Won500 million.
2 The Fair Trade Commission may impose on an enterpriser engaged in practices violating any provision of Article 26 (1) a surcharge of not more than five percent of turnover as prescribed by the Presidential Decree. In the absence of turnover, however, a surcharge of not more than Won500 million may be imposed.

Chapter 7 Restrictions on Resale Price Maintenance

Article 29 (Restrictions on Resale Price Maintenance)

1 No enterpriser shall engage in resale price maintenance. Note, however, that this provision shall not apply to cases wherein there are justifiable reasons in terms of the maximum price maintenance preventing the transactions of commodities or services in excess of the specified prices.
2 The provisions of Clause (1) shall not apply to literary works prescribed by the Presidential Decree or to those commodities meeting the following conditions and receiving designation in advance from the Fair Trade Commission as being eligible for resale price maintenance:
   1. The uniformity in quality of the commodity concerned is easily identifiable.
   2. The commodity concerned is used daily by ordinary customers.
   3. Free competition exists with respect to the commodity concerned.
3 Any enterpriser wishing to be designated as per Clause (2) shall apply with the Fair Trade Commission under the conditions prescribed by the Presidential Decree.
4 Whenever it designates a commodity as eligible for resale price maintenance under Clause (2), the Fair Trade Commission shall make such fact public.

Article 30 (Modification of Resale Price Maintenance)

If an enterpriser producing or selling a commodity designated and made public by the Fair Trade Commission under Article 29 (4) concludes a contract to determine and maintain the resale price of such commodity, but the contract threatens to cause serious harm to the interest of consumers or contradicts public interest, the Fair Trade Commission may order the modification of such contract.

Article 31 (Corrective Measures)

When an act violates the provisions of Article 29 (1), the Fair Trade Commission may order the enterpriser concerned to discontinue such act, announce the receipt of corrective order to the public, or take other necessary corrective measures against such act.

Article 31-2 (Surcharge)

For resale price maintenance in violation of Article 29, the Fair Trade Commission may impose on the enterpriser concerned a surcharge of not more than two percent of the turnover as prescribed by the Presidential Decree. In the absence of turnover, however, a surcharge of not more than Won500 million may be imposed.

Chapter 8 Restrictions of the Conclusion of International Contracts

Article 32 (Restrictions on the Conclusion of Unfair International Contracts)

1 No enterpriser or enterprisers' organization shall enter into an international agreement or an international contract as prescribed by the Presidential Decree (hereinafter referred to as 'international contract') if such agreement or contract contains provisions concerning improper cartels, unfair business practices, or resale price maintenance. When the Fair Trade Commission deems the effect of said agreement on competition in a particular business area to be negligible, or in case of other unavoidable reasons to validate such contract, however, this provision shall not apply.

2 The definition of policies regarding improper cartels, unfair business practices, and resale price maintenance as referred to in Clause (1) may be determined, and public notice, given by the Fair Trade Commission.

Article 33 (Request for the Review of International Contracts)

Upon entering into an international contract, the enterpriser or enterprisers' organization may request that the Fair Trade Commission determine whether the contract violates any of the provisions of Article 32 (1) in accordance with the procedure set forth by the Presidential Decree.

Article 34 (Corrective Measures)

When an international contract violates the provisions of Article 32(1), or there is a likelihood of such, The Fair Trade Commission may order the enterpriser or the enterprisers' organization concerned to cancel the contract, amend or revise the contract, or take other necessary corrective measures.

Article 34-2 (Surcharge)

In the case of conclusion of international contracts in violation of Article 32 (1), the Fair Trade Commission may impose on the relevant enterprisers' organization surcharges of not more than Won500 million or on the enterpriser concerned surcharges of not more than two percent of turnover as determined by the Presidential Decree. In the absence of turnover, however, surcharges of not more than Won500 million are imposed.

Chapter 9 Enforcement Agency

Article 35 (Establishment of the Fair Trade Commission)

1 The Fair Trade Commission shall be established under the jurisdiction of the Prime Minister for the purpose of independently promoting the objectives of this Act.

2 The Fair Trade Commission shall carry out its function as one of the central administrative organizations pursuant to Article 2 (Establishment and Structures of the Central Administrative Organization) of the Government Organization Act.

Article 36 (Matters Under the Jurisdiction of the Fair Trade Commission)

The following matters shall be placed under the jurisdiction of the Fair Trade Commission:

1. Matters related to regulating the abuse of Market Dominance.
2. Matters related to restricting the combination of enterprises and preventing the concentration of economic power.
3. Matters related to regulating improper cartels and anti-competitive behavior on the part of an enterprisers' organization.
4. Matters related to regulating unfair business practices and resale price maintenance.
5. Matters related to preventing the conclusion of unfair international contracts.
6. Matters related to competition encouragement policies through consultation and coordination with respect to Acts, subordinate statutes, and administrative measures that restrict competition.
7. Matters other than Acts and subordinate statutes to be established.

Article 36-2 (International Cooperation of the Fair Trade Commission)

1 The government may sign an agreement for the enforcement of this Act with foreign governments, provided the laws and interests of the Republic of Korea are not violated.

2 Pursuant to the agreement signed as per the provision of Clause 1, the Fair Trade Commission shall support law enforcement by a foreign government.

3 Even when the agreement as per the provision of Clause 1 is not signed, the Fair Trade Commission shall support a foreign government's law enforcement activity if there is any guarantee from the requesting country that it shall support the same or similar cases requested by the Korean government in the future.

Article 37 (Composition of Fair Trade Commission and Related Matters)

1 The Fair Trade Commission shall consist of nine commissioners including a chairman, a vice chairman, and four commissioners who shall serve as non-standing members of the Fair Trade Commission.

2 The standing and non-standing commissioners of the Fair Trade Commission (hereinafter referred to as 'Commissioners') shall be appointed from among those persons with experience or specialized knowledge in the field of monopoly regulation and fair trade or consumers and who meet the following qualifications the President shall appoint the chairman and vice chairman at the recommendation of the Prime Minister, and the other commissioners, at the recommendation of the chairman:

   1. Grade II public officials or higher with experience in monopoly regulation and fair trade.
   2. Judges, prosecutors, or attorneys with at least fifteen years' experience.
   3. Associate professors, professors, or their equivalent at certified research institutes with at least fifteen years' experience and who majored in law, economics, or business administration at their respective universities.
   4. Business managers or individuals engaged in consumer protection activities with at least fifteen years' experience.

3 The chairman and vice chairman shall be considered political appointees; other standing commissioners shall be considered Grade I public officials.

4 Notwithstanding the provisions of Article 10 (Executive Representative) of the Government Organization Act, the chairman, vice chairman, and chief officer of the Secretariat as per Article 47 (Establishment of a Secretariat) shall serve as executive representative.

Article 37-2 (Types of Meetings)

Meetings of the Fair Trade Commission shall fall into 2 categories: meetings consisting of all members (hereinafter referred to as 'Plenary Session') and meetings consisting of three members including a standing commissioner (hereinafter referred to as 'Chamber').

Article 37-3 (Subjects of Plenary Session and Chamber)

1 The Plenary Session shall deliberate on and determine the following matters:
   1. Matters related to the interpretation and application of Acts and subordinate statutes and public notices under the jurisdiction of the Fair Trade Commission.
   2. Matters involving an appeal as per Article 53.
   3. Matters whose resolutions have not been made in a Chamber, or those that have been decided to be referred to the Plenary Session by a Chamber.
   4. Matters required to establish or amend regulations or public notices.
   5. Matters having substantial economic impact or those that should be dealt with by the Plenary Session itself.

2 A Chamber may deliberate or decide on matters in addition to those falling within the items of Clause (1).

Article 38 (Chairman)

1 The chairman shall represent the Fair Trade Commission.

2 The chairman may attend the state council and take the floor.

3 If the chairman is unable to perform his/her duties due to poor health or emergency, the vice chairman shall act on his/her behalf. If both the chairman and the vice chairman are unable to perform their duties due to emergency, the standing commissioners shall act on their behalf according to seniority.

Article 39 (Term of Office of the Commissioner)

The terms of office of the chairman, vice chairman, and commissioners of the Fair Trade Commission shall be three years, and they may be renewed only once.

Article 40 (Guarantee of the Commissioner's Status)

No commissioner shall be removed from his/her office against his/her will except under the following cases:

1. He/She has been sentenced to imprisonment without labor or slapped with a severer punishment.
2. He/She has become incapable of performing his/her duties due to prolonged physical or mental illness.

Article 41 (Prohibition on the Commissioner's Political Activities)

No commissioner may enter a political party or participate in any political activity.

Article 42 (Proceedings and Quorum of Meetings)

1 The proceedings of the Plenary Session shall be presided over by the chairman. Resolutions shall be made in the presence of all members based on the majority vote.

2 The proceedings of a Chamber shall be presided over by one of the standing members, and resolutions shall be made in the presence of all the members based on a unanimous vote of the members in attendance.

Article 43 (Disclosure of Trial and Resolutions and Confidentiality of Agreement)

1 All trials and resolutions made by the Fair Trade Commission shall be disclosed. Note, however, that this provision shall not apply when deemed necessary by the Fair Trade Commission to protect the trade secrets of an enterpriser or an enterprisers' organization.
2 The Fair Trade Commission shall conduct oral trials; if necessary, however, written trials may be conducted.
3 An agreement on the resolution of a case by the Fair Trade Commission shall not be disclosed.

Article 43-2 (Maintenance of Good Order in the Venue of Adjudicatory Proceedings)

The chairman of the Plenary Session or a Chamber may give the necessary orders to maintain good order in the adjudicatory proceedings with respect to the parties, those with an interest in the outcomes of the proceedings, witnesses, and those in attendance.

Article 44 (Challenge, Discharge, and Withdrawal of Members)

1 Any member may be challenged in relation to the deliberation or resolution of any of the following cases:
   1. The challenged member himself/herself or his/her spouse or ex-spouse is one of the parties whose rights or obligations are held jointly with other persons.
   2. The challenged member has a personal relationship with one of the parties, or the challenged member himself/herself or a juristic person for whom the member is working is providing advisory or consulting services on legal or managerial matters to any party.
   3. The member or a juristic person for whom the member is working has testified.
   4. The member or a juristic person for whom the member is working has acted (or is acting) as an agent of one of the parties.
   5. The member or a juristic person for whom the member is working has participated in any act, or its omission has been the subject matter of cases.
   6. The Fair Trade Commission official himself/herself is involved in the investigation or review of the case concerned.

2 One of the parties may apply for the discharge of members if he/she deems the fair deliberations or resolutions to be impossible. An application for the discharge of members shall be evaluated by the chairman without any resolution from the Plenary Session.
3 Any member may withdraw himself/herself from the deliberation and resolution of cases if there are conflicts of interest as described in the items in Clause (1) or (2).

Article 45 (Signatures and Seals by Commissioners)

1 Any and all decisions on matters in violation of the provisions of this Act shall be made in writing by the Fair Trade Commission, and the reasons for such, specified. The written decision shall be signed and sealed by the commissioners who have participated in the decision making.
2 Based on official authority or application, the Fair Trade Commission may determine whether there are written errors in the letter of resolution, error in calculation, or other similar errors, if any.

Article 46 [Deleted]

Article 47 (Establishment of the Secretariat)

A secretariat shall be established in the Fair Trade Commission to carry out the affairs of the Fair Trade Commission.

Article 48 (Provisions on Organization)

1 Matters other than those provided for in this Act but deemed necessary for the organization of the Fair Trade Commission shall be prescribed by the Presidential Decree.
2 Matters other than those provided for in this Act but deemed necessary for the operation of the Fair Trade Commission shall be prescribed by the Rules of the Fair Trade Commission.

Chapter 9-2 Establishment and Conflict Mediation of the Korea Fair Trade Mediation Committee

Article 48-2 (Establishment of the Korea Fair Trade Mediation Committee)

1 The Korea Fair Trade Mediation Committee (hereinafter referred to as 'committee') shall be established to carry out the following:
   1. Mediation of conflict related to acts in violation of Clause 1, Article 23.
   2. Mediation of conflict between franchises under the Fair Franchise Transactions Act.
   3. Research and analysis on the trading practice of businesses and market and industry analyses.
   4. Other businesses entrusted by the Fair Trade Commission.
2 The committee shall be a corporation.
3 The head of the committee shall be designated as the chairman of the Fair Trade Commission as per Clause 2, Article 37.
4 The government may allocate funds or subsidize the expenses incurred in the establishment and management of the committee within the range of the budget.
5 Matters other than those specified in this act shall be governed by the regulations on foundation in the Civil Code.

Article 48-3 (Establishment and Operation of the Korea Fair Trade Mediation Committee)

1 A committee shall be established to mediate conflicts and acts in violation of Clause 1, Article 23.
2 The committee shall consist of 7 people including one head.
3 The head of the commission shall serve as the head of the committee.
4 Committee members shall be appointed from among persons with experience or specialized knowledge in the field of monopoly regulation and fair trade or consumers and who meet the following qualifications as prescribed by the head of the commission (more than 1 of the following persons must be included):
   1. Public officials meeting the requirements prescribed by the Presidential Decree.
   2. Judges, prosecutors, or attorneys with longer experience than the period specified by the Presidential Decree.
   3. Associate professors, professors, or their equivalent at certified research institutes with longer experience than the period specified by the Presidential Decree and who majored in law, economics, or business administration at their respective universities.

4. Business managers or individuals engaged in consumer protection activities and with longer experience than the period specified by the Presidential Decree.
5. Those with longer experience in corporate management and consumer protection activities than the period specified by the Presidential Decree.

5 The term of office of committee members shall be three years, and they may be reappointed.

6 Any vacancy can be filled based on Clause 4; the term of office of the vacancy shall be the remaining term of the predecessor.

Article 48-4 (Meetings of the Committee)

1 The chairman of the committee shall convene a meeting and preside over the meeting.

2 The meeting shall start when majority of the committee members are present. Decisions shall be upheld based on the vote of the majority of the committee members in attendance.

3 If the chairman of the committee cannot perform his/her duties after figuring in an accident, he/she shall be replaced by the committee member he/she appointed.

4 Any of the subjects of conflict (hereinafter referred to as 'subjects of conflict') can make a statement in the committee.

Article 48-5 (Removal, Exemption, and Avoidance of Committee Member)

1 A committee member is removed from the mediation of conflict under the following cases:

1. The committee member or his/her spouse or ex-spouse is the subject of conflict for mediation or rightful person or related to the responsible person.
2. The committee member is a relative of the subject of conflict for mediation.
3. The committee member or the company where he/she belongs is a legal or a managerial adviser for the subject of conflict.
4. The committee member or company where he/she belongs is a witness, or he/she has participated as a representative of the subject of conflict for the mediation.

2 The subject of conflict may apply for evasion of the committee members in case securing fairness in the mediation is deemed difficult.

3 If the committee members fall under Clause 1 or 2, they may not mediate the conflict.

Article 48-6 (Application of Mediation)

1 A company sustaining damages as a result of a violation of Clause 1, Article 23 may apply for mediation of conflict by submitting to the Fair Trade Commission and committee a letter specifying the matters prescribed by the Presidential Decree (hereinafter referred to as 'conflict mediation application'). Note, however, that this provision shall not apply under the following cases:

1. Acts falling under the criteria prescribed by the Presidential Decree and conforming to Articles 24 and 51, taking into account the content, characteristics, and extent of violation of the law.
2. Case being researched by the Fair Trade Commission under Article 49 prior to receiving an application for conflict mediation.

2 Upon receiving the application for mediation as per Clause 1, the Fair Trade Commission must notify the committee accordingly within the period prescribed by the Presidential Decree by examining whether or not the case falls under Clause 1 and attaching a conflict mediation application form.

3 When receiving the application as per Clauses 1 or 2, the committee must notify the subject of conflict or Fair Trade Commission in accordance with the Presidential Decree.

Article 48-7 (Mediation, Etc.)

1 The committee may prepare and present a mediation plan or advise the subjects of conflict to reach an agreement themselves.
2 If deemed necessary to check the fact of conflict mediation, the committee may request for the attendance or submission of materials from the subjects of conflict or research on the matter.
3 The committee must reject an application for mediation for the case or act specified in Clause 1, Article 48-6. The same shall apply to conflict deemed by the Fair Trade Commission to fall under the case or act described in Clause 1, Article 48-6.
4 The committee must stop the mediation procedure under the following cases:
  1. The subjects of conflict accept the mediation plan or advice of the committee and carry out mediation themselves.
  2. Mediation is not realized even after 60 days following the receipt of a notice from the Fair Trade Commission.
  3. A subject of conflict refuses mediation or files a lawsuit in court regarding the mediation of conflict.
5 When stopping mediation or rejecting an application for mediation, the committee must immediately report in writing to the Fair Trade Commission the reason for stopping the mediation or rejecting the application for mediation and details of mediation as required by the Presidential Decree aside from attaching the relevant documents and notify the subjects of conflict accordingly.
6 The Fair Trade Commission may not recommend correction as per Clause 1, Article 51 and corrective measures as per Article 24 to the subjects of conflict until the mediation of the conflict has ended.

Article 48-8 (Writing of Mediation Protocol and its Validity)

1 The committee shall write a mediation protocol signed by the subjects of conflict and participating committee members in case mediation is realized. In this case, an agreement shall be deemed to have been reached as in the mediation protocol.
2 The committee may write a mediation protocol in case the subjects of conflict mediate their conflict by themselves prior to mediation and request for a mediation protocol.
3 The subjects of conflict must execute matters agreed upon in the mediation and submit the result to the Fair Trade Commission.
4 Once an agreement is reached based on Clause 1 and is enforced, the Fair Trade Commission shall not recommend correction according to Clause 1, Article 51 and corrective measures as per Article 24.

Article 48-9 (Organization and Management of the Committee)

The necessary matters related to the organization, management, and mediation procedure of the committee in addition to those regulated in Articles 48-3-48-8 shall be prescribed by the Presidential Decree.

Chapter 10 Investigation Procedures and Other Related Matters

Article 49 (Identification and Reporting, Etc., of Violations)

1 If it suspects that a violation of the provisions of this Act has been committed, the Fair Trade Commission may conduct the necessary investigation ex officio.
2 Any person discovering a violation of the provisions of this Act may report the occurrence of such to the Fair Trade Commission.

3 For the investigation under Clause (1) or (2), the Fair Trade Commission shall serve to the parties concerned a written notice specifying the results of the investigation (including any and all corrective measures to be implemented as a result of the investigation).

4 If five years has passed since a violation of the provisions of this Act was committed, the Fair Trade Commission shall not issue orders for corrective measures or impose surcharges as prescribed by this Act against such offense. Note, however, that this provision shall not apply in case a corrective measure or the imposition of surcharge is cancelled by a judgment of court and if a new disposition is made based on the relevant reasons for judgment.

Article 50 (Investigation, Etc., of Violations)

1 The Fair Trade Commission may take the following measures in accordance with the procedures set forth by the Presidential Decree as necessary to enforce this Act:

1. Summon the parties concerned, interested parties, or witnesses to a hearing and get their testimonies.
2. Designate and invite expert witnesses.
3. Issue an order to an enterpriser or an enterprisers' organization or its officer or employee to report on the business situation, present other necessary information or materials, or report on maintaining custody of the presented materials or information.

2 The Fair Trade Commission may have a public official under its control (including those under the control of an agency as commissioned under Article 65) enter the office or business place of an enterpriser or an enterprisers' organization to examine the business and management situation, records, documents, electronic materials, voice-recording materials, video materials, and other materials or matters prescribed by the Presidential Decree as necessary to enforce this Act as well as get the statements of the parties concerned, interested parties, and witnesses at a designated place under the conditions prescribed by the Presidential Decree.

3 Any public official conducting an examination as per Clause (2) may order an enterpriser or an enterprisers' organization or its officer or employee to present materials or matters necessary for such examination or maintain custody of the presented materials or matters in accordance with the procedures set forth by the Presidential Decree.

4 Any public official conducting an examination as per Clause (2) shall show to the appropriate person a certificate indicating his/her competency.

5 If confirming whether to provide money or other forms of assistance without any financial transaction-related information or data (hereinafter referred to as 'financial transaction information') is impossible in connection with an investigation of a company subject to the publication of internal trading suspected of violating the provisions of Article 23 (1) 7, the Fair Trade Commission shall ask the head of a certain branch of a financial institution to submit the financial transaction information based on the document specifying the information described below through voting to the committee stipulated in Article 37-3, notwithstanding the provision of Article 4 of the Act on Real Name Financial Transactions and Guarantee of Secrecy. The requested head of the branch concerned shall not decline such request.

1. Personal data of the trader.
2. Transaction period for any requested information.
3. Legal basis for the request.
4. Purpose of use.
5. Financial transaction information requested (limited to financial transaction information for persons under suspicion in connection with unfair assistance activities with the financial institution).
6. Personal data of persons and officials in the requesting organization.

6 Requesting for the submission of financial transaction information pursuant to the provision of Clause 5 shall be limited to investigation purposes only.

7 When providing financial transaction information to the Fair Trade Commission in accordance with the provision in Clause 5, the financial institution concerned shall serve a written notice to trader regarding the major contents of the submitted financial transaction information, its purpose of use, the recipient, and the date of provision within 10 days of submission. In this case, the cost of serving the notice shall apply mutatis mutandis to the provision in Clause 4, Article 4-2 of the Act on Real Name Financial Transactions and Guarantee of Secrecy.

8 In accordance with the provision of Clause 5, the Fair Trade Commission shall record the fact of requesting for financial transaction information from financial institutions and save such record for three years starting from the date of such request.

9 In accordance with the provision of Clause 5, the person receiving the financial transaction information shall neither disclose nor provide it to others nor use it for purposes other than its main purpose.

Article 50-2 (Prohibition on the Abuse of Investigation Right)

Investigative officials should conduct investigation within the minimum scope as necessary to enforce the law without abusing the investigation right for other purposes.

Article 50-3 (Application for Delaying the Investigation, Etc.)

1 In accordance with the provision in Clause 1 or 3, Article 50, an enterpriser or an enterprisers' organization subject to the investigation and any measure taken by the Fair Trade Commission and deemed to face difficulties in undergoing investigation or establishing measures for reasons specified by the Presidential Decree, e.g., natural disaster, etc., may ask the Fair Trade Commission to take measures or delay the investigation in accordance with the Presidential Decree.

2 When the Fair Trade Commission receives any application for delaying the investigation, etc., as per the provision in Clause 1, the measure and investigation shall be delayed if they are deemed to be appropriate after reviewing the reasons.

Article 51 (Recommendation for the Correction of Violation)

1 If a violation of the Act has been committed, the Fair Trade Commission may establish the standards for correction and recommend that the enterpriser or enterprisers' organization concerned comply with those standards.

2 Any person receiving such recommendation as per Clause (1) shall notify the Fair Trade Commission within ten days of receiving the notice of recommendation for correction as to whether or not he/she will comply with such recommendation.

3 If a person receiving a recommendation for correction as per Clause (1) complies with it, corrective measure shall be considered to have been taken under this Act.

Article 52 (Opportunity to State Opinion)

1 Before issuing corrective measures or imposing surcharges in response to violations of this Act, the Fair Trade Commission shall give the parties concerned and interested parties the opportunity to state their opinions.

2 The parties concerned and interested parties may attend a hearing of the Fair Trade Commission to state their opinions or present relevant materials.

Article 52-2 (Request for Access to Data)

Any party or interested person may request the Fair Trade Commission for access to or authorization to make copies of data related to measures taken under this Act. If deemed necessary for public interest, or in case consent is granted by the person providing such data, the Fair Trade Commission shall comply with such request.

Article 53 (Appeal)

1 Any party dissatisfied with the measures taken by the Fair Trade Commission pursuant to this Act may file an appeal stating the reasons with the Fair Trade Commission within thirty days of receiving a notice of said measure.

2 The Fair Trade Commission shall make a decision with respect to an appeal as per Clause (1) within sixty days. If making a decision within such period is impossible for unavoidable reasons, however, such period may be extended by not more than thirty days.

Article 53-2 (Suspension of Enforcement of Orders for Corrective Measures)

1 In case an appeal as per Article 53 (Appeal) (1) has been made by a person who has been ordered to take corrective measures under this Act, or if deemed necessary by the Fair Trade Commission to prevent irrevocable damage or harm caused by the enforcement of such orders or continuance of procedures, the Fair Trade Commission may decide to suspend the enforcement of such orders or continuance of procedures at the request of one of the parties or on an ex officio basis (hereinafter referred to as 'suspension of enforcement').

2 The Fair Trade Commission may revoke a decision granting the suspension of enforcement at the request of one of the parties or on an ex officio basis in case the grounds for the suspension of enforcement no longer exist following the decision of suspension of enforcement.

Article 53-3 (Serving of Document)

1 The serving of document in Article 14 or 16 of the Administrative Procedure Act shall apply mutatis mutandis.

2 Notwithstanding the provision of Clause 1, an enterpriser or an enterprisers' organization maintaining an overseas address (hereinafter referred to as 'address') shall appoint a domestic representative to whom it shall serve the document.

3 For a business that needs to appoint a domestic representative, or if the business group does not appoint a domestic representative, Clause 1 shall apply.

Article 54 (Filing of Lawsuit)

1 Any person wishing to file a lawsuit in response to any measure taken by the Fair Trade Commission under this Act may do so within thirty days of the date of receipt of a notice of the disposition in question or a written decision of the Fair Trade Commission against the appeal.

2 The period referred to in Clause (1) may not be extended.

Article 55 (Exclusive Jurisdiction over Lawsuits for Appeal)

The Seoul Appellate Court having jurisdiction over the seat of the Fair Trade Commission shall have exclusive jurisdiction over any and all appellate cases filed pursuant to Article 54 (Filing of Lawsuit).

Article 55-2 (Procedures for Dealing with Cases, Etc.)

Matters related to the procedures for dealing with cases in violation of this Act shall be prescribed by the Fair Trade Commission.

Chapter 10 Imposition and Collection of Surcharges, Etc

Article 55-3 (Imposition of Surcharges)

1 In imposing surcharges under this Act, the Fair Trade Commission shall take into account the following factors:
 1. Nature and extent of the unlawful practice.
 2. Duration and frequency of the unlawful practice.
 3. Benefit accrued by the unlawful practice.

2 If a company merges with a company violating this Act, surcharges may be imposed or collected on the grounds that the company concerned has engaged in the unlawful practices engaged in by the existing company.

3 The standards for the imposition of surcharges in Clause 1 shall be prescribed by the Presidential Decree.

Article 55-4 (Extension of Period of Surcharge Payment and Payment in Instalments)

1 The Fair Trade Commission may extend the period of surcharge payment or allow the surcharge to be paid in instalments for a person on whom a surcharge has been imposed (hereinafter referred to as 'person subject to surcharge payment') when he/she is deemed to have difficulty paying the surcharge in lump sum because such surcharge is more than the amount prescribed by the Presidential Decree and under any of the following cases (under these circumstances, security may be required):
 1. Substantial damage has been inflicted on the properties due to fire, theft, etc.
 2. A business is at considerable risk because of unfavorable business conditions.
 3. A lump sum payment of the surcharge is likely to cause considerable financial difficulties.
 4. Other relevant factors falling under Items 1-3 occur.

2 When applying for the extension of the period of surcharge payment or for payment in instalments, a person subject to surcharge payment shall apply with the Fair Trade Commission within 30 days of the date of receiving a notice of surcharge payment.

3 If a person subject to surcharge payment and for whom the period of surcharge payment is extended or who is permitted to pay the surcharge in instalments violates the following matters, the Fair Trade Commission may revoke its decision to extend the period of surcharge payment or accept payment in instalments and collect such surcharge in lump sum:
 1. Instalments of a surcharge are overdue.
 2. Orders by the Fair Trade Commission regarding the modification or preservation of security are not observed.
 3. Collecting all or the remaining amount of surcharge through enforcement, commencement of an auction, declaration of insolvency, dissolution of a juristic person is impossible, or national or local taxes are in arrears.

4 In relation to the extension of the period for surcharge payment or payment in instalments pursuant to Clauses (1)–(3), the relevant policies shall be established based on the Presidential Decree.

Article 55-5 (Obligation of Aligned Payment of Surcharge)

1 When a company obligated to pay the surcharge is divided or merged by division (including cases of division or merger by division as of the date of imposition), the following companies are obligated to pay the surcharge jointly:
 1. Divided company.
 2. Company established through division or merger by division.
 3. When part of the divided company is merged with another company, obligation to fall on the other company concerned.

2 When the enterpriser of the company faced with surcharge is dissolved through division or merger by division (including the date of dissolution as of the date of imposition), the following companies are obliged to pay the surcharge:
1. Company established through division or merger by division.
2. When part of the divided company is merged with another company, obligation to fall on the other company concerned.

Article 55-6 (Collection of Surcharge and Surcharge in Arrears)

1 The Fair Trade Commission may collect additional or extra surcharge equal to the amount derived by applying the interest rate set and announced by the Fair Trade Commission considering the interest rates in arrears of financial institutions as per the provision of Article 2 of the Banking Act but not exceeding 40/100 per year based on the number of days from the day after the expiration of the period for surcharge payment including the date of payment, except when the person subject to surcharge payment pays the sum of the surcharge within the period of payment.
2 Unless a person subject to the surcharge payment pays the sum of surcharge within the period of payment, the Fair Trade Commission may serve a notice specifying the period of payment and collect surcharges similar to national taxes in arrears except when original and additional surcharges as per Clause (1) are paid within the period of payment.
3 The Fair Trade Commission may delegate to the Commissioner of the National Tax Office its functions related to surcharges, collection of additional surcharges, and procedures for surcharges in arrears as per Clauses (1) and (2).
4 The Fair Trade Commission may request the Commissioner of the National Tax Office to furnish information on the imposition of national taxes on persons who failed to pay the surcharges as deemed necessary for the collection of the deferred surcharges.
5 The public officials in charge of the affairs of surcharges may request the heads of registry offices and other relevant administrative agencies to allow them to have access to the required documents or to deliver their transcripts or abstracts without compensation as necessary for the collection of surcharges.
6 All relevant matters concerning the collection of surcharges shall be prescribed by the Presidential Decree.

Article 55-7 (Additional Payment for the Refund of Surcharge)

When issuing a refund of surcharge following the adjudication of appeal or ruling of the court, the Fair Trade Commission shall make an additional payment of refund for the period from the date of paying the surcharge to the date of refund under the conditions prescribed by the Presidential Decree.

Article 55-8 (Disposal of Deficits)

1 The Fair Trade Commission may dispose of deficits with the payer of the collected surcharge and fine (hereinafter referred to as 'collection amount') under the following cases:
1. The delinquency disposition has been completed, and the distributed amount does not meet the amount in arrears.
2. The right to collect the collection amount has been terminated.
3. The whereabouts of the defaulter are not clear, or the defaulter is judged to have no assets or property.
4. The estimated total assets of the delinquency disposition are confirmed to appropriate the delinquency disposition, but there is no remainder.

5. The estimated total assets of the delinquency disposition are confirmed to appropriate the payment of debt based on mortgage or national tax, local tax, or right of pledge that takes priority, but there is no remainder.
6. The collection is impossible and falling under the Presidential Decree.

2 When disposing of deficits as per Clause 1, the whereabouts of the defaulter and whether he/she has property or assets must be checked by the related institution, e.g., local administrative institution.

3 When disposing of deficits as per Items 4-5, Clause 1, the delinquency disposition must be stopped, and the attachment of property must be unattached.

4 When the Fair Trade Commission finds other property that can be attached after disposing of deficits according to Clause 1, the deficit must be disposed of, but the delinquency disposition must be cancelled. If Item 2, Clause 1 is invoked, however, this provision does not apply.

Chapter 11 Damages

Article 56 (Liability for Damages)

1 Any enterpriser or enterprisers' organization violating the provisions of this Act and consequently causing damage to a person shall be liable for compensating such person for damage. If the enterpriser himself/herself or the enterprisers' organization itself proves that he/she/it did not intend to commit any fault, and no error is found on his/her/its part, however, this provision shall not apply.

2 [Deleted]

Article 56-2 (Transmission of Records)

In case a lawsuit for liability for damage is instituted as per Article 56 (Liability for Damages), the court may request the Fair Trade Commission to transmit the records of the case in question (including protocols and stenographic records of examination of the persons concerned and references and expert witnesses as well as all judicial evidences).

Article 57 (Deciding the Amount of Damages)

When proving the necessary facts to verify the amount of damage considering the characteristics of such facts is extremely difficult even though the occurrence of damage is deemed to be the result of a violation of the provision, the court shall decide the substantial amount of damage based on the result of evidentiary investigation and intent of overall pleading.

Chapter 12 Exemptions

Article 58 (Legitimate Actions Taken Pursuant to Acts and Subordinate Statutes)

This Act shall not apply to acts of an enterprise or an enterprisers' organization as committed in accordance with any Act or any of its decrees.

Article 59 (Exercise of Right to Intangible Property)

The provisions of this Act shall not apply to any act deemed to be an exercise of rights under the Copyright Act, Patent Act, Utility Models Act, Design Act, or Trademark Act.

Article 60 (Act of Specified Associations)

The provisions of this Act shall not apply to any act of an association (including a federation of associations) established in accordance with the following requirements (note, however, that this provision shall not apply to unfair business practices or price hikes by unfairly restricting competition):

1. The association shall aim at providing mutual aid among small-scale enterprisers or consumers.
2. The association shall be established voluntarily; its members may join and withdraw at will.
3. Each member shall have an equal voting right.
4. In case profits are distributed to members, the limits on such shall be set by the Articles of Incorporation.

Article 61 [Deleted]

Chapter 13 Supplementary Provisions

Article 62 (Duty to Maintain Confidentiality)

Any commissioner or public official performing (or has performed) his/her duties under this Act may neither divulge any and all secrets of an enterpriser or an enterprisers' organization as learned in the course of carrying out his/her duties nor use it for purposes other than to enforce this Act.

Article 63 (Consultation on Enactment of Acts Restricting Competition)

1 The chief officer of the competent administrative authority shall consult with the Fair Trade Commission in advance when wishing to propose legislation or amend enactments containing anti-competitive regulations such as restrictions on the fixing of prices or terms of transaction, entry to markets, business practices, improper cartels, prohibited practices of an enterpriser or an enterprisers' organization, etc., and to approve or establish other measures involving anti-competitive factors against an enterpriser or an enterprisers' organization.

2 When planning to enact or amend rules or regulations involving anti-competitive factors, the chief officer of the competent administrative authority shall serve advance notice to the Fair Trade Commission.

3 With regard to the approvals or other measures involving anti-competitive factors as per Clause (1), the chief officer of the competent administrative authority shall serve a notice to the Fair Trade Commission regarding the contents of the relevant approval or other measures.

4 In relation to the notice prescribed in Clause (2), if the rules or regulations to be enacted or amended are deemed to contain anti-competitive provisions, the Fair Trade Commission may give advice to the chief officer of the competent administrative authority regarding the modification of such anti-competitive provisions. This provision shall also apply to enactments made or amended without notifying the Fair Trade Commission as prescribed by Clause (1), Acts, and subordinate statutes enacted or amended without notice, approvals, or other measures given without prior notice.

Article 64 (Cooperation from the Chief Officer of a Competent Authority, Etc.)

1 If deemed necessary for the enforcement of this Act, the Fair Trade Commission may solicit the opinions of the heads of the relevant administrative authorities, other authorities, or associations.

2 If necessary for the enforcement of this Act, the Fair Trade Commission may entrust the heads of competent administrative authorities, other authorities, or associations with the necessary investigations or request for the relevant materials from them.

3 If necessary to secure compliance with a corrective measure under this Act, the Fair Trade Commission may request for the necessary cooperation from the chief officers of competent administrative authorities, other authorities, or associations.

Article 64-2 (Payment of Compensation)

1 The Fair Trade Commission may pay compensation within its budgetary limit to any person reporting any violation of this Act to the Fair Trade Commission and providing proof of such violation.

2 The detailed certification of any practice in violation of this Act and qualification of whistle-blowers eligible for compensation as well as the scope of and procedure for paying compensation as per the provision of Clause 1 shall be set by the Presidential Decree.

Article 65 (Delegation and Entrustment of Authority)

The Fair Trade Commission may delegate part of its authority as prescribed by this Act to the head of an agency under its control, the Seoul Special Metropolitan City Mayor, a Metropolitan City Mayor, or a provincial governor or entrust such to the head of another administrative agency in accordance with the procedures set forth by the Presidential Decree.

Article 65-2 (Public Officials' Agenda in Applying the Penal Clauses)

1 In applying the penal clauses in the Penal Code and other laws, a Fair Trade Commission member who is not a public official shall be regarded as a public official.

2 In applying the penal clauses in Articles 129–132 of the Penal Code, those who took charge (or taking charge) of mediation of conflict as per Articles 48-3–48-9 shall be regarded as public officials.

Chapter 14 Penal Provisions

Article 66 (Penal Provisions)

1 The following persons shall be slapped with a jail term of not more than three years or a fine of not more than Won200 million:

1. Person who has committed an abusive act in violation of the provisions of Article 3-2.
2. Person who has combined enterprises in violation of Article 7(1).
3. Person who has violated the provisions of Article 8-2(2) or (5).
4. Person who has established a holding company or converted a company into a holding company in violation of Article 8-3.
5. Person who has acquired or owned stocks in violation of the provisions of Article 9 or 10 (1), excluding the person subject to an order of prohibition as per Article 17-2 (1) (including the applicable case as per Article 4 of the Addenda) from among those violating Article 10 (1).
6. Person who has guaranteed a debt in violation of the provisions of Article 10-2 (1).
7. Person who has exercised his/her voting rights in violation of the provisions of Article 11 or 18.
8. Person who has evaded the law in violation of the provisions of Article 15.
9. Person who has engaged in unfair collaborative practices or encouraged others to participate in such in violation of the provision of Article 19 (1).
10. Person who has engaged in prohibited practices involving an enterprisers' organization in violation of Article 26 (1) 1.

2 Both a jail term and a fine as referred to in Clause (1) may be imposed concurrently.

Article 67 (Penal Provisions)

The following persons shall be slapped with a jail term of not more than two years or a fine of not more than Won150 million:

1. [Deleted]
2. Person who has engaged in unfair trade practice in violation of Article 23 (1).

3. Person who has violated the provisions of Article 26 (1) 2-5.
4. Person who has engaged in resale price maintenance in violation of Article 29 (1).
5. Person who has concluded an international contract in violation of Article 32 (1).
6. Person who has failed to comply with the corrective measures or order of prohibition, etc., as per Articles 5, 16 (1), 17-2 (1), 21, 24, 27, 30, 31, or 34.
7. Person who has failed to undergo audit by a certified public accountant in violation of the provisions of Article 14 (5).

Article 68 (Penal Provisions)

The following persons shall be slapped with a fine of not more than Won100 million:

1. Person who fails to make a report on the establishment of a holding company or conversion of an existing company into a holding company or makes a false report in violation of Article 8.
2. Person who fails to make a report on the business activities of a holding company, a subsidiary, and a business-related sub-subsidiary or makes a false report in violation of Article 8-2 (7).
3. Person who fails to make a report on the status of stockholding or debt guarantee or makes a false report in violation of Articles 13 (1) and 13 (2).
4. Person who has refused to submit the requested data as per Article 14 (4) without justifiable reason or submitted false data.
5. Providing false appraisal in violation of Item 2, Clause (1), Article 50 (Investigation of and Hearing on Violation).
6. [Deleted]
7. [Deleted]
8. [Deleted]

Article 69 (Penal Provisions)

1 Notwithstanding the provision of Clause 5, Article 50, the person who requests the head of a certain branch of a financial institution to submit the financial transaction information by abusing his/her authority or one who violates the provision of Clause 9, Article 50 shall be slapped with a jail term of less than 5 years or a fine of less than Won30 million.

2 A person who violates the provisions of Article 62 shall be slapped with a jail term of not more than two years or a fine of not more than Won2 million.

Article 69-2 (Fine)

1 An enterpriser or an enterprisers' organization shall be slapped with a fine for negligence of not more than Won100 million for the cases described in Items 1-6 and 8 or not more than Won200 million for the case described in Item 7. Officers, employees, and other interested parties of a company or an enterprisers' organization shall be slapped with a fine for negligence of not more than Won10 million for the cases described in Items 1-6 and 8 or not more than Won50 million for the case described in Item 7.

   1. In making the publication required by Article 11-2, any party that has not obtained a resolution of the board of directors or has failed to make such publication, person who has omitted the major contents of such publication or published false information.
   2. Person who fails to issue a notice of the combination of enterprises as required by Article 12 (1) or (6) or issues false notice, person who violates Clause (7), Article 12.
   3. With regard to the request for documents as per Article 14-2 (2), person who fails to submit the requested documents without justifiable reason or submits falsified documents.
   4. Person who has violated the provisions of Article 17-2 (4).
   5. Failure to appear without just cause in violation of Item 1, Clause (1), Article 50 (Investigation of and Hearing on Violation).

6. Person who has failed to make a report or present the necessary materials or matters prescribed in Article 50 (1) 3 or (3) or made a false report or presented falsified materials or matters.
7. Person who has refused, interfered with, or evaded the investigation prescribed in Article 50 (2).
8. Person who has refused to submit financial transaction information as per Article 50 (5).

2 A person who has not complied with the orders for the maintenance of good order in violation of Article 43-2 shall be punished by a fine for negligence of not more than Won1 million.

3 The fine for negligence referred to in Clause (1) or Clause (2) shall be imposed and collected by the Fair Trade Commission in accordance with the procedures set forth by the Presidential Decree.

4 Any person wishing to contest the disposition of a fine for negligence referred to in Clause (3) may file an objection with the Fair Trade Commission within thirty (30) days of receiving a notice of the fine.

5 If a person subject to the disposition of a fine for negligence raises an objection as per Clause (4), the Fair Trade Commission may bring the case immediately to the competent court. Upon receiving the notification, the competent court shall bring the issue regarding the fine for negligence to trial under the Non-Contentious Case Litigation Procedure Act.

6 If no objection is made, and no fine for negligence is paid in the period referred to in Clause (4), the fine shall be collected in accordance with the procedures for collecting national taxes in arrears.

Article 70 (Concurrent Punishment)

If the representative of a juristic person (including a non-incorporated association; the same shall apply herein), an agent, an employee, or any other person working for a juristic person, or an individual has committed any of the offenses specified in Articles 66–68 in relation to the business of the juristic person or individual, a fine prescribed by the relevant Article shall be imposed on the juristic person or individual as well as on the person who actually committed the violation.

Article 71 (Filing of Complaint)

1 Any offense in violation of Articles 66 and 67 shall be prosecuted through public action only after a complaint is filed by the Fair Trade Commission.

2 If necessary, the Fair Trade Commission shall file complaints together with the Prosecutor General for cases involving the offenses listed in Articles 66 and 67 because the violation is deemed gross and considerable it may substantially suppress competition.

3 The Prosecutor General may notify the Fair Trade Commission of the existence of factors requiring the filing of a complaint as per Clause (2) and may request for the cooperation of the Fair Trade Commission in filing a complaint based on such factors.

4 The Fair Trade Commission may not withdraw the complaint after prosecution has commenced.

APPENDIX 4

Vietnam: Law on Competition

THE STATE PRESIDENT

ORDER No 23/2004/L-CTN OF DECEMBER 14, 2004 ON THE PROMULGATION OF LAW

THE PRESIDENT OF THE SOCIALIST REPUBLIC OF VIETNAM

PROMULGATES:

The Competition Law,
which was passed on December 3, 2004 by the XIth National Assembly of the Socialist Republic of Vietnam at its 6th session.

COMPETITION LAW

(No. 27/2004/QH11)

Pursuant to the 1992 Constitution of the Socialist Republic of Vietnam, which was amended and supplemented under Resolution No. 51/200 1/QH10 of December 25, 2001 of the Xth National Assembly, the 10th session;

This Law provides for competition.

Chapter I General Provisions

Article 1 Scope of regulation

This Law provides for competition-restricting acts, unfair competition acts, order and procedures for settling competition cases, measures to handle violations of competition legislation.

Article 2 Subjects of application

This Law shall apply to:

1. Business organizations and individuals (hereinafter referred collectively to as enterprises), including also enterprises producing, supplying products, providing public-utility services, enterprises operating in the State-monopolized sectors and domains, and foreign enterprises operating in Vietnam.
2. Professional associations operating in Vietnam.

Article 3 Interpretation of terms

In this Law the following terms are construed as follows:

1. Relevant market means relevant market of products and relevant geographical market.
   Relevant market of products means a market of goods, services which are interchangeable in terms of characteristics, use purposes and prices.

Relevant geographical market means a specific geographical area in which exist goods, services which are interchangeable under similar conditions of competition, and which is considerably differentiated from neighboring areas.

2. Professional associations include commodity line associations and trade associations.
3. Competition restriction acts mean acts performed by enterprises to reduce, distort and prevent competition on the market, including acts of competition restriction agreement, abusing the dominant position on the market, abusing the monopoly position and economic concentration.
4. Unfair competition acts mean competition acts performed by enterprises in the process of doing business, which run counter to common standards of business ethics and cause damage or can cause damage to the State's interests, legitimate rights and interests of other enterprises or consumers.
5. An enterprise's market share of a certain kind of goods or service means the percentage between sale turnover of this enterprise and aggregate turnover of all enterprises dealing in such kind of goods or service on the relevant market or the percentage between purchase turnover of this enterprise and aggregate purchase turnover of all enterprises dealing in such kind of goods or service on the relevant market on a monthly, quarterly or yearly basis.
6. Combined market share means aggregate market share on the relevant market of enterprises participating in the competition restriction agreement or economic concentration.
7. Total cost of production of goods or services consists of:
   (a) Cost of production of products or services; purchasing price of goods;
   (b) Cost of circulation to bring goods, services to consumers.
8. Competition case means a case showing signs of violation of the provisions of this Law, which is investigated and handled by a competent state agency according to law provisions.
9. Competition procedures mean activities carried out by agencies, organizations and individuals according to the order and procedures for settling and handling competition cases prescribed by this Law.
10. Business secret means information that fully meets the following conditions:
    (a) Being other than common knowledge;
    (b) Being applicable to business and, once used, placing the holder of such information at an advantage over the non-holder or non-user of such information;
    (c) Being kept confidential by the owner by applying necessary measures to keep such information from disclosure and easy access.
11. Multi-level sale means an approach of marketing to retail goods, which meets the following conditions:
    (a) The marketing to retail goods is conducted through a multi-level and multi-branch network of participants in the multi-level sale;
    (b) Goods are marketed by participants in the multi-level sale directly to consumers at the customers' homes, working places or other places other than regular retail places of the enterprises or participants;
    (c) Participants in the multi-level sale enjoy commissions, bonuses or other economic benefits from the sale results of their own and of lower-level multi-level sale participants within the network which is organized by themselves and approved by the multi-level sale enterprises.

Article 4 Right to business competition

1. Enterprises enjoy freedom to competition within the legal framework. The State protects the lawful right to business competition.
2. Competition must be implemented on the principles of honesty, non-infringement upon the interests of the State, public interests, legitimate rights and interests of enterprises, consumers and compliance with the provisions of this Law.

Article 5 Application of this Law, other relevant laws and international agreements

1. Where there is any disparity between the provisions of this Law and those of other laws on competition restriction acts or unfair competition acts, the provisions of this Law shall apply.
2. Where international agreements which the Socialist Republic of Vietnam has signed or acceded to contain provisions different from those of this Law, the provisions of such international agreements shall apply.

Article 6 Acts that State management agencies are prohibited from performing

State management agencies are prohibited from performing the following acts to prevent competition on the market:

1. To force enterprises, organizations or individuals to buy, sell goods, provide services to enterprises which are designated by these agencies, except for goods and services in the State-monopolized domains or in emergency cases prescribed by law;
2. To discriminate between enterprises;
3. To force professional associations or enterprises to align with one another with a view to precluding, restricting or preventing other enterprises from competing on the market;
4. Other acts that prevent lawful business activities of enterprises.

Article 7 State management responsibilities for competition

1. The Government performs uniform State management over competition.
2. The Trade Ministry shall be responsible to the Government for performing the State management over competition.
3. Ministries, ministerial-level agencies, provincial/municipal People's Committees shall, within the scope of their respective tasks and powers, have to coordinate with the Trade Ministry in performing the State management over competition.

Chapter II Control of Competition Restriction Acts

Section 1 Competition Restriction Agreements

Article 8 Competition restriction agreements

Competition restriction agreements include:

1. Agreements on directly or indirectly fixing goods or service prices;
2. Agreement on distributing outlets, sources of supply of goods, provision of services;
3. Agreements on restricting or controlling produced, purchased or sold quantities or volumes of goods or services;
4. Agreements on restricting technical and technological development, restricting investments;
5. Agreement on imposing on other enterprises conditions on signing of goods or services purchase or sale contracts or forcing other enterprises to accept obligations which have no direct connection with the subject of such contracts;
6. Agreements on preventing, restraining, or disallowing other enterprises to enter the market or develop business;
7. Agreements on abolishing from the market enterprises other than the parties of the agreements;
8. Conniving to enable one or all of the parties of the agreement to win bids for supply of goods or provision of services.

Article 9 Prohibited competition restriction agreements

1. Competition restriction agreements prescribed in Clauses 6, 7 and 8 of this Law are prohibited.
2. Competition restriction agreements prescribed in Clauses 1, 2, 3, 4 and 5, Article 8 of this Law the parties of which have combined market share of 30% or more on the relevant market are prohibited.

Article 10 Cases of exemption with regard to prohibited competition restriction agreements

1. Competition restriction agreements defined in Clause 2, Article 9 of this Law shall enjoy exemption for a definite term if they meet one of the following conditions in order to reduce costs to benefit consumers:
   (a) Rationalizing the organizational structure, business model, raising business efficiency;
   (b) Promoting technical and technological advances, raising goods and service quality;
   (c) Promoting the uniform application of quality standards and technical norms of products of different kinds;
   (d) Harmonizing business, goods delivery and payment conditions, which have no connection with prices and price factors;
   (e) Enhancing the competitiveness of small- and medium-sized enterprises;
   (f) Enhancing the competitiveness of Vietnamese enterprises on the international market.
2. The order, procedures for granting exemptions and exemption terms shall comply with the provisions of Section 4 of this Chapter.

Section 2 Abuse of Dominant Position on the Market, Abuse of Monopoly Position

Article 11 Enterprises, groups of enterprises holding the dominant position on the market

1. Enterprises shall be considered to hold the dominant position on the market if they have market shares of 30% or more on the relevant market or are capable of restricting competition considerably.
2. Groups of enterprises shall be considered to hold the dominant position on the market if they take concerted action to restrict competition and fall into one of the following cases:
   (a) Two enterprises having total market share of 50% or more on the relevant market;
   (b) Three enterprises having total market share of 65% or more on the relevant market;
   (c) Four enterprises having total market share of 75% or more on the relevant market;

Article 12 Enterprises holding the monopoly position

An enterprise shall be considered to hold the monopoly position if there is no enterprise competing on the goods or services dealt in by such enterprise on the relevant market.

Article 13 Prohibited acts of abusing the dominant position on the market

Enterprises, groups of enterprises holding the dominant position on the market are prohibited from performing the following acts:

1. Selling goods, providing services at prices lower than the aggregate costs in order to eliminate competitors.
2. Imposing irrational buying or selling prices of goods or services or fixing minimum re-selling prices causing damage to customers;

3. Restricting production, distribution of goods, services, limiting markets, preventing technical and technological development, causing damage to customers;
4. Imposing dissimilar commercial conditions in similar transactions in order to create inequality in competition;
5. Imposing conditions on other enterprises to conclude goods or services purchase or sale contracts or forcing other enterprises to accept obligations which have no direct connection with the subject of such contracts;
6. Preventing new competitors from entering the market.

Article 14 Prohibited acts of abusing the monopoly position

Enterprises holding the monopoly position are prohibited from performing the following acts:

1. Acts defined in Article 13 of this Law;
2. Imposing unfavorable conditions on customers;
3. Abusing the monopoly position to unilaterally modify or cancel the contracts already signed without plausible reasons.

Article 15 Control of enterprises operating in the State monopolized domains, enterprises producing, supplying public-utility products, services

1. The State controls enterprises operating in the State-monopolized domains with the following measures:
   (a) Deciding on the buying prices, selling prices of goods, services in the State-monopolized domains;
   (b) Deciding on the quantities, volumes and scope of market of goods, services in the State monopolized domains.
2. The State controls enterprises producing and supplying public-utility products, services with measures of ordering goods, assigning plans or bidding according to prices or charges set by the State.
3. When undertaking other business activities outside the State-monopolized domains and producing, providing public-utility products, services, enterprises shall not be subject to the application of the provisions of Clause 1 and Clause 2 of this Article but still be subject to the application of other provisions of this Law.

Section 3 Economic Concentration

Article 16 Economic concentration

Economic concentration means acts of enterprises, including:

1. Merger of enterprises;
2. Consolidation of enterprises;
3. Acquisition of enterprises;
4. Joint venture between enterprises;
5. Other acts of economic concentration prescribed by law.

Article 17 Merger, consolidation, acquisition of enterprises and joint venture between enterprises

1. Merger of enterprises means an act whereby one or several enterprises transfer all of its/their property, rights, obligations and legitimate interests to another enterprise, and at the same time terminate the existence of the merged enterprise (s).
2. Consolidation of enterprises means an act whereby two or more enterprises transfer all of their property, rights, obligations and legitimate interests to form a new enterprise and, at the same time, terminate the existence of the consolidated enterprises.

3. Acquisition of enterprises mean an act whereby an enterprise acquires the whole or part of property of another enterprise sufficient to control or dominate all or one of the trades of the acquired enterprise.
4. Joint venture between enterprises means an act whereby two or more enterprises jointly contribute part of their property, rights, obligations and legitimate interests to the establishment of a new enterprise.

Article 18 Prohibited cases of economic concentration

Economic concentration shall be prohibited if the combined market shares of enterprises participating in economic concentration account for over 50% on the relevant market, except for cases specified in Article 19 of this Law or the case where enterprises, after implementing economic concentration, are still of small or medium size as prescribed by law.

Article 19 Cases of exemption from prohibited economic concentration

Prohibited economic concentration prescribed in Article 18 of this Law may be considered for exemption in the following cases:

1. One or more of the participants in economic concentration is/are in danger of dissolution or bankruptcy;
2. The economic concentration has an effect of expanding export or contributing to socio-economic development, technical and technological advance.

Article 20 Notification of economic concentration

1. If enterprises participating in economic concentration have combined market shares of between 30 and 50% on the relevant market, their lawful representatives must notify the competition managing agency before implementing economic concentration.

   Where combined market shares of enterprises participating in economic concentration are lower than 30% on the relevant market or where enterprises, after implementing economic concentration, are still of small or medium size as prescribed by law, such notification is not required.
2. Enterprises participating in economic concentration eligible for exemption prescribed in Article 19 of this Law shall submit exemption application dossiers under the provisions of Section 4 of this Chapter instead of notification of economic concentration.

Article 21 Economic-concentration notification dossiers

1. An economic-concentration notification dossier shall comprise:
   (a) The written notification of economic concentration, made according to a form set by the competition-managing agency;
   (b) Valid copies of the business registration certificates of all enterprises participating in economic concentration;
   (c) Financial statements of the latest two consecutive years of each enterprise participating in economic concentration, with the certification of audit organizations according to law provisions;
   (d) The list of dependent units of each enterprise participating in economic concentration;
   (e) The list of kinds of goods, services dealt in by each enterprise participating in economic concentration and by its dependent units;
   (f) Reports of the latest two consecutive years of each enterprise participating in economic concentration on their market shares on the relevant market.
2. Enterprises submitting the economic concentration notification dossiers shall be accountable for the truthfulness of their dossiers.

Article 22 Acceptance of economic concentration notification dossiers

Within seven working days after receiving the economic-concentration notification dossiers, the competition-managing agency shall have to notify in writing the dossier-submitting enterprises of the validity and completeness of their dossiers; where a dossier is incomplete, the competition-managing agency shall have to clearly point out the contents that have to be supplemented.

Article 23 Time limit for reply to economic concentration notification

1. Within forty five days after receiving complete economic-concentration notification dossiers, the competition-managing agency shall have to reply in writing to the dossier-submitting enterprises. Written replies of the competition-managing agency must determine whether economic concentration falls into one of the following cases:
   (a) Economic concentration does not fall into the prohibited cases;
   (b) Economic concentration is prohibited under the provisions of Article 18 of this Law; the prohibition reason must be clearly stated in the written reply.
2. Where economic concentration involves many complicated circumstances, the head of the competition-managing agency may extend the time limit for reply specified in Clause 1 of this Article no more than twice, each time for no more than thirty days and notify such in writing to the dossier submitting enterprises no later than three working days before the expiration of the time limit for reply, clearly stating the extension reason.

Article 24 Implementation of economic concentration

Lawful representatives of the enterprises participating in economic concentration subject to notification as prescribed in Clause 1, Article 20 of this Law may only carry out economic concentration procedures at the competent State agencies prescribed by legislation on enterprises after the competition-managing agency replies in writing that such economic concentration does not fall into any prohibited cases.

Section 4 Procedures For Execution Of Exemption Cases

Article 25 Competence to decide on exemption

1. The Trade Minister shall consider and decide in writing on the exemption prescribed in Article 10 and Clause 1, Article 19 of this Law.
2. The Prime Minister shall consider and decide in writing on the exemption prescribed in Clause 2, Article 19 of this Law.

Article 26 Subjects submitting exemption application dossiers

The subjects submitting exemption application dossiers are the parties intending to participate in competition restriction agreements or economic concentration.

Article 27 Lawful representatives of parties of competition restriction agreements or economic concentration

1. The parties of the competition restriction agreements or economic concentration may appoint a representative to carry out the procedures to apply for exemption. The appointment of representatives must be made in writing and certified by the involved parties.
2. Rights and obligations of the representative party shall be determined by the involved parties;
3. The parties shall be responsible for acts of the representative party within the scope of authorization.

Article 28 Dossiers of application for exemption for competition restriction agreements

1. A dossier of application for exemption for a competition restriction agreement shall comprise:
   (a) The application, made according to the form set by the competition-managing agency;
   (b) The valid copies of the business registration certificates of each enterprise participating in the competition restriction agreement and the charter of the association for cases where the competition restriction agreement is participated by such association;
   (c) Financial statements of the latest two consecutive years of each enterprise participating in the competition restriction agreement, with the certification of audit organizations according to law provisions;
   (d) Reports of the latest two consecutive years of each enterprise participating in the competition restriction agreement on their market shares on the relevant market;
   (e) A report elaborating the satisfaction of the cases eligible for exemption prescribed in Article 10 of this Law;
   (f) The written authorization of the representative party by the parties of the competition restriction agreement.
2. The dossier submitters and the parties of the competition restriction agreements shall be accountable for the truthfulness of their dossiers.

Article 29 Dossiers of application for exemption for economic concentration

1. A dossier of application for exemption for economic concentration shall comprise:
   (a) The application, made according to the form set by the competition-managing agency;
   (b) The valid copies of the business registration certificates of each enterprise participating in economic concentration;
   (c) Financial statements of the latest two consecutive years of each enterprise joining in economic concentration, with the certification of audit organizations according to law provisions;
   (d) Reports of the latest two consecutive years of each enterprise participating in economic concentration on their market shares on the relevant market;
   (e) A report elaborating the satisfaction of the cases eligible for exemption prescribed in Article 19 of this Law;
   (f) The written authorization of the representative party by the parties of economic concentration.
2. The dossier submitters and the parties of economic concentration shall be accountable for the truthfulness of their dossiers.

Article 30 Acceptance of exemption application dossiers

1. The competition-managing agency shall be responsible for accepting exemption application dossiers, putting forward its opinions to the Trade Minister for decision or submission to the Prime Minister for decision.
2. Within seven working days after receiving exemption application dossiers, the competition managing agency shall have to notify in writing the dossier submitters of the completeness of their dossiers. Where a dossier is incomplete, the competition-managing agency must point out the contents that have to be supplemented.
3. The dossier submitters must pay a fee for evaluation of exemption application dossiers according to law provisions.

Article 31 Requests for supplementation of exemption application dossiers

The competition-managing agency may request the submitters of exemption application dossiers to supplement necessary documents and information related to their intention to implement the competition restriction agreements or economic concentration and give additional explanation on unclear matters.

Article 32 Supply of information by related parties

1. The competition-managing agency may request related organizations and individuals to supply information on competition restriction agreements or economic concentration which it is handling.
2. Within fifteen days after receiving the requests of the competition-managing agency, related organizations and individuals shall have to reply in writing to the requests.

Article 33 Withdrawal of exemption applications

1. If wishing to withdraw their exemption applications, the dossier submitters must notify in writing the competition-managing agency thereof.
2. The competition-managing agency shall not refund the fee for evaluation of exemption application dossiers in the case prescribed in Clause 1 of this Article.

Article 34 Time limit for issuance of decisions

1. Within sixty days after receiving complete exemption application dossiers, the Trade Minister shall issue one of the following decisions:
   (a) Approving the exemption for the parties;
   (b) Disapproving the exemption for the parties.
2. For cases involving many complicated circumstances, the Trade Minister may extend the time limit for issuance of decisions prescribed in Clause 1 of this Article no more than twice, each for thirty days at most.
3. In case of economic concentration falling under the Prime Minister's competence to grant exemption, the time limit for issuance of decisions approving or disapproving exemption shall be ninety days as from the date of receipt of complete exemption application dossiers; for cases involving many complicated circumstances, the time limit for issuance of such decisions shall be one hundred and eighty days.
4. In case of extension of the time limit for issuance of decisions, the competition-managing agency shall notify in writing the dossier submitters not later than three working days before the expiration of such time limit, clearly stating the reason therefor.

Article 35 Decisions on grant of exemption

1. A decision on grant of exemption must contain the following principal details:
   (a) Names and addresses of the parties approved to perform the act;
   (b) The details of the act to be performed;
   (c) The time limit for enjoyment of exemption, conditions and obligations of the parties.
2. The competition-managing agency shall have to publicize the decisions on grant of exemption according to the Government's regulations.

Article 36 Implementation of competition restriction agreements, economic concentration for cases of enjoyment of exemption

1. The parties of the competition restriction agreements that enjoy exemption may implement their competition restriction agreements only after the decisions on grant of exemption are issued by the Trade Minister.
2. Lawful representatives of enterprises participating in economic concentration eligible for exemption may carry out procedures for economic concentration only at the competent Stage agencies prescribed by enterprise legislation after the decisions on grant of exemption are issued by the Prime Minister or the Trade Minister.

Article 37 Cancellation of decisions on grant of exemption

1. The agency competent to issue decisions on grant of exemption shall be entitled to cancel decisions on grant of exemption.
2. Decisions on grant of exemption shall be cancelled in the following cases:
   (a) Frauds in the exemption application are detected;
   (b) Enterprises enjoying exemption fail to abide by the conditions and obligations within the time limit stated in the decisions on grant of exemption;
   (c) The conditions for grant of exemption no longer exist.

Article 38 Complaints about decisions related to grant of exemption

Enterprises which disagree with the decisions on grant or non-grant of exemption or decisions canceling the decisions on grant or exemption may lodge complaints according to law provisions on complaints and denunciations.

Chapter III Unfair Competition Acts

Article 39 Unfair competition acts

Unfair competition acts in this Law include:

1. Misleading indications;
2. Infringement upon business secrets;
3. Constraint in business;
4. Discrediting other enterprises;
5. Disturbing business activities of other enterprises;
6. Advertising for the purpose of unfair competition;
7. Sale promotion for the purpose of unfair competition;
8. Discrimination by associations;
9. Illicit multi-level sale;
10. Other unfair competition acts according to the criteria determined in Clause 4, Article 3 of this Law and prescribed by the Government.

Article 40 Misleading indications

1. Enterprises are forbidden to use instructions containing information causing confusions about trade names, business mottoes, business logos, packing, geographical indications and other elements as prescribed by the Government to mislead customers about goods or services for the purpose of competition.
2. It is forbidden to do business in goods or services using misleading information prescribed in Clause 1 of this Article.

Article 41 Infringement upon business secrets

Enterprises are forbidden to perform the following acts:

1. Accessing and collecting information belonging to business secrets by counteracting the security measures applied by lawful owners of such business secrets;
2. Disclosing, using information belonging to business secrets without the permission of owners of such business secrets;
3. Breaching security contracts or deceiving or taking advantage of the trust of persons having the security duty in order to access, collect or disclose information belonging to business secrets of owners of such business secrets;
4. Accessing, collecting information belonging to business secrets of other persons when such persons carry out procedures according to law provisions concerning business, carry out procedures

for product circulation, or by counteracting the measures applied by State agencies, or using such information for business purposes, application for licenses related to business or product circulation.

Article 42 Constraint in business

Enterprises are forbidden to constrain customers, business partners of other enterprises by performing acts of threatening or forcing them not to enter in transactions or to stop transactions with such enterprises.

Article 43 Discrediting other enterprises

Enterprises are forbidden to discredit other enterprises by performing acts of directly or indirectly issuing untruthful information badly affecting the latter's reputation, financial status and business activities.

Article 44 Disturbing business activities of other enterprises

Enterprises are forbidden to disturb lawful business activities of other enterprises by performing acts of directly or indirectly preventing, disrupting the latter's business activities.

Article 45 Advertising for the purpose of unfair competition

Enterprises are forbidden to carry out the following advertising activities:

1. Comparing their goods, services directly with those of the same kind of other enterprises;
2. Imitating other advertising products to mislead customers;
3. Issuing false or misleading information to customers on one of the following contents:
   (a) Prices, quantities, quality, utilities, designs, categories, packing, date of manufacture, use duration, goods origin, manufacturers, places of manufacture, processors, places of processing;
   (b) Usage, mode of servicing, warranty duration;
   (c) Other false or misleading information.
4. Other advertising activities prohibited by law.

Article 46 Sale promotion for the purpose of unfair competition

Enterprises are forbidden to carry out the following sale promotion activities:

1. Organizing sale promotion with prize frauds;
2. Organizing sale promotion which is dishonest or causes confusion about goods, services in order to cheat customers;
3. Discriminating between similar customers at different sale promotion places under the same sale promotion program;
4. Presenting goods free to customers for trial use but requesting customers to use their goods in exchange for similar goods manufactured by other enterprises and currently used by such customers;
5. Other sale promotion activities prohibited by law.

Article 47 Discrimination by associations

Professional associations are forbidden to perform the following acts:

1. Refusing to admit enterprises eligible for admission or refusing to allow enterprises to withdraw from the associations in a discriminatory way, placing such enterprises at a competitive disadvantage;

2. Irrationally restricting business activities or other business-related activities of member enterprises.

Article 48 Illicit multi-level sale

Enterprises are forbidden to perform the following acts to gain illicit profits from the recruitment of participants into the multi-level sale networks:

1. Requesting those who wish to participate to pay a deposit, buy an initial volume of goods or pay a sum of money for the right to participate in the multi-level sale network;
2. Not to commit to buy back goods at 90% at least of the price at which the goods were sold to participants for re-sale;
3. To give participants commissions, bonuses or other economic benefits which are gained mostly from the enticement of other people to participate in the multi-level sale network;
4. Supplying false information on the benefits of the participation in the multi-level sale network, false information on the nature and utilities of goods in order to entice the participation of other people.

Chapter IV Competition-Managing Agency, Competition Council

Section 1 Competition-Managing Agency

Article 49 Competition-managing agency

1. The Government shall decide to establish, and prescribe the organization and apparatus of, the competition-managing agency.
2. The competition-managing agency shall have the following tasks and powers:
   (a) To control the process of economic concentration according to the provisions of this Law;
   (b) Accepting exemption application dossiers; put forward opinions to the Trade Minister for decision or submission to the Prime Minister for decision;
   (c) Investigating competition cases related to competition-restricting acts and unfair competition acts;
   (d) Handling and sanctioning unfair competition acts;
   (e) Other tasks prescribed by law.

Article 50 Head of the competition-managing agency

1. The head of the competition-managing agency shall be appointed or dismissed by the Prime Minister at the proposal of the Trade Minister.
2. The head of the competition-managing agency shall have to organize and direct the competition-managing agency to perform the tasks and powers defined in Clause 2, Article 49 of this Law.

Article 51 Investigators of competition cases

1. Investigators of competition cases (hereinafter called investigators) shall be appointed by the Trade Minister at the proposal of the head of the competition-managing agency.
2. Investigators shall investigate specific competition cases under decisions of the head of the competition-managing agency.

Article 52 Criteria of investigators

Persons who fully meet the following criteria may be appointed investigators:

1. Possessing good ethical qualities, being honest, impartial;
2. Having the degree of bachelor of law, economics or finance;

3. Having worked at least five years in one of the domains defined in Clause 2 of this Article;
4. Having been trained in professional investigation skills.

Section 2 Competition Council

Article 53 Competition Council

1. The Competition Council is an agency established by the Government.

   The Competition Council shall be composed of between eleven and fifteen members appointed or dismissed by the Prime Minister at the proposal of the Trade Minister.
2. The Competition Council shall have to organize the handling and settlement of complaints about competition cases involving competition-restricting acts under the provisions of this Law.

Article 54 Chairman of the Competition Council

1. The Competition Council chairman shall be appointed or dismissed by the Prime Minister among the Competition Council members at the proposal of the Trade Minister.
2. The Competition Council chairman shall have to organize the operation of the Competition Council.
3. The Competition Council chairman shall decide to set up the Competition Case-Handling Council composed of at least five members of the Competition Council, one of whom shall chair hearings to deal with a specific competition case.

Article 55 Criteria of Competition Council members

1. Persons who fully meet the following criteria may be appointed as Competition Council members:
   (a) Possessing good ethical qualities, being honest, impartial, and having the sense of protecting socialist legality;
   (b) Having the degree of bachelor of law, economics or finance;
   (c) Having worked at least nine years in one of the domains defined at Point b, Clause 1 of this Article;
   (d) Being capable of fulfilling the assigned tasks.
2. Competition Council members shall have a five-year term of office and may be re-appointed.

Chapter V Investigation, Handling of Competition Cases

Section 1 General Provisions

Article 56 Principles for competition procedures

1. The settlement of competition cases involving competition-restricting acts shall comply with the provisions of this Law.
2. The settlement of competition cases involving unfair competition acts shall comply with the provisions of this Law and legislation on handling of administrative violations.
3. In the process of carrying out competition procedures, investigators, the head of the competition-managing agency and Competition Council members must, within the scope of their respective tasks and powers, keep confidential business secrets of enterprises, respect legitimate rights and interests of the related organizations and individuals.

Article 57 Language and script used in competition procedures

The language and script used in competition procedures is Vietnamese. Participants in competition procedures shall be entitled to use their native language and script; in this case interpretation is required.

Article 58 Complaints about competition cases

1. If organizations and individuals deem that their legitimate rights and interests are infringed upon by acts in violation of the provisions of this Law (hereinafter referred collectively to as complainants), they may lodge complaints with the competition-managing agency.
2. The statute of limitations for lodging complaints is two years, as from the date the acts involving signs of violation of competition legislation are committed.
3. Complaint dossiers must comprise the following principal documents:
   (a) The written complaint, made according to a form set by the competition-managing agency;
   (b) Evidences on the violation act.
4. Complainants shall be accountable for the truthfulness of evidences they supply to the competition-managing agency.

Article 59 Acceptance of complaint dossiers

1. The competition-managing agency shall have to accept complaint dossiers.
2. Within seven working days after receiving complaint dossiers, the competition-managing agency shall have to notify in writing the complainants of the acceptance of their dossiers.
3. Complainants must pay an advance for the cost of handling the competition case according to law provisions.

Article 60 Evidences

1. Evidences are facts used by investigators and the Competition Case-Handling Council as grounds for determining whether or not exist acts of violating the provisions of this Law.
2. Evidences are determined from the following sources:
   (a) Exhibits, which are things used as tools or means for commission of violations, money and other things having the effect of proving acts of violating the provisions of this Law;
   (b) Testimonies of witnesses, explanations of related organizations and individuals;
   (c) Original documents, copies and translations of original documents which are lawfully notarized or authenticated or supplied and certified by competent agencies or organizations.
   (d) Expertise conclusions.

Article 61 Application of administrative preventive measures

1. The head of the competition-managing agency, the Competition Council chairman may apply some administrative preventive measures prescribed by legislation on handling of administrative violations in the cases specified in Clause 6, Article 76 and Clause 4, Article 79 of this Law.
   The Government shall specify administrative preventive measures that the head of the competition-managing agency and the Competition Council chairman may apply.
2. The following persons may propose the application of administrative preventive measures:
   (a) Complainants may make such a proposal to the head of the competition-managing agency and the Competition Council chairman;
   (b) Investigators may make such a proposal to the head of the competition-managing agency;
   (c) Presidents of hearings may make such a proposal to the Competition Council chairman.
3. In case of application of administrative preventive measures at the proposals of complainants, the complainants shall have to pay a guaranty money according to the Government's regulations.
   In cases of wrong application of administrative preventive measures, causing damage to the investigated parties, the complainants must pay compensation therefor. The compensation level shall be agreed upon by the complainants and the investigated parties; if the two parties cannot reach agreement thereon, they may initiate lawsuits at court to claim for damages according to the provisions of civil legislation.

4. Where the administrative preventive measures are applied at variance of the requests of investigators or the hearing presidents, thereby causing damage to the investigated parties, the competition-managing agency or the Competition Council must pay compensation therefor. The level of compensation shall be agreed upon by the investigated parties and the competition-managing agency or the Competition Council; if they cannot reach agreement thereon, the investigated parties may initiate lawsuits at courts to claim for damages according to the provisions of civil legislation. If compensation must be paid, the competition managing agency or the Competition Council must identify the responsibility, also including material responsibility, of the proposers and related persons so as to impose proper disciplinary forms on such persons and force them to indemnify for the money amounts the competition-managing agency or the Competition Council has compensated to the investigated parties.
5. The parties subject to the application of administrative preventive measures may lodge complaints about the decisions thereon according to the law provisions on complaints and denunciations.

Article 62 Competition case-handling charges

Competition case-handling charges shall be used for the handling of competition case. The Government shall prescribe the levels, collection, payment, management and use of such charge in accordance with legislation on charges and fees.

Article 63 Liability to competition case-handling charges

1. The party that is concluded to have violated the provisions of this Law must pay competition case-handling charges.
2. Where the invested party does not violate the provisions of this Law, the complainant shall have to pay competition case-handling charges.
3. Where a competition case is conducted under the provisions of Clause 2, Article 65 of this Law, if the investigated party does not violate the provisions of this Law, the competition-managing agency shall have to pay competition case-handling charges.

Section 2 Competition Procedure Participants

Article 64 Competition procedure participants

Competition procedure participants include:

1. The complainant;
2. The investigated party;
3. Lawyers;
4. Witnesses;
5. Experts;
6. Interpreter;
7. Persons with related interests and obligations.

Article 65 Investigated parties in competition cases

The investigated parties in competition cases (hereinafter called investigated parties) are organizations or individuals that are investigated under decisions of the competition-managing agency in the following cases:

1. Being complained against under the provisions of Article 58 of this Law;
2. Being detected by the competition-managing agency to be committing or have committed acts involving signs of violation of competition legislation within two years as from the date such acts were committed.

Article 66 Rights and obligations of involved parties

1. The investigated party shall have the following rights:
   (a) To produce documents, things; to know documents and things produced by the complainants or the competition-managing agency;
   (b) To participate in hearings;
   (c) To request the change of investigators, Competition Case-Handling Council members if detecting that they fall into one of the cases prescribed in Article 83 of this Law;
   (d) To authorize lawyers to participate in competition procedures;
   (e) To request witnesses;
   (f) To propose the competition-managing agency to request expertise;
   (g) To propose the change of competition procedure-conducting persons and competition procedure participants under the provisions of this Law.
2. The complainant shall have the following rights:
   (a) The rights prescribed in Clause 1 of this Law;
   (b) To propose the head of the competition managing agency or the Competition Council chairman to apply administrative preventive measures related to the competition cases.
3. The investigated party and the complainant shall have the following obligations:
   (a) To supply full, truthful, accurate evidences in a timely manner related to their proposals or requests;
   (b) To appear in response to the summonses of the competition-managing agency or the Competition Case-Handling Council. Where they are summoned but fail to appear without plausible reasons, the Competition Case-Handling Council shall proceed with handling the cases based on available information;
   (c) To abide by decisions of the competition managing agency and the Competition Case-Handling Council.

Article 67 Lawyers of the complainants, the investigated parties

1. Lawyers who fully meet the procedure-participating conditions prescribed by legislation on lawyers and are authorized by the complainants or investigated parties may participate in competition procedures to protect the legitimate rights and interests of the parties which they represent.
2. When participating in competition procedures, lawyers shall have the following rights and obligations:
   (a) To participate in all stages of the process of competition procedures;
   (b) To verify and collect evidences and supply them in order to protect the legitimate rights and interests of the parties which they represent;
   (c) To study documents in the competition case dossiers and to take notes and copy necessary documents in such dossiers in order to protect the legitimate rights and interests of the parties which they represent;
   (d) To propose on behalf of the parties they represent the change of competition procedure–conducting persons and/or competition procedure participants under the provisions of this Law;
   (e) To render legal assistance to the parties they represent in order to protect their legitimate rights and interests;
   (f) To respect truth and law; not to bribe, force or incite other persons to give false testimonies or supply untruthful documents;
   (g) To appear in response to the summonses of the Competition Case-Handling Council;
   (h) Not to disclose investigation secrets they know in the process of participating in competition procedures; not to use their notes and copies of documents in the competition case dossiers for the purpose of infringing upon the State's interests or legitimate rights and interests of organizations and individuals.

Article 68 Witnesses

1. Persons who know about circumstances related to the competition cases may be summoned by the Competition Case-Handling Council to participate in competition procedures in the capacity as witnesses or invited by the competition-managing agency in the capacity as witnesses at the requests of the involved parties. Persons who have lost their civil act capacity must not act as witnesses.
2. Witnesses shall have the following rights and obligations:
   (a) To supply all documents, papers and things they have, which are related to the settlement of competition cases; give testimony verbally or in writing to the competition-managing agency or the Competition Case-Handling Council on all circumstances they know, which are related to the settlement of competition cases;
   (b) To participate in hearings and give testimony to the Competition Case-Handling Council;
   (c) To be allowed to take leave when they are summoned by, or give testimony to, the competition-managing agency or the Competition Case-Handling Council if they are working for State agencies, organizations or enterprises;
   (d) To be paid for travel expenses and enjoy other regimes as prescribed by law;
   (e) To refuse to give testimony if such testimony is related to State secrets, professional secrets or personal privacy or badly, disadvantageously affects the complainants or investigated parties that are their close relatives;
   (f) To honestly report on circumstances they know, which are related to the settlement of competition cases;
   (g) To pay damages and take responsibility before law for their false testimony causing damage to the complainants, investigated parties or other persons;
   (h) To appear at the hearings in response to the summonses of the Competition Case-Handling Council if they must give testimony publicly at the hearings;
   (i) To pledge before the competition-managing agency or the Competition Case-Handling Council to exercise their rights and fulfill their obligations, except for minor witnesses.
3. Witnesses who refuse to give testimony, give false testimony, supply false materials or are absent without plausible reasons when being summoned by the Competition Case-Handling Council shall have to bear responsibility according to law provisions, except for the case prescribed at Point e, Clause 2 of this Article.
4. Witnesses shall be protected according to law provisions.

Article 69 Experts

1. Experts are those who have necessary knowledge about the matters to be expertised at the request of the head of the competition-managing agency or the Competition Case-Handling Councilor at the request of the involved parties after it is accepted by the head of the competition-managing agency or the Competition Case-Handling Council according to law provisions.
2. Experts shall have the following rights and obligations:
   (a) To read documents in the competition case dossiers which are related to the expertised subject; to request the expertise-requesting agency to supply materials necessary for expertise;
   (b) To raise questions to the competition procedure participants on matters related to the expertised subject;
   (c) To appear in response to the summonses of the expertise-requesting agency, give answers on matters related to the expertise as well as expertise conclusions in an honest, grounded and objective manner;
   (d) To notify in writing the expertise-requesting agency of the impossibility to expertise because the matters requested to be expertised fall beyond their professional capability or the supplied documents are not enough or are of no use for expertise;

(e) To preserve the received documents and return them to the expertise-requesting agency together with the expertise conclusions or the notice on the impossibility to expertise;
(f) Not to collect by themselves documents for expertise, not to privately contact other competition procedure participants if such contact affects the impartiality of the expertise results; not to disclose information they know in the expertising process, not to notify the expertise results to other persons, except for the signees of the expertise-requesting decisions;
(g) To write their opinions on the written general conclusions if disagreeing with the general conclusions in the case of collective expertise;
(h) To be paid for travel expenses and enjoy other regimes according to law provisions.

3. Experts who refuse to give expertise conclusions without plausible reasons or give false expertise conclusions or are absent without plausible reasons when summoned by the expertise-requesting agency shall have to bear responsibility according to law provisions.
4. Experts must refuse to participate in competition procedures or be changed in the following cases:
   (a) They fall into one of the cases prescribed in Article 83 of this Law;
   (b) They have participated in competition procedures in the capacity as lawyers, witnesses or interpreters in the same competition case;
   (c) They have conducted procedures in such competition case in the capacity as Competition Case-Handling Council members.

Article 70 Interpreters

1. Interpreters are those who are capable of translating a language other than Vietnamese into Vietnamese and vice versa in case where competition procedure participants cannot use Vietnamese. Interpreters shall be selected according to the agreement of the involved parties and accepted by the Competition Case-Handling Councilor shall be appointed by the Competition Case-Handling Council.
2. Interpreters shall have the following rights and obligations:
   (a) To appear in response to the summonses of the Competition Case-Handling Council;
   (b) To interpret in an truthful, objective and accurate manner;
   (c) To ask competition procedure-conducting persons and competition procedure participants to explain the contents more clearly for interpretation;
   (d) Not to contact other competition procedure participants if such contact may affect the truthfulness, objectivity and accuracy of the interpretation;
   (e) To be paid for travel expenses and enjoy other regimes according to law provisions;
   (f) To pledge before the Competition Case-Handling Council to exercise their rights and fulfill their obligations.
3. Interpreters who deliberately give false interpretation or are absent without plausible reasons when summoned by the Competition Case-Handling Council shall have to bear responsibility according to law provisions.
4. Interpreters must refuse to participate in competition procedures or be changed in the following cases:
   (a) They fall into one of the cases prescribed in Article 83 of this Law;
   (b) They have participated in competition procedures in the capacity as lawyers, witnesses or experts in the same competition case;
   (c) They have conducted procedures in such competition case in the capacity as Competition Case-Handling Council members.
5. The provisions of this Article also apply to those who understand the signs given by dumb or deaf competition procedure participants.

   Where only the representatives or relatives of dumb or deaf competition procedure participants can understand the latter's signs, they may be accepted by the Competition Case-Handling Council to act as interpreters for such dumb or deaf persons.

Article 71 Persons with interests, obligations related to competition case

1. Persons with related interests, obligations may file independent claims or participate in competition procedures on the side of the complainants or investigated parties.
2. Persons with related interests, obligations who file independent claims or participate in competition procedures on the side of the complainants or persons with interests only shall have the complainant's rights and obligations prescribed in Article 66 of this Law.
3. Persons with related interests, obligations who participate in competition procedures on the side of the investigated parties or persons with obligations only shall have the investigated party's rights and obligations prescribed in Article 66 of this Law.

Article 72 Procedures for refusing expertise, interpretation or requesting change of experts or interpreters

1. The refusal of expertise or interpretation or request for change of experts or interpreters before the opening of hearings must be made in writing, clearly stating the reasons therefor.
2. The refusal of expertise or interpretation or request for change of experts or interpreters during a hearing must be written in the hearing's minutes.

Article 73 Deciding on change of experts or interpreters

1. Before opening a hearing, the change of experts or interpreters shall be decided by the Competition Council chairman.
2. During a hearing, the change of experts or interpreters shall be decided by the Competition Case-Handling Council after hearing the opinions of the persons requested to be changed and other competition procedure participants.

   If it is necessary to change experts or interpreters, the Competition Case-Handling Council shall issue a decision to postpone the hearing. The request for expertise by other experts or the appointment of other interpreters shall comply with the provisions of Articles 69 and Article 70 of this Law.

Section 2 Competition Procedure – Conducting Agencies, Competition Procedure-Conducting Persons

Article 74 Competition procedure-conducting agencies

Competition procedure-conducting agencies include the competition-managing agency and the Competition Council.

Article 75 Competition procedure-conducting persons

Competition procedure-conducting persons include Competition Council members, the head of the competition-managing agency, investigators and the hearing's clerks.

Article 76 Tasks and powers of the head of the competition-managing agency when conducting competition procedures

When conducting competition procedures, the head of the competition-managing agency shall have the following tasks and powers:

1. To decide to assign investigators to investigate specific competition cases;
2. To inspect investigative activities of competition case investigators;
3. To decide to modify or cancel groundless and illegal decisions issued by competition case investigators;
4. To decide to change competition case investigators;

5. To decide to request expertise;
6. To decide to apply, change or cancel administrative preventive measures pending the transfer of competition case dossiers to the Competition Council for handling;
7. To decide to conduct preliminary investigation, stop investigation, conduct official investigation of competition cases falling under the competence of the competition-managing agency;
8. To invite witnesses at the requests of the involved parties at the investigation stage;
9. To sign written conclusions on the investigation of competition cases, submitted by the assigned investigators;
10. To transfer competition case dossiers to the Competition Council in cases where the competition cases involve competition-restricting acts;
11. To settle complaints and denunciations falling under the competence of the competition-managing agency.

Article 77 Powers of investigators when conducting competition procedures

When conducting competition procedures, investigators shall have the following powers:

1. To request related organizations and individuals to supply necessary information and documents concerning competition cases;
2. To request the investigated parties to supply documents and give explanations concerning competition cases;
3. To propose the head of the competition-managing agency to request expertise;
4. To propose the head of the competition-managing agency to apply administrative preventive measures to competition cases.

Article 78 Obligations of investigators when conducting competition procedures:

When conducting competition procedures, investigators shall have the following obligations:

1. To hand the investigation decisions of the head of the competition-managing agency to the investigated parties;
2. To keep confidential business secrets of enterprises;
3. To preserve the supplied documents;
4. To investigate competition cases assigned by the head of the competition-managing agency;
5. To make investigation reports upon termination of preliminary investigation or official investigation of competition cases;
6. To take responsibility to the head of the competition-managing agency and before law for the performance of their tasks and powers.

Article 79 Tasks and powers of the Competition Council chairman when conducting competition procedures

1. To set up the Competition Case-Handling Council under the provisions of Clause 3, Article 54 of this Law.
2. To decide to change Competition Case-Handling Council members, the hearing's clerks, experts or interpreters before opening a hearing according to the provisions of Clause 1 of Article 73, Article 83 and Clause 1 of Article 85 of this Law.
3. To decide to appoint Competition Case-Handling Council members, the hearing's clerks to replace those who are changed during the hearing according to the provisions of Clause 2, Article 85 of this Law.
4. To decide to apply, change or cancel administrative preventive measures when receiving competition case dossiers.

Article 80 The Competition Case-Handling Council

1. When settling competition cases, the Competition Case-Handling Council shall work independently and only abide by law.
2. Decisions on handling competition cases shall be adopted by the Competition Case-Handling Council by majority vote; where the numbers of votes for and against are equal, decisions shall be made according to the side sharing the opinion of the hearing's president.

Article 81 Tasks and powers of the president of a hearing

The president of a hearing shall have the following tasks and powers:

1. To organize the study of competition case dossiers;
2. On the basis of the decision of the Competition Case-Handling Council, to sign the proposal to the Competition Council chairman to apply, change or cancel administrative preventive measures; decide to return the competition case dossier to the competition-managing agency and request additional investigation; decide to stop the settlement of the competition case;
3. On the basis of the decision of the Competition Case-Handling Council, to sign the decision to open the hearing;
4. To decide to summon participants to the hearing;
5. To sign and announce the decision on the handling of the competition case and other decisions of the Competition Case- Handling Council;
6. To carry out other activities under his/her competence prescribed by this Law when handling the competition case.

Article 82 Clerks of hearings

1. The clerk of a hearing shall have the following tasks and powers:
   (a) To prepare necessary professional jobs before the opening of a hearing;
   (b) To announce the rules of the hearing;
   (c) To report to the Competition Case-Handling Council on the presence or absence of those summoned to the hearing;
   (d) To write the minutes of the hearing;
   (e) To perform other jobs assigned by the president of the hearing.
2. The clerk of a hearing must refuse to conduct competition procedures or be changed in the cases prescribed in Article 83 of this Law.

Article 83 Cases of refusal or change of Competition Case-Handling Council members, investigators, the hearing's clerks, experts, interpreters

Competition Case-Handling Council members, investigators, the hearing's clerks, experts, interpreters must refuse to perform their tasks or shall be changed in one of the following cases:

1. They are relatives of the complainants or investigated parties;
2. They are persons with interests, obligations related to the competition cases;
3. There are other explicit grounds to deem that they shall not be impartial when performing their tasks.

Article 84 Procedures for refusal to conduct competition procedures or request for change of Competition Case-Handling Council members, the hearing's clerks

1. The refusal to conduct competition procedures or request for change of Competition Case-Handling Council members, the hearing's clerks before the opening of the hearings must be made in writing, clearly stating the reasons and grounds therefor.

2. The refusal to conduct competition procedures or request for change of Competition Case-Handling Council members, the hearing's clerks during the hearings must be recorded in the hearing's minutes.

Article 85 Deciding on change of Competition Case-Handling Council members or the hearing's clerks

1. Before a hearing is opened, the change of Competition Case-Handling Council members, the hearing's clerk shall be decided by the Competition Council chairman.
2. During a hearing, the acceptance of the change of Competition Case-Handling Council members or the hearing's clerk shall be decided by the Competition Case-Handling Council after hearing the opinions of the refusing persons or the persons requested to be changed. The Competition Case-Handling Council shall discuss behind closed doors and make decision by majority vote.

   If it is necessary to change Competition Case-Handling Council members or the hearing's clerk, the Competition Case-Handling Council shall issue a decision to postpone the hearing. The appointment of Competition Case-Handling Council members or a hearing's clerk to replace those who must be changed shall be decided by the Competition Council chairman.

Section 4 Investigation of Competition Cases

Article 86 Preliminary investigation

The preliminary investigation of competition cases shall be conducted under decisions of the head of the competition-managing agency in the following cases:

1. Competition case dossiers have been accepted by the competition-managing agency;
2. The competition-managing agency detects signs of violation of the provisions of this Law.

Article 87 Time limit for preliminary investigation

1. The time limit for preliminary investigation is thirty days as from the date of issuance of preliminary investigation decisions.
2. Within the time limit specified in Clause 1 of this Article, investigators assigned to investigate competition cases must complete the preliminary investigation and propose the head of the competition-managing agency to issue a decision to stop investigation or conduct official investigation.

Article 88 Decisions to stop investigation, decisions to conduct official investigation

On the basis of the preliminary investigation results and the proposals of investigators, the head of the competition-managing agency shall issue one of the following decisions:

1. To stop investigation if the preliminary investigation results show that there are no acts of violation of the provisions of this Law;
2. To conduct official investigation if the preliminary investigation results show that there are acts of violation of the provisions of this Law.

Article 89 Contents of official investigation

1. For cases of competition restriction agreement, abuse of the dominant position on the market or abuse of the monopoly position, or economic concentration, investigation shall covers:
   (a) Identifying the relevant market;
   (b) Verifying the investigated party's market share on the relevant market;
   (c) Collecting and analyzing evidences on violation acts.

2. For cases of unfair competition, investigators must identify the grounds to deem that the investigated parties have performed or are performing unfair competition acts.

Article 90 Time limit for official investigation

The time limit for official investigation is prescribed as follows:

1. For cases of unfair competition, the time limit for official investigation shall be ninety days as from the date of issuance of decisions; in case of necessity, this time limit may be extended by the head of the competition-managing agency for another sixty days at most;
2. For cases of competition restriction agreement, abuse of the dominant position on the market or abuse of the monopoly position, or economic concentration, the time limit for official investigation shall be one hundred and eighty days, as from the date of issuance of decisions; in case of necessity, this time limit may be extended by the head of the competition-managing agency no more than twice, each time for sixty days at most;
3. The extension of the investigation time limit must be notified by investigators to all related parties not later than seven working days before the expiration of the investigation time limit.

Article 91 Investigation minutes

1. When conducting investigation, investigators must make investigation minutes, clearly indicating the investigation time and place, investigators, investigated party, investigated contents and complaint and/or claim of the investigated party.
2. Investigation minutes must be read out by investigators to the investigated party before they both sign the minutes.
3. If the investigated party refuses to sign the minutes, investigators must record such in the minutes together with the reason therefor.

Article 92 Request to invite witnesses in the investigation process

1. In the process of investigation, the involved parties may request the competition-managing agency to invite witnesses. The requestors shall be obliged to state the reasons for inviting witnesses to the competition-managing agency for decision.
2. The competition-managing agency's invitation to a witness must clearly indicate the full name and address of the invitee, time and place for giving testimony, the parties and subject involved in the case.
3. Testimonies of witnesses must be recorded in minutes by investigators, which shall be read out to the witnesses before they both sign the minutes.

Article 93 Investigation reports

1. After the termination of investigation, the head of the competition-managing agency must transfer the investigation reports together with the whole competition case dossiers related to competition-restricting acts to the Competition Council.
2. An investigation report shall contain the following principal contents:
   (a) A brief account of the case;
   (b) Verified circumstances and evidences;
   (c) Proposed handling measures.

Article 94 Transfer of dossiers of competition cases involving criminal signs

If, through investigation, it is detected that a competition case shows criminal signs, investigators must promptly propose the head of the competition-managing agency to consider and transfer the relevant dossier to competent State agencies for institution of criminal cases.

Article 95 Return of dossiers in case of availability of grounds for non-institution of criminal cases

Where state agencies with competence to institute criminal cases find that there are grounds for non-institution of criminal cases under the provisions of the Criminal Procedure Code, they must return the dossiers to the competition-managing agency for further investigation according to the procedures prescribed in this Law. The investigation time limit prescribed in Article 90 of this Law shall be counted as from the date the dossiers are received back.

Article 96 Additional investigation, time limit for additional investigation

1. Competition case investigators must conduct additional investigation if it is so requested in writing by the Competition Case-Handling Council.
2. The time limit for additional investigation is sixty days, as from the date of issuance of the Competition Case-Handling Council's written requests for additional investigation.

Article 97 Responsibilities for coordination and support in the investigation process

Local administrations, police agencies, other agencies and organizations shall have to coordinate and support the investigation process at the request of the head of the competition-managing agency.

Section 5 Hearings

Article 98 Competition cases must be considered and handled through hearings

Competition cases falling under the settling competence of the Competition Council must be considered and handled through hearings.

Article 99 Preparation for opening a hearing

1. After receiving the investigation report and the complete competition case dossier, the Competition Council chairman shall decide to set up a Competition Case-Handling Council.
2. Within thirty days after receiving the competition case dossier, the Competition Case-Handling Council must issue one of the following decisions:
   (a) To open a hearing;
   (b) To return the dossier for additional investigation;
   (c) To stop settling the competition case.
3. Within fifteen days after the date of issuance of the decision to open a hearing, the Competition Case-Handling Council must open a hearing.
4. In case of returning the dossier for additional investigation, within fifteen days after the date of receiving back the dossier, the Competition Case-Handling Council must issue one of the decisions defined in Clause 2 of this Article.

Article 100 Return of dossiers for additional investigation

If finding that the collected evidences are not enough for determining acts of violation of the provisions of this Law, the Competition Case-Handling Council shall decide to return the dossiers for additional investigation.

Article 101 Stoppage of settlement of competition cases falling under the settling competence of the Competition Council

1. The Competition Case-Handling Council shall decide to stop settling competition cases falling under the settling competence of the Competition Council in the following cases:
   (a) The head of the competition-managing agency proposes to stop settling the competition case if there are not enough evidences of acts of violation of the provisions of this Law and the Competition Case-Handling Council deems such proposal justified;
   (b) The investigated party has voluntarily terminated its violation acts, remedied consequences and the complainant has voluntarily withdrawn its written complaint;
   (c) The investigated party has voluntarily terminated its violation acts, remedied consequences and the head of the competition-managing agency proposes to stop settling the competition case, for cases where investigation has been conducted under the provisions of Clause 2, Article 65 of this Law.
2. Decisions to stop settling competition cases must be sent to the investigated parties and the complainants (if any) as well as the competition-managing agency.

Article 102 Decisions to open hearings

1. A decision to open a hearing must be handed to the parties named therein not later than ten days before the date of opening of the hearing.
2. A decision to open a hearing must contain the following contents:
   (a) The investigated party;
   (b) The complainant or the competition-managing agency, for cases where investigation has been conducted under the provisions of Clause 2, Article 65 of this Law;
   (c) Violated articles and/or clauses of this Law;
   (d) Time and place of opening of the hearing;
   (e) The hearing is to be held in public or behind closed doors;
   (f) Full names of Competition Case-Handling Council members;
   (g) Full names of investigators who have investigated the competition case, the hearing's clerk;
   (h) Full names of lawyers;
   (i) Full name of the interpreter;
   (j) Full names of witnesses;
   (k) Full names of experts;
   (l) Persons with related interests and obligations.

Article 103 Summoning of persons who must appear at the hearings

On the basis of the decisions to open the hearings, the Competition Case-Handling Council shall send summonses to persons who must appear at the hearings not later than ten days before the date of opening of the hearings.

Article 104 Hearings

1. Hearings shall be held in public. Where the contents of a hearing are related to national secrets or business secrets, the hearing shall be held behind closed doors.
2. Participants to a hearing include:
   (a) Competition Case-Handling Council members, the hearing's clerk;
   (b) The investigated party;
   (c) The complainant;
   (d) Lawyers;
   (e) Investigators who have investigated the competition case;
   (f) Other persons named in the decision to open the hearing.

3. After hearing the opinions and arguments presented by the participants to the hearings, the Competition Case-Handling Council shall discuss, cast secret votes and make decision by majority vote.

Section 6 Effect of Competition Case-Handling Decisions

Article 105 Competition case-handling decisions

1. A competition case-handling decision shall contain the following principal contents:
   (a) A brief account of the case;
   (b) Analysis of the case;
   (c) Conclusion on the handling of the case.
2. The hearing presidents must sign competition case-handling decisions.
3. Competition case-handling decisions must be sent to the related parties within seven working date after the date of its signing.

Article 106 Effect of competition case-handling decisions

Competition case-handling decisions shall come into force thirty days after the date of its signing provided that during this period they are not complained about under the provisions of Article 107 of this Law.

Section 7 Settlement of Complaints About Competition Case-Handling Decisions Which have not Yet Come into Force

Article 107 Complaining about competition case-handling decisions

1. If the involved parties disagree with part or the whole of the competition case-handling decisions issued by the Competition Case-Handling Council, they may lodge complaints with the Competition Council.
2. If the involved parties disagree with part or the whole of the competition case-handling decisions issued by the head of the competition-managing agency, they may lodge complaints with the Trade Minister.

Article 108 Written complaints about competition case-handling decisions

1. A written complaint about the competition case-handling decision must contain the following principal contents:
   (a) Date of making;
   (b) Name and address of the maker;
   (c) Serial number and date of the complained competition case-handling decision;
   (d) The reason for complaining and the complainant's claim;
   (e) The signature and seal (if any) of the complainant.
2. Written complainants must be addressed to the agencies issuing the competition case-handling decisions in question together with supplementary evidences (if any) proving that the complaints are grounded and lawful.

Article 109 Acceptance of written complaints about competition case-handling decisions

Within five working days after receiving the written complainants about the competition case-handling decisions, the agencies which have issued such decisions must check the validity of the written complaints according to the provisions of Article 108 of this Law.

Article 110 Consequences of complaints about competition case-handling decisions

1. The complained parts of competition case-handling decisions shall not be executed.
2. Within fifteen days after receiving the written complaints about competition case-handling decisions, the agency accepting such written complaints shall have to consider and transfer them together with the whole competition case dossiers as well as their proposals on the written complaints to the Competition Council or the Trade Minister according to the provisions of Article 107 of this Law.

Article 111 Time limit for settling complaints about competition case-handling decisions

Within thirty days after receiving the complaint dossiers, the Competition Council or the Trade Minister shall have to settle the complaints according to competence; in specially complicated cases, the time limit for settling complaints may be extended for another thirteen days at most.

Article 112 Powers of the Competition Council when settling complaints about competition case-handling decisions of the Competition Case-Handling Council

When considering and settling complaints about competition case-handling decisions of the Competition Case-Handling Council, the Competition Council shall have the following powers:

1. To hold up the competition case-handling decisions if deeming that the complaints are not sufficiently grounded;
2. To amend part or whole of the competition case-handling decisions if such decisions are illegal;
3. To cancel the competition case-handling decisions and transfer the competition case dossiers to the Competition Case-Handling Council for resettlement in the following cases:
   (a) Evidences have not yet been fully collected and verified;
   (b) The composition of the Competition Case-Handling Council contravenes the provisions of this Law or other serious violations of competition procedures were committed.

Article 113 Powers of the Trade Minister when settling complaints about competition case-handling decisions of the competition-managing agency

When considering and settling complaints about competition case-handling decisions of the competition-managing agency, the Trade Minister shall have the powers defined in Clause 1 and Clause 2, Article 112 of this Law, the power to cancel the competition case-handling decisions and request the competition-managing agency to resettle the cases according to the procedures prescribed in this Law in cases where evidences have not yet been fully collected and verified.

Article 114 Effect of complaint-settling decisions

Decisions to settle complaints about competition case-handling decisions shall come into force as from the date of signing.

Article 115 Initiation of lawsuits against complaint-settling decisions

1. If the involved parties disagree with the decisions to settle complaints about competition case-handling decisions, they may initiate administrative lawsuits against part or the whole of the contents of such decisions at the competent provincial/municipal People's Courts.
2. Where the courts accept the written lawsuits against the decisions to settle complaints about competition case-handling decisions according to the provisions of Clause 1 of this Article, the

Trade Minister and the Competition Council chairman shall have to direct the transfer of the competition case dossiers to the courts within ten working days after receiving the court's requests.

Article 116 Consequences of lawsuits

Those parts of competition case-handling decisions which are not sued against at court shall continue to be executed.

Section 8 Handling of Violations of Competition Legislation

Article 117 Forms of sanctioning violations of competition legislation and measures to remedy consequences

1. For each act of violation of competition legislation, violating organizations or individuals shall be subject to one of the following principal sanctioning forms:
   (a) Warning;
   (b) Fine.
2. Depending on the nature and seriousness of their violations, the organizations or individuals violating competition legislation may be subject to one of the following additional sanctioning forms:
   (a) Revocation of the business registration certificates, deprivation of licenses and practicing certificates;
   (b) Confiscation of exhibits and means used for commission of violations of competition legislation.
3. In addition to the sanctioning forms prescribed in Clause 1 and Clause 2 of this Article, organizations or individuals violating competition legislation may be subject to the application of one or more than one of the following consequence remedying measures:
   (a) To restructure the enterprises having abused their dominant position on the market;
   (b) To divide or split the merged or consolidated enterprises; to force the resale of the acquired enterprise parts;
   (c) To make public corrections;
   (d) To remove illegal provisions from the business contracts or transactions;
   (e) Other necessary measures to overcome the competition restriction impacts of the violation acts.

   If organizations or individuals violating competition legislation cause damage to the interests of the State, legitimate rights and interests of other organizations or individuals, they must pay compensation therefor according to law provisions.

Article 118 Levels of fine imposed for acts of violating competition legislation

1. For acts of violating the provisions on competition restriction agreements, abuse of dominant position on the market, abuse of monopoly position or economic concentration, the agencies with sanctioning competence may impose fines of up to 10% of total turnover earned by the violating organizations or individuals in the fiscal year preceding the year when they commit violation acts.
2. For acts of violating the provisions on unfair competition and other acts of violating the provisions of this Law other than those prescribed in Clause 1 of this Article, the agencies with sanctioning competence shall impose fines according to law provisions on handling of administrative violations or relevant law provisions.
3. The Government shall specify the levels of fine imposed for acts of violating the provisions of this Law.

Article 119 Competence to sanction, handle violations of competition legislation

1. The Competition Case-Handling Council and the Competition Council shall have the following powers:
   (a) To issue caution;
   (b) To impose fines according to the provisions of Clause 1, Article 118 of this Law;
   (c) To confiscate exhibits and means used for commission of violations of competition legislation;
   (d) To apply the measures prescribed at Points c, d and e, Clause 3, Article 117 of this Law;
   (e) To request competent state agencies to revoke business registration certificates, deprive of licenses and/or practicing certificates;
   (f) To request competent state agencies to apply the measures prescribed at Points a and b, Clause 3, Article 117 of this Law.
2. The competition-managing agency may apply the measures prescribed at Point a of Clause 1, Point b of Clause 2, Point c of Clause 3, Article 117 and Clause 2, Article 118 of this Law.
3. Other agencies with sanctioning competence shall sanction intellectual property-related unfair competition acts according to law provisions on handling of administrative violations.

Article 120 Handling of violations committed by state officials and employees

State officials and employees who commit acts of violation of competition legislation shall, depending on the nature and seriousness of their violations, be disciplined or examined for penal liability; if causing any damage, they must pay compensation therefor according to law provisions.

Article 121 Execution of competition case-handling decisions

1. After thirty days as from the date the competition case-handling decisions come into force, if the parties obliged to comply with such decisions fail to voluntarily comply with and do not initiate lawsuits at court according to the provisions of Section 7 of this Chapter, the parties in favor of which the competition case-handling decisions are executed may request in writing the competent state agencies to organize the execution of the competition case-handling decisions falling within the scope of their functions, tasks and powers.
2. Where the competition case-handling decisions are related to the property of the parties bound to comply with the decisions, the parties in favor of which the competition case-handling decisions are executed may request the civil judgment-executing agencies in the provinces or centrally run cities where the parties obliged to comply with the decisions are headquartered, reside or their property is located to organize the execution of the competition case-handling decisions.

Chapter VI Implementation Provisions

Article 122 Implementation effect

This Law shall take effect as from July 1, 2005.

Article 123 Implementation guidance

The Government and the Supreme People's Court shall detail and guide the implementation of this Law.

This Law was passed on December 3, 2004 by the XIth National Assembly of the Socialist Republic of Vietnam at its the 6th session.

Chairman of the National Assembly

NGUYEN VAN AN

BIBLIOGRAPHY[1]

BOOKS

Alese, F, *Federal Antitrust and EC Competition Law Analysis* (Aldershot: Ashgate Publishing Limited, 2008).
American Bar Association, *Antitrust Law Developments (Sixth)* (Chicago Ill: ABA, 2007).
Cheng, LK and Wu, C, *Competition Policy and the Regulation of Business* (Hong Kong: City University of Hong Kong Press, 1998).
Chung, Y-I, *South Korea in the Fast Lane: Economic Development and Capital Formation* (Oxford: Oxford University Press, 2007).
Cook, P, Fabella, R, and Lee, C (eds), *Competitive Advantage and Competition Policy in Developing Countries* (Cheltenham: Edward Elgar, 2007).
Dabbah, MM and Lasok, P, *Merger Control Worldwide* (Cambridge: Cambridge University Press, 2005).
Eichengreen, B, Wyplosz, C, and Park, YC (eds), *China, Asia, and the New World Economy* (Oxford: Oxford University Press, 2008).
Faull, J and Nikpay, A (eds), *The EC Law of Competition* (Oxford: Oxford University Press, 2nd edn, 2007).
Gao, Y and Cao, D (eds), *Anti-Unfair Competition Law: Understanding, Application and Case Studies* (Beijing: Peoples Court Publishing House, 2nd edn, 1997).*
Gittings, J, *The Changing Face of China: From Mao to Market* (Oxford: Oxford University Press, 2006).
Hoa, TV (ed), *Competition Policy and Global Competitiveness in Major Asian Economies* (Cheltenham: Edward Elgar, 2003).
Hovenkamp, H, *Federal Antitrust Policy: The Law of Competition and its Practice*, (St Paul Minn: West Publishing Co, 3rd edn, 2005).
Hu, R, *Competition and monopoly; micro-economic analysis of socialism* (Shanghai: Shanghai Shanlian Publishing House, 1998).*
Huang Qi, Cao, Q, and Tu, T (eds), *Anti-Unfair Competition Law Cases* (Hunan People Publishing House, 1998).*

[1] This bibliography excludes regular publications by official bodies, such as the KFTC newsletters, or the OECD annual reports on competition policy in the various States. Items marked with an '*' are not available in English. The practice in Asia is for the family name to precede the given name. This can cause confusion when authors write in both Western and non-Western journals. For example, Professor Wang Xiaoye is cited as such in China, but as Professor Xiaoye Wang in the *Antitrust Law Journal* (Wang being her family name). Throughout this bibliography references are to family name and to given name initials (or full given names when there is the possibility of confusion between authors) irrespective of the source of original publication or the nationality of the writer. If I have made any mistakes in transcribing names I apologize. Journal titles and book titles are translated from the original where the publication is not in English.

Ilzkovitz, F and Meikeljohn, R (eds), *European Merger Control: Do we Need an Efficiency Defence?* (Cheltenham: Edward Elgar, 2006).

Jin, C and Luo, W, *Competition Law in China* (Buffalo NY: William S Hein & Co Inc, 2002).

Lam, P-L, *Competition in Energy* (Hong Kong: City University of Hong Kong Press, 1997).

—— and Chan, Y-C, *Privatizing Water and Sewage Services* (Hong Kong: City University of Hong Kong Press, 1997).

Noonan, C, *The Emerging Principles of International Competition Law* (Oxford: Oxford University Press, 2008).

Rowley, JW and Baker, DI, *International Mergers: The Antitrust Process*, Looseleaf (London: Sweet & Maxwell).

Shin, HY, *Korean Competition Law* (Seoul: Bubmunsa, 2007).*

Tondel, LM (ed), *The International Position of Communist China: Background Papers and Proceedings of the Fifth Hammarskjold Forum* (Dobbs Ferry NY: Oceana Publications Inc, 1965).

Williams, M, *Competition Policy and Law in China, Hong Kong and Taiwan* (Cambridge: Cambridge University Press, 2005).

ARTICLES, ESSAYS, REPORTS, AND PAPERS

American Bar Association's Sections of Antitrust Law and International Law and Practice, *Joint Submission on the Proposed Anti-Monopoly Law of the People's Republic of China* (2003).

Areeda, P and Turner, DF, 'Predatory Pricing and Related Practices under Section 2 of the Sherman Act' (1975) 88 *Harvard Law Review* 697.

Bush, N and Zhou, Z, 'Chinese Antitrust—Act II, Scene 1', *theantitrustsource* <http://www.antitrustsource.com>, October 2008.

Charney, JI, and Prescott, JRV, 'Resolving Cross-Strait Relations between China and Taiwan' (2000) 94 *American Journal of International Law* 453.

Chen, AHY, 'Competition Law and Hong Kong' (1993) 23(3) *Hong Kong Law Journal* 412.

Chiang, LM, 'Enforcement of Competition Law—Taiwan Experience', <http://www.ftc.go.kr/data/english/20010809-f.doc>.

Commerce and Economic Development Bureau, *Detailed Proposals for a Competition Law—A Public Consultation Paper*, May 2008, CEDB, Hong Kong <http://www.cedb.gov.hk>.

Connor, JM and Bolotova, Y, 'Cartel Overcharges: Survey and meta-analysis', *International Journal of Industrial Organisation* (2006) vol 24, 1109.

Consumer Council (Hong Kong), *Competition Policy: The Key to Hong Kong's Future Economic Success* (1996) <http://www2.consumer.org.hk/trd96/TRD96_E.HTM>.

CUTS International, *A Guide to Competition Issues in Vietnam* [now renamed *Competition Law in Vietnam: A Toolkit*] <http://www.cuts-international.org/HRC/pdf/Vietnam_Toolkit-en.pdf>.

——*Promoting Competition Policy & Law in Vietnam* [now renamed *Fairplay please! Advocacy and capacity building on competition policy and law in Asia*] <http://www.cuts-international.org/7up2/7Up2_Vietnam.pdf>.

Dabbah, MM, 'The Development of Sound Competition Law and Policy in China: An (Im)possible Dream?' (2007) 30:2 *World Competition* 341.

Deng, F, and Leonard, GK, 'Incentives and China's New Antimonopoly Law' (2008) *Antitrust*, Spring, 73.

Economic Development and Labour Bureau, *Promoting Competition—Maintaining our Economic Drive* (2006) <http://www.edlb.gov.hk>.

——*Report on Public Consultation on the way forward for Hong Kong's Competition Policy* (2007) <http://www.edlb.gov.hk>.

Emch, A, 'Abuse of dominance in China: a paradigmatic shift?' (2008) *European Competition Law Review* 615.

Fox, EM, 'An Anti-Monopoly Law for China—Scaling the Walls of Government Restraints' (2008) 75 *Antitrust Law Journal* 173.

Furse, M., 'Competition Law Choice in China' (2007) 30:2 *World Competition* 323.

——'Competition Law and Reform in Hong Kong' (2007) *European Competition Law Review* 401.

——'Excessive Prices, Unfair Prices and Economic Value: The Law of Excessive Pricing under Article 82 EC and the Chapter II Prohibition' (2008) *European Competition Journal* 59.

Haley, JO, 'Competition Law for the Asia-Pacific Economic Cooperation Community: Designing Shoes for Many Sizes' (2002) *Washington University Global Studies Law Review*, vol 1, (1 & 2), 1.

Harris, SH, 'The Making of an Antitrust Law: The Pending Anti-Monopoly Law of the People's Republic of China' (2006–2007) 7 *Chicago Journal of International Law* 169.

—— and Ganske, RJ, 'The Monopolization and IP Abuse Provisions of China's Anti-Monopoly Law: Concerns and a Proposal' (2008) 75 *Antitrust Law Journal* 213.

—— and Yang, KL, 'Draft Anti-Monopoly Legislation and the SAIC Report' (2004) *International Antitrust Bulletin* (Spring/Summer), 16.

Harvie, C, 'Competition and SMEs in Vietnam', in Hoa, TV (ed), *Competition Policy and Global Competitiveness in Major Asian Economies* (2003) at 170.

Hu, W, 'Anti-monopoly law is a necessity in China' (1995) 3 *Jurisprudence* 35.*

Huang, X and Zhou, J, 'Research on the legislative control of administrative monopoly and monopoly practices' (2001) 3 *China Jurists Journal* 99.*

Huang, Y, 'Pursuing the Second Best: The History, Momentum, and Remaining Issues of China's Anti-Monopoly Law' (2008) 75 *Antitrust Law Journal* 117.

Hung, VM-Y, 'China's WTO Commitment on Independent Judicial Review: Impact on Legal and Political Reform' (2004) 52 *American Journal of Comparative Law* 77.

Hwang, T-L, 'Recent Competition Law Development in Taiwan' <http://www.jftc.go.jp/eacpf/06/6_03_05.pdf>.

Jenny, F, 'Competition Policy and the Asian Economic Crisis' (1999) 1:2 *OECD Journal of Competition Law and Policy* 13.

Jiang, X, 'Promoting Competition and Maintaining Monopoly: Dual Functions of Chinese Industrial Policies During Economic Transition' (2002) *Washington University Global Studies Law Review*, vol 1, (1 & 2), 49.

Junfeng, L, 'Foreign-Invested Companies: More Risky Facing up to China's Anti-Monopoly Law' (2008), Symposium, Shanghai University/Liverpool John Moore's University (unpublished).

Jung, Y, 'Korean Competition Law: First Step Towards Globalisation' (2005) 4:2 *Journal of Korean Law* 177.

Jung, Y and Chang, SW, 'Korea's Competition Law and Policies in Perspective' (2005–2006) 26 *Northwestern Journal of International Law and Business* 687.

Jung, Y and Hao, Q, 'The New Economic Constitution in China: A Third Way for Competition Regime?' (2003) 24 *Northwestern Journal of International Law and Business* 110.

Kim, W-K, 'The Extraterritorial Application of US Antitrust Law and its Adoption in Korea' (2003) 7 *Singapore Journal of International & Comparative Law* 386.

Kim, Y-H, 'A Guide to Korean Antitrust Law' (2002) 2 *Journal of Korean Law* 161.

Kwon, O, 'Retrospect and Prospect on Korean Antitrust Law' (2005) 4:2 *Journal of Korean Law* 1.

Lee, BE, 'Prohibition of Abuse of Market-Dominating Undertakings under the Monopoly Regulation and Fair Trade Act' (2005) 4:2 *Journal of Korean Law* 61.

Lee, H-H, 'Korea's Competition Policy and Its Applications to Other Asian Economies', in Hoa, TV (ed), *Competition Policy and Global Competitiveness in Major Asian Economies* (2003).

Lee, HY, 'Regulation of Undue Internal Dealings under the Monopoly Regulation and Fair Trade Act' (2005) 4:2 *Journal of Korean Law* 83.

Lee, KJ, 'Towards a more comprehensive international competition forum in Asia and worldwide', Conference presentation, Asia International Competition Conference, 4 September 2008, Seoul.

Lee, KU, 'Economic Development and Competition Policy in Korea' (2002) *Washington University Global Studies Law Review*, vol 1, (1 & 2), 67.

Lee, LLC, 'Taiwan's Antitrust Statutes: Proposals for a Regulatory Regime and Comparison of US and Taiwanese Antitrust Law' (1995–1996) 6 *Indiana International and Comparative Law Review* 583.

Lee, MH, 'Recent Developments in the Treatment of Collusion by the Korean Courts' (2005) 4:2 *Journal of Korean Law* 155.

Li, KX and Du, M, 'Does China Need Competition Law?' (2007) *Journal of Business Law* 182.

Lin, G-L, 'Taiwan's Competition Law Enforcement Experience and Cases in Retailing Business', <http://www.jftc.go.jp/eacpf/05/APECTrainingProgram2003/LINGin.pdf>.

Liu, LS, 'Fostering Competition Law and Policy: A Façade of Taiwan's Political Economy' (2002) *Washington University Global Studies Law Review*, vol 1, (1 & 2), 77.

Lloyd, PJ, 'Competition Law in APEC Economies and in Vietnam', in Hoa, TV (ed), *Competition Policy and Global Competitiveness in Major Asian Economies* (2003) at 29.

Lorenz, M, 'The New Chinese Competition Act' (2008) *European Competition Law Review* 257.

McBratney, A, 'The Nine Lives of Vietnam's new Competition Law' (2004) *European Competition Law Review* 485.

Owen, BM, Sun, S, and Zheng, W, 'Antitrust in China: The Problem of Incentive Compatibility' (2005) 1 *Journal of Competition Law and Economics* 123.

——'China's Competition Policy Reforms: The Anti-Monopoly Law and Beyond' (2008) 75 *Antitrust Law Journal* 231.

Park, S-E, 'Korean Competition Statute: Its Limits and Measures for Improvements' (2005) 4:2 *Journal of Korean Law* 139.

Pate, RH, 'What I Heard in the Great Hall of the People—Realistic Expectations of Chinese Antitrust' (2008) 75 *Antitrust Law Journal* 195.

Pham, A, 'The Development of Competition Law in Vietnam in the face of Economic Reforms and Global Integration' (2005–2006) 26 *Northwestern Journal of International Law and Business* 547.

Phillips Fox, *Competition Law Update*, July 2006 (<http://www.phillipsfox.com>).

Qi, D, 'Research Problems in Chinese Anti-Monopoly legislation' (1994) 4 *Chinese Journal of Law* 54.*

Robertson, JR, 'Symposium: The Anti-Monopoly Law of the People's Republic of China—Editor's Note' (2008) 75 *Antitrust Law Journal* 67.

Ross, L, 'China's Anti-Monopoly Law' (2008) *Antitrust*, Spring, 66.

Shi, J, 'Follow the objective requirement of competition: two basic questions of the concept and object of Chinese anti-monopoly law' (1998) 4 *Intertrade* 10.*

Shieh, M-Y, 'A discussion of the relationship between the patent law and the Fair Trade Law in Taiwan with a review of the *Phillips CD-R* decisions', in Hwang, T-L and Chen, C (eds), *The Future Development of Competition Framework* (The Hague: Kluwer Law International, 2004).

Song, B 'Competition Policy in a Transitional Economy: The Case of China' (1995) 31 *Stanford Journal of International Law* 387.

Spratling, GR and Arp, DJ, 'Making the Decision: What to do when Faced with International Cartel Exposure—Developments Impacting the Decision in 2008', Conference presentation, Asia International Competition Conference, Seoul, 4 September 2008.

Stigler, GJ, 'A Theory of Oligopoly' (1964) 72 *Journal of Political Economy* 44.

Suh, DW, 'Enforcement Direction of Competition Law' (2005) 4:2 *Journal of Korean Law* 29.

Thai, LV, Hong, VXN, and Hoa, TV, 'Anti-trust Law and Competition Policy in Vietnam', in Hoa, TV, (ed) *Competition Policy and Global Competitiveness in Major Asian Economies* (2003) at 139.

The Frontier and the Hong Kong Democratic Foundation, *Competition Policy in Hong Kong* (1993) <http://www.hkdf.org/pr.asp?func=show&pr=123>.

Urata, S, 'Competition Policy and Economic Development in East Asia' (2002) *Washington University Global Studies Law Review*, vol 1, (1 & 2), 15.

Vietnam Competition Administration Department, *Report on Economic Concentration in Vietnam in 2008—Current Situation and Outlook* (2009) VCAD.

Wang, B, 'Comments upon anti-trust law application to administrative monopoly' (1998) 5 *Journal of the Graduate School of the Chinese Academy of Social Sciences* 49.*

Wang, Chundi, 'Monopoly through merger' (1998) 3 *Jurists' Review* 72.*

Wang, Cunxue, 'Price cartels and their regulation in China's market economy' (1998) 2 *Modern Law Science Review* 64.*

Wang, Xianlin, 'An approach to the establishment of an anti-monopoly law enforcement authority and its functions' (August 2000) *China Administrative Supervision Journal.**

Wang, Xiaoye, 'Anti-Monopoly Law under the conditions of the socialist market economy' (1996) *Social Sciences in Chinese* 72.*

——'Anti-monopoly law should regulate the activities of public companies in the market' (1997) *Chinese Academy of Social Science Journal of Law* 92.*

——'The Prospect of Antimonopoly Legislation in China' (2002) *Washington University Global Studies Law Review*, Vol 1, (1 & 2), 201.

——'Highlight's of China's New Anti-Monopoly Law' (2008) 75 *Antitrust Law Journal* 133.

——'The need for a non-governmental, international competition forum in Asia', Conference presentation, Asia International Competition Conference, 4 September 2008, Seoul.

Wang, X and Tao, Z, 'WTO Competition Policy and Its Influence in China' (2004) Spring, *Social Sciences in China* 43.*

Wen, X, 'Market Dominance by China's Public Utility Enterprises' (2008) 75 *Antitrust Law Journal* 151.
Williams, M, 'Cartels and Collusion: Failing Competition Policy in Hong Kong' (2005) 28:3 *World Competition* 313.
Williamson, O, 'Economies as an Antitrust Defense: the Welfare Trade-Offs' (1968) 58 *American Economic Review* 18.
Wise, M, 'Review of Competition Law and Policy in Korea' (2000) 2 *OECD Journal of Competition Law and Policy* 127.
Wu, H, 'A discussion on China's Administrative Monopoly and avoidance' (2000) 6 *Jurists' Journal* 60.
Wu, P and Thomas, C, 'Taiwan's Fair Trade Act: Achieving the "Right" Balance?' (2005–2006) 26 *Northwestern Journal of International Law and Business* 643.
Wu, Z, 'Perspectives on the Chinese Anti-Monopoly Law' (2008) 75 *Antitrust Law Journal* 73.
Xu, S, 'Talks on American anti-monopoly law' (1994) 1 *Political Science and Law, Shanghai Academy of Social Sciences* 58.*
Yun, S-R, 'Regulation of Business Combination under the Antimonopoly Regulation and Fair Trade Act with Emphasis on the Case Law' (2002) 2 *Journal of Korean Law* 1.
—— and Hong, DS, 'Merger Regulations under the Korean Competition Law—Based on M&A Review Guidelines and KFTC's Decisions' (2005) 4:2 *Journal of Korean Law* 103.
Zhang, D, 'Monopoly and anti-monopoly legislation in China' (1995) *Study on China Administration for Industry and Commerce* 16.*
Zhen, F, 'An economic constitution; a discussion of some ideas and problems in legislating a Chinese anti-monopoly law' (1998) 4 *Intertrade* 4.*

INDEX

abuse of dominance and monopolistic practices
see also **abuse of dominant position/ monopolistic practices under Article 82 (EC Treaty and) Sherman Act; China monopoly and abuse of dominance; Korea monopoly and abuse of dominance; Taiwan monopoly and abuse of dominance; Vietnam monopoly and abuse of dominance**
Hong Kong 1-1.19, 3-1.06, 3-1.09
merger control 1-2.38
standards 1-2.02, 1-2.21–1-2.34
substantial market power, abuse of 3-1.09
abuse of dominant position/monopolistic practices under Article 82 (EC Treaty) and Sherman Act
bundling 1-2.34
condemned conduct 1-2.25–1-2.34
definition of monopoly 1-2.22
essential facilities doctrine 1-2.32
evidence 1-2.24
excessive pricing 1-2.31
exploitative pricing 2-3.07
full line forcing 1-2.34
market
power 1-2.22–1-2.26
relevant market 1-2.23–1-2.24
share 1-2.24
merger control 1-2.38
predatory pricing 1-2.27–1-2.29
prices 1-2.21, 1-2.22, 1-2.25, 1-2.27-1-2.30, 2-3.07
refusal to supply 1-2.32
relevant market 1-2.23–1-2.24
standards 1-2.02, 1-2.21–1-2.34
Taiwan 4-3.07, 4-3.09
tying 1-2.34
access to files
Korea 5-5.10
Taiwan 4-5.20
administrative monopolies
abuse of monopolies 1-1.07, 2-3.01, 2-3.10–2-3.15
China
abuse of monopolies 1-1.07, 2-3.01, 2-3.10–2-3.15
antitrust law regime 2-1.16
Law against Unfair Competition 1993 1-1.12
administrative preventive measures (APMs)
Vietnam 6-5.11, 6-5.22, 6-5.27
anticompetitive agreements *see* **anti-competitive agreements under Article 81 (EC Treaty) and Sherman Act; China agreements; Korea agreements; Taiwan agreements; Vietnam agreements**
anticompetitive agreements under Article 81 (EC Treaty) and Sherman Act 1-2.02, 1-2.04–1-2.20
block exemptions 1-2.10–1-2.11, 1-2.18, 1-2.20
cartels 1-2.14–1-2.15
concerted practices 1-2.07, 1-2.09
contracts between companies 1-2.06
control of anti-competitive agreements 1-2.04–1-2.20
effects doctrine 2-1.19
efficiencies 1-2.16, 1-2.19
exclusive distribution agreements 1-2.19
exemptions or exceptions 1-2.10–1-2.12, 1-2.18, 1-2.20
forms of agreements 1-2.06–1-2.09
hard core restrictions 1-2.13–1-2.15
Hong Kong 3-1.06, 3-1.08
horizontal agreements 1-2.02, 1-2.10, 1-2.13–1-2.17, 3-1.08
information, exchange of 1-2.17
inter-brand competition 1-2.19
intra-brand competition 1-2.19
leniency programmes 1-2.15
minimum price-setting 1-2.20
oligopolies 1-2.07
parallel behaviour 1-2.08
research and development agreements 1-2.13, 1-2.16
rule of reason 1-2.10–1-2.12, 1-2.18
selective distribution schemes 1-2.20
specialization agreements 1-2.13, 1-2.16
standard setting agreements 1-2.16
standards 1-2.02, 1-2.04–1-2.20
territorial restraints 1-2.19, 1-2.20
trade associations 1-2.09

anticompetitive agreements under Article 81 (EC Treaty) and Sherman Act (*cont.*)
vertical agreements 1-2.02, 1-2.05, 1-2.10, 1-2.18–1-2.20, 3-1.06
vitamins cartel 1-2.15
anti-counterfeiting technologies
China 2-3.11
Anti-Monopoly Committee (AMC) (China) 2-1.09–2-1.11
Anti-Monopoly Investigation Bureau (China) 2-1.11
Anti-Monopoly Law Enforcement Agency (AMEA) (China)
abuse of dominance 1-1.15
antitrust regime 2-1.13
appeals 2-5.15, 2-5.17
commitments and undertakings 2-5.09
complaints 2-5.07
enforcement 2-5.01
investigations 2-5.02–2-5.07, 2-5.09
merger control 2-4.03, 2-4.07, 2-4.12–2-4.15, 2-4.18, 2-4.22–2-4.23
penalties 2-5.10–2-5.14
rectification 2-5.05
antitrust law regimes *see* **China antitrust law regime; Hong Kong antitrust law regime; Korean antitrust law regime; Taiwan antitrust law regime; Vietnam antitrust law regime**
antitrust policy
China 1-1.15, 1-2.01
economic development 1-1.01
Hong Kong 1-1.18–1-1.23
industrial policy, relationship with 1-1.01
international organizations 1-1.02
Korean 1-1.27–1-1.30
trade 1-1.02
World Trade Organization (WTO) 1-1.02
APEC (Asia Pacific Economic Cooperation)
Competition Policy and Law Database 1-1.25
Vietnam antitrust law regime 6-1.20
appeals
China 2-5.15–2-5.17
EC competition law 1-2.41
Hong Kong 3-1.14, 3-1.19
Korea 5-5.24–5-5.27
merger control 1-2.41
Taiwan 1-1.25, 4-5.31, 4-5.37
Vietnam 6-5.04, 6-5.18, 6-5.25, 6-5.36–6-5.39
approvals
Korea 5-4.01
Taiwan 4-2.08–4-2.18
arbitration
Korea 5.3.29, 5-5.29
Article 81 (EC Treaty) *see* **anti-competitive agreements under Article 81 (EC Treaty) and Sherman Act**
Article 82 (EC Treaty) *see* **abuse of dominant position/monopolistic practices under Article 82 (EC Treaty) and Sherman Act**
ASEAN 6-1.20
Asia Pacific Economic Cooperation (APEC)
Competition Policy and Law Database 1-1.25
Vietnam antitrust law regime 6-1.20
Asian economic crisis 1997 1-1.01, 5-4.54
Australia
Korea, bilateral agreement with 5-1.14
Taiwan, bilateral agreement with 4-1.18

barriers to entry
China 2-3.12
Korea
merger control 5-4.38, 5-4.44
monopoly and abuse of dominance 5.3.06, 5-3.15–5-3.17
merger control 4-4.30, 4-4.36, 5-4.38, 5-4.44
monopoly and abuse of dominance 2-3.12, 5.3.06, 5-3.15–5-3.17, 6-3.04, 6-3.08, 6-3.11
Taiwan 4-4.30, 4-4.36
Vietnam 6-3.04, 6-3.08, 6-3.11
behavioural remedies
China 2-4.22
Hong Kong 3-1.22
Korea 5-4.55–5-4.56
merger control 1-2.43, 2-4.22, 5-4.55–5-4.56
bid-rigging
Korea agreements 5-2.14, 5-2.18, 5-2.20
Vietnam agreements 6-2.02, 6-2.06
bilateral agreements
Australia 4-1.18, 5-1.14
Korean 5-1.14
Taiwan 1-1.25, 4-1.17–4-1.18
United States 1-1.33
Vietnam 1-1.33
block exemptions 1-2.10–1-2.11, 1-2.18, 1-2.20, 3-1.08
brands 1-2.19
bundling 1-2.34, 5-3.20, 5-4.56
business certificates, revocation of
Vietnam 6-5.28
business secrets *see also* **confidentiality**
China 2-5.06
Korea 5-5.10
Taiwan 4-2.36, 4-5.07
Vietnam 6-5.26

cartels
China
agreements 2-2.07
anti-trust regime 1-1.08, 1-1.09, 2-1.23
crisis cartels 2-2.07, 4-2.09, 4-2.15
economic principles 1-2.51
experts 1-2.45
export cartels 1-2.14, 4-2.09
hard core infringements 1-2.14–1-2.15, 1-2.51, 1-2.52
horizontal agreements 1-2.14–1-2.15
international cooperation 1-2.52
Korea
agreements 5-2.02–5-2.21
antitrust law regime 1-1.30, 1-1.31, 5-1.12
merger control 5-4.20
procedure 5-5.06, 5-5.14, 5-5.19, 5-5.21–5-5.23
merger control 1-2.39, 5-4.20
tacit coordination 1-2.39
Taiwan agreements 4-2.05, 4-2.09, 4-2.15, 4-2.36
United States 4-2.09
vitamins cartels 1-2.15, 5-1.12
***chaebols* (Korea)** 1-1.27–1-1.29, 5-2.01, 5-3.02, 5-4.31
China *see* **China agreements; China antitrust law regime; China merger control; China monopoly and abuse of dominance; China procedure**
China agreements 2-2.01–2-2.09
Anti-Monopoly Law 2-2.01, 2-2.04–2-2.08
cartels 1-2.14, 2.2.07
crisis cartels 2-2.07
definition of monopoly agreement 2-2.01
exemptions 2-2.05–2-2.08
export cartels 1-2.14
horizontal agreements 2-2.02
international trade or economic cooperation 2-2.07
penalties 2-2.09
price-fixing 2-2.02, 2-2.03, 2-2.04
public interest 2-2.07
resale price maintenance 2-2.03
research and development agreements 2-2.07
rule of reason 2-2.05
trade associations 2-2.04
vertical agreements 1-2.18, 2-2.03
China antitrust law regime 1-1.06–1-1.15, 2-1.01–2-1.24
abuse of dominant position 2-1.06, 2-1.16, 2-1.23
administrative monopolies 2-1.16
agricultural producers, exemption of 2-1.18
Anti-Monopoly Committee (AMC) 2-1.09–2-1.11
Anti-Monopoly Investigation Bureau 2-1.11
Anti-Monopoly Law (AML) 2-1.01–2-1.07
background 1-1.11–1-1.12
contents 2-1.03
enforcement 2-1.14
guidelines 2-1.02
implementation 1-1.15, 2-1.01
importance of 1-1.03
institutional structure 2-1.08–2-1.15
intellectual property rights 2-1.17
legislation preceding AML 2-1.22–2-1.24
purpose 2-1.05, 2-1.06
state-owned enterprises 2-1.16
territorial application 2-1.19–2-1.20
text App 1
Anti-Monopoly Law Enforcement Agency (AMEA) 2-1.13
antitrust policy 1-1.15, 1-2.01
business operators, definition of 2-1.07
cartels 1-1.08, 1-1.09, 2-1.23
cases, reporting of 2-1.15
collusion 1-1.09
concentrations 2-1.06
Constitution 1-1.06
courts, involvement of the 2-1.14
EC competition law 1-2.03, 2-1.21
economy in transition, as 1-1.06
effects doctrine 2-1.19
enforcement 2-1.13–2-1.14, 2-1.20
essential facilities doctrine 2-1.23
European Union, cooperation with 2-1.21
exemptions 2-1.16–2-1.18
guidelines 2-1.02
information sources 2-1.15
institutional structure 2-1.08–2-1.15
intellectual property 2-1.15, 2-1.17
international companies, unfair trading by 1-1.08
international cooperation and agreements 2-1.21
international standards 1-1.11
Korea, trade agreement with 1-2.52
Law against Unfair Competition 1993 1-1.09–1-1.10
legislation 1-1.09, 2-1.01–2-1.24
Ministry of Commerce (MOFCOM) 2-1.10–2-1.12
monopolies 2-1.06, 2-1.16, 2-1.23
National Development and Reform Commission (NDRC) 2-1.10–2-1.12
price-fixing cartels 1-1.08
regional protectionism 1-1.07

China antitrust law regime (*cont.*)
relevant market
definition of 2-1.07
guidance on assessment of 2-1.07
rural economic organizations, exemption of 2-1.18
Russia, memorandum of understanding with 2-1.21
self-disciplinary practices 1-1.08
socialist market economy, China as 1-1.06, 1-2.01, 2-1.04
standards 1-2.01
State Administration for Industry and Commerce (SAIC) 2-1.10–2-1.13
State Council 2-1.09–2-1.10
State Economic and Trade Commission (SETC) 1-1.08, 1-1.11
state-owned enterprises 1-1.07, 1-1.12, 2-1.16
territorial application 2-1.19–2-1.20
World Trade Organization (WTO) 1-1.02
China merger control 2-4.01–2-4.22
'actual controller', definition of 2-4.04
Anti-Monopoly Law 2-4.01–2-4.05, 2-4.10–2-4.11, 2-4.20–2-4.24
Anti-Monopoly Law Enforcement Agency (AMLEA) 2-4.03, 2-4.07, 2-4.12–2-4.15, 2-4.18, 2-4.22–2-4.23
behavioural remedies 2-4.22
concentrations 2-1.06, 2-4.03, 2-4.18–2-4.19
conditions 2-4.22
control, definition of 2-4.04
definition of concentrations 2-4.03
discrimination 2-4.01
efficiencies 2-4.21
expedited review 2-4.16
failing firm defence 2-4.21
fines 2-4.23
foreign mergers 2-4.10–2-4.11, 2-4.19
guidance 2-4.02, 2-4.04, 2-4.09, 2-4.18–2-4.19
horizontal mergers 2-4.09
jurisdiction 2-4.05–2-4.11
market power 2-4.18
market share 2-4.18
Ministry of Commerce (MOFCOM) 2-4.11, 2-4.24
national security 2-4.20
nationality discrimination 2-4.01
notification 2-4.03, 2-4.08, 2-4.11, 2-4.12–2.4.15
one-shop-stop 2-4.01
penalties 2-4.22–2-4.24
positive impact of concentrations 2-4.18–2-4.19
pre-notification review 2.4.16
procedure 2-4.12–2-4.17
protectionism 2-4.01
public interest test 2-4.19
remedies 2-4.22–2-4.24
reviews 2-4.12–2.4.16
structural remedies 2-4.22
substantive test 2-4.18–2-4.20
Taiwan 4-4.04
turnover thresholds 2-4.02, 2-4.05–2-4.06
vertical mergers 2-4.09
China monopoly and abuse of dominance 2-1.06, 2-3.01–2-3.15
abuse of administrative monopolies 1-1.07, 2-3.01, 2-3.10–2-3.15
administrative monopolies 2-1.16
abuse of 1-1.07, 2-3.01, 2-3.10–2-3.15
Law against Unfair Competition 1993 1-1.12
anti-counterfeiting technologies 2-3.11
Anti-Monopoly Law 1-1.07, 1-1.13–1-1.14, 2-3.01
administrative power, abuse of 2-3.10–2-3.11
drafting 1-1.13–1-1.15
intellectual property 2-3.09
socialist market economy 1-2.01
text App 1
Anti-Monopoly Law Enforcement Agency (AMLEA) 1-1.15
antitrust law regime 2-1.06, 2-1.16, 2-1.23
assessment of dominance 2-3.02–2-3.05
barriers to entry 2-3.12
collusion 2-3.05
conditions, imposing unreasonable 2-3.06
counterfeiting 2-3.11
definition of dominance 2-3.02
EC competition law 1-1.13
essential facilities doctrine 2-3.06
excessive pricing 2-3.06
exclusionary abuses 2-3.07
exclusivity, compelling 2-3.06
exemptions 2-3.08
exploitative abuses 2-3.07
fines 2-5.13
forms of abuse 2-3.06
guidelines 2-3.08
intellectual property 2-3.09
Law against Unfair Competition 1993 1-1.09–1-1.10, 1-1.12
local protectionism 2-3.10
market
relevant market 2-3.03–2-3.05
segmentation of internal market 2-3.12
share 2-3.04–2-3.05
monopolistic conduct, definition of 2-1.06
nationality discrimination 2-3.12
oligopolies 2-3.05

penalties 2-3.15, 2-5.10–2-5.14
price-fixing 2-3.12
protectionism 2-3.10, 2-3.12–2-3.14
refusal to supply 2-3.06
refusal to trade 2-3.06
regional protectionism 2-3.12–2-3.14
relevant market 2-3.03–2-3.05
remedies 2-5.08
rule of reason 2-3.08
segmentation of internal market 2-3.12
selling below cost 2-3.06
socialist market economy 1-2.01
state-owned enterprises 1-1.12, 2-3.10
tying 2-3.06

China procedure 2-5.01–2-5.21
administrative reconsideration 2-5.15–2-5.16
Anti-Monopoly Law 2-5.01–2-5.14, 2-5.18–2-5.21
Anti-Monopoly Law Enforcement Agency (AMEA)
appeals 2-5.15, 2-5.17
commitments and undertakings 2-5.09
complaints 2-5.07
enforcement 2-5.01
investigations 2-5.02–2-5.07, 2-5.09
penalties 2-5.10–2-5.14
rectification 2-5.05
appeals 2-5.15–2-5.17
business secrecy 2-5.06
civil courts, actions in 2-5.18–2-5.21
commitments and undertakings 2-5.09
complaints 2-5.02, 2-5.07, 2-5.16
confidentiality 2-5.02, 2-5.06
confiscation 2-5.11, 2-5.13
cooperate, duty to 2-5.05
damages 2-5.19
enforcement 2-5.01, 2-5.03, 2-5.11, 2-5.18
final decisions 2-5.08–2-5.09
fines 2-5.05, 2-5.11–2-5.13
foreign antitrust agencies, agreements with 2-5.03
investigations 2-5.02-2-5.07, 2-5.09–2-5.10
judicial review 2-5.16
merger control 2-4.12–2-4.17
obstruction 2-5.05
penalties 2-5.03, 2-5.05
rectification 2-5.05
remedies 2-5.05, 2-5.08
statements 2-5.04
structural remedies 2-5.08
third party rights 2-5.18–2-5.21
trade associations, penalties against 2-5.13
trade secrets 2-5.06

civil actions *see* **private actions**

Clayton Act (United States) 1-2.38

collusion
China 1-1.09, 2-3.05
Hong Kong 3-1.08
Korea 5-2.05, 5-4.39

commitments 1-2.41, 2-5.09

commodity line associations
Vietnam 6-1.06

Competition Administration Department (VCAD) (Vietnam)
agreements 6-2.07–6-2.08
antitrust law regime 1-1.34, 6-1.03, 6-1.05, 6-1.08, 6-1.10–6-1.13, 6-1.20
merger control 6-4.04, 6-4.06–6-4.14
monopoly and abuse of dominance 6-3.03
procedure 6-5.02, 6-5.06, 6-5.09–6-5.12, 6-5.16, 6-5.21–6-5.22, 6-5.25–6-5.26, 6-5.30–6-5.39

Competition Case-Handling Council (CCHC) (Vietnam)
antitrust law regime 6-1.14
procedure 6-5.14–6-5.17, 6-5.20, 6-5.29, 6-5.32, 6-5.36

Competition Commission (Hong Kong) 3-1.03, 3-1.06–3-1.12, 3-1.14–3-1.26

Competition Council (VCC) (Vietnam)
antitrust law regime 6-1.03, 6-1.14
monopoly and abuse of dominance 6-4.16

Competition Policy Advisory Group (COMPAG) (Hong Kong) 1-1.18–1-1.19

Competition Policy Review Committee (CPRC) (Hong Kong) 1-1.22, 3-1.13

Competition Tribunal (Hong Kong) 3-1.11, 3-1.14, 3-1.16, 3-1.19–3-1.23, 3-1.26, 3-1.28

complaints
China 2-5.02, 2-5.07, 2-5.16
Hong Kong 3-1.14, 3-1.17
Korea 5-5.11–5-5.12
Taiwan 4-1.12–4-1.13, 4-5.11
Vietnam 6-1.14, 6-2.08, 6-5.02, 6-5.06, 6-5.21–6-5.24

concerted practices
anti-competitive agreements 1-2.07, 1-2.09
Article 81 (EC Treaty) 1-2.07, 1-2.09
definition 1-2.07
Hong Kong 3-1.08
Korea 5-2.08–5-2.11, 5-2.16, 5-2.21
oligopolies 1-2.07
Sherman Act 1-2.07, 1-2.09
Taiwan
agreements 4-2.02–4-2.04, 4-2.09–4-2.11, 4-2.14, 4-2.16, 4-2.40
monopoly and abuse of dominance 4-3.11

concerted practices (*cont.*)
Taiwan (*cont.*)
merger control 4-4.27
procedure 4-5.21
trade associations 1-2.09
confidentiality *see also* **business secrets**
China 2-5.02, 2-5.06
Taiwan 4-5.17
confiscation
China 2-5.11, 2-5.13
Vietnam 6-5.28
conglomerate mergers
Korea 5-4.42–5-4.45
merger control 1-2.35, 4-4.31, 5-4.42–5-4.45
portfolio effects 1-2.35
Taiwan 4-4.31
coordinated effects
Korea 5-4.39
merger control 1-2.35, 4-4.26–4.4.27, 5-4.39
Taiwan 4-4.26–4.4.27
cooperation *see* **international cooperation**
corrective measures
Korea
agreements 5-2.24, 5-2.31, 5-2.33, 5-2.37
merger control 5-4.21, 5-4.50
monopoly and abuse of dominance 5-3.13, 5-3.28
procedure 5-5.04, 5-5.13–5-5.23, 5-5.25, 5-5.28
Taiwan
agreements 4-2.23
procedure 4-5.21–4-5.30
counterfeiting 2-3.11
criminal prosecutions
Korea 5-5.20, 5-5.23
crisis cartels 2-2.07, 4-2.09, 4-2.15

damages
China 2-5.19
Hong Kong 3-1.24, 3-1.28
Korea 5-5.28
Taiwan
merger control 4-4.43
procedure 4-5.02, 4-5.33–4-5.37
de minimis **principle**
Hong Kong 3-1.10–3.1.12
Korea 5-3.05
Taiwan 4-3.04
Vietnam 6-2.03
directors
disqualification 3-1.21
Hong Kong 3-1.21
penalties 3-1.21
discrimination
abuse of dominant position/monopolistic practices 1-2.25, 1-2.30, 2-3.05, 4-3.07, 4-3.10, 6-3.11
Article 82 (EC Treaty) 1-2.25, 1-2.30
China 2-3.05, 2-4.01
EC competition law 1-2.25, 1-2.30
Korea 1-2.30, 5-3.11, 5-3.27
merger control 2-4.01
pricing
Article 82 (EC Treaty) 1-2.25, 1-2.30
Korea 1-2.30, 5-3.11, 5-3.27
Sherman Act 1-2.25, 1-2.30
Taiwan 4-2.36, 4-3.07, 4-3.10
Vietnam 6-2.05, 6-3.11
distribution agreements
exclusive distribution agreements 1-2.19
Korea 5-2.31
selective distribution agreements 1-2.20
Vietnam 6-2.02
divestiture
EC competition law 1-2.43
Korea 5-4.53
merger control 1-2.43, 5-4.53, 6-4.13
Vietnam 6-4.13
doi moi **policy (Vietnam)** 1-1.32, 1-1.34
dominance *see* **China monopoly and abuse of dominance; Korea monopoly and abuse of dominance; Taiwan monopoly and abuse of dominance; Vietnam monopoly and abuse of dominance**

EC competition law *see also* **abuse of dominant position/monopolistic practices under Article 82 (EC Treaty) and Sherman Act; anti-competitive agreements under Article 81 (EC Treaty) and Sherman Act**
appeals 1-2.41
China 1-1.13, 1-2.03, 2-1.21
commitments, offer of 1-2.41
divestiture 1-2.43
dominant position 1-2.38
economic principles 1-2.45–1-2.48, 1-2.51
efficiency 1-2.03, 1-2.44
failing firm defence 1-2.44
guidance 1-2.39
Herfindahl-Hirschman Index 1-2.39
injunctions 1-2.41
Korea
agreements 5-2.01, 5-2.05
antitrust law regime 1-1.28, 5-1.14
merger control 1-2.38–1-2.44
Merger Regulation (ECMR) 1-2.37–1-2.38, 1-2.41
modernization of EC competition law 1-2.11

notification 1-2.41
private rights of action 1-2.42
significant impediment of effective competition (SIEC) test 1-2.38
structural remedies 1-2.43
Taiwan antitrust law regime 4-1.01
United States 1-2.35, 1-2.38
Vietnam antitrust law regime 6-1.04
economic crisis 1997 1-1.01, 5-4.54
economic data 1-1.04
economic principles
antitrust policy 1-1.01
application of, 1-2.45–1-2.51
cartels 1-2.51
EC competition law 1-2.45–1-2.48, 1-2.51
economists, use of 1-2.51
experts 1-2.45, 1-2.51
geographic market 1-2.49
hard core infringements 1-2.45, 1-2.51
interchangeability 1-2.46
judiciary, expertise of 1-2.51
market
power 1-2.50
product market 1-2.46, 1-2.48
relevant market 1-2.46, 1-2.48–1-2.50
modelling 1-2.51
product market 1-2.46, 1-2.48
relevant market 1-2.46, 1-2.48–1-2.50
relevant time period 1-2.50
socialist market economies 1-1.01, 1-1.06, 1-1.32, 1-2.01, 2-1.04
SSNIP test 1-2.47–1-2.48
standards 1-2.45–1-2.51
substitutability 1-2.46, 1-2.48
supply side substitution 1-2.48
United States 1-2.47–1-2.48, 1-2.51
economists, use of 1-2.51
education
Korea 5-5.14, 5-5.19
effects doctrine
anti-competitive agreements 2-1.19
Article 81 (EC Treaty) 2-1.19
China 2-1.19
merger control 1-2.37
Sherman Act 2-1.19
efficiencies
China 2-4.21
EC competition law 1-2.03, 1-2.44
horizontal agreements 1-2.16
Korea
agreements 5-2.05, 5-2.16
antitrust law regime 5-1.06
merger control 5-4.02, 5-4.45–5-4.49
merger control 1-2.44, 2-4.21, 5-4.02, 5-4.45–5-4.49
standards 1-2.01, 1-2.03
Taiwan
agreements 4-2.11, 4-2.16, 4-2.19
antitrust law regime 4-1.02
merger control 1-2.44, 4-4.32–4-4.33, 4-4.35
United States 1-2.03, 1-2.44
vertical agreements 1-2.19
Vietnam 6-2.02, 6-3.12, 6-4.01
employees, liability for acts of
Korea 5-5.06
enforcement
China
antitrust law regime 2-1.13–2-1.14, 2-1.20
procedure 2-5.01, 2-5.03, 2-5.11, 2-5.18
Hong Kong 3-1.17–3-1.19, 3-1.25–3-1.28
Korea
agreements 5-2.17–5-2.21, 5-2.25, 5-2.27
antitrust law regime 1-1.27, 1-1.31, 5-1.02–5-1.03, 5-1.07, 5-1.13
merger control 5-4.01, 5-4.11
monopoly and abuse of dominance 5-3.02
merger control
Korea 5-4.01, 5-4.11
Taiwan 4-4.01, 4-4.08, 4-4.17, 4-4.24
monopoly and abuse of dominance
Korea 5-3.02
Taiwan 4-3.01, 4-3.02–4-3.06
Taiwan
agreements 4-2.10–4-2.11, 4-2.34, 4-2.36
antitrust law regime 1-1.25, 4-1.01–4-1.02
merger control 4-4.01, 4-4.08, 4-4.17, 4-4.24
monopoly and abuse of dominance 4-3.01, 4-3.02–4-3.06
procedure 4-5.01, 4-5.22, 4-5.27, 4-5.32
Vietnam
antitrust law regime 1-1.34, 6-1.05, 6-1.07, 6-1.11, 6-1.13–6-1.14
procedure 6-5.12
entry, barriers to *see* barriers to entry
essential facilities doctrine
abuse of dominant position/monopolistic practices 1-2.32, 2-3.06, 4-3.08, 6-3.11
Article 82 (EC Treaty) 1-2.32
China 2-1.23, 2-3.06
Sherman Act 1-2.32
Taiwan 4-3.08
Vietnam 6-3.11
European Union *see* EC competition law
evidence
abuse of dominant position/monopolistic practices 1-2.24

evidence (*cont.*)
Article 81 (EC Treaty) 1-2.08
Article 82 (EC Treaty) 1-2.24
experts 1-2.45, 1-2.51
failing firm defence 1-2.44
Korea procedure 5-5.05–5-5.07, 5-5.12
parallel behaviour 1-2.08
relevant market 1-2.49
Sherman Act 1-2.24, 1-2.08
Vietnam 6-5.07, 6-5.10–6-5.11, 6-5.14, 6-5.25
excessive pricing
abuse of dominant position/monopolistic practices 1-2.31, 2.3.06, 5-3.08
Article 82 (EC Treaty) 1-2.31
China 2.3.06
Korea 5-3.08
Sherman Act 1-2.31
exclusive distribution agreements 1-2.19
exclusive purchasing arrangements 6-2.02
exclusivity, compelling
China 2-3.06
exemptions
agricultural producers 2-1.18
anti-competitive agreements
Article 81 (EC Treaty) 1-2.10–1-2.12
China 2-2.05–2-2.08
Sherman Act 1-2.10–1-2.12
Article 81 (EC Treaty) 1-2.10–1-2.12
block exemptions 1-2.10–1-2.11, 1-2.18, 1-2.20, 3-1.08
China
agreements 2-2.05–2.2.08
agricultural producers 2-1.18
antitrust law regime 2-1.16–2.1.18
monopoly and abuse of dominance 2-3.08
rural economic organizations 2-1.18
Hong Kong 3-1.10–3-1.12
Korea
agreements 5-2.04, 5-2.26
antitrust law regime 5-1.09
merger control 6-4.01, 6-4.05–6-4.08
modernization of EC competition law 1-2.11
monopoly and abuse of dominance 2-3.08
rural economic organizations 2-1.18
Sherman Act 1-2.10–1-2.12
Taiwan
agreements 4-2.01, 4-2.08, 4-2.17
antitrust law regime 4-1.09–4-1.10
vertical agreements 1-2.10, 1-2.18, 1-2.20
Vietnam
agreements 6-2.01, 6-2.03–6.2.09
antitrust law regime 6-1.04, 6-1.08, 6-1.11, 6-1.15–6-1.16
merger control 6-4.01, 6-4.05–6-4.08
experts 1-2.45, 1-2.51, 6-5.14
exploitative pricing
abuse of dominant position/monopolistic practices 2-3.07
Article 82 (EC Treaty) 2-3.07
Sherman Act 2-3.07
Taiwan monopoly and abuse of dominance 4-3.09, 4-4.16
exports
cartels 1-2.14, 4-2.09
Taiwan agreements 4-2.09, 4-2.13
United States 4-2.09
extraterritoriality
antitrust law regime 1-1.31, 5-1.10
EC Merger Regulation (ECMR) 1-2.37
merger control 1-2.37
United States 1-2.37
Vietnam 6-1.18

failing firm defence
China 2-4.21
EC competition law 1-2.44
evidence 1-2.44
Korea 5-4.02, 5-4.46–5-4.49
merger control 1-2.44, 2-4.21, 4-4.32–4-4.33, 5-4.02, 5-4.46–5-4.49
Taiwan 4-4.32–4-4.33
United States 1-2.44
Vietnam 6-4.01
Fair Trade Commission (Korea)
anticompetitive agreements 5-2.04–5-2.07, 5-2.14, 5-2.17–5-2.37
antitrust law regime 1-1.27, 1-1.31, 5-1.03, 5-1.06–5-1.13
composition 5-1.06
enforcement 1-1.31, 5-1.07, 5-1.13
meetings 5-1.03
merger control 5-4.01, 5-4.07–5-4.14, 5-4.17, 5-4.20–5-4.57
monopoly and abuse of dominance 5-1.07, 5-3.03–5-3.13, 5-3.18–5-3.29
procedure 5-5.01–5-5.28
structure 1-1.27, 5-1.02, 5-1.07
website 1-1.27, 5-1.08
Fair Trade Commission (Taiwan)
agreements 1-2.20, 4-2.04–4-2.06, 4-2.16–4-2.19, 4.2.23,4-2.25, 4-2.37–4-2.39
antitrust law regime 1-1.25, 4-1.05–4-1.08, 4-1.12–4-1.19
merger control 1-2.44, 4-4.03, 4-4.07–4-4.16, 4-4.20–4-4.43
monopoly and abuse of dominance 4-3.03, 4-3.05–4-3.12, 4-3.16
procedure 4-5.01, 4-5.03–4-5.34

Fair Trade Commission (United States) 1-2.41
Fair Trade Mediation Committee (Korea) 5-1.02, 5-3.29, 5-5.29
fees
Taiwan 4-4.19
Vietnam 6-5.03, 6-5.21–6-5.22
financial institutions
Korea 5-4.01
Financial Supervisory Commission (KFSC) (Korea) 5-4.01
fines
China
merger control 2-4.23
monopoly and abuse of dominance 2-5.13
procedure 2-5.05, 2-5.11–2-5.13
Hong Kong 3-1.20
Korea
agreements 5-2.18–5-2.21, 5-2.31–5-2.33, 5-2.38
antitrust law regime 1-1.31
merger control 5-4.14
monopoly and abuse of dominance 5-3.19, 5-3.28
procedure, 5-5.20
merger control 2-4.23, 4-4.39, 5-4.14
monopoly and abuse of dominance 2-5.13, 4-3.12, 4-3.16, 5-3.19, 5-3.28
Taiwan
agreements 4-2.06, 4-2.23, 4-2.40, 4-2.41
antitrust law regime 4-1.16
investigations 4-5.08
merger control 4-4.39
monopoly and abuse of dominance 4-3.12, 4-3.16
procedure 4-5.08, 4-5.22, 4-5.25
Vietnam procedure 6-5.28–6-5.29, 6-5.32
fora, proposal for development of competition 1-2.53
foreclosure
Korea 5-4.40–5-4.41
Taiwan 4-4.30
Vietnam 6-2.02
foreign mergers
China 2-4.10–2-4.11, 2-4.19
Korea 5-4.08, 5-4.19–5-4.20
Taiwan 4-1.12–4-1.16, 4-1.17, 4-4.09, 4-4.11–4-4.12
Vietnam 6-4.15
franchises
Korea
agreements 5-2.01, 5-2.30, 5-2.34–5-2.38
antitrust law regime 5-1.05
monopoly and abuse of dominance 5-3.29
Taiwan 4-4.05, 4-4.34
full line forcing 1-2.24

Gao, Y and Cao, D. *Anti-Inappropriate Competition Law* 1-1.10
geographic market
economic principles 1-2.49
Korea 5-4.25
relevant market 1-2.49
Vietnam 6-3.04
groups of companies
Taiwan 4-4.10, 4-4.22
Vietnam 6-3.07

hard core infringements
anticompetitive agreements 1-2.13–1-2.15
cartels 1-2.14–1-2.15, 1-2.51, 1-2.52
economic principles 1-2.45, 1-2.51
Hong Kong 3-1.06
horizontal agreements 1-2.13–1-2.15
OECD recommendation 1-2.13
rule of reason 1-2.14
Taiwan agreements 4-2.04
Vietnam 6-2.01–6-2.09, 6-5.12
hearings
confidentiality 4-5.17
guidelines 4-5.13, 4-5.18
initiation 4-5.16
Korea 5-5.09–5-5.10
notification 4-5.14, 4-5.17, 6-5.20
oral hearings 4-5.13–4-5.16
preliminary hearings 4-5.18
public hearings 4-5.12, 4-5.15–4-5.16, 4-5.18, 6-5.20
publicity 4-5.17
records 4-5.19
Taiwan 4-5.12–4-5.20
Vietnam 6-5.14, 6-5.16–6-5.20, 6-5.25
witnesses 6-5.14
Herfindahl-Hirschman Index 1-2.39
holding companies
Taiwan 4-4.23
Hong Kong antitrust law regime 1-1.16–1-1.23, 3-1.01–3-1.28
abusive conduct
examples of 1-1.19
guidelines 3-1.06
substantial market power, abuse of 3-1.09
anticompetitive agreements 3-1.06, 3-1.08
antitrust law, proposal for 1-1.03, 1-1.16, 1-1.20–1-1.23, 3-1.01–3-1.28
antitrust policy 1-1.18–1-1.23

Hong Kong antitrust law regime (*cont.*)
appeals 3-1.14, 3-1.19
behavioural remedies 3-1.22
block exemptions 3-1.08
collusion 3-1.08
Competition Commission 3-1.03, 3-1.06–3-1.12, 3-1.14–3-1.26
Competition Policy Advisory Group (COMPAG) 1-1.18–1-1.19
Competition Policy Review Committee (CPRC) 1-1.22
Detailed Proposals for a Competition Law 3-1.01, 3-1.05–3-1.28
guidelines 1-1.20
Statement on Competition Policy 1-1.18, 1-1.19, 3-1.02
Competition Policy Review Committee (CPRC) 1-1.22, 3-1.13
Competition Tribunal 3-1.11, 3-1.14, 3-1.16, 3-1.19–3-1.23, 3-1.26, 3-1.28
complaints 3-1.14, 3-1.17
concerted practices 3-1.08
damages 3-1.24, 3-1.28
de minimis provisions 3-1.10–3-1.12
Detailed Proposals for a Competition Law 3-1.01, 3-1.05–3-1.28
directions 3-1.22
directors
disqualification 3-1.21
penalties against 3-1.21
enforcement 3-1.17–3-1.19, 3-1.25–3-1.28
exclusions and exemptions 3-1.10–3-1.12
fines 3-1.20
free trade policy 1-1.16
guidelines 3-1.06, 3-1.08
hardcore conduct 3-1.06
horizontal agreements 3-1.08
injunctions 3-1.23, 3-1.28
institutional arrangements 3-1.15–3-1.16
interim orders 3-1.23, 3-1.26
international standards 3-1.01
investigations 3-1.14–3-1.15, 3-1.17
leniency programme 3-1.24
market share 3-1.12
merger control 1-2.02, 3-1.07, 3-1.13
notification 3-1.11
penalties 3-1.14–3-1.15, 3-1.20
persuasion, system of 1-1.17
private actions 3-1.14, 3-1.16, 3-1.24
private enforcement 3-1.25–3-1.28
procedure 3-1.14–3-1.28
Promoting Competition. Economic Development and Labour Bureau (EDLB) 1-1.22–1-1.23
remedies 3-1.22–3-1.23, 3-1.28
representative actions 3-1.14, 3-1.27
sector specific approach 1-1.16
senior managers, penalties against 3-1.21
services of general economic interest 3-1.10
settlements 3-1.18
small businesses 3-1.03, 3-1.12, 3-1.20, 3-1.26–3-1.27
Statement on Competition Policy 1-1.18, 1-1.19, 3-1.02
structural remedies 3-1.22
substantial market power, abuse of 3-1.09
supervision 1-1.18
vertical agreements 3-1.08

horizontal agreements
anti-competitive agreements
Article 81 (EC Treaty) 1-2.02, 1-2.10, 1-2.13–1-2.17
Sherman Act 1-2.02, 1-2.10, 1-2.13–1-2.17
Article 81 (EC Treaty) 1-2.02, 1-2.10, 1-2.13–1-2.17
block exemptions 1-2.10
cartels 1-2.14–1-2.15
China 2-2.02
efficiency 1-2.16
exemptions 1-2.10
export cartels 1-2.14
hard core restrictions 1-2.13–1-2.15
Hong Kong 3-1.08
information, exchange of 1-2.17
Korea agreements 5-2.02–5-2.21, 5-2.29
leniency programmes 1-2.15
research and development agreements 1-2.13, 1-2.16
Sherman Act 1-2.02, 1-2.10, 1-2.13–1-2.17
specialization agreements 1-2.13, 1-2.16
standard setting agreements 1-2.16
standards 1-2.02
Taiwan agreements 4-2.01–4-2.18, 4-2.33–4-2.40
vitamins cartel 1-2.15

horizontal mergers 1-2.35, 1-2.39
China 2-4.09
Korea 5-4.32
Taiwan 4-4.22, 4-4.26–4-4.29, 4-4.31

industrial policy 1-1.01

information
antitrust law regime 5-1.08
China 2-1.15
horizontal agreements 1-2.17
Taiwan 4-2.16, 4-2.39, 4-5.08
Vietnam 6.2.07, 6-4.06

injunctions
EC competition law 1-2.41
Hong Kong 3-1.23, 3-1.28
merger control 1-2.41, 4-4.43

Taiwan 4-4.43
United States 1-2.41
inspections
Korea procedure 5-5.05–5-5.06
intellectual property
China 2-1.15, 2-1.17, 2-3.09
Taiwan 4-1.10, 4-2.01, 4-2.20, 4-2.25–4-2.32
Vietnam 6-1.21-6.1.22
inter-brand competition 1-2.19
interchangeability 1-2.46
International Competition Network (ICN) 1-1.32, 1-2.52
international cooperation 1-2.52–1-2.53
bilateral contacts 1-2.52
China
agreements 2-2.07
antitrust law regime 2-1.21
foreign antitrust agencies, agreements with 2-5.03
Korea, trade agreement with 1-2.52
fora, proposal for development of competition 1-2.53
hard core cartels 1-2.52
International Competition Network (ICN) 1-2.52
international organizations 1-2.52
Korea
antitrust law regime 5-1.13–5-1.14
China, trade agreement with 1-2.52
standards 1-2.52–1-2.53
Taiwan 1-1.25, 1-2.52, 4-1.17–4-1.20
Vietnam 6-1.16, 6-1.20
international organizations 1-1.02
intra-brand competition 1-2.19
investigations
China 2-5.02–2-5.07, 2-5.09–2-5.10
fines 4-5.08
Hong Kong 3-1.14–3-1.15, 3-1.17
Korea 1-1.31, 5-5.04–5-5.08, 5-5.11
on-site investigations 4-5.07
Taiwan
fines 4-5.08
materials, submission of 4-5.03, 4-5.06
notice 4-5.05
on-site investigations 4-5.07
procedure 4-5.03–4-5.11, 4-5.20
rights of persons subject to investigations 4-5.20
statements 4-5.03, 4-5.05
Vietnam
antitrust law regime 6-1.02–6-1.03, 6-1.10–6-1.12
merger control 6-4.14
procedure 6-5.06–6-5.20, 6-5.31
Japan, Vietnam's partnership with 6-1.20
joint ventures
Taiwan 4-4.01
Vietnam 6-4.02
judicial review
China 2-5.16
judiciary, expertise of 10-2.51
jurisdiction
China 2-4.05–2-4.11
Korea 5-4.08
merger control 1-2.37, 2-4.05–2-4.11, 4-4.05–4-4.12, 4-4.16, 5-4.08
service outside the jurisdiction 4-1.15
Taiwan 4-4.05–4-4.12, 4-4.16

Korea *see* **Korea agreements; Korean antitrust law regime; Korea merger control; Korea monopoly and abuse of dominance; Korea procedure**
Korea agreements 5-2.01–5-2.38
administrative guidance 5-2.04, 5-2.20
bid-rigging 5-2.14, 5-2.18, 5-2.20
cartels 5-2.02–5-2.21
chaebols 5-2.01
collusion 5-2.05
concerted practices 5-2.08–5-2.11, 5-2.16, 5-2.21
corrective measures 5-2.24, 5-2.31, 5-2.33, 5-2.37
distribution agreements 5-2.31
EC competition law 5-2.01, 5-2.05
efficiency 5-2.05, 5-2.16
enforcement 5-2.17–5-2.21, 5-2.25, 5-2.27
enterprisers' organizations 5-2.22–5-2.25
exemptions 5-2.04, 5-2.26
Fair Trade Commission (KFTC) 5-2.04–5-2.07, 5-2.14, 5-2.17–5-2.37
fines 5-2.18–5-2.21, 5-2.31–5-2.33, 5-2.38
franchise agreements 5-2.01, 5-2.30, 5-2.34–5-2.38
guidelines 5-2.02, 5-2.04–5-2.05, 5-2.16, 5-2.20, 5-2.26, 5-2.28
hard core conduct 5-2.05, 5-2.31
horizontal agreements 5-2.02–5-2.21, 5-2.29
international contracts 5-2.28
leniency tariff 5-2.31
list of condemned practices 5-2.03
market
power 5-2.05, 5-2.29
relevant market 5-2.05
share 5-2.05, 5-2.12, 5-2.27, 5-2.30
Monopoly Regulation and Fair Trade Act 1980 (MRFTA) 5-2.01–5-2.33
notification 5-2.02
parallel conduct 5-2.09, 5-2.29

Korea agreements (*cont.*)
penalties 5-2.16–5-2.21, 5-2.24, 5-2.27, 5-2.31–5-2.33, 5-2.38
price-fixing 5-2.05, 5-2.10, 5-2.18–5-2.20
refusal to supply 5-2.26
relevant market 5-2.05
resale price maintenance 5-2.23, 5-2.26–5-2.27, 5-2.32
research and development agreements 5-2.05
reviews 5-2.15
specialization agreements 5-2.05
territorial protection 5-2.30
trade associations 5-2.22–5-2.25
United States 5-2.01
vertical agreements 5-2.29–5-2.30
vitamins cartel 1-2.15
Korean antitrust law regime 1-1.26–1-1.31, 5-1.01–5-1.14
antitrust policy 1-1.27–1-1.30
Australia, bilateral agreement with 5-1.14
bilateral agreements 5-1.14
cartels 1-1.30, 1-1.31, 5-1.12
chaebol, role of the 1-1.27–1-1.29
China, trade agreement with 1-2.52
Constitution 5-1.01
EC competition law 1-1.28, 5-1.14
efficiency 5-1.06
enforcement 1-1.27, 1-1.31, 5-1.02–5-1.03, 5-1.07, 5-1.13
enterprisers, definition of 5-1.04
EU/Korea Competition Dialogue 5-1.14
exemptions 5-1.09
extraterritoriality 1-1.31, 5-1.10
Fair Franchise Transactions Act 5-1.06
Fair Trade Commission (KFTC) 5-1.06–5-1.12
composition 5-1.06
enforcement 1-1.31, 5-1.07, 5-1.13
meetings 5-1.03
structure 1-1.27, 5-1.02, 5-1.07
website 1-1.27, 5-1.08
Fair Trade Mediation Committee 5-1.02
fines 1-1.31
franchises 5-1.05
guidelines 5-1.03, 5-1.09
information sources 5-1.08
international cooperation and agreements 5-1.13–5-1.14
investigations 1-1.31
legislation, review of 1-1.30
Monopoly Regulation and Fair Trade Act 1980 (MRFTA) 5-1.01–5-1.13
amendments 1-1.27, 1-1.30, 5-1.01
contents 5-1.01–5-1.02
enforcement 1-1.31, 5-1.03
purpose 1-1.26, 5-1.01
reform roadmap 1-1.30
text App 3
OECD-Korea Regional Centre for Competition 5-1.13
Omnibus Cartel Repeal Act 1-1.30
penalties 1-1.31
prices 1-1.27
publication of decisions 5-1.08
reform roadmap 1-1.30
small and medium-sized enterprises (SMEs) 1-1.29
sub-contracting 1-1.29
territorial application 5-1.10–5-1.12
United States 1-2.03, 5-1.14
vitamins cartel 5-1.12
Korea merger control 5-4.01–5-4.57
approvals 5-4.01
barriers to entry 5-4.38, 5-4.44
behavioural remedies 5-4.55–5-4.56
bundling 5-4.56
cartels 5-4.20
chaebols 5-4.31
collusion 5-4.39
competitive assessments 5-4.31
conglomerate mergers 5-4.42–5-4.45
coordinated effects 5-4.39
corrective measures 5-4.21, 5-4.50
divestiture 5-4.53
economic crisis 1997 5-4.54
efficiencies 5-4.02, 5-4.45–5-4.49
enforcement 5-4.01, 5-4.11
failing firm defence 5-4.02, 5-4.46–5-4.49
Fair Trade Commission (KFTC) 5-4.01, 5-4.07–5-4.14, 5-4.17, 5-4.20–5-4.57
financial institutions 5-4.01
Financial Supervisory Commission (KFSC) 5-4.01
fines 5-4.14
foreclosure 5-4.40–5-4.41
foreign mergers 5-4.08, 5-4.19–5-4.20
geographic market 5-4.25
guidelines 5-4.01, 5-4.42, 5-4.46–5-4.53
assessment of competition 5-4.31
controlling relationships 5-4.03
foreign mergers 5-4.08
horizontal mergers 5-4.32–5-4.35
market definition 5-4.24, 5-4.26
notification 5-4.09, 5-4.14–5-4.21
substantive test, application of 5-4.22–5-4.26
vertical mergers 5-4.40–5-4.41

horizontal mergers 5-4.32
interlocking directorates 5-4.03
jurisdiction 5-4.08
market
definition 5-4.24–5-4.29
power assessment 5-4.30
product market 5-4.34
relevant market 5-4.25, 5-4.42
share 5-4.30, 5-4.34, 5-4.40, 5-4.42
Ministry of Information and Communication (MIC) 5-4.01
Monopoly Regulation and Fair Trade Act 1980 (MRFTA) 5-4.01–5-4.02, 5-4.06–5-4.21, 5-4.41, 5-4.49–5-4.50
notification 5-4.01, 5-4.08–5-4.20
penalties 5-4.14, 5-4.20
pre-merger contacts 5-4.09
procedure 5-4.09–5-4.21, 5-5.01
product market 5-4.34
relevant market 5-4.25, 5-4.42
remedies 5-4.20, 5-4.45, 5-4.50–5-4.57
reporting requirements post-merger 5-4.57
reviews 5-4.09, 5-4.19, 5-4.22–5-4.32, 5-4.55
SSNIP test 5-4.24–5-4.25, 5-4.29
structural remedies 5-4.51
substantive test, application of 5-4.22–5-4.49
substitutability 5-4.34
telecommunications 5-4.01
vertical mergers 5-4.31, 5-4.40–5-4.41
Korea monopoly and abuse of dominance 5.3.01–5.3.29
abusive conduct 5-3.08–5-3.18
arbitration 5-3.29
assessment of dominance 5-3.04–5-3.07
barriers to entry 5-3.06, 5-3.15–5-3.17
bundling 5-3.20
case examples 5-3.20–5-3.23
chaebols 1-1.28, 5-3.02
clean market project 5-1.07
corrective measures 5-3.13, 5-3.28
de minimis rule 5-3.05
enforcement 5-3.02
examination of industries 5-1.07
examples of abuse 5-3.04
excessive prices 5-3.08
Fair Trade Commission (KFTC) 5-1.07, 5-3.03–5-3.13, 5-3.18–5-3.29
Fair Trade Mediation Committee (KFTMC) 5-3.29
fines 5-3.19, 5-3.28
franchising 5-3.29
guidance 5-3.06–5-3.08, 5-3.11, 5-3.17, 5-3.26–5-3.27
illegal conduct 5-3.15, 5-3.18
market
share 5-3.05–5-3.06, 5-3.17–5-3.18
structures 5-3.03
Monopoly Regulation and Fair Trade Act 1980 (MRFTA) 1-2.30, 5-1.01, 5-3.01–5-3.19, 5-3.24–5-3.29, App 3
penalties 5-3.19, 5-3.28
predatory pricing 5-3.18
price discrimination 1-2.30, 5-3.11, 5-3.27
price-fixing 5-3.08–5-3.09, 5-3.19
refusal to deal 5-3.13–5-3.14, 5-3.27
refusal to supply 5-3.11–5-3.14
remedies 5-3.19, 5-3.21
tying 5-3.11, 5-3.20–5-3.22, 5-3.27
unfair trade practices 5-3.24–5-3.26
Korea procedure 5.5.01–5.5.29
access to files 5-5.10
appeals 5-5.24–5-5.27
arbitration 5-5.29
cartels 5-5.06, 5-5.14, 5-5.19, 5-5.21–5-5.23
case handling 5-5.01–5-5.02
complaints 5-5.11–5-5.12
corrective measures 5-5.04, 5-5.13–5-5.23, 5-5.25, 5-5.28
criminal prosecutions 5-5.20, 5-5.23
damages 5-5.28
deliberation preparation process 5-5.01
documents by post, delivery of 5-5.03
education and compliance programmes 5-5.14, 5-5.19
employees, liability for acts of 5-5.06
evidence 5-5.05–5-5.07, 5-5.12
examinations 5-5.10
Fair Trade Commission (KFTC) 5-5.01–5-5.28
Fair Trade Mediation Committee (KFTMC) 5-5.29
fines 5-5.20
guidelines 5-5.14
hearings 5-5.09–5-5.10
inspections 5-5.05–5-5.06
investigations 5-5.04–5-5.08, 5-5.11
leniency programmes 5-5.21–5-5.23
merger control 5-4.09–5-4.21, 5-5.01
Monopoly Regulation and Fair Trade Act 1980 (MRFTA) 5-5.04, 5-5.07–5-5.24, 5-5.28–5-5.29
notifications 5-5.12, 5-5.24
penalties 5-5.04, 5-5.06, 5-5.13–5-5.23
public interest 5-5.10
rewards, offering of 5-5.12
trade secrets 5-5.10
warnings 5-5.16

leniency programme
Hong Kong 3-1.24
horizontal agreements 1-2.15
Korea 5-2.31, 5-5.21–5-5.23
penalties 1-2.15
Taiwan 4-5.30
Vietnam 6-5.34

market *see* **geographic market; market definition; market power; market share; product market; relevant market**
market definition
Korea 5-4.24–5-4.29
Taiwan 4-4.24
Vietnam 6-3.02
market power
abuse of dominant position/monopolistic practices 1-2.22–1-2.26
Article 82 (EC Treaty) 1-2.22–1-2.26
China 2-4.18
economic principles 1-2.50
Korea 5-2.05, 5-2.29, 5-4.30
merger control 1-2.02, 1-2.39, 2-4.18, 5-4.30
Sherman Act 1-2.22–1-2.26
standards 1-2.02
substantial market power, abuse of 3-1.09
Taiwan 4-4.25
Vietnam 6-2.01–6-2.11, 6-3.01, 6-3.06
market share
China 2-3.04–2-3.05, 2-4.18
Hong Kong 3-1.12
Korea
agreements 5-2.05, 5-2.12, 5-2.27, 5-2.30
merger control 5-4.30, 5-4.34, 5-4.40, 5-4.42
monopoly and abuse of dominance 5-3.05–5-3.06, 5-3.17–5-3.18
merger control
China 2-4.18
Korea 5-4.30, 5-4.34, 5-4.40, 5-4.42
Taiwan 4-4.06, 4-4.07, 4-4.22–4-4.27, 4-4.29, 4-4.34
Vietnam 6-4.01, 6-4.03–6-4.04, 6-4.08–6-4.12, 6-4.14–6-4.15
monopoly and abuse of dominance
China 2-3.04–2-3.05
Korea 5-3.05–5-3.06, 5-3.17–5-3.18
Vietnam 6-3.05–6-3.06, 6-3.09
Taiwan merger control 4-4.06, 4-4.07, 4-4.22–4-4.27, 4-4.29, 4-4.34
Vietnam
agreements 6-2.02, 6-2.03, 6-2.06–6.2.07
merger control 6-4.01, 6-4.03–6-4.04, 6-4.08–6-4.12, 6-4.14–6-4.15
monopoly and abuse of dominance 6-3.05–6-3.06, 6-3.09
procedure 6-5.27–6-5.34
merger control 1-2.35–1.2.44 *see also* **China merger control; Korea merger control; Taiwan merger control; Vietnam merger control**
appeals 1-2.41
behavioural remedies 1-2.43
cartels 1-2.39
Clayton Act 1-2.38
commitments, offer of 1-2.41
conglomerate mergers 1-2.35
coordinated effects 1-2.35
defences 1-2.44
divestiture 1-2.43
dominant position 1-2.38
EC competition law
appeals 1-2.41
commitments, offer of 1-2.41
divestiture 1-2.43
dominant position 1-2.38
efficiency defence 1-2.44
failing firm defence 1-2.44
guidance 1-2.39
Herfindahl-Hirschman Index 1-2.39
injunctions 1-2.41
notification 1-2.41
private rights of action 1-2.42
significant impediment of effective competition (SIEC) test 1-2.38
structural remedies 1-2.43
United States 1-2.35, 1-2.38
EC Merger Regulation (ECMR) 1-2.37–1-2.38, 1-2.41
effects doctrine 1-2.37
efficiency defence 1-2.44
extraterritoriality 1-2.37
failing firm defence 1-2.44
guidance 1-2.39
Herfindahl-Hirschman Index 1-2.39
Hong Kong 1-2.20, 3-1.07, 3-1.13
horizontal mergers 1-2.35, 1-2.39
injunctions 1-2.41
jurisdiction 1-2.37
market power 1-2.02, 1-2.39
notification 1-2.37, 1-2.41
oligopolies 1-2.35
portfolio effects 1-2.35
private rights of action 1-2.42
remedies 1-2.43
significant impediment of effective competition (SIEC) test 1-2.38
standards 1-2.02, 1-2.35–1-2.44
structural remedies 1-2.43
substantially lessen competition test 1-2.38

tacit coordination 1-2.39
turnover threshold 1-2.37
unilateral anti-competitive effects 1-2.35
United States
Clayton Act 1-2.38
Department of Justice (DOJ) 1-2.41
EC competition law 1-2.35, 1-2.38
efficiency defence 1-2.44
extraterritoriality 1-2.37
failing firm defence 1-2.44
Fair Trade Commission (FTA) 1-2.41
guidance 1-2.39
Herfindahl-Hirschman Index 1-2.39
injunctions 1-2.41
notification 1-2.41
private rights of action 1-2.42
substantially lessen competition test 1-2.38
vertical mergers 1-2.40
Ministry of Commerce (MOFCOM) (China)
antitrust regime 2-1.10–2-1.12
merger control 2-4.11, 2-4.24
Ministry of Industry and Trade (MIT) (Vietnam)
agreements 6-2.07
antitrust law regime 1-1.34, 6-1.08–6-1.14
merger control 6-4.05, 6-4.07
Ministry of Information and Communication (MIC) (Korea) 5-4.01
Mongolia, Taiwan's memorandum of understanding with 4.1.19
monopoly *see* **abuse of dominance and monopolistic practices; abuse of dominant position/ monopolistic practices under Article 82 (EC Treaty) and Sherman Act; China monopoly and abuse of dominance; Korea monopoly and abuse of dominance; Taiwan monopoly and abuse of dominance; Vietnam monopoly and abuse of dominance**
multi-level sales arrangements
Taiwan 4-2.01, 4-2.22–4-2.24
Vietnam 6-2.11

National Development and Reform Commission (NDRC) (China) 2-1.10–2-1.12
national security
China 2-4.20
notification
China merger control 2-4.03, 2-4.08, 2-4.11, 2-4.12–2.4.15
EC competition law 1-2.41
hearings 4-5.14, 4-5.17
Hong Kong 3-1.11
Korea
agreements 5-2.02
merger control 5-4.14, 5-4.20
procedure 5-5.12, 5-5.24
merger control 1-2.37, 1-2.41
China 2-4.03, 2-4.08, 2-4.11, 2-4.12–2.4.15
Korea 5-4.14, 5-4.20
Taiwan 4-4.05–4-4.06, 4-4.14, 4-4.17, 4-4.19
Taiwan merger control 4-4.05–4-4.06, 4-4.14, 4-4.17, 4-4.19
United States 1-2.41
Vietnam 6-4.01, 6-4.08–6-4.12, 6-4.14, 6.5.20

obstruction
China 2-5.05
OECD 1-1.25, 1-2.13, 4.1.20, 5-1.13
oligopolies 1-2.07, 1-2.35, 2-3.05
oral hearings
Taiwan 4-5.13–4-5.16

parallel behaviour 1-2.08, 5-2.09, 5-2.29
penalties *see also* **fines**
China
agreements 2-2.09
confiscation 2-5.11, 2-5.13
merger control 2-4.22–2-4.24
monopoly and abuse of dominance 2-3.15, 2-5.10–2-5.14
procedure 2-5.03, 2-5.05
confiscation 2-5.11, 2-5.13, 6-5.28
directors 3-1.21
Hong Kong 3-1.14–3-1.15, 3-1.20–3-1.21
Korea
agreements 5-2.16–5-2.21, 5-2.24, 5-2.27, 5-2.31–5-2.33, 5-2.38
antitrust law regime 1-1.31
merger control 5-4.14, 5-4.20
monopoly and abuse of dominance 5-3.19, 5-3.28
procedure 5-5.04, 5-5.06, 5-5.13–5-5.23
leniency programmes 1-2.15
merger control
China 2-4.22–2-4.24
Korea 5-4.14, 5-4.20
Taiwan 4-4.38–4-4.43
Vietnam 6-4.13
monopoly and abuse of dominance
China 2-3.15, 2-5.10–2-5.14
Korea 5-3.19, 5-3.28
Taiwan 4-3.12
senior managers, penalties against 3-1.21
Taiwan
agreements 4-2.06, 4-2.23, 4-2.40–4-2.41
merger control 4-4.38–4-4.43
monopoly and abuse of dominance 4-3.12
procedure 4-5.02, 4-5.08, 4-5.21–4-5.30

penalties (*cont.*)
Vietnam
agreements 6-2.06, 6-2.11
confiscation 6-5.28
merger control 6-4.13
People's Republic of China *see* **China abuse of dominance; China agreements; China antitrust law regime; China merger control; China monopoly; China procedure**
portfolio effects 1-2.35, 4-4.31
predatory pricing
abuse of dominant position/monopolistic practices 1-2.27–1-2.29, 5-3.18
Article 82 (EC Treaty) 1-2.27–1-2.29
Korea 5-3.18
Sherman Act 1-2.27–1-2.29
price-fixing
China
agreements 2-2.02, 2-2.03, 2-2.04
antitrust regime 1-1.08
monopoly and abuse of dominance 2-3.12
Korea
agreements 5-2.05, 5-2.10, 5-2.18–5-2.20
monopoly and abuse of dominance 5-3.08–5-3.09, 5-3.19
monopoly and abuse of dominance 2-3.12, 5-3.08–5-3.09, 5-3.19, 6-3.11
Taiwan agreements 4-2.04–4-2.06, 4-2.16, 4-2.40
Vietnam 6-2.02, 6-2.06, 6-3.11
pricing *see also* **price-fixing; resale price maintenance; SSNIP (Small but Significant and Non-transitory Increase in Price) test**
abuse of dominant position/monopolistic practices 1-2.21, 1-2.22, 1-2.25, 1-2.27–1-2.31, 2-3.07
Article 82 (EC Treaty) 1-2.21, 1-2.22, 1-2.25, 1-2.27–1-2.31, 2-3.07
China 2-3.06
discrimination 1-2.25, 1-2.30, 5-3.11, 5-3.27
excessive pricing 1-2.31, 2.3.06
exploitative pricing 2-3.07, 4-3.09, 4-3.16
Korea 1-1.27, 1-2.30, 5-3.08, 5-3.11, 5-3.27
minimum price-setting 1-2.20
monopoly and abuse of dominance
China 2-3.06
Taiwan 4-3.07–4-3.09, 4-3.14–4-3.16
Vietnam 6-3.11
predatory pricing 1-2.27–1-2.29
Sherman Act 1-2.21, 1-2.22, 1-2.25, 1-2.27–1-2.31, 2-3.07
Taiwan 4-3.07–4-3.09, 4-3.14–4-3.16
Vietnam 6-3.11
private actions
China 2-5.18–2-5.21
EC competition law 1-2.42
Hong Kong 3-1.14, 3-1.16, 3-1.24
merger control 1-2.42
Taiwan 4-5.37
United States 1-2.42
privatization 1-1.01
procedure *see also* **China procedure; Korea procedure; Taiwan procedure; Vietnam procedure**
Hong Kong 3-1.14–3.1.28
product market
economic principles 1-2.46, 1-2.48
Korea 5-4.34
relevant market 1-2.46, 1-2.48
protectionism
China
anti-trust regime 1-1.07
merger control 2-4.01
monopoly and abuse of dominance 2-3.10, 2-3.12–2-3.14
public hearings
Taiwan 4-5.12, 4-5.15–4-5.16, 4-5.18
Vietnam 6-5.20
public interest
China 2-2.07, 2-4.19
Korea 5-5.10
Taiwan 4-4.23, 4-4.37, 4-5.03
public utility services
Vietnam 6-1.06

refusal to supply
abuse of dominant position/monopolistic practices 1-2.32, 2-3.06, 4-3.11, 5-3.11–5-3.14
Article 82 (EC Treaty) 1-2.32
China 2-3.06
Korea 5-2.26, 5-3.11–5-3.14
Sherman Act 1-2.32
Taiwan 4-3.11
refusal to trade
China 2-3.06
Korea 5-3.13–5-3.14, 5-3.27
relevant market
abuse of dominant position/monopolistic practices 1-2.23–1-2.24, 2-3.03–2-3.05, 4-3.03, 6-3.02–6-3.09
Article 82 (EC Treaty) 1-2.23–1-2.24
China 2-1.07, 2-3.03–2-3.05
definition 2-1.07
economic principles 1-2.46, 1-2.48–1-2.50
evidence 1-2.49
geographic market 1-2.49

Korea 5-2.05, 5-4.25, 5-4.42
merger control 4-4.23, 5-4.25, 5-4.42, 6-4.14
product market 1-2.46, 1-2.48
Sherman Act 1-2.23–1-2.24
Taiwan 4-3.03, 4-4.23
Vietnam 6-3.02–6-3.09, 6-4.14, 6-5.08
remedies
China
damages 2-5.19
merger control 2-4.22–2-4.24
monopoly and abuse of dominance 2-5.08
rectification 2-5.05, 2-5.08
damages
China 2-5.19
Hong Kong 3-1.24, 3-1.28
Taiwan 4-4.43, 4-5.02, 4-5.33–4-5.37
Hong Kong 3-1.23–3-1.24, 3-1.28
injunctions
EC competition law 1-2.41
Hong Kong 3-1.23, 3-1.28
merger control 1-2.41
Taiwan 4-4.43
United States 1-2.41
Korea
merger control 5-4.20, 5-4.45, 5-4.50–5-4.57
monopoly and abuse of dominance 5-3.19, 5-3.21
merger control 1-2.41, 1-2.43
China 2-4.22–2-4.24
Korea 5-4.20, 5-4.45, 5-4.50–5-4.57
Taiwan 4-4.03, 4-4.11, 4-4.38–4-4.43
Vietnam 6-4.13–6-4.14
monopoly and abuse of dominance
China 2-5.08
Korea 5-3.19, 5-3.21
Taiwan 4-3.12
Taiwan
merger control 4-4.03, 4-4.11, 4-4.38–4-4.43
monopoly and abuse of dominance 4-3.12
procedure 4-5.02, 4-5.33–4-5.37
United States 1-2.41
Vietnam
merger control 6-4.13–6-4.14
procedure 6-5.27–6.5.34
representative actions
Hong Kong 3-1.14, 3-1.27
resale price maintenance
China 2-2.03
Korea 5-2.23, 5-2.26–5-2.27, 5-2.32
Taiwan 4-2.20–4-2.21, 4-2.35
Vietnam 6-3.11
research and development agreements
China 2-2.07
horizontal agreements 1-2.13, 1-2.16
Korea 5-2.05
Taiwan 4-2.09, 4-2.12
reviews
China 2-4.12–2-4.16
Korea
agreements 5-2.15
merger control 5-4.09, 5-4.19, 5-4.22–5-4.32, 5-4.55
merger control
Korea 5-4.09, 5-4.19, 5-4.22–5-4.32, 5-4.55
Taiwan 4-4.13, 4-4.16, 4-4.21–4-4.25
Taiwan 4-4.13, 4-4.16, 4-4.21–4-4.25
rewards
Korea 5-5.12
rule of reason
anti-competitive agreements 1-2.10–1-2.12, 2-2.075
Article 81 (EC Treaty) 1-2.10–1-2.12
China 2-2.075, 2-3.08
hard core restrictions 1-2.14
Taiwan 4-2.09
United States 1-2.10–1-2.12, 2.2.05, 4-2.09
vertical agreements 1-2.10, 1-2.18
Vietnam 6-1.04
Russia, memorandum of understanding between China and 2-1.21

sales below cost
China 2-3.06
secrecy *see* **business secrecy**
selective distribution schemes 1-2.20
senior managers, penalties against 3-1.21
services of general economic interest
Hong Kong 3-1.10
settlements
Hong Kong 3-1.18
Taiwan 4-5.29
Sherman Act *see* **abuse of dominant position/ monopolistic practices under Article 82 (EC Treaty) and Sherman Act; anti-competitive agreements under Article 81 (EC Treaty) and Sherman Act**
significant impediment of effective competition (SIEC) test 1-2.38
small businesses
Hong Kong 3-1.03, 3-1.12, 3-1.20, 3-1.26–3-1.27
Korea 1-1.29
Taiwan 4-2.16
Small but Significant and Non-transitory Increase in Price test *see* **SSNIP (Small but Significant and Non-transitory Increase in Price) test**
socialist market economies 1-1.01, 1-1.06, 1-1.32, 1-2.01, 2-1.04

South Korea *see* **Korea agreements; Korea merger control; Korea monopoly and abuse of dominance; Korea procedure; Korean antitrust law regime**
specialization agreements 1-2.13, 1-2.16, 4-2.09, 5-2.05
SSNIP (Small but Significant and Non-transitory Increase in Price) test
  economic principles 1-2.47–1-2.48
  Korea 5-4.24–5-4.25, 5-4.29
  Taiwan 4-4.24
  Vietnam 6-3.03
standard setting agreements 1-2.16
standards in antitrust law 1-2.01–1-2.53
  abuse of dominant position/monopolistic practices 1-2.02, 1-2.21–1-2.34
  anti-competitive agreements 1-2.02, 1-2.04–1-2.20
  Article 82 (EC Treaty) 1-2.02, 1-2.03, 1-2.21–1-2.34
  China 1-1.11, 1-2.01
  economic principles and evidence, application of, 1-2.45–1-2.51
  efficiency standard 1-2.01, 1-2.03
  Hong Kong 3-1.01
  international cooperation 1-2.52–1-2.53
  merger control 1-2.02, 1-2.35–1-2.44
  Sherman Act 1-2.02, 1-2.03, 1-2.21–1-2.34
  Vietnam as socialist market economy 1-2.01
standstill period
  Taiwan 4-4.17
State Administration for Industry and Commerce (SAIC) (China) 2-1.10–2-1.13
State Economic and Trade Commission (SETC) (China) 1-1.08, 1-1.11
state-owned enterprises (SOEs)
  China 1-1.07, 1-1.12, 2-1.16, 2-3.10
  Vietnam 1-1.33, 1-1.34, 6-1.06, 6-3.01, 6-3.15
structural remedies
  China 2-4.22, 2-5.08
  EC competition law 1-2.43
  Hong Kong 3-1.22
  Korea 5-4.51
  merger control 1-2.43, 2-4.22, 5-4.51
  Vietnam 6-5.32
substantially lessen competition test 1-2.38
substitutability 1-2.46, 1-2.48, 5-4.34
supply side substitutability 1-2.47-1.2.48, 1-2.51

tacit coordination 1-2.39
Taiwan *see* **Taiwan agreements; Taiwan antitrust law regime; Taiwan merger control; Taiwan monopoly and abuse of dominance; Taiwan procedure**
Taiwan agreements 4-2.01–4-2.41
  approvals 4-2.08–4-2.18
  cartels 4-2.05, 4-2.09, 4-2.15, 4-2.36
  concerted actions 4-2.02–4-2.04, 4-2.09–4-2.11, 4-2.14, 4-2.16, 4-2.40
  conditions 4-2.29
  corrective action 4-2.23
  crisis cartels 4-2.09, 4-2.15
  deceptive or unfair conduct 4-2.38–4-2.40
  discrimination 4-2.36
  efficiency 4-2.11, 4-2.16, 4-2.19
  enforcement 4-2.10–4-2.11, 4-2.34, 4-2.36
  exemptions 4-2.01, 4-2.08, 4-2.17
  export agreements 4-2.13
  export cartels 4-2.09
  Fair Trade Act (TFTA) 4-2.01–4-2.40
  Fair Trade Commission (TFTC) 1-2.20, 4-2.04–4-2.06, 4-2.16–4-2.19, 4.2.23, 4-2.25, 4-2.37–4-2.39
  fines 4-2.06, 4-2.23, 4-2.40, 4-2.41
  guidelines 4-2.01, 4-2.16, 4-2.20, 4-2.25–4-2.27, 4-2.37–4-2.38
  hard core restrictions 4-2.04
  horizontal agreements 4-2.01–4-2.18, 4-2.33–4-2.40
  illegal agreements 4-2.35, 4-2.36–4-2.38
  importation of foreign goods 4-2.14
  information transparency 4-2.16, 4-2.39
  intellectual property rights 4-2.01, 4-2.20, 4-2.25–4-2.32
    black clauses 4-2.25, 4-2.28
    conditions 4-2.29
    factors to be considered 4-2.26
    grey list 4-2.29
    list of clauses not presumed to be anti-competitive 4-2.27
    technology licensing 4-2.25–4-2.32
  multi-level sales arrangements 4-2.01, 4-2.22–4-2.24
  penalties 4-2.06, 4-2.23, 4-2.40–4-2.41
  price-fixing 4-2.04–4-2.06, 4-2.16, 4-2.40
  resale price maintenance 4-2.20–4-2.21, 4-2.35
  research and development agreements 4-2.09, 4-2.12
  rule of reason 4-2.09
  small and medium-sized enterprises 4-2.16
  specialization agreements 4-2.09
  technology licensing 4-2.25–4-2.32
  trade associations 1-2.09, 4-2.19
  trade secrets 4-2.36
  transaction stability, principle of 4-2.16

undertakings 4-2.17
unilateral conduct 4-2.01
United States 4-2.09
vertical agreements 1-2.20, 4-2.01, 4-2.20–4-2.40

Taiwan antitrust law regime 1-1.24–1-1.25, 4-1.01–4-1.20
APEC (Asia Pacific Economic Cooperation) Competition Policy and Law Database 1-1.25
appeals 1-1.25
Australia, bilateral agreement with 4-1.18
bilateral international agreements 1-1.25, 1-2.52, 4-1.17–4-1.18
complaints 4-1.12–4-1.13
definition of competition 4-1.04
EC competition law 4-1.01
efficiency 4-1.02
emanations of the state 4-1.09
enforcement 1-1.25, 4-1.01–4-1.02
enterprises, definition of 4-1.03
exemptions 4-1.09–4-1.10
Fair Trade Act 1992 4-1.01–4-1.02, 4-1.09–4-1.16
amendment 4-1.01
contents 1-1.24, 4-1.02
drafting 1-1.24
Fair Trade Commission (TFTC) 1-1.25
purpose 4-1.02
text App 2
Fair Trade Commission (TFTC) 4-1.05–4-1.08, 4-1.12–4-1.19
appeals 1-1.25
composition 4-1.07
departments 4-1.06
enforcement 1-1.25, 4-1.01–4-1.02
Executive Cabinet 4-1.05
Guidelines on Cases Involving Foreign Elements 4-1.12–4-1.15, 4-1.17
independence 1-1.25
information sources 4-1.08
international activities 1-1.25
role 1-1.25
website 4-1.08
workload 4-1.07
fines 4-1.16
foreign mergers 4-1.12–4-1.16, 4-1.17
information sources 4-1.08, 4-1.14
intellectual property rights 4-1.10
international cooperation and agreements 4-1.17–4-1.20
merger control 4-1.12
mixed economy, Taiwan as 1-1.24
Mongolia, Memorandum of Understanding with 4-1.19
OECD 1-1.25, 4-1.20
service outside the jurisdiction 4-1.15
telecommunications 4-1.01
territorial application 4-1.11–4-1.16
United States 4-1.01

Taiwan merger control 4.1.12, 4-4.01–4-4.43
barriers to entry 4-4.30, 4-4.36
case records 4-4.34–4-4.37
China, prohibition of investment from 4-4.04
concerted action 4-4.27
conglomerate mergers 4-4.31
coordinated effects 4-4.26–4-4.27
countervailing power 4-4.26, 4-4.28
damages 4-4.43
definition of merger 4-4.01, 4-4.11
efficiency defence 1-2.44, 4-4.32–4-4.33, 4-4.35
enforcement 4-4.01, 4-4.08, 4-4.17, 4-4.24
enterprise, definition of 4-4.02
entry 4-4.26, 4-4.30, 4-4.36
failing firm defence 1-2.44, 4-4.32–4-4.33
Fair Trade Act (TFTA) 4-4.01, 4-4.04, 4-4.06, 4-4.14, 4-4.17, 4-4.20–4-4.21, 4-4.32, 4-4.38–4-4.39, 4-4.43
Fair Trade Commission (TFTC) 1-2.44, 4-4.03, 4-4.07–4-4.16, 4-4.20–4-4.43
fees 4-4.19
fines 4-4.39
foreclosure 4-4.30
foreign mergers 4-4.09, 4-4.11–4-4.12
franchise agreements 4-4.05, 4-4.34
groups of companies 4-4.10, 4-4.22
guidelines 4-4.11, 4-4.21–4-4.27, 4-4.31
Herfindahl-Hirschman Index 1-2.39
holding companies 4-4.23
horizontal mergers 4-4.22, 4-4.26–4-4.29, 4-4.31
injunctions 4-4.43
joint ventures 4-4.01
jurisdiction 4-4.05–4-4.12, 4-4.16
market
definition 4-4.24
power assessment 4-4.25
relevant market 4-4.23
share 4-4.06, 4-4.07, 4-4.22–4-4.27, 4-4.29, 4-4.34
notification 4-4.05–4-4.06, 4-4.14, 4-4.17, 4-4.19
penalties 4-4.38–4-4.43
portfolio effects 4-4.31
pre-merger contacts 4-4.13
procedure 4-4.13–4-4.19, 4-5.23
public interest 4-4.23, 4-4.37
publication of decisions 4-4.18
relevant market 4-4.23
remedies 4-4.03, 4-4.11, 4-4.38–4-4.43

Taiwan merger control (*cont.*)
removal of certain persons from positions 4-4.40
reports 4-4.14–4-4.15
reviews 4-4.13, 4-4.16, 4-4.21–4-4.25
SSNIP test 4-4.24
standstill period 4-4.17
structural mergers 4-4.01
subsidiary mergers, simplified procedure for 4-4.22–4-4.23
substantive test, application of 4-4.20–4-4.37
turnover thresholds 4-4.06, 4-4.08, 4-4.34
unilateral effects 4-4.26–4-4.27
United States 4-4.11
vertical mergers 4-4.22, 4-4.30–4-4.31
Taiwan monopoly and abuse of dominance 4-3.01–4.3.16
abusive conduct 4-3.07–4-3.11
Article 82 (EC Treaty) 4-3.07, 4-3.09
assessment of dominance 4-3.03–4-3.06
case examples 4-3.13–4-3.16
collective dominance 4-3.03
concentration ratio 4-3.04
concerted action 4-3.11
de minimis rule 4-3.04
discrimination 4-3.07, 4-3.10
enforcement rules 4-3.01, 4-3.02–4-3.06
essential facilities doctrine 4-3.08
exclusionary conduct 4-3.07–4-3.08
exploitative pricing 4-3.09, 4-3.16
factors to be taken into consideration 4-3.06
Fair Trade Act (TFTA) 4-3.01–4-3.03, 4-3.06, 4-3.12
Fair Trade Commission (TFTC) 4-3.03, 4-3.05–4-3.12, 4-3.16
fines 4-3.12, 4-3.16
guidelines 4-3.02, 4-3.03
penalties 4-3.12
pricing 4-3.07–4-3.09, 4-3.14–4-3.16
procedure 4-5.21, 4-5.25
refusal to supply 4-3.11
relevant market 4-3.03
remedies 4-3.12
United States 4-3.07, 4-3.09
Taiwan procedure 4-5.01–4-5.37
access to files 4-5.20
Administrative Settlement Agreements 4-5.29
appeals 4-5.31, 4-5.37
business secrets 4-5.07
complaints 4-5.11
concerted actions 4-5.21
confidentiality 4-5.17
corrective measures 4-5.21–4-5.30
damages 4-5.02, 4-5.33–4-5.37
disclosure 4-5.07, 4-5.17
enforcement 4-5.01, 4-5.22, 4-5.27, 4-5.32
Fair Trade Act (TFTA) 4-5.01–4-5.03, 4-5.07, 4-5.15, 4-5.21–4-5.25, 4-5.32–4-5.34
Fair Trade Commission (TFTC) 4-5.01, 4-5.03–4-5.34
fines 4-5.08, 4-5.22, 4-5.25
guidance 4-5.09, 4-5.13, 4-5.18, 4-5.20, 4-5.27
hearings 4-5.12–4-5.20
confidentiality 4-5.17
guidelines 4-5.13, 4-5.18
initiation 4-5.16
notification 4-5.14, 4-5.17
oral hearings 4-5.13–4-5.16
preliminary hearings 4-5.18
public hearings 4-5.12, 4-5.15–4-5.16, 4-5.18
publicity 4-5.17
records 4-5.19
information gathering 4-5.08
investigations 4-5.03–4-5.11, 4-5.20
fines 4-5.08
materials, submission of 4-5.03, 4-5.06
notice 4-5.05
on-site investigations 4-5.07
rights of persons subject to investigations 4-5.20
statements 4-5.03, 4-5.05
leniency programme 4-5.30
merger control 4-4-13–4-4.19, 4-5.23
monopolies 4-5.21, 4-5.25
penalties 4-5.02, 4-5.08, 4-5.21–4-5.30
private actions 4-5.37
public hearings 4-5.12, 4-5.15–4-5.16, 4-5.18
public interest 4-5.03
publication of judgments 4-5.36
settlements 4-5.29
third party rights, damages and 4-5.32–4-5.37
warnings 4-5.28
technological progress, agreements impeding 6-2.02
technology licensing 4-2.25-4.2.32
technology transfer 6-1.22
telecommunications
Korea 5-4.01
Taiwan 4-1.01
territorial application
China 2-1.19–2-1.20
Korea 5-1.10–5-1.12, 5-2.30
Taiwan 4-1.11–4-1.16
Vietnam 6-1.18–6.1.19, 6-4.15
territorial restraints 1-2.19, 1-2.20, 6-2.02

third parties
China 2-5.18–2-5.21
Taiwan 4-5.32–4-5.37
Vietnam 6-5.24, 6-5.35
trade associations
China 2-2.04, 2-5.13
concerted practices 1-2.07
Korea 5-2.22–5-2.25
Taiwan 1-2.09, 4-2.19
Vietnam 6-1.06, 6-2.04–6-2.05
trade secrets *see* **business secrets**
turnover thresholds
China 2-4.02, 2-4.05–2-4.06
merger control 1-2.37
China 2-4.02, 2-4.05–2-4.06
Taiwan 4-4.06, 4-4.08, 4-4.34
Taiwan 4-4.06, 4-4.08, 4-4.34
tying
Article 82 (EC Treaty) 1-2.34
China 2-3.06
Korea 5-3.20–5-3.22, 5-3.27
Sherman Act 1-2.34
Vietnam 6-3.11

undertakings
China 2-5.09
Taiwan 4-2.17
United States *see also* **abuse of dominant position/ monopolistic practices under Article 82 (EC Treaty) and Sherman Act; anti-competitive agreements under Article 81 (EC Treaty) and Sherman Act**
bilateral agreements 1-1.33
Clayton Act 1-2.38
Department of Justice (DOJ) 1-2.41
EC competition law 1-2.35, 1-2.38
economic principles 1-2.47–1.2-48, 1-2.51
efficiency defence 1-2.03, 1-2.44
export cartels 4-2.09
extraterritoriality 1-2.37
failing firm defence 1-2.44
Fair Trade Commission (FTA) 1-2.41
guidance 1-2.39
Herfindahl-Hirschman Index 1-2.39
injunctions 1-2.41
Korea 1-2.03, 4-4.11, 5-1.14, 5-2.01
merger control 1-2.35, 1-2.37–1-2.44, 4-4.11
notification 1-2.41
private rights of action 1-2.42
rule of reason 4-2.09
standards 1-2.03
substantially lessen competition test 1-2.38
Taiwan 4-1.01, 4-2.09, 4-3.07, 4-3.09
Vietnam 1-1.33, 6-1.04

vertical agreements
anti-competitive agreements 1-2.02, 1-2.05, 1-2.10, 1-2.18–1-2.20
Article 81 (EC Treaty) 1-2.02, 1-2.05, 1-2.10, 1-2.18–1-2.20
block exemptions 1-2.10, 1-2.18, 1-2.20
China 1-2.18, 2-2.03
efficiency 1-2.19
exclusive distribution agreements 1-2.19
Hong Kong 3-1.08
inter-brand competition 1-2.19
intra-brand competition 1-2.19
Korea 5-2.29–5-2.30
minimum price-setting 1-2.20
rule of reason 1-2.10, 1-2.18
selective distribution schemes 1-2.20
Sherman Act 1-2.02, 1-2.05, 1-2.10, 1-2.18–1-2.20
standards 1-2.02
Taiwan 1-2.20, 4-2.01, 4-2.20–4-2.40
territorial restraints 1-2.19, 1-2.20
Vietnam 6-2.10–6-2.11
vertical mergers
challenges 1-2.40
China 2-4.09
Korea 5-4.31, 5-4.40–5-4.41
Taiwan 4-4.22, 4-4.30–4-4.31
Vietnam *see* **Vietnam agreements; Vietnam antitrust law regime; Vietnam merger control; Vietnam monopoly and abuse of dominance; Vietnam procedure**
Vietnam agreements 6-2.01–6-2.11
bid-rigging 6-2.02, 6-2.06
Competition Administration Department (VCAD) 6-2.07–6-2.08
complaints 6-2.08
conditions or obligations, agreements imposing 6-2.02
de minimis threshold 6-2.03
discrimination 6-2.05
distribution agreements 6-2.02
efficiencies 6-2.02
eject market participants, agreements to 6-2.02
exclusive purchasing arrangements 6-2.02
exemptions 6-2.01, 6-2.03–6-2.09
foreclosure 6-2.02
formal decisions 6-2.08
hard core conduct 6-2.06
horizontal agreements 6-2.01–6-2.09
information from related parties, power to request 6-2.07
Law on Competition 2005 (VLOC) 6-2.01–6-2.11

Vietnam agreements (*cont.*)
market
market-sharing agreements 6-2.02, 6-2.06
power 6-2.03
share 6-2.02, 6-2.03, 6-2.06–6-2.07
Ministry of Industry and Trade (MIT) 6-2.07
multi-level sales 6-2.11
output restrictions 6-2.02
penalties 6-2.06, 6-2.11
price-fixing 6-2.02, 6-2.06
socialist market economy 1-2.01
technological progress, agreements impeding 6-2.02
territorial exclusivity 6-2.02
trade associations 6-2.04–6-2.05
vertical agreements 6-2.10–6-2.11
Vietnam antitrust law regime 1-1.32–1-1.34, 6-1.01–6-1.22
acts of the state 6-1.17
administrative sanctions 6-1.11
APEC (Asia Pacific Economic Cooperation) 6-1.20
ASEAN 6-1.20
command and control system 1-1.34
commodity line associations 6-1.06
Competition Administration Department (VCAD) 1-1.34, 6-1.03, 6-1.20
committees 6-1.12
composition 6-1.12
establishment 6-1.08
role 6-1.05, 6-1.10–6-1.13
structure 6-1.05
Competition Case-Handling Council (CCHC) 6-1.14
Competition Council (VCC) 6-1.03, 6-1.14
complaints 6-1.14
compulsory licensing 6-1.22
decrees 6-1.05
doi moi policy 1-1.32, 1-1.34
EC competition law 6-1.04
economic growth 1-1.33
enforcement 1-1.34, 6-1.05, 6-1.07, 6-1.11, 6-1.13–6-1.14
exemptions 6-1.04, 6-1.08, 6-1.11, 6-1.15–6-1.16
extraterritoriality 6-1.18
foreign enterprises 6-1.06
foreign investment 1-1.32
framework 1-1.01
institutional arrangements 6-1.10–6-1.14
intellectual property 6-1.21–6-1.22
International Competition Network (ICN) standards 1-1.32
international cooperation and agreements 6-1.16, 6-1.20
investigations 6-1.02–6-1.03, 6-1.10–6-1.12
Japan, partnership with 6-1.20
language 6-1.19
Law on Competition 2005 (VLOC) 6-1.01–6-1.22
contents 6-1.03
drafting 1-1.33, 6-1.04
purpose 6-1.02
scope 1-1.32
text App 4
market oriented economy 1-1.32, 1-1.34
Ministry of Industry and Trade (MIT) 1-1.34, 6-1.08–6-1.14
political intervention 1-1.34
public utility services 6-1.06
rule of reason 6-1.04
socialist market economy, Vietnam as 1-1.32
state management agencies 6-1.17
state-owned enterprises (SOEs) 1-1.33, 1-1.34, 6-1.06
technology transfer 6-1.22
territorial application 6-1.18–6-1.19
trade associations 6-1.06
United States 1-1.33, 6-1.04
World Trade Organization (WTO) 1-1.33
Vietnam merger control 6-4.01–6-4.15
acquisitions, definition of 6-4.02
Competition Administration Department (VCAD) 6-4.04, 6-4.06–6-4.14
Competition Council (VCC) 6-4.14
concentrations, definition of 6-4.02
consolidation, definition of 6-4.02
Decree on Competition 6-4.02, 6-4.05
definition of merger 6-4.02
divestiture 6-4.13
economic considerations 6-4.01
efficiency defence 6-4.01
exemptions 6-4.01. 6-4.05–6-4.08
failing firm defence 6-4.01
foreign mergers 6-4.15
growth in activity 1-1.33
information from third parties 6-4.06
investigations 6-4.14
joint ventures 6-4.02
Law on Competition 2005 (VLOC) 6-4.01–6-4.02, 6-4.05, 6-4.10, 6-4.14–6-4.15
Law on State-Owned Enterprises 6-4.01
market share 6-4.01, 6-4.03–6-4.04, 6-4.08–6-4.12, 6-4.14–6-4.15

Ministry of Industry and Trade (MIT) 6-4.05, 6-4.07
notification 6-4.01, 6-4.08–6-4.12, 6-4.14
penalties 6-4.13
procedure 6-4.08–6-4.12
relevant market 6-4.14
remedies 6-4.13–6-4.14
territorial application 6-4.15
Vietnam monopoly and abuse of dominance 6-3.01–6-3.15
assessment of dominance and monopoly 6-3.02–6-3.09
barriers to entry 6-3.04, 6-3.08, 6-3.11
Competition Administration Department (VCAD) 6-3.03
conditions, imposition of 6-3.11, 6-3.13
countervailing power 6-3.08
Decree on Competition 6-3.03–6-3.13
definition of monopoly 6-3.09
discrimination 6-3.11
efficiencies 6-3.12
essential facilities doctrine 6-3.11
geographic market 6-3.04
groups of enterprises 6-3.07
irrational prices 6-3.11
Law on Competition 2005 (VLOC) 6-3.01–6-3.03, 6-3.06, 6-3.08, 6-3.10, 6-3.14–6-3.15
market
definition 6-3.02
power 6-3.01, 6-3.06
relevant market, determination of 6-3.02–6-3.09
share 6-3.05–6-3.06, 6-3.09
modification or cancellation of contracts 6-3.13
price-fixing 6-3.11
prices lower than aggregate costs, selling at 6-3.11
prohibited conduct 6-3.10–6-3.15
relevant market, determination of 6-3.02–6-3.09
resale price maintenance 6-3.11
SSNIP test 6-3.03
state-owned enterprises (SOEs) 6-3.01, 6-3.15
tying 6-3.11
Vietnam procedure 6-5.01–6-5.39
administrative law 6-5.02
administrative preventive measures (APMs) 6-5.11, 6-5.22, 6-5.27
appeals 6-5.04, 6-5.18, 6-5.25, 6-5.36–6-5.39
business certificates, revocation of 6-5.28
business secrets 6-5.26
compensation 6-5.35
Competition Administration Department (VCAD) 6-5.02, 6-5.06, 6-5.09–6-5.12, 6-5.16, 6-5.21–6-5.22, 6-5.25–6-5.26, 6-5.30–6-5.39
Competition Case Handling Council (CCHC) 6-5.14–6-5.17, 6-5.20, 6-5.29, 6-5.32, 6-5.36
Competition Council (VCC) 6-5.02, 6-5.06, 6-5.11, 6-5.15, 6-5.17, 6-5.19, 6-5.25–6-5.26, 6-5.29–6-5.38
complaints 6-5.02, 6-5.06, 6-5.21–6-5.24
confiscation 6-5.28
corrective action 6-5.33
dawn raids 6-5.11
decisions, contents of 6-5.18
Decree on Competition 6-5.01, 6-5.07, 6-5.11, 6-5.19
Decree on Dealing with Breaches in Competition Sector (DDB) 6-5.01, 6-5.28–6-5.32, 6-5.35
detention 6-5.11
enforcement 6-5.12
evidence 6-5.07, 6-5.10–6-5.11, 6-5.14, 6-5.25
experts 6-5.14
fees 6-5.03, 6-5.21–6-5.22
fines 6-5.28–6-5.29, 6-5.32
hard core conduct 6-5.12
hearings 6-5.16–6-5.20
appeals 6-5.18
decisions, contents of 6-5.18
experts 6-5.14
notification 6-5.20
president, powers of 6-5.17
public hearings 6-5.20
rights of parties 6-5.25
witnesses 6-5.14
investigations 6-5.06–6-5.20, 6-5.31
cooperation 6-5.13
notification 6-5.12
official 6-5.08
preliminary 6-5.08
reports 6-5.12
Law on Competition 2005 (VLOC) 6-5.01–6-5.02, 6-5.06–6-5.08, 6-5.21–6-5.27, 6-5.35–6-5.36
legal representation 6-5.25
leniency 6-5.34
market
relevant market 6-5.08
share 6-5.08
merger control 6-4.08–6-4.12
penalties 6-5.27–6-5.34
procedural infringements 6-5.30
public hearings 6-5.20

Vietnam procedure (*cont.*)
relevant market 6-5.08
remedies 6-5.27–6-5.34
rights of the parties 6-5.25–6-5.26
searches 6-5.11
structural remedies 6-5.32
third parties 6-5.24, 6-5.35
voluntarily termination of infringement 6-5.31
warnings 6-5.28, 6-5.30
witnesses 6-5.14

warnings
Korea 5-5.16
Taiwan 4-5.28
Vietnam 6-5.28, 6-5.30

Williams, M. ***Competition Policy on China, Hong Kong and Taiwan*** 1-1.15, 1-1.24, 4-1.09

witnesses
Vietnam 6-5.14

World Trade Organization (WTO) 1-1.02, 1-1.33